THE PAPERS OF
ZEBULON BAIRD VANCE

Zebulon Baird Vance, ca. 1859. Photograph by Julian Vannerson in the Library of Congress Prints and Photographs Division, Washington, D.C.

THE PAPERS OF
ZEBULON BAIRD Vance

• Volume 3 •

1864-1865

Joe A. Mobley

Editor

Assisted by
Anne Miller and Kenrick N. Simpson

Raleigh
Office of Archives and History
North Carolina Department of Cultural Resources
2013

North Carolina Department of Cultural Resources
Susan W. Kluttz
Secretary

Office of Archives and History
Kevin Cherry
Deputy Secretary

Historical Publications Section
Donna E. Kelly
Administrator

CONTENTS

FOREWORD

The first volume of *The Papers of Zebulon Baird Vance* was published in 1963 during the centennial commemoration of the Civil War. It is fitting that this third volume, which includes Vance's correspondence in the last eighteen months of the conflict, is published fifty years later during the sesquicentennial commemoration of that war.

Joe Mobley, former administrator of the Historical Publications Section and longtime employee of the Office of Archives and History, edited the second volume of the Vance Papers series and both selected and transcribed the documents in this third volume. Kenrick N. Simpson and Anne Miller, former and current employees of the section respectively, served as assistant editors and prepared the manuscript for publication. Other members of the Historical Publications Section who worked on this publication include Susan M. Trimble, who typeset the work, and Lisa D. Bailey who, along with the section administrator, helped proofread it.

Mr. Mobley received both his B.A. and M.A. degrees in history at North Carolina State University, where he currently serves as a lecturer. He is author of a number of other works published by the Office of Archives and History, including *James City: A Black Community in North Carolina, 1863–1900* and *Ship Ashore! The U.S. Lifesavers of Coastal North Carolina*. His *"War Governor of the South": North Carolina's Zeb Vance in the Confederacy* (University Press of Florida) won the North Caroliniana Society Book Award for 2006. Other Civil War books include *Weary of War: Life on the Confederate Home Front* (Praeger) and *Confederate Generals of North Carolina: Tar Heels in Command* (History Press). Mr. Mobley served as editor of the present edition of *The Way We Lived in North Carolina* (University of North Carolina Press) and wrote *Raleigh, North Carolina: A Brief History* (History Press). He served as editor of the *North Carolina Historical Review* for many years and wrote articles and numerous book reviews for the journal. He also served as president of the North Carolina Literary and Historical Association and of the Historical Society of North Carolina.

Many changes have occurred in the past half century. The first volume of the Vance Papers was published in a print edition in 1963, the second volume in 1995. Both of these volumes remain in print and are available for purchase. In recognition of the public's reading habits today, this third volume is also being issued in a digital e-book edition. Although times change, Zebulon Baird Vance continues to hold a significant place in North Carolina history.

Donna E. Kelly, *Administrator*
Historical Publications Section

INTRODUCTION

In January 1864, Zebulon Baird Vance could look forward with some trepidation to the remaining eight months of his first term as governor of North Carolina. As part of the Confederate States of America, North Carolina had been at war with the United States since the state's secession in May 1861. By the beginning of 1864, the state was experiencing the stress of waging a war with dwindling resources and success.

Within the Tar Heel State, Vance increasingly had to deal with the ever-pressing problems of enforcing Confederate conscription, arresting deserters, and addressing citizens' complaints about shortages, inflation, speculation, tax-in-kind, and the impressment of forage and supplies. By late 1863, dissatisfaction and disillusionment with the war had led disaffected North Carolinians to consider the possibility of peace negotiations. They found a spokesman in William W. Holden, editor of Raleigh's *North Carolina Standard*, a member of the Conservative Party, and promoter of Vance in the gubernatorial election of 1862. In the autumn of 1863, Holden began calling for a convention of delegates to consider peace negotiations with the Federal government.[1]

In early 1864, Vance committed himself to run for reelection as governor and based his platform upon support for the war and Confederate independence, as well as denunciation of Holden and his allies. In late 1863, Holden had let Vance know in no uncertain terms that he and his allies would oppose Vance's reelection if he did not support the peace convention. "I can not of course favour such a thing for any existing cause," Vance wrote to his adviser, former governor and Confederate senator William A. Graham. "I will see the Conservative party blown into a thousand atoms and Holden and his understrappers in hell . . . before I will consent to a course which I think would bring dishonor and ruin upon both State & Confederacy!"[2] The governor also wrote to David L. Swain, president of the state university, former governor, and adviser and father figure to Vance. He asked for Swain's advice about running for reelection to the governorship. As governor, he asserted, he could never lead North Carolinians back into the Union "humbled and degraded."[3]

Vance, however, did not immediately proclaim publicly his opposition to Holden and the peace movement. He vacillated for several weeks, perhaps because he was uncertain about how to proceed in his race for reelection, or perhaps to wait for advice from his Conservative supporters. Such advice was not long in coming. John D. Hyman—a friend and former coeditor of the *Asheville Spectator* who soon became editor of the pro-Vance Raleigh *Conservative*—wrote to Vance on February 17, 1864: "By your silence you are daily losing friends. The Democratic and secession party allege that Holden is your spokesman & that you are in favor of a convention while a large number of Conservatives are committing themselves to a convention, whether by signing petitions or participating in public meetings held at Holden's suggestion—whereas they would commit themselves in opposition to a convention, if they knew you were opposed to it."[4] Vance finally publicly denounced Holden's peace convention five days later, on February 22, when he made his first campaign speech in Wilkesboro, the seat of Wilkes County.

In the meantime, the peace movement in North Carolina received some additional support when the Confederate Congress, at the urging of President Jefferson Davis, passed a law suspending the writ of habeas corpus in thirteen specific cases. The eleventh clause of the act was intended to suppress peace activities in the Confederacy. That provision suspended the writ of habeas corpus for anyone arrested for "advising or inciting others to abandon the Confederate cause, or to resist the Confederate States, or to adhere to the enemy."[5]

Upon hearing of the bill, and convinced that it was directed at North Carolina's disaffected citizens, Vance wrote to President Davis urging him to be "chary of exercising the power" of the new law. Such actions, Vance cautioned, would play right into the hands of the dissenters. The problems in North Carolina, he insisted, could not be solved by suppression of civil rights. North Carolina would remain loyal to the Confederacy so long as Davis dealt fairly and cautiously with its residents. Vance pointed out that he and other supporters of the Confederacy were already working in the state to prevent the calling of a peace convention.

Vance then launched into a long explanation of why some North Carolinians had become disenchanted with the Confederate war effort. He maintained that from the beginning, the Davis government had been suspicious of the Old North State because it had been reluctant to leave the Union. As a result, the governor complained, those Tar Heels who had originally opposed secession had been excluded from high civil and military positions in the Confederacy. He also contended that the Confederate policies of conscription, impressment, and tax-in-kind had been harshly and unfairly imposed upon North Carolinians.[6] Davis angrily responded that he had no intention of suspending the writ of habeas corpus without just cause, "But should the occasion unhappily arise when the public safety demands their employment, I would be derelict in duty, if I hesitated to use" such powers. Davis went on in great detail to defend himself against Vance's charges that he and his officials had been biased against North Carolina because of its strong Unionist sentiment prior to secession.[7]

A series of angry letters ensued between Davis and Vance, in which each blamed the other for the disaffection in North Carolina. Throughout the war, the relationship between the president and the governor remained strained and sometimes antagonistic, and their correspondence often disintegrated into petulant quarreling. Nevertheless, Vance made conscientious efforts to cooperate and compromise with the Davis government. On two occasions he visited Richmond in order to talk personally with Davis to smooth out difficulties between the state and the Confederacy. Shortly after taking office in 1862, he traveled to the Confederate capital to discuss with the president how the two governments could best operate together to prosecute the war. Again in August 1863 he called on Davis to talk over the dissatisfaction in North Carolina about certain Confederate policies and appointments. He came away encouraged by Davis's response. "I trust things will be better now that we are understood at Richmond," he reported after the meeting.[8]

To be sure, Davis frequently argued with Vance. Davis's stubborn and quarrelsome nature, however, was not confined to his discourses with Vance but levied at other officials as well.[9] Vance's temper, on the other hand, displayed a certain insecurity and immaturity. He sometimes fired off angry missives to Davis or the secretary of war about alleged Confederate injustices before he took time to reflect on his comments or to verify facts about reported outrages such as impressment or other abuses of North Carolina soldiers or civilians.[10] But neither man ever denounced the other as a demagogue, and Davis never openly questioned Vance's loyalty to the cause of a free and independent Confederate States of America.

The governor did, however, manage to turn the issue of the suspension of the writ of habeas corpus to his advantage in the gubernatorial election of 1864. After he launched his 1864 campaign, a number of his advisers encouraged him to speak out strongly against suspension, which reportedly had created some outrage in the Tar Heel State. Holden and his peace proponents had seized on the issue of suspension as fuel for their crusade to defeat Vance. Responding to the advice of his associates, Vance did defend the writ of habeas corpus in an April speech in Fayetteville, in the columns of the *Fayetteville Observer* in that same month, before the legislature in May, and thereafter in the campaign. But the governor tempered his defense of the principle of habeas corpus by insisting that North Carolina should support the Davis government and accept nothing short of Confederate independence. Responding to his remarks in May, the legislature passed a resolution against the suspension of the writ of habeas corpus and a bill making it a high misdemeanor to ignore a writ issued by a state judge. But the legislature also passed a resolution expressing its "most hearty approval and cordial sympathy" for Vance's position and stating that any peace negotiations should be made only on the basis of Confederate independence.[11] Vance was politically astute enough not to ignore the habeas corpus issue, and he denied Holden and his allies that weapon with which to assail him, but it does not necessarily follow that Vance strongly opposed the 1864 Confederate law suspending the writ. In 1863, Vance had defended the right of Chief Justice Richmond M. Pearson to issue writs of habeas corpus for men that he ruled were illegally conscripted into the Confederate army, and the governor had refused to allow Confederate authorities to ignore the writs. Although Vance accepted and defended Pearson's rulings as state law, he did not agree with the chief justice's decisions that denied the legality of the arrests of deserters and recusant conscripts by the militia or Home Guard, and he attempted to have the full North Carolina Supreme Court overturn them.[12]

Vance began his campaign for reelection in the midst of a stronghold of peace sentiment, for Wilkes County stood in the west and at the edge of the area of war disaffection and antislavery Unionist sentiment known as the Quaker Belt. In his speech at Wilkesboro on February 22, the governor set the tone and agenda that would prevail throughout his campaign. He denounced the secessionists who had started the war but at the same time condemned the movement calling for a peace convention. He asserted that the Confederacy could win its independence if the people would only persist in supporting the Confederate government. He told the crowd of two thousand onlookers that he had "no more doubt about the establishment of the independence of the Southern Confederacy than I have of my own existence, provided we remain true to the cause we have solemnly undertaken to support." He went on to chastise the Davis government for its recent law authorizing the suspension of habeas corpus. But he qualified his remarks with an appeal to the citizens of North Carolina to obey the laws of the state and the Confederacy. He also defended the conscription laws. "I have come among you," he told the crowd, "to beg you in the name of reason, of humanity, to obey the law; to recognize order and authority; to do nothing except in the manner prescribed by the Constitution; to bear the ills you have rather than fly to evils you know not of; in short . . . to implore you 'to do nothing rash.' "[13]

Following his speech at Wilkesboro, the governor delivered it again at Statesville, Taylorsville, and Salisbury. Upon Vance's return to Raleigh, Holden—seeing plainly that the man he previously supported for the office of chief executive was not going to support a peace convention—announced his intention to run against him in the gubernatorial race. "The man who has been deepest in my confidence and whom my friends have persisted in apologizing for, has at length shown his purpose," Vance wrote to Graham.[14] The race for the office of governor continued through the spring and summer.

The governor stumped the state vigorously, responding to many invitations to speak and drawing large crowds. He also visited the North Carolina troops in Virginia and addressed several brigades. He continued to attack Holden and his peace convention, while at the same time leaving the impression that he was open to peace negotiations if such negotiations recognized Confederate independence. He also implied that he was a protector of habeas corpus and the civil liberties of the people. He accused Holden of being affiliated with the Heroes of America or Red Strings, a radical Quaker Belt Unionist organization working to undermine the Confederacy. He also insisted that Holden wanted North Carolina to negotiate a separate peace with the Federals. Having much of his political thunder stolen, Holden could only respond to Vance's platform by accusing the governor of having a wasteful and corrupt administration and of neglecting the state's business by staying so long on the campaign circuit. He also claimed that the governor was really the candidate of the Confederate or Democratic Party and not a true Conservative. More war, not peace, was Vance's objective, Holden maintained. The editor of the *Standard* declined to debate Vance and had to spend much of his effort defending himself against the charges that he was a member of the Heroes of America and desired a separate peace for North Carolina.[15]

In the end, Vance's strategy paid off. He won both the Democratic and Conservative vote and carried the August election by an overwhelming margin, receiving 77.2 percent of the popular vote. From the soldiers' vote, Holden garnered only 1,824 votes of the nearly 15,000 cast. There is evidence of possible fraud in some of the army vote, but it would not have changed the outcome of the election. In North Carolina, Vance carried all but three counties: Wilkes (the site of the governor's opening campaign speech), Randolph, and Johnston. His votes totaled 57,873, while Holden received only 14,432.[16] With this vote of confidence from the electorate, Vance would in the coming months continue steadfastly to lend his support to the Confederacy's efforts to win its independence.

In the autumn of 1864, the war increasingly turned against the Confederate states as Atlanta fell, Gen. William T. Sherman began his march northward into the Carolinas, and the Army of the Potomac tightened its grip on the Army of Northern Virginia in the trenches around Petersburg and Richmond. Lincoln's reelection in November meant a continuation of the Federal campaign to see the war through until victory. The fall of Fort Fisher at the port of Wilmington in January 1865 added to the despondency in North Carolina. Those events resulted in a revival of peace sentiment in North Carolina and other Southern states. But amid the renewed clamor for peace negotiations, Vance stood firm in his support of the government in Richmond and his commitment to continuing the hostilities until Confederate independence was won. In August 1864, he had issued a proclamation enticing deserters to return to their regiments with only mild punishment and promising to pursue relentlessly those who did not. He then called for a conference of Confederate governors east of the Mississippi to revive their waning efforts for Southern independence. At the conference, held in Augusta, Georgia, in October 1864, he suggested that the governors urge their state legislatures to make greater efforts to support the war effort, including breaking up "The great evil of desertion" and permitting the conscription of some state officials, who "could constitute quite a material reinforcement to our hard pressed armies." Back in North Carolina, Vance called together his Council of State and asked it to endorse an immediate session of the state legislature in order to approve the conscription of some state officials and the Home Guard to be sent to Robert E. Lee's army in Virginia. The council, however, refused. At the regular session of the legislature in November, the governor further demonstrated his concern for bolstering the Confederate army by asking the state lawmakers to extend the age of conscription to fifty-five. The assembly declined his request.[17]

Vance also continued to oppose vehemently any further talk about a peace convention, even after he became virtually certain that the Confederacy stood no chance of achieving a military victory. On January 18, 1865, he wrote to Gov. Joseph E. Brown of Georgia that "The March of Sherman through Georgia his threatened advance through So. Carolina and the recent disasters involved in the defeat of Genl Hood and the fall of the principal defensive work of Wilmington, have necessitated the desire of a State Convention for vague and indefinable purposes. I do not think however that a Convention can be called in North Carolina unless your State should lead in the movement, and I see many indications of such an intention among your people. . . ." Vance went on to admonish Brown to do all he could to prevent such a convention in Georgia. "I suppose you are aware of my opinion in regard to the danger of such a movement," he wrote Brown. "I regard it as simply another revolution and by which we would incur not only the danger attendant upon a disunited Confederation, but also of domestic strife and bloodshed."[18]

In late January 1865, Vance learned that the Hampton Roads Peace Conference would be held on February 3. At that conference, three Confederate commissioners and critics of Jefferson Davis—Alexander Stephens, John A. Campbell, and Robert M. T. Hunter—would attempt to negotiate a peace with the Federal government. To a friend, Vance expressed his opinion of the pending conference. "Never was there a greater error," he declared. "It is most unwise to suspend our preparations [*for the public defense*] in the hour of negotiations. We should really double our dilligence, & present to our enemies the energetic determination of a great people, driven to the wall in the last stages of desperation and ready to dare every thing! But alas! Alas! We hail the first step of our enemies toward negotiation, on any terms, as an act of gracious condescension and tacitly accept our degradation beforehand!" As far as Vance was concerned, the peace meeting was "a great swindle, and we are so anxious to be duped that we can never plead *rape*. I believe however it will result in peace but such a peace as I for one will blush to accept."[19] But the governor soon learned that he had no reason to fear the success of the peace talks. The Hampton Roads conference failed quickly when the Confederate commissioners learned that President Lincoln would not compromise on his stipulations that the Confederate states lay down their arms, renounce their independence, and accept emancipation of their slaves.[20] After the failure of negotiations at Hampton Roads, Senator William A. Graham approached Vance on behalf of a group of Confederate senators and representatives who had concluded that further resistance in the war was useless and would result only in additional bloodshed. They wanted North Carolina to begin unilateral peace negotiations with the Federal government. As their spokesman, Graham suggested to Vance that he recall North Carolina's troops from Virginia and thereby force Gen. Robert E. Lee to surrender his army and conclude the war. Vance refused to do what Graham suggested and vowed to fight on to the end along with the other Confederate states.

Indeed, the Tar Heel war governor resisted capitulation to the very end, even when the troops of Sherman were at the gates of the state's capital. On April 10, 1865, Gen. Joseph E. Johnston, whose troops were defending against the advance of Sherman's army toward Raleigh, informed Vance that he intended to evacuate the Raleigh area and retreat to the west. He would meet at Greensboro with Jefferson Davis, who was fleeing southwestward from Richmond with his cabinet. Lee's army had been trapped by U. S. Grant's troops at Appomattox on April 9, and rumors spread that Lee had surrendered. Vance began transferring out of Raleigh the state records and the stores of supplies that he had on hand.[21]

At around that same time, Graham and Swain proposed to the governor a plan for securing peace and avoiding further destruction at the hands of Sherman. Both Graham and Swain were convinced that the cause of Confederate independence was hopeless and that "through the administration of Mr. Davis we could expect no peace, so long as he shall be supplied with the resources of war. . . ." Their scheme called for Vance to convene the legislature and have it pass a resolution calling for a conclusion to the war and inviting the other Confederate states to do likewise. The legislature would elect commissioners to treat with the Federal government and report to a state convention to be called "to wield the sovereign power of the State in any emergency that may arise out of the changing state of events." If Sherman drew near to Raleigh, however, Vance should dispatch commissioners to Sherman to request that Union troops suspend fighting until the governor could determine what further action the state would take regarding continuing the war. Again Vance rejected the idea of unilateral peace negotiations by North Carolina. But he did concur in the plan to send commissioners to meet with Sherman, after first receiving permission from Confederate general William J. Hardee, whom Johnston had left in command at Raleigh.[22]

On April 12, Vance dispatched Graham and Swain to negotiate with Sherman, who was then fast approaching Raleigh from the east. Graham and Swain, accompanied by several other state officials, left Raleigh by train, but before they reached Sherman, they were detained by Federal officers. When Vance learned that his two emissaries had been captured, he prepared a letter to Sherman, which he left with city officials. The letter stated that Mayor William H. Harrison was authorized to surrender the city of Raleigh and asked for Sherman's "protection for the charitable institutions of the State located here filled as they are with unfortunate inmates, most of whose natural protectors would be unable to take care of them in the event of their destruction." The governor also asked that Sherman not allow the destruction of "The Capitol of the State with its Libraries, Museum and most of the public records. . . ." Around midnight, the governor fled from Raleigh and rode to the encampment of Gen. Robert F. Hoke, about eight miles west of the city.[23]

On the following day, he traveled to Hillsborough, where he stopped at Graham's house. In the meantime, Graham and Swain had met with Sherman and returned to Raleigh with the Union commander's promise to protect the city from destruction. Finding Vance gone, they took over state affairs at the State Capitol. Mayor Harrison surrendered the city to the advance guard of the Federal army. On April 14, Graham and Swain set out to find Vance, carrying with them a pass from Sherman (who had taken up residence in the Governor's Palace) giving Vance safe conduct back to Raleigh. They proceeded to Hillsborough, where they attempted to persuade Vance to return to the capital city, but Vance refused, even though he also received for the first time definite news that Lee had surrendered. Shortly before Graham and Swain arrived, Vance had received a message from Jefferson Davis requesting a meeting at Greensboro. Still clinging to the shreds of a legitimate Confederate government, Vance departed on April 15 for Greensboro; but upon arriving, he found that Davis had left for Charlotte. Vance then returned to Hillsborough accompanied by Confederate secretary of war John C. Breckinridge.

At Hillsborough, General Johnston had convened a council of Confederate generals and cabinet officials to discuss possible peace terms between Sherman and Johnston. The two leaders had begun talks at the farmhouse of James Bennett, near Durham Station. Egged on by Gen. Wade Hampton, the Confederate authorities snubbed Vance because they felt he might have been willing to negotiate with Sherman on his own. Wounded by such an accusation, Vance strongly denied it. He then left Hillsborough and returned to Greensboro, where he hoped to established a temporary state capital.[24]

On April 23, Davis wired Vance to meet with him and his cabinet at Charlotte. Vance arrived shortly, and Davis began to talk of a plan to unite with Gen. Edmund Kirby Smith in the Trans-Mississippi. According to Vance, the president wanted Vance and the remaining North Carolina troops to join him and the remnants of Johnston's army in a flight to the West, where they would continue the fight. The cabinet, however, convinced Davis that such a scheme had no chance of success. Davis reluctantly instructed Johnston to accept the surrender terms that he and Sherman had reached at the Bennett farmhouse. Vance then returned to Greensboro. But word soon reached the Confederate president that the government in Washington had refused to accept the generous surrender terms that Sherman had offered Johnston. The Confederate government had forty-eight hours to accept the same terms that General Lee had been given at Appomattox. Davis then ordered Johnston to begin moving his army southward. Instead, Johnston met with Sherman at the Bennett farm and on April 26 surrendered his army according to the Federals' terms, effectively ending the war. Davis was eventually captured in southwestern Georgia on May 10. At Greensboro, Vance attempted, without success, to reestablish a state government. On May 2, he surrendered to Union general John M. Schofield, who had replaced Sherman. Not sure what to do with Vance, Schofield told him to go home. Vance went to Statesville, where earlier he had sent his family, and on May 13, Federal soldiers arrested him there. He was transported to Washington, D.C., and placed in the Old Capitol Prison, where he remained until released on July 6.[25]

[1]William C. Harris, *William Woods Holden: Firebrand of North Carolina Politics* (Baton Rouge: Louisiana State University Press, 1987), 127-136, 138-142.

[2]ZBV to William A. Graham, January 1, 1864, William Alexander Graham Papers, Private Collections, State Archives, Office of Archives and History, Raleigh.

[3]ZBV to David L. Swain, January 2, 1864, Zebulon Baird Vance Papers, Private Collections, State Archives.

[4]John D. Hyman to ZBV, February 17, 1864, Vance Papers, Private Collections, State Archives.

[5]Richard E. Yates, "Governor Vance and the Peace Movement," part 2, *North Carolina Historical Review* 17 (April 1940): 92-93.

[6]ZBV to Jefferson Davis, February 9, 1864, Zebulon B. Vance, Governors Papers, State Archives.

[7]Jefferson Davis to ZBV, February 29, 1864, Vance, Governors Papers, State Archives.

[8]ZBV to James A. Seddon, January 6, 1863, Zebulon B. Vance, Governors Letter Books, State Archives; ZBV to Edward J. Hale, August 11, 1863, Edward Jones Hale Papers, Private Collections, State Archives.

[9]The most complete treatments of Davis and his personality are William J. Cooper Jr., *Jefferson Davis, American* (New York: Vintage Books, 2001), and

William C. Davis, *Jefferson Davis: The Man and His Hour* (New York: HarperCollins, 1991).

[10]For examples of Vance's temper, see ZBV to Jefferson Davis, July 6, 1863, and ZBV to James A. Seddon, July 26, 1863, Vance, Governors Letter Books, State Archives.

[11]Yates, "Vance and the Peace Movement," part 2, 92-93, 109.

[12]ZBV to Richmond M. Pearson, October 7, 26, 1863, Vance, Governors Letter Books, State Archives; ZBV to William H. Battle, October 6, 1863, Pearson to ZBV, August 11, November 2, 1863, all three in Vance, Governors Papers, State Archives. For a discussion of habeas corpus in North Carolina, see Mark E. Neely, *Southern Rights: Political Prisoners and the Myth of Confederate Constitutionalism* (Charlottesville: University Press of Virginia, 1999), 64-79.

[13]*Conservative* (Raleigh), April 16, 20, 1864; Yates, "Vance and the Peace Movement," part 2, 96-97.

[14]Yates, "Vance and the Peace Movement," part 2, 97-99; ZBV to William A. Graham, March 3, 1864, in Max R. Williams, J. G. de Roulhac Hamilton, and Mary Reynolds Peacock, eds., *The Papers of William Alexander Graham*, 8 vols. (Raleigh: Office of Archives and History, Department of Cultural Resources, 1957-1992), 6:36.

[15]Frontis W. Johnston and Joe A. Mobley, eds., *The Papers of Zebulon Baird Vance*, 2 vols. to date (Raleigh: Office of Archives and History, Department of Cultural Resources, 1963-), 1:lxxiii.

[16]North Carolina Gubernatorial Election Returns, 1864, Compiled Election Returns, Miscellaneous Papers, State Archives.

[17]Proclamation by ZBV, August 24, 1864, Vance, Governors Letter Books, State Archives; Glenn Tucker, *Zeb Vance: Champion of Personal Freedom* (New York: Bobbs-Merrill, 1965), 367-370; *Laws of North Carolina, 1864*, as cited in Richard E. Yates, "Governor Vance and the End of the Civil War in North Carolina," *North Carolina Historical Review* 18 (October 1941): 316.

[18]ZBV to Joseph E. Brown, January 18, 1865, Vance, Governors Letter Books, State Archives.

[19]ZBV to Anonymous, January 31, 1865, Vance Papers, Private Collections, State Archives.

[20]Patricia L. Faust et al., eds, *Historical Times Illustrated Encyclopedia of the Civil War* (New York: HarperCollins, 1986), 335-336.

[21]Yates, "Vance and the End of the Civil War," 325-328; Gordon B. McKinney, *Zeb Vance: North Carolina's Civil War Governor and Gilded Age Political Leader* (Chapel Hill: University of North Carolina Press, 2004), 246-247.

[22]David L. Swain to William A. Graham, April 8, 1865, Graham to Swain, April 8, 9, 1865, in Williams, Hamilton, and Peacock, *Papers of Graham*, 6:292-297; Yates, "Vance and the End of the Civil War," 328-329; McKinney, *Zeb Vance*, 247.

[23]ZBV to William T. Sherman, April 11, 1865, Cornelia P. Spencer Papers, Southern Historical Collection, Wilson Library, University of North Carolina at Chapel Hill.

[24]Mark L. Bradley, *This Astounding Close: The Road to Bennett Place* (Chapel Hill: University of North Carolina Press, 2000), 108-121, 126-129, 198-201; McKinney, *Zeb Vance*, 249-250; ZBV to William T. Sherman, April 11, 1865, Spencer Papers.

[25]Jefferson Davis to ZBV, April 23, 1864, Vance, Governors Papers, State Archives;

ZBV, "Lecture—The Last Days of the War in North Carolina," in Clement Dowd, *Life of Zebulon B. Vance* (Charlotte, N.C.: Observer Printing and Publishing House, 1897), 485-486; Cooper, *Jefferson Davis*, 568-569; John G. Barrett, *The Civil War in North Carolina* (Chapel Hill: University of North Carolina Press, 1963), 385; William C. Davis, *An Honorable Defeat: The Last Days of the Confederate Government* (New York: Harcourt, 2001), 192-193; Joseph E. Johnston to ZBV, April 24, 1865, Vance Papers, Private Collections, State Archives.

EDITORIAL METHOD

The number of documents currently known to exist in the papers of Zebulon Baird Vance for the period January 1864 to June 1865 totals approximately 3,582. The largest single repository for those materials is the State Archives, North Carolina Office of Archives and History, Raleigh. That agency houses three major collections pertaining to Vance: the Governors Papers, the Governors Letter Books, and Vance's private papers. The rest of the Vance papers reside in various collections throughout the United States. Of the number extant, 502 have been transcribed and printed in this volume. The rest are listed in a calendar at the end of the book. The calendar catalogs the papers chronologically in the order in which they are arranged within a collection. Listed first are the Governors Papers, then the Governors Letter Books, followed by Vance's private papers, and lastly all other repositories.

In this volume the editors have selected and transcribed materials that pertain to the major political, military, and administrative decisions of Governor Vance from January 1864 until the end of the Civil War and the governor's imprisonment in Washington, D.C. The predominant topics are states' rights, war disillusionment and the peace movement, conscription, desertion, the gubernatorial election, blockade-running, supplies and shortages, and the final events leading to the surrender of the Confederacy. But the editors have also included a sampling of letters that reflect the hardships and fears of Confederate soldiers and the home-front population. Of the 502 letters, telegrams, proclamations, and memorandums published herein, nearly half of them are *from* Vance. Virtually all surviving correspondence known to have been created by Vance has been printed. The few exceptions include routine commissions, appointments, and other documents merely requiring his signature. The editors have made transcriptions for this volume from manuscript sources only. None comes from printed matter such as newspapers, published records, or other documentaries, although some of the same documents might be found in other printed works.

Although the Vance papers have been transcribed and printed as exactly as feasible, a number of editorial adjustments and devices appear throughout volume 3 to provide continuity and assist the reader. Margins, indentation, and placement of elements have been standardized. Misspellings and punctuation have been retained except when the misspelling was so flagrant or the punctuation so erratic or bizarre as to be unintelligible or misleading. In such cases silent emendations have been made. Flourishes and other extraneous marks have been eliminated. Small dashes, at the bottom of a line or at the end a sentence (_), have been converted to periods. Long dashes (—) are retained whether they come within or at the end of a sentence. [*Sic*] indicates only factual errors and words that are repeated in error ("the the," for example). Superscript characters have been brought down to the line and followed by a period. Angle brackets (< >) enclose letters and words canceled by the writer but still legible. Interlinear insertions appear within (/ /), and all editorial insertions have been italicized and placed in square brackets ([ ]). Inferred readings also are in square brackets but in Roman type. [*Illegible*] indicates words that cannot be deciphered, and such terms as [*faded*] and [*torn*] appear where appropriate. All notes follow immediately the document to which they refer.

Zebulon B. Vance frequently made endorsements on the backs of letters he received. In those notations he usually gave instructions to clerks or aides for responding to the letter or for filing the correspondence. Because those endorsements (some brief, others having several sentences) include significant information about Vance and his mind-set, the editors have placed them—with the designation [*Endorsed*]—at the end of the document on which they were written. Some letters received have been published herein mainly on the basis of what Vance's endorsement reveals. Endorsements other than those by the governor also have been included when they provide information not already given in the item. The editors have noted enclosures with the heading [*Enclosures*] and placed them immediately after the correspondence that they accompanied, regardless of the date on which the enclosure was written.

LIST OF PAPERS PRINTED IN THIS VOLUME

ABBREVIATIONS OF REPOSITORIES

A&H:GA
: General Assembly Session Records, State Archives, Office of Archives and History, Raleigh

A&H:GLB
: Zebulon Baird Vance, Governors Letter Books, State Archives, Office of Archives and History, Raleigh

A&H:GP
: Zebulon Baird Vance, Governors Papers, State Archives, Office of Archives and History, Raleigh

A&H:GraPC
: William Alexander Graham Papers, Private Collections, State Archives, Office of Archives and History, Raleigh

A&H:Hale
: Edward Jones Hale Papers, Private Collections, State Archives, Office of Archives and History, Raleigh

A&H:VanPC
: Zebulon Baird Vance Papers, Private Collections, State Archives, Office of Archives and History, Raleigh

A&H:Whit
: John D. Whitford Papers, Private Collections, State Archives, Office of Archives and History, Raleigh

A&H:Wiley
: Calvin H. Wiley Papers, Private Collections, State Archives, Office of Archives and History, Raleigh

Duke:Dav
: Jefferson Davis Papers, David M. Rubenstein Rare Book and Manuscript Library, Duke University, Durham, North Carolina

Duke:Holm
: Theophilus Hunter Holmes Papers, Special Collections Department, Duke University Library, Durham

Duke:Van

Zebulon Baird Vance Papers, Special Collections Department, Duke University Library, Durham

Har:Brown

Joseph Emerson Brown Papers, Manuscript Department, Harvard College Library, Harvard University, Cambridge

Har:Clin

Thomas Lanier Clingman Papers, Manuscript Department, Harvard College Library, Harvard University, Cambridge

Har:Dav

George Davis Papers, Manuscript Department, Harvard College Library, Harvard University, Cambridge

Mich:Sch

Schoff Collection, William L. Clements Library, University of Michigan, Ann Arbor

SHC:BattFM

Battle Family Papers, Southern Historical Collection, Wilson Library, University of North Carolina at Chapel Hill

SHC:Car

David Miller Carter Papers, Southern Historical Collection, Wilson Library, University of North Carolina at Chapel Hill

SHC:Gree

Wharton J. Green Papers, Southern Historical Collection, Wilson Library, University of North Carolina at Chapel Hill

SHC:Mall

Peter Mallett Papers, Southern Historical Collection, Wilson Library, University of North Carolina at Chapel Hill

SHC:Russ

Daniel Lindsay Russell Papers, Southern Historical Collection, Wilson Library, University of North Carolina at Chapel Hill

SHC:Set

Thomas Settle Papers, Southern Historical Collection, Wilson Library, University of North Carolina at Chapel Hill

SHC:Sha   John McKee Sharpe Papers, Southern Historical Collection, Wilson Library, University of North Carolina at Chapel Hill

SHC:Spen   Cornelia P. Spencer Papers, Southern Historical Collection, Wilson Library, University of North Carolina at Chapel Hill

SHC:Swain   David Lowry Swain Papers, Southern Historical Collection, Wilson Library, University of North Carolina at Chapel Hill

SHC:SWBatt   Mrs. Samuel Westray Battle Papers, Southern Historical Collection, Wilson Library, University of North Carolina Library at Chapel Hill

SHC:Yel   Edward Clements Yellowley Papers, Southern Historical Collection, Wilson Library, University of North Carolina at Chapel Hill

SHC:Van   Zebulon Baird Vance Papers, Southern Historical Collection, Wilson Library University of North Carolina at Chapel Hill

Windsor No. Ca.
Jany 1st. 1864

His Excelly.
Zeb. B. Vance
Raleigh No. Ca.

Dear Sir,

I have had an opportunity to day, to see and converse with man[y] of the prominent citizens of this county at their request, I address you this communication—The past season was a most disastrous one to us. The entire crop of the Roanoke river, was utterly destroyed by the freshets, and in addition to that calamity, our low-lands yielded an exceedingly small crop—Beside this, more probably than one half of the effective labor of the country, has left it, either by being in the army—having gone to the enemy; or by being removed to places supposed to be more secure than this. And yet the country is swarming with Confederate, State, and other agents buying up and carrying from the county all its provisions—We have agents here from Virginia, professing to have authority from you to buy in the county of Bertie, where we are probably as destitute as any other community in the State—If my memory serves me correctly the General Assembly passed resolutions requesting you to use your influence and authority to prevent provisions from being carried from [thi]s State—The exigencies of this community imperiously demand in my judgment this should be done—Corn here now is selling at $35 per bushel and what these agents will run pork to, if they go unchecked there is no telling—Why these cormorants should be allowed to make Bertie, the scene of their operations I cannot imagine. Certainly not because, there is any superfluity here—Our country for the want of adequate protection is fast becoming a solitude, and if all the provisions are carried away, we shall be still worse off the coming year because our people will not have the means of making a crop—From these considerations we respectfully ask the [sic] you will issue your proclamation, prohibiting the carrying of provisions out of the State, except by the Confederate Government, and also to use your influence to have the tenth commuted for many ex-[*portion missing*] in so far as they may be needed [*blotted*] the troops in this section—

This has been written very hurriedly and at night, and I see so badly I cannot read it. But I think Col. Barnes[1] will assure you the picture which I have drawn of our situation is not too highly colored. Wishing you many happy returns of this once <y> joyful season I remain

> Very truly & Resy.
> Your Obt. Sert.
> David Outlaw[2]

[*Endorsed*] Ansr. that I will do all I can to have the tything commuted but that as we are drawing large supplies from S.C. I can not issue the proclamation he desires &c

ZBV

[1]David Alexander Barnes, ZBV's aide. *Dictionary of North Carolina Biography*, s.v. "Barnes, David Alexander."

[2]Bertie County lawyer, legislator, and congressman. He served in the state senate, 1862-1864. *Dictionary of North Carolina Biography*, s.v. "Outlaw, David"; John L. Cheney, ed., *North Carolina Government, 1585-1979: A Narrative and Statistical History* (Raleigh: Department of the Secretary of State, 1981), 329.

Thomas W. Ritter to ZBV   A&H:GP

Carthage
Jan the 1st. 1864

His Excellency
Governor Vance

Dear Sir

I received yours of the 23rd. December/63[1] as for Maj. Dowd[2] having given orders to burn those Still houses I know nothing about as I stated to you that the men that burned the houses stated that they were acting under orders from the maj. and maj. Dowd said that he give no such orders I dont know that maj. Dowd knew anything at all about it I was asked to state the facts to you which I did and as for the two men that was shot Davis & Brewer[3] as for their being shot trying to Escape from the guard that I do not think is so they certainly were parted from the other two <illegible> conscripts that were taken at the same time and carried a different road to the camp and before they got to the camp they Davis & Brewer were parted and found Shot and were fast tied when found and no doubt were seperated on purpos to be shot Davis I supose was found Shot by a log as if he was setting on the log when Shot and fell over by the side of the log with his brains shot out and as for being ring leaders of a band of Robers I now nothing about I have no doubt from report that they were both bad men and were concerned in a great deal of the Stealing that has been Done in this county There has ben a man by the name of George Moore[4] Kiled Since by Adams Brewer Moore was a poore man with a large familly was conscripted under the last call and did not choose to go to the war and took the thicket there was some bad reports on Moore but I think he was accused of moore that he was gilty he was just trying to keep out of the way becaus he did not want to go the war and Brewer and a man by the name of Peter Garner[5] sliped up to Moore & two others and without saying a word presented and fired killing Moore and wounding one <other> of the others there was a man standing talking to them when they were Shot who give the facts as they were Brewer Shot Moore and had Swore before on several occasions <tha> I supose that he would Shoot him if he ever come up with him Brewer is an old man dont belong to the army no the Militia and Peter Garner is a conscript himself and has so managed to be detailed I believe to cetch conscripts and Deserters he shot the other and wounded him very badley they had no armes nor nothing to fight with I supose and could have been <illegible> taken very easy without shooting the people are geting tired of Peter Garners condict any way and want him gone sent to the army where he should be and as for Brewer the majority of the people want him delt with as <he> a murderr should be Moore lived in Moore County but was Shot just over the line in Randolph County it is two bad for men to be murderd up in that Style any other information that is wanting in the premacies can be had at any time

most respectfully yours
Thos. W. Ritter[6]

[*Endorsed*] Ex. Dept. of N.C. Jany 4th./64 Res. referred to the Solicitor Buxton[7], Fayetteville N.C. with the request that he will examine into the killing of these men & the burning of some distillaries alleged to have been done in Moore County by Confederate Soldiers & Home Guards, & report results to me

Z. B. Vance

[*Endorsed*] File carefully

Z B V

[1]Not extant.

[2]Clement Dowd of Moore County, a major in the Home Guard. Formerly he had been an officer in ZBV's regiment, Twenty-sixth North Carolina Troops. After the war he became a biographer of ZBV, mayor of Charlotte, a congressman, revenue collector, and banker. *Dictionary of North Carolina Biography*, s. v. "Dowd, Clement."

[3]Adams Brewer, a slaveholder and vigilante who tracked down men he considered disloyal to the Confederacy, accompanied Capt. Nathan A. Ramsay's 61st Regiment into Chatham, Moore, and Randolph counties to arrest deserters. Brewer lived in the Brower's mill neighborhood of Randolph County. His neighbors considered him a "hot head secesh." Victoria E. Bynum, *The Long Shadow of the Civil War: Southern Dissent and Its Legacies* (Chapel Hill: University of North Carolina Press, 2010), 43-45. U.S. Bureau of the Census, Federal Manuscript Census, Randolph County, Moore County, N.C. Bynum found no record of Brewer in the 1870 census.

[4]George Moore resided in Moore County. See Bynum, *The Long Shadow of the Civil War*, 44.

[5]According to Bynum (who cites William Auman), Peter Garner was an "extreme secessionist." (see Notes, p. 158). Bynum, *The Long Shadow of the Civil War*. See also William Trotter, *Silk Flags and Cold Steel: The Piedmont*, vol. 1 of *The Civil War in North Carolina* (Winston-Salem, N.C.: John F. Blair, 1991) for Adams Brewer and Peter Garner.

[6]Moore County legislator, 1862-1864. Cheney, *North Carolina Government*, 330, 357n.

[7]Ralph Potts Buxton, judge and politician, was solicitor of the Fayetteville Judicial District until the war's end. *Dictionary of North Carolina Biography*, s.v. "Buxton, Ralph Potts."

ZBV to William A. Graham A&H:GraPC

State of North Carolina,
Executive Department,
Raleigh, Jany. 1st. 1863[4]

Confidential

My Dear Sir,[1]

It seems that all my efforts to preserve the unity of our party and the harmony of its counsels are to be frustrated at last. I have heard since the adjournment of the Legislature, that it was resolved to agitate the calling of a Convention to take the State out of the Confederacy. Last night I learned that Holden[2] had proposed a sett of resolutions and sent down to Johnson County to be passed at a public meeting next week, and that a series of similar meetings are to follow with a view to forcing the Legislature into calling the Convention in May. I also learn that a Convention Candidate is to oppose me unless I agree to the scheme &c &c. Now Sir, what should I do? I can not of course favour such a thing for any existing cause. I will see the Conservative party blown into a thousand atoms and Holden and his understrappers in hell (if you will pardon the violence of the expression) before I will consent to a course which I think would bring dishonor and ruin upon both State & Confederacy! We are already ruined, almost, but are not yet dishonored, neither have we been the cause of ruin to others. With my help we never shall be. Is Holden the leader of the Conservative party? If so I dont belong to it. Why will old whigs and Union men surrender the leadership of their party to a man who has denounced them all his life, who has done more to produce our present troubles than any man in it, and who is moreover a known demagogue & a man of bad character?

If such is to be the case, a split is inevitable, to say nothing of the other & more serious consequences likely to ensue to the country. I regret exceedingly that you have resigned yr seat in the Senate, but as you are happily out of this trouble I hope you will not refuse me your advice as heretofore.

Very truly yrs
Z. B. Vance

[1]William Alexander Graham, planter, lawyer, and political leader in the state—U.S. and Confederate senator, governor, and U.S. secretary of the navy. *Dictionary of North Carolina Biography*, s.v. "Graham, William Alexander."

[2]William Woods Holden, editor of the *North Carolina Standard* and leader of the peace movement. He became provisional governor after the war. *Dictionary of North Carolina Biography*, s.v. "Holden, William Woods."

John White to ZBV   A&H:GP

Hamilton Bermuda
January 2nd. 1864

His Excellency
Gov. Z B. Vance
Raleigh N.C.

Sir

On the 31st. Octr. last I wrote you from Manchester acknowledging the receipt of all State Bonds which had been forwarded to me $400,000 & $600,000 at Same time Stating that I had the business for the State so arranged as to be able to leave what was unfinished in the hands of Mess Collie & Co.[1] to compleate. At that time I Expected to have left for home soon after the middle of November the Steamer however was not ready so soon as Expected & did not Sail until the 12th. Decr. & arrived here, all safe, on the 26th. here I shall await the arrival of the Ad-Vance,[2] which I understand is Expected every day, her second cargo of Cotton had arrived at Liverpool a few days before I left London, the price had gone down from 1½ to 2. per pound. I consequently directed Mr Collie to hold it for a short time, hoping it would recover, the decline was attributed to the high rate of Bank interest.

The Ship "Arbutes" by which I had shipd. a good many goods arrived about a week since, I understand in rather a leaky condition & I fear some of the packages may in consequence have sustained some injury, to that I will attend, as soon as the goods are discharged & will make a claim for any damages, the invoices for this Shipment have been forwarded you & hope have been received. The last Shipment made was per Ship "Carl Emile" which is daily Expected to arrive the invoice for her Cargo I will send in a copy of as soon as it can be got ready.

The Steamer "Vesta" is Expected to leave for Wilmington tomorrow She takes in a package of Clothes for Col. D. A. Barnes. I have written to Mess Crenshaw & Brother to forward and also to forward to you a dispatch Box a present from Mr. Collie, hoping all may go in safely & that I may have the pleasure of seeing you soon in Raleigh.

I am
Your Obt. Servt.
Jno. White[3]

P.S. If you think it best for the State that I should remain in England until the business is entirely finished, try to let me know before I leave here for N.C. the risk of running in & out is now very much increased & if I am required to go back I prefer not taking the chance of capture, notwithstanding /my/ anxiety to get home, I am ready to do what I can for the benefit of the State in our present difficulties.

J. W.

[1]Alexander Collie and Company of England. It remained North Carolina's financial agent for securing supplies from Britain until the last days of the war. John G. Barrett, *The Civil War in North Carolina* (Chapel Hill: University of North Carolina Press, 1963), 254.

[2]The blockade steamer *Advance*, owned by the State of North Carolina, was a Wilmington partner of Alexander Collie and Company. The partnership and the company's contract with the Confederacy ended in February 1864. Stephen R. Wise, *Lifeline of the Confederacy: Blockade Running during the Civil War* (Columbia: University of South Carolina Press, 1988), 136-137.

[3]North Carolina merchant dispatched to England by ZBV as agent to purchase supplies for state troops. *Dictionary of North Carolina Biography*, s.v. "White, John."

ZBV *to David L. Swain*   A&H:VanPC

Raleigh, Jan'y 2d./64

Private

My dear Sir,[1]

The final plunge which I have been dreading and avoiding, that is to separate me from a large number of my political friends is about to be made. It is now a fixed policy of Mr. Holden and others to call a convention in May to take N.C. back to the United States, and the agitation has already begun. Resolutions advocating this course, were prepared a few days ago in the Standard office and sent to Johnson County to be passed at a public meeting next week: and a series of meetings are to be held all over the State.

For any cause now existing or likely to exist, I can never consent to this course. Never. But should it be inevitable and I be unable to prevent it—as I have no right to suppose I could—believing that it would be ruin alike to State and Confederacy, producing war and devastation at home, and that it would steep the name of North Carolina in infamy and make her memory a reproach among the nations, it is my determination to quietly retire to the army and find a death which will enable my children to say that their father was not consenting to their degradation. This sounds no doubt, a little wild and bombastic, not to say foolish, but is for your eye only. I feel Sir in many respects as a son towards you, and when the many acts of kindness I have received at your hands is remembered, and the parental interest you have always manifested for my welfare, the feeling is not unnatural. I therefore approach you frankly in this matter.

I will not present the arguments against the proposed proceeding. There is something to be said on both sides. We are sadly pushed to the wall by the enemy on every side it is true. That can be answered by military men and a reference to history; many peoples have been worse off, infinitely, and yet triumphed. Our finances and other material resources are not worse off than were those of our fathers in 1780-81, though repudiation is inevitable. Almost every <question> /argument/ can be answered, against the chances of our success, but one. That is, the cries of women and little children for bread! Of all others, that is hardest for a man of humane sentiments to meet, especially when the sufferers rejoin to your appeals to their patriotism, "You Governor have plenty; your children have never felt want." Still, no great political or moral blessing ever has been or can be attained without suffering. Such is our moral Constitution, that liberty and independence can only be gathered of blood and misery sustained and fostered by devoted patriotism and heroic manhood. This requires a deep hold on the popular heart, *and our people will not pay this price* I am satisfied for their national independence! I am convinced of it. But Sir, in tracing the sad story of the backing down, the self imposed degradation of a great people, the historian shall *not* say it was due to the weakness of their Governor and that Saul was consenting unto their death! Neither do I desire for the sake of a sentiment, to involve others in a ruin which they might avoid by following more ignoble councils. As God liveth, there is nothing which I would not do or dare, for the people who, so far beyond my merits, have honored me. But in resisting this attempt to lead them back, humbled and degraded, to the arms of their enemies who have slaughtered their sons, outraged their daughters, and wasted their fields with fire; and lay them bound at the feet of a master who promises them *only life*, provided they will swear to justify and uphold his own perjury and surrender to the hangman those whom they themselves placed in the position which constitutes their crime, in resisting this I say, I feel that I am serving them truly, worthily.

In approaching this, the crisis of North Carolinas fate—certainly of my own career—I could think of no one to whom I could more appropriately go for advice than yourself, for the reasons before stated. If you can say anything to throw light on my paths, or enable me to avoid the rocks before me I shall be thankful My great anxiety now, as I can scarcely hope to avoid the contemplated action of the State, is to avoid civil war and to preserve life and property as far as may be possible. With due consideration on the part of public men, which I fear is not to be looked for, this might be avoided. It shall be my aim under God, at all events.

All the circumstances considered, do you think I ought again to be a candidate? It is a long time until the election it is true, but the issue will be upon the country by Spring. My inclination is, to take the stump early and to spend all my time and strength in trying to warn and harmonize the people. If I go down before the current I shall "—Perish if it must be so, At bay, destroying many a foe"[2]

> Believe me my dear Sir,
> respectfully & sincerely
> Yours
> Z. B. Vance

[1]David Lowry Swain, president of the University of North Carolina, lawyer, former judge, legislator, and governor. *Dictionary of North Carolina Biography*, s.v. "Swain, David Lowry."

[2]Quotation from Lord Byron's *Mayeppa*, a Romantic narrative poem written in 1819.

James A. Seddon to ZBV   A&H:GP

> Confederate States of America,
> War Department,
> Richmond, Va. January 4 1864

His Excellency
Z B Vance
Governor of North Carolina
Raleigh N.C.

Sir

Your letter of the 29th ult,[1] with the resolutions of the Legislature of North Carolina relative to impressments in that State has been received.

The Department has taken the utmost care by its General Orders, and by its instructions in writing and otherwise, to mitigate as far as practicable the evils consequent upon the execution of the law relative to impressments. These orders provide that, "necessary supplies which any person may leave for the consumption of himself, his family, employees, slaves, or to carry on his ordinary mechanical, manufacturing or agricultural employments, shall not be impressed, until further orders, which will not be given unless under imperative exigencies for the supply of the army, not to impress necessaries of subsistence to man, owned by producers in transitu to market, or after arrival at market, unless retained an unreasonable time from sale to consumers."

The 7th Section of the Act of Congress of the 26th March last, which has been published as a part of the instructions, requires, that the supplies to be exempt as family supplies, shall be ascertained by appraisers and that the judgement of the appraisers is to be conclusive on the impressing officer. Each citizen who claims to hold the property impressed for his family supply, is entitled to claim the benefit of an appraisement and to designate one of the appraisers, who shall act with an appraiser to be appointed by the impressing officer, and who is entitled to aid in the selection of an umpire in case of their disagreement.

The Department has enjoined upon the Commissary Department, that the powers entrusted to it should be employed with discrimination and care, and that all the directions of the Act of Congress and of this Department for the execution of the Act should be scrupulously fulfilled. This Department is constantly employed in correcting irregularities in the execution of these regulations, and the 11th Section of the Act furnishes a remedy to every citizen aggrieved.

In the report from this Department which has been submitted to Congress, a copy of which is sent to your Excellency with this letter, you will find a statement of the difficulties under which the Government labors in providing for the subsistence of the army, and how much of the evils complained of is the result of inexorable necessity. The Department /has/ heretofore, and will in future exert itself, to <limit> /confine/ these evils within the exact limits of that necessity.

Very Respectfully
Your Obdt Servt.
James A Seddon[2]
Secretary of War

[1]In Frontis W. Johnston and Joe A. Mobley, eds., *The Papers of Zebulon Baird Vance*, 2 vols. to date (Raleigh: Division of Archives and History, Department of Cultural Resources, 1963-), 2:356.

[2]James Alexander Seddon, Confederate secretary of war, November 1862-February 1865. *Dictionary of American Biography*, s.v. "Seddon, James Alexander."

James A. Seddon to ZBV   A&H:GP

Confed States of America
War Department
Richmond Jany 4 1864

His Excellency
Z. B. Vance
Gov of N.C.
Raleigh

Your Excellency'

I have the honor to acknowledge the receipt of your letter of the 23d. ulto[1] in relation to cotton kindly loaned by the State of North Carolina to the War Department.

I am not informed at what points the cotton was delivered, but it would gratify me if I could meet your wishes and make immediate delivery at Wilmington, or at such other place as would be most agreeable to you.— but the difficulties of rail-road transportation are such now that I can only hope to discharge the debt in partial payments from time to time as this transportation will admit.

If however, it will be agreeable to you to allow the cotton to be paid for I will direct that this shall be done immediately and at such price as you may consider just and proper.

The Ordnance Dept, for which the cotton was borrowed, have a supply at Augusta and if it would suit your purpose to receive the cotton there I can order that it shall be turned over immediately to such officers as you may designate.

I appreciate your promptness in making the loan and desire as far as possible to meet your wishes fully in making such return as may be most agreeable to you.

I have the honor to be
Very Respy
Yr obt svt
James A Seddon
Secy of War

[1]In Johnston and Mobley, *Papers of Vance*, 2:349.

Paul F. Faison to ZBV   A&H:GP

Hd. Qrs. 56th. Regt. NCT
Asheboro NC Jany 4th./64

Gov Vance

Dear Sir

We have now been in this section some three weeks & so far have accomplished but little—I have my men scattered over the adjoining counties at the most suitable points—the deserters have numerous friends which makes it more difficult to catch them—it will require time to do so—and probably an increase of my force to occupy the whole section at once to prevent their evading the troops by going from one place to another as they /(the soldiers)/ change their <(the soldiers)> stations—This would not be necessary could we live upon the country—which is impossible as it does'ent afford the supplies. We then have to draw them from Greensboro & wagon them some fifty miles & makes it necessary for small detachments to return to their comp'y Hd. Qrs. every three days—I learned a few days ago that the deserters sent from Wilkes were rapidly returning thinking our forces withdrawn—also that an entire company of cavalry had deserted from Tennesse with horses arms & accoutrements—these men have given confidence to others who are now becoming very bold—Cap't Whites comp'y of my reg't about (50) men was left there—I think this too small a force & shall start another comp'y for that county to morrow. I shall then certainly need the two (2) comp'y's of mine now at Weldon—they were included in the order detaching the reg't for this duty—but Gen'l Ransom[1] retained them & has since declined sending them. You will oblige me by applying for them. I certainly need them to fully accomplish the duty assigned me. I shall make an application myself but do not expect it to be granted—My men are behaving themselves remarkably well I have not heard of a single misdemeanor & hope I will not. This is decidedly disagreable service—but I hope we will be allowed to remain here during the winter as it is too late to prepare winter quarters elsewhere

Very Resptly
Your Obt. Servt & friend
P. F. Faison
Col 56th. NC Troops

The deserters /of Wilkes/ (cavalry) killed one of men last week & wounded one or two of the home guard

P. F. F.

[*Endorsed*] I have written as he desired

Z B V

[1]Matt Whitaker Ransom, *Dictionary of North Carolina Biography*, s.v. "Ransom, Matt[hew] Whitaker."

ZBV to James A. Seddon   A&H:GLB

State of North Carolina
Executive Department
Raleigh Jany. 4th. 1863[4]

Hon. Jas. A. Seddon
Secy. of War
Richmond Va.

Dear Sir

I wrote you a few days ago[1] about some Cotton which this State had loaned the Confederacy at Wilmington, and was now refused to be returned. Since my letter my difficulties have become so much increased that I am compelled to appeal to you again. I have telegraphed to the Rail Roads in S.C. & Ga. and can get no cotton hauled, because the Confederacy has monopolized all the transportation. I have now three steamers bringing in our Army Stores from Bermuda, and as the Confederacy will neither allow me to transport my own cotton or pay me what it owes me, they will be compelled to stop or take cotton for Speculators. Now Sir, I submit that is not right, and will greatly injure the public service. The Confederacy has plenty of Cotton and the control of the Roads, and should at once deliver me 1800 Bales at Wilmington or permit me to transport my own from Georgia to keep the vessels running—I have a large supply of valuable stores at Bermuda, and heavy contracts for bacon.

If not got in this winter, they will not get in at all.

Your prompt action in this matter will greatly promote the public good and will much oblige

Very Respectfully Yrs.
Z. B. Vance

[1]See ZBV to James A. Seddon, December 23, 1863, in Johnston and Mobley, *Papers of Vance*, 2:349.

ZBV *to William A. Graham*   A&H:GraPC

[*Telegram*]

Raleigh
Jan 4th. 1863[4]

Hillsboro

Gov. Graham—

Mr. Geo. Davis[1] having been made Attorney General has resigned his seat in Senate—I will appoint you to fill the unexpired term If you will accept it—Let me know immediately as I desire to convene my Council of State

Z. B. Vance

[1]Confederate senator who became last attorney general of the Confederacy. *Dictionary of North Carolina Biography*, s.v. "Davis, George."

ZBV *to Theodore Andreae*   A&H:GLB

State of North Carolina
Executive Department
Raleigh Jany. 5th. 1863[4]

Mr. T. Andreae[1]
Wilmington N.C.

Yrs[2] is recd., I regret very much that you did not send the Hansa to Bermuda, as I have no freight at Nassau. The only object I had in view in purchasing an interest in her was to get my cargoes brought in from Bermuda. I would not risk one dollar in any vessel to bring in freight for other parties. I telegraphed you to take the States Coal, 90 tons and send her to Bermuda and I learn that you took 40 tons of it and still sent the vessel to Nassau. This will not do. If I cannot have the inward cargo, I shall have to decline proceeding with Mr. Collie any further. The Don will probably come in without sufficient coal and will have the same excuse for returning to Nassau. Thus time is lost and I am compelled to run two risks of capture to get one cargo.

It seems to me that we misunderstood each other about the Cotton. I told you I would deliver two thousand (2000) Bales at Wilmington, out of my stores at Raleigh, if you would furnish me with a guarantee that Mr. Collie would claim no damage or indemnity if, in consequences of this loan, I failed to comply with the terms of the bonds he holds on this State to deliver this amount promptly after peace.

I expected of course you would replace it at some more remote point, and as I cannot control transportation in other States, I might not be able to deliver it as agreed upon. Or if this was not acceptable, I would deliver the Cotton in Wilmington in discharge of the bonds, as proposed by Mr. Collie in a letter to Mr. John White, Agent of N.C. in Manchester dated [blank] 1863.[3]

This was intended to accommodate Mr. Collie with Cotton for his Steamers in case you failed to get transportation from Augusta, which I have failed to do so far. You have as yet furnished me no such guarantee and decline to take it in satisfaction of the bonds. I cannot sell it to you of course, as I have it safely housed for Mr. Collie's benefit. Mr. Carter[4] will be instructed, will be instructed [sic] to replace that which you advanced to load the Hansa, and the other as it goes down will remain in his possession until we come to a more definite understanding. I do not think it practicable to import an engine for our purpose alone. Hope we shall be able to get along without it.

Very Respectfully Yours
Z. B. Vance

[1]Theodore Andreae, agent in Wilmington for Alexander Collie and Company. See Alexander Collie to ZBV, December 7, 1863, in Johnston and Mobley, *Papers of Vance*, 2:337.

[2]Theodore Andreae to ZBV, January 1, 1864, A&H:GP.

[3]October 28, 1863, A&H:GLB.

[4]Thomas Carter, special agent for supplying the *Advance*. See ZBV to Power Low and Company, January 6, 1864, in this volume.

John A. Gilmer to ZBV　　　　　　　A&H:VanPC

Greensboro N C.
Jany 5th. 1864

Govr. Vance

Dear Sir.

Your confidential note,[1] dated the 1st. but mailed this morning, was received today—I think it Exceedingly dangerous to give any countenance to the calling of a convention at this time—I had a long conversation with one of these convention men last night—I asked him what good purposes he Expected to Effect by a convention—He replied that the convention would protest, remonstrate, & propose the terms on which N.C was willing to agree for peace—ask the Sister Southern States to call conventions & come into conference with N.C &c—I asked him then, Suppose Lincoln & the U. S. Congress, gave no attention, or refused to reply, What then?—He answered, that in that Event, he would have N.C Secede from the Confederacy, & then make the very best terms with Lincoln & the Congress of the U.S. that she could—In fact when he came to run out his results he became confused, & ran away upon another Subject—

You & thousands of old Whigs conservatives had nothing to do with bringing on this terrible crisis—Before God & the world our consciences will forever stand acquitted—But we were beaten down—and trodden under foot by the precipitators of our own section—We were forced by the madness, which they engengered and fostered, to join them in a common declaration for nationality—We are pledged to the fight—Our word, our honor is pledged to the fight—There is no room for us to fight jockey—We ought, & I hope will all be good and true to the Cause we have pledged ourselves, and in which are now so clearly involved the issues of life & death to us—If we make good our nationality we must stand together with stout hearts and unflincing nerves—If we desired the most favorable terms, we must do the same thing—In this great Struggle to doubt, is to be damned— At least this should be the Watch word, & on Every tongue, seared to Every heart—Eight Millions of Southern freemen, sustained by the labor of four millions of slaves, scattered over 900,000 square miles of the best Territy in the world, properly aroused, and, appealing to Giver of all good things, never can & never will be conquered—United under the blessing of Providence, we must prevail—The Southern people properly advised of the dangers that await them, will become united, and stand a strong pull, a long pull, and a pull altogether—If not they have greatly degenerated from the Spirit of their noble Sires—I cannot for a moment cherish the mortifying thought that /the/ Southern people of this generation, have so degenerated as ever to entertain the proposition of of [sic] submission to Lincoln's proclamation, & make for themselves such a degrading history, from the pages of which our children will turn with scorn & contempt—

To attempt to settle this matter by the separate action of N.C. or the separate action of N.C & other States, will certainly end in civil war among ourselves, & make our State & condition indescribably worse—

If our foolish Congress, would restore the franking privalege, and address every man, woman, and child in the Confederacy, and thereby arouse in every Southern heart the true Southern Spirit the work would be done—we would lack nothing of men or the Senews of War—The whole South might Easily be aroused to a sense of our danger, & of our duty—Appeals of love and inspiriting patriotism, are worth more than all the devices of force, and harsh Enactments—The people must be induced to love their Lawgivers & their Government—They must believe & feel that these are not only their agents, but their best friends—Then the yoke & burdens of the laws & of the Government, which they love & respect /will/ rest Easily on their shoulders—There should be no legislation, tinctured with a suspicion of the people—The Government should scrupulously adhere to its plighted faith to all her Citizens—But as a true and devoted friend to Southern happiness & prosperity, I do verily believe our President and Congress are deficient & wanting in these considerations, and the results may be more ruinous to us than the power of our Enemy—

I have an abiding confidence that God does not intend to let us sacrifice ourselves or our Enemies to destroy us—

I have already given my opinion as to State conventions—we must sleep on our arms until we get peace—

If however Congress should pass a resolution, prefaced with the most solemn pledge and assurance that we are united on nationality, that for the sake of avoiding the shedding of human blood, and the horrors of the war, <that> /we/ were ready and anxious to unite in a commission, to see whether the two sections could not agree upon proper terms of separation, intimating a willingness to form a Diet between the two Governments, in which there should only be two votes, & Northern & Southern ones and the Suggestions or recommendations of this Diet only to be binding when ratified by both Governments—I say should something of this kind be suggested by our Congress, it would introduce a new subject for consideration on the part of both Sections, and lead to terms of peace and safe terms of nationality—I think thus the South might safely & easily propose—The people of the North are anxious that the war should end—This new idea might, and doubtless /would/ seize the popular mind of the North & South—They already know how the people of Each Section are embittered against Each other—That in Consequence they are not likely ever to live any more at peace under the same Government &c &c. that by Such an arrangement, safe & consistant with perfect independence of Each, neither side is Exactly Whipped, & some great good including peace may grow out of it—

My advice would be to have no rupture with Holden—But to treat him with all the common civilities of life, but on all suitable occasions to speak freely of my political views & opinions—

The Secessionists in the State are too weak <in the State> to have any candidate,—If you pursue the course, which I suggest, improved by your better judgement, we shall reelect you next August with an increased Majority—If [Bedford] Brown had appeared on the stump against me, & had taken ground against my views, I should have beaten him in this District at least 4000 votes

I was determined, when I saw that secession was likely to succeed, never to have it said that I did it—So now we have separated and set up for ourselves, and if we fail of nationality, I am Equally determined that it shall never be said that I failed in the performance of my part—

Please pardon the great haste with which I have written, but as I have written only for your inspection, I have written with perfect freedom—

> Yours truly
> John A Gilmer[2]

When Mr. Holden begins his machine some friend must write you a letter & by answer you can get into the papers in proper time & manner

[Endorsed] File—private

ZBV

[1]Not extant.

[2]John Adams Gilmer, lawyer, large slaveholder, former state senator (Whig), and U.S. congressman, strongly opposed to secession. He became a Confederate congressman in the last year of the war. *Dictionary of North Carolina Biography*, s.v. "Gilmer, John Adams."

James A. Seddon to ZBV   A&H:VanPC

Confederate States of America,
War Department,
Richmond, Va. Jan 5 1864.

His Excellency
Z. B. Vance,
Governor of N.C.
Raleigh, N.C.

Sir,

I have received your letter[1] proposing to place certain State troops under the command of Col. W. J. Clark,[2] provided he be made a Brigadier General.

In reply I have the honor to say, that I do not understand you as proposing to transfer the troops of the State to the Confederate service, and yet without such transfer, I do not see how they could be placed under the command of a Confederate Brigadier. As there is no vacant North Carolina Brigade to which Col. Clark could be assigned, if promoted, the proposed action would withdraw him from his regiment and leave him unemployed.

Very Respecfully
Your obdt. servt.
James A Seddon
Secretary of War

[1]December 16, 1863, in Johnston and Mobley, *Papers of Vance*, 2:343-344.

[2]William John Clarke, prewar army officer, lawyer, and state comptroller, commander of Twenty-fourth Regiment North Carolina Troops, and postwar Republican state senator and judge. *Dictionary of North Carolina Biography*, s.v. "Clarke, William John."

ZBV *to William A. Graham*   A&H:GraPC

[*Telegram*]

Raleigh
Jany 5 1864

Gov Graham

Senator George Davis has been made attorney General & has resigned[1]—I will appoint you to fill the unexpired term if you will accept and can go on <at once> immediately—Please let me know at once by Telegraph.

Z. B. Vance

[1]From the Confederate Senate.

Theodore Andreae to ZBV   A&H:GP

Wilmington
6 January 64

To His Excellency
Governor Vance
Raleigh

Dear Sir

I received your telegram[1] dated yt. day.—I had already *written* to you that the Don had arrived, they will not allow arrivals of Steamers to be telegraphed.—In reply to your telegr. I sent the following message: ["]D. arrived all safe and will leave to'morrow for Bermuda. I wrote to you about her. It would be advisable that you should telegraph to the Secretary of War that you have charge of the Don and Hansa and have to load them by contract—that he is to inform his agent /here/by wire not to interfere with them."—The agent of the war Department wrote to me that he claimed one third of the room in the Don for the Government. I replied that by your order I was loading her with Cotton & won't send her out—that you had by contract acquired the management of the Steamer of which you were part owner & I have no doubt this must put matters all right—but in order to avoid delay I thought it best to settle it by wire.

Expecting your reply to my last I remain Dear Sir

Your obdt. Servt.
Th. Andreae

P.S. I just received your telegram[2] about purchase of Bacon for you in Nassau. I'll write out pr Steamer to morrow to buy it if it can be got & if not to apply to the Government agent for a cargo of Bacon for them.

Trly yours
T.A.

[1]Not extant.
[2]Not extant.

James A. Seddon to ZBV   A&H:GP

[Telegram]

Richmond
Jany 6th. 1864

Gov. Vance
Raleigh

I regret to learn that because of an interest of your state in the Steamer Don objection is made to its conformation to the regulations about taking out government cotton the necessities of the Govt really require adhearance to this regulation & really hope that you will not encourage or allow in your name the infringement of it

J. A. Seddon
sec War

ZBV to Theodore Andreae   A&H:GLB

State of North Carolina
Executive Department
Raleigh Jany 6th. 1864

Mr. T. Andreae
Wilmington

Dr. Sir

I am glad to hear of the arrival of the Don at Wilmington, I consider her as partly mine as per agreement. You will proceed at once to load her with Cotton, one fourth for the State to be furnished by Mr. Carter and send her to Bermuda as soon as possible, to return with Cargo of freight for the State &c. When can she get off? And what is the chance for getting down more coals? I will send another load of cotton this week.

Yours respectfully
Z. B. Vance

ZBV to Power, Low and Co.   A&H:GLB

State of North Carolina
Executive Department
Raleigh Jany. 6th. 1864.

Messrs Power Lowe & Co.[1]
Wilmington N.C.

Gentlemen,

Your favors[2] are rec'd., I regret exceedingly the long delay of the Advance both on your account and my own. But I shall confidently expect her by the 10th. or 12th., and every preparation must be made to send her out instantly. I have not sufficient coals on hand and the prospect for getting more is bad on account of the accident to the mines. Can you assist me in getting them? I have a Special Agent in Wilmington for this purpose, Mr. Thos. Carter, but fear he will be unable to supply her. I will send another load of Cotton down immediately.

As to lightening the vessel by cutting away her upper works, I see no objection to it except the one /of/ time. If carpenters could be put at work in transitu and while in port I should be willing. I learn also that there is a vast accumulation of dirt & rubbish in her hold and coal bunks which should be removed. Telegraph her condition, cargo &c. promptly on her arrival. As at present informed, I think I should prefer having the Cotton in S. W. Georgia, as it seems to me that region is safer & more accessible.

I will let you hear further on this subject before long, as also the making of your friends the consignees of the vessel in Europe.

> Very Respectfully
> Yr. obt. svt.
> Z. B. Vance

[1]Owned a half interest in the *Advance*, as of December 1863. Wise, *Lifeline of the Confederacy*, 157, 286.
[2]Power, Low and Co. to ZBV, January 1, 1864, A&H:GP.

ZBV *to James A. Seddon*   A&H:GP

> State of North Carolina
> Executive Department
> Raleigh Jany. 7th. 1864

Hon James A Seddon

Sir

Your dispatch of the 6th.[1] asking me not to object to making the Steamer "Don" conform to the regulations of the Confederate Authorities in regard to transporting Government Cotton, requires a more detailed reply than I can transmit by telegraph.

I have now at Bermuda and on the way there, Eight or ten Cargoes of Supplies of the very first importance to the army and the people. Consisting chiefly of some 40,000 blankets, 40,000 pairs shoes, large quantities of army cloth, leather and 112,000 pairs of Cotton Cards, machinery & findings to refit twenty six of our principal Cotton & woolen factories, dye stuffs, lubricating oils &c. In addition to which I have made large purchases of bacon. Knowing that our steamer could not bring these cargoes in before Spring, at which time I anticipate the closing of the port, if not sooner, and that the risk was increasing daily, I sold one half of the State Steamer "Ad'Vance" and purchased of Messrs Collie & Co one fourth interest in four Steamers the "Don" & the "Hansa" and two others now building for the purpose of hurrying these supplies in. The terms of sale give the State one fourth the outward Cargo and the *whole* of the inward—Nothing being carried for speculators whatever. The "Hansa", which recently left Wilmington, not having coal enough to take her to take her [sic] to Bermuda, where my freight is, was instructed to load at Nassau with Confederate bacon, so determined was I that the whole capacity of these steamers should be employed for the public good. In return for this Messrs. Collie & Co. did expect they would be relieved from the burden of giving one third of their outward capacity to the Confd. Govt. and I did also.

Should one third be given to the Confederacy and one fourth to the State outward and to the latter the whole of the return cargo, I submit that it would amount to a prohibition of the business, neither would it comport with justice or sound policy.

It is a little remarkable to me that the entire importing operations of this State, which have been so successful and so beneficial to the cause, seems to have met with little else than down right opposition, rather than Encouragement from the Confederate Government. In its very inception, Mr. Mason[2] our Comr. in England laid the strong hand on my agents and positively forbad them putting a bond on market for five months after they landed in England. Then came vexations and irritating quarantine delays at Wilmington (enforced by the military, not the civil authorities) though our foreign depot was at great cost and inconvenience made at Bermuda instead of Nassau to avoid this. Then seizing of my coal at Wilmington occurred, and the denial of facilities to get it from the mines &c. It was not until after my decided remonstrance to you in November, that I met with any thing else than an evident hostility in the operations of my steamers And now if the regulations in regard to private blockade runners are enforced, I think it highly probable that this line will be stopped entirely, as the profits will scarcely justify the risk. A great deal of this I am aware is attributable to the want of discretion on the part of Subordinate officers as well as the want of foresight displayed in the oppression of every industrial interest of the country by Army Officers. Yet I have had it to contend with. After this statement I leave it with you to say whither the regulations referred to shall be enforced. If they are I shall certainly countermand the Sailing of the two other Steamers now expected, and would suggest for the benefit of the Dpt. that it would be much better to *purchase* than to *seize* an interest in the property of Strangers, who are engaged in bringing us indispensible Supplies through a most rigorous and dangerous blockade.

> Very Respectfully,
> Yr. obt. svt.
> Z. B. Vance

[1]In this volume.

[2]James Murray Mason remained Confederate diplomatic commissioner to England until the war's end. *Dictionary of American Biography*, s.v. "Mason, James Murray."

Theodore Andreae to ZBV   A&H:GP

Wilmington
7 January 64.

To His Excellency
Governor Vance
Raleigh

Dear Sir

Your favor of 5 inst[1] is to hand and I regret you are disappointed at the Hansa going to Nassau.—I gave you the reason—She had no coal for the trip & if you were informed that she took 40 tons of your coal you were misinformed—for she took none. The coal you have here is very small and dusty & the engineers are afraid of it for that reason—the captains because it smokes very much. The "Don" has taken some of your coal & will as telegraphed to you—proceed to Bermuda for a cargo of your goods there. The Hansa shall on her return proceed there as well & both steamers will continue on this route until your stores there are exhausted.—

As regards the 2000 Bales of Cotton I am ready to furnish you with a guaranty that Mr. Collie will claim no damages or indemnity if in consequence of this accomodation you fail to comply with the terms of your bonds—to deliver this amount promptly after peace. I will replace the Cotton at Augusta *at once*. There is communication with Savannah by water from Augusta & transportation to the Sea will thereby be comparatively easy.—If you will get drawn up a guaranty such as will be quite satisfactory to you I will sign it & return it.—As soon as the "Don" has left, I'll call upon you at Raleigh as I am desirous of having a conversation with you respecting the account keeping of this venture &c. In the meantime I should thank you to instruct Mr. Carter to get about 700 Bales of your Cotton *compressed*—the Cotton I furnished for you was all compressed & for the Steamers we have running we must ship all Cottons compressed. I'll not have Cotton enough without these 700 B. for the Steamers when they return.—I hear from the agent of the Secretary of War that he has (the Secretary of War) telegraphed to you with respect to shipping of Government Cotton. I hope you have been able to settle this point.—

> Believe me Dear Sir
> Your obdt. servt.
> Th. Andreae

[1]In this volume.

ZBV to James A. Seddon   A&H:GLB

> State of North Carolina
> Executive Department
> Raleigh Jany. 7th. 1864

Hon. J. A. Seddon
Secy. of War

Dr. Sir

Yours of the 4th[1] in relation to the Cotton due this State from the Confederacy, is to hand.

Unless it was delivered somewhere within N.C. it would be of no use to me whatever, as I cannot command transportation beyond the limits of this State. My demand for its return now arises from the fact that I cannot get a bale brought from Georgia to supply my steamers.

The turning over to me of Cotton in Georgia therefore would not relieve me of my present difficulty in the slightest degree, unless you could furnish me transportation for it. If but 500 bales could be sent me per month, I would try to make out. Should it be found impossible to deliver me the Cotton at Wilmington I would designate a point at which I would receive the amount borrowed, as it is out of the question for me to receive pay for it now. The State is obliged to have that amount and it could not be bought for any price the Gov't. would be willing to give.

> Very Respectfully
> Yr. obt. svt.
> Z. B. Vance

[1]In this volume.

ZBV to Theodore Andreae A&H:GLB

State of North Carolina
Executive Department
Raleigh Jany 7th. 1864

Mr. Thomas Andreae
Wilmington, N.C.

Dr. Sir,

There are about 1000 prisoners of the troops of this State in Northern prisons who are suffering for clothing. Mr. Commissioner Ould[1] of the office of Exchange, informs me that money can be sent to them to purchase clothing, and for this purpose I desire a bill of exchange on London. My own check on Mr. Collie (for Cotton Sales) might not be received. Could you give me a check on your house, which is doubtless well known in N York, and take my check on Mr. Collie? The amount I desire is six thousand dollars, in two bills of three thousand dollars each. If you can manage this for me, I shall be greatly obliged. Let me hear immediately.

Yrs &c
Z B. Vance.

[1]Robert Ould, Confederate agent for exchange of prisoners of war. Jon L. Wakelyn, *Biographical Dictionary of the Confederacy* (Westport, Conn.: Greenwood Press, 1977), 336.

Jefferson Davis to ZBV A&H:GP

Executive Office
Richmond,
January 8th. 1864.

His Exceley
Z. B. Vance
Govr. of N.C.
Raleigh

Dear Sir;

I have received your letter of 30th. ulto.[1] containing suggestions of the measures to be adopted for the purpose of removing "the sources of discontent" in North Carolina. The contents of the letter are substantially the same as those of the letter[2] addressed by you to Senator Dortch,[3] extracts of which were by him read to me.

I remarked to Mr. Dortch that you were probably not aware of the obstacles to the course you indicated, and without expressing any opinion on the merits of the proposed policy, I desired him in answering your letter to invite suggestions as to the method of opening negotiations, and as to the terms which you thought should be offered to the enemy. I felt persuaded you would appreciate the difficulties as soon as your attention was called to the necessity of considering the subject in detail. As you have made no suggestions touching the manner of overcoming the obstacles I infer that you were not apprised by Mr. Dortch of my remarks to him.

Apart from insuperable objections to the line of policy you propose, (and to which I will presently advert) I cannot see how the mere material obstacles are to be surmounted. We have made three distinct efforts to communicate with the authorities at Washington, and have been invariably unsuccessful. Commissioners were sent before hostilities were begun, and the Washington government refused to see them or hear what they had to say. A second time I sent a military officer with a communication addressed by myself to President Lincoln. The letter was received by General Scott, who did not permit the officer to see Mr. Lincoln, but who promised that an answer would be sent. No answer has ever been received. The third time, a few months ago, a gentleman was sent whose position, character, and reputation were such as to ensure his reception, if the enemy were not determined to receive no proposal whatever from the government. Vice-President Stephens made a patriotic tender of his services in the hope of being able to promote the cause of humanity, and although little belief was entertained of his success, I cheerfully yielded to his suggestion that the experiment should be tried. The enemy refused to let him pass through their lines or to hold any conference with them. He was stopped before he even reached Fortress Monroe on his way to Washington. To attempt again, (in the face of these repeated rejections of all conference with us,) to send commissioners or agents to propose peace, is to invite insult and contumely, and to subject ourselves to indignity without the slightest chance of being listened to. No true citizen, no man who has our cause at heart can desire this, and the good people of North Carolina would be the last to approve of such an attempt, if aware of all the facts. So far from removing "sources of discontent" such a course would receive, as it would merit, the condemnation of those true patriots who have given their blood and their treasure to maintain the freedom, equality and independence which descended to them from the immortal heroes of King's Mountain and other battle-fields of the revolution.

If then proposals cannot be made through envoys because the enemy would not receive them, how is it possible to communicate our desire for peace otherwise than by the public announcements contained in almost every message I ever sent to Congress? I cannot recall at this time one instance in which I have failed to announce that our only desire was peace, and the only terms which formed a *sine qua non* were precisely those that you suggest, namely, "a demand only to be let alone."

But suppose it were practicable to obtain a conference through Commissioners with the government of President Lincoln, is it at this moment that we are to consider it desirable, or even at all admissable. Have we not just been apprised by that despot that we can only expect his gracious pardon by emancipating all our slaves, swearing allegiance and obedience to him and his proclamations, and becoming in point of fact the slaves of our own negroes? Can there be in North Carolina one citizen so fallen beneath the dignity of his ancestors as to accept, or to enter into conference on the basis of these terms? That there are a few traitors in the State who would be willing to betray their fellow citizens to such a degraded condition in hope of being rewarded for their treachery by an escape from the common doom, may be true. But I do not believe that the vilest wretch would accept such terms for himself.

I cannot conceive how the people of your State, than which none has sent nobler or more gallant soldiers to the field of battle, (one of whom it is your honor to be,) can have been deceived by any thing to which you refer in "the recent action of the Federal House of Representatives"—I have seen no action of that House that does not indicate by a very decided majority the purpose of the enemy to refuse all terms to the South except absolute, unconditional subjection or extermination—But if it were otherwise, how are we to treat with the House of Representatives? It is with Lincoln alone that we ever could confer and his own partisans at the North avow unequivocally that his purpose in his message and proclamation was to shut out all hope that he would *ever* treat with us on *any* terms. If we will break up our government, dissolve the Confederacy, disband our armies, emancipate our slaves, take an oath of allegiance binding ourselves to obedience to him and to disloyalty to our own states, he proposes to pardon us and not to plunder us of any thing more than the property already stolen from us and such slaves as still remain. In order to render his proposals so insulting as to secure their rejection, he joins to them a promise to support with his army one tenth of the people of any state who will attempt to set up a government over the other nine-tenths, thus seeking to sow discord and suspicion among the people of the several states, and to excite them to civil war in furtherance of his ends.

I know well that it would be impossible to get your people, if they possessed full knowledge of these facts to consent that proposals should now be made by us to those who control the government at Washington. Your own well known devotion to the great cause of liberty and independence to which we have all committed whatever we have of earthly possessions would induce you to take the lead in repelling the bare thought of abject submission to the enemy. Yet peace on other terms is now impossible. To obtain the sole terms to which you or I could listen this struggle must continue until the enemy is beaten out of his vain confidence in our subjugation. Then and not till then will it be possible to treat of peace. Till then, all tender of terms to the enemy will be received as proof that we are ready for submission and will encourage him in the atrocious warfare which he is waging.

I fear much from the tenor of the news I receive from North Carolina that an attempt will be made by some bad men to inaugurate movements which must be considered as equivalent to aid and comfort to the enemy, and which all patriots should combine to put down at any cost. You may count on my aid in every effort to spare your State the scenes of civil warfare which will devastate its homes, if the designs of these traitors be suffered to make head. I know that you will place yourself in your legitimate position in the lead of those who will not suffer the name of the old North State to be blackened by such a stain. Will you pardon me for suggesting that my only source of disquietude on the subject arise from the fear that you will delay too long the action which now appears inevitable; and that by an over-earnest desire to reclaim by conciliation men whom you believe to be sound at heart, but whose loyalty is more than suspected elsewhere, you will permit them to gather such strength as to require more violent measures than are now needed. With your influence and position, the promoters of the unfounded discontents now prevalent in your State, would be put down without the use of physical force, if you would abandon a policy of conciliation and set them at defiance. In this course, frankly and firmly pursued, you would rally around you all that is best and noblest in your State, and your triumph would be bloodless. If the contrary policy be adopted, I much fear you will be driven to the use of force to repress treason. In either event however, be assured that you will have my cordial concurrence and assistance in maintaining with you the honor, dignity and fair name of your State, and in your efforts to crush treason whether incipient as I believe it now to be, or more matured as I believe, if not now firmly met, it will in our future inevitably become.

I have the honor to be
very respectfully your's
Jeffn. Davis

[1] In Johnston and Mobley, *Papers of Vance*, 2:357-358.

[2] Not extant.

[3] William Theophilus Dortch, legislator and Confederate senator, lent support to programs to strengthen the Confederacy and opposed peace schemes. *Dictionary of North Carolina Biography*, s.v. "Dortch, William Theophilus."

James A. Seddon to ZBV   A&H:GP

Confederate States of America,
War Department,
Richmond, Va.
January 8 1864

His Excellency
Z B Vance
Governor of North Carolina
Raleigh N.C.

Sir

I have the honor to acknowledge the receipt of your letter of the 4th inst.[1] again asking the return of certain cotton borrowed by the Confederate States, and to state that on the 4th inst I expressed to you in a letter of that date,[2] my willingness to replace the cotton as promptly as possible, and offering in preference to pay its value in money or cotton in Augusta if agreeable to you, and if not, in cotton at Wilmington in partial payments made necessary by difficulties in RailRoad transportation.

I can only, at this time, reiterate the sentiments expressed in that communication and add that the debt will be paid as speedily as practicable

Very Respectfully
Your Obdt Servt
James A Seddon
Secretary of War

[1] In this volume.

[2] In this volume.

ZBV to George E. Pickett   A&H:GP

State of North Carolina,
Executive Department,
Raleigh, 8 Jany 1864

Majr Genl.
George E. Pickett[1]
Head Qrs.
Petersburg Va.

Dear Sir—

At a meeting of the Board of Trustees of the University of North Carolina held at the Executive Office a Resolution was passed, a copy[2] of which is herewith enclosed directing "That the President of the Board be requested to adopt such measures as he may deem best calculated," to carry into effect, the objects, of the meeting.

I respectfully request therefore, you will allow all provisions purchased in pursuance of said Resolution, to be brought out from the localities, where obtained and transported to Chapel Hill North Carolina—

It may not be out of place for me to state in this connection, that the University of North Carolina has allways been, the pride of our State; to sustain and cherish it has been the constant aim of every North Carolinian— Its members have been greatly thinned out by the War and but few remain now, to receive its benefits, or sustain its deservedly high character.

By granting the privileges asked for, you will confer a great public benefit, and aid in sustaining an Institution which is still worthy of its ancient renown.

I am very respectfully
Your obt. servt.
Z. B. Vance
Pres. Ex officio of the
Board Trustees

[1]George Edward Pickett, commanding the Department of Virginia and North Carolina. Mark Mayo Boatner III, *The Civil War Dictionary* (New York: David McKay Co., 1959), 651-652.

[2]Not extant.

ZBV to James A. Seddon   A&H:GP

Copy

State of North Carolina
Executive Department
Raleigh Jany. 8th. 1864

Hon James A. Seddon
Secty. of War

Dear Sir

One Archibald McPhail formerly a private in Co. E. 63d. N.C. Troops, (Cavalry) was recently regularly discharged from service on Habeas Corpus, by his Honor Judge Heath,[1] by reason of having furnished a Substitute. He was notwithstanding arrested a short time since by order of Captain Harris, his Comdg. officer and taken back into service with the fiat of the Judge in his pocket. Being officially informed of this, and it being my duty to execute the laws of this State, I have the honor to demand the immediate discharge of the said McPhail from the custody of the Confederate officers

Very Respectfully
Your obt. servt.
Z. B. Vance

[1]Robert R. Heath, superior court judge. Cheney, *North Carolina Government*, 362, 371n.

ZBV to John T. Bourne   A&H:GLB

Raleigh N.C. Jany 8th.

Mr J T. Bourne,[1]
St. Georges Bermuda

Dear Sir

By an arrangement with Mr. Collie the entire inward cargoes of his Steamers sailing from Bermuda to Wilmington are at the service of the State of North Carolina, Please load them as they arrive with the following articles, first Cotton Cards (if there) Second Shoes and leather, third blankets, fifth [*sic*] army cloth. Sixth machinery and whatever else remains.

Z B. Vance
Gov of N.C.

[1]John Tory Bourne, commission merchant at St. George, Bermuda. Wise, *Lifeline of the Confederacy*, 95-96, 134-135

ZBV to Theodore Andreae   A&H:GLB

Raleigh Jany 8th. [*1864*]

Mr. Theo. Andrea[e].
Wilmington.

Please instruct the Supercargo of the Don to load at Bermuda with Shoes, blankets & Cotton Cards if there in preference to anything else, After taking in all of these articles, then fill up with such other articles as may be there belonging to the State

Z. B. Vance

Theodore Andreae to ZBV   A&H:VanPC

Wilmington 8 January 64

My Dear Sir

I just received your letter of 6 inst[1] & will order the 2 B. & Hansa & 2 I am going to put on the Don for you to be sold in England for your account. Collie I know will attend to it with pleasure for you. Lend me 10 or 15 B. down & I'll squeeze one or two in whenever I can—after Steamers are loaded.

The detention of the Don here may loose her a trip. A serious loss but I want the question of carrying Cotton for the Govrnt. brought to an issue—Amongst the mercantile class here the result is looked for with great interest—like every thing else every body seems to know all about it. God knows how they ferret these things out—I suppose thro' employ'es at the agent's for the war Department.

As soon as the Don is off I hope to see you in Raleigh.

Believe me Dear Sir
Yours very truly
Th. Andreae

[1]Not extant.

James A. Seddon to ZBV   A&H:VanPC

Confederate States of America,
War Department,
Richmond, Va. January 8, 1864

His Excellency
Z. B. Vance
Governor of North Carolina
Raleigh N.C.

Sir

Your letter of the 11th ult[1] asking that the 1st; 3rd; & 55th Regts N C.T belonging to Brigade of Genl Lane[2] be formed into a new Brigade was referred to Genl Lee with an expression of my desire that when the interests of the service will permit, troops of the same state may be brigaded together.

I have the honor now to communicate the reply of Genl Lee and respectfully to invite your attention to it.

He states, that on several occasions when this subject has been referred to him, he has stated that the 1st and 3d Regiments N C. Troops were brigaded with three Virginia regiments: the whole under Genl Geo Stewart,[3] an officer of experience of the old army from the State of Maryland. This at the time was rendered necessary from the fact that He had no N.C regts to brigade with them. All the other N.C brigades having been filled. These troops have been serving together for some time; their Commander cannot be disposed to treat them unfairly and is very attentive to their comfort and interests. He cannot withdraw them without breaking up that Brigade. The 55th N.C. regt was brigaded with three Missi regts before it joined this army and while serving in the vicinity of Richmond or south of James River—To take it away now would break up that Brigade (Davis')[4] Genl Lane's brigade by the last return numbered 2398 aggregate, to take from it the 33d N.C;

one of the largest in the brigade, would reduce it to about 1900 men. This Brigade is composed entirely of N.C. regts: is one of the oldest in service & he thinks it would be disadvantageous to reduce it. Unless he had more NC regts: the only change that could be made, if there is any advantage in so doing, would be to join the 55th to Stewart's Brigade. There would then be three N.C. and three Va regts: together, but that would break up Davis' brigade. He sees no public benefit that would result from the changes proposed by you, and therefore cannot recommend them. The men, he believes would be satisfied if let alone.

> Very Respectfully
> Your Obdt Servt
> James A Seddon
> Secretary of War

[*Endorsed*] File & send copy to Col C M Avery 33d. N C T.

ZBV

[1] In Johnston and Mobley, *Papers of Vance*, 2:39.
[2] James Henry Lane, whose brigade comprised five North Carolina regiments. Patricia L. Faust et al., eds., *Historical Times Illustrated Encyclopedia of the Civil War* (New York: HarperCollins, 1991), 424.
[3] George Hume Steuart. Faust et al., *Encyclopedia of Civil War*, 717.
[4] Joseph Robert Davis, nephew of Jefferson Davis. Faust et al., *Encyclopedia of Civil War*, 209.

Power, Low and Co. to ZBV   A&H:GP

Wilmington
8 Jany. 1863[4]

To his Excely.
Gov. Zeb. B. Vance
Raleigh

Dear Sir

We are in receipt of your favor of 6th. Inst.[1]—We regret our inability at the moment to help you with Coals, we loaned our neighbor Andreae the small surplus we had—We trust the AdVance will not require any here, if so her detention may be protracted—

Our own ships always bring sufficient for the voyage in and out—

In reference to any lightening of the ship, we shall advise you more particularly after consultation with some of the knowing ones on board & a more full investigation of the matter.

We look for Col. Fitzhugh[2] here tomorrow, shall write you in reference to Cotton from advices recd. from him we suspect that some ports in Florida are about being opened that will offer a good oppt. for ships to run in & out with some safety—

The Lucy, Wild [Darrel, Pat & Harvine] all left yesterday The Index is just in to us from Bermuda, shall advise you of any thing interesting from that point after reading h[er] letters.

Yours respt.
Power Low & Co.

The Presto not the Index arrd. from Bermuda sailed on 4th. Advance not arrived there—when she sailed—I have just seen Mr. Carter has about 60 tons Coal here, not likely to get any more at present, there were plenty of Coals at Bermuda and we hope the ship would take a full supply—We shall find you storage for 600 Bales Cotton at Mr. Carters request—

[1]In this volume.
[2]H. Fitzhugh, Virginia agent for the purchase of cargo from the *Advance*.

Theodore Andreae to ZBV　　　　A&H:GP

Wilmington
10 January 1864

To His Excellency
Governor Vance
Raleigh

Dear Sir

Your favor of 7 January[1] has come to hand and I shall be happy to send you the exchange on England.

I telegraphed as follows:

"I will send you the drafts or order gold or drafts to be sent from Nassau to anybody you may appoint. Telegraph which you prefer. No decision from

Richmond yet. Don left on Friday night all right. The question at issue is left in suspense"

I have gold at my disposal sufficient for your purpose which I can send you at once if desired. I have ordered 1000 B. Cotton to be bought at Columbia & will send you all documents to enable you to move it in due time. The Hansa will be back I expect on Wednesday. We have the "Presto" in from Bermuda. The A.D. Vance has not arrived in B'a yet.—Your telegram for Bourne[2] came too late for the "Don" I had however sent orders to our agent to ship first the articles you telegraphed to me about & have no doubt these will be attended to.—The Presto is the only Steamer now here.—She is going to Nassau to morrow. The gales must have been fearfull—the Coquette returned to Bermuda with cylinder bottom blown out, the "Flora" & "Will of the Wisp["] returned crippled & have to go for repairs to "Halifax," the "Vesta" and "Dare" left on the 3d. for here & are not in yet. I have a few young Englishmen here to help me to manage the bussiness if the "foreigner expulsion act" passes I Suppose I'll have no difficulty to get them exempted thro' your assistance?

> I am Dear Sir
> Yours [illegible] obd.
> Th. Andreae

[1]In this volume.
[2]ZBV to John T. Bourne, January 8, 1864, in this volume.

James A. Seddon to ZBV   A&H:GP

> Confederate States of America,
> War Department,
> Richmond Va. Jan 11th. 1864

His Excellency
Z B Vance
Governor of North Carolina

Sir

I have the honor to acknowledge the receipt of your letter of the 21st. ulto.[1] and regret exceedingly that the citizens of North Carolina have been subjected to any annoyance by the ill-conduct of Confederate Cavalry. It has been the effort of this Department to restrain all troops in service within proper limits of military discipline; and the uniform practice is, when outrages perpetrated by them have been reported, to require a prompt investigation, with the view to bring the perpetrators before a Court under proper charges and specifications. As your communication is general in its terms, and does not implicate any officer or command by name, that rule cannot be enforced in the grievances you mention. It is believed, the Articles of War, and the Regulations and General Orders from the Adjt. & Inspr. Genl's Office are sufficient to restrain troops from committing depredations upon property and outraging the rights of citizens of the Confederacy. The 32d. Article of War punishes any officer who, upon complaint made to him, "refuses or omits to see justice done to the offender or offenders and reparation made to the party or parties injured, as far as part of the offender's pay shall enable him or them, by cashiering or otherwise as a Court Martial shall direct." And the Regulation for the government of the Army and General Orders are in accordance with the Articles of War cited. Any further orders relating to the subject would seem to be supererrogatory, since they could not more emphatically forbid or punish disorders and outrages committed by troops. Of course if the crime committed be cognizable by a civil tribunal, the offender is subject to the demand of the Executive of the State where the act is done.

It is suggested when depredations are committed by troops of the Confederacy, that the names of the perpetrators, designating the commands to which they belong, be communicated to this Department that they may be brought to trial.

> I am, Sir
> Very respectfully
> Your obedient Servant
> James A Seddon
> Secty of War

[1]In Johnston and Mobley, *Papers of Vance*, 2:344-345.

James A. Seddon to ZBV   A&H:GP

War Department
Richmond Va. Jany. 11/64

Gov. Z B. Vance
Raleigh, N.C.

Your Excellency,

I am in rcpt. of your favor of the 7th. inst.,[1] and have directed its reference to Mr. Seixas,[2] special agent of the Depmt. at Wilmington, with the following endorsement:

"The reports made here do not show where this cotton was delivered. The Secty. War wishes to meet the views of Gov. Vance, and to return the Cotton as promptly as possible, at places where it was delivered, or at Wilmington. Mr. Seixas will return this Cotton, 500 bales per month, if possible, taking up rcpts. for Same given by himself and Capt. Archer, and will give notice to Gov. Vance."

According to statements on file here, the amt. of cotton due you is only about 1300 bales, but I cannot be positive as to the accuracy of these figures The a/c can be adjusted exactly by Mr. Seixas, and Some State officer charged by you with the duty.

I have experienced great difficulty in transporting to Wilmington an adequate supply of Cotton, but I hope that arrangements recently inaugurated will enable me to put at that point all that may be required for shipment, and to repay your generous loan

Very Rspctly
Yr. obt. Servt
James A Seddon
Secty War

[1] In this volume
[2] Sent by the Confederate War Department to Wilmington to find blockade-runners. Encyclopedia of Southern Jewish Communities, Goldring/Woldenberg Institute of Southern Jewish Life, http://www.isjl.org/history/archive/nc/wilmington. html.

Richmond M. Pearson to ZBV   A&H:GP

Richmond Hill
Jany 11th. 1864.

His Excellency
Gov. Vance

Dear Sir,

I am satisfied, you possess the talents & qualities of a politician; & having long since withdrawn from the arena, I can see no useful purpose, that will be effected by a continuation of our correspondence—but a few remarks are called for, in reply to your last letter.

It seems then, that with a knowledge that judges Battle & Manly[1] did not concur with me, & knowing that I had invited them to assist me at the hearing of Austins case[2]—before the matter had become "res adjudicata,"[3] so far at least as I was concerned,—you, had a case prepared, in order to have my decision reviewed & reversed by them. There is no precedent for such a proceeding, & my sense of duty did not allow me to join in it— For, certain it is, unless the judges conform to prior decisions, (except when there is palpable error) & each of the eleven thinks himself at liberty to decide according to his own notion—there must be utter confusion & the usefulness of the judiciary be greatly impaired—And yet this suicide on the part of the judiciary, was to be committed, in order to relieve you from the embarrassment in which you found yourself involved, by an eagerness on your part to take a hand with the president, in executing the acts of congress—a duty which by this constitution is confided exclusively "to the president of the Confed. States"—So far as I am concerned personally, it would have been gratifying to know the grounds on which it is thought, there is *palpable error* in Austins case, but in the name of the judiciary, I thank you for withdrawing your case at the suggestion of Judge Battle—

I should be exceeding sorry to think myself obnoxious to the charge of a want of forbearance towards a young and inexperienced governor, who had my warm support. It is true, I took it for granted, you had seen or heard of my decision in "Whitehearts case"[4]—The proceeding in which [faded] interesting questions, & was published in full in one newspaper and noticed by two or three others & as a bench warrant issued, & two of the parties were bound over to the Superior court of Guilford for a violation of "the peace & dignity of the State," it was reasonable to suppose, "the militia officer" had reported the fact to the Gov.—Besides I had no right to assume that you were ignorant of a plain principle of the constitution, which forbids the arrest of any citizen for an indictable offence, except on a States warrant issued by a judge or justice of the peace on probable cause shown on oath—

I did not expect the "militia officers" were to be left to judge whether cases fell under the principles decided by the Supreme court. But I did expect that after the Sec. of war, upon your remonstrance had given assurance, that the principles settled by the court would be respected, & the orders constraining them be revoked; that you would not become accessory, & aid in the execution of such orders, by putting the "Militia officers" under the absolute control of the Confd. officers; with a knowledge, as was notorious, that such orders instead of being revoked, had been specially renewed—I supposed rather, that you would have refused your aid & revoked your orders to the "Militia officers"—unless the assurance given to you by the Sec. of war was carried out.

I was pleased to find you concur with me in the hope, that we may discharge the duties of our positions without any unkind feeling—& readily accept the assurance that on your part there is no unkind feeling—I must confess I did feel somewhat aggrieved that instead of adopting my suggestion to recommend to the legislature, to allow appeals in habeas corpus cases, & under certain circumstances to make it *the duty* of the ch. justice to call an extra session of the court, you proposed to put it in the power of the Gov. & council, or to require the ch. justice at *the request of the Gov.* to call an extra session,—in other words to make the Supreme Court subject to "the beck & call" of the executive in violation of the constitutional provision, that the judiciary shall be independent of the executive—And candor, also requires me to say,—I thought your letter in reply to mine in reference to the "*protest*" you had seen proper to make against what you supposed might be my action in the discharge of the duties of my office, which trenched upon a judges oath of office—(see Rev. Code 439, oath of a judge of the Superior court" showing the exteme jealousy of the law in respect to communication of that character)—was objectionable in this—that you do not make a direct disclaimer—but a general indefinite sort of one, connected with a dissertation, upon your stock of patience, carried so far as to shadow forth a menace—that the stock altho ample; might be exhausted—

However, let it all pass—I take occasion to renew the assurance, that I have no unkind feeling towards you—I regret that in some instances, our correspondence has assumed somewhat a tone of asperity—altho that seems to be almost unavoidable, when there is a radical difference of opinion— Indeed I have observed that even ministers of the gospel fall into it, which may be some excuse for us, but it is useless to squabble as boys are apt to do—about "who struck the first lick" I am approaching my three score years & have no political aspirations—you are just entering upon your career— which I sincerely hope will be one of distinction & usefulness to our country, you have talents which, if properly directed, will in these stiring times enable you to take a high position.

Respectfully &c yours &c
R M. Pearson[5]

[1]William Horn Battle and Matthias Evans Manly, state supreme court justices. *Dictionary of North Carolina Biography*, s.v. "Battle, William Horn" and "Manly, Matthias Evans."

[2]Case of Richard M. Austin, who refused to obey ZBV's order for the Home Guard in Davie County to arrest deserters. Austin was jailed and brought before Chief Justice Pearson, who ordered the defendant released on the ground that the governor had no authority to order home guards to arrest deserters and conscripts. The Home Guard (or Guard for Home Defense), established by a legislative act of July 7 and composed of men not eligible for conscription, had supplanted the state militia. J. G. De Roulhac Hamilton, "The North Carolina Courts and the Confederacy," *North Carolina Historical Review* 4 (October 1927): 376-377; Memory F. Mitchell, *Legal Aspects of Conscription and Exemption in North Carolina, 1861-1865* (Chapel Hill: University of North Carolina Press, 1965), 59; *Public Laws of North Carolina, 1863* (called session), c. 10; Louis H. Manarin, ed., *Guide to Military Organizations and Installations, North Carolina, 1861-1865* (Raleigh: North Carolina Confederate Centennial Commission, 1961), 2.

[3]A common misspelling of *res judicata*, which refers to a controversy or dispute that has been settled by the decision of a court.

[4]Case in which Pearson "discharged the petitioner on the ground, that a Militia officer, could not lawfully arrest a man for harboring a conscript." See ZBV to Pearson, December 26, 1863, in Johnston and Mobley, *Papers of Vance*, 2:351-352.

[5]Richmond Mumford Pearson, chief justice of the North Carolina Supreme Court. *Dictionary of North Carolina Biography*, s.v. "Pearson, Richmond Mumford."

ZBV to David L. Swain   A&H:VanPC

Raleigh Jany 11 1864.

Gov Swain

My Dear Sir,

Mr Graham has declined to accept the appointment of Senator for Mr. Davis' unexpired term. I desire very much that you should accept it. In the first place, I believe that above all men in the State your age, position, and character would enable you to modify & soften the present violent & desperate temper of Congress: and that you could really be of great service to the State. In the next place it would afford me infinite satisfaction for you to receive this mark of confidence (The greatest it may ever be in my power to bestow) at *my* hands.

If you can go, the sooner the better.

Most Truly Yours
Z B. Vance

James A. Seddon to ZBV   A&H:GP

Confederate States of America,
War Department,
Richmond, Va. Jan 12 1864

His Excellency Z. B. Vance
Governor of North Carolina.
Raleigh N.C.

Sir,

On the receipt of your letter of the 31st ult.[1] relating to the consumption of grain in North Carolina in the manufacture of whiskey, I called upon the Surgeon General to report whether he had any contracts for the distillation of spirits in your State, and if so, the quantity of grain required, and the necessity for the supply. I annex a copy of his reply: "The Medical Department has no contract for alcoholic stimulants in the State of North Carolina. The distillery at Salisbury, referred to by Gov. Vance, is owned by the Medical Department, and is engaged in the manufacture of whiskey and alcohol for the sole use of the sick and wounded of the Army. This distillery was purchased by this Department for the purpose of dispensing with the system of contracting for alcoholic stimulants, as it has been found that a large quantity of whiskey manufactured by contractors is of an inferior quality, and their contracts were not in other respects faithfully carried out. It is also believed that a large quantity of whiskey made by contractors has been sold to private parties, when it should have been delivered to the Government, thereby consuming more grain than was required to fill their contracts. Maj. Badham[2] has been instructed to turn over grain to the Medical Purveyor in charge of the Government distillery at Salisbury, in order to obviate the necessity of this Department going into market to purchase, which would enhance the price paid for grain by the Quarter Master's Dept., and the thirty thousand bushels referred to in the within communication, is for a whole year's supply for the distillery. There is no distillery at Charlotte belonging to this Department, nor am I aware that there is one there. The Attorney General has decided that the Confederate Government has the express power to 'support armies,' that any means may be used which are necessary and proper to obtain supplies for that support. Therefore a State has no power to interfere with the Confederate Government in the manufacture or even contracting for such supplies. In conclusion, I would state that it is absolutely necessary for the comfort and welfare of the sick and wounded of our army, that the Government distillery at Salisbury should not be interfered with or the supply of grain cut off."

I may add to the above that on enquiry I learn that a greater coolness of temperature than for many months of the year prevails in the Southern States, where corn is more abundant, is essential to the ready and proper distillation of spirits and that this circumstance presents the easy solution of the difficulties presented by your remonstrance which I should have sought in the removal of the Govt. Labratory. I trust your objections will under the circumstances be withdrawn

Very Truly Yrs
James A Seddon
Secty. of War

[1]In Johnston and Mobley, *Papers of Vance*, 2:360.
[2]Chief collector of tax in kind in North Carolina. See ibid.

Francis C. Lawley to ZBV   A&H:VanPC

Box 321. Richmond.
Jan 12. 1864.

Private

H.E. Governor Vance

My Dear Sir
I have read with the greatest interest your instructive letter of Dec 26[1] and instead of finding it too long I should have rejoiced if you had found it necessary to extend your area of paper from nine sheets to eighteen. There is I allow much truth in what you say about the suspicion entertained in regard to the loyalty of N.C. towards the South. But believe me that the

behaviour of many of your noblest sons both officers & men upon many a bloody field has been not without its effect, & I do not think you will have occasion to complain of want of appreciation during the coming year. The recent appointment to the vacant office in the Confed. Cabinet & some other trifling indications of the spirit prevailing in high quarters here are an Earnest of bitter feeling towards your State. And forgive me if I point out to you the natural exasperation of men who have suffered as have the Virginians—with at least one third of their State in the hands of the enemy—with damaging raids continually recurring—with negroes stolen by hundreds, & more or less demoralised all over the State. Altogether after 16 months experience of the Confederacy, after travelling for thousands of miles through its length & breadth, and after being a good deal behind the scenes, I have come to the conclusion that when the events of this stirring crisis are surveyed with impartial & dispassionate eyes the luster of the fame of every prominent /Southern/ man—even of Stonewall Jackson & Robert E. Lee—will pale its ineffectual fires before that of Jefferson Davis. I know that this sentiment will not meet with your approbation & concurrence; it may possibly even provoke your indignation: but when all the world knows how President Davis has been tried, when the correspondence between him & his Generals sees the light, when the intrigues & personal self-seeking of nine tenths of those with whom he is surrounded are exposed (as Exposed they will certainly be) to the glare of day, I cannot doubt that the patience, the magnanimity, the forbearance, the courage, moral & physical, which he has shown will raise him at least to the level of the Washingtons of history & will be honoured & extolled to a degree of which we, who live by his side & know only the weariness and sacrifices of the struggle, can form but an imperfect conception.

I own that it does move my scorn & indignation to see some of the little men who swarm in this city—who have contributed not one cent either morally or materially to the war, but who think that in the midst of this agonising conflict loyalty to the South means acrimony & backbiting for Jeff. Davis—sharpening their pens & filling their ink with gall, instead of thanking God for giving them to so staunch, so pure, so firm a man, as the Atlas of this Revolution! It is hardly necessary that I should tell you that I have no personal relations which bind me at all to Mr. Davis. I hardly ever see him, & have judged him with the cold & impartial eyes of a stranger who has been allowed to judge of the materials which, when gathered together, will form the History of this great Revolution, & who has come to the conclusion that the verdict of posterity will be what I say. You will I trust be spared to see my prophecy realized; for long before you have attained the allotted term of man, the words which I have now written will have been brought to a practical test.

I repeat what I stated in my last letter, that my firm & unalterable conviction is that, if you struggle with any thing like such an equality of force as you have hitherto maintained until August next, the agony will be over. I do not pretend to conceal from you that *every* effort you can make will be needed to resist Grant & Meade in the Spring. The former is by far the most formidable General the Federals have yet found. I own I have little faith, from what I saw /last October,/ in the army now commanded by Gen Johnston.[2] I *have* the greatest faith in the small body under Longstreet,[3] & in Longstreet himself. If they are strong enough to make any impression upon Grant's flank next spring, the advantage will be enormous. If in any way you can strengthen Longstreet, by throwing State troops or stragglers up to his assistance, through Ashville, believe me that you have no idea how much you will <b> assist the entire cause.

My principal object in going now to England is to do my utmost to procure for you that recognition which is your right, & which would wonderfully inspirit you if extended to you at this moment. If I can be of any assistance to you or your State in England, I pray you always to command me. My address is 29 Berkeley Square, London.

> With my best wishes,
> Believe me, my Dr. Sir
> Very truly yours
> Francis Lawley[4]

[1]Not extant. But see ZBV to Francis Lawley, March 4, 1863, and Lawley to ZBV, December 22, 1863, in Johnston and Mobley, *Papers of Vance*, 2:78, 347-348.

[2]Joseph Eggleston Johnston, commanding the Army of Tennessee against the Federal advance from the West. Faust et al., *Encylopedia of Civil War*, 400-401.

[3]James Longstreet, serving in the Army of Tennessee in the West from September 1863 until his return to Virginia in April 1864. Boatner, *Civil War Dictionary*, 490-491.

[4]Francis C. Lawley, an English correspondent covering the war for the *London Times*, whom ZBV once considered employing as an agent to secure a loan in England for North Carolina. See William Stanley Hoole, *Lawley Covers the Confederacy* (Tuscaloosa, Ala.: Confederate Publishing Co., 1964).

ZBV to William H. C. Whiting   A&H:GLB

Raleigh Jany 13th.

Genl. Whiting[1]
Wilmington

I have a lot of negroes started to you from Iredell county who are detained at Salisbury by the Commandant of Post to put up ice and bale hay. Please order them on to Wilmington and punish the officer for stopping them.

Z. B. Vance

[1]William Henry Chase Whiting, commander of military district of Wilmington. *Dictionary of American Biography*, s.v. "Whiting, William Henry Chase."

David L. Swain to ZBV   A&H:GP

[*With enclosure*]

Chapel Hill,
1<2>3 Jan 1864

My dear Sir,
The enclosed note designed for your letter book was prepared yesterday just too late for the evening mail. I did not very much regret the departure of the hack at an earlier hour than I anticipated, as it afforded me a day for consideration, and opportunity to observe the effect of remedies for the health of my children, neither of whom is well enough to justify my immediate departure for Richmond.

In accordance with your request[1] I have carefully and intensively considered the question, who may with most propriety be called upon to take the vacant seat in the Senate. I greatly regret Gov. Grahams declination. His predecessor ought to be a gentleman of equal abilities, age experience and prestige if such an one can be found, and in addition to these qualities, it is very important that he should not be obnoxious to either of the political parties at present striving for supremacy in the State. Judge Ruffin, Gov. Morehead and Col. Brown,[2] seem to me to present higher claims than any others. The two former were members of the Peace Congress, both disapprove the repeal of the law in relation to substitutes, both I suppose would advocate more moderate measures in general and especially in relation to the suspension of the Habeas Corpus act, than extremists at Richmond. Gov. Morehead is a manufacturer, and an advocate for a Currency system, which was not received with favor by his friends at home, when first proposed, and which will soon become odious to the great body of the people. I know [noth]ing of Judge Ruffin's opinions on this subject. He is supposed however to have made large investments in Confederate bonds, and prejudicious in [*illegible*] to the Currency system, have [*torn*] of it. Personally I would approve the selection of either

Under all the circumstances however, I incline to the opinion that the tender of the [stake] to Col. Brown, will be most judicious. He has neither the learning nor ability of Judge Ruffin, or the great strength of intellect of Morehead. He has age, experience, prestige, and high character for integrety. He is a favorite of that portion of the Conservative party, to which you are least acceptable, and while he has few warm friends and admirers, among moderate Conservatives and secessionists, he is less obnoxious to them, than the two other gentlemen, to the party with which he is indentified. His selection would I suspect be grateful to him and to his political friends, he would probably be able to exercise a salutary influence at Richmond, and if unsuccessful, his adherents, would be estopped from blaming you. At present it is in their power to complain of every thing, while responsible for nothing. If he shall assume the reins, the condition of things will change at once.—I doubt moreover whether Ruffin or Morehead can be induced to accept, and the tender would subject you to concur with or consecrate supporters of your former friends. I am by no means certain that Col. Brown will be willing to vacate his seat in the General Assembly and enter upon a months service in the Confederate Senate. If he does not, I think the offer would give more general satisfaction, than to any one else. And in relation to this I have conferred freely with Judge Battle & other friends who concur with me in opinion. If he should decline, please give me immediate notice.

After full consideration, I see no reason to change the opinion expressed in Raleigh on the subject of your letter of the 2d. The Johnston resolutions <*illegible*>/serve/ to look to a call of the General Assembly and a Convention, but they handle both so gingerly, that unless they are followed by much more decided action elsewhere, they need occasion no great concern. The General Assembly having determined to convene in May, very important causes must present themselves, in the meantime, to require or justify y[*torn*]ng it at an [earlier] day.

Yours very sincerely
D. L. Swain

¹January 11, 1864, in this volume.

²Thomas Ruffin, former chief justice of the North Carolina Supreme Court and member of the state secession convention; John Motley Morehead, wealthy railroad promoter and textile entrepreneur, former governor, state senator, and member of Confederate Provisional Congress; and Bedford Brown, prewar Democratic U.S. senator and state senator, whose wartime service in the state senate was from 1861 to 1864. *Dictionary of North Carolina Biography*, s.v. "Ruffin, Thomas," "Morehead, John Motley," and "Brown, Bedford."

[*Enclosure*]

David L. Swain to ZBV   A&H:GP

Chapel Hill,
12 Jan. 1864.

His Excellency
Governor Vance

My dear Sir,

Your letter of yesterday was received by this mornings mail

I regret exceedingly to find myself compelled, at this momenteous crisis in our public affairs, to decline the acceptance of the high public trust the proper discharge of which you consider me competent, and propose in such flattering terms. The health of my /family/ however will not admit of my leaving home immediately and the session of Congress, is too near its close, and occupied with too important subjects to admit of any delay.

I am very truly & Sincerely
Your friend & sevt.
D. L. Swain

James A. Seddon to ZBV   A&H:GP

War Department
Richmond Va.
Jany. 14/64

Gov. Z. B. Vance
Raleigh N.C.

Your Excellency

I am duly in rcpt. of your letter of 7th inst.[1] Before it came to hand, I had directed that the following telegram be sent to the Agent of the Department at Wilmington: "No reply yet from Gov. Vance—the Secty. War wishes you to arrange to let "Don" go out leaving the question of ownership of One Third of her cargo to be determined after full conference with Gov. Vance," and had recd. a reply as follows: "Suggestion in your telegram relative to "Don" anticipated—she has proceeded to Sea."

I am most anxious, in reference to the blockade trade, to do whatever will most subserve the use of the army and people. After I found that the few steamers owned by the Government were inadequate to carry out cotton to purchase supplies and munitions urgently needed, I sent an officer to Wilmington and Charleston to confer with owners of steamers, and make the best arrangements possible to secure a portion of the carrying capacity of their steamers for the Government; and wrote, at the same time, to Gens. Beauregard & Whiting, placing the necessities of the Govmt. before them. Arrangements were then made whereby the several owners conceded at least one third of their carrying capacity, on payment of reasonable freights therefor. Under these arrangements the "Don" & "Hansa" have heretofore been loaded. I am aware that the owners and agents of this line (who are all foreigners, as I am advised) were prepared to make any concession as to inward freight to be relieved from carrying out any cotton for the Govmt, their sole interest lying in getting out of the country as much cotton as possible. Indeed, I have found no difficulty in securing as much <cotton> /freight room/ inward as I desire from the ports from which the strs. run. Under these circumstances, I think you will agree with me, Governor, that the arrangements with Messrs Collie & Co with which you propose to supercede mine are less advantageous to the Country than those established by me. We are both laboring in the same cause and for the same end, and I will not willingly allow any conflict with you, thro' officers acting under my authority, and I feel that I may ask the same of you. Our wants for meat, lead, saltpetre, shoes clothing &c are most urgent at this time, and every bale of cotton that I could send out has been directed to such purchases for the use of all the troops in the field. When I learned that you had purchased the Str. "Ad-Vance," I did not wait for an application, but at once directed the Agent at Wilmington to exempt her from the requirements made of all other Steamers. The "Don" and "Hansa" are upon a different footing, they were already engaged in carrying out one third of cargo for a/c of the Govmt. The owners made overtures to you, in order to be relieved from what they regarded as an onerous obligation. When advised of these facts, I do not think you will insist on thus relieving them by your contract, from their engagements with the Government, engagements they were actively executing at the time you entered into contract with them. If for special temporary purposes connected with our supplies at Bermuda you wish the exemption of the "Hansa" & "Don" for present trip, or indeed longer time, I shall give orders to meet your wishes.

I am sure that you will agree with me, that as a general thing, it will be better for the Confederate Govern. to send out <supplies> /cotton/ to procure supplies for our armies, than for the individual states to undertake the matter. Some states have no ports, others are within the occupation of the enemy. The troops from such states must be supplied by the Confederate Govmt. only. If each State undertakes the export of Cotton and the import of all supplies necessary, we shall have great jealousy among the troops from the different States and great embarrassment in questions connected with rail road transportation. There can be no objection to a State's exerting every effort for the comfort and well being of its soldiers and people, but such efforts should be outside of, and not interfere with, those of the Confederate Govmt. for the comfort and well being of the whole army and country.

I will, in this full representation of the considerations that control the Department, leave it entirely to your own judgment and patriotism to determine whether any, and what, allowance should be made the Govmt. of the last cargoes of the "Hansa" and "Don"; but trust that, upon their return, you will consent to have them resume their places in carrying out one third for the Govmt., and will so advise me on rcpt. of this.

I ought, in addition, to intimate to you that Gen Whiting, from some correspondence he has seen with Mr Andreae has formed unfavorable opinions as to his interest in our Cause and the purely selfish ends at which he is aiming.

> I have the honor, Sir, to remain
> Very Respctly.
> Yr. obt. Servt.
> James A Seddon
> Secty. War.

[1] In this volume.

ZBV to Edwin G. Reade   A&H:GLB

State of North Carolina
Executive Department
Raleigh Jany. 14th. 1864

Hon. E. G. Reade[1]
Roxboro N.C.

My Dear Sir

I enclose you herewith a commission as Senator from N.C. to the Confederate States Congress for the remainder of the unexpired term of the Hon. Geo. Davis. I trust you will accept it and proceed at once to Richmond. The term is short it is true, but yet I regard it of importance that we should be represented at such a crisis as this; and perhaps our calm voice amid the reckless and desperate legislation of the day, might be heard warning and expostulating.

Very Truly Yours
Z. B. Vance

[1]Edwin Godwin Reade, lawyer and former Whig and U.S. congressman who favored peace with the North. He served as a Confederate senator and after the war became associate justice of the state supreme court. *Dictionary of North Carolina Biography*, s.v. "Reade, Edwin Godwin"; Cheney, *North Carolina Government*, 361, 362, 369n, 371n, 388, 403n, 575, 588, 689, 832.

Robert Ould to ZBV   A&H:GP

Confederate States of America,
War Department,
Richmond, Va. Jany. 15th. 1864

Hon. Z. B. Vance
Governor of No. Ca.

My dear Sir,

The North Carolina troops are within the provisions of the Cartel,[1] and are fully entitled to the protection of the Confederate authorities. If any cruelties not warranted by the laws of war are inflicted upon them, prompt retaliation will follow. Moreover as these troops are acting upon your orders, I see nothing to prevent you from retaliating upon any Yankees whom they may capture, for any outrages which they may inflict upon your people.

Respectfully
Yr. Obt. Svt.
Ro. Ould
Agent of Exchange

[1]Of prisoner exchange. See ZBV to Robert Ould, December 29, 1863, in Johnston and Mobley, *Papers of Vance*, 2:357.

Joseph E. Brown to ZBV　　　　　A&H:VanPC

Executive Department
Milledgeville
January 16th 1864

His Excellency
Z. B. Vance

Dear Sir

Your letter of 30th December[1] reached my office while I was absent in upper Georgia and this is the first moment since my return which I have been able to devote to a reply. I regret to hear of the condition of affairs in your State. While there is considerable discontent at the action of the Confederate authorities in this State, and a sincere desire for peace, there is not a great deal of disloyalty, and no disposition manifested to take any course by separate state action to correct the errors or abuses of the Confederate Government, at so critical a period in our struggle. I agree with you that too little effort has been made on our part to conciliate and build up the party in the North who are hostile to the Lincoln policy, and who desire peace upon honorable terms. The action of the administration at Richmond seems to have had the effect to repel rather than encourage the advances made by the Constitution men in the United States. This ought to be corrected <by the> by the President, and I trust your letter to him[2] may have had a good effect.

I believe with you that it is not probable that the Lincoln Government would now receive commissioners sent by our Government, or hear any proposition made by them. But the effort on our part and the refusal by them would show to the world, and /especially/ to that portion of our own people who believe that such propositions would be entertained, that we are not responsible for the continuance of the war. In this view of the question I can see no good reason why the Government at Richmond should not make the effort, by sending Commissioners and offering such terms of adjustment as we could accept, without lowering our dignity or compromitting our Independence

But while I would approve this course on the part of the Confederate Government I think a State Convention in any one of the States at the present, looking to seperate State action, would be very unfortunate and would create divisions and party strife, at a time when harmonious action is indispensable to the achievement of our Independence

I expect in a few days to write the President upon questions connected with the prosecution of the War, and I will with pleasure call his attention to this subject, and unite with your suggestions as I see no harm that can result from such a course, and it may and will do much good, if it has the effect to unite our own people more firmly and resolutely in their resistance to the outrages of the enemy, and to build up a party in the North hostile to the policy of the present abolition administration.

I think it quite probable I shall be under the necessity of convening the Legislature of this State in extra session early in the spring. If so, I expect to review this question, and hope to be able to mature and offer some suggestions which I trust may meet the approval of your judgment.

I shall be gratified at all times to confer freely with you and to receive any suggestions you may think proper to submit. If the President adopts the policy you propose I hope his action will stop the proposed State Convention in your State and relieve you from embarrassment. Wishing you a long life of usefulness.

I am Very Repectfully
Your obt Servt
Joseph E. Brown[3]

[1]Not extant.

[2]December 30, 1863, in Johnston and Mobley, *Papers of Vance*, 2:357-358.

[3]Joseph Emerson Brown, governor of Georgia. *Dictionary of American Biography*, s.v. "Brown, Joseph Emerson."

ZBV to John T. Bourne   A&H:GLB

State of North Carolina
Executive Office
Raleigh Jany. 18th. 1864

Mr. J. T. Bourne
St Georges Bermuda

Dr. Sir

Having made arrangements with Messrs Collie & Co by which the entire inward cargoes of the Don and Hansa (with two other Steamers not yet arrived from Europe) is to be at my disposal, you will please load them with such freight for this State as may be on hand in the following order viz.

1st. Cotton Cards and Machinery for making them

2d. Shoes & Leather 3d. Blankets 4th. Factory Machinery 5th Army Cloth, 6th. Dye Stuffs findings for No 4 &c.

Should there be any vessel of this line at Bermuda & no State freight on hand, you will load with any freight of Army stores for the Confederacy that may be on the Island, giving preference to Bacon, Salt petre and shoes. I despatched you to this effect to go by the Don but she sailed before it reached her.

Very respectfully
Yr. obt. Servt.
Z. B. Vance

Edwin G. Reade to ZBV   A&H:GLB

Roxboro
Jany. 18th 1864

His Excellency
Z. B. Vance

I have this day received your favour,[1] enclosing my appointment and commission to a seat in the Senate of the Confederate States. I am arduously engaged in preparation for the judgeship, the duties of which, I have to enter upon in March. The Session of Congress is near its close, with many important measures before it, involving the very life of the country—which have been considered in secret Session and upon which Senators have formed their opinions. Distrusting my abilities for the position at any time, I feel, as I fear others will think, that it is presumptuous to take it now. But I have to choose between this and the alternative of embarrassing you and having the State unrepresented. I do not hesitate, therefore, to accept the appointment and I will repair immediately to the Senate, and do my duty. I do not doubt the indulgent consideration of a generous public. I thank you for the distinguished honor and for the kind manner in which it is conferred. With high regard, I am,

Very truly yours
E G. Reade.

[1]January 14, 1864, in this volume.

William M. Browne to ZBV   A&H:GP

Confederate States of America
Executive Department
Richmond Va. Jan. 18th. 1864

His Excellency Z B Vance
Governor of N. Carolina

Sir.

I have the honor by direction of the President to acknowledge the receipt of yours of the 29th. ulto,[1] asking information as to the arrest & imprisonment of W D. Wynns.[2]

His Excellency caused enquiry to be made and has been informed that W. D. Wynns was reported to the War Dept. on the 7th. ulto, through Genl. Winder[3] as having been sent to this city by Colonel Griffin commanding at Blackwater on 21st. Novr. '63 with the statement that "he was disloyal; that he had acted as poll keeper at a bogus election, & had put a substitute into the army who had deserted. His case was examined by J. H. Carrington Esqr & on his report Genl. Winder was instructed to send Wynns to a Conscript Camp to have his liability to service or his right to exemption determined.

Hon. W. N. H. Smith,[4] MC. also made enquiries respecting him & the foregoing facts were communicated to him by letter from the War Dept. on the 21st. ulto. Since the receipt of the above mentioned instructions to Genl. Winder that officer has reported that Wynns has been in hospital & would be sent to camp as soon as his condition would permit. On the suggestion of Mr. Smith on the 20. inst. Genl. Winder was ordered to send Wynns to the N. Car Hospital to be sent when well enough to Camp Holmes at Raleigh.

> Very respectfully
> Yr. Obt. Servt.
> Wm. M. Browne
> Col & A.D.C.

[1]In Johnston and Mobley, *Papers of Vance*, 2:355.

[2]William D. Wynne, arrested by Confederate soldiers. Resolution in Relation to William D. Wynne, House Resolutions, Session of November-December, 1863, A&H:GA.

[3]John Henry Winder, Confederate provost marshal general. Boatner, *Civil War Dictionary*, 940.

[4]William Nathan Harrell Smith, Confederate congressman, former U.S. representative, and future chief justice of the North Carolina Supreme Court. *Dictionary of North Carolina Biography*, s.v. "Smith, William Nathan Harrell."

ZBV to Robert Ould   A&H:GLB

[*With enclosure*]

> State of North Carolina
> Executive Department
> Raleigh Jany 20th. 1864

My Dear Sir

Your long promised letter in regard to transmitting funds to the N.C. prisoners, not having come to hand I enclose you herewith a letter to Gov. Seymour of N. York covering three bills of Exchange on A Collie & Co. London two for £500 each and one for £200, which please transmit to its destination if practicable. Without your advice this was the best plan I could fix upon. Please have a receipt from the Officer receiving it.

> Very Respectfully
> Yr. obt. Svt.
> Z. B. Vance

[*Enclosure*]

ZBV to Horatio Seymour A&H:GLB

State of North Carolina
Executive Department
Raleigh Jany. 20th. 1864

His Excellency
Horatio Seymour
Gov. of N. York

Sir

There are quite a number of the Soldiers of this State prisoners of War in the United States confined principally within your State. I learn that they are suffering greatly for want of winter clothing, and that the regulations of your Government do not forbid their purchasing if they had the means. Presuming upon your known humanity, I have ventured to enclose to you by flag of truce, three Stirling bills of exchange drawn by Theo Andreae upon Messrs A. Collie & Co 17 Leadenhall St. London amounting to £1200 (Twelve hundred pounds Sterling), which I desire you will have expended in the purchase of the most necessary clothing for the prisoners of War from North Carolina in whatever prison confined. I presume at the quoted rates of exchange the bills will produce near nine thousand dollars. In venturing to ask you to take so much trouble upon your hands, I feel sure that the suggestion of humanity and the common courtesy existing between honest enemies will be a sufficient apology. I can but hope you will accept the trouble and that you will not hesitate to allow me an opportunity of reciprocating your kindness should it become possible for me to do so. I am Sir,

With proper respect
Yr. obt. Svt.
Z. B. Vance

ZBV to Anonymous   A&H:VanPC

State of North Carolina,
Executive Department.
Raleigh, Jan'y 20, 1864.

My dear Sir,

As I expected Majr. P. very readily agreed to carry out that arrangement and only wanted Capt Deweys receipts.

Hoping that he would hear me, though he would not hear Moses and the Proph[ets] I have just written him (C[apt.] D.) to send me the receipts for Jone's corn by return mail. I think you may regard the matter as settled—

very truly yours
Z. B. Vance

Calvin J. Cowles to ZBV   A&H:VanPC

Wilkesboro
Jany. 20/64

Gov. Vance

Dr Sir

You are to be invited to join the people of this Co in Celebrating Washingtons birthday. A committe of citizens have the matter in hand & will probably let you hear from them by next mail. Every body except Lee Martin[1] as far as I have heard is anxious to *meet* you & *greet* you once more on our red hills. The day selected it is hoped will suit you—what an inspiration there is in the name of Washington!—we should never give up the celebration of his natal day nor the celebration of the glorious 4th.— the natal day of a nation—but we of the South seem inclined to neglect both—Washington was ours if any section can claim him. Every thing will be done /that can be/ to make your visit a pleasant one—you will find a Carriage awaiting you at Statesville & from the hour you enter it till you are returned there you will be the guest of the people of Wilkes Co. If the weather is good hundreds—yes thousands, will come out to see you & hear you speak—I verily believe if an amnesty /of two days/ was granted most of the Deserters would come out & hear your warning & entreaty which some no doubt could not withstand.

If Congress persists in enacting certain Laws, you have a stern duty to perform or State sovreignty is "a dead Cock in the pit"[3]

Hoping you may consent to come & partake of our humble fare I am Dear Governor

> Your obliged humble Svt.
> Calvin J. Cowles[2]
> one of the Committe of
> Arrangements

[1]Identity unknown

[2]Calvin Josiah Cowles, Wilkes County merchant and Union sympathizer who served as Confederate postmaster in Wilkesboro until his refusal to take a loyalty oath to the Confederacy led to his removal from that office in 1863. After the war he was an active Republican and superintendent of the U.S. Branch Mint at Charlotte. *Dictionary of North Carolina Biography*, s.v. "Cowles, Calvin Josiah."

[3]A dead cock in the pit. An informal description of something that was considered as good as dead. From John D. Wright *The Language of the Civil War* (Wesport, Conn.: Oryx Press, 2001), 83.

Alexander R. Lawton to ZBV   A&H:GP

> Confederate States of America
> Quartermaster General's Office
> Richmond, Januy 21 1864

Govr. A. [sic] Vance
Raleigh N.C.

Sir:

I am informed that the authorities of the State of North Carolina hold a large quantity of Woolen goods, partly imported, beyond what can possibly be needed, for some time to come, to meet the wants of the troops from that State. As all the manufacturing resources of the State have been devoted to the Service of the Soldiers therefrom; & the State, besides has enjoyed, through its enterprise, unusual facilities for drawing supplies from abroad, it occurs to me that there may be on hand an excess of other necessary articles such as shoes & blankets that can be spared for a while to aid the service at large, during the stress of the Winter months. At all events, I venture to bring the matter to your attention confident that your public spirit will lead you to do whatever you can to aid the troops of the Confederacy.

Just at this time we are greatly in want of Woolen goods & Cloth (heavy) of any description & Blankets; & Shoes too would be acceptable. The recent heavy losses experienced by this Dept., in connection with the blockade, has restricted somewhat its resources; & if you can advance for a while any of the supplies referred to, they will be acceptable & I will come under an obligation to return the same, early in the Spring, when the pressure now upon /me/ shall, in part, have passed by.

> I am respectfully
> Your obt Servt
> A R Lawton[1]
> Q. M. Genl

[*Endorsed*] Copy & file—Say that we have already made large advances to Gen Johnstons army & promised to advance also to Longstreets, of clothing—Shoes & blankets we have not enough of for our own troops—

Z B V

[1]Brig. Gen. Alexander Lawton replaced Col. Abraham C. Myers as Confederate quartermaster general in August 1863. Faust et al., *Encyclopedia of Civil War*, 427.

William J. Clarke to ZBV   A&H:GP

Camp Near Tarboro N.C
Jany. 21st. 1864

Hon. Z. B. Vance

Governor:

I received yours of 9th. inst.[1] two days ago, in consequence of the countermanding of the order for us to go to Weldon. I cannot see how the Prest. can, with any regard for the protection of this section of the State, decline acceding to your proposition, by which the objection raised by him is obviated. Altho' I am desirous of promotion, and think it due me in justice, still I would not procure it at the price of our State's truckling to the national Executive.

I regret that we are debarred from doing the good we proposed, and I pray that the evils which I too truly foresee may be averted from the good people of this section.

Situated as I am I can do nothing toward raising troops, tho' I feel confident that had I been commissioned I could have raised two or three regiments. If I could have been left in this section occupying that position, and if the Brigade of Roanoke could have been organized the 17 counties which it would have protected would, in August next, have voted for you almost unanimously. I hope they will do so *any way*; but by that time burning under a sense of neglect, knowing the Confederate Govt. only by the burdens which it imposes, noticed only to collect taxes or take away men, desperate of our success and lashed into fury by a licentious and treasonable press it will be a wonder if they do not support a "peace on any-terms" candidate; and I fear that such an one will be in the field.

Already many are declaring that they will not pay any more taxes to a Govt. which takes no steps to protect them.

If my plan had been adopted, all these cavillers would have been silenced, and the volunteer spirit of the country would have been raised to the pitch of enthusiasm.

I do not think that you will have any cause to regret your connection with this matter, and I only hope I may be able to address the people in your behalf when the canvass opens. I think I will be able to show that few men have more influence. Accept my thanks for the kind interest you have taken in me individually, for the generous support you have given to me, and rest assured that I will bear it in grateful remembrance, and that one at least will stand by and support you "thro' good report and thro' evil report," against all opposers.

> Very truly and respectfully
> Your obedient servant
> William J. Clarke

[1]Not extant, but see James A. Seddon to ZBV, January 5, 1864, in this volume, and ZBV to Seddon, December 16, 1863, in Johnston and Mobley, *Papers of Vance*, 2:343-344.

Jefferson Davis to ZBV   A&H:GP

Executive Office
Richmond
Jan. 22d. 1864

His Excy. Z. B. Vance
Governor of North Carolina—

Sir,

Your letter of 29th. December,[1] requesting, in pursuance of a Resolution of the General Assembly of the State of North Carolina, that I would direct Eli Swanner, named in the Resolution, to be returned to North Carolina to be tried for the offence alleged against him, was duly received and was referred to the Secretary of War for inquiry and report in the case. You will see from the reports, (copies of which are herewith enclosed)[2] that the prisoner Swanner is avowedly disloyal and hostile to the cause of his State and of the Confederacy. He resides in a portion of the State overrun by the enemy, and if discharged will have the ability, as he unquestionably has the disposition, to do us much injury. Scarcely an attack is made upon our pickets or our troops, or a plundering expedition undertaken, in Eastern No. Ca., but the information reaches us that the enemy were advised and guided by disloyal citizens peculiarly acquainted with the country, and the position of our forces. If such persons are to be put upon a footing with the most loyal citizens, and treated with the tenderest regard to the strict law of treason, you see how impossible it will be to procure testimony sufficient for their conviction. Before an overt act committed they must not be touched, out of a nice and scrupulous regard for the rights of the citizen. After the commission of the act, they are screened and protected within the enemy's lines. I cannot conceal from Your Excellency my opinion of the inexpediency of permitting such persons to go at large unmolested. Still, in deference to the declared wishes of the General Assembly of North Carolina, and with an earnest desire of promoting harmony and good feeling between the State and Confederate authorities, I have acceded to your request and have directed the said Eli Swanner to be returned to North Carolina for examination and trial.

Very respectfully
Your obt. servant
Jeffn. Davis

[1]In Johnston and Mobley, *Papers of Vance*, 2:355-356.
[2]Not extant.

ZBV to Sion H. Rogers A&H:GLB

State of North Carolina
Executive Department
Raleigh Jany 22d. 1864

Hon. Sion H. Rogers
Atty. General NC

Dear Sir

It has been officially notified to me that certain employees of the Confederate States Government, are engaged by order of that Govt. in distilling grain into spirits at Salisbury in this State in defiance of the laws and ordinances thereof. Will you please give me your opinion as to the power of that Government to disregard and violate in this manner the laws of N.C. and to suggest such proceedings as you may think would be proper to be taken in regard thereto.

Very Respectfully
Yr. obt. Svt.
Z. B. Vance

ZBV to Edward J. Hale A&H:Hale

Private

State of North Carolina,
Executive Department.
Raleigh, Jany 22, 1864.

Mr. Hale[1]

Dr. Sir,

There is great talk among the disaffected about the danger of losing our liberties, Habeas Corpus &c. Many good men are alarmed in this regard. Please read the document[2] I sent you yesterday—"the overthrow of the ballot" in Ky. You can show these timorous gentlemen where we are to go to, to have our civil rights respected! It will repay you to read it.

In haste yours
Z B Vance

1Edward Jones Hale, confidant of ZBV and politically influential editor and publisher of the *Fayetteville Observer*, a leading Whig newspaper before the war. *Dictionary of North Carolina Biography*, s.v. "Hale, Edward Jones."

2Not extant.

ZBV to James A. Seddon   A&H:GP

Copy

State of North Carolina
Executive Department
Raleigh Jany 25th. 1864

Hon Jas. A Seddon
Secty. of War
Richmond Va.

Dear Sir

To obviate any further difficulty in regard to carrying Cotton by the Collie line of Steamers, the Agent of the owners proposes to sell an interest to the Confederacy in these Steamers of one fourth, which would give one half of the Cotton for the Confederacy and this State. I hope you will accept this proposition

Yrs. Respectfully
Z. B. Vance

Congressional Delegation to ZBV   A&H:GP

House of Representatives
Jany. 25 1864

His Excellency
Z B Vance
Raleigh NC

Sir

In a consultation of our delegation this morning with the President in regard to public affairs in North Carolina the President read to us a communication made by himself to you,[1] in reply to a letter of yours[2] upon the subject of negotiating with the U States Government for the termination of the war. He did not read your letter to him, to which his was a response and we do not know what were the views expressed by you to him, in your letter. The letter of the President to you, contains information, which would be interesting to our people and we are of the opinion that its publication would have a happy effect <illegible> not only in our state, but upon public opinion throughout the Confederacy.

There may be something in your letter to the President, which you do not care to make public & if so the letter of the President alone would effect our object in geting his views before the public.

The President informed us that the letter was a public paper, in the hands of yourself & that its publication was a matter for your consideration, that he certainly had no objection to its being made public.

In that state of facts, we have thought proper to suggest the publication of this correspondence, or at least the letter of the President. Thinking that it will remove much prejudice against the President now existing in our State, upon the subject of Peace and peace propositions.

We have the honor to be,

> Your ob. svts.
> B. S. Gaither
> Thos. S. Ashe
> A. H. Arrington
> E. G. Reade
> J. R. McLean
> A. T. Davidson
> W. N. H. Smith
> R. R. Bridgers
> Tho D. McDowell
> O R Kenan
> William Lander

P.S. The question of the publication you must judge for yourself If you publish the Presidents letter without yours, your letter may be called for & place you in an unpleasant position, provided there is any thing in yours, which you would not like to make public.

[1]January 8, 1864, in this volume.
[2]December 30, 1863, in Johnston and Mobley, *Papers of Vance*, 2:357-358.

ZBV to Jefferson Davis   A&H:GLB

State of North Carolina
Executive Department
Raleigh Jany. 27th. 1864

His Excellency
President Davis

Dr. Sir

The delegation in Congress from this State have applied to me for the publication of your recent letter to me on the subject of negotiation. They state that you did not object to the proposition. If you think it not objectionable I will have my letter and yours published. Please let me know at once.

Very Truly &c
Z. B. Vance

ZBV to Joseph E. Brown   A&H:GLB

State of North Carolina
Executive Department
Raleigh Jany. 28th. 1864

His Excellency Joseph Brown
Governor of the State of Georgia

Dear Sir

The State of North Carolina has purchased and now has in yr State two thousand bales of Cotton. I respectfully request that you will inform me at your earliest convenience what tax is to be paid upon it and to whom the amount should be remitted.

With sentiments of great respect

Your obedient servant
Z. B. Vance

ZBV to Edward J. Hale   A&H:Hale

State of North Carolina,
Executive Department.
Raleigh, Jany 28, 1864.

My dear Sir,

Yr note of yesterday[1] recd. Judge [*Edwin* G.] Reade is all right, unless he deceived me. In a private talk with [*him*] he assured me that my position was correct & met his support. Since going to Richmond he has signed a request to me to publish a letter from the Prest.[2] in reply to mine[3] on the subject of negotiations, in the hope that it will do good. I tendered it to him as a matter of policy, after consulting with the best advice at hand. I am waiting for the Presidents permission to publish his letter. It will please you.

Hyman[4] agrees to come here to edit a paper,[5] but no arrangements are yet made for it. I believe I would like [*Clement*] Dowd better though. More of this hereafter.

The Wilks speech[6] is to come [*torn*] 22 of Feb'y as this and preparat[ion] [*torn*] done, though the time is rather too far off.

There is plenty of clothing & blankets for our soldiers now, if they are not supplied it is the fault of their Quarter Masters. The Ad-Vance brought 10,000 prs shoes, 12,000 blankets 8,000 prs cards &c. The "Don" is expected this week with more. Holden & Pennington[7] are much alarmed, but I don't anticipate any radical reform.

In haste yours
Z. B Vance

[1]Not extant.

[2]January 8, in this volume

[3]December 30, 1863, in Johnston and Mobley, *Papers of Vance*, 2:357-358.

[4]John Durante Hyman, a friend of ZBV, lawyer, and co-editor of the *Asheville Spectator*, in which ZBV was a partner. Johnston and Mobley, *Papers of Vance*, 1:50n.

[5]Becomes the pro-ZBV Raleigh *Conservative*.

[6]A gubernatorial campaign speech by ZBV in Wilkesboro, Wilkes County.

[7]John L. Pennington, editor of the Raleigh *Progress* and a peace advocate. *Dictionary of North Carolina Biography*, s. v. "Pennington, John L." See also ZBV to Edward J. Hale, September 20, 1863, in Johnston and Mobley, *Papers of Vance*, 2:282.

ZBV to Pierre G. T. Beauregard　　　　　　　　A&H:GP

State of North Carolina,
Executive Department,
Raleigh, 29th. Jany. 1864.

Genl. G. T. Beauregard[1]
Charleston So. Ca.

General.

I have been informed, only a day or two since, that a valuable package (a trunk I think), sent to me from England, was on the Steamer "Dare," which was beached on the coast of South Carolina, near Georgetown, some weeks since. It was in charge of a Mr. Edward Hamblinton, who landed it safely, but it was afterwards forcibly taken from him by the troops of the 61st. Georgia Regiment, at the time under the command of Major White—as I am informed. Mr. Hambleton protested, but was forced to give it up.

Will you do me the kindness to have the matter officially enquired into? I wish, if possible, to recover the package or its value.

A list of the contents of package can be furnished if necessary

Very Respectfully
Yr. obt. Servt.
Z. B. Vance

[1]Pierre Gustave Toutant Beauregard commanded the coastal defense of the Carolinas and Georgia until April 1864, when he was transferred to Virginia to assist in the defense of Richmond. Faust et al., *Encyclopedia of Civil War*, 51-52.

ZBV *to John White*   A&H:GP

[*With enclosure*]

State of North Carolina,
Executive Department
Raleigh, Jany 30, 1864

Mr. John White
Warrenton N.C.

Dr. Sir,

In estimating Col Crossans[1] account we find it to stand about as follows,
15 months pay as Capt in C.S. Navy at $4,500

per annum	$5625.00
Traveling expenses in England	485.00
For bounty money, running four trips through blockade $1000 ea	4,000.00
	10,110.00
Recd. from your obt. & Capt Hughes[2]	4,110.00
Due him	6,000.00

You will please give him an order on Mr. Collie for this amount—& take
his receipt.

Yours Truly
Z. B. Vance

[1]Thomas Morrow Crossan, captain of the blockade-runner *Advance*. *Dictionary
of North Carolina Biography*, s.v. "Crossan, Thomas Morrow."

[2]Theodore J. Hughes, an agent operating with White from whom White secured
a loan for North Carolina. Walter Clark, ed., *Histories of the Several Regiments and
Battalions from North Carolina in the Great War, 1861-'65*, 5 vols. (Raleigh: State of
N.C., 1901), 5:455.

[*Crosshatched*]

Preserve this letter—
I have drawn on Messrs. A. Collie & Co. England
for L 400—in favour of Col. Crossan, in
part of this bill—equal to $1,920.00

    June 15th. 1864 drawn for the further sum—
    of One Hundred pounds—equal to   480.00

    July 6—1864 drawn for the further sum—
    of Three Hundred pounds—equal to   1,440.00

    July 6—1864 drawn for the further sum—
    of Two Hundred pounds—equal to   960.00

    July 6—1864 drawn for the further sum—
    of One Hundred & fifty pounds—equal to   720.00

    July 6—1864 drawn for the further sum—
    of One Hundred pounds   480.00
                                              $6,000.00

JNW.

At the request of Mr. Crossan several of these drafts were taken back by
me and others of different amounts given in Stead without changing the
amount in the agregate

JNW.

Received of John White the above mentioned drafts drawn by him, in
my favour on Messrs. Alexr. Collie & Co. 17 Leadenhall Street London
amounting to Twelve Hundred & fifty pounds Sterling. Equal to Six
Thousand Dollars

Thos. M. Crossan

Jefferson Davis to ZBV   SHC:Van

[*Telegram*]

Richmond
Jany 30 1864

Gov Z B Vance
Raleigh

Your letter of twenty seventh (27th)[1] inst recd. I have no objection to the publication referred to if you think it advisable

Jeffn. Davis

[1]In this volume.

ZBV to Thomas J. Boykin   A&H:GLB

State of North Carolina
Executive Department
Raleigh Feby. 1st. 1864.

Dr. T J Boykin[1]
Purser of Str. Advance
Wilmington

You are hereby appointed Purser & Supercargo of State Strmr. Advance, and will apply to Messrs Power, Lowe & Co for instructions as to the disbursements of the Ship. In case the part owners, Messrs. P. L & Co. have no freight at Bermuda, The State will be entitled to have the entire inward capacity of the vessel. You will load her there with the following articles, assorting the cargo. First, cotton cards & machinery and wire for making them. Secondly, Shoes & leather. Third blankets, then card cloth for factories, cloth, ready made clothing &c &c. The importance of this arrangement you will readily comprehend

Very respectfully Yrs.
Z. B. Vance.

[1]Thomas J. Boykin was surgeon of the Twenty-sixth Regiment North Carolina Troops when ZBV was colonel of that regiment. In the autumn of 1862 he had been appointed chief surgeon of the Department of the Cape Fear and transferred to Wilmington. Louise H. Manarin, Weymouth T. Jordan, Matthew B. Brown, and Michael W. Coffey, comps., *North Carolina Troops, 1861-1865: A Roster*, 18 vols. to date (Raleigh: Division of Archives and History, Department of Cultural Resources, 1966-), 7:464.

ZBV to Alexander Collie   A&H: GLB

State of North Carolina
Executive Department
Raleigh Feby. 1st. 1864

Mr. Alexr. Collie
17 Leadenhall St.
London

My dear Sir

I have to acknowledge the reception of a very handsome Despatch Box, per Steamer Vesta, a present from you. Your kind note[1] enclosing a check upon Mr. T. Andreae for Twenty Thousand dollars, for the benefit of the poor of N. C., was also received.

Permit me to return you my thanks for your personal remembrance of myself, and in the name of the poor women and children who will be the recipients of your bounty, my warmest acknowledgements. It will relieve the patriotic suffering of many, who will I trust in days to come of returning peace and prosperity, learn to bless the munificence of the stranger who remembered them in the hour of adversity and distress. With sentiments of the highest esteem and regard.

I am Sir
Very Truly Yours
Z. B. Vance

[1]See Alexander Collie to ZBV, December 7, 1863, in Johnston and Mobley, *Papers of Vance*, 2:337.

ZBV to Alexander Collie A&H:GLB

State of North Carolina
Executive Department
Raleigh Feby 1st. 1864.

Mr Alexr. Collie
17. Leadenhall Street
London

Dr. Sir

Mr John White having returned home, I have deemed it best to send out another special agent to represent the interest of this State in your Country. You will therefore please recognize the bearer Mr Joseph H. Flanner[1] in that capacity. I desire no change made in the present management of the States affairs. The Cotton shipped will be consigned to you as heretofore, the net proceeds I wish placed in Bank subject to the order of the Governor of No. Carolina, retaining what may be necessary to meet such orders as I may heretofore have sent out &c. Mr Flanners instructions will confine him to the mere looking after and superintending of the States interest leaving the details of business in your hands. I refer you to him for further particulars as he fully understands my situation and wishes, and have the honor to commend him to your favor as a man of business and a gentleman.

Very Respectfully
Yr. obt. servt.
Z. B. Vance

[1]President of the Wilmington Steamship Company and a purser of the blockade-runner *Advance*. Johnston and Mobley, *Papers of Vance*, 1:354n; ZBV to John White, September 3, 1863, in Johnston and Mobley, *Papers of Vance*, 2:261.

ZBV to Joseph H. Flanner   A&H: GLB

State of North Carolina
Executive Department
Raleigh Feby. 1st. 1864

J. H. Flanner Esq.
Wilmington

Having appointed you a Special Agent of the State of N. Carolina to represent her commercial interests in Europe, you will proceed by the first Steamer to your destination. You are instructed to visit Bermuda on your way and look into the business of this State in the hands of John T. Bourne, Lemmon & Co[1] and the Consignees of Power Lowe & Co Wilmington, who will henceforth be the Agents of the Steamer Advance, and give such instructions to them as you may deem most condusive to States interest, and advise me fully. On arriving in England you will see and confer with Mr. Alexr. Collie, 17 Leadenhall Street London, who was left in charge of Mr John Whites' business and to whom, all of our Cotton heretofore shipped has been consigned. In conjunction with him you will exercise a general superintendence over the shipments of Cotton, its sale and the investments of its proceeds in a Solvent Bank as heretofore instructions have been given to Mr Collie and Mr White. The Cotton to be hereafter shipped by the "Advance" will as a matter of convenience be consigned to Lawrence & Co. Liverpool,[2] the correspondents of Power Lowe & Co. part owners of that Vessel. I desire you to enquire into the solvency of this house, change the consignment should it be necessary, not otherwise. The proceeds of this Cotton I desire put in Bank also in the same manner.

Col. McRae[3] also left some unfinished business in the hands of I. A. Weston, 110 Burnhill Row London. You will call upon him and investigate his accounts also. In a word whilst I do not wish any change made of the parties who are now acting for us without the best of reasons, I desire to know that all continue to deal fairly with the state and obey my instructions, and to this end you are invested with power to investigate their transactions from time to time, and to give fresh instructions should it be deemed necessary. You will advise me of your progress and observations by every steamer.

Very respectfully
Yr. obt. Servt.
Z. B. Vance

Confederate States of America
State of North Carolina

Know all men by these presents that Joseph H Flanner of the town of Wilmington, and state of North Carolina, is hereby constituted & appointed an agent for the general Superintendence of the affairs of said State in England in relation to the sale of Cotton, the depositing of the proceeds in Bank and the shipping of goods & stores, as per instructions contained in explanatory letter of this date to said Flanner, copied in the letter Book of the Executive Department of said state page 439. All acts of said Flanner in pursuance of & in conformity with said instructions are hereby ratified and confirmed

Witness Z. B. Vance Governor of said State, at the city of Raleigh with the attestation of the Great Seal this 1st. day of February A.D. 1864

Z. B. Vance
Gov. of N.C.

[1]J. S. Lemmon's Bermuda shipping company. J. S. Lemmon to ZBV, February 26, 1864, A&H: GP.

[2]Edward Lawrence and Company. Wise, *Lifeline of the Confederacy*, 112.

[3]Duncan Kirkland McRae, lawyer, politician, and Confederate colonel appointed by ZBV as special envoy to Europe to sell North Carolina naval stores bonds and procure supplies. *Dictionary of North Carolina Biography*, s.v. "McRae, Duncan Kirkland."

ZBV to John J. Guthrie   A&H: GLB

State of North Carolina
Executive Department
Raleigh, Feb. 1st. 1864

Capt. Guthrie[1]
Comdg. Str. Ad-Vance
Wilmington N.C.

Dr. Sir,
You will proceed to Sea as soon as possible & sail for Bermuda, where you will take in freight, as per instructions to T. J. Boykin, Purser, of this date.

In consequence of the great abuse of the vessel by the carrying of private freight it becomes necessary to order that nothing shall go aboard without my consent in writing, or that of the consignees & part owners, Messrs Power Lowe & Co. I shall look to you to see this order rigidly carried out.

I need hardly warn you Captain of the great importance of not despairing of the ship too hastily. The prema-& culpable beaching of the Don & Vesta furnish a useful warning of the timidity of pilots & commanders, who merely serve for money.

You will receive the same compensation which was allowed Col. Crossan.

> Very truly &c.
> Z. B. Vance

[1]John Julius Guthrie, a Confederate naval officer who replaced Thomas M. Crossan as captain of the *Advance*. Clark, *Histories of Regiments from North Carolina*, 1:59, 5:471; ZBV to John J. Guthrie, October 18, 1863, in Johnston and Mobley, *Papers of Vance*, 2:303.

ZBV to Power, Low and Co　　　　　　　　　A&H:GLB

> State of North Carolina
> Executive Department
> Raleigh Feby. 1st. 1864

Messrs Power Lowe & Co
Wilmington N.C.

Gents

Your will please load the Steamer with Cotton as soon as possible and start her to Sea. Mr [*Thomas*] Carter will furnish the States share, let it be compressed if possible. Capt Guthrie goes in command & Dr. Boykin as Purser, which I hope will be satisfactory. The former will receive the same pay allowed Capt. Crossan, viz monthly pay as a Captain in C.S. Navy, and one thousand dollars per trip, round. I have ordered him not to let a pound of freight for private parties go onboard without my written consent or yours and hope you will assist in executing the order. You will please give such instructions to Dr. Boykin as to his duties as he may require.

Should you have no freight in Bermuda of course I desire that the vessel shall take her entire cargo there for State account paying you the usual freight. In case the vessel should be unable to reenter the port of Wilmington, I leave it to you to give such instructions to your Agents aboard as may best suit the interest of both parties, desiring of course to be consulted before she is sold &c. The Cotton I suppose should be weighed and sent forward on joint account in the manner agreed upon at our interview.

Yrs Respectfully
Z. B. Vance

ZBV to Kemp P. Battle and Sion H. Rogers   SHC:BattFM

State of North-Carolina,
Executive Department.
Raleigh Febry. 1st. 1864

Kemp P. Battle Esq[1]
Hon S H. Rogers

Gentlemen

I request that you will investigate the circumstances connected with the negotiation in England by Col. D. K. McRae of naval store scrip of this state and purchase of arms clothing &c. for the use of the State, and report what in your judgment would be just compensation for his services.

My letter-book & all papers in my possession throwing light on the question are subject to your inspection.

Very respectfully Z. B. Vance

[1]Kemp Plummer Battle, lawyer, president of Chatham Railroad during the Civil War. He became a trustee of the University of North Carolina, Chapel Hill, in 1862 and its president in 1876. *Dictionary of North Carolina Biography*, s.v. "Battle, Kemp Plummer."

W. H. Hatch to ZBV A&H:GP

Office of Exch of Prisoners
Richmond Va. Feby 2nd. 1864

His Excellency
Z. B. Vance

Sir

I have the honor to acknowledge receipt of yours of 30th. ult.[1] On the 29th. ult Judge Ould forwarded to Maj Genl E. A. Hitchcock[2] Comr for Exch of Prisoners, Surg Genl Warren's[3] letter[4] requesting permission to visit the Northern prisons for the purpose of alleviating the condition of N. Carolina prisoners. On the same day he addressed to Genl Hitchcock a letter of which the enclosed[5] is a copy, and to which he respectfully requests your attention. The replies to these letters when received shall be promtly communicated to you. Without the consent of the U.S. Govt, it is impracticable to send such an agent as you propose.

Respectfully
Your obt servt
W. H. Hatch[6]
Capt & A. A. Genl

[*Endorsed*] File—

ZBV

[1]Not extant.

[2]Union general Ethan Allen Hitchcock. Beginning in 1862, he served as commissioner for exchange of war prisoners. Boatner, *Civil War Dictionary*, 403.

[3]Edward Warren, surgeon general of North Carolina. *Dictionary of North Carolina Biography*, s.v. "Warren, Edward."

[4]Not extant.

[5]Not extant.

[6]Assistant agent of exchange for the Confederate army. Clark, *Histories of Regiments from North Carolina*, 5:624.

ZBV to Theodore Andreae   A&H: GLB

State of North Carolina
Executive Department
Raleigh Feby. 2d. 1864

Mr. T. Andreae
Agent for Stmr. Hansa & Don
Wilmington

Dear Sir

In order to have the accounts of the State properly before the Auditor of public accounts, as I am required to do by law, it will be necessary that I should have a detailed statement of the disbursements of each steamer for every trip. The disbursements on this side you can submit yourself, those at Bermuda & Nassau you can obtain by directing our Agents there to forward duplicate copies by each steamer. Please attend to this

Very Respectfully Yours
Z. B. Vance

James A. Seddon to ZBV   A&H:GP

Confederate States of America
War Department,
Richmond, Va. February 3, 1864

His Ex. Z. B Vance.
Gov. of No Ca

Sir

In accordance with your request[1]—communicating resolutions of the Legislature of North Carolina to the same effect—The President has ordered that Eli Swanner be sent to Raleigh for examination before the civil authorities—He is clearly liable to military service & if discharged from prosecution must be enrolled for duty under the Act of Congress.[2] He has been twice subjected to examination since his arrest by the Confederate authorities: once by a Commissioner sent to Salisbury N C in January 1863 for the special purpose of examining all political prisoners there confined &

once since he was brought to the City of Richmond. Upon each occasion he avowed his adhesion to the cause of the enemy & demanded to be sent to the North—Though he offered to pledge his word that he would not return South during the war—it seemed more than probable that his real purpose was—as soon as permitted to enter the lines of the enemy—to claim the full protection of the United States authorities to enable him to resume his residence in that portion of your State then & now unfortunately in their occupancy—Had he been enabled to do this it can not be doubted that the vengeance of the enemy would have been promptly directed towards his loyal neighbors—& the calamities to which they are unavoidably subject very seriously enhanced.

> Very Resp Yrs
> James A. Seddon
> Sec War

[*Endorsed*] File & copy.

ZBV

[1] ZBV to Jefferson Davis. December 29, 1863, in Johnston and Mobley, *Papers of Vance*, 2:355-356. See also Jefferson Davis to ZBV, January 22, 1864, in this volume.

[2] In April 1862, the Confederate Congress passed the first conscription law, requiring a three-year enlistment for white males between the ages of 18 and 35. The upper age limit was raised to 45 in September 1862. In February 1864 Congress passed a law conscripting all white males who were 17 to 50 years of age and requiring all enlisted men to remain in the army regardless of whether they had fulfilled their initial three-year contract. James M. McPherson, *Ordeal by Fire: The Civil War and Reconstruction*, 2nd ed. (New York: McGraw Hill, 1992), 184, 185. See also Albert Burton Moore, *Conscription and Conflict in the Confederacy* (New York: Macmillan Co., 1924).

Joseph E. Johnston to ZBV   A&H:GLB

Dalton Feby. 3d. 1864

His Excy. Z. B. Vance
Gov. of N. Carolina

Sir:
    I have had the honor to receive your letter of the 29th. ulto.[1]—& that of Col Palmer[2] to you enclosed with it.

I regret very much the capture of an officer so valuable as Genl. Vance.[3] Col Palmer has reported it, with the circumstances as well as the orders given to Colonels Thomas[4] & Henry.[5] He had been directed to have the conduct of these officers investigated by a Court Martial.[6]

Most respectfully
Your obt. svt
J. E. Johnston

[1]Not extant

[2]Col. John B. Palmer, commanding the Fifty-eighth Regiment North Carolina Troops in East Tennessee. Clark, *Histories of Regiments from North Carolina*, 3:432-445; Barrett, *Civil War in North Carolina*, 201.

[3]Brig. Gen. Robert Brank Vance (brother of ZBV), commanding the District of Western North Carolina. He was captured during a raid in eastern Tennessee. Palmer replaced him as district commander. *Dictionary of North Carolina Biography*, s.v. "Vance, Robert Brank"; Barrett, *Civil War in North Carolina*, 199-201.

[4]Col. William Holland Thomas, white chief of the Eastern Band of the Cherokee Indians and former legislator who commanded Thomas's Legion North Carolina Troops, which included Cherokee companies. During the raid into eastern Tennessee, General Vance dispatched Thomas's troops to Gatlinburg. *Dictionary of North Carolina Biography*, s.v. "Thomas, William Holland"; Barrett, *Civil War in North Carolina*, 200-201. See also Volume 16 of Manarin et al., *North Carolina Troops*, on Thomas's Legion.

[5]Lt. Col. James L. Henry, commanding Fourteenth Battalion North Carolina Cavalry, which eventually was expanded and redesignated the Sixty-ninth Regiment North Carolina Troops (Seventh Regiment North Carolina Cavalry). He had accompanied Thomas to Gatlinburg. Manarin et al., *North Carolina Troops*, 2:61, 560-561.

[6]As General Vance conducted his raid into Tennessee, Thomas, "commanding the party left at Gatlinburg[,] had been ordered to fall back with his infantry and to send Lieutenant-Colonel Henry with his cavalry and artillery to Schultz' Mill where they were directed to take up position and await the arrival of General Vance." But Henry fell back with Thomas and therefore was unable to assist Vance. Apparently. Henry subsequently was placed under arrest for disobeying orders but remained present or accounted for until September 1864. Barrett, *Civil War in North Carolina*, 200-201. Manarin et al., *North Carolina Troops*, 2:560-561.

ZBV to Burgess S. Gaither et al.   A&H:GLB

State of North Carolina
Executive Department
Raleigh Feb. 4th. 1864

Hon. B. S. Gaither
& others M.C.
Richmond Va.

Gents

Your letter[1] asking me to publish the letter of the President[2] in regard to the troubles in N.C. has been recd.

After careful consideration I am doubtful of the propriety of so doing, for the reason that it contains an intimation of *force* to be applied in certain contingencies which I think better calculated to increase than to allay irritation. However so great is my respect for the opinion you express that if after a reexamination of the letter you should still advise it I will publish it. I have no earthly objection to the publication of my own to the President.[3]

Very Resply yrs.
Z. B. Vance

[1]January 25, 1864, in this volume.
[2]January 8, 1864, in this volume.
[3]December 30, 1863, in Johnston and Mobley, *Papers of Vance*, 2:357-358.

ZBV to Edward J. Hale   A&H:Hale

Private

State of North Carolina,
Executive Department.
Raleigh, Feb 4, 1864.

My dear Sir,

You no doubt have noticed that in answering yr letters I hardly ever reply to yr questions? In looking over your last two favors tonight I find several flagrant instances. You ask who will supply [*William A.*] Grahams place in the Senate? I don't know—it cant be supplied. The legislature is a very weak body at best and after Graham is taken out it is a catfish without a head! The ablest men left, Warren[1] [*Bedford*] Brown &c in Senate, & Grissom[2] in the House I fear will all be against us. Amis[3] is a capital man however & so is Carter.[4] I hope opportunity will bring out others.

You have before this an explanation of the sale of the Journal[5] I had nothing to do with it of course, though I am glad it has got into more decent hands & hope it will do the country more service. The editorials as you will see are now respectful and in good temper, which like a soft voice in woman "is an excellent thing."

Holden has quit coming to see me, though his friends break to me to protect him whenever a few soldiers are at the depot. I had a long talk with [*John L.*] Pennington this afternoon, and worked upon his fears considerably. He is a time [saver] and a coward and must be appealed to accordingly. Holden is in constant terror & alarm, sleeps I am told away from home every night. Alas, alas!

By the way, seeing that Holden and you were getting up an issue about the preparation of the Johnson resolutions in Raleigh, I traced up my authority for so stating. [*Sion H.*] Rogers told me that he was informed by Fowle[6] that they were either prepared or *revised* in Raleigh, but that he was not at liberty to say so & hoped you would let the matter drop, as he could not make public what he had recd. from Fowle privately. There is no doubt of the truth of this statement. The Johnson resolutions of last summer were revised by Holden for I saw the bearer in Holdens office with them. But it matters not.

Yours truly
Z B Vance

[1]Edward Jenner Warren, Beaufort County lawyer and state senator who supported ZBV. *Dictionary of North Carolina Biography*, s. v. "Warren, Edward Jenner."

[2]Eugene Grissom, physician, former Confederate army officer, and member of the state House, 1862-1865. *Dictionary of North Carolina Biography*, s.v. "Grissom, Eugene."

[3]James S. Amis, state legislator from Granville County. J. G. de Roulhac Hamilton, Max R. Williams, and Mary Reynolds Peacock, eds., *The Papers of William Alexander Graham*, 8 vols. (Raleigh: Division of Archives and History, Department of Cultural Resources, 1957-1992), 6:419.

[4]David Miller Carter, Beaufort County lawyer, planter, former Confederate army officer, and state legislator, 1862-1865. Williams, Hamilton, and Peacock, *Papers of Graham*, 6:44-45.

[5]*State Journal*, a Raleigh newspaper.

[6]Daniel Gould Fowle, who had quarreled with ZBV and resigned his office as state adjutant general in August 1863. He began serving in the state legislature in 1864. *Dictionary of North Carolina Biography*, s.v. "Fowle, Daniel Gould."

ZBV *to Edward J. Hale*   A&H: Hale

Private

State of North Carolina,
Executive Department.
Raleigh, Feb 4, 1864.

E. J. Hale Esq

My dear Sir,

I can not conceal my satisfaction at Judge [*Robert S.*] French's decision. Not that I am entirely satisfied with it, but that it gives me a complete triumph over Pearson. According to his doctrine, that the decision of a single judge in chambers is binding & settles the law,[1] he is forestalled & bound by French's decision though I have it from most reliable authority that he thinks the law unconstitutional and was waiting to decide so. He is now obliged to respect French's decision, and can neither get the Supreme Court together until June, nor sit with the other Judges on a case agreed— Good. I wish you could see the correspondence between him & myself You would then appreciate how completely I am justified by his having over reached himself.

The expedition to New Bern was a fizzle, as most expeditions in N.C. are. I see many good men from the coast who are all right and will work for the cause. What do you think of [*Edwin G.*] Reade's remarks in the Senate? I like it except the delicacy /with/ which he speaks of the Convention.[2] Altogether I am hopeful. You heard of the Greensboro meeting—it was a miserable failure.

Do you observe that Holden gives me very little credit for my blockade running enterprize? Every body else gives me due praise but him, of course. I am sorry to have no more cards (10,000) for distribution, but look for more every week. Will send these to the Co. courts according to white population. The Advance goes out to night with 720 bales cotton. Success to her.

In haste yrs
Z B Vance

¹See Richmond M. Pearson to ZBV, January 11, 1864, in this volume, and Pearson to ZBV, November 2, 1863, in Johnston and Mobley, *Papers of Vance*, 2:314-316.
²The statewide peace convention proposed by William W. Holden.

David A. Barnes to David L. Swain   SHC: Swain

State of North-Carolina,
Executive Department.
Raleigh, Feb 4th, 1864

Hon: David L. Swain

Dear Sir

His Excellency Governor Vance directs me to inform you that Colonel Mallett¹ says there will be no change in /the/ existing order in regard to the conscription of the students of the University.

Yours very truly
David A Barnes
Aid de Camp to the Governor

¹Peter Mallett, Confederate commandant of conscription in North Carolina. Johnston and Mobley, *Papers of Vance*, 1:175n.

James A. Seddon to ZBV   Mich:Sch

Confederate States of America,
War Department,
Richmond, Va. Feb 5 1864

His Excellency Z. B. Vance
Governor of N.C.
Raleigh, N.C.

Sir,

I have received your letter¹ asking a renewal of the furlough of S. P. Arrington² for sixty days.

In reply I have the honor to say, that a long indulgence has already been extended to the gentleman and no reason being assigned for the extension now asked, I have no ground on which to base my action. If you will state the reasons for your application, there will be every disposition on my part to meet your wishes, so far as the interest of the public service will permit.

> Very Respectfully
> Your obdt. servt.
> James A Seddon
> Secretary of War

[1]Not extant.

[2]Samuel Peter Arrington, son-in-law of John White, supply agent for North Carolina in England. See ZBV to Jefferson Davis, March 7, 1863, in Johnston and Mobley, *Papers of Vance*, 2:83.

Theodore Andreae to ZBV   A&H:GP

[*With enclosure*]

Private

Wilmington 8 February 1864

Dear Sir

Your telegram[1] reading: "The Don must go to B'muda as it seems *impossible to get* the Hansa there—if my orders are not obeyed I will have to change my agent" has just come to hand.

This message implies that the Hansa was sent to Nassau *willingly* or *intentionally*. If you are under such an impression you are wrong and I only hope that after knowing me a little longer you will not come as readily to a similar conclusion. I enclose an original dispatch from the Capt of Hansa last trip to which I replied that if he had not coal enough after he was out he would as a matter of course have to go to Nassau or even Green Turtle Key. You had no coal here at the time to give her any more, to come back up the river take coal, go down again would have lost her half a trip & if she had had to wait here for coal from the mines—it would have taken her longer than going to Nassau.—The facts will confirm this & I was therefore right to let her go the road she did. As long as I am agent for you & A Collie & Co. I will do what I consider right and nothing else.—As I telegraphed to you the Hansa has plenty of coal now & shall go to B'muda. The A. D. Vance & her will bring nearly all—if not all in, you have at B'muda. The Don in the contrary has from what captain and engineers say lost a deal of her speed by being foul & I would not act up to what I consider profitable &

fair towards all interested if I was not to send her out to a place where she can be put into the required condition again.—I would be sorry if what I am going to add would displease you but there is nothing like making a clear breast of it. I do not consider the conclusion of your message "if my orders are not obeyed I'll have to change my agent" quite fair. Your know that by Mr. Collie's orders the managemt of the Strs. was to remain in his hands & I only agreed to let you have nominal control because I thought it would look more the thing if the Steamers in which the State has an interest were under the management of the State nominally.—I have no particular interest to send the Strs. to Nassau. Collie has agents in B'muda as well as in Nassau & therefore my actions regarding the destination of the boats can not be influenced by Collies interest viz. Governor Vances interest. I shall manage the Steamers in the way in which I consider they'll pay best. If I displease you I am very sorry but can not help it.— Should you perhaps regret the contract you made I am ready to cancel it at any time you like or sell you the Steamers at a fair price.—Mr Collie I know—and I act for him here—would be sorry to see you continuing engaged in Steamers with him if you were for a moment under the impression that his interest was looked after and not yours at same time.

Excuse the scribbling but as Mr Flanner who takes this had to leave by train a few minutes after receipt of your dispatch I could not make it any better.

Yours vy truly
Andreae

[1]See ZBV to Theodore Andreae, February 8, 1864, A&H:GLB.

[*Enclosure*]

F. Atkinson to Theodore Andreae   A&H:GLB

Smithville 28th.

Mr. Andreae

We grounded last night and burned so much coal we will not be able to make Bermuda without more. Shall we go to Nassau. Answer at once

F. Atkinson
Master
Approved W. D. Hardeman
Capt. & A.A.G.

Leonidas F. Siler to ZBV   A&H:GP

Franklin N.C.
Febr. 8th 1864

My dear Sir;

On the 2nd. inst. about one thousand Yankees & tories came to my brother's (T. P. Siler)[1] arrested him and two negro men, took them and several old men on to where they met up with some of [*William H.*] Thomas' forces, whom they attacked and fought for a little while. The Indians fought nobly, under the surprise, until their ammunition failed. The loss on either side was not heavy. Our loss two killed and eighteen prisoners. Yankees lost six killed & several wounded. The raiders then returned to John Dehart's and camped, destroying corn, apple trees, bacon, household furniture &c. In the morning they went on to T. P. Siler' s where they fed & carried away all his corn. poured his rye in the sand, took his wife's money and all the arms and horses they could find, placed a wounded man in my brother's carriage and drove off to Tennessee. That night T. P. escaped from them and is now at home. I suppose he will accept the commission of Col. of Home Guards and is in a good humor for disturbing the rest of tories and deserters. His negro boys also escaped. Several old citizens were captured and carried off. The wildest excitement prevailed through the county and the most exaggerated stories were in circulation. But they did not come nearer the village than Dehart.[2]

I have to night written to Col [*John B.*] Palmer at Ashville, requesting him to make some disposition of his forces at Ashville, so as to secure our protection. A few of the right sort of men will effectually prevent a repetition of this thing. If our people are to live, they must have protection. Give us the companies we have sent to the war, and we defy the Yankees & tories in that direction. But I know the authorities cannot do everything. But you can cause a scattering of the forces which are doing nothing at Ashville and we need them. Your brother Robt. wrote me, while on his way to Tennessee, that he intended to defend our frontier. He is gone. We appeal to you to stir up the authorities in our behalf.

We are generally a well up here. All stronger for the South than ever. Have no use for Holden & his peace programme. Deem it best to fight for peace now. I would be glad to hear from you.

Yours truly
L. F. Siler[3]

[*Endorsed*] File

ZBV

[1]Thaddeus P. Siler, former captain in Ninth Regiment North Carolina Troops (First Regiment North Carolina Cavalry). He was wounded in Maryland in 1862 and imprisoned by the Federals. Paroled, he became major of the Seventh Battalion North Carolina Cavalry and then of the Sixty-fifth Regiment North Carolina Troops, from which he resigned and subsequently became colonel of the Sixth Regiment North Carolina Home Guard. Manarin et al., *North Carolina Troops*, 2:89, 457, 516; Clark, *Histories of Regiments from North Carolina*, 3:673-674, 4:650.

[2]For an account of the raid, see Barrett, *Civil War in North Carolina*, 232-233.

[3]Leonidas Fidelis Siler, lawyer, journalist, teacher, minister, and fellow university student with ZBV in 1851. Johnston and Mobley, *Papers of Vance*, 1:5n.

ZBV *to Alexander Collie*   A&H:GLB

State of North Carolina
Executive Department
Raleigh, Feb. 8th. 1864.

Mr. Alexr. Collie
17 Leadenhall St.
London.

Dr. Sir

I sent out last month an order for one hundred thousand pairs of hand cards & machines & wire for making them. Mr White informs me that he gave the order to the manufacturer in September for the cards & that the machines (5 of them) had been purchased and were waiting shipment.

As yet only eight thousand pairs have been received, and the Don just in reports none in Bermuda. Do you know why this delay occurs. It is of the utmost importance to the people of N.C. that these cards should be obtained speedily. I have repeatedly urged the hastening of them forward but without avail. Please investigate the cause of this delay and hold responsible the defaulting party. If the cards & machinery are not already shipped please forward them without regard to expense, for if I do not get them in by the 1st. of May I despair of getting them at all.

I have just cause of complaint against your agent here Mr Andreae. By the terms of the contract entered into between us in regard to the Steamers Don

& Hansa, I was to have all the inward capacity of the vessels for the bringing in of my freight from Bermuda. But in defiance of my express commands Andreae has on one pretence or another sent the Hansa both trips since my part ownership to Nassau where I had no freight.[1] I am consequently running all the risks of the blockade for the benefit of the other part owners, and getting none of my supplies in. This course I shall not submit to, and should I conclude to exercise the powers vested in me by the contract and take charge of the vessels when arriving at Wilmington to the exclusion of your agent, you must not regard it as evincing any disregard of your interests, but as only a necessary attempt to protect those of this State.

Should your connection with the blockade running business in N.C. be continued long I respectfully advise that you substitute for Mr. A. an agent who would inspire more confidence & respect than this gentleman has been able to do.

Hoping to hear from you often

> I am Sir
> Very resply & truly
> Yr. obt. svt.
> Z. B. Vance

[1]See Theodore Andreae to ZBV, February 8, 1864, in this volume.

ZBV to William H. C. Whiting   A&H:GLB

Raleigh Feb. 8th.

Genl. Whiting
Wilmington,

Why do you object to a Signal officer & pilot going out for the new Steamer at Bermuda? She cannot come in without them, and I hope you will permit them to go. The State is part owner in two Steamers expected at Bermuda daily.

Z. B. Vance

ZBV to Jefferson Davis   A&H:GP

State of North Carolina
Executive Department
Raleigh Feby. 9th. 1864

His Excellency
Jefferson Davis

My Dear Sir

Since receiving your letter of the 8th. Ult.[1] to which it was my intention to have replied before this, reports have reached me from Richmond, which if true would render my reply unnecessary. I hear with deep regret that a bill is certainly expected to pass the Congress, suspending the writ of Habeas Corpus, throughout the Confederacy, and that certain arrests will immediately be made in North Carolina.[2] Of course if Congress and Your Excellency be resolved upon this, as the only means of repressing disaffection in this State it would be a mere waste of time for me to argue the matter. And yet I should not hold myself guiltless of the consequences which I fear will follow did I not add yet another word of expostulation to the many which I have already spoken. If the bill referred to, about which I can form no opinion until I see it—be strictly within the limits of the Constitution I imagine the people of this State will submit to it—so great is their regard for law. If it be adjudged, on the contrary, to be in violation of that instrument and revolutionary in itself, it will be resisted. Should it become a law soon, I earnestly advise you to be chary of exercising the power with which it will invest you. Be content to try, at least for a while, the moral effect of holding this power over the heads of discontented men before shocking all worshipers of the common law throughout the world by hurling freemen into sheriffless dungeons for opinions sake. I do not speak this factiously, or by way of a flourish, nor do I believe that as an enlightened lawyer, and a Christian Statesman you would feel any pleasure in the performance of such an ungracious task. I am on the contrary convinced that you believe it to be the only way to secure North Carolina in the performance of her obligations to her Confederates. The misfortune of this belief is yours, the shame will light upon those unworthy sons who have thus sought to stab their Mother because she cast *them* off. If our citizens are left untouched by the arm of military violence, I do not dispair of an appeal to the reason and patriotism of the people at the ballot box. Hundreds of good and true men now acting with and possessing the confidence of the party called Conservatives are /at work/ against the dangerous movement for a Convention; and whilst civil law remains intact will work zealously and with heart. I expect myself to take the field as soon as the proprieties of my position will allow me and shall exert every effort to restrain the revolutionary tendency of public opinion—Never yet Sir, have the people of North Carolina refused to listen to their public men if they show right and reason on their side. I do not fear to trust the issue now to these potent weapons in the hands of such men as will wield them next summer. I do fear to trust bayonets and dungeons. I endeavored soon after my accession to the Chief Magestracy of North Carolina, to make you aware of both the fact of disaffection in the State and the cause of it. In addition to the many letters to you, I have twice visited Richmond expressly to give you information on this point. The truth is, as I have often said before, that the great body of our people have been *suspected* by their Government, perhaps because of the reluctance with which they gave up the old Union: and I know you will pardon me for saying that this conciousness of their being suspected has been greatly strengthened by what seemed to be a studied exclusion of the anti-secessionists from all the more important offices of the government, even from those promotions in the army, which many of them had won with their blood. Was this suspicion just? And was there sufficient effort made to disprove that it existed if it really did not exist at Richmond? Discussion it is true has been unlimited and bitter and unrelenting criticism upon your Administration has been endulged in, but where and when have our people failed you in the battle, or withheld either their blood or their vast resources? To what exaction have they not submitted, what draft upon their patriotism have they yet dishonored? Conscription, ruthless and unrelenting has only been exceeded in the severity of its execution by the impressment of property, frequently entrusted to men unprincipled, dishonest and filled to overflowing with all the petty meaness of small minds dressed in a little brief authority. The files of my office are piled up with the unavaling complaints of outraged citizens to whom redress is impossible. Yet they have submitted and so far performed with honor their duty to their country, though the voice of these very natural murmurs is set down to disloyalty. I do not hold you responsible for all the petty annoyances—"the insolence of office" under which our people lose heart and patience. Even if I did, I cannot forget that it is *my country* that I am serving, not the rulers of that country. I make no threat, I desire only, with singleness of purpose and sincerity of heart to speak those words of soberness and trust which may with the blessing of God best subserve the cause of my suffering country. Those words I now believe to be the advice herein given, to refrain from exercising the extraordinary power about to be given you by Congress, at least until the last hope of moral influence being sufficient, is extinct. Though you expressed a fear in your last letter[3] that my continued efforts to concilliate were injudicious,

I cannot yet see just cause for abandoning it. Perhaps I am unduly biased in my judgement concerning a people whom I love and to whom I owe so much. Though I trust not. Our success depends not on the number engaged to support our cause, but upon their zeal and affection. Hence I have every hope in persuading, not one in *forcing* the sympathy of an unwilling people. The Legislature of this state meets next May. Two thirds are required by our constitution to call a convention. This number cannot be obtained, a bare majority vote for submitting the proposition will in my opinion be impossible. Under no circumstances can a convention be assembled in No. Ca. during the present year, in my judgment, and during next summer the approaching state elections will afford an opportunity for a full and complete discussion of all the issues, the result of which I do not fear if left to ourselves. If there be a people on earth given to the sober second thought, amenable to reason and regardful of their plighted honor, I believe that I may claim that it is the people of North Carolina.

> Very Respectfully
> Yr. obt. Servt.
> Z. B. Vance

[1]In this volume.

[2]For a summary of the suspension of habeas corpus in the Confederacy, see Faust et al., *Encyclopedia of Civil War*, 331. For North Carolina and ZBV's response, see Glenn Tucker, *Zeb Vance: Champion of Personal Freedom* (New York: Bobbs-Merrill Co., 1965), 285-290; and Hamilton, "The North Carolina Courts and the Confederacy," 389–391.

[3]January 22, 1864, in this volume.

ZBV to James A. Seddon   A&H: GLB

> State of North Carolina
> Executive Department
> Raleigh Feb. 9th. 1864

Hon. Jas. A. Seddon
Secy of War

Dr. Sir.

Three or four of the extreme western mountain counties of this State are almost in a state of starvation. There short crops were badly frost bitten and the roving bands of my old friend the cavalry with constant depredations of the enemy have consumed everything they had.

Can some arrangements not be made to furnish them a few thousand bushels of tithe grain in Pickens & Anderson districts S.C. I will give bacon in exchange for it if it cannot be otherwise procured—please answer soon.

Yrs. Resptly
Z. B. Vance

ZBV to Seth M. Barton   A&H:VanPC

Copy

State of No Ca
Executive Dept.
Raleigh Feby 9th./64

Gen Barton[1]
Kinston N C

I am informed by Mr. Parrott who has procured for me a thousand pounds of bacon or salted pork near Kinston, that you "positively refused" to let it be brought to me.

I am not willing to accept this extraordinary statement, from any less authority than yourself—If such is your determination, be pleased to let me know it—

very Respectfully
your obt servt.
Z. B. Vance

[1]Brig. Gen. Seth Maxwell Barton, commanding a brigade in eastern North Carolina. Faust et al., *Encyclopedia of Civil War*, 299.

Edwin G. Reade to ZBV A&H:VanPC

Richmond Feby 10th. '64

Gov. Z. B. Vance

My Dear Sir:

On the next day but one after my arrival here, the N. C. delegation were summoned to meet the President. He opened the conference by reading to us a very long letter from somebody in Raleigh of "considerable inteligence" whose name he withheld, giving a bad account of the state of things in N.C. & advising the suspension of the writ of _habeas corpus_ & that prompt & vigorous measures should be taken to "over awe & silence" the people, <& saying that your policy was temporising & inefficient>. He also read us some scribbling upon the margin of a newspaper, anonomous even to him, of the same character. These two were all that he exhibited. Messrs McLean Arrington & Lander sustained the letter writer, & some of them said a convention would be called forthwith, if let alone, by 30,000, majority & go right back in the old Union. I characterized the letter as mischievous— doing the writer no credit & the state gross injustice—that if that letter were published in the state & known to be the basis of any unfavorable action against the state that instead of 30000 there would be 100000 majority to rise up against it,—that her people were sensitive & spirited & could be easily controled by Gov. Vance Gov. Graham & others who had their confidence, but if attempted to be over awed or silenced by force, N. C. would be the bloodiest field of the South. I told Mr. President that N. C. had the right to expect that he would form his estimate of her from what was said & done by her constituted authorities & not from partizan letter writers & anonimous scribblers who were always malicious & seldom truthful. At this he flared up a little & said "Well but Mr. Reade we had better understand what it is that you censure so strongly in this letter." I answered that the whole of it was mischievous, that it advised that N. C. should be "over-awed & silenced" He said I had mistaken the letter. He turned to the letter & there was the language. He said "Well, but he only means the leaders" I told him the writer did not so qualify it, but if he did it was all the same, I told him it advised that he should be made military dictator. He said "There you are mistaken again" I asked "does not the letter advise the suspension of the writ of _habeas corpus?_" He said "Yes." "Well does not that clothe you with dictatorial powers"? He replied "Well if it does, it does not show that I would abuse the power" I told him I had not intimated that he would, but that the people of N. C. were unwilling to trust any body with the power. We were both getting up our pluck, & Mr. Smith told me afterwards that there would probably have been a scene, but that my manner was so entirely respectful as to afford no excuse. The interview lasted I suppose some two hours & I have given you a very poor account of it. Mr. Smith sustained me fully in what I said of the loyalty of our people & he instanced the ease with which you stopt the meetings last summer. Mr. Gaither also properly defended the state. When about leaving we all formed a sort of long circle with Mr. Davis at one end of it. I extended my hand & walked up towards him & said with emphasis "Mr President, trust North Carolina *& let her alone.*" He grasped my hand cordially & said "I earnestly hope that your strong faith in your state may be realized."

The interview got out by some means & several sought an introduction & expressed much satisfaction & hoped good would come of it—among them Mr. W. C. Rives[1] who expressed the liveliest satisfaction <of> at learning that there was not the mischief in the state which every body seemed disposed to charge upon her, & he begged me to follow up the assurance I had given the President & he was sure it would disabuse the Presidents mind & remove the unfavourable impressions which had been made.

But, Governor, I do not think they can be removed. I have the best reason for knowing, outside of that interview that the President is deeply prejudiced against the state. He said in the interview that he would not be alarmed about the state if all her people were at home but the best of them were in the army.

The interview was not confidential but you will see from the nature of it that it was not intended for the crowd.

I have been a little tedious in detailing but I thought that in that way I could give you the best idea of the state of things here.

I have been informed that it was charged that, from my remarks in the Senate, I was in favour of a convention. That could only be inferred from the fact that I did not *denounce* it. But to have denounced the movement as disloyal would have been inconsistent with my proposition that the dissatisfaction in N. C. *did not mean disloyalty.* I said distincly that I spoke neither for or against any party, that I spoke only for the state & that no matter whether the state called a convention or not, she would do right. I on purpose ignored any opinion upon the subject—1st. because I did not think it suitable for the occasion that called forth the remarks—it being a compliment to soldiers, 2d. because it would have been unbecoming in the Senate & 3d. because I was soon to go upon the Bench & I did not wish to ally myself to any party. I did not mean to express any opinion at all.

It was stated to the President that one of the causes of dissatisfaction among our people was the impression on their part that nothing had been done on our part to make peace. He said he had done all that he could do & that he had made three deliberate efforts & had been repulsed, & that he had so informed you by letter. We said that our people were not unreasonable & if satisfied that we had done all that we could it would tend to satisfy them—that if it were known that he had tried to make peace & could not, it might do good. He said there was no restraint upon publishing his letter to you. The delegation thought it might do good & we so advised you. But upon reflection & for the reason you mention in your letter to Mr. Gaither I doubt the propriety of publishing it.

Since writing above I have been shown the "Confederate" in which is said that I made a speech in caucus at Raleigh abusing the Government & in favour of a convention. It is wholy false. I said not a word against the Government or for a convention. The facts are: Resolutions were introduced in the House of Commons which gave some uneasiness. It was thought that the assembly would be obliged to vote upon some resolutions, a caucus was called, several sets of resolutions were introduced into caucus, the most moderate was about as follows: Resolved that N.C. is undivided in her devotion to the Confederate cause, that her aim is independence & the freedom & safety of her citizens; with these she earnestly desires <peace> peace & that the arbitrament of the sword may give place to negociation.

I was invited by a committee of gentlemen to address the caucus. I did so, & advised the adoption of that resolution, as being the least that could be said, & as not embarrassing the Government or any body. I urged as the reason for adopting it, that, in my opinion, the people were determined that something should be said about peace, that if they would only say that much the people would see that they had had the matter under consideration & would be satisfied; & they would retain the confidence & lead of the people, & yet embarrass nobody, but that if they ignored the whole subject, the people would drop them & take up other leaders who without their prudence might do mischief. I thought that would be the result. Recent events show that I was not entirely wrong.

I have not any where, at any time, to any person, by word or letter, advised a single meeting, or a convention. And especially since my election to the Bench I have stood aloof from every thing partizan. I have nothing to say for or against the meetings or for or against a convention. But I thought it allowable to speak for the *state*.

Doctr Hoge[2] has been invited to deliver his Lectures in Raleigh & will be with you next week. The proceeds of his Lectures will be charitably distributed.

I do not know how I can better describe the feeling here than by saying in your own language that it is "reckless & desperate."

very truly yours
E. G. Reade

Please ask Mr. [*William H.*] Battle to send my commission as Judge
to Roxboro, & to inform me what circuit I will ride I have seen no
announcement in the papers

E. G. R.

[1]William Cabell Rives, former U.S. diplomat, member of the Washington Peace
Conference of 1861, and Confederate congressman from Virginia. Richard N.
Current et al., *Encyclopedia of the Confederacy*, 4 vols. (New York: Simon and
Schuster, 1993), 3:1335-1338.
[2]The Reverend Moses Drury Hoge, Presbyterian minister in Richmond who
preached to Confederate soldiers and ran the blockade to secure Bibles and religious
books for the troops. *Dictionary of American Biography*, s.v. "Hoge, Moses Drury."

ZBV to Theodore Andreae   A&H:GLB

State of North Carolina
Executive Department
Raleigh Feby. 11th. 1864

Mr. Theo. Andreae
Wilmington N.C.

Dear Sir
Your letter[1] and despatches explaining why the Hansa went to Nassau
instead of Bermuda, have been received and I beg leave to submit the
following remarks in regard thereto.
After the Hansa first came into port after my purchase of an interest in
her, I ordered that she should be sent to Bermuda where my freight was. My
reason for making the purchase was to get in this freight as you well know,
and the getting out of Cotton was of secondary importance. You replied that
she could not go to Bermuda for the want of coal, but she should bring in
enough coal to go certainly next trip. I replied that the State had ninety tons
on the wharf, to take that and send her to Bermuda. You answered that the
Engineers were afraid of my Coal and sent her to Nassau in defiance of my
wishes. Was this fairly regardful of the interest of the State, knowing as you
did that the return cargo of army supplies was my *main* object? Your interest
was to get out Cotton, which could be best subserved by going to the nearest
port, but could be served *well* by going to either. My interest or rather that
of the State could only be subserved at all by going to Bermuda. The States'

interest was sacrificed. The vessel could have used N.C. Coal of course, since the Advance and all other vessels use [it] when necessary with perfect safety.

But again the Hansa returned without freight for the State or Confederacy, but without coal enough to go to Bermuda as you inform me, this time certainly she clears for Bermuda and *after her return to port*, I am informed that she again had not coal enough in consequence of having got aground in the river, and her destination was again changed without consulting me. This time you say I had no coal at Wilmington and if there had been it would have delayed the Steamer too long to have returned for it. To this I reply that I had at that moment in Wilmington 120 tons of coal which you could have had on application. See Carters despatch 19th. Jany. Was it fair that rather than lose two days, if indeed it would have required that time to run back and take in coal, the State should lose again the reception of an entire cargo, having already lost one under similar circumstances? Was this showing a due or even decent regard to the interest of the State, or any thing like a compliance with the contract with Mr. Collie? It looks to me rather like a very flagrant violation of the rights of N.C. in the Steamers whether intentional or unintentional, it makes no difference. On both occasions the Steamer *could* have gone to Bermuda had there been a desire to send her there, and fair dealing and the spirit of the contract of purchase both required it to be done. In reply to all my complaints on this subject, you finally decline, in substance, in your letter of the 8th., that the management of the vessels is in your hands, that my claim to control them is merely nominal, and that you will run the vessels as you think best. To this very respectful and conciliatory assertion I have only one reply to make. If you have not a copy of the agreement with Mr. Collie, I beg leave to quote the following passage from it on this point & will send you a copy in full if you desire it.

"The appointment of the Captains and other officers of such steamers will remain with Alexander Collie, and the general control of the steamers whilst aboard, but whilst such steamers may be in Confederate waters, the general control of them shall rest in the State of North Carolina." For the proof that you acknowledged the full power of this clause, I refer <you> to my letter of the 23d. Dec.[2] of which a copy is enclosed, which you solicited me to give you to enable you to act. If this constitutes only a nominal power of control, please to give me your ideas of what would be an actual power. I delegated this power to you as my Agent, you accepted it and cannot now deny it. I preferred you should do the business at Wilmington both as a matter of convenience & because I thought you could do it better than I could. But if I find a continued disregard to my interests in this matter, if the vessels are to risk the blockade at the expense of the State without any return, I shall certainly assume the powers which belong to me and take control of the Steamers in Confederate waters. I do not wish to buy them or to dissolve the contract, but to carry it out strictly and in good faith. I am confident Mr. Collie will concur in what I ask and that if time permitted an appeal to him would be satisfactory to me. I have telegraphed permission to the Don to go to Nassau to be scraped if such is the decree of the Engineers. The Hansa cannot leave Wilmington except for Bermuda and with such an amount of coal as all the world shall pronounce sufficent to take her there. I call your attention to enclosures[3] of letters and despatches.

> Very Respectfully
> Yr. obt. servt
> Z. B. Vance

[1]February 8, 1864, in this volume.
[2]In Johnston and Mobley, *Papers of Vance*, 2:350.
[3]Not extant.

ZBV *to Edward J Hale*   A&H:Hale

Private.

> State of North Carolina,
> Executive Department.
> Raleigh, Feb 11, 1864.

My dear Sir,

Your letter[1] in relation to Judge Reade and the formation of three parties, deserves a longer reply than I shall be able to give you, for in addition to being overwhelmed with business, I shall have to be all night with my wife by the bedside of a very dangerously ill child.

You are mistaken I think of several of your views. I yet believe that Reade is sound on the main issues, though I did not like the timidity with which he spoke of a convention. Yet I think it arose more from state pride and a desire to have our people appear in the best possible light than from any sympathy with the prospect of a convention. His speech in the caucus has certainly been misrepresented either to you or myself. As I heard of it, a Convention was not spoken of at all in that caucus, and the only difference between his speech & Grahams was that he thought it wise to make some concession to the popular feeling in regard to peace by taking some steps toward negotiations and Graham did not think the time had come. If I was correctly informed his position in this respect was scarcely different from yours and mine, & in private conversations he assured me that my administration "had given him great pleasure." I quote his very words. He is however a bitter hater of the Secessionists and inclined to cover the sins of his own party and denounce those of his opponents beyond the point of candor. I may have erred but thought I was doing for the best. To show you how men differ, many men here as sound as any on the war urged me to appoint Bedford Brown or Bob Dick[2] as a matter of policy!

I don't agree with you about the the [sic] Secessionists running the third man. They are as dead as a door nail—they will be obliged to vote for me, and the danger is in pushing off too big a slice of the old union men with Holden. By coming square out with the secessionists this would be done and I should get very little support except from them. I hope you understand my policy. I desire to lead my party friends into the support of the war if possible, and intend to try to show Holden to be no fit leader & associate for old union whigs. I do not intend to allow him to read me out of the party if I can help it, for this would be ruinous. The old union men are in large majority, without them we would be powerless, and I humbly conceive that the best way I can serve my country will be to preserve my influence with them, and hold them up to the war notch. To do this requires some tact of course, and I make no doubt but the Convention issue will force everything asunder and form a new party—two of them rather. I do not wish this rupture to be upon any *minor* issue. In other words and to make myself plain, I do not wish to fritter away any strength or lose a friend by fighting the ultra *conservatives* upon any but the *main points*. Let them abuse Jeff Davis and the secessionists to their hearts contents so they but oppose this Convention movement & keep to their duty on the war question. And whilst I would disapprove of all this as vexatious <& mischievous>, I hold it would be bad policy to waste my strength by quarreling with them.

However, so far, I have not courted the Secessionists or quarreled with many friends for things that even threatened to compromise me, but have suffered them in silence. I wish much I could see you to explain more fully my views. I do not believe the Convention is gaining ground. Pennington is badly scared & says he intends to go with Gov Vance against the field. Thomas[3] of Davidson has recanted and now urges me to stand firm—a few weeks ago he was the other way. Many things are encouraging. I am invited to speak at Statesville, Taylorsville & Salisbury as I go to Wilks—ought I to do it? Will they not say I am trying to dictate to the people? Dr. Leach[4] Holden's right hand man, came into my office to day & begged me not to commit myself against a Convention in my Wilksboro speech & intimated that it would not be becoming in the Governor to say a word! That is the cry with Holdens friends here & I suppose will be the cue throughout.

Don't be uneasy about my blockade running business. I assure you that I shall be able to show the most brilliant financial operation ever performed in the State. In addition to the enormous quantity of army supplies brought in I have already about $400,000 to the credit of the State in Bank of England. I have now at Bermuda 40,000 prs cotton cards, machinery for making them, card clothing for 20 factories, dyestuffs, factory findings, rail road iron and fixtures in abundance & ten thousand scythe blades &c for the farmers— Besides other army stores. All this is based upon $2,400,000 which the state gave me. There is it is true a considerable degree of extravagance & wasteful expenditure about the ship which is common to the reckless business of blockade running and *cant be avoided*, but the general results will astonish you. Though not much of a business man you may rest assured I keep my eyes open. After making five round trips, I have sold half the Ad-vance for $350,000 in State bonds-she cost originally $90,000 all told! I have recently sent £1200. sterling to our Northern prisoners to buy winter clothing-have loaned Gen Johns[t]on & Longstreet 10,000 suits of clothes, complete. I have on hand now 14,000 pairs English shoes 24,000 English blankets & 5,000 over coats & some 50,000 suits of ready made clothes. But I will stop blowing.

I had a letter by Flag of Truce today from my brother Gen Vance. He is / in/ Camp Chase, Ohio, quite well. My English correspondent writes me that the Confed. loan is 45—going up a little & that N.C. warrants command a premium! What do you think of that?

But I'll stop.

Yrs truly

Z. B. Vance

[1]Not extant.

[2]Robert Paine Dick, jurist and state senator. *Dictionary of North Carolina Biography*, s.v. "Dick, Robert Paine."

[3]John W. Thomas, former state senator and contractor for the North Carolina Railroad. Johnston and Mobley, *Papers of Vance*, 1:310-311.

[4]James Thomas Leach, physician and Confederate congressman, who supported peace negotiations. *Dictionary of North Carolina Biography*, s.v. "Leach, James Thomas."

James A. Seddon to ZBV   A&H:GP

Confederate States of America War
Department
Richmond Va.
Feby. 12/64

His Excellency
Z B Vance
Governor of North Carolina

Your Excellency

In the pressure of business I have postponed for several days a reply to your last letter[1] suggesting that difficulties in relation to steamers Don and Hansa might be solved by the Government acquiring one fourth interest in these steamers. It has been our policy /not/ to acquire less than a controlling interest heretofore in any contracts made—the recent legislation confirms me in this view.

I am willing to place the state on the same footing with the Confederate Government in the shipments that have been made—that is to credit to the owners the quantity taken out for the state just as if it had been taken for the Confederate states—The Don and Hansa have taken one fourth for your State; the agents will be called upon to turn over to our agent at Bermuda and Nassau the difference between one fourth and one third which the vessels would have been compelled to take if they had continued to run under arrangements with the Confederate Government.

For the future it will be necessary to make the terms upon which cotton is taken out for the states and for the Confederate Govt uniform, or the result will be a competition ruinous to each.

Upon application from the authorities of the State of So. Ca. for Steamer Alice and of State of Virginia for Str City of Petersburg, I have at once directed the agent that cotton taken out by these steamers, for a/c of the states named on the same terms as fixed for the Confed Govt will be considered as if taken for the Confed Govt and credited accordingly.

This arrangement has been satisfactory here & to Gov. Bonham[2] and I earnestly hope will be so to you.

Congress has just legislated on the subject, authorizing shipment by private individuals, only under license granted by Confed Government, reserving to states the right to ship out on their steamers their own cotton.

Uniform regulations will be drawn up as required by this law and it shall be my effort to make them such as to facilitate the efforts of the state and

Confederate Governments in exporting cotton and introducing supplies and munitions of war.

> Very Respectfully Yrs
> James A. Seddon
> Secy of War

[*Endorsed*] Copy & file & send copy to Theo. Andrea[e]

ZBV

¹January 25, 1864, in this volume.
²Milledge Luke Bonham, South Carolina governor, 1863-1864. *Dictionary of American Biography*, s.v. "Bonham, Milledge Luke."

ZBV to James A. Seddon   A&H:GLB

> State of North Carolina
> Executive Department
> Raleigh Feb. 17th. 1864

Hon J. A. Seddon
Secty. of War

Dr. Sir
  You will see by the enclosed letter[1] from J. M. Seixas[2] the result of my efforts to get back the Cotton loaned the Confederate Government and which you ordered to be returned. It amounts practically to a refusal of payment and to a stoppage of my shipments altogether, as it is utterly impossible to get a train to bring Cotton from Georgia or any where else. If the Confederate government is determined to impose upon the owners of these Steamers the tax of one third of their capacity, it seems unreasonable to deprive them of the means of running them altogether. That I have been always anxious to accommodate the General Government in every possible way, I think may be safely asserted, but that I have been disinterested in doing so, my reward will testify beyond a doubt

> I am Sir
> Very respectfully
> Z. B. Vance

[1]Not extant.
[2]See James A. Seddon to ZBV, January 11, 1864, in this volume.

Theodore F. Davidson to ZBV			A&H:VanPC

Asheville. Feby 17th 1864

Gov. Z. B. Vance
Raleigh No. Ca.

Dear Gov:

Cousin Hattie[1] wishes you to send her one bunch of thread no 12 if possible or if not, any you can get. She also wishes a pr of cards. The latter and (I suppose the former) she is much in need of.

I think she will be able to get along pretty well, as she has a supply of corn, Bacon, & almost flour enough to do until harvest. She recd. a letter a day or two ago from the Genl[2] dated "Camp Chase[3]: Prison No. 1. Mess No. 4 Jany 28." He & Lucius were quite well—fixing up their quarters &c. Altho' he evidently endeavored to put as pleasant a face upon it as possible, it was clearly to be seen that he was /not/ faring so very well.

Did Congress pass the act giving officers rations?

The court martial[4] for the trial of Frisby met to-day. The ground upon which his counsel rests his defence, is that the order issued to Gen McElroy[5] to report to Gen Vance is not legal, that the calling out of the H.G.[6] by Gen V is void-& that no one has authority to call them out except yourself, and the officers so authorized by you.

No news—very cold—coldest we have had since New Year.

My kindest regards to cousin Hattie & the boys.

Yours very truly
Theo. F. Davidson[7]

[1]Harriett Espy Vance, ZBV's wife.
[2]Robert Brank Vance.
[3]Federal prison in Fort Chase, Ohio.
[4]Of William Holland Thomas and James L. Henry. See Joseph E. Johnston to ZBV, February 3, 1864, in this volume.
[5]John W. McElroy, brigadier general of Home Guard, with headquarters in Burnsville. Clark, *Histories of Regiments from North Carolina*, 4:651.

[6]Home Guard.
[7]Theodore Fulton Davidson, ZBV's cousin. He later became attorney general of North Carolina. *Dictionary of North Carolina Biography*, s.v. "Davidson, Theodore Fulton."

Jefferson Davis to ZBV   A&H:VanPC

Private

Camp near Petersburg Va.
Richmond 17th February 1864

To Governor Z. B. Vance

Dr. Sir

I am in receipt of your private letter of 4th. inst.[1] informing me that upon reflection you doubt the propriety of publishing in full my letter[2] according to the permission given in answer to your request, and that you propose to have the substance of it published in the Fayetteville Observer.

You must pardon me for declining to have my correspondence thus changed for presentation to the public. You can use your discretion as to the publication of my letter as it was sent to you.

Your letter of 4th inst was laid on my table with a mass of other correspondence and escaped my attention, which fact must form my apology for the delay in this answer.

I remain
Very truly & resply. Yours
Jeffn. Davis

[1]Not extant, but see ZBV to Burgess S. Gaither, February 4, 1864, in this volume.
[2]Jefferson Davis to ZBV, January 8, 1864, in this volume.

John D. Hyman to ZBV   A&H:VanPC

Hendersonville
Feby 17/64

His Excellency
Z. B. Vance

Dear Governor—

Your favor of 4th. inst.[1] came duly to hand. Allow me to suggest that if a rupture between yourself & your branch of the Conservative party /and Holden/ is to become a *conceded* fact by both sides—a fact that all intelligent minds in the state are bound to recognize—the sooner the avowal is made the better. By your silence you are daily losing friends. The Democratic and secession party allege that Holden <are> /is/ your spokesman & that you are in favor of a convention[2]: while a large number of Conservatives are committing themselves to a convention, either by signing petitions or participating in public meetings held at Holden's suggestion—whereas they would commit themselves in opposition to a convention, if they knew you were opposed to it. You know how far pride of opinion will carry men, even in opposition to their judgment, when they have fully committed themselves to particular measures.

You now have a good occasion to make known your views in response to the public meetings that have been holden and the petitions that have been sent to you. Come out at once and I believe the people will stand by you. The public mind needs to be enlightened. The stump is your forte and you should not wait long in mounting it. Prepare your budget, fling your banner to the breeze, and treason will stand aghast!

As I wrote you before,[3] I am ready to undertake the enterprise concerning which you wrote me,[4] whenever the necessary arrangements can be made.

I am, Dear Governor,
Yours most truly
Jno. D. Hyman

[1]Not extant.

[2]For plans and delegates to negotiate peace with the Federal government.

[3]About demoralizing influence of Holden and potential for counterinfluence through pamphlets and speeches. John D. Hyman to ZBV, February 13, 1864, A&H:GP.

[4]Presumably about efforts to combat Holden's influence. Hyman subsequently came to Raleigh to edit the pro-ZBV newspaper, the *Conservative*.

ZBV to James A. Seddon   A&H:GP

(Copy)

State of North Carolina
Executive Department
Raleigh Feby. /18th./ 1864

Hon Jas. A Seddon
Secty of War.

If the State of N.C. were to buy a third of the Steamers Don and Hansa, would they be released from the existing regulations in regard to carrying cotton for Confederacy?

They are already under my control by virtue of the within contract.

What permit is now required for shipping cotton under the recent act of Congress?

The steamer "Advance" has again arrived

Respectfully Yrs.
Z. B. Vance

ZBV to Alexander Collie   A&H:GLB

State of North Carolina
Executive Department
Raleigh Feb. 18th. 1864

Alex. Collie Esq.
17 Leadenhall Street
London

Dear Sir

Since writing you last, I have come to a definite and satisfactory arrangement with Mr. Andreae and I apprehend no further misunderstanding. Your favor of the 16th ult[1] was duly & promptly received and its statements relative to the condition of North Carolina matters very satisfactory.

You are doubtless aware by this time that you misapprehended my wishes in the purchase of the iron as contemplated in your proposition to Mr White. I do not desire any more at present though we need it here of course, yet the great difficulty of getting it in quantities sufficient to meet our wants, and the greater necessity for other articles, induces me to decline shipping it. My intention was to deposit in Bank in your country as much as possible of the net proceeds of my Cotton shipments for the purpose of giving confidence to my bond holders and strengthening our credit, giving you orders from time to time for such supplies as our variously arising necessities may require. Bacon will be our great want this spring & summer, though I fear to keep much at the Islands as it easily spoils. Your suggestion about the method of shipping Cotton has recd. attention. Our prospects have improved materially since the beginning of the winter. Our troops are better clothed and equipped than at any time since the beginning of the war, and nearly two thirds of our entire army have already voluntarily reenlisted for the war, disdaining to be conscribed. We shall enter on the spring campaign with largely inferior numbers it is true, but with an army largely increased, excelling in discipline and baptized in the fires of three years of constant strife and with the spirit of resistance in the people strong and determined. I beg to assure you that the statements you see in Yankee newspapers about disaffection in N.C. are entitled to little weight. Our people are very fearful of a destruction of their civil rights & liberties and are struggling to preserve them, our enemies will take this for disaffection. With sentiments of sincere regard, I am sir,

> Yrs. Respectfully
> Z. B. Vance

[1]A&H: GP.

Thomas L. Clingman to ZBV   A&H:VanPC

> Camp near Petersburg Va.
> February 18th. 1864

His Excellency
Z. B. Vance

My dear Sir
 Your letter of the 15th. inst[1] reached me yesterday and I have no hesitation in expressing to you my opinions freely on the subject of your letter. I am clearly of the opinion that you should be reelected without opposition, and I am ready to write a letter advising that course to the Confederate at Raleigh or any other paper in which it might appear with more propriety. Before

doing so however I would like to know, as you are in a better position to Judge, at what time it should be done. I have no doubt but that all the true men in the State can be brought to your support.

With reference to Holden's course I have this to say, I have seen but one number of his paper in many months and while that contained a number of articles against the Confederate Government there was not a single one against that of Lincoln atrocious as are its acts. If his paper generally accords with this single number then he is against us and for Lincoln, but that paper may not be a fair index and he ought to be allowed to take his true position. He for years advocated the right of secession, repeatedly stated that the election of a black republican was cause for resistance, as a member of the convention voted the State out of the Union, and into the Confederacy then at war with Lincoln and in addition to these things insisted that the "last man and the last dollar" should if necessary be given to secure our Independence. He stimulated our citizens to volunteer and contributed his whole influence to get the entire body of capable men into the field. After having done all this in addition to other motives which ought to influence every citizen he is bound by his personal honor to sustain the cause. He cannot abandon the men in the field without the deepest *personal disgrace*. I have no hesitation in saying that we cannot permit a Lincoln organ to exist in the state. If I am willing to give up my own life, and what is much more, sacrifice the lives of the patriotic soldiers I command for the good of the country, then certainly I would not hesitate to give up to the same cause the lives of a few traitors to secure the same end. If the conduct of any man gives encouragement to our enemies and thus induces them to continue to destroy our brave and patriotic men, then *let him die* for the safety of the community. Mr. Holden advocated your election as well as that of Davis & Stephens[2] on the platform of a zealous prosecution of the war for Independence, and he must therefore either sustain the cause, or share the fate of John Brown and Judas Iscariot and have perhaps a Yankee song made over him as the last martyr in the cause of "*nigger freedom.*" One of these contingencies is immediately before him and the time has come for him to make his decision between honor and ignominy. I should myself no more hesitate to act out these views than to order my Brigade to fire into Lincolns black & white hirelings.

Should Holden make a proper choice as I hope he will then there will be no division in the State as he can in a few weeks bring the body of his party to take the right view. The fact that the Lincoln government has in its Congress voted down all conciliatory measures, will fully justify Holden in abandoning the peace movement until we have changed by a vigorous campaign, the feelings of the north. I hope some of your friends will submit these matters to his consideration as I would do if I were to see him and

I sincerely trust that he will take the proper course and relieve us from difficulty the State. Should he do wrong while he might be the first sufferer, many others would be sacrificed perhaps.

An united and vigorous prosecution of the war by all who originally encouraged it will in a short time convince our enemies of the impossibility of our being subjugated.

From what I have hastily written you will see what my impressions are, and I think they are those of the soldiers generally.

I am much gratified to know that you will take the field early and if you will advise me as to what you think I ought to do you may calculate on all the aid I can give you. I hope soon to hear of your brother the General's release from the hands of the enemy.

> Very truly yours &c
> T. L. Clingman[3]
> Brig. Gen.

[1]Not extant.
[2]Jefferson Davis and Alexander Stephens.
[3]Thomas Lanier Clingman, former Whig, legislator, and U.S. congressman and senator, who commanded a North Carolina brigade. *Dictionary of North Carolina Biography*, s.v. "Clingman, Thomas Lanier."

Augustus S. Merrimon to ZBV   A&H:VanPC

> Asheville N.C.
> Feby. 22d. 1864.

His Excellency,
Gov. Vance.

My Dear Sir:

I beg to make a suggestion for your consideration, and I venture to hope that our friendly relations personal and political are sufficient warrant for such intrusion.

There is wide spread alarm among the people here and elsewhere, growing out of the constant exercise of high and questionable powers on the part of Congress and the President. The whole action of the Conf'd Gov. seems to tend to the concentration of the whole military power of the country in the hands of the President. He exercises such power frequently, unwisely and manifests a fondness for it, that does not comport with the feelings and purposes of a devoted friend of free government. Believe me, when I tell you, that the people are really alarmed, and this alarm is going far toward precipitating the South upon a fearful doom.

I make these remarks in view of the Military Act lately passed by Congress. I understand that the Act provides, among other things, for the conscription of all persons between the ages of 17 & 18 and 45 & 50 years for the purpose of *State-defence*, and that this Army for *State-defence*, is to be under the control, command and direction of the President. If I am correct in this statement, the Act, if xecuted, will strip the Governors of the several states of power and leave them at the will & pleasure of the President.

Now, I respectfully suggest, that the Executives of the states ought not to allow the provision of the law referred to, to be xecuted. If it is necessary to place the class of our population designated, in the Army, the Legislature has power to do so and to place them under the direction of *state authority*. The Conf'd Gov. ought not at any time to be allowed to take the whole military <authority> power of the country <at any time>, and especially not now, when there is a manifest purpose to subvert state authority.

I undertake to say, that the Conf'd Gov. cannot legitimately demand the whole military force of the State, if the latter see proper to have military organizations. If our Legislature through our Executive, has organized a force for State defence, or shall here after do so, the Conf'd Gov. cannot legitimately dissolve such state organization and place the state soldiery in the Conf'd Army. Indeed, when persons within the conscript age, are recruited into our *State Army* now, the Conf'd authorities have no legitimate power to take these recruits out, although they claim the right to do so.

What I beg to suggest is, that you ought to notify President Davis promptly, that the Conf'd. Army for *state defence*, as proposed by the late act of Congress, cannot be <xecuted> organized in this State and that our state military organizations must stand as they are, until our Legislature shall see proper to change them. If you allow the whole fighting population of the state to be taken, you will be a mere formal officer and the state a formal organization, without power, subject to the insults and tyranny of President Davis and his subordinates. If he gets the State Army proposed what can you do but submit to his order, though he should *order you* into the army and *imprison the Judges* of our Courts? Hold at least a part of the military power of the State in your own hands. The integrity and dignity of the State requires, *demands* that you shall do so.

I don't object to [*illegible*] all possible defence, but I do object to a concentration of power in hands of the President, especially, to placing the great power spoken of, in the hands of President *Davis*.

I would be gratified to have a line from you touching the prospects, and present condition of our unhappy country. Can't you find leisure to write me at least a hasty note.

Pardon the liberty I have thus taken and the haste of this letter.

> I am &c. Yrs. truly,
> A. S. Merrimon[1]

[1]Augustus Summerfield Merrimon, lawyer and future U.S. senator and chief justice of the state supreme court. During the war he served as solicitor of the state's Eighth District. *Dictionary of North Carolina Biography*, s.v. "Merrimon, Augustus Summerfield."

James A. Seddon to ZBV   A&H:GLB

> Confederate States of America
> War Department
> Richmond Feby. 25th 1864

Gov. Z. B. Vance
Raleigh N.C.

Your Excellency

I have the honor hereby to acknowledge receipt of your letter of 18th. inst.[1] and to say in reply thereto, that the President has now under consideration certain uniform regulations in conformity with the recent legislation of Congress—a copy of same will be sent you as soon as they are promulgated

> Very Respectfully
> Your Obt. Servt.
> Jas A. Seddon
> Secty. of War.

[1]In this volume.

ZBV to Power, Low and Co. A&H:GLB

State of North Carolina
Executive Department
Raleigh Feby. 26th. 1864

Messrs Power Lowe & Co
Wilmington N.C.

Gents

Your several favors reached this place in my absence. I have pretty well arranged all matters with Dr. Boykin, who will fully explain all things now necessary to the sailing of the vessel [*Advance*]. I desire her to run once more to Bermuda for my cards and machinery—after that I am willing for her to go to Nassau. Some other matters present themselves for consideration about which I will write you in a few days. I learn that Capt. Guthrie is dissatisfied with his pay, although the same that Capt. Crossan got, explain to him what it is and if he declines to take it send the vessel out in charge of Capt Wylie.[1] I will not consent to give Morse the pilot any more than your bargain promised him. We have already kept him from being forced to Genl. Whiting terms and if he is not satisfied, I propose letting him try the Conscript Camp at $11. per month. I hope you will not pander to his unpatriotic greed.

In spite of my express orders to Capt. Guthrie, I learn that considerable Cotton was found aboard beyond what appears on the Manifest & that the principal sinner was the Captain himself, of course the crew would do no better with such an example. This thing *must* be stopped. I have agreed with Dr. Boykin that an arrangement may be made by you for the officers & crew to take twenty four bales, divided among them according to rank. All other Cotton over this found on board at the Island must be seized for the ship, any officer transgressing shall be discharged, the crew shall be conscribed, those of them at least who are North Carolinians. I can get plenty of men to replace them. I have written Capt. Guthrie, and refer you to Boykin for particulars.

Yrs truly
Z. B. Vance

[1] Joannes Wylie, captain who had commanded the *Lord Clyde* on its initial voyage from Glasgow, Scotland, to Wilmington, where its name was changed to *Advance*. Wise, *Lifeline of the Confederacy*, 106, 200, 211.

ZBV to John J. Guthrie   A&H:GLB

State of North Carolina
Executive Department
Raleigh Feby 26th. 1864

Capt Guthrie
Stmr. Advance
Wilmington N.C.

Dr. Sir

I have to repeat my former order concerning the shipment of Cotton on private account. Messrs Power Lowe & Co are authorized to make an arrangement which it is hoped will be satisfactory to officers and crew. All cotton not appearing on the manifest will be seized and it is earnestly hoped the officers will set an example to their subordinates of promptly and cheerfully obeying orders. I learn that you were dissatisfied with your pay. I cannot afford to give you the same pay as is paid by blockade runners to their Captains, who merely work for the pay, yet I will pay you what Capt. Crossan worked for. I paid him the regular pay of a Captain in the C.S. Navy per month and one thousand dollars in gold per trip. Beside this you will be allowed the privilege of taking out four bales of Cotton. If this is not satisfactory, fully and amply so, please telegraph me. Consider your former orders as to destination, cargo &c as repeated. Congratulating and thanking you for your recent speedy & successful trip, which I fully appreciate, and wishing you a like happy issue

I remain yours &c
Z. B. Vance

Nathaniel Boyden to ZBV   A&H:GP

Salisbury Feb 27th. 1864

To His Excellency
Gov Vance
Raleigh

Dear Gov

I have learned here to day, that orders have been received by the enrolling officer in Salisbury directing him to pay no regard to the decision of the

Chief Justice,[1] but to conscribe all those that were before the Chief Justice & have the certificates directed by the Chief Justice & consented to by Gov Bragg[2] on the part of the government. You learned the arrangement and have seen the certificates putting in the custody of the law until the supreme court shall have decided the case in the matter of Walton.[3] Every man you know is under a recognizance to the Confederate States in the sum of $1,000 to abide the decision in that case & to report to the enrolling officer of his county or district within three days after he shall receive notice of the decision of the supreme court in the matter of Walton; provided the decision is against Walton. Could any thing be fairer than this This secures to the Government every man as soon as the supreme court make the decision, should the reverse the decision of the Chief Justice. I trust in God that there is a mistake about the enrolling officers having received order to disregard the decision of the chief Justice. So my dear Sir use every exertion in your power to prevent such a course Great trouble will certainly come yet, if men are to be thus treated after the court has decided that the particular man is not liable to be conscribed I send you the decision of the chief justice. The paper has not yet issued & the opinion is on separate pieces of paper The opinion is an able one & unanswerable in my humble judgement

Respectfully
Nathaniel Boyden[4]

[1]Richmond M. Pearson, who ruled that the December 1863 Confederate law abolishing the practice of substitution was null and void. Pearson concluded that the previous substitution act, which provided for substitution, "authorized a contract which could not be impaired by any subsequent law." Hamilton, "The North Carolina Courts and the Confederacy," 389-391.

[2]Thomas Bragg, lawyer, U.S. senator, former governor, and Confederate attorney general from November 22, 1861, to March 18, 1862. Returning to North Carolina from Virginia in November 1862, he continued to work in support of the Confederate government, including an association with the Confederate district attorney. *Dictionary of North Carolina Biography*, s.v. "Bragg, Thomas"; Hamilton, "North Carolina Courts and the Confederacy," 371, 374, 394.

[3]Edward S. Walton, who on January 27 applied for a writ of habeas corpus on the ground that he was exempted from conscription because he had furnished a substitute. Chief Justice Pearson ordered him discharged but bound him in a recognizance to appear at the next term of the supreme court in June. Hamilton, "North Carolina Courts and the Confederacy," 389-391.

[4]Nathaniel Boyden, lawyer, legislator, postwar state supreme court justice and congressman. *Dictionary of North Carolina Biography*, s.v. "Boyden, Nathaniel."

John A. Gilmer to ZBV   A&H:GP

Greensboro NC
February 27th. 1864

Gov. Vance

My dear friend—

Very great increased troubles will certainly appear & be realized in N.C. if the understanding between Judge Pearson & Gov. Bragg at Salisbury, is not Concurred in by the Secretary of War.

It is a matter of small moment, whether the principals of substitutes go into the army *now*, or in June next. Peace & harmony, as well as unity in N.C. is a matter of the first importance to us and to our nationality. The agreement of Gov. Bragg is a wise & good one. All will acquiesce in the decision of the Supreme Court N. C [*illegible*]. My friend Col. Mallett[1] can carry this out *if he will*. For the peace & happiness of our beloved state, I ask you to see Col. Mallett at once, & make him see that Gov. Bragg's arrangement [*illegible*] agreed to shall be carried out. Mark, what I say to you—Judge Pearson is still issuing writs of Habeas Corpus—& we will have a conflict of a most serious character in this State if Col. Mallett advises the Secretary of War to hold out & send the principals of substitutes into the army before they have had what they concieve is a fair & impartial trial. I suggest that you see & have a conference with Col. Mallett at your very earliest convenience.

Yours truly
John A. Gilmer

[1]Peter Mallett, commandant of conscripts in North Carolina. See Johnston and Mobley, *Papers of Vance*, 1:175n.

Peter Mallett to ZBV   A&H:GP

Conscript Office,
Raleigh, N.C.,
February 27th. 1864

His excellency Z. B. Vance,
Governor of North Carolina,
Raleigh,

Governor:

I have the honor most respectfully to inform your Excellency that I am directed by the Superintendent of Conscription[1] to enforce the entire requisitions of the Law of Congress suspending the Writ of Habeas Corpus, and in answer to writs served to make return that the person or persons are detained for attempt to avoid military service.

While determined to obey orders literally and discharge my duty faithfully, I most respectfully and earnestly solicit your aid, support and co-operation.

To avoid the possibility of a conflict, or misunderstanding with the State authorities, I most respectfully request that your Militia and Home Guard officers be instructed not to interfere or resist officers acting under orders from this Office, in the faithful discharge of their duties.

I am, Governor
With high regard
Your Obedient Servant Peter Mallett
Col. Comdt. of Conscripts for N.C.

[*Endorsed*] File and copy

ZBV

[1]Gabriel James Rains, native North Carolinian, superintendent of Bureau of Conscription, and explosives expert. W. Davis Waters, " 'Deception is the Art of War': Gabriel J. Rains, Torpedo Specialist of the Confederacy," *North Carolina Historical Review* 66 (January 1989): 29-60.

ZBV to Edward J. Hale   A&H:Hale

Private

State of North Carolina,
Executive Department.
Raleigh, Feb 28, 1864

E. J. Hale Esq

My dear Sir,

I returned on Thursday from my trip up country & have been too busy since to let you hear the result. I was delighted. So far as I could judge the Convention is dead, _dead dead_, if our public men will only be a little bold. I spoke at Salisbury, Statesville, Taylorsville & Wilkesboro' with great acceptance as the preachers say. At Salisbury & <Statesville>/Taylorsville/ I spoke at night to only the people of the vicinity but at the other two points the crowds were enormous. At Wilkesboro 2,000 & at Statesville 3,000 people at the very lowest. I am confident great good has been done— Delegations from Burke, Caldwell, Ashe, Surry, Yadkin, Davie, Mclenburg & Forsythe, came to me & entreated me to visit & speak to them.

I have secured an excellent report of my Wilks speech and it will appear Tuesday morning in the Progress. I thought it better to publish it first here or I would have sent you the copy. Holden will publish it in an extra & send to all his subscribers-his own offer. I had to cut off much of it and it is still too long. I hope you will appreciate my line of argument, and understand why I say something that you may not approve.

Troubles are brewing for me I fear about Pearsons decisions again, and I am on the verge of being forced into conflict with [_Col. Peter_] Mallett. He lacks brains. But I shall act cautiously and hope to steer safely. The news all round from the army is good and I feel generally quite cheerful & hopeful. My child is well.

Write me when you see my speech, if you think it worth while to publish in pamphlet form.

Yours truly
Z B Vance

Jefferson Davis to ZBV   A&H:GP

Executive Office
Richmond Feb. 29, 1864

Sir:

Your letter of 9th. instant[1] was received on the 13th., but the close of the Congressional Session imposed on me duties too engrossing to permit a prompt reply.

Your counsels upon matters of grave import to the success of our cause in North Carolina have received from me the consideration to which they are entitled as emanating from the governor of a Sovereign State. But I regret that you have deemed proper in urging your views to make unjust reflections upon my official conduct and to accompany them by assertions which you would in vain attempt to sustain by proof.

In my earnest desire to avoid every possible controversy with all whose co-operation can be made valuable in the defense of the country, I would have preferred to remain silent under these reflections, and to have left to time and the sober judgment of my countrymen the vindication of my course from your arraignment. But public interests are involved which preclude this course, for some of your statements if uncontradicted would tend to create hostility to the government and undermine its power to provide for the public defense. I therefore deem it a duty to respond.

When you assert that there has been "what seemed a studied exclusion of the anti-secessionists from all the more important offices of the government, even from those promotions in the army which many of them had won with their blood," I am compelled to characterise the statement as unjust to my conduct, my feelings and my character. You cannot expect me to receive such a charge from the Governor of a State without insisting on a specification. I must therefore request that you give the name, not of "many," but of one officer whose promotion has been refused on the grounds or for the reason you mention. If unable to maintain this assertion, I leave to your own sense of justice to determine how best to repair the wrong done. In the meantime I assert that there exists not to my knowledge in the files of the War Department a single case among the thousands there to be found, in which the promotion of an officer has ever been recommended on the ground of his party or political opinions or relations: and I am as certain as one can be of the occurrences of three years that no objection has ever been suggested to me by any of my advisers civil or military against the appointment or promotion of any officer of the army on the ground of his opposition to secession or other political opinion held prior to the war. I further affirm that the promotions of officers have been guided *exclusively* by military considerations, and that they have almost invariably been made upon the recommendations received from their fellow-soldiers and Commanders, as I have, in the large majority of cases no other source of reliable information concerning the relative merits of the officers.

Having thus been forced, from considerations of public duty, to abandon that reserve in relation to my official conduct which I had hoped to maintain at least till my retirement to private life, it becomes necessary to mark as unfounded some other disparaging statements of your letter, lest I be supposed to admit their truth.

1st. you say: "The truth is, Sir, as I have often said before that the great body of our people have been *suspected* by their government, perhaps because of the reluctance with which they gave up the old union." If by the words "their government" you refer to the Executive Department of the Confederate States, I deny that there is any ground for the assertion, and invite you to specify the facts to which you refer, and the persons to whom your frequent communications were made.

2d. "That this consciousness of their being suspected has been greatly strengthened by what seemed to be a studied exclusion of the anti-secessionists from all the more important offices of the government, even from those promotions in the army which many of them had won with their blood." To the second part of this charge, I have already adverted: the first part is equally without foundation.

3rd. You ask in reference to a suspicion of the people of North Carolina, which you seem to impute to me "Was this suspicion just? And was there sufficient effort made to disprove that it existed, if it really did not exist at Richmond?" I reply that your knowledge of the injustice of such a suspicion, should have prevented your imputing to me the possibility of entertaining it, or at least have prompted, before such imputation, an enquiry which would have made known to you that no such suspicion was entertained. I admit that I made no effort to disprove the existence of such suspicion, nor did you inform me of any necessity for doing so. I should have left this, like many other similar misrepresentations, to be answered by the sound judgment and the patriotism of the people, if it had not been endorsed by the Governor of the State, or some equally respectable authority.

4th. You complain that "Conscription ruthless, and unrelenting has only been exceeded in the severity of its execution by the impressment of property frequently entrusted to men unprincipled, dishonest, and filled to overflowing with all the petty meanness of small minds, dressed in a little brief authority. The files of my office are piled up with the unavailing complaints of outraged citizens to whom redress is impossible." I will not assume to say that in North Carolina as elsewhere, subordinate officers may not have been guilty of misconduct and harshness. I have lamented such abuses and done my utmost to correct them whenever brought to my knowledge. But I am at a loss to conceive how you can assert that these complaints were "unavailing" and that "redress was impossible" if you kept the papers on your files in Raleigh. I know that no complaint has ever been received from you on any subject, without meeting respectful consideration and redress, as far as it was within my power to have justice done. I am sorry that the complaints of the citizens of North Carolina were addressed through a channel by which they failed to reach me. On what fact then do you base the assertion that redress was impossible for just complaint?

5th. You do not "hold me responsible for all the petty annoyances, the insolence of office under which our people lose heart and patience." I make no comment on this language, as I must suppose, that you deem it becoming our mutual positions, and simply invite you to state what portion of these "petty annoyances" and this "insolence of office" you do impute to me, and the facts on which the imputation rests.

I cannot close without adverting to the singular misconstruction of my letter to you of the 8th. ultimo,[2] which pervades the close of your reply. In that letter I expressed, for I felt, no distrust whatever of the noble people of North Carolina, nor did I allude to your efforts to conciliate *them* as injudicious, for it did not enter my mind that *they* were at all in question. I warned you of the error of warming *traitors* into active life by ill-timed deference or timid concession, instead of meeting their insidious attempts to deceive the people, by tearing the mask from the faces of the conspirators. Your present letter is the first intimation I have had from any source, that the *people* of North Carolina were suspected of disloyalty, and your needless defence of them takes me by surprise. In my letter of 8th. ultimo I spoke of attempts that would be made "by some bad men" to inaugurate treacherous movements; of the danger of suffering the designs "of these traitors" to make head; of your over-earnest desire to reclaim by conciliation "men whom you believe to be sound at heart, but whose loyalty is more than suspected elsewhere"; of your permitting "them" to gather strength; of the necessity for putting down the "promoters of unfounded discontent." I never did and do not now, notwithstanding your misdirected defence of them, entertain aught but respect and admiration for the people of North Carolina and her gallant sons, who have on the battlefields of this war won for her so glorious a name. I did and do suspect a knot of traitors who have been conspiring at home, while the mass of the State's true sons were at their posts of duty in the army. This was the import of my letter of 8th. ultimo, and I find in it nothing to justify your answering it, as though I had counselled you to avoid conciliating the *people* of your State.

I again express my regret at being compelled to send you this reply, extracted from me solely by a sense of duty to the country, not by personal considerations. Your arraignment of my conduct would, I repeat, have been received in silence, but for your position of Governor of a State, which seemed to me to impose the necessity of an answer.

In respect to your general recommendations touching the exercise of any extraordinary powers conferred on me by Congress, I can only say that they will be used, if at all, with a due regard to the rights of the citizen as well as to the public safety. Arbitrary measures are not more congenial to my nature than to the spirit of our institutions. But should the occasion unhappily arise when the public safety demands their employment, I would be derelict in duty, if I hesitated to use them to the extent required by the exigency. Should that contingency occur, I shall confidently rely for support on the mass of the good people of North Carolina, in spite of the threats or blandishments of those who would persuade them that their liberties are endangered, not by the wicked invaders of their country, but by their own government and their own fellow citizens.

> I have the honor to remain
> very respectfully yrs. &c.
> Jeffn. Davis

¹In this volume.
²In this volume.

K. J. Kenedy to ZBV   A&H:GP

Old Furnace
Gaston County N C
Feb 29th. 1864

His Exelency Z. B. Vance
Govenor of the State of North Carolina

Dear Sir

I hope you will excuse me for intrudeing on your valueable time as I have been a strong advocate of your election and administration and being solicited by several friends I have concluded to drop you a few lines concerning the present excited condition of the country the late military law enacted by the congress of the confederate states placing all men between the ages of seventeen and fifty years of age in the military service and at the disposal of the president and the suspension of the habeas corpus has produced a great

[d]eal of excitement in this section the people are verry anxious to know what position you will take in the present emergency you have proved equal to every emergency up to the present time and it is natural to expect that the people will look to you for aid and protection in this there time of need the suspension of the writ of habeas corpus alone allmost effects a revolution in our system of Government it has been represented to the people for the last two months by the press of the south to be one of the most dangerous enemies to a free government the first step of a tyrant and the death blow to civil liberty the Richmond Examiner caracterizes it in the folowing maner it says arrest on mere suspition has allways been regarded as the most odious exertion of arbitrary power the pratice has produced more revolution than it has ever repressed it further says and in this case we have the additional apprehension that the power woul not be used to public advantage but be abused to purposes of personal malignancy it is a mournful fact placed beyond doubt by conspicuous evidence that the Executive is capable of employing the great powers of Government for the unworthy graification of animosity the Examiner further says there is not one man in every hundred citizens in the confederacy who does not entertain this opinion in this I fully concur so far as North carolina is concerned I also read from your first message to the legislature the folowing in speaking of the citizens confined in Salisbury by confederate authority you said I have not seen an official coppy of the act but learn from the news papers that congress has confered upon the president the power to suspend the writ of habeas corpus in all cases of arrest made by confederate authority if it be once admited no man is safe from the power of one individual he could at pleasure seize any citizen with or without excuse throw him in prison and permit him to languish there without relief a power that I am unwiling to see entrusted to any liveing man to submit to its exercise would in my opinion be establishing a precedent dangerous and pernicious in the extreme you further said in that admirable document a free republic that must needs cast off its freedom in every time of trouble <must> will soon cast it off for ever freedom can not be embraced to day: and spurned tomorow a steadfast and constant worship can alone secure her countless blessing her chosen instrument the constitution and the laws were made the sure covenant of her ever lasting residence among us our delight in times of peace and prosperity and our /guide &/ sheild in the day of trouble and calamity deeply impress by these great truths I [can] not help but beleive it is your duty to convene the legislature at an early day to take in consideration the condition of the country the military law if fully executed which I have no doubt it will be will leave at least one half the farms in western North Carolina to lie out the present year a large portion is allready grown up in broom sage for the last two years for the want of its owners to cultivate it and the truth is which you know as well as any other

man that if we are to submit to the drain of our whole male population from seventeen to fifty years of age that starvation will be the inevitable result and that in less than two years I beleive this is the opinion of a large majority of the people of this county I will close for the present

yours with the greatest respect
K J Kenedy
a private citizen

[*Endorsed*] Thank him for his advice I dont see how these ills are to be remedied

Z B V

ZBV to Christopher G. Memminger   A&H:GP

Copy

State of North Carolina
Executive Department
Raleigh 29th. Feby. 1864

To C. G. Memminger[1]
Secty of Treasury
Richmond Va.

Dear Sir

Upon a recent visit to the county of Wilkes in this State, I was informed that a number of inoffensive citizens in that and the adjacent counties had been robbed of their property and effects by the 56 Regt. N.C.T. employed there for the purpose of arresting deserters. It has occurred to me that some compensation should be made to these people for the losses they have sustained, in many cases a large part of their property having been taken away. And the mode I propose is to appoint a Commissioner or Commissioners in the region where the depredations have been committed and ascertain the loss of each individual and credit the amount on his current taxes. Should this proposition meet your views and the measure be carried into effect promptly, I feel satisfied it will go far to compose the dissatisfaction of my people who have suffered so severely in that section and bring to the

Support of the Government a large class of persons, who think and feel they are out of the pale of its protection.

Your early consideration of this measure will enable me to effect much in the restoration of confidence amongst the people where its benefits are to be received. I am

> Very Respectfully
> Yr. obt. servt.
> Z. B. Vance

[1]Christopher Gustavus Memminger, Confederate secretary of the treasury. *Dictionary of American Biography,* "Memminger, Christopher Gustavus."

ZBV to James A. Seddon   A&H:GP

Copy

State of North Carolina
Executive Department
Raleigh Feby. 29th. 1864

Hon Jas. A. Seddon
Secty. of War

Dear Sir

I desire to call yr. attention most earnestly to the difficulties and complications arising from the conscription of principals of substitutes in this State. Chief Justice Pearson has decided recently that the law is unconstitutional and further that the act of Congress suspending the privilege of the writ of Habeas Corpus does not apply to these men.[1] He therefore continues to grant the writ, and the execution being resisted by the enrolling officers by orders from the Conscript Bureau the result will be a direct and unavoidable collision of State and Confederate authorities. I have taken the ground that the decision of a single Judge at Chambers, does not possess the binding force and effect of an "adjudicated case" but it only operates to discharge the individual. It certainly does this much and until it is overruled it is final and absolute, made so expressly by the statutes of this state. It cannot be overruled except by the Supreme Court which does not meet until June next. In the meantime if a man is discharged, I am bound to protect him and if the process of the court is resisted I am forced by my oath of office to summon the military power of the State to enforce it. There is no Escape from this conclusion. An agreement was proposed by Chf Justice Pearson at Salisbury and accepted by Gov. Bragg as counsel for the Govt., subject to the approval or disapproval of the same, to remove one case to the Supreme Court by *certiorari*[2] and to bind over all others applying for writs to appear and abide the decision there to be rendered. This gave general satisfaction and had a quieting effect upon the whole state. Since it has been understood, however, that the Confederacy would not recognize the arrangement, the excitement is becoming very great and I fear much trouble will result. Knowing, as I trust you do, my great anxiety to avoid collision with the Confederate Authorities and every thing else that might tend to hinder its efficiency, yet it cannot be supposed that I am to omit a plain and obvious duty, prescribed by my official oath. I therefore earnestly request that you will order a suspension of the enrollment of the principals of substitutes in No. Ca., at least until time sufficient be allowed to exhaust all efforts at an amicable arrangement. I do not know a better one than that made at Salisbury, and which though it would deprive the Govt. of the services of these men until June, would yet give still greater advantages by preserving that peace and harmony between the respective Governments, without which all our labors will be in vain. You will observe /that/ I make no comment whatever upon the correctness of the Chief Justice's opinions. As an Executive officer I consider I have no right to do so. Neither, with all due respect, do I consider you to have any such discretion. And however unfortunate it may be to the efficient and equal working of the Government, that the laws of Congress are at the mercy, so to speak, of the various Judges of the various states. I submit that it is not possible to avoid it in the absence of a Supreme Court of the Confederacy to give harmony and uniformity of construction.

We can only obey the Judges we /now/ have and even this is infinitely preferable to the assumption of judicial powers by Executive officers and making their will the law. Hoping an early response, I am Sir

> Very Respectfully
> Z. B. Vance

[1]See Nathaniel Boyden to ZBV, February 27, 1864, in this volume.
[2]Writ for review.

James A. Seddon to ZBV   A&H:GP

Richmond Va
War Depmt
March 2/64

Gov. Z. B. Vance
Raleigh, N.C.

Your Excellency

I am duly in receipt of yours of 17th ulto.[1] I have already written you of the difficulty of transporting to Wilmington a sufficiency of cotton to meet our urgent and pressing wants. Lt. Col. Sims,[2] chief of the Rail Road Bureau, to whom I had referred your letter, returns it endorsed: "All the rolling stock that can be found is now employed in running cotton to Wilmington; and instructions have been sent out to load all trains with Govmt. cotton to the exclusion of that owned by private parties. Nothing more can be done, without diverting some of the corn trains." You will see, therefore, that every effort is being made to transport the Govmt. cotton to Wilmington. On 26th ulto. Mr. Seixas was enabled to borrow 600 bls from some parties in Wilmington, and I at once telegraphed him to pay over 300 of them to your Agent. The balance of the debt will be cancelled as rapidly as possible.

Yr. obdt. servt.
Very Rspctly
James A. Seddon
Secty. War

[*Endorsed*] File & copy

Z B V

[1]In this volume.
[2]Frederick William Sims.

ZBV to Peter Mallett A&H:GLB

State of North Carolina
Executive Department
Raleigh March 3d. 1864

Col. P. Mallett
Comdt. of Conscripts

Dear Sir

The recent act of Congress having left it to the discretion of the Governors of States to exempt such state officers as they may deem necessary to the due administration of the laws thereof, I hereby enclose you an "act to exempt certain officers and employees of the State from Conscription" ratified by the Legislature of North Carolina Decr. 14th. 1863, which for the present will govern my action in this regard. You will please to order yr. enrolling officers to respect all named therein.

Very Respectfully Yours
Z. B. Vance.

ZBV to William A. Graham A&H:GraPC

<State of North Carolina>
<Executive Department.>
Raleigh, March 3, 1864

Gov. Graham,

My Dear Sir

You will see by this morning's papers that I have opposition—The man who has borne deepest on my confidence and whom my friends have persisted in apologising for, has at length showed his purpose.[1]

As this development gives a new face to affairs, I would be greatly obliged if you could spare time to come down and advise with me as to the best course to be persued. I am sadly in need of advice on several important matters—at the urgent request of Mr. Worth[2] I have summoned my Council, for the 11th. inst, & would like to see you before that day—

Yrs truly
Z B Vance

[1]William Woods Holden, who had announced his candidacy for governor in opposition to ZBV. See Joe A. Mobley, "Zebulon B. Vance: A Confederate Nationalist in the North Carolina Gubernatorial Election of 1864," *North Carolina Historical Review* 77 (October 2000): 434-454.

[2]Jonathan Worth, treasurer of North Carolina, 1862-1865, and postwar governor. *Dictionary of North Carolina Biography*, s.v. "Worth, Jonathan."

James A. Seddon to ZBV   A&H:GP

War Dept. Mch 5th 1864

His Excy Z B Vance
Gov. of N.C

Sir

I have the honor to acknowledge your letter of the 29th Ultimo[1] relative to an apprehended collision between the Confederate and state authorities in the enforcement of the recent Law of Congress abolishing Conscription—You cannot deprecate /more/ a collision of such a character nor be more anxious to avoid it than myself, and yet I am unable to perceive how naturally or rightfully in the enforcement of the Law such collision can occur. The decision of Judge Pearson on the unconstitutionality of the Law abolishing substitution appears to my humble Judgment strange and clearly incorrect, and being contrary to the general course of decision and [received] opinion, and only in a case at Chambers cannot be considered as settling the Law an appeal has therefore been directed in the particular case and the enrolling officers directed to proceed in enrolling under the law. Judge Pearson's decision, however inaccurate, is of course until reversed the Law of the particular case, and will be respected as such—No effort will therefore be made to arrest or enrol the man temporarily discharged by him, and how then can any possible obligation <raise> be imposed on you to execute the Judgment or protect that man—You have I presume been inaccurately informed or have incorrectly presumed the action of the Enrolling officers would be against that man—

In other cases arising under that special Law or others imposing military service, when persons seeking to avoid military service sue out writs of Habeas Corpus, officers are instructed not to appear with the person, but to make return according to the precise and clear provision of the Late Law that the person is held by authority of the President for attempting to avoid military service—The act then by its plain language, not susceptible of doubt or misconstruction, suspends the writ so long as the act is in force—It cannot be presumed that any Judge will be guilty of the Judicial usurpation of disregarding such return and attempt to enforce the writ. Should such assumption be practised, collision would only result from the wanton unauthorized attempt by violence to take from the Confederate /officer/ the person of the petitioner or to take the officer himself for punishment—In such event, the state authorities could surely not be Justified in such acts of aggressive violence, and it is not deemed necessary to advert to what under his oath of office would be the plain duty of the President to see to the due enforcement of the Laws and the protection of Confederate officers acting in Conformity to them.

You will the more readily appreciate this obligation, because in another aspect, under a mistaken conception of the proposed action of the Conf Govt, you have seen no alternative to the discharge of a kindred duty.

In view of the facts as they exist and of the proposed action of the Conf. Govt I trust all apprehension of collision may be dismissed, and yet there will not be the necessity of foregoing during the ensuing critical campaign (in which the Civil Liberties of all may depend) the services of the considerable number of efficient soldiers, which the arrangement you suggest would withdraw to await a Judicial adjudication, which I am happy to think cannot be doubtful.

> Very Truly Yrs
> James A. Seddon
> Secy of War.

[*Endorsed*] Copy & file

Z B V

¹In this volume.

ZBV to James A. Seddon   A&H:GP

[*Telegram*]

Copy

Raleigh March 5th. 1864

Hon James A. Seddon
Secty. of War
Richmond

You have not yet answered my proposition[1] about the vessels carrying cotton. The Hansa is in port waiting to load and I should like to have the matter definitely settled

Please reply at once

Z. B. Vance

[1]ZBV to Seddon January 25, 1864, A&H:GP. Seddon had responded on February 12, 1864, in this volume.

James A. Seddon to ZBV   A&H:VanPC

War Dept Mch 5th. 64

Private

His Ecy Z B Vance

Dear Sir

I have been grateful to receive your Private Letter[1] explaining more fully than the formality of official communication would allow your views in relation to the dangers to be apprehended from the enforcement in your state of the Law abolishing substitution. I have every disposition to defer to your Judgment and meet your wishes as far as they may be consistent with my conviction of the public interests. Unfortunately I do not find myself able to yield in respect to the present Enforcement of the Law. I do not really see how unless collision between the Conf and State authorities can be induced unless a foregone factious purpose exist to force it and then such purpose cannot be too soon developed and suppressed However I may censure and differ from Judge Pearson, I have no disposition to misjudge him nor will I ascribe to him in his past decisions (mischievous as several have been) a traitorous or even factious purpose, but if after the recent act suspending the Habeas Corpus writs, to the return of the officers in exact conformity to the Law, the Judge should decide to proceed to enforce the writ or attack the officer making the return, it will be impossible to resist the conclusion that he is violating duty and is resolutely bent on traitorous designs. In such event, it is Just plainly impossible for the Govt. to yield to his usurpation (tho' vested under Judicial forms) and for its own dignity and to maintain a proper tone and confidence among the people of North Carolina as well as other States, it will be necessary to resist by the strict enforcement of the Law and by defending the officers executing it. I am thoroughly convinced that much has already been lost in your State by over tolerance and concession to the few bad men who are busy breeding disaffection and sowing discontent. A more decided & firmer course of dealing is necessary and it would be weakness not to resort to it.

Of course it is very important not to startle even honest prejudices much more conservative opinions and I hope sincerely the Judgment of the other Judges will as you assure me overrule Judge Pearson and give the moral effect of casting the Prestige of Law & the Judiciary on the right side. Tho the court may not sit till June, could not the Judgments of the other two Judges be obtained at once by Cases of Habeas Corpus brought before them. Surely two men who have put in substitutes might be found in N C sufficiently patriotic and really indifferent to discharge to present their petitions for <illegible> writs of Habeas Corpus to the other two Judges respectively. The cases could thus be made and the opinions of the Judges opposite to those of Judge Pearson be obtained & published. The unanimous opinion of the Court of Appeals of Va and those of the majority of your Supreme Court would probably at once suppress all objections and reconcile the <people> / principals/ to the enforcement of this. I think this a much better plan than the arrangement you suggest which appears to give up the Law temporarily—to be a withdrawal by the Govt from its position and must with/hold/ from the army many valuable recruits. I commend it to your favourable consideration & hope it will solve the difficulty & avoid the ends you fear

Very Cordially
J A Seddon

[*Endorsed*] File—private

ZBV

[1]Not extant.

ZBV *to Edward J. Hale*   A&H:Hale

[*Burned*]

State of North Carolina,
Executive Department.
Raleigh, March 6, 1864.

[*Burned*] Hale Esq

My dear Sir,

Your letter[1] is recd. I believe I may assure you that your fears about the effect of my speech on the Secessionists are groundless—the leaders here are as well satisfied with it as I desire them to be. I did make a mistake in saying that the "movers of this question" are sound & honest—I should have said the "mass" or "majority" of them were &c. It is not very important however, I don't think.

You see Holdens card & his game to couple me with the "destructives." I shall make some rare devellopments on him when I take the stump. Where do you think I ought to begin? He does not want people to leave their crops to hear fearmongers—not him! Although he wanted them to line up and hold peace meetings in [*burned*] of last harvest. I had [*burned*] invitation, from 15 or 20 [*burned*] to go & address them, and [*burned*] insist on loosing the time. [*Burned*] cant complain.

I want you if you can get time soon, to make for me, a compilation from his old files, for ten years back, showing his advocacy of secession, his abuse of Graham, [John G.] Gilmer, Reade, & myself and also his praise of us. "Kiss him Giddings"[2] &c. You will find in the spring of [*burned*] some extracts in the Standard about Gilmer & myself [*burned*] the Boston Atlas with appropriate comments. If he likes old extracts let him have them. Especially show his denunciations of Yancey & Co[3] in the Charleston Convention[4] & what he after said. You will see what [*burned*] of papers it should be. [*Burned*] is making up here to pay [*burned*] 50,000 of them—my aim will be to prove him the dady of secession in N.C., who gets people into scrapes and then backs out himself—that he has abused and praised every man in the State &c. &c.

I do not know how I am to canvass much—the duties of my office are now exceedingly arduous. The blockading running is especially troublesome & keeps me constantly anxious and busy—I have three steamers now running & the fourth expected—Still my cotton cards do not come—it's the only bad luck I have had.

> Write me often
> Yrs truly
> Z. B. Vance

I have still a sick child—which distracts my attention greatly

[1]Not extant.

[2]It is not certain to whom ZBV is referring but possibly to the Ohio abolitionist congressman and consul general Joshua Reel Giddings, who died in 1864. *Dictionary of American Biography*, s.v. "Giddings, Joshua Reel."

[3]William Lowndes Yancy, radical secessionist and Confederate congressman from Alabama. Faust et al., *Encyclopedia of Civil War*, 845.

[4]Of the Democratic Party in 1860.

ZBV to James A. Seddon   A&H:GP

[*Telegram*]

Copy

Raleigh 7th. March 1864

Hon James A. Seddon
Richmond

No reply to my letter of the 29th.[1] The enrolling Officers are arresting men who have been discharged by competent Judicial Authority. Will you for the sake of about Eighty (80) men force me to resist? I warn you of the consequences. Please answer immediately.

Z. B. Vance

[1]In this volume. Seddon had responded to ZBV in a letter of March 5, which apparently had not yet reached the governor. See Seddon to ZBV, March 5, 1864, in this volume.

James A. Seddon to ZBV   A&H:GP

Confederate States of America
War Department,
Richmond, Va. March 8th. 1864

His Excellency Z. Vance
Gov of North Carolina

Sir.

Your letter of the 29th. Ult.[1] addressed to the Secry of the Treasury, proposing that a commissioner be appointed to enquire of the depredations committed by the 50th. reg't[2] of the N.C. troops, and to allow the amount of loss sustained by any citizen to be credited, on the claim of the Treasury for taxes has been referred by him to this department "for consideration & reply." The only reply this department can make is, that it has no authority to comply with the terms of the proposition—All that this department can do is to direct an inquiry to be made for the purpose of ascertaining the persons who have committed the injuries & to control their pay & allowances, for the purpose of affording compensation, if they belong to the service—

Very resp
Your obt svt
James A. Seddon
Secy of War

[*Endorsed*] Copy & file

ZBV

[1] In this volume. See also Christopher G. Memminger to ZBV, March 8, 1864, A&H:GP.

[2] In a letter to Memminger on February 29, 1864 (in this volume), Vance notes that depredations were committed by the 56th Regiment N.C.T.

ZBV to James A. Seddon A&H:GP

[*With enclosure*]

Copy

State of North Carolina
Executive Department
Raleigh March 8th. 1864

Hon. J. A. Seddon
Secty of War
Richmond Va.

Sir

I call your attention to the enclosed copy of a letter from the Agent of the Navy Department to my agent in Wilmington Is it possible that such an unblushing outrage is intended by the Government?

I have no comment to make on such a proceeding further t[h]an that I will fire the ship before I will agree to it.

Very Respectfully
Yr. obt. svt.
Z. B. Vance

[*Enclosure*]

William H. Peters to Theodore Andreae A&H:GP

"Copy"

Agency Navy Department
Wilmington N.C.
March 5th. 1864

Theo Andrea Esqr.
Agent Stmr. "Hansa"
Wilmington

Sir

In pursuance of instructions received late this evening from the Honorable Secretary of the Navy,[1] I inform you that instead of the one third capacity hitherto occupied in private steamers by the Government, we henceforth claim one half the carrying capacity of all private steamers. And you are hereby notified that I claim one half the capacity of the Hansa on her next outward trip. I respectfully request to be informed when this Steamer will be in readiness to take in the quantity of Cotton I am entitled to under this claim.

Very respectfully
Your obt. servt.
Wm. H. Peters[2]
Agent Navy Department

[1]Stephen Russell Mallory. Faust et al., *Encyclopedia of Civil War*, 470-471.

[2]William H. Peters, paymaster, Confederate States navy. U.S. Navy Department, Naval History Division, *Civil War Chronology, 1861-1865* (Washington, D.C.: Government Printing Office, 1961), 6:303.

ZBV *to Jefferson Davis*   Duke:Dav

State of North-Carolina,
Executive Department.
Raleigh, March 9th, 1864

To His Excellency
Jefferson Davis,
Richmond Va

Sir:

Your letter of the 29th. Ult.[1] has been recd. Several portions of it were read with any thing but pleasure, as it was very far from my intention, in my letter of the 9th ult.,[2] to raise any issues of a disagreeable & unprofitable character with you.

Before proceeding to the specifications you invite me to make in support of my statements in the letter of the 9th. of Febry., I desire especially to correct your apprehension in regard to the subject of the 5th item of your letter—when quoting from my letter—"I do not hold you responsible for all the petty annoyances, 'the insolence of office' under which our people lose heart & patience"—you say "I make no comment on this language, as I must suppose that you deem it becoming our mutual positions, and simply invite you to state what portion of these 'petty annoyances' and this 'insolence of office' you do impute to me and the facts upon which the imputation rests." I desire to say, in brief, that I intended no such imputation at all & deny that my language can be fairly so interpreted.

I simply meant to say that I did not hold you responsible for *these things*—this harshness and cruelty of subordinates, and in using the word "all" I intended to convey no implication of *a part*, for which you were responsible. I trust I am incapable of wantonly & needlessly insulting the Chief Magistrate of the Confederate States; and I have ever endeavored in making unpleasant statements to you to avoid discourtesy, while expressing myself with candor. If I have made a different impression in my last, or any former letter, I now assure you, once for all, that it has resulted from my misfortune in the employment of terms, and not from any want of the respect due you personally or officially.

You object seriously to that part of my letter, which alleges that there seemed to have been a studied exclusion of all, once termed *anti-secessionists*, from office in this State, even from promotions in the army which many of them had purchased with their blood; and you deny the allegation, affirming that all your appointments in the Army have been influenced by military considerations alone, & generally made upon the recommendations of the superior officers.

As your denial of the allegation relates only to the army appointments, I presume that you admit its justice in regard to the civil appointments, and I need cite no cases of the latter character. You will please observe that I only charged that there "seemed" to have been a studied exclusion &c. It is of course impossible for me to prove that any other than military considerations have governed your army appointments; but I desire to call your attention to the fact that of twenty-five or thirty generals appointed from North Carolina, only three were anti-secessionists—two of whom Baker[3] & Gatlin[4] were old army officers & the other was my brother, a civilian. Now does it not seem strange, when it is remembered that two thirds of the people of this State were opposed to secession until Lincoln's Proclamation, that God should have endowed the remaining one third with *all* the military talent?—that "military considerations" should divest two thirds of our citizens, however brave, patriotic & intelligent of the capacity to serve their country except in the ranks or subordinate offices? Branch,[5] Clingman, <Scales> Scales,[6] Ransom[7] & Gordon,[8] all politicians are promoted at once! What representatives of the old Unionists was thought fit to receive similar favors? Col. [*Duncan K.*] McRae of the 5th N.C. Regt. was the Senior Colonel of his Brigade; on the first vacancy a junior officer from another state[9] was put over him! He was a Douglas Democrat. Col Garrett[10] his successor was an old Unionist Whig previous to the War, had fought for three years & was covered with wounds—On the next vacancy in the Brigadiership *Lt. Col.* Johnston,[11] a secessionist was put over him. Col. McElroy[12] of the 16th N.C.T., who had fought his glorious regiment from 1200 down to 150 men, & was himself disfigured with wounds, and who was, I learn, recommended by Genl. Pender[13] for promotion, was superseded by Genl. Scales, a Secessionist. I make no complaint against any of these gentlemen, but can only wonder at the passing strangeness of this singular freak of nature, in so partially and arbitrarily distributing the military capacity of the country.

As to the allegation that the great body of the people of N.C. have been "suspected" by their government, which you deny & invite me to specify wherein it is evidenced, I deem the facts just alluded to—the exclusion of the anti-secessionists from office both civil & military—sufficient proof. But proof of this, direct & positive was given in the refusal to reappoint R. P. Dick Esq.,[14] District Attorney under the late U.S. Govt.—for the avowed reason that he "was slow to leave the old government." A majority of forty thousand were quite as laggard as Mr. Dick, and among them the writer is not ashamed to class himself. If these facts taken together do not constitute a case of "suspicion" against the great body of our people, I am unable to conceive what would.

In a long letter which I addressed your Excellency in October 1862[15] I earnestly endeavored to impress this idea upon you. I afterwards followed it up still more earnestly on the two occasions, when I had the honor to visit you in Richmond,[16] and when (on the last visit especially) I was so anxious to give you a true insight into the condition of N.C., to candidly state the causes & suggest the remedy, that I feared you would consider me importunate if not discourteous.

To add the weight of action to the assurances I gave you of my desire to ignore *party* feelings, a considerable majority of the recommendations for office, both civil & military, which I have made to you, have been of my heretofore political enemies.

In reference to my remarks about the outrages of the military upon the citizens, you desire to know why the complaints are on my files in Raleigh, instead of being forwarded to Richmond, and assert that no complaint has been made to you of such a character without redress being granted, when possible &c.

I reply that I have sent up to the Sect'y of War's Office many complaints of wrong & outrage, and, to my knowledge, no case whatever has been redressed. Others, having been referred to the General commanding, instead of the War Dept., after going through the circumlocution of military reference for several weeks, or perhaps months are finally "respectfully returned to Gov. Vance for his information"—that is, the matter stops in the acceptance of the story of the accused party as a full exculpation from all accusation. Hence my office becomes piled up with these unavailing complaints.

One of two instances where unavailing complaint was made to Head Quarters will suffice for explanation. Some time last year a company of Cavalry went into Tyrrell County, in this State, & stole (for they were not authorized to impress & made no attempt to do so under the law) a lot of horses from owners who actually had them in the plough. The poor farmers, thus robbed, put their means together and employed a neighbor, by the name of Lewis to go to Richmond to get the horses back or pay for them. Lewis was paid for the horses by a lodgement in Castle Thunder,[17] upon the accusation of the men, who had taken the horses!

In the Winter of 62-63, a squad of Cavalry were sent into Cherokee Co. N.C., by Col. Lee of Atlanta, Georgia. They seized a number of old citizens, beyond the age of Conscription, one of them at least not under sixty years old, chained them together like galley-slaves and drove them before their horses 120 miles to Atlanta.[18] There they were thrown into prison & told that they could volunteer in the army or remain in prison during the War! Upon my earnest remonstrance they were finally liberated. Was that wrong redressed? Was any body punished for that outrage?

The 56th Regt. N.C.T. was lately sent to Wilkes County to arrest deserters & conscripts, in a section where some disorders existed & some disloyalty had been manifested. On my recent visit to the County, complaint by loyal citizens of most outrageous conduct was made to me. Whole districts were represented to have been robbed & the inhabitants reduced to the verge of starvation. Cattle & horses belonging to the loyal men were seized, carried into the neighboring counties & sold and the money divided—with much more to the same effect. At the instance of several respectable farmers, who had been rendered by these robberies unable to pay their taxes, without selling real estate, I applied to the Sect'y of the Treasury[19] to make an arrangement for these damages to be assessed by the tax collectors for the county & have their taxes credited with the amount. The Sect'y replies that he has nothing to do with it & refers it to Mr Seddon.[20] The latter, in a reply recd. since I commenced writing this letter, says he can do nothing in the matter except to withhold the salaries of the officers, if they be convicted of permitting it![21] For that complaint I consider it impossible to get redress; and the women & little children ruined by this conduct must be fed by the State or starve to death.

Do not, I pray you misunderstand me in this regard. I know these things, in a greater or less degree, are inseparable from a State of War, & that it is utterly impossible for you to prevent them or adequately redress them. But they *do* add to the discontents in North Carolina (to show which I alluded to them in my letter) and prompt & kindly *efforts* to redress would cause these poor <poor> people to love their government and support its laws, far more than the terrors of the Suspension of the Writ of Habeas Corpus and a display of force. To impress you with this was the object aimed at in my letter of the 9th. ulto.

In conclusion I would say that your letter should have received earlier attention at my hands, but for a press of official business since my return to Raleigh, after a short absence & an indisposition, for several days past, which has hardly allowed me to attend to my ordinary duties.

Very resptly.

Yr. obt. Svt.

Z. B. Vance

[*Endorsed*] Govr. of N.C. Raleigh, N.C. March 9, 1864 Reply to the President's letter of the 29th. utl. Answer in the letter book dated March 31-1864

B. N. H.[22]

Recd. March 19/64

[1]In this volume.

[2]In this volume.

[3]Brig. Gen. Laurence Simmons Baker. *Dictionary of North Carolina Biography*, s.v. "Baker, Laurence Simmons."

[4]Brig. Gen. Richard Caswell Gatlin. He replaced Daniel Gould Fowle as state adjutant general following Fowle's resignation in August 1863. *Dictionary of North Carolina Biography*, s.v. "Gatlin, Richard Caswell."

[5]Brig. Gen. Lawrence O'Bryan Branch, a prewar Democratic congressman. He had been killed at the Battle of Antietam in September 1862. *Dictionary of North Carolina Biography*, s.v. "Branch, Lawrence O'Bryan."

[6]Brig. Gen. Alfred Moore Scales, a prewar member of the state House of Commons and Democratic congressman. He served as governor after the war. *Dictionary of North Carolina Biography*, s.v. "Scales, Alfred Moore."

[7]Brig. Gen. Matt W. Ransom, a Whig and then antisecession Democrat who served as state attorney general before the war. He was a U.S. senator after the war. *Dictionary of North Carolina Biography*, s.v. "Ransom, Matt W."

[8]Brig. Gen. James Byron Gordon, an antebellum state legislator. *Dictionary of North Carolina Biography*, s.v. "Gordon, James Byron."

[9]Brig. Gen. Alfred Iverson of Georgia, former commander of the Twentieth Regiment North Carolina Troops. After the Battle of Gettysburg in July 1863, he was transferred back to Georgia and subsequently served in the western theater. Faust et al., *Encyclopedia of Civil War*, 387.

[10]Thomas Miles Garrett. Manarin et al., *North Carolina Troops*, 4:127.

[11]Robert Daniel Johnston, Twenty-third Regiment North Carolina Troops. *Dictionary of North Carolina Biography*, s.v. "Johnston, Robert Daniel"; Manarin et al., *North Carolina Troops*, 7:143. No evidence has been found that Johnston held political office.

[12]John S. McElroy, who had resigned from the army in December 1863. Manarin et al., *North Carolina Troops*, 6:10.

[13]Maj. Gen. William Dorsey Pender, who had died of wounds sustained at the Battle of Gettysburg in July 1863. Faust et al., *Encyclopedia of Civil War*, 569.

[14]Robert Paine Dick, a prewar Douglas Democrat, served in ZBV's Council of State but in 1864 joined the peace movement led by William W. Holden, ZBV's opponent in the gubernatorial election of that year. Dick was then elected to the state senate on the peace platform. During Reconstruction he supported the Republican Party and served on the state supreme court and as a federal district judge. *Dictionary of North Carolina Biography*, s.v. "Dick, Robert Paine"; Cheney, *North Carolina Government*, 179, 193.

[15]See ZBV to Jefferson Davis, October 25, 1862, in Johnston and Mobley, *Papers of Vance*, 1:275-278.

[16]ZBV had visited Richmond in October 1862, ostensibly to deliver—in company with Surgeon General Edward Warren—medical supplies to North Carolina troops returning from the Battle of Antietam. He returned to Richmond in August 1863 to discuss William Woods Holden's criticism of the war and the broadening support in North Carolina for peace resolutions. Johnston and Mobley, *Papers of Vance*, 1:lx, 275n; Tucker, *Zeb Vance*, 207.

[17]Confederate prison in Richmond.

[18]See ZBV to James A. Seddon, May 23, 1863, in Johnston and Mobley, *Papers of Vance*, 2:166-167.

[19]See ZBV to Christopher G. Memminger, February 29, 1864, in this volume.

[20]See Christopher G. Memminger to ZBV, March 8, 1864, in this volume.

[21]See James A. Seddon to ZBV, March 8, 1864, in this volume.

[22]Burton N. Harrison, Jefferson Davis's private secretary.

ZBV to Peter Mallett   SHC:Rus

State of North-Carolina
Executive Department.
Raleigh, March 11th., 1864

I claim the exemption of Daniel L. Russell jr:[1] the county commissioner of Brunswick County, from conscription as an officer necessary to the civil administration of the State Government.

Z. B. Vance

[*Endorsed*] Conscript office Raleigh N.C. March 12/64 Resp'y ref'd to C.O. 4th. Dist. who will inspect claims of Gov. Vance until further orders By order of Col. P. Mallet Josiah Jones Lt & Aide AG

[1]Daniel Lindsay Russell Jr., future Republican governor of North Carolina. He had enlisted at age 18, on May 5, 1862, in the Thirty-sixth Regiment North Carolina Troops (Second Regiment North Carolina Artillery). He was promoted to captain on January 8, 1863. A general court martial reduced him to ranks for his assault on enrolling officer William M. Swann, at Wilmington. While Russell was home on furlough, ZBV appointed him a county commissioner for Brunswick County and therefore requested that Russell be excused from Confederate service. Manarin et al., *North Carolina Troops*, 1:280-281; Jeffrey J. Crow and Robert F. Durden, *Maverick Republican in the Old North State: A Political Biography of Daniel L. Russell* (Baton Rouge: Louisiana State University Press, 1977), 4-7.

James A. Seddon to ZBV　　　　　　　A&H:GP

Confederate States of America,
War Department,
Richmond, Va. Mar 15 1864

His Excellency Z. B. Vance
Governor of N.C.
Raleigh, N.C.

Sir,

The notice to which reference is made in your letter of the 8th. inst.[1] having been given by the authority of the Navy Department, your communication was transmitted to the Secretary of the Navy, who, in his response, expresses some surprise that a notice given in conformity to regulations adopted by the President, under the authority and in pursuance of an Act of Congress, should cause indignation on your part. He presumes the vessel referred to is the Hansa, and adds that the nature of the interest owned by the State of North Carolina in her is not explained by you.

Under the late regulations, I have no authority over the subject, which rests now mainly with the Secretary of the Treasury, and any remonstrance you deem requisite should appropriately be addressed to him.

Very Respectfully
Your obdt. servt
James A. Seddon
Secretary of War

[*Endorsed*] File & copy

Z B V

[1]In this volume.

ZBV to William H. C. Whiting   A&H:GLB

State of North Carolina
Executive Department
Raleigh March 16th. 1864

Genl Whiting

Dr. Sir

In regard to slaves for work on the fortifications at Wilmington, I directed [*Adj.*] Genl [*Richard C.*] Gatlin some weeks ago to inform you that I could furnish you no more after the 1st. /of/ April. Your reply to him is before me. I hope you will at least return all who have been sent to Wilmington by my orders, as I promised the people they should not be detained longer than two months and they hold me responsible for the delay. I am aware of the importance of the works for the defence of our only remaining port, but respectfully submit that it is a *Confederate port*, and the labor for defending it should not all fall upon North Carolina. We have sent many slaves to Petersburg Va. on this principle. Besides I do not consider any thing of greater importance than the question of Supplies which cannot be produced except by the aid of these negroes. After the ploughing season begins it seems to me that the necessary labor should be performed by the soldiers whilst the negroes make bread. Entertaining these views I must decline furnishing more slaves upon your requisition after this month.

Very Respectfully
Yr. obt. svt.
Z. B. Vance

James A. Seddon to ZBV   A&H:GP

Confederate States of America,
War Department,
Richmond, Va. Mar 17 1864

His Excellency Z. B. Vance
Governor of N.C.
Raleigh, N.C.

Sir,

I have received your letter of the 27th. ult.,[1] and regret to find there is any opposition to the appropriation of the iron of the Wilmington, Charlotte & Rutherford Railroad for the use of the Confederate States. The removal of the iron had been duly considered by me, and I should not have sanctioned it, had I not considered its use on other roads of more vital importance to the Confederacy.

The removal of the iron will be suspended for further investigation, but there are other roads in your State from which efforts will be made to secure iron, and I hope you will give all the aid in your power to the Confederate Government in this important matter.

My information derived from all the officers having control of Railroad transportation, is that the condition of the principal roads on which we mainly depend for our supplies is very bad, and the necessity for iron to repair them at an early day is imperative. The state of the roads is daily growing worse and their wants more urgent.

Very Respectfully
Your obdt. servt.
James A. Seddon
Secretary of War

[*Endorsed*] Copy & file

ZBV

[1]In this volume.

William Smith to ZBV   A&H:GP

State of Virginia
Executive Department,
Richmond.
March 17th. 1864

His Excellency Z. B. Vance
Governor of N.C.

Dear Sir

In reply to your telegram[1] for my principles of exemptions, I respectfully state that I mean to certify as exempt all persons *necessary* to the preservation and operation of the State Government. This of course includes all her institutions, such as cities, towns, colleges, Banks, asylums, &c. &c., holding that bodies politic have an inherent right of self preservation and that the State authorities have a right to designate, *without question*, all persons they may think needful & requisite for the purpose. While, however, I lay down this broad proposition, I acknowledge my anxiety as well as my duty to be, to send all persons into the army not *indispensable* to state purposes.

Exemption from military service should . . . attach to no person who is *not* in the performance of civil duties. An officer, even though named in the Constitution and in the laws, without any duty to perform in consequence of the presence of the enemy in his county, should be required to join in the public defence. In this there is no inconsistent nor incompatible duty. It cannot be said that in any sense he is needful to the State Government, when he cannot perform the duties for which he was elected or appointed. For instance—take the case of sheriffs, clerks of courts or justices of the peace. Their duties are local & are to be performed in their several counties and it would be incompatible with the discharge of those duties for these officers to be placed in the army—as in such event the civil duties required of them would have to be abandoned. In such cases the duties being so incompatible with military service, such officers are entitled to exemption. But where such officers are prevented from the discharge of the duties of their respective offices by reason of the occupancy of their county by the public enemy, the reason for their exemption ceases, can there be any reason why they should not go into the army as soldiers? There is no incompatibility of duty—no stoppage of the State Government. It may be said that their counties may be recovered from the enemy this is true—and when the event occurs such officers will have an undoubted right to be restored to their offices & discharged from the army.

In reference to the Banks I have concluded to exempt the Presidents, cashiers & tellers of all such, in which the State is a stockholder, as necessary to the protection of her interests therein, but I do not exempt their clerks, as they are mere ministerial officers, whose places may be supplied from those outside of the conscript age. To this there is, however, an exception in the case of the State Banks in this City, who are the fiscal agents of the State without charge & who are by law the receivers, custodians and disbursers of the revenue & other public funds. These banks are allowed to retain their whole corps of officers and clerks as necessary as well to the interests of the State as to the execution of the laws touching the public fisc. But I have wholly refused exemptions to the employees of the Independent Banks [those in which the state is not a stockholder]—officers as well as clerks. These Banks are founded upon associated surplus capital and are operated entirely for the advantage of private interests of the stockholders and they have no more right to exemption from the military service due to the country for their overseers and managers than other individual owners of real and personal estate. Indeed, capital, thus associated, is less entitled to favour than when invested in land and negroes, embracing generally the whole of one's private fortune, and operated almost exclusively in raising bread and meat—yet I cannot pretend to give these exemption.

The two great principles which guide my action are first to exempt all persons who are really necessary to the preservation of the State Government in all her parts & institutions—but, secondly, to exempt nobody who is not practically necessary thereto. Officers who are refugees from their counties having no civil duties to perform are left to the requisitions of military authority. Commissioners of the Revenue, having nothing to do—the Legislature having forborne to levy any taxes for the present year—are for the time being subject to military duty.

I am now considering the propriety of withholding my certificate from all justices of the peace under forty five years of age. Our Constitution provides that there shall be four justices to each magisterial district. That number is certainly not necessary to the administration of justice and the enforcement of the laws within their district & county & I have almost concluded, as I have said, to withhold my certificate as stated & leave it to the Confederate Government to exempt or not.

I have thus very hastily stated my purposes & principles of action and in return would gladly receive your views on the subject.

Respectfully yours
Wm Smith[2]

¹Not extant.
²Former Confederate general and governor of Virginia from January 1864 to the end of the war. Faust et al., *Encyclopedia of Civil War*, 698.

ZBV to Jefferson Davis   Har:Van

State of North-Carolina,
Executive Department.
Raleigh, March 17, 1864.

To His Excellency
Jefferson Davis,

Sir,

I beg your attention to a matter of great importance to this State and the entire Confederacy—I allude to the business of blockade running. I learn that the new "Regulations upon Foreign Commerce" are to be imposed as rigidly upon the Ships of this State as upon those of private individuals; and I beg leave most respectfully but earnestly to enter my protest against such action and to state some of the many and obvious reasons which induce me to persist in the trade which the State has so successfully established.

The *right* of the State to engage in the exportation of its own productions and the importation of articles needed for the welfare of its soldiers and people, is too plainly recognized to require discussion—I presume it was less to establish a right new to the States, than to recognize and affirm the policy and utility of the enterprise, that the law "Imposing regulations upon Foreign Commerce " declared "that nothing in this act shall be construed to prohibit the Confederate States or *any* of *them* from exporting any of the articles herein enumerated on their own account."

I learn therefore, it is conceded in conformity with the letter of the law, that a Ship owned wholly by the State may sail unmolested by the claims of the Confed. Govt. Under these regulations, which it is asserted, as I believe, in derogation from the spirit of the law as well as the rights of the States independent of the law of Congress, that ships owned jointly by the State and individuals, & though sailed under contract with the State and with the whole benefit which the individual can afford to surrender already conceded, must suffer the imposition of the "regulations" as to the individual share, and be made to surrender more than as much more to the Confed. States.

In the experience and practice of N. Carolina it has been found that convenience, economy and success have been best attained by inducing individuals with the ships and capital to conduct the enterprise of exporting & importing on joint ac't. If the Confed. Govt. seizes the shares of individuals in the ships thus dedicated to the enterprise of the State, it not only destroys the means & power for performing these contracts, but by indirection prohibits the State from exporting on her own account and in the way most convenient & advantageous to her, while it constrains on the State a breach of contract & of faith with the individual & exposes her to claim for damages—In these cases, the State of North Carolina, having by well considered contracts secured to herself an adequate benefit and advantage, as great as the enterprise will permit from the individuals shareholders for the portion of the vessels secured to them is warranted in asserting an interest in the whole voyage, and claiming that it is a voyage of exportation as well as of importation "on her own account."

Seeing nothing in the law requiring the State to surrender these contracts or to suffer them to be interfered with by these "Regulations," is there anything in *policy* or the public interest to induce the abandonment of her enterprises? The State undertook them when the Confed. Govt. with the offer of liberal contracts to individuals had failed to obtain the requisite ships and supplies, and when the necessities of our armies were pressingly great. Now that the Confed. Govt. has no ships, little money abroad, and inflexible terms which will drive the fleet now so usefully employed in evading the blockade away and prevent others from entering the trade, it is more than ever necessary for this State to continue to relieve her troops and people by persisting in her own enterprises—While it would be a grateful relief to the Govt. of this State from responsibility and risk to discontinue the trade and leave a monopoly of Govt. commerce in the hands of the Confd. Govt., the evident operation & tendency of the Regulations to diminish commerce would make a cessation of the State's enterprise more severely felt and complained of by her troops & people now than ever before. I only desire to be allowed to adhere to a system long since entered into—without interference by these "Regulations" or otherwise, which has given so much success & done so much good.

It is said that one scheme is at variance, or in competition with the Confederate one & destroys its chance for success, so in like manner it appears to me, the scheme of the Regulations offers an opportunity and alternative in the 13th. Section for individuals to buy the cotton bonds, now at near fifty per cent of depreciation & to export the cotton paid on them at about half the Regulation price, without benefit to the Govt. in the outward voyage and without importation of needed goods in return, much more out of harmony with the general system sought to be established by the Regulations than the separate traffic of N Carolina & infinitely less useful.

The trade capable of being based on these bonds alone would exceed the entire exportation of cotton through the blockade so far—

As therefore the Regulations (perhaps without so intending) permit exportation under two distinct systems by individuals, the State of N Carolina proposes to enlarge the traffic and increase the supplies of the country by another, less at war with either of the Confederate systems than they are with each other, and which is cumulative & not competitive. I beg leave in this connection to ask you to cause yr Quarter Master General to institute a comparison both as to quality & price, of the articles furnished the Confed. Govt. by this State & those furnished by speculators and contractors.

It might perhaps be proper in <considering> conceding the right to N.C. to continue the trade in connection with individuals upon the system mentioned to require her to abstain from contracting hereafter with any vessel now trading to our ports & subject to the duties imposed by the Regulations, but to add to the fleet, the commerce and the supplies by obtaining such new vessels from abroad & as additions to the present exporting & importing capacity in the trade. There is supply of cotton ample enough to support the enterprise of both Confed. and State Govts. and a want broader than both can supply—And although the Confederate Govt. may contemplate increased traffic, in which I trust they may be successful, it can not be yet pretended that the limited enterprise accomplished or contemplated of this State is in the way.

I deem it hardly necessary to add that the Regulations if persisted in will destroy the trade absolutely, except it may be under the 13th. Section as alluded to. A few weeks trial will I am sure convince you of this. The vessels in which N.C. is interested can not and will not operate under those terms. Money would be lost by each trip, and of course the State can not incur losses for the benefit of the whole which are not to be shared by the whole.

I could add much more to these reasons and could give you many particulars of my own experience, but forbear. Earnestly hoping that these views may meet your favor and that I shall hear from you soon, as my ships are idle at the wharf. I beg to assure you of the great respect &c &c of

Yr. obt. Sevt
Z. B. Vance

William H. C. Whiting to ZBV   A&H:GLB

Hd. Qrs. Wilmington
March 18th. 1864

To His Excellency Gov Vance
Raleigh

Sir

I have received your letter of 16th. inst.[1] consirning negroes at work on the defenses here. While I regret your inability to furnish me with any more labor after the 1st. April, I feel myself bound in consideration for your position and especially for the assistance you have given me theretofore to return the slaves which have been furnished by your order, upon that date. In the mean time however it is manifest that the work here must go on. I will apply to the War Dept. and to the Govr. of Virginia for a supply of labor. If that cannot be furnished from Virginia, I shall be compelled to resort to the power of impressment conferred on the Comdg. General of Departments by act of Congress—though I shall do so with great reluctance with the endeavor to burden this people as little as possible.

Very Respectfully
W. H. C. Whiting
Maj. Genl.

[1] In this volume.

ZBV to Edward J. Hale   A&H:Hale

Private

Raleigh March 20 [1864]

E. J. Hale Esq

My dear sir,

I start to Virginia tomorrow to visit the army upon the urgent invitation of five or six brigades. I shall be absent about ten days and shall go to your place as soon as I get back. Will telegraph you the day. Things appear wonderfully well in all directions—better than I could have thought. Holdens friends say he is much discouraged and would come off, but that it would be suicide. If he runs through it will be murder I hope. I beg to call your attention to Gov Browns message it is much praised by the Holdenites. You will see that his manner of getting peace is the same as mine—viz, hard fighting and negotiations through the legal channels—the [burned] Senate. In a letter to the [burned] [Jefferson Davis] December [30] last[1] I urged [burned] views— nearly three [burned] before he spoke. I consulted you by letter about it. A good point might be made for me by publishing that letter at the proper time, together with the Presidents reply.[2] Gov Graham advised me not to publish it some time ago. Cant Waddell[3] & Taylor[4] be got off and let Foster[5] have the track? He is all right & is the only man that stands any chance to beat [James T.] Leach. The latter *refused to say* who he was for for Govr. at Wadesboro! I fear he will be against me. That & [Burgess S.] Gaithers districts are my dangerous places. Orange County is almost unanimous for me –Six candidates were out for the Legislature & all for Vance! By the way, I will see that reporter in Richmond and bring him to Fayetteville if you insist on it. Having to make so many speeches in the State it embarrasses [*me gre*]atly to have them printed [burned] & language anticipa[*ted.*] My vanity is not sufficient to cause me to make a new speech every day.

I feel the need of a newspaper here every day. The Progress is a poor concern & is in fact edited by Holden, and I cant go into the arms of McRae[6] & Co. I *must* have a paper here, and yet our friends are slow to move in the matter. I think we will buy the Spirit of the Age and convert it into an organ.

By the way I may have done Judge Pearson injustice in my private letter to you. To my astonishment I recd. a letter[7] from him last week acknowledging that he had been too hasty on me about the Austin case, that perhaps he was wrong, and expressing himself highly pleased with my speech and my position in regard to sustaining the judiciary. I also learn privately that he will support me warmly & that Gen [Daniel G.] Fowle will also! Is that not astounding?

The best judges I can see here tell me I will beat Holden badly in this county.

I thank you for your kind invitation to stop with you, but guess I had better go to the Hotel where every one can see me. They want me to speak in Harnett as I go through There is the trouble of it; when I leave home once on a speaking tour I can with difficulty get back again. There is one thing very flattering in it however, and which affords me great hopes of success; and that is, the immense crowds which turn out everywhere, even on the shortest notice to hear me speak—

But my letter is too long—Adieu till my return—

Very truly yours
Z B Vance

[1]In Johnston and Mobley, *Papers of Vance*, 2:357-358.
[2]January 8, in this volume.
[3]Alfred Moore Waddell, Wilmington politician and newspaper editor who originally opposed secession. He served for a time as lieutenant colonel of the Forty-first Regiment North Carolina Troops. *Dictionary of North Carolina Biography*, s.v. "Waddell, Alfred Moore."
[4]James Fauntleroy Taylor, lawyer and former state librarian. *Dictionary of North Carolina Biography*, s.v. "Taylor, James Fauntleroy."
[5]Albert Gaither Foster, lawyer and legislator from Davidson County who became a member of the Council of State in 1864. Johnston and Mobley, *Papers of Vance*, 1:431.
[6]Duncan Kirkland McRae, who, having ended his service as supply agent to Europe, became editor of the Raleigh *Confederate*, which strongly supported Jefferson Davis and the war effort. Johnston and Mobley, *Papers of Vance*, 1:163n-164n.
[7]Not extant. But see Richmond M. Pearson to ZBV, January 11, 1864, in this volume.

ZBV to James A. Seddon　　　　　　　　　　A&H:GP

Copy

State of North Carolina
Executive Department
Raleigh March 21st. 1864

Hon James A. Seddon
Secty. of War

Dear Sir

A large lot of Artillery Horses from Longstreet's Army, under the command of Lt. J. W Born are now in Burke County N.C. impressing corn and eating out the country.[1] Large sums of money have been appropriated by that county and agents sent to So. Ca. to buy corn to keep the poor from starvation. If these men and horses remain there, actual starvation to many of the women and children must ensue.

Please remove them South to where corn is more abundant.

Yours Most Respectfully
Z. B. Vance

[1]See Tod R. Caldwell to ZBV, March 18, 1864, A&H:GP.

David A. Barnes to George V. Strong　　　　　A&H:GP

Copy

State of North Carolina
Executive Department
Raleigh March 23d. 1864

Geo. V. Strong Esqr.[1]
District Attorney for North Carolina

Dear Sir

The General Assembly at its late extra session passed certain resolutions directing His Excellency Governor Vance to correspond with the President and demand the return of Eli W. Swanner[2] to this State for trial. I am directed by His Excellency to inform you he has corresponded with the President upon the subject and the said Eli W. Swanner has been returned and is now in prison in Salisbury. If you have any charges to prefer against him you are respectfully requested to do so at an early day and notify this Department of the fact: Otherwise he will be discharged

Yrs. very Respectfully
David A. Barnes
Aid de Camp to Gov. Vance

[1]George Vaughn Strong, Confederate district attorney. Cheney, *North Carolina Government*, 387, 825.

[2]See ZBV to Jefferson Davis, December 29, 1863, in Johnston and Mobley, *Papers of Vance*, 2:355-356, and Jefferson Davis to ZBV, January 22, 1864, in this volume.

George V. Strong to ZBV   A&H:GP

Goldsboro March 24th. 1864

His Excellency Z. B Vance
Raleigh

Sir—

Your favor of yesterday, by Col. D. A. Barnes, as to Eli W. Swanner has been recd.—I have written to the Secretary of War on the subject, knowing nothing of the matter myself, and beg you to detain the prisoner till I can hear from him—I am, Dear Sir,

> Respectfully your obedt. Servt
> George V. Strong
> C. S. Atto for N.C.

Jefferson Davis to ZBV   A&H:GP

Richmond, 26 March 1864.

His Excellency
Governor Z. B. Vance

Sir.

Your letter of 17th. instant,[1] urging reasons why the "Regulations," lately adopted under the authority and by the direction of Congress, should not be enforced in the case of vessels in part owned by the State of North Carolina, has been duly received.

The Regulations were adopted after much consideration, and a careful comparison of the necessities of the public service with the benefits to be derived from leaving commerce as little trammeled as possible. They do not operate upon a State's right of exportation. But exemption from their operation was not given, and under the law could not be given, to vessels owned in part by a State, nor to individuals shipping in such vessels. The declared policy of the Act of Congress was, to prevent the exportation of cotton, tobacco, &c by private persons, except in such way as would make them most available for the public service. And in accomplishing this end the hardship of the policy was equalized by requiring that the regulations to be made by the President should be *uniform*,—that is to say, that they should bear upon all classes of persons alike. But if certain persons had been exempted because they were part-owners with a State in a vessel, or because they were shippers in a vessel owned in part by a State, while others were left to the strict government of the regulations, such regulations would have been in direct contravention of the law.

Nor has the President any power to modify the regulations or dispense with them in such cases or any others. No such discretion has been given by Congress; and to assume it, would be to violate its declared purpose of uniformity.

Even if this could be done, you will readily see how injurious would be the effect. Such consideration could not be extended to North Carolina alone. All the other States would have to be put upon the same footing. And thus a premium would be offered to ship owners to dispose of part interests to States on such terms, that all the ships engaged in running the blockade would ere long be owned in part by States; and there would be nothing left for the Confederate Government to regulate. I am informed that this has already been contemplated by owners of vessels as the means of escaping from the effect of the law and regulations.

It is not pretended that the regulations are perfect. But they are such as the experience of the several Departments, and those connected with running the blockade on the part of the Government has suggested. Their practical operation may show that they will require modification, but no modification can properly be made affecting their character of uniformity. Being unauthorized, in the view which I have taken of the law, to make the exceptions which you desire, it is needless to examine particularly the reasons which you have urged in that behalf; and I can only express the hope that the injurious results you apprehend, may not ensue.

I would remark, however, in reference to the evils you suggest, as likely to arise under the 13th. section, by speculation in the cotton bonds of the Government, that, having sold those bonds upon the expectation and understanding that this Government would do nothing to embarrass the exportation of the cotton, it would have been an act of bad faith, eminently injurious to the public credit, to subject the bondholders to any restrictions in furtherance of a subsequent policy. And even if the effect you anticipate should, to some extent, result, I cannot but think it will be more than counterbalanced by the consequent enhancement of the public credit and resources abroad.

The exportations thus permitted in order to protect the faith and credit of the Government are in fact made on behalf of the Government. And although the bondholders are thereby benefitted, this is an indirect effect of the regulations made in conformity with the policy declared in the law, to make the exports contribute to the public defence.

Very Respectfully
yr. obt. sevt. &c
Jeffn. Davis

[1] In this volume.

James A. Seddon to ZBV   A&H:GP

Confederate States of America,
War Department,
Richmond, Va. Mar 26 1864

His Excellency Z. B. Vance,
Governor of N.C.
Raleigh, N.C.

Sir,

I regret to learn from your letter of the 21st. inst.[1] of the necessity for the impressment of corn in Burke County, N.C., to sustain the Artillery horses of Genl. Longstreet's command, and that such impressment may cause inconvenience and perhaps some suffering to the people of the county. Genl. Longstreet, however, I know from recent communication with his Chief Quarter Master, has directed essential supplies to be left in all cases, and it is certain that the Artillery cannot with safety be removed to a greater distance. Some compensation for the loss, it is hoped, will be found by the people of the county in the reflection that to the presence of Genl. Longstreet's forces, to which this Artillery is essential, is due their protection from greater ills.

Very Respectfully
Your obdt. servt.
James A. Seddon
Secretary of War

[1] In this volume.

Jefferson Davis to ZBV   A&H:GP

[*With enclosures*]

Richmond, 31. March 1864.

To/Gov. Z. B. Vance,
Raleigh, No. Ca.

Sir.

It has been necessary to call for information from the Secretary of War, before answering your letter of 9th. instant,[1] received on the 19th.

In reply to my invitation to specify even one case in which officers of your state had been "excluded from promotion which had been purchased with their blood, because they had been anti-secessionists," you name three cases, Col. McRae, Col. Garrett, and Col. McElroy. Not knowing the political antecedents of those gentlemen, I assume that you state correctly that they were anti-secessionists, and reply briefly to each case.

From the copies of the papers on file in the War Department which have been furnished by my direction and are enclosed herewith, it appears that in the *first instance*, that of Col. McRae, his name, that of Col. Iverson and those of three other Colonels were presented with recommendations for promotion by General D. H. Hill, a North Carolinian, who commanded the division, and that the recommendation closed with this emphatic statement, "Col. Iverson is in my opinion the best qualified by education, courage and character, of any Col. in the service for the appointment of Brigadier General." It further appears that the lamented General T. J. Jackson, in forwarding the recommendation of the five Colonels with his approval, endorsed on it the request, "that Colonel Iverson be the first promotion," and the recommendation thus endorsed was sent to me by General Robert E. Lee with a recommendation for its "favorable consideration." With reference to your remark that Colonel Iverson was "a junior officer from another State," I have simply to say that it was not I who placed this gallant son of Georgia in command of North Carolina troops, but that a regiment of your State adopted him, elected him for its Colonel, and was commanded by him on many bloody fields. I did not consider myself at liberty to set aside this North Carolina Colonel, because of his nativity in a sister State, when I had every reason to believe that he was recognized with pride by the North Carolina Generals and soldiers who had witnessed his bearing in battle.

In the *second instance*, that of Col. Garrett, no recommendation for his promotion is found on file in the War Office. The gentleman who was promoted to command the Brigade, although styled by you *Lt. Col.* was by right the Colonel of the 23rd. No. Ca, in consequence of the death of Col. Christie.[2] The papers show that his Division Commander, Major Genl. [*Robert Emmett*] Rodes reported of Lt. Col. Johnston that "the good of the service demands that he shall be placed in command of the Brigade in preference to all others." This recommendation was endorsed and approved by the Corps Commander, Lt. Genl. [*Richard Stoddert*] Ewell, and by the Commanding General Robert E. Lee. It bears my endorsement in the following words: "appoint as recommended, J. D."

The *third instance* is that of Col. McElroy who is stated by you to have been superseded by Col. Scales, although "as you learn the former was recommended by Gen. Pender." No recommendation of Col. McElroy is on file in the War Office, but Gen. Pender's recommendation of Col. Scales is appended. That noble soldier whose name is a glorious legacy to his mother State, North Carolina, twice urged the promotion of Col. Scales, but there was no vacant brigade at the date of the first recommendation. On the second occasion General Pender's request that Col. Scales should be preferred as being worthy of promotion and as being the senior Colonel of the Brigade, was endorsed by Lieut. General A. P. Hill, and the Commanding General Robert E. Lee. It may be added that Col. Scales was also recommended by the officers of his regiment and by the North Carolina delegation in both Houses of Congress.

I have thus stated the facts as to the three cases you specify, and refrain from comment on the contrast between these facts and your accusations.

You further specify the case of one civilian, the former District Attorney of the United States, Robert P. Dick, who was not re-appointed by me, and as you aver "for the avowed reason that he was slow to leave the old government." If any such expression was used by me, of which I have no recollection whatever, and which I do not believe was made by me, it was simply the mildest form of indicating my distrust of this person, who, if my information is correct, is not considered in North Carolina to be well affected to the cause to which her honor is committed, and I do you the justice to declare my disbelief that you are right in associating yourself and a majority of the people of North Carolina as being on the same footing of "suspicion" as this man.

You state in your letter that "as my denial of the allegations relates only to the army appointments, you presume I admit its justice with regard to the civil appointments, and you need cite no cases of the latter character." My letter on the contrary distinctly denied your whole charge, both as to civil and military appointments in the passage marked II., and you thus compel me reluctantly to the statement, that, I made this distinct denial on both points for the reason that I foresaw from the tone of your correspondence that you would put on my language the most uncharitable construction that it would bear.

In answer to my request for specification of the basis of your complaint that redress of grievances for the citizens of North Carolina was impossible, you cite three cases, none of which ever came to my knowledge before, and in none of which do you forward any papers or point out the redress that you deem it in my power to give. If I have no power to grant redress, as seems to be intimated by some of your expressions, it is difficult to understand why such acrimonious complaints should have been addressed to me. If the remedy lies in my power, the papers necessary to put me in possession of the cases should have been forwarded with the complaints, if they were designed to be an appeal from the action of the Secretary of War.

There are other passages of your letter in which you have so far infringed the proprieties of official intercourse as to preclude the possibility of reply. In order that I may not again be subjected to the necessity of making so unpleasant a remark, I must beg that a correspondence so unprofitable in its character and which was not initiated by me may here end, and that your future communications be restricted to such matters as may require official action.

[1]In this volume.
[2]Daniel Harvey Christie, who died of wounds on July 17, 1863, Manarin et al , *North Carolina Troops*, 23:142-143.

[Enclosures]

[The enclosures are recommendations from various generals (including North Carolinians Daniel H. Hill and William D. Pender) for promotions of Colonels Iverson, McRae, Johnston, and Scales. Also included is a certificate from the secretary of war that no recommendations for Garrett or McElroy could be located among War Department records.]

ZBV to Jefferson Davis   A&H:GP

Copy

Richmond April 5th. 1864

To His Excellency
Jefferson Davis
Prest. of the Confederate States

Sir

I have the honor to state that the steamship "Ad'vance" is detained at Wilmington under a claim that the new Regulations of the President regarding commerce shall be imposed on her.

This ship was purchased in Europ by the State of N.C. and entered a Confederate Port in June 1863. She carried on a successful commerce for the State, importing supplies for our troops until in February 1864, when one half of her was sold to Messrs Davis & Fitzhugh.[1] These purchasers had a contract for importing supplies for the Confederate Govt. and the sale to them was encouraged by the letter of the Secty. of War to me, as favorable to the wants and interests of the Confederacy.

After the sale the vessel continued to sail without the imposition of the carriage of one third of her outward cargo for the Govt. or any other claim on her by the same. Her trade however, was devoted by the private owners so far as they shared in the same, towards getting means to execute their contract and her whole importing capacity was employed in bringing into the country army and other useful stores. The State of N. Carolina has retained and enjoyed the control and management of the whole ship and a substantial & valuable interest & benefit in her whole bottom outward and inward, about eighteen hundred bales of goods, of clothing, shoes, blankets machinery &c, ordered for this Steamer for this Steamer [sic] are at the Islands awaiting transportation into the Confederacy by her. To arrest her departure and to claim the carriage of cotton on her for the Govt. either by the State or the individual owners, will so seriously interfere with the arrangements made to promote these importation[s], as to brake them up and destroy the enterprise. These arrangements exact from the individual owners all the burdens they are able to bear & were entered into & respected, before the new regulations or those which proceeded them, were in force. To alter them so as to adapt them to the unexpected terms of the regulations in all is impossible. This enterprise, having proceeded all regulations and being entitled at least to as much favor as pre existing contracts with individuals,

I respectfully request she may be allowed to go on uninterrupted. I know of no other ship in the same condition and to allow the continuance of the enterprise may be suffered & the required "uniformity" be still observed.

If the privilege cannot be accorded to her promptly, I beg that she may be allowed to go out on this "moon" reserving any claim of the Govt. on her for deliberate adjudication, the burden of which I will engage to make good out of her further trips. The latest period at which the ship can safely go out is not later than the last days of this week. I have the honor to be,

> Very Respectfully
> Your obt. Servt.
> Z. B. Vance

[1]A. L. Davis and H. Fitzhugh. See Power, Low and Co. to ZBV, January 8, 1864, in this volume, H. Fitzhugh to ZBV, December 2, 1863, and ZBV to H. Fitzhugh, December 3, 1863, in Johnston and Mobley, *Papers of Vance*, 2:335, and Wise, *Lifeline of the Confederacy*, 289.

ZBV to Thomas Bragg A&H:GP

Copy

Telegram

Goldsboro April 7th. 1864

Gov Bragg
Raleigh

An order[1] is here from Hoke's[2] Provost Marshal for the arrest of James A. Everett. It does not profess to be from the President or Secretary of War, and unless it is and in the manner prescribed by the law I shall resist it. Please telegraph Genl. Hoke at Kinston how he should proceed if you desire to avoid trouble—answer

Z. B. Vance

[1]See R. E. Wilson to John B. Griswold, April 7, 1864, A&H:GP.
[2]Gen. Robert Frederick Hoke, commanding Confederate forces in eastern North Carolina. *Dictionary of North Carolina Biography*, s.v. "Hoke, Robert Frederick."

ZBV to Robert F. Hoke   A&H:GLB

[*Telegram*]

Goldsboro April 7th. 1864

To Genl. Hoke, Kinston

An order comes here from your Provost Marshal for the arrest of James A. Everett with no reason assigned or authority given. As such arrests can only be made in a certain manner, and by order of the President or Secty of War, I shall resist it unless satisfied of its legality and that it is ordered by proper authority. Please answer immediately to Goldsboro.

Z. B. Vance

H. Fitzhugh to ZBV   A&H:GP

Richmond Apl. 9th. 1864

His Excellency,
Gov. Z. B. Vance,

Dear Sir,
Your letter to the Prest. dated on the 5th inst.[1] (a copy of which I sent you) was referred by him to the Secy. of War, & afterwards to the Secy. of the Treasury. In spite of the utmost importunity, I did not get action until today, when the Secy. of the Treasury telegraphed to the Collector at Wilmington to let the whole ship go free on our undertaking to make good to the Govt. any claim upon her which it might hereafter establish.

Influenced no doubt by the endorsement of the Secy. of War to that effect, Mr. Memminger first decided that your state interests in ships shall go free from claim of the Govt. on the same, of any sort, either for carriage of cotton out, or for bond &c; but that the share owned by individuals shall carry one half for the Govt. & give bond to import goods &c. He consents however, that where the individuals receive Cotton of the Govt. for freight or in payt. for goods, under the 13th Section of the Regulations, this Cotton shall go out free from Govt. claim—We propose to put our half of the AdVance on this basis; & for the purpose can buy say £3,000 worth of goods, the payt. for which & the freights & profit of 50 pr. ct. on invoice cost, will produce cotton enough at 6 pence per pound to load her for us—or say 500 bales—Or if you say so, we can bring in your goods to her entire capacity, for £3,000 worth of which you can receive cost, profit & freight in Cotton at 6 pence pr. pound, & turn the <same> /cotton so recd./ over to us at Cost (viz.: 6 pence), by which you will receive more for the lot of goods so disposed of, than you have hitherto recd. by one hundred per cent. So you may treat the Collies in your other ships, with this difference, that in those cases you will be paid cotton at 10 pence per pound, it being by the terms of the *Contract* of Davis & Fitzhugh, that we are paid in Cotton at 6 pence. The Regulations fix the price of cotton paid for freights & goods at 10 pence—Or the Collies can procure Govt. Cotton Bonds, the cotton paid on which goes out free. I have had several interviews with the Secy. of War & Treasury to get these terms so settled; & obstinately refused to agree to any which did not concede to you, the unrestricted use of your own share in all ships—I congratulate you that this at least is finally settled. Allow me respectfully to suggest that in the alternatives above suggested, & others based on the principles announced, which will occur to your mind, you can find extrication from the entanglements of the Regulations, & room for an unrestricted commerce for yourself & with very light burdens on your associate individual co-owners—Indeed calculation will show it to be the most profitable course of trade for them—

I saw today the letter from Mr. Memminger to Gov. Brown, who claimed freedom from obligation to the Govt. for certain ships when *whole* bottoms were under charter parties to him, & which told him that he must so arrange his charters as to admit the Govt. into the benefits & preserve one half of the cargo room outward for Govt. cotton! Gov. Smith has also written Mr. Memminger a letter claiming a like freedom for the "City of Petersburg" & for the same reason. He has not been answered: but the letter to Gov. Brown covers his case. They will have ugly collisions with the Govt. which I think you will escape, while you will still enjoy your commerce to the same extent & as profitably as ever.

I shall go to Europe in about 20 days. If I can serve you there, or here while I remain, do not hesitate to command me. I go abroad to accelerate the execution of our Govt. Contract—

May I ask you to send me a few copies of your speech?

With my best wishes for you,

> I am, Respectfully & truly
> H. Fitzhugh
> care R. H. Maury & Co.
> Richmond—

Col Power² will see you in a day or two—

[*Endorsed*] File—

ZBV

¹In this volume.
²Thomas B. Power of Power, Low and Co.

ZBV to William A. Graham   A&H:GraPC

State of North-Carolina,
Executive Department.
Raleigh, April 9, 1864

Hon W A Graham
Hillsboro

Govr.

I have just returned from a very agreeable & profitable trip to the army—I find on my return that the only damage doing to me is by making the impression that I have "gone over" to the secessionists. This is busily circulated. Our news paper¹ will be out next week which being my organ will to some extent avoid this charge. What would do more than all else however, would be for you, Gilmer, Reade, Boyden & others to seek some fitting opportunity of letting the public know your sentiments. Every one concurs in the importance of this step, for its effect on the old Whig Party, and I hope you will think favorably of it.

Should it not be convenient or proper to make any extended exposition of your sentiments a brief note would suffice.

Very truly yrs.
Z. B. Vance

¹*Conservative* (Raleigh).

ZBV to Alexander Collie   A&H:GLB

State of North Carolina
Executive Department
Raleigh, April 11th. 1864

Alexr. Collie Esq.
17 Leadenhall St.
London

Dr. Sir

Your several favors are acknowledged, and the gratifying condition of N.C. affairs on your side of the water appreciated.

Since my last,[1] you have doubtless been informed of the complication to our trade arising from the very illiberal—not to say stupid & destructive—regulations imposed by the Confederate authorities. The States are illegally put upon the same footing as private parties, and both are subjected to such restrictions as will if persisted in, destroy the trade entirely. My remonstrances, joined to those of the almost entire mercantile community of this country, have so far proved unavailable to procure a modification of these regulations, and I am of opinion that our ships had best stop at the Islands, where the expence will be least until new arrangements can be made. Other parties in the trade speak of doing the same thing.

I send you a copy of the Regulations, and suggest that you purchase Confederate cotton warrants; under the 13th. Article, you can export cotton delivered on such bonds, and I hope as soon as Congress meets (next month) to save the State's interest in the ships untrammeled. This will enable us to get along, though much valuable time will be lost in the meanwhile.

I desire to send you further orders for supplies, but in the present uncertainty of matters will not do so. Should everything be arranged satisfactorily, I will send you some heavy orders.

Mr. Andreae is absent at Nassau, and should the pressure drive us out of the business entirely, I will depend upon you & Mr. Flanner to make such disposition of the vessels as may be best for all concerned.

We are extremely hopeful of the Spring campaign. Our Army though small, is in magnificent condition physically & morally. We have high hopes of winding up the matter with the year 1864.

> With high regard
> I am Sir
> Yr. obt. svt.
> Z. B. Vance

[1]February 18, 1864, in this volume.

ZBV to James A. Seddon   A&H:GP

Copy

> State of North Carolina
> Executive Department
> Raleigh April 11th. 1864

Hon J. A. Seddon
Secty. of War

Sir

I beg leave again to call your earnest attention to the importance of suspending the execution of the Conscript law in the mountain counties of Western N. Carolina

They are filled with tories and deserters, burning, robbing and murdering: they have been robbed and eaten out by Longstreets command and have lost their crops by being in the field nearly all the time trying to drive back the enemy. Now that Longstreets command is removed, their condition will be altogether wretched, and hundreds will go to the enemy for protection and bread

Please consider their condition and relieve them if possible

> Yrs &c
> Z. B. Vance

ZBV to James A. Seddon   A&H:GP

Copy

State of North Carolina
Executive Department
Raleigh April 11th. 1864

Hon J. A. Seddon
Secty. of War

Dear Sir

Permit me to express the hope that you will suspend for the present at least, the enrollment and conscription of the State reserves in No. Ca. from 17 to 18 and from 45 to 50 years.[1] Their enrollment now with the present prospect of their being called to the field from their crops, causes the most general consternation and gloom. I have no hesitation in assuring you that the partial abstraction even, of these men from their crops at any time between this and August would be followed by the most distressing consequences. In addition to these considerations I beg leave to remind you that the authorities of this State would be left powerless, without the shadow of a military organization to enforce obedience to law or respect. Having no second class militia, as most of the states have, I presume it cannot be the intention of the Confederate Government to reduce a Sovereign State to this dangerous and humiliating condition. Such a course would be utterly at war with the genius of our new government and repugnant to all the professions of the Administration

Our Legislature will convene again in the latter part of May, when I have no doubt Steps will be taken to provide such a military force as the exhaustion of the country will allow. Till that time I insist that you leave the present organization untouched. In the mean time the Home Guard,[2] now thoroughly organized and pretty will officered, are entirely at your service in case of emergency

Very Respectfully
Yr. obt. Servt.
Z. B. Vance

[1]The Conscription Act of February 17, 1864—the third conscription act passed by the Confederacy—drafted all eligible men between the ages of 17 and 50. The previous age limit had been 18 to 45. Under the new act, boys of 17 years and men

between 45 and 50 years old were organized under Confederate authority as junior and senior reserves for local defense in order to release other Confederate troops to fight on the major battlefields. Albert Burton Moore, *Conscription and Conflict in the Confederacy* (New York: Macmillan Co., 1924), 240, 308.

²The Home Guard (or Guard for Home Defense) had been established by a legislative act of July 7, 1863, and was composed of men not eligible for conscription. It supplanted the state militia after the members of that organization became liable to Confederate conscription. *Public Laws of North Carolina, 1863* (called session), c. 10; Louis H. Manarin, ed., *Guide to Military Organizations and Installations, North Carolina, 1861-1865* (Raleigh: North Carolina Confederate Centennial Commission, 1961), 2.

ZBV to William H. C. Whiting   A&H:GLB

State of North Carolina
Executive Department
Raleigh, April 11th. 1864

Genl. Whiting
Wilmington N.C

Genl.

Great complaints are being made daily about the detention of slaves at Wilmington & I am held responsible for it. If you keep them you have now, it will cause their owners to do more than their share & work unequally. I hope you will send them all home as you promised me, and if compelled to have more, that you began a regular system of impressment from this time on, bearing equally on all the counties.

Very truly yours
Z. B. Vance

Joseph E. Brown to ZBV   A&H:GP

[*Telegram*]

Milledgeville Apl 13 1864

To Gov Z. B. Vance

Confederate Gov't Refuses to permit the states to export their own productions upon their own Ships unless they will allow th<at> /e/ govt to occupy half the room of the vessels will you unite with me & either govern in asking Congress when it assembles to remove this restriction—

Jos E Brown

ZBV to Edward J. Hale　　　　　　　　　　A&H:Hale

State of North Carolina,
Executive Deparment.
Raleigh, April 13, 1864

E J Hale Esq

My dear Sir,

I have agreed to speak at Summerville on Thursday the 21st. and at Egypt on Saturday following[1]—Please make these appointments public, making such changes as you may think best—provided you notify me.

The contest is beginning to assume shape—Holdens friends will try to hold me responsible for every obnoxious act of Davis, the Congress, every General, impressing officer, enrolling officer or strolling thief in the country and lastly for the deprecia[tion] of the currency and the [burned] of provisions! All these [burned] be laid on my broad [burned]

You have seen a long article (editorial) in the Progress of April 10th. which was written by Holden in which he abuses my proclamation against the peace meetings. Look back to his first paper after the mob at his office & see how completely he endorsed it! Great Heavens what a low down scoundrel he is! He says if I had convened the Legislature the act suspending the Writ of H. C. [*habeas corpus*] could have been repealed. How? By the Legislature?

Our paper is just waiting an Editor—I have written for Hyman, having failed to do any better, but it will be ten days before he gets here.[2]

The great effort as I foresaw would be the case, is to couple [burned] with the Destructives. This [burned] the necessity for the next [burned] as I don't wish McRae to become my organ.[3] Another thing also is necessary, and that is for the old Union men of position in the state to come out for me. I have written to Gov. Graham asking him to make his views known & shall write to others. You could assist me I think in the same way. It is *due to me* and the country. It would strengthen me in the country & the Legislature, for it could hardly be said that Gilmer, Graham, Boyden, Mebane,[4] Puryear,[5] & such men, had joined the destructives. I hear of no prominent Whig whose position is doubtful except Dockery[6]—and I hardly think he will go for

Holden. [*Robert P.*] Dick is out for him, but [*Thomas*] Settle [*Jr.*], [*Bedford*] Brown & Brogden[7] say nothing! I set them down against me how[ever.] Hoping to see you soon I [*burned*]

Yours truly
Z B Vance

[1]Summerville in Harnett County. Egypt a community in Lee County; name changed to Cumnock in 1895. William S. Powell, *The North Carolina Gazetteer* (Chapel Hill: University of North Carolina Press, 1968), 131, 481-482.

[2]See ZBV to Edward J. Hale, January 28, 1864, in this volume.

[3]See ZBV to Edward J. Hale, March 29, 1864, in this volume.

[4]Giles Mebane, speaker of state senate. Williams, Hamilton, and Peacock, *Papers of Graham*, 6:84n.

[5]Richard Clanselle Puryear, former state legislator, United States congressman, and delegate to Confederate Provisional Congress. Williams, Hamilton, and Peacock, *Papers of Graham*, 6:100n.

[6]Alfred Dockery, former legislator, congressman, unsuccessful gubernatorial candidate, and member of postwar Reconstruction government. Although his associates referred to him as general, he never served in the military. *Dictionary of North Carolina Biography*, s.v. "Dockery, Alfred."

[7]Curtis Hooks Brogden, comptroller for North Carolina, former state legislator, and future governor. *Dictionary of North Carolina Biography*, s.v. "Brogden, Curtis Hooks."

Christopher G. Memminger to ZBV   A&H:GP

Treasury Department C.S.A.
Richmond April 14, 1864.

His Excellency
Z. B. Vance,
Governor of No. Ca.

Sir,

I have been directed by the President to inform you that your letter of 5 instant[1] has received his attentive consideration. In order that the delay incident to such consideration should not effect any injury to the State of North Carolina, I adopted your proposal to authorize the clearance and sailing of the Steamer Advance without prejudice to the final adjustment, and gave orders accordingly.

Since those orders, a conclusion has been reached which was communicated to you in the following telegram.[2]

"Since the permission to sail granted to the Advance, the question raised in her case has been fully considered, and it has been decided, that the authority to make regulations in relation to the export of Cotton so as to render it available for public defence, impose the restriction that the regulations should be uniform. Therefore the requirement that one half the cargo of every outward bound vessel should be for account of the Confederate States cannot be relinquished as an exception in your favor."

This decision renders it necessary to recur to the case of the Advance, in order that the claim of the Government to the stowage room in her last voyage may be adjusted. I accordingly addressed a letter to [H.] Fitzhugh Esq. your agent, suggesting this claim, and that in our last conference, he had stated certain facts which might avail to bring in operation the 13th Regulation, and thereby satisfy the claim of the Government. I requested him to present those facts, if thus available, or propose some arrangement whereby the Government may receive the benefit of one half the last cargo, or an equivalent for the same.

> Very respectfully,
> Yr. ob. servant,
> C G Memminger,
> Secretary of Treasury.

[1]In this volume.
[2]Christopher G. Memminger to ZBV, April 13, 1864, A&H:GP.

ZBV to James A. Seddon   A&H:GLB

> State of North Carolina
> Executive Department
> Raleigh, 14th. April, 1864

Hon J. A. Seddon
Secy. of War,

Dear Sir:

I beg to call your attention to the case of Private H. Bradford[1] of Co. F 26th. Regiment N.C.T. He was received into the regiment as substitute for one D. M. P[r]uett[2] who had at the organization of the regiment volunteered for 12 months, at the reorganization in the spring of 1862 & was to serve during the balance of the three years for which his principal was held to service by conscription. The term is now expired & Bradford is sixty one years of age, & I would respectfully ask whether he be not entitled to discharge.

> Very respectfully
> Yr. obt. svt.
> Z. B. Vance

[1]Hosea Bradford enlisted as a substitute at Petersburg, Va., on June 22, 1862, at age 60. He was discharged on December 3, 1864. Manarin et al., *North Carolina Troops*, 7:535.

[2]D. M. Pruett enlisted July 15, 1861. He was present and accounted for through July 1, 1862, and subsequently discharged after providing a substitute. Manarin et al., *North Carolina Troops*, 7:544.

John A. Gilmer to ZBV   A&H:VanPC

Greensboro N.C.
April 14th. 1864

Dear Govr.

Had it not been that my Superior Courts are now on hand, & ten thousand things pressing upon me preparatory to my going to Richmond, I would have /been/ to see you some weeks ago.

If your friends are not up & doing, we will be beat at the next August elections. Mr. Holden & his friends are moving Heaven & Earth to identify you with the ultra & Extreme men of the Confederacy. They are now on the Brown & Stephens Platform[1]—after having lauded & published the proceedings of meetings, in which nothing is said about fighting & unitedly standing in defence of our nationality. The meetings which Mr. Holden's peculiar friends figured in, substantially said nothing about maintaining our nationality. It was all convention, and North Carolina state action for peace. We have never understood you to favor the suspension of the Writ of Habeas Corpus or to make the people of North Carolina, loyal by force. But on the contrary you have on all occasions Expressed your Confidence in the patriotism & loyalty of the great mass of our people, and have relied on the proper appeals, to cheer the few that might despond and move slowly.

That whilst you were for peace on the basis of our seperate nationality, and that the strength of the Confederates, should be unitedly Exerted to this<e> End<s>, that you were anxious for a national assurance of our reluctance to shed more blood, and a commission to see whether the war could not be brought to a close, & the further destruction of life stayed, on proper terms of seperation and Nationality.

In your forthcoming message, you must be prepared to set yourself right before the State—and, in fact, if you could do so at a much Earlier day, it would be very desirable <to do so>.

A Strong game is now being played against you, by crying out that you have changed, and adducing Evidence of this by pointing out original Secessionists as being your friends & warm advisers.

Your letter to President Davis,[2] suggesting that in your opinion, that national proposals for peace, and the sparing of the further effusion of blood & the destruction of property might under circumstances, & with proper Explanations, be safely & properly made—if now in the papers, might do much good.

Those in the State, who now admit & boast that they were Original Secessionists are few. If in what you have hereafter to say, you would have a few words to say about their old arguments <of them> that secession would be most peaceful & bloodless—that Cotton was King, & that the loss of it would ruin, & force to terms not only the North but England & France too /and that we would get all our rights in the territories &c/ this would not hurt. The secessionists are now willing to be told of their past Errors, by any one who declares himself ready & willing to stand up for his country, in this her time of <fear> peril, regardless of the question, as to who are to blame for bring[ing] on the War. They are willing to be curried for their past faults, by those <that> /who/ are known to be honest in their wishes for unanimity in the fight, <which can be [*illegible*]>.

The idea of allowing Mr. Holden, who so long fanned the flame & Excited the spirit of disunion, /to/ become the head & leader, of those, who withstood the Storm, which he and others, caused to fall on our heads, is ridiculous.

It strikes me that with prudent management nearly the whole of the old Democratic party and two thirds of the old Whig party, can yet be induced to vote for you—altho, things are now getting very wrong.

<If> I see in Mr. Stephens speech,[3] he says that the Excuse in Georgia for voting for the Suspension of the Writ of Habeas Corpus is that it was deemed necessary to keep down disloyalty in N.C. & to carry Elections. If in any thing you should favor this Suspension, this Excuse of its advocates in Georgia, will do you much harm

The man, who would lead & control the popular mind successfully, must be familiar, with their opinions, feelings, & prejudices. This knowledge is essential to get the people out of their errors—Thousands of good people in this state, have an honest idea that a national proposition for commissioners, to settle on the terms of seperation & peace, would be properly received, & that great good would grow out of it. This idea has a fast hold on them. By designing men it is being ingrained in them. Deference can safely be shewn to them—and I believe in the Expediency of doing it. I have lately been among the people of Yadkin, Surry, Stokes, & Forsyth, and feel satisfied in writing to you as I do.

Yours truly
John A. Gilmer

[*Endorsed*] File—private

Z B V

[1]Of Gov. Joseph E. Brown and Confederate vice-president Alexander H. Stephens of Georgia. They opposed suspension of habeas corpus by the Confederate government, and they advocated peace negotiations. With the aid of Stephens's brother, Linton, they introduced and defended resolutions passed by the Georgia Legislature that condemned the suspension of habeas corpus and proposed peace negotiations. Current et al., *Encyclopedia of the Confederacy*, 4:1540-1541.

[2]December 30, 1863, in Johnston and Mobley, *Papers of Vance*, 2:357-358.

[3]On March 16, 1864, before the Georgia legislature. See note 1 above.

George V. Strong to David A. Barnes   A&H:GP

Goldsboro April 16th. 1864

Col D. A. Barnes—

I have just recd. from the Department of War, at Richmond, the papers in the case of Eli Swanner.[1] Although it is evident that Swanner is a very dangerous & disloyal man, yet I do not see that he can be convicted of any overt act of Treason, and shall not therefore proceed in the case—

With great respect,
Yours Truly
George V. Strong

[1]See David A. Barnes to George V. Strong, March 23, 1864, and George V. Strong to ZBV March 24, 1864, in this volume.

ZBV to Christopher G. Memminger   A&H:GP

[*Telegram*]

Copy

Raleigh April 18th.

Hon C. G. Memminger
Richmond

In pursuance of a contract made last December with the holders of N.C. Cotton Warrants in Europe, the new steamer "Edith" has arrived at Wilmington to carry out the cotton due on the Warrants. Can she do so? I send particulars[1] by mail

Z. B. Vance

[1]Not extant.

ZBV to Commandant of Military Prison   A&H:GP

Copy

State of North Carolina
Executive Department
Raleigh April 18th. 1864

To the Commandant
of the Military Prison
Salisbury

Sir
Eli Swanner now confined in prison at Salisbury was by direction of the Secretary of War, returned to this state, in order that he might be proceeded against by the civil tribunals if guilty of any offence within their jurisdiction

George V. Strong Esq. the District Attorney for the State has informed me that he shall institute no proceedings against him:[1] it is therefore respectfully requested that you will discharge said Swanner from confinement

Yrs. Very Respectfully
Z. B. Vance

[1]See George V. Strong to David A. Barnes, April 16, 1864, in this volume.

ZBV to Jefferson Davis A&H:GP

Copy

State of North Carolina
Executive Department
Raleigh April 18th. 1864

His Excellency
Jefferson Davis

Sir

I enclose you a copy of a letter[1] from an entirely reliable source in Wilkes County No. Ca. It is a sample of many I am daily receiving and about which I have lately complained to the Secretary of War without effect.[2] It is strange that disaffection to the government should be engendered by such conduct.

I can only say Sir, that if no steps on the part of the Confederate Authorities are taken to protect our citizens from illegal impressments of this kind, I shall be compelled to take such measures myself as may be in my power for that purpose

Very Respectfully
Yr. obt. Servt.
Z. B. Vance

[1]Not extant.
[2]See two letters of ZBV to James A. Seddon, April 11, 1864, in this volume.

ZBV to James A. Seddon   A&H:GLB

State of North Carolina
Executive Department
Raleigh April 18, 1864

Hon J A Seddon

Dr. Sir

If it is possible let me beg you to send one regiment at least of regular troops to Col [John B.] Palmer in Western N. Carolina. I enclose you a letter[1] from Brig Genl Mc. Elroy[2] of the N.C. Militia which I beg you to read—The condition of that country is truly deplorable, and if the militia could be depended on, starvation must ensue by the wholesale if they are kept from their crops, in a country where there are no slaves. Time will not suffice to tell you of all the horrors to which they are exposed. I beg you to relieve them and quickly by sending some troops there.

Very truly yours
Z. B. Vance

[1]Not extant.
[2]John W. McElroy, Yancey County merchant and father-in-law of Robert B. Vance. He commanded the Yancey County militia and then a brigade of Home Guard against raids, Unionists, and deserters in western North Carolina. Clark, *Histories of Regiments from North Carolina*, 4:651, 5:7.

ZBV to James A. Seddon   A&H:GP

State of North Carolina
Executive Department
Raleigh, April 19th. 1864

Hon. James A. Seddon
Secty of War

Dear Sir:

I bring to your attention the case of David Mahaley,[1] a private in Co. F. 57th. Regt. N. C. T. Mr. Mahaley was discharged by Judge Pearson at Salisbury on the 22nd. of Feby. last under a writ of Habeas Corpus And his is one of those cases referred to in your letter to me,[2] as being permitted by the Government to be discharged until the Supreme Court of North Carolina shall decide the case.

There is no difference in Mahaleys case and all the others then discharged. Enclosed is a statement[3] from Gov. [Thomas] Bragg that Mahaley ought to be returned. Under this state of facts I respectfully demand the immediate discharge of David Mahaley

David Mahaley was arrested in defiance of this discharge and in opposition to your letter to me on the subject.

Very Respectfully
Yr. obt. svt.
Z. B. Vance

[1]A conscript from Rowan County. See Manarin et al., *North Carolina Troops*, 14:167, Peter Mallett to ZBV, March 22, 1864, A&H:GP, and David A. Barnes to Peter Mallett, April 16, 1864, A&H:GP.

[2]Not extant.

[3]Not extant.

Braxton Bragg to ZBV   A&H:GLB

Head Quarters
Confederate States
Richmond, April 21 1864

His Excellency
Z. B. Vance
Governor N.C.
Raleigh

Sir:

I have the pleasure to congratulate you upon the recent brilliant affair at Plymouth under the leadership of the young North Carolinian Brig. Gen. Hoke. May we have many more such to refer to hereafter as part of the history of the campaign of 1864.

The President directs that the negroes captured by our forces, be turned over to you for the present, and he requests of you that if, upon investigation, you ascertain that any of them belong to citizens of North Carolina, you will cause them to be restored to their respective owners. If any are owned in other States, you will please communicate to me their number, & the names and places of residence of their owners, and have them retained in strict custody, until the President's views in reference to such may be conveyed to you.

To avoid as far as possible all complications with the military authorities of the United States in regard to the disposition which will be made of this class of prisoners, the President respectfully requests your Excellency to take the necessary steps to have the matter of such disposition kept out of the newspapers of the State, and in every available way to shun its obtaining any publicity as far as consistent with the proposed restoration.

I have the honor to enclose to your Excellency a copy of a telegram[1] just received by the President from Col. Wood of his Staff telling of some of the avails of our victory in the way of materials & personnel captured from the enemy.

> I am, Sir,
> With high regard
> Yr. obt. servt.
> *Braxton Bragg*[2]
> General

[1]See John T. Wood to ZBV, April 21, 1864, following.

[2]Confederate military advisor to Jefferson Davis. He formerly had commanded the Army of Tennessee. Current et al., *Encyclopedia of Confederacy*, 1:203-206.

John T. Wood to ZBV   A&H:GP

[*Telegram*]

Rocky Mt Apl 21 1864

To Gov Z B Vance
Raleigh

The land & water attack upon Plymouth under Gen Hoke & Comr. Cooke[1] was complete Success twenty five hundred prisoners thirty pieces or ordnance two gun boats Sunk one Small Steamer captured Stores & supplies of all Kinds.

> J. Taylor Wood
> col & adc

[1]Commander James W. Cooke, CSN, commanding the ironclad *Albemarle*. Robert G. Elliot, *Ironclad of the Roanoke: Gilbert Elliott's Albemarle* (Shippensburg, Pa.: White Mane Publishing Co., 1994), 1-7.

William H. C. Whiting to ZBV   A&H:GP

Hd. Qrs. Wilmington
Apr. 22 1864

To His Excellency Gov. Vance
Raleigh—

Sir,
Last night the enemy landed at the State Salt Works & destroyed one of them taking off a number of the conscripts—I do not regret it—I consider that the whole affair was done with the complicity & on the information of parties engaged there—The enemy undoubtedly were made aware of the withdrawal of Martin's brigade[1]—The establishment has long been a nuisance & the circumstantial evidence of their intercourse with the enemy is very strong & combined with the known character of many of the conscripts, is sufficient to induce me to remove what may have been spared—In this connection I rsply. refer to my letter of 22 ult.[2] to you—
If the Works are regarded as indispensable to the State, it will be necessary to remove them to the Cape Fear river—
No more salt works will be permitted on Masonboro Sound. The men left a number of letters to be distributed—

Very Resply
W. H. C. Whiting
Maj. Genl.

[1]Brig. Gen. James Green Martin, former state adjutant general and former commander of District of North Carolina. In fall of 1863 he had formed a brigade of three North Carolina regiments and encamped at Wilmington. He had departed the Wilmington area in January 1864 to create a diversion at Morehead City during the Battle of New Bern. *Dictionary of North Carolina Biography*, s.v. "Martin, James Green"; Barrett, *Civil War in North Carolina*, 211.
[2]Not extant.

Pierre G. T. Beauregard to ZBV   A&H:GP

[*Telegram*]

Weldon Apl 23 1864

To Gov Vance
Raleigh

By order from the War Dept I will have delivered to you the negro prisoners captured at Plymouth & with your consent send the slaves captured to Wilmington N C have written <to> you today

G T Beauregard[1]

[1]On the day of this telegram, Beauregard had taken command of the department that included "Virginia south of the James and Appomatox, and all that portion of North Carolina east of the mountains." He referred to the area as the "Department of North Carolina and Southern Virginia," but its boundaries and command responsibilities were ambiguous. Barrett, *Civil War in North Carolina,* 221, 433n.

James A. Seddon to ZBV   A&H:GP

Confederate States of America,
War Department,
Richmond, Va. Apl. 23 1864

His Excellency Z. B. Vance
Governor of N.C., Raleigh, N.C.

Sir,

I have received your letter of the 11th. inst.[1] calling attention to the importance of suspending the execution of the Conscript Law in the mountain counties of Western North Carolina.

In reply I have the honor to say, that grave doubt is entertained by the Department of the expediency of such apparent yielding to the disaffected classes which are said by your Excellency to exist in those districts, and in this view the President, to whom your communication was submitted, concurs. It is hoped that the organization of the "Reserve Forces" will, when brought into unity of action with the active army, give defence, and, without interfering with agricultural pursuits, /afford a source of/ <add> security.

> Very Respectfully
> Your obdt. servt.
> James A. Seddon
> Secretary of War

[*Endorsed*] Copy & file

[Z B V]

[1]In this volume.

ZBV to David G. Worth   A&H:GP

Copy

> State of North Carolina
> Executive Department
> Raleigh, April 27th. 1864

D. G. Worth Esq.[1]
Salt Comr., Wilmington

Dr. Sir,
Your letters[2] in relation to the destruction of the salt works, & Genl Whiting's order[3] for their removal have been duly recd.
For the present I see nothing better to be done, than to repair the works as rapidly as possible, & get to work again—The works cannot be removed at present—I have written Gen. Whiting[4] to this effect.

> Very rsply. yours
> Z. B. Vance

[1]David Gaston Worth, state salt commissioner. *Dictionary of North Carolina Biography*, s.v. "Worth, David Gaston."
[2]April 22, 23, 25, 1864, A&H:GP.
[3]James H. Hill to David G. Worth, April 22, 1864, A&H:GP.
[4]April 27, 1864, following.

ZBV to William H. C. Whiting   A&H:GP

Copy

State of North Carolina
Executive Department
Raleigh, April 27th. 1864

Genl,

Mr. Worth, state salt comr. writes me that you ordered the removal of the salt works from Masonboro Sound & have forbidden their remaining there any longer—I am at a loss both to know both the reason why this is necessary, and where you get the authority to control this important state work! Certainly the state cannot exist without salt, & certainly you cannot legally stop the making of it—

If there exists any pressing military necessity for the removal of the works, I will hear it & comply most cheerfully, if satisfied of the propriety of so doing, as I claim to have done in regard to all your suggestions

Very resply. yours
Z. B. Vance

ZBV to James A. Seddon   A&H:GLB

State of North Carolina
Executive Department
Raleigh, April 28th. 1864

Hon. J. A. Seddon
Secy of War

Dr. Sir:

I sent Genl Whiting of lot of negroes for the fortifications several months ago, to be returned at the end of sixty days in accordance with an act of our Legislature. He persistently defers returning them to their owners, in the face of my repeated solicitations.

I can therefore only appeal to you to have them returned. Genl Whiting can press others on his own motion, if he sees proper. If I can not control the impressments as contemplated by the Legislature, of course I desire to have nothing to do with it.

Very respectfully
Z. B. Vance

William H. C. Whiting to ZBV   A&H:GP

Copy

Hd. Qrs. Wilmington
Apr. 29 1864

To His Excellency Govr. Vance
Raleigh N.C.

Sir,

I have received your letter of the 27 ulto.,[1] from which I perceive you could not have been aware of my letters of Mar 22[2] & Apr 22[3] on the subject of the State Salt Works.

I am anxious & willing always to aid & protect any State enterprise, but at present & ever since the attack of the enemy on these works my men have been engaged in daily & nightly contest, from Masonboro to Ft. Fisher—The enemy are sounding every day & landing every night for information—I have no doubt of the disloyalty of many men employed at the salt works—I cannot trust them at that point of the coast—I am entirely willing however to aid in placing the State Salt Works at any point which may be selected under the control of my batteries & where communication with the enemy cannot be had.

With regard to the men employed at the salt works, whose places I think should be supplied by negroes, I have called the attention of the conscript Bureau to them—The authority to detail them is, I believe, vested in the War Dept. & by it in the comdg. Genls. of Depts.

Very Respl.
W. H. C. Whiting
Maj. Genl.

[1]In this volume.
[2]Not extant.
[3]In this volume.

ZBV to Christopher G. Memminger   A&H:GP

[*Telegram*]

Copy

Raleigh April 30th

Hon C. G. Memminger
Richmond Va.

Two weeks ago I wrote[1] to know if the "Edith" and other vessels demanding Cotton due upon N. Ca Cotton Warrants should be allowed to load free of the regulations on the same footing as those holding Confederate Cotton Warrants, I have as yet recd. no reply and the vessel meantime eats her head off at the wharf. Please answer at once

Z. B. Vance

[1]See ZBV to Christopher G. Memminger, April 18, 1864, in this volume.

Peter Mallett to ZBV   A&H:GP

Conscript Office,
Raleigh, N.C.,
April 30 1864.

His Ex'cy Z. B. Vance
Gov. of N.C.

Governor:
I have the honor to request that you will cause to be furnished to this Office a list of the different *classes* of Officers for whom you intend to claim exemption

Such a list will enable me to issue instructions that will prevent any unauthorized action on the part of my enrolling officers—

I am Governor
Very respectfully
Your ob'dt sv't
Peter Mallett Col.
Comm'dt of Conscripts for N.C.

Christopher G. Memminger to ZBV   A&H:GP

[*Telegram*]

Richmond May 1 1864

To Gov Vance
Raleigh

In reply to your telegram of thirtieth 30th.[1] I state that on 22nd. April I sent you telegram[2] that president would issue a regulation authorizing shipment of your cotton in the "Edith" on 26th. telegram was sent to the collector directing him to allow her to be loaded & cleared without hindrance from the regulations

C. G. Memminger
Secty Treary

[1]In this volume.
[2]A&H:GP.

James A. Seddon to ZBV   A&H:GLB

Confederate States of America
War Department
Richmond Va. May 2d. 1864

His Excellency Z. B. Vance
Governor of North Carolina
Raleigh N.C.

Sir

Maj. Genl. Whiting has referred to this Department the correspondence between yourself and him relative to the exemption of D. L. Russell,[1] under your claim for his discharge that he is an officer of the State of North Carolina.

No act of Congress has provided for the discharge of any person belonging to the Army from services, in consequence of his election to an office either by the State or Confederate Government except the act of the 2nd. April 1863. That act provides that any person who has been elected or appointed since entering the military services, or who may be thereafter elected or appointed a Senator or Representative in Congress, or in any State Legislature, Judge of the Circuit, District or Superior Courts of law, or equity in any State of the Confederacy, district attorney, Clerk of any Court of record, Judge of any Court of probate, Collector of State taxes, not to exceed one for each county, parish recorder, upon proof of his election or appointment shall be permitted to resign if he be an officer, or if a noncommissioned officer or private shall be discharged. All the Conscription Acts provide for the continuing in the army those who belong to it, and the exemptions allowed by the Acts plainly refer to persons who are not in the army, but who are made liable to conscription. The Acts relative to the exemption of State officers refer only to such persons. The 4th. [*section*] of the Act of May 1st. 1863 provided that in addition to the enumerated officers mentioned in previous Acts, there should be exempted all State officers whom the Governor of the State may claim to have exempted for the due administration of the laws and government thereof; but this exemption shall not continue in any State after the adjournment of the next regular session of its Legislature, unless such Legislature shall by law exempt them from military duty in the Provisional Army of the Confederate States. By the military act of the 17th. of February last, Congress repealed all laws exempting persons from military service, and provided that none should be exempt but those enumerated in that Act. The question presented then is, what is the condition of Mr. Russell under this act?

The 2nd. Section of the Act continued all men between 18 and 45 who were in the army at its passage, with the same organisation and officers during the present war with the United States. The 1st. Section of the Act placed in the Service those between 17 and 50 all residents in the Confederate States not belonging to the Army for the War. From this class exemptions are to be made. Among the exemptions are such State officers as the Governor of any state might certify to be necessary to the proper administration of the State government. The Department does not in any case go behind the certificate of the Governor of the State to ascertain, whether the person be an officer, or whether his services are required for the administration of the government. But the person claimed must be one who does not belong to the Army. The person in the army is already in the service of the Confederate States under the laws of the Confederacy, and no power exists to withdraw him from that service, except in the cases provided by their laws. This power has not been delegated to the State Executive under the act aforesaid, or under any other act. The facts disclosed by the papers show that Russell was in the service at the date of the passage of the Act of 17th. February 1864 and held no office in the State at that time. That he was reduced to the ranks by the Sentence of a Court Martial and under the Army regulations became liable to service in the Brigade to which he belonged. That subsequent to this he procured his election and that upon that election this claim was made on his behalf by you This question has been repeatedly presented to the Department and when the laws and regulations have been explained, the decisions of the Department have been acquiesced in

Very Respectfully
Your obt. Servt.
James A. Seddon
Secretary of War

[1] Not extant, but see ZBV to Peter Mallett, March 11, 1864, in this volume. Whiting contended that Russell had never been discharged from service, and ZBV maintained that he was a state officer and not subject to Confederate authority. The question was ultimately resolved when Russell was restored to his former rank of captain in the Thirty-sixth Regiment North Carolina Troops (Second Regiment North Carolina Artillery) on December 30, 1864. He then submitted his resignation on February 7, 1865. Manarin et al., *North Carolina Troops*, 1:280-281.

James A. Seddon to ZBV   A&H:GP

Confederate States of America,
War Department,
Richmond, Va. May 3rd 1864

His Excellency Z. B. Vance
Governor of North Carolina
Raleigh N.C.

Sir

I have the honor to acknowledge the receipt of your letter of the 28th ult[1] relative to Genl Whiting's action, in regard to the return of slaves to their owners in obedience to an Act of the Legislature, and to state that I have referred the paper through the Adjt and Insp Genl's Office to Genl Whiting with the following endorsement.

"The authority to make impressments of slaves to work on fortifications or other public works was given in § 9 of the bill relative to impressments published in General Orders No 37. /[65]/ That section requires the observance of the rules and regulations of the State wherein such impressments are made, if such rules have been adopted. The attention of Maj Genl Whiting is called to the Act of Congress as the guide to his action."

> Very Respectfully
> Your Obdt Servt
> James A. Seddon
> Secretary of War

[*Endorsed*] Copy & file—

ZBV

¹ In this volume.

ZBV to Peter Mallett   A&H:GP

Copy

State of North Carolina
Executive Department
Raleigh 11th. May 1864

Col. Peter Mallett
Comdg. Conscripts for No. Ca.

Dear Sir

Your favor of the 30th. Ult.¹ requesting me to furnish you with a list of the different classes of officers I claim as exempt from Conscription, has, in consequence of my absence from the city for several days, been just received. I am guided in my claim of exemptions for State officers by the act of Assembly passed at the late extra Session.² The following is the list embraced in that act.

All Justices of the Peace whose appointments were made previous to the 11th. May 1863 County Trustees, County Solicitors, Registers. Tax Collectors, One Deputy Sheriff in each County where there is no Tax Collectors, Coroners, Constables, who entered into bonds previous previous [*sic*] to the 11th. of May 1863 or their Successors in office. One Deputy Clerk for each Court requiring it. One County Commissioner for each County for distributing money and provisions amongst soldiers' families. Agents appointed under an act of Assembly for any duty. Commissioned Officers of the Militia of this State, and Commissioned Officers of the Home Guard. Mayors and Police of Raleigh, Wilmington Salisbury, Charlotte Fayetteville and Goldsboro. Counsellors of State. Board of Internal Improvements and Literary Board and Employees of the State Government in the different Departments. This list is expressed to be in addition to the State Officers exempted by the Act of Congress passed October 11th. 1862, who are of course now claimed also

> Very Respectfully
> Your obt. Servt.
> Z. B. Vance

¹In this volume.

²The exemption act was ratified December 14, 1863. See "Resolutions Exempting State and Other Officers from Conscription," *Public Laws of North Carolina, 1863,* p. 26.

ZBV to James A. Seddon   A&H:GLB

> State of North Carolina
> Executive Department
> Raleigh May 11th. 1864

Hon Jas. A. Seddon
Secty of War
Richmond

Sir

Circumstances have arisen which make it necessary that I should again call your attention to the claim which the State of North Carolina has against the Confederate Government for Cotton loaned it some twelve months since. The Cotton loaned was part of that purchased by the State and pledged to parties in Europe who upon such pledges advanced the money necessary to purchase and bring our Army supplies. The terms upon which this cotton was so pledged were that the party holding the obligation might at any time on Sixty days notice receive the Cotton from the State. This notice has now been given and the credit of the State requires that the Cotton shall be delivered. The Cotton loaned to the Confederate Government was loaned with the distinct understanding that it was to be returned at any time when called for and at the port of Wilmington, and yet in answer to repeated applications I have received but three hundred (300) bales leaving fifteen hundred still due. In the present juncture of military affairs it is impossible to command transportation and unless you order your Agent in Wilmington to pay the debt due the State her credit must suffer. Should the credit of the State abroad receive this blow it will very seriously cripple me in my efforts to bring in supplies of food & clothing which efforts up to this time have been attended with a fair portion of success, and this blow will <be> most unnecessarily be inflicted by the Confederate Government. The Government has now lying in the town of Wilmington in charge of the Navy Department a large amount of Cotton and the War Department I am informed has also a large amount here. I submit to you Sir, that I should not be met by the answer that the Cotton was loaned to the "War Department" & that cotton belonging to the "Navy Department" cannot be used. The loan was made to the "Government" and justice demands that it be paid even at some inconvenience. I will be most entirely satisfied with an order on your Agent at Wilmington to deliver to my Agent five hundred (500) bales of Cotton per month until the debt is discharged and as I am so moderate in my demands I have every hope that I will not be disappointed.

> I am Very Respectfully
> Your obt. Servt.
> Z. B. Vance

ZBV *to William A. Graham*   A&H:GraPC

> State of North-Carolina,
> Executive Department,
> Raleigh, May 11 1864.

Hon. W. A. Graham
Richmond

Dr Sir,

Let me beg you to try what legislation can be had to relieve the State from the inequities and absurd "regulations" upon the blockade trade. As they at present exist it will be impossible to continue our business. I have directed all our ships not to return unless the restrictions are removed, and large quantities of merchandize & machinery are lying at the Islands and will I fear cause great loss to the state. The Confed. Govt. claims that States are liable to the regulations as individuals.

Very resptly
Yr obt svt
Z. B. Vance

ZBV *to James A. Seddon*   SHC:Rus

State of North Carolina
Executive Department
Raleigh May 19th.1864

Hon. James A. Seddon
Secretary of War

Dear Sir,

Your letter[1] relative to the claim of exemption for D. L. Russell, Jr., as a State Officer has been received, and as I dissent from the conclusion at which you have arrived, I beg leave most respectfully to present the reasons which have influenced my Judgment.

In the first place I am unwilling to concede that the exemption of State officers depends upon the action of Congress, believing as I do that each State has the unqualified right to exempt from military service such officers as the General Assembly "may declare necessary for the due administration of the Government and laws of the State." The act of Congress declaring there shall be exempted "all State officers whom the Governor of the State may claim to have exempted for the due administration of the laws and government thereof" was not to *confer* power on the Governor to exempt State officers; for the Governors derive their power from the Constitution and Laws of the State, and not from Congress; but, to make the operation of the act of Congress depend upon the action of the Governors in claiming certain State Officers for the due administration of the laws of the State (See Jones Reports 9th. vol. page 186, in the matter of Kirk[)]

The Supreme Court of Appeals of Virginia in the cases of Burroughs vs Peyton, and Abrahams vs Peyton, has decided that "Congress can have no right to deprive a State of the services of any officer necessary to the action of its government, and the State itself is the sole judge as to the officers that are necessary for this purpose."

Again, I am unwilling to concede that the Confederate Government has the right to retain in its service and refuse to discharge any conscripted citizen of a State who has been elected or appointed to an office which the Legislature has declared to be necessary for the due administration of the government and Laws thereof.

You make no question as to the fact that Mr. Russell was elected to an office which I had declared necessary, but you assume that he was at the time of his election in the military service, and that "the Conscription Acts provide for the continuing in the army those belong/ing/ to it, and the exemptions allowed by the Acts plainly refer to persons who are not in the army, but who are made liable to conscription." In my opinion you are mistaken both as to the fact assumed and the construction placed upon the law. You say that Mr Russell "was reduced to the ranks by the sentence of a Court Martial." Such is not the language of the sentence of the Court. It is as follows: "And the Court does therefore sentence the said Capt Daniel L. Russell Jr., Co. G. 36th. N.C.T. to be dismissed from the service, and on account of his extreme youth, the Court recommends the said Capt Daniel L. Russell to the clemency of the Commanding General." What then was his status? The Court sentenced him to be dismissed from the service, the Commanding General approved the sentence, and the War Department directed it to be carried out, and yet you hold that he *is now*, was then and had previously been in the military service. To dismiss means "to send away," to give leave of departure, not to retain, not to reduce to the ranks. The language of the Court, the recommendation to clemency in consequence of the extreme youth of the party plainly shows that it was not the purpose of the Court to subject him to the humiliation of being reduced to the ranks and it is respectfully submitted that no action of the Commanding General could modify or change the sentence. He could only approve or disapprove it.

You say that the first section of the Act of Congress approved the 17th. day of Feb. 1864, entitled "An Act to organize forces to serve during the war," placed in the service those between 17 and 50 all residents in the Confederate States not belonging to the army for the War. From this class exemptions were to be made." This restricted operation of the Act cannot be admitted. The 10th. section of the 1st. Clause of the Act is as follows: "that all laws granting exemptions from Military service be and the same are hereby repealed, and hereafter none shall be exempted except the following." After enumerating certain exemptions, it proceeds, "and such other Confederate and State Officers as the President or Governors of the respective States may certify to be necessary for the proper administration of the Confederate or State Governments as the case may be." The Act continues in the service those between eighteen and forty-five who were then in the army, and declared "all white men residents of the Confederate States, between the ages of seventeen and fifty to be in the military service from and after the passage of the act during the war." From the date of the passage of the Act, therefore, the latter class, namely, those between seventeen and fifty are *in the military service* as well as those then actually in. The clause of exemption is general in its terms, and not restricted to any particular class, either those *placed* or *continued* in service by said Act. In the matter of Bradshaw,[2] Chief Justice Pearson, in commenting upon the previous exemption act, the language of which was, "there shall be exempted all State officers whom the Governor of any State may claim" & says, "I can see no good ground to except from the operation of these general words State officers who were in the Military service. If such was the intention a proviso to that effect would have been made, and there is no rule of law by which it can be made, under construction. It was suggested in the argument that the exception should be made by implication from the use of the words, "shall be exempted," and it was said that the word exempted is restricted in its meaning to persons who are not in the military service, and "discharged" is the proper word when referring to persons who are in the military service. This distinction may obtain in military circles, but the word "to exempt" is not a technical term, it is a plain English word, and means, literally, "to take out of or from," and its ordinary signification is "to free from, not to subject to" any service or burthen to which others are made liable; as to "exempt" from military service, to "exempt" from taxation; and it is a settled rule of construction that words in a Statute are to be construed according to their ordinary meaning, unless there is something to show that they are used in a different sense.

You concede the right of the Governor of a State, from whatever source that right may be derived, to claim the exemption of such State Officers as he may deem necessary, provided the exempted person be between seventeen and fifty years of age, and "not in the army." The act of the 17th. of Feb. 1864 declares that "all white men, residents of the Confederate States, between the ages of seventeen and fifty shall be in the military service from and after the passage of the act." If your construction be correct, the States cannot rightfully place in office (except certain Officers enumerated by Congress) any citizen, except he be one under seventeen or over fifty years of age. This power being conceded, Congress may extend indefinitely upwards and downwards the age of conscription, and thus absorb the whole male white population, place them in the military service, leave the States without an officer, and thus blot them out of existence.

Upon consideration of the whole case my conclusion is, that by the sentence of the Court, Mr Russell was dismissed from the service and became liable to be enrolled as a conscript; that before his enrollment he was duly elected to an office which I deemed necessary, namely a "Commissioner for distributing money and provisions to soldiers families." I am aware of the existence of an order of the War Department which provides "that officers of the army cashiered by Courts Martial, and who may thus become liable to military duty under the conscription Acts, will, when present with their commands, be at once enrolled by their respective Brigade Commanders, when not so present, their names will be furnished by their commanding officer to the proper enrolling officer of the district to which they belong." This proves the position which I hold, that Mr. Russell was not in the service when elected to the office of Commissioner, but by being cashiered he become a conscript. You concede my right to claim the exemption of persons liable to conscription who have not been in actual service, although declared to be *in* service by act of Congress. Why then may I not claim the exemption of one declared *in the service* by the order of a Commanding General or the War Department? I can see no difference. State officers have been enrolled and placed in Camp of Instruction, and yet the Commandant of Conscripts and the Bureau of Conscription have uniformly discharged them upon my claim for exemption. What difference can it make if the party has been enrolled by a Commanding General after being dismissed from the service by the sentence of a Court Martial? General Whiting, in a letter to the Adjutant General of this State, says that Mr. Russell "had been allowed a short leave to make his choice of a Company in which to be enrolled, but I endorsed upon it a positive order directing him to remain at his home until further orders, viz (those of the 7th.) In a subsequent letter to me, General Whiting says, "Previous to his receipt of these orders (of the 7th. Inst.) which directed him to report to General Hebert,[3] at Smithville, I am informed that he had been elected a County Commissioner or Trustee by the Bench of Magistrates of Brunswick Co. The order of the 7th. directed him to report at once to Genl Hebert "or Genl [*James G.*] Martin, for assignment or selection as you may choose." He had not therefore been enrolled as a conscript at the time of his election, but had simply been ordered to report for enrollment, which order had not been received by him.

    Should I be in error upon the law of the case, I must earnestly urge upon you not to wound the spirit of this gallant and promising young officer by sending him into the ranks. At the age of sixteen he left the University of the State, raised a Company, served in such an acceptable manner as to win the admiration and applause of his Superior Officer Major General Whiting, in approving the sentence of the Court bore testimony to his very good character as an officer, Col Lamb,[4] under whom he served, gave most flattering testimony as to his capacity and efficiency. His aged father feels most keenly and sensitively upon the subject, and on his account in behalf of the promising young officer himself and as a matter of justice and right, I again most respectfully insist that my claim of exemption for him be allowed.

Very respectfully
Yr. Obt. Svt.
Z. B. Vance

[1]May 2, 1864, in this volume.

[2]Apparently a case involving the legality of Confederate conscription of state officials.

[3]Brig. Gen. Louis Hebert, commanding heavy artillery in the Fort Fisher area and serving as the War Department's chief engineer in North Carolina. Faust et al., *Encyclopedia of Civil War*, 355.

[4]William Lamb, Confederate commander at Fort Fisher since July 1862. *Dictionary of North Carolina Biography*, s.v. "Lamb, William."

William A. Graham to ZBV   A&H:VanPC

Richmond
May 22nd 1864

His Excely. Z. B. Vance

My Dear Sir

I avail myself of a private opportunity to address you this line—to say, that I read your message[1] today with great satisfaction. The topics are well chosen, and treated in a becoming manner.

I had moved on the subject of our state commerce before receiving your letter in conjunction with Col. Orr[2] of S. C. and hope to get a bill reported tomorrow, by the committee on commerce in accordance with our views. I regret /that/ by repeated interruptions on the eve of leaving home, I did not address a letter to Thomas[3] as I designed, but the session of Congress will probably end in ten days, and /I/ shall have opportunities to communicate with the people.

Every thing is in a state of excitement here. Genl. Lee has fallen back to Hanover junction as we learn this evening in consequence of Grants landing troops at Port Royal to outflank him. But great confidence is felt in his ability to defeat Grant and drive him back in the end.

The slaughter in the late actions has been immense on the part of the enemy, and very considerable to us—and as usual exceedingly heavy on N. C.

very truly Yours
W. A. Graham

[1]Not extant.

[2]James Lawrence Orr, Confederate congressman from South Carolina, who had served briefly in the army. He became governor of South Carolina and a Republican after the war. Faust et al., *Encyclopedia of Civil War*, 549.

[3]It is not certain to whom Graham is referring. But it is probably Thomas Settle Jr., a prewar Douglas Democrat, legislator, and state solicitor. During the war he served as a Confederate army officer and again as solicitor. After the war, he helped establish the Republican Party, became a state senator and supreme court justice, then served as ambassador to Peru and district court judge in Florida. He ran unsuccessfully against ZBV for governor in 1876. *Dictionary of North Carolina Biography*, s.v. "Settle, Thomas, Jr."

James A. Seddon to ZBV   A&H:GP

[*With enclosure*]

Confederate States of America
War Department,
Richmond, Va. May 26 1864

His Excellency Z. B. Vance
Governor of North Carolina
Raleigh, N.C.

Sir,
I have the honor to enclose a copy of a letter just received from Genl. Lee.

The Department takes pleasure in expressing its high appreciation of the gallantry displayed by the 20th. N.C. Regiment on the occasion referred to, and in complying with their wish that the flag captured by them be presented to you, to be preserved among the honorable trophies won by the valor and devotion of the troops of North Carolina.

The flag is held subject to your order, and will be transmitted in such manner as you may suggest.

> Very Respectfully
> Your obdt. Servt.
> James A. Seddon
> Secretary of War

[*Enclosure*]

Robert E. Lee to James A. Seddon

Copy

> Head Qrs. A. N. Va.
> 11th. May 1864

Hon. Secretary of War,

Sir,

Yesterday evening the enemy penetrated a part of our lines and planted his colors upon the temporary breastwork erected by our troops. He was immediately repulsed, and among the brave men who met him, the 20th. N.C. Regt. under Col. Toon,[1] of the Brigade commanded by Brig. Genl. R. D. Johnston, captured his flag. It was brought to me by Major John S. Brooks[2] of that Regiment, who received his promotion for gallantry in the battle of Chancellorsville, with the request that it be given to Gov. Vance. I take great pleasure in complying with the wish of the gallant captors, and respectfully ask that it be granted, and that these colors be presented to the State of North Carolina as another evidence of the valor and devotion that have made her name eminent in the armies of the Confederacy.

> Very Respectfully
> Your obdt. Servt.
> R. E. Lee
> Genl.

[1] Thomas Fentress Toon. Manarin et al., *North Carolina Troops*, 6:432.

[2] Brooks had been promoted to lieutenant colonel on November 2, 1863. He was killed at Spotsylvania Courthouse on May 12, 1864. Manarin et al., *North Carolina Troops*, 6:433.

ZBV to James A. Seddon   A&H:GLB

State of North Carolina
Executive Department
Raleigh May 28th. 1864

Hon James A. Seddon
Secretary of War

Dear Sir

I have recd. your letter of the 26th. instant[1] enclosing a copy of a letter from Genl Lee complimenting the gallant conduct of the 20th. Regiment N.C. T. and stating that they had captured a flag from the enemy, which they desired to be presented to the State. The complimentary terms in which Genl Lee speaks of the brave and gallant soldiers of that Regiment should be a source of pride to every citizen of the State, and it will afford me much pleasure as the Executive of the State to accept the present and place it among the many other trophies which attest the valor of our troops. I will thank you to deliver the flag to the Hon. Josiah Turner[2] member of Congress from this State who will take charge of it and see that it is delivered.

With very great respect
Your obedient servant
Z. B. Vance

[1] In this volume.
[2] Former Confederate army captain and postwar newspaper editor and heated opponent of Congressional Reconstruction. *Dictionary of North Carolina Biography*, s.v. "Turner, Josiah, Jr."

William H. C. Whiting to ZBV   A&H:GP

Hd. Qrs. Wilmington
June 7, 1864

To His Excellency
Gov. Vance
Raleigh

Sir,

It is absolutely necessary for the security of this port & this part of the state that all public & private salt works be removed from Masonboro Sound.

This measure is more especially required now than heretofore owing to the absence of troops in the field.

I have therefore notified salt workers. Please to give directions as to the disposition of the state property. I have already received orders to send all conscripts to their proper camps.

In this connection I beg leave to remind you of my letters on this subject of the 22 Mar[1]. & order of 22 of April.[2] During my absence in Va. I find that the salt works had been resumed.

The constant communication kept up with the enemy from this locality, their increased force, their daily landings for the purpose of abducting slaves & procuring information together with the proximity of this sound to the city, make it imperative to occupy this belt of sounds solely for military purposes.

> Very Resply.
> W. H. C Whiting
> Maj. Genl.

[1]Not extant.
[2]In this volume.

ZBV to James A. Seddon   A&H:GLB

> State of North Carolina
> Executive Department
> Raleigh June 7th. 1864

Hon. Jas A Seddon
Secty of War

Sir

Enclosed you will find affidavits of Majr. Walton of No. Ca. Home Guards and the Messrs Corpening concerning the stealing of three mules & other outrages by Col. Ashby 2d. Tenn Cavalry & his men.

I respectfully demand that Col. Ashby and the men engaged in this outrage be delivered up to me for trial by the Courts of this State. I am well satisfied that no punishment will be visited upon them by military authority, and such conduct is well calculated to ruin country and our cause

> Very Respectfully
> Z. B. Vance

ZBV to George Little   A&H:GP

[*Telegram*]

Charlotte
June 9 1864

Col Little[1]
I will be here again tonight. Telegraph me any news today

Z. B. Vance

[1]Aide to ZBV.

ZBV to George Little   A&H:GP

[*Telegram*]

Charlotte
June 9 1864

Col Little
Gen Gatlin is correct about the Home Guards they are all absorbed except State officers & they must be Subject to my control

Z. B. Vance

George Little to Peter Mallett   A&H:GP

[*With enclosure*]

State of North Carolina,
Executive Department,
Raleigh, 18 June 1864

Col P. Mallett
Comdt. of Conscripts

Sir—
    Some weeks ago, I transmitted to you, the application for exemption, as a Constable, of Jos S Latta with the endorsement of the Governor that he was

exempt. The applicant has not yet received your decision on the subject. I am very respectfully

> Your obt. servt,
> Geo. Little
> Col & adc

[*Endorsed*] Conscript Office—Raleigh, N.C. June 22/64 Respectfully returned to His Ex'cy Gov. Vance. This man was not a "successor in office" having been the first constable <in his> *ever appointed* in his district. He was accordingly enrolled and assigned to the 6th. N. C. T. on the 31st. March. Being *in the army* this office has no longer any authority /over him/. His *discharge* should be demanded of his commanding officer. It is understood that he has been ordered to rejoin his Reg't from the hospital where he has been for treatment but has not yet done so—If this be the case he is a deserter or an absentee without leave and liable to be arrested accordingly His papers were referred to the Bureau for instruction

> Peter Mallett
> Col Comm'dt of Conscripts

[*Enclosure*]

ZBV to Peter Mallett   A&H:GP

[*Ca. May 20, 1864*]

Col P. Mallett
Conscript Office—

Col,
    What have you done with the case of Joseph Latta—a constable from Orange? Some time ago I demanded his discharge & I learn he is here in the hospital—No reply has been made to my application.

> Resptfully yours
> Z. B. Vance

[*Endorsed*] Conscript Office Raleigh, N.C. May 20/64 Resp'y ret'd to His Ex'cy Gov. Vance Latta was assigned to the 6th. N. C. T. some time since and in consequence this office has no authority to discharge him—When his

certificate was received with Your Ex'cy's endorsement claiming his discharge
as a State Officer (this *subsequent* to his assignment) it was at once referred
to the Enrolling Officer to report why the man had been enrolled—If upon
its return it is ascertained that Latta was a constable /as claimed/ at the time
of enrollment in regular succession, it will be forwarded to his commanding
officer recommending his discharge—As before stated this office has no
authority to grant the discharge and at present there is not sufficient ground
to recommend it The matter has been explained to Mr Latta twice

> Peter Mallett
> Col Comm'dt of Conscripts
> for N.C.

[Endorsed] File

> Z. B. V.

ZBV to James A. Seddon[1]   A&H:GP

> State of North Carolina,
> Executive Department,
> Raleigh, 27th. June 1864.

Hon. J. A. Seddon
Sect'y of War

Dear Sir:

You are perhaps aware that this State has works for the manufacture of
salt, near Wilmington, that have been in operation more than two years.
They constitute now the principal dependence of our people for a supply of
salt, & in case of accident to the Va. Salt works they would constitute our
entire dependence.

For some cause or other, especial hostility has been displaced towards
them by Genl. Whiting. Frequent attempts have been made to conscribe
the hands employed & other petty annoyances have been offered. Not long
since he issued an order to Mr. Worth, the State Superintendent, in the most
peremptory terms; to remove the works from their location on Masonboro
Sound. I ordered the Superintendent not to do so, but to continue his
operations; & I respectfully requested Genl. Whiting, if there existed so great
a military necessity as to require North Carolina to suspend the manufacture

of salt, please to inform me of it. Instead of doing so, after his return from Petersburg, he issued another peremptory order to the Superintendent to remove the works immediately, & seized the boats by which they were supplied with wood—thus absolutely stopping the manufacture of salt, in defiance of the laws of this State, in contempt of my authority & to the very great injury of the State at large. If any military reason, sufficient to justify this, exists he has not seen fit to inform me of it. Copies of this order & of his letter to the Adjt. Genl. /& myself/ are enclosed.

Before submitting to this outrage upon the rights & dignity of the State, as well as its vital interests, I deem it proper to appeal to you, in the hope that this officer can be made to do both what is right & <decent> /proper/. If he can, then I have no objection to his remaining in command at Wilmington. Otherwise I shall be compelled to ask his removal. The State must have salt, & the removal of the works from their present position is equivalent to the abandonment of its manufacture—as there is no other point available on the coast of this State, where salt could be manufactured at a price, that would put it at all in the reach of the poor.

To be compelled to change their present commodious location at a cost of from $60,000 to $75,000, at the mere bidding of an officer, who has not sufficient respect for the Chief Magistrate of the State, in which he commands, to ask his consent or assign a reason therefor, is more than I feel called upon to bear.

If a military guard for the protection of these works, or for the prevention of communication with the enemy by the employees, cannot be furnished by Genl. Whiting, I will furnish it myself.

Asking your earnest attention to this at as early a day as possible—as the teams, hands &c. are all idle—

I remain very respectfully

> Yr. Obt. Servant
> Z. B. Vance

[1]Deleted from GLB with the notation, "This letter was not sent."

Samuel Cooper to ZBV   A&H:GLB

Adjutant and Inspector
General's Office
Richmond Va. June 29th. 1864.

(No 48)
His Excellency
Governor Z. B. Vance
Raleigh, N.C.

Sir

I have the honor to bring to your attention a question, already made the subject of correspondence between your Excellency and the War Department, as to the authority of the Executive of North Carolina to appoint promote and commission the officers of certain regiments of the Confederate States Army, known as North Carolina State Troops.

Upon a review of the grounds upon which the exercise of this power is claimed to be one of your Excellency's powers and duties, the Department, adheres to its former opinion that these regiments having been transferred from the State to the Confederate Service, are subject to the laws of Congress and the general regulations which govern appointments and promotions in the Army of the Confederate States. Such was the conclusion when the subject was originally presented, although, for obvious considerations, it was not then deemed expedient to abrogate the practice which had obtained, hitherto, allowing officers in these regiments to be designated by the Governor of North Carolina. It has accordingly been acquiesced in, so far, as to continue to refer questions touching these appointments to your Excellency. It is proper however, to state, that the Secretary of War was misunderstood, if it has been inferred from this acquiescence that he admitted the claim of the Executive of North Carolina: or consented to waive the legal right to make these appointments which is vested, in his judgement, in the Confederate authorities alone.

The Department would be reluctant now, to disturb the attitude which the subject has been permitted to assume were it not impelled, by considerations of an imperative character, to exercise the authority devolved upon it by law. Recently a number of cases have arisen, which present, very forcibly, the practical evils and inconvenience that result from a divided control over the organization of the regiments referred to; and exhibit the necessity of all promotions and appointments of their officers, being made, hereafter, in the mode prescribed by the Confederate Laws, as enforced in all other regiments of the provisional army.

It cannot but be apparent to Your Excellency that the exercise of this power by a State, in regard too, to only a portion of its troops, must prove both inexpedient and practically injurious to the service. It is certainly clear that it prevents uniformity of organization; that it places officers serving, possibly in the same brigades, in different relations to the service. That the immediate responsibility of officers, so appointed and commissioned, is, practically, to the Executive of the State and not to the Confederate Authority; that obedience, on their part, to the articles of war and the army regulations cannot be direct and absolute as required by the inflexibility of military discipline, that frequent and vexatious questions of rank will arise, not promptly determinable by Confederate authority; that the laws enacted by Congress with a view to secure a more efficient organization of the Army and intended to apply, without exception to all troops in the service, cannot be thoroughly and uniformly executed, thereby occasioning serious dissatisfaction and complaint; and that injurious delays and irregularities will constantly occur, in filling vacancies and making promotions, because of the indirectness of the relation which the regiments bear to the authority by which the appointments and promotions are made.

This summary, though brief, exhibits some of the evils and difficulties which are presented by cases submitted for the action and decision of the Department: other examples of a similar character, are not wanting; but, it is believed, they will be readily suggested to your consideration. They are of so frequent occurrance and occasion such constant embarrassment, that the Department can no longer ignore the necessity of taking that action which will prevent their recurrence in the future. Your Excellency will perceive that the only remedy to be applied, is that the Confederate Government shall exercise the power and perform the duties which are devolved upon it in regard to the organization of these and all other regiments in its service.

The Secretary of War, has therefore determined in view of the foregoing considerations and of the necessity which renders such action imperative, that the North Carolina State Troops must be placed on the same footing with other regiments in the provisional Army in regard to their organization: and that all questions connected with the appointment and promotion of their officers, shall be determined by the Department, without being referred, as formerly to the consideration of the Governor of the State.

In formilly communicating this decision, I beg to express my confidence that the action of the Department will meet the approval of your Excellency as it has been prompted solely by considerations which refer to the general benefit of the service and the increased efficiency of that Army, in whose struggles and success the North Carolina State Troops, have borne so conspicuous a part. I have the honor to be,

> Very Respectfully,
> Yr. obt. Servt.
> S. Cooper[1]
> Adjt. & Insptr. Genl.

[1]Samuel Cooper, Confederate adjutant general. Faust et al., *Encyclopedia of Civil War*, 165.

ZBV to William H. C. Whiting   A&H:GLB

> State of North Carolina
> Executive Department
> Raleigh, June 30 1864

Genl. Whiting

Dr. Sir

Having at length got the time I address you on the subject of the Salt Works.

I was greatly astonished to find that you had again peremptorily ordered the suspension of the works & seized the boats which supplied them with wood.

Passing over the question of your right to do this for the present, I desire to urge a few reasons against the stopping these works. Their removal now would be equivalent to abolishing them altogether. From all I can gather there is no other point than Masonboro Sound where salt can be made at a price within the reach of the poor. If there was it would require $50,000 or $60,000 according to the estimate of the Superintendent, and there is not a dollar appropriated for that purpose. The Legislature at its recent session, declared that the work must be continued and passed a resolution asking for military protection. In short, the State must have salt and it cannot be supplied on time, if the works are removed.

I am willing & anxious that any of the hands on whom disloyalty may be proved shall be arrested & dealt with, and if you fear their communication with the enemy, I will send a company of State troops to guard them & their boats which shall be under your command. There is nothing now short of the protection of Wilmington itself of more importance to our people than the making of salt.

As all communication is for the present, suspended between this & Richmond I have to ask that you surrender Mr. Worth's boats & allow him to proceed with his operations until the matter can be submitted to the Secy of War.

> Very respectfully
> Yr. obt. Servt.
> Z. B. Vance

ZBV to Theodore J. Hughes   A&H:GP

"Executive Department"
Raleigh N.C. July 1st. 1864

Captain Theo. J. Hughes a.q.m

Captain
    You will proceed without delay to purchase all the Rosin lying west of the Wilmington & Weldon Rail Road for account of the State of North Carolina, and report your purchases regularly to Major Jno D Ervaux a.q.m. You will make a requisition for Ten Thousand Dollars ($10,000.00) in gold, which you will convert into Confederate Treasy. notes to be used in paying for the Rosin.

> Z. B. Vance

Pardon by ZBV for Slave Sam   A&H:GLB

(Pardon)
Zebulon B. Vance
Governor, Captain General & Commander-in-chief
of the State of North Carolina

To
    All who shall see these presents, Greeting:
    Whereas, Sam a slave of Amanda M. Moses of Franklin County, at the Court of Oyer & Terminer, held for the County of Franklin on the 3d. Monday in June A.D. 1864, was convicted upon an indictment for Rape, charged to have been committed upon the person of one Malitia Pullen, a

free woman of color, & by the judgement of this said Court, was sentenced to be taken to the Jail of Franklin County, whence he came, there to remain until the 5th. day of August A.D. 1864, & that on that day he be taken by the Sheriff of said County to the place of public execution of said County, between the hours of 12 o'clock M & 2 o'clock PM & there be hanged by the neck till he be dead. And whereas it has been made to appear to me that the case is one fit for the exercise of Executive clemency

Now therefore in consideration of the premises, by virtue of the power and authority in me vested, by the Constitution of the State

I do, by these Presents Pardon the said Sam of the penalty of death & of so much of his term of imprisonment as shall be unexpired on the 15th. of July inst. upon condition that the said Sam immediately thereafter be removed from the State not to return or be brought back, & that all the costs be paid by his said owner Amanda M. Moses, before the release of him, the said Sam from imprisonment, and upon the further condition that this pardon shall not extend to any other offence of which the said Sam may have been guilty.

Given under my hand & attested by the Great Seal of the State

Done at the City of Raleigh this the the [sic] first First [sic] day of July, one thousand Eight hundred & sixty four & in the eighty-eighth year of our Independence

Z. B. Vance

(By the Governor)
R. H. Battle Jr.
Private Secretary

ZBV to Peter Mallett   A&H:GLB

State of North Carolina
Executive Department
Raleigh, July 1st. 1864

Col. P. Mallett
Comdt. of Conscripts
Raleigh N.C.

Col,

If at all compatable with your sense of duty I earnestly beg that you will send Lt. Hines' command back to the Mountains. That country is in a most deplorable & unfortunate condition, & that command, I am sure, could render more important service there than any where else.

Very resptly. Yrs.
Z. B. Vance

ZBV *to Christopher G. Memminger*   A&H:GP

Copy

State of North Carolina
Executive Department
Raleigh July 4th. 1864

Hon C. G. Memminger
Secty. Treasury Confd. States
Richmond

Sir

As the Steamer "Ad'Vance", in which Messrs Power Low & Co, Genl. Davis & Col. Fitzhugh are half interested with the State, will soon be in St. Georges, Bermuda ready for business, having completed her repairs in England, I, in accordance with your invitation to Col. Fitzhugh to place her under the "Davis and Fitzhugh contract" give my consent to such an arrangement in behalf of the State interest and have so notified Messrs Power, Low & Co, Wilmington, who manage the business of the ship in that city.

You will please notify Messrs Power Low & Co officially that the management has been consummated in accordance with your invitation as above, so that no delay will take place in her business, which will no doubt work to the mutual advantage of the Genl. and State governments, as well as for the private interest in the ship.

Very Respectfully
Your obedient Servt.
Z. B. Vance

William H. C. Whiting to ZBV   A&H:GLB

Hd. Qrs. Wilmington
July 4th. 1864.

To His Excellency Gov. Vance
Raleigh

Sir

The War Dept. has decided that the claim on the part of the State to Mr. Danl Russell cannot be admitted he having been "in the service already at the date 17th Feb of the act to organize forces for the War—That act continued in it all persons belonging to it till the termination of the War". The exemption clauses in that act do not apply to the class whose position had already been determined. They apply only to those who were not in service but were made liable by universal expression of 1st. Sect of the Act and an exception to the operations of that Section." "The Governors authority to claim as exempts those in service does not extend to a person in service."

I have accordingly notified Mr Russell that in accordance with the sentence of the Court Martial he will be required to select one of the N.C. Companies for service.

Very Respectfully
W. H. C. Whiting
Maj. Genl.

Peter Mallett to ZBV   A&H:GLB

Conscript Office
Raleigh N.C.
July 4th. 1864

Hon Z. B. Vance
Governor No. Ca.

Sir

Your communication of the 1st. instant[1] urging that the Command of Lt. Hines be sent back to the Mountains, has been received. Upon the strength of your representations, and in view of the utterly defenceless condition of the Counties through which the riders passed, I have assumed the responsibility of sending Lt. Hines back, and he accordingly left with his two Companies on yesterday, not having been able to get transportation sooner. I am Sir

Yr. obt. Servt.
Peter Mallett
Col. & Comdr. Cons N.C.

[1]In this volume.

William H. C. Whiting to ZBV   A&H:GLB

Hd. Qrs. Wilmington
July 4th. 1864

To His Excellency Gov. Vance
Raleigh

Sir

Your letter of the 30th. ult.[1] about Salt Works of the State is recd. While I fully acknowledge the need the State has to procure salt for the poor, I see no reason to change any thing I have reported concerning the prejudice of these establishments to a much more important matter, the safety of this place, which concerns not only No. Ca. but the whole country—On the contrary, from the movements of the enemy at this very time, what I advocate with regard not only to these works but to all families living on that belt of Sound viz their entire and absolute removal. This has been approved by Genl Beauregard and no doubt will be so by the War Dept. In consideration of your request however the works may still proceed until the War Dept. is heard from, unless indeed, which is more than likely the enemy attempt the coast. Some other means than boats must be had to procure fuel, for two reasons, one that I am filling all the channels of the Sound with torpedoes and obstructions, and no reliance can be had that the boats may not be improperly used. Private works use no boats. There is another matter in connection with these Salt Works to which I again call attention and that is the employment of a large number of able bodied men in the making of Salt. This labor can be done as well by negroes, as in the case of all private

Salt works. If this is continued it will furnish an additional reason for doing away with these works.

Very Respectfully
W. H. C. Whiting
Maj. Genl.

[1]In this volume.

ZBV to James A. Seddon   A&H:GLB

State of North Carolina
Executive Department
Raleigh July 4th. 1864.

Hon J A. Seddon
Secty of War

Dear Sir,

You are perhaps aware that this State has had Salt works in operation near Wilmington that have been our principal source for a supply for more than two years past. In case of an accident to the salt works in Va. these works would be our sole dependence for an article of indispensable necessity to our people.

Genl Whiting has recently issued a most peremptory order to the Superintendent of the works to suspend his operations, has addressed me a letter suggesting that I have the State property removed from the Sound where they are located, & he has impressed the boats that have been used in supplying the works with wood.

Considering the vast importance of this manufacturing of Salt to the people of this State, it appears to me that the reasons Genl Whiting has given for his course in regard to it are unsatisfactory. His principal reason is that the operatives are in many cases disloyal, & there is danger of their communicating with the enemy. This objection to the continuance of the works might be easily obviated by having a guard of soldiers stationed at the point where they are located and I have offered to spare a guard for the purpose, from my State troops, in case Genl. Whiting cannot detail a sufficient number from the troops under his command. I am willing of course that this guard shall be subject to his orders.

The State must have Salt & I know of no other point on our coast available for its manufacture, or at any rate where it could be made at a price to put it within the reach of the majority of our people.

I earnestly request that you will give this subject of such importance to the State your early attention & hope you will see proper to forbid any interference on the part of Genl Whiting with the States manufacture of Salt.

The General Assembly at its recent session again recognized the importance of these works & ordered their continuance

> Very respectfully
> Yr obt Servant
> Z. B. Vance

ZBV to William H. C. Whiting   SHC:RUS

> State of North-Carolina,
> Executive Department.
> Raleigh, July 5, 1864

Genl Whiting,

Some six weeks ago I addressed a letter to the Sec'y of War in regard to the exemption of D. L. Russell Jr., County Commissioner for Brunswick County. No answer has yet been received, & I learn that young Russell has been ordered by you to go into camp.

Mr. Russell was "dismissed the service," was not a conscript <previous to this enrolment> until he was enrolled; previous to his enrollment he received this appointment which made him a State Officer, "necessary to the due administration of the laws," in accordance with the act of Congress and the resolutions of the Legislature of this state I have given him a certificate of exemption. This I cannot recede from, and especially in favor of a government that will not answer a respectful letter on the subject.

I therefore notify you that your offer to arrest Mr. Russell or to disturb him in the discharge of his official duties will be taken as a deliberate & unwarranted usurpation of authority & will be resisted accordingly.

> Very respectfully
> Yr. Obt. Svt.
> Z. B. Vance

ZBV to James A. Seddon   A&H:GLB

State of North Carolina
Executive Department
Raleigh, July 5 1864

Hon J. A. Seddon
Secy of War

Sir,

I have waited anxiously for a reply to my letter of the [*blank*][1] in regard to the exemption of Danl. L. Russell Jr. as an officer of this State. None has been recd., but I am told that that Genl Whiting has orders to conscribe him immediately.

I simply wish to inform you that I cannot & will not submit to this being done without resisting it by every means at my command

Very Resptly.
Yr. obt. Svt.
Z. B. Vance

[1]See ZBV to James A. Seddon, May 19, 1864, in this volume.

William H. C. Whiting to ZBV   A&H:GLB

Headquarters Wilmington N.C.
July 8th. 1864

To His Excellency
Gov. Vance
Raleigh N.C.

Sir—

I have recd. your communication of July 5th. I presume when you wrote you had not received my letter of the 4th. Inst. relative to the case of Mr. Russell. That letter is respectfully referred to you as expressing all I have to say upon the subject. Your letter of the 5th. has been forwarded to the War Dept. and in regard to it, considering the manner in which you have addressed me you will permit me to inform you, that I do not admit the propriety of your animadverting to me upon the Government of the Confederate States or its conduct of its correspondence.

My own correspondence with the authorities of the State of N.C. has been carried on not only with courtesy, as may be seen from the record, but with an entire deference to your wishes in the case of Mr. Russell very much beyond the deserts of that individual in his attempts to evade service.

Very Respectfully
W. H. C. Whiting
Maj. Genl.

ZBV to James A. Seddon   A&H:GLB

State of North Carolina
Executive Department
Raleigh 16th. July 1864

Hon Jas. A Seddon
Secy of War
Richmond Va.

Sir

The Western border of North Carolina requires protection from the inrodes of the Yankees and Tennessee tories and I am greatly in want of Arms to supply the militia. I have loaned to the Confederate Government all the arms I had and find myself now without any. I must now urgently request that you return me two or three thousand stands immediately to enable me to give that protection the people of the Western counties require and the interest of the Government demands. Let me hear from you without delay, as the exigencies of the occasion demands of me prompt action. I have the honor to be

Very Respectfully
Your obt. Servt.
Z. B. Vance

ZBV to John D. Whitford　　　　　　　A&H:GLB

State of North Carolina
Executive Department
Raleigh July 16th. 1864

Col. J. D. Whitford
Pres. A & N.C. R Rd.

Dear Sir

Mr. Elliott[1] informs me that his Company is desirous of contracting for rail road iron to build a Gun Boat upon the terms proposed by your Company, that is to say, to pay for the iron in funds which can be made available to pay the debt of the Company to the State. The Treasurer of the State will receive State Bonds or Treasury Notes. Mr. Elliott visits you to make a contract and I hope you can come to some Satisfactory arrangement.

Yours Very Respectfully
Z B. Vance

[1]Apparently Gilbert Elliott, an engineer who had previously constructed the ironclad gunboat, *Albemarle*. *Dictionary of North Carolina Biography*, s.v. "Elliott, Gilbert."

Robert E. Lee to ZBV　　　　　　　A&H:GP

[*Telegram*]

Headquarters
July 20 1864

To Gov Z B. Vance
Raleigh

Col Gorgas[1] informs me a portion of arms required by you go forward from Richmond to Salisbury tomorrow

R. E. Lee

[1]Josiah Gorgas, chief of the Confederate Ordnance Bureau. Faust et al., *Encyclopedia of Civil War*, 316.

Samuel J. Person to ZBV   A&H:GLB

Wilmington N.C.
July 20th. 1864

His Excellency
Z. B. Vance

Dear Sir
    In answer to a resolution, introduced by me and passed by the House of
Commons, in May last, requesting you to furnish that body with the whole
of the correspondence between the President and yourself upon the subject
of the Habeas Corpus, you sent in three letters—two from the President
to you[1] and one from you to him[2]—in addition to what accompanied your
message at the beginning of the Session. They were rec'd; and thinking it
but just that the whole correspondence should in some way go before the
public, and not that part only which was to be printed with your message I
moved the printing of these additional letters as a House document and after
a good deal of discussion it was so ordered upon a call of the yeas and nays.
But that order has never been executed for the reason, it is said, that it did
not pass the Senate also, and thus a public judgement upon the question and
the conduct of the persons connected with it, is to be made up without any
opportunity of seeing the whole case. Who made this decision I know not,
but it seems to have had authority sufficient to prevent the printing. And as
it appears to be settled that the House of Commons has no power of itself to
order the printing of documents, which are called for and obtained by the
action of that body alone. The motion to print was never intended to go to
the Senate under the belief of its author that it was perfectly competent for
the House of Commons to have matter properly before it printed, whether
bills, letters or papers of any sort, without having or asking the concurrence
of the Senate. Under these circumstances and as an act of justice to all
concerned, I respectfully request that you will furnish me for publication
a copy of the three letters above mentioned. This application would have
been made at an earlier day but for reasons which need not be now stated.

                          Very respectfully
                          Saml. J. Person

[1]January 8 and February 29, 1864, in this volume.
[2]February 9, 1864, in this volume.

ZBV to Samuel Cooper   A&H:GLB

State of North Carolina
Executive Department
Raleigh July 20th. 1864

Genl. S. Cooper
Adjt & Insp. Genl

General

I have recd. your letter of the 29th. ulto.[1] in which you say the Secretary of War has determined "that the North Carolina State Troops must be placed on the same footing with other regiments in the provisional army in regard to their organization and that all questions connected with the appointment and promotion of their officers should be determined by the Department without being referred as formerly to the consideration of the Governor of the State."

Soon after my accession to the Chief Executive Office of the State, this matter was the subject of a correspondence between the Secretary of War and myself. In that correspondence the Secretary of War disclaimed any purpose to entrench upon my perogative in this regard and asked me to state the regiments to which my power of appointment extended and on what ground the claim rested. In my reply I stated the ground upon which I deemed it not only my right, but my duty to make such appointments, namely that those regiments were organized originally for the period of the War under a State Law, and the Governor was required by that Law to commission the officers and to fill vacancies. This claim of right was then acquiesced in, if not admitted and since that period (Feb. 1863) I have continued as I had before done to make these appointments.

The reasons given by you for this determination on the part of the Secretary of War existed with as much force then as now. The Confederate Authorities appoint the officers of what are known as conscript regiments, whilst I appoint those of the State Troops. Can it be said that the former are more efficient that the latter? Are they more obedient to the Articles of War and army regulations: is there less dissatisfaction and complaint among them? are there fewer injurious irregularities and delays in filling vacancies in the former than the latter? Yet such are among the reasons which you assign for this change in the mode of appointment. I cannot fully appreciate many of them. I entertained the opinion that no troops in the Confederate service were better organized or had rendered more efficient service than the North Carolina State Troops, and I cannot believe their efficiency will be improved or the public interest be subserved by the change, neither do I believe that it will prevent vexatious questions of rank from arising or give more general satisfaction, but on the contrary the evils which you seek to avoid will be greatly aggravated. I have heard no complaints of the mode of appointment and supposed the system was working harmoniously.

If however I could see the subject in the light in which you view it, still my path of duty as the Chief Executive of the State is plain. The Law requires me to make the appointments and I must discharge that duty.

Fully appreciating the motive which prompts this action on the part of the Department, I can but regret the presentation of this question at so late a day. I shall be happy at any and all times to cooperate with you in all measures which may advance our cause in the great struggle in which we are engaged, whenever I can consistently do so, with my sense of official duty.

> With Sentiments of great respect
> Your Obedient Servant
> Z. B. Vance

[1]In this volume.

James A. Seddon to ZBV   A&H:GP

War Department
Richmond July 23rd. 1864

His Excellency
Z B Vance
Governor of N.C.

Sir

Your letter of the 5th. Ins't[1] has been rec'd, having been delayed for some time in its coming by the interruption of the postal communications. This department stated to you in its letter of the 5th May last[2] the principle which regulated its conduct. That principle is that Congress by the Act of the 17 february last continued in the service all the persons who were then in service for the war who belonged to the class, between 18 & 45 years That Mr Russell was of that class, & was not withdrawn from it by any of the sections of the same act or of any previous act

In your letter of the 19th of May[3] you contested that rule <upon>with assumptions and arguments that did not carry conviction to the mind of the department. If the department were to admit the assumptions it would admit that the legislature of North Carolina could withdraw from the military service the troops of that State, whenever in their judgement they were necessary for State Service. This would be to reverse the rule established in the Constitution of the Confederate States & paralyze the faculties of the Confederate government for the carrying on of the war. The department has conceded many things to the government of North Carolina with the view to secure a cordial cooperation of the government & people in the defence of the country in the great struggle in which it is now engaged, but it cannot make a concession of a principle so vital as the one contained in the question under discussion

If Mr. Russell be legally liable to military service he should render it, & the department cannot in justice to others similarly situated bend the law so as to discharge him

Very Respectfully
Your obt Svt
James A Seddon
Secy of War.

[1] In this volume.
[2] Not extant.
[3] In this volume.

ZBV to Samuel J. Person   A&H:GLB

State of North Carolina
Executive Department
Raleigh July 23d. 1864

Hon S. J. Person

Sir

Yr. letter of the 20th.[1] requesting me to furnish you a copy of certain letters of mine & President Davis' which were read to the House in accordance with a resolution introduced by yourself, has been recd. You say these letters were afterwards ordered to be printed and that it has not been done for the reason as you learn, that the Senate did not concur in the proposition to print. You then argue to show that the Senates' concurrence was not necessary &c. In reply I have to state, that the publication of these letters was not declined for the reason you assign. I am perfectly aware of the fact, that either house of the General Assembly can order the publication of whatsoever it may please. My only reason for withholding the letters from the Public Printer was the simple one that *I have never yet been furnished with the order of the House.* I heard verbally from members that such a resolution had passed the House and waited for a copy. When about to leave for the west I left orders with my Private Secretary to furnish the copies when called for by any one having the authority, which has never been done. About ten days ago I applied to Mr. Stanley the reading Clerk in relation to it and he informed me that he knew nothing about it and did not <think> believe it would be found on the Journals. Mr. Cotton the principal clerk, I have not seen. I am still ready Sir, to obey the resolution of the House of Commons whenever officially informed of it. I am Sir

> Very Respectfully
> Yr. obt Servt.
> Z. B. Vance

[1]In this volume.

William H. C. Whiting to ZBV   A&H:GLB

> Hd. Qrs. Wilmington
> July 28th. 1864

To His Excellency Gov Vance

Sir

I have at length positive information that at least two thirds of the Conscripts at the State Salt Works belong to the treasonable organization called the "H.O.A."[1] Their mode of communicating with the enemy has also been ascertained. I have also trustworthy information that this "order" musters very strong in Randolph Co. where the deserters armed are in strong force & associated with it. They state if arrested they will rebel. Instructions have been given them from their Chiefs to advocate your election if spoken to on the subject of politics to disarm suspicion. Many of those on the public works will not vote at all for a like reason. I have many times called attention to these men heretofore only on suspicion. Now I know what I state. I recommend strongly that the whole force be turned over to the Conscript Camp for distribution in the Army and their places be supplied by free negro or slave labor. As I am still pursuing my investigations into this traitorous association and hope to be able to detect some in overt act, you will see the reason for making this letter personal & confidential.

Very Respectfully,
W. H. C. Whiting
Maj Genl.

[1]Heroes of America.

William R. Cox to ZBV   A&H:VanPC

Camp near Bunker Hill Va
Aug 1st. 1864.

Dear Sir.

I have the pleasure to inform you that my Brigade gave you 508 votes[1] to 15 for Holden, & 5 of the men, who voted for Holden, deserted on the succeeding night, when it was understood that a second invasion of the enemy's country was in contemplation And thus you see, I have a model brigade in voting as well as, in fighting. It is however small, but voted more fully than others here, indeed it is generally difficult to get the soldiers to take interest enough in elections, to vote.

I would prefer that you would not make any permanent appointments among the field officers of this brigade until you hear from me as many of them, will require thorough examinations

I am
Very respectfully Yours &c
Wm. R. Cox[2]

[*Endorsed*] File—private

ZBV

[1]In gubernatorial election.
[2]Brig. Gen. William Ruffin Cox, postwar jurist and Democratic politician. *Dictionary of North Carolina Biography*, s.v. "Cox, William Ruffin."

ZBV to James A. Seddon   A&H:GLB

State of North Carolina
Executive Department
Raleigh Augt. 3d. 1864

Hon James A Seddon
Secretary of War
Richmond Va.

Sir

I have the honor to recommend that a Military Court be appointed at an early day for the Western District of North Carolina. It is deemed important that deserters taken with arms in their hands, in that District, should be there tried and punished. First, for the moral effect and secondly, to prevent the escape of desperate men from poorly guarded prisons or while being transferred to some distant point for trial. Many have escaped from the county jails, and not long since a number of deserters, while being transferred from Ashville to Camp Vance, overpowered the Guard, composed of Junior Reserves, killed two of the boys, and made their escape

I remain Very respectfully
Your obt. Servant
Z. B. Vance

William A. Graham Jr. to ZBV   A&H:GP

[*Telegram*]

Hillsboro 5 Aug 1864

To Gov Z B Vance

Official vote[1] of Orange Vance 1252 Holden one hundred & ninety four (194)

W. A. Graham Jr

[1] In gubernatorial election.

ZBV *to Alexander Collie*   A&H:GLB

State of North Carolina
Executive Department
Raleigh Augt. 5th. 1864

Mr. Alexr. Collie
17 Leadenhall St.
London

Dr. Sir

Your several favors since the date of my last[1] have been duly recd. and considered. The great labor and loss of time imposed upon me by the Canvass for re-election which closed yesterday, has rendered it impossible for me to give them prompt attention, and I was compelled to refer these to my Quarter Master. I am hardly in a proper condition for business today, the excitement of yesterdays polling being still kept up by the returns receiving from all parts of the State, but as the Steamer Advance sails tomorrow carrying out our Commissioner Mr John White, I can not lose the opportunity. All efforts to remove those most unjust and absurd restrictions upon commerce imposed by the "Regulations" of the Confederate Govt.[2] have been so far unavailing. Upon the application of myself and four governors of other States Congress repealed the "Regulations" but the President vetoed the bill. They then provided by another bill that no restrictions should be placed upon the States and this the President defeated by retaining until the adjournment of Congress. So here we are. My only hope now lies in the good sense of Mr. Trenholm[3] the new Secretary of the Treasury to whom it is my intention forthwith to address myself. I will inform you of the result. At present the business does not pay and if no relief is obtained I have instructed Mr White to ask your consent to dissolve our contract and sell out. White is making some arrangement for bringing our remaining purchases on freight. He is fully authorized to act in the matter as may be thought best on consultation with you and Mr. Flanner. I have been greatly at a loss to know why Mr. T. Andreae was not permitted by our authorities to return. Genl. Whiting in Command at Wilmington does not know and the Secretary of War is silent. I have to assure you that it arose from no complaint of mine. I had only the one difficulty with him which I mentioned to you in a former letter[4] and which I afterwards informed you was happily adjusted.[5] He was however for some reason exceedingly obnoxious to all of our people with whom he came in contact, and but for his acknowledged ability I should not regret his absence. I am therefore without those new views and propositions of yours which I learn he was authorized to submit. I was surprised to learn from Mr. Flanner's recent favors that the State was probably behind with you. I cannot account for it. We have shipped over 4100 bales of cotton, which if all was safely received should according to our calculations leave quite a balance in our favor. I fear it has been unreasonably delayed somewhere. I have given Mr. White only some small orders until the account can be properly ascertained as we do not desire to tax your kindness too far. I have felt greatly outraged by the most extortionate charges of agents and consignees at Nassau & Bermuda. Two and a half per cent on the invoices for receiving and forwarding which is the usual charge there, it strikes me is little better than robbing. Is there no way to avoid it? Can not an agency of our own be established at Hamilton Bermuda, I commend this subject to you and Mr White. The scythes have been recd., those for grass in good time, the grain harvest was over. Every thing shipped in fact has been safely recd. and I have cause to expect our vessels in and out with almost as much regularity as the trains. I am very uneasy about the bacon now at the Islands, it will spoil if not got in soon. What has become of the iron bought by you under the contract with Mr. White before I forbade it? Is it at Nassau? You wrote me that if not desired by the State you could realize a profit on it, as the price had advanced. If so please dispose of it immediately. I cannot close without saying a word in regard to the "Situation," I am happy to say that it is promising. Grants great and bloody campaign against Richmond is an acknowledged failure. Instead of our Capitol being in danger, Genl. Lee spares 25000 men under a new & rising General (Early)[6] are now in Pennsylvania avenging in the ashes of their towns the desolation of many a Southern village. There is hardly the semblance of a Yankee army west of the Mississippi and Genl Sherman has been halted in front of Atlanta by a severe and bloody check. Our army is in good spirits well equipped *and abundantly fed.* Crops of Indian corn are fine and our people are more hopeful than ever. It has been supposed that there was much disaffection in this State particularly, but the recent election contradicts it. My competitor a bold and popular demagogue made the issue distinctly of peace on terms less than independence and I have beaten him worse than any man was ever beaten in North Carolina. Our people will stand fair and square by their new Government and abide the common fate. Rest assured of it. Peace "feelers" have already been put forth by both sides and people begin to breathe again. Hoping to hear from you frequently and assuring you of high esteem & regard,

I am very sincerely
Your friend & obt. servt.
Z. B. Vance

[1]The last extant letter from ZBV to Collie was February 18, 1864, in this volume.

[2]Under the "regulations," the Confederate government claimed cargo space on blockade-runners, except those vessels that were exclusively owned by the states. ZBV maintained that blockade-runners only partially owned by the states should also be exempted from the Confederacy's commandeering of space. For a discussion of the regulations and the controversy, see Wise, *Lifeline of the Confederacy*, 145-146, 157-158, and Tucker, *Zeb Vance*, 234-237.

[3]George Alfred Trenholm, of Fraser, Trenholm and Co., Confederate financial agent. He replaced Memminger as secretary of treasury in July 1864. Faust et al., *Encyclopedia of Civil War*, 762.

[4]February 8, 1864, in this volume.

[5]See ZBV to Collie, February 18, 1864, in this volume.

[6]Lt. Gen. Jubal Anderson Early had undertaken an unsuccessful raid to threaten Washington, D.C., in order to relieve pressure on Lee's defenses around Richmond. In retreat, Early's troops burned Chambersburg, Pa., in retaliation for Federal destruction in the Shenandoah Valley. Faust et al., *Encyclopedia of Civil War*, 233-234.

ZBV to John White   A&H:GLB

State of North Carolina
Executive Department
Raleigh Augt. 5th. 1864

Mr. John White
[Present]

Dr. Sir

As special Agent of the State of North Carolina for the purpose of conducting the blockade running operations we are now engaged in, I desire to give you the following instructions. As I have given you my views in detail verbally it will only be necessary to say generally. That the main object of your mission at present will be to buy upon the best possible terms the Rosin and Cotton warrants of the State now outsanding in Europe. For this purpose you will consult Mr. Flanner as to the best method of operating and in case shipments of Cotton should not arrive fast enough you may borrow money, if you can, or use the credit of the State in any other way to secure your object. No limitation is placed upon the price which you may pay, this is left to your discretion, provided you do not make the cost so great as the fulfilment of the face of the warrants would be to the State. I have great confidence in Mr. Flanner's judgement in this matter & hope you will consult him freely. I desire if possible, that some arrangement may be made to avoid the outrageous charges of Agents & Consignees in the Islands and to facilitate the shipment of cargoes from them, especially of the bacon belonging to this State which will spoil unless removed soon. I desire all transactions whatsoever closed as rapidly & completely as possible, as I do not wish any unsettled matters to remain over for my successor in office if it can be avoided.

I desire a complete and accurate statement of our accounts with Mr. Collie to be made out and sent me as soon after your arrival in England as possible, Also with J. S. Livermore & Co & all other persons with whom we have dealings abroad and a monthly statement of all our transactions in Europe regularly thereafter, to include amount of our indebtedness there, articles purchased and shipped commissions and charges expended, pounds of Cotton received and sold, price, disposition of the money &c. &c.

You will also get in Wilmington statement of the different shipments of Cotton, No. of pounds &c & trace it up to see if it has all arrived in England safely and by whom received.

You will also give particular attention to bills for disbursements on board the several Steamers in which the State is part owner, and see that no imposition is practiced [or] unusual charges are made. Other instructions will be forwarded as occasion may arise.

> Very Respectfully
> Yr. obt. svt.
> Z. B. Vance

Milledge L. Bonham to ZBV   A&H:GP

[*Telegram*]

Columbia Aug 6th. 1864

To Gov. Z. B. Vance
Raleigh

Hurrahs for the Glorious Old North State & Govr. Vance I feel assurd & told your people you would

M. L. Bonham

Edward J. Hale to ZBV   A&H:VanPC

Fayetteville, Aug 11, 1864

My Dear Sir:

I am sorry & surprised to hear that you have had no letter from my son Edward,[1] & can only account for it on the supposition that he has not received my letters on the subject of your offer. I wrote him, enclosing a copy of Gov. Swain's letter on the subject & your letter[2]; & in none of his subsequent letters has he alluded to them. But he had written me, before he could have received them, that he had heard from his Sister, at Chapel Hill, that you had made him the offer; & that "of course" he could not, in his present state of good health, leave the field to take an office elsewhere. I had expected such a decision, & though regretting, could not but approve of it. I did not feel at liberty to communicate this to you as his decision, for I knew that he had then had no direct offer of the position, & took it for granted that when he did receive such a one he would write you a formal letter of thanks & declension. Changes of position, from the South to the North side of the James may have made my letter miscarry. I will write him; but in the mean time it will be better that you should not wait, but make some other appointment. His expression was so strong as to leave no doubt whatever that he would remain where he is.

We have indeed gained a great victory over disaffection at home & confident hopes & expectations in Yankee land. I confess that the thoroughness of the defeat, the using up, of Holden, has surprised me. His incessant boasts of strength, with the universal desire for peace, had misled me into a belief, not that he would come near being elected, but that he could not be beaten out of sight. God be praised! What a terrible blow it would have been to the cause if he had received a respectable vote! Look at the conduct of the deserters even as it is. I hope, by the way, that you will be able to send a force into Moore or Montgomery to give them a thorough drubbing—kill two or three dozen of them & the rest will cast off very quickly. There has been no signal defeat & punishment of the rascals—only here & there one or two—and that is the reason they are so bold.

I think that if Holden & [John L.] Pennington should continue their course of stirring up disaffection, the law should be appealed to. There has been just enough forbearance.

Yours truly,
E. J. Hale

[1]Edward Joseph Hale, son of Edward Jones Hale. He served in the Confederate army throughout the war. Apparently, ZBV had offered him a government office. *Dictionary of North Carolina Biography*, s. v. "Hale, Edward Joseph.

[2]Not extant.

Robert E. Lee to ZBV   A&H:VanPC

Private

Hd. Qrs. A N Va
12th. Aug. 1864

His Excy. Z. B. Vance
Governor of N Carolina,
Raleigh.

Governor,

Your letter of the 8th. inst.[1] was received, and afforded me great satisfaction. The result of the late election in N Carolina is well calculated to cheer and sustain the people of the Confederacy. It dissipates the hopes that our enemies had cherished of a division of our efforts and councils, and convinces them that three years of war have in no degree shaken the resolution of our people to resist, as long as they present them no alternative but that of a degrading submission.

I cannot but believe that its effect upon the northern mind will be salutary in demonstrating the futility of force as a means of adjusting the pending controversy.

My pleasure at this auspicious result is enhanced by the patriotic sentiments declared by yourself. Your desire to promote in every way that harmony of action which is essential to our success, and to devote the power and influence of your position to the attainment of the great end of our labors, evinces the spirit that should actuate us all.

The disposition to sacrifice party and personal considerations to the public good, of which North Carolina has just presented so striking an example, will, I trust, be found to pervade all classes of our people.

I learned with much regret that you considered there had been evidence of an opposite tendency in any quarter.

So far as my knowledge of the subject extends, I believe the official to whom you refer,[2] has been actuated by the single desire of advancing the interests of the country by the best means his judgment could devise.

That he has erred in some instances, or that his advisers have been mistaken, was to be expected under any circumstances, but particularly amidst the vast cares and responsibilities that surrounded him. Such errors however are only subjects of regret, not of censure, and I am sure you will always be ready to extend to them that forbearance and indulgence which the best and wisest men are sometimes constrained to ask.

If it be in my power, by any advice I can give or by any other means, to aid him in the discharge of his arduous duties, to enable him to conciliate and harmonize conflicting interests and opinions, and thus secure the best interests of the country, it will be my duty, as I need not say, it will be my pleasure, to place all my efforts at his disposal.

Congratulating you upon the deserved approval of your course which your fellow citizens have expressed, and with the conviction that under your administration, the cause of Southern independence will continue to receive the powerful support of the brave people of North Carolina as fully and efficiently as heretofore,

> I am with great respect
> Your obt. servt.
> R E Lee

[1]Not extant.
[2]It is not certain who the official was, but Lee may have been referring to Jefferson Davis.

ZBV to John White   A&H:GP

> State of North Carolina,
> Executive Department,
> Raleigh, Aug 18 1864.

Mr John White,

Dr Sir,

Please buy at Halifax & send in on act of the state fifty boxes of sperm candles, 4's—They are needed for lighting the capitol—

> Yrs truly
> Z B Vance

ZBV to Jeremy F. Gilmer   A&H:GLB

State of North Carolina
Executive Department
Raleigh Augt. 18th.1864

Maj. Genl. J. F. Gilmer[1]
Chief of Engr. Bureau

Genl.

I have received your communication[2] asking my consent to the removal of a portion of the iron from the Wilmington, Charlotte & Rutherfordton R. Rd. and you urge as a reason that this iron is required for the repair of the Wilmington & Manchester R Rd., which is at present so necessary for the transportation of Government supplies.

I have at all times endeavored to further the interest of the Confederate Government and shall continue to do so, while I continue to occupy my present position, but at the same time I must guard and protect the interest of North Carolina. If I were fully satisfied that this iron was absolutely necessary for the purpose indicated and that it could not be *otherwise* obtained, I would unhesitatingly give my consent. I am however not so satisfied.

Two thirds of the Wilmington & Manchester R. Rd is located in the State of South Carolina and there are no doubt, many branch roads in that State, from which iron could be spared with less detriment to the public interest. Until this impression is shown to be erroneous, I must with hold my consent, as the road proposed to be broken up is one of vast importance to a large number of people who have hitherto been cut off from all rail road facilities.

With Sentiments of great respect
Your obedient Servant
Z. B. Vance

[1]Jeremy Francis Gilmer, head of the Confederate Bureau of Engineers. Faust et al., *Encyclopedia of Civil War*, 311.
[2]August 5, 1864, A&H:GP.

ZBV to Stuart Buchanan and Co.   A&H:GLB

State of North Carolina
Executive Department
Raleigh 18th. Augt. 1864

Messrs Stuart Buchanan & Co
Saltville N.C. [Va.]

Gentlemen

I have this day received a letter from N. W. Woodfin Esq. the State Salt Agent informing me that you desired to deliver at once, twelve or fourteen thousand bushels of the Salt contracted to be delivered by you, to the State of North Carolina and that you wished some money to be paid for it, at least $25,000—to be placed to your credit in the Bank of the Commonwealth at Richmond. I regret to state that it is not in my power to do so immediately, but I hope to be able to comply with your request in a very short time. In consequence of the failure of the Confederate Government to pay the claims of North Carolina which are very large, there is no money in the Treasury, except old issue which I presume you could not conveniently use. We have an Agent now in Richmond, urging the settlement of these claims, and I trust that in a very short time, he will effect their payment and receive the new issue—when the arrangement you desire shall be made, and the sum stated, placed to your credit in the Bank of the Commonwealth at Richmond.

I am very respectfully
Your obt. Servt.
Z. B. Vance

ZBV to David G. Worth   A&H:GLB

State of North Carolina
Executive Department
Raleigh Augt. 18th. 1864

D. G. Worth Esqr.

Dr. Sir

It will be with some difficulty that the State can furnish the two Companies required by Genl. Whiting as a guard for the Salt Works and I am induced to adopt another course if practicable.

1st. Can you remove the works to Confederate Point or any other place under protection of our guns & if so at what cost of convenience or money?

2nd. Can you designate the disloyal men in your employ for dismission or conscription, whose removal would satisfy Genl Whiting that no guard is necessary?

I can get you other hands in place of all such. If any of your men are actually disloyal, I dont wish to protect them and Genl Whiting avers most positively that he has proof of their constant communication with the enemy. *But we must have Salt.* Let me know how these propositions would work immediately.

> Yrs Truly
> Z. B. Vance

David G. Worth to ZBV   A&H:GP

> Wilmington N C
> Augt 20th. 1864.

To His Excellency
Gov Z. B. Vance
Raleigh N.C.

Dr. Sir,

Yours of the 18th inst[1] is just to hand.

In reply to your first inquiry, I have to say the removing & running of the works at Confederate Point is impracticable. They cannot be removed for want of means & could not be run to any advantage if at all, for want of wood. The wood within reach of there that has not already been consumed for fire wood & building purposes, is wanted for these purposes, by the military authorities at the Fort.

The cost of removing would exceed the means at my command. I think it would not fall short of $40,000. The loss of time would amt. to at least two or three months.

As to 2d. inquiry: I would long since have designated the disloyal men if it had been in my power & have offered to coöperate with Genl Whiting & with detectives who have been sent here to ferret out the matter & discover the offenders. There is a detective now here on this 'special business who I offered to assist in any & every way I could.

I doubt, & in fact I do not believe, that the men have constant communication with the enemy. I do not believe they have communication at all, further than by occasional desertions. If Genl Whiting has *proof* of their *constant* communication, why does he not exercise his authority in bringing that proof to bear on the guilty ones. If I had the proof, I do not think I should be long in finding out the offenders & committing them to the tender mercies of Col Mallett.

As to question of disloyalty, I confess my opinions have undergone a change since the election. I would not now say, as I said before, that I do not believe there are disloyal ones among these men. I do not believe as a *general* thing that the supporters of Mr Holden are *strictly* loyal men. For this reason & no other that I am aware of, I fear that at least a part of those who voted for him, are not loyal. It would not be difficult to tell who they are.

I have no wish or desire to protect these men, nor would I ask you to do so for any reason, other than the prosecution of the works. To this extent I have a deep interest in it for being responsible beyond any one else connected with it I desire to see the work prosecuted with vigor & success.

The works are in condition to be run with success & economy at their present location for at least six months to come.

As I stated in a former communication the losses in money from delays & interruptions, in the past three months, has been at least $30,000, & in production of salt not less that 5000 bushels, & possibly 6 or 7000. I have continued to sell salt at $12 per 50 lbs. though at a loss, hoping daily to be able to resume the whole work when it can be easily made at that price. Market price for salt $35.

Very Respectfully
Your obt sevt.
D. G. Worth salt comr

[*Endorsed*] Copy & file

Z B V

[1]In this volume.

ZBV to Anonymous   A&H:VanPC

Raleigh Augst. 22d.

My dear Sir,

I send you by Dr. [*Edward*] Warren quite a file of the "London Times" which I have had only time to glance at & send you now for fear they will get scattered if I keep them longer—

I don't believe I have had one word of congratulation from you on my reelection! Whats the matter? Did you bolt the track & turn Holden man on the last quarter? If so I am sorry for you. Pardon this paper. I write at my house & found only this scrap when I took up my pen—My kind regards to Mrs S—who I hope is fully restored—& the young ladies & believe me most sincerely

Yours
Z. B. Vance

Cornelia A. Spencer to ZBV   A&H:VanPC

Chapel Hill
Aug 22, '64

My dear Governor

While my Mother was in Raleigh I wrote to her enclosing $30.00 & begging her to see if she could not get for me two or three pairs of cards at government price. You see, I presumed to hope that you would let me have them for that! I wanted them dreadfully, to give away to two or three very poor women in the country, who tho' widows had not had husbands in the army, & were not entitled to apply for government cards. One of them however has lost two sons in the army & has a third there now.

You were gone from Raleigh when my Mother received my letter, but that was matter of less consequence as she informed me you had *given* her five pairs of cards for distribution. On her return home, she gave me one pair, which I forthwith bestowed upon the poor woman I have mentioned, and if you, Governor, could have see[n] the tears with which she received them, you would have felt amply repaid for anything it may have cost you to get them here. I hope it sweetens your sleep at night to know how many poor women daily bless you for providing those cards.

The object of my troubling you now is to thank you very heartily, & to beg you to allow me to pay you for this pair. You have a right to the luxury of bestowing them on those who are unable to pay for them, but it certainly is not fair that those should accept them as a gift who are able & glad to pay at least the government price. Getting them *at that*, makes me unspeakably your debtor. Please find $10.00 enclosed, that you may the more freely give to the next poor woman that begs you for cards.

I cannot close without expressing my own individual pleasure & exultation at your re-election. It was so triumphantly carried that we are a little ashamed now of having ever been uneasy. I only hope you will be our Governor till the war is over.

Please present me very kindly to Mrs. Vance. I am much obliged to her for her kindness to my Mother—for to confess the truth we were all a little cross about her going to Raleigh. Ma thinks however, like many other old ladies, that her age entitles her to be exempted from some conventionalities, & that the end sanctifies the means!

Tell Mrs. Vance if she will promise that her boys shall turn out any ways like their Father, I'll engage to save up my daughter for one of them.

I am dear Governor

> Most cordially & truly
> your friend
> Cornelia A. Spencer[1]

[1]Cornelia Ann Phillips Spencer, author, proponent of education and the University of North Carolina, who after the war defended ZBV's role as wartime governor in the book, *The Last Ninety Days of the War in North Carolina.* Annette C. Wright, " 'The Grown-up Daughter': The Case of North Carolina's Cornelia Phillips Spencer," *North Carolina Historical Review* 74 (July 1997): 260-283.

Jeremy F. Gilmer to ZBV   A&H:GP

> Confederate States of America,
> War Department,
> Engineer Bureau,
> Richmond, Va.
> 23 August 1864

His Excellency
Z. B. Vance
Governor of North Carolina

Sir,

Your communication of the 18th. inst.[1] In regard to the removal of a portion of the rails from the Eastern Division of the Wilmington, Charlotte & Rutherford R. R. has been duly received.

It is not proposed, as you seem to think, to remove the whole of the Eastern Division of the above Road, but only ten miles beyond Laurenburg, where the Company's shops are situated. Thus the large community of which you speak in your letter, would be only somewhat incommoded by an increased distance to R. R. transportation—not altogether deprived of it. The difficulty of transporting, heavy articles, such as R. R. iron is so great, that a most important consideration in the removal of R. R. iron from Roads of secondary importance to those of first class importance is that they should be as near to each other as possible. In this point of view the transfer from the Road under consideration to the W. & M. R. R. presents peculiar facilities.

The condition of the main trunk lines of South Carolina (other than the portion of the Wilmington & Manchester R. R. lying in that State) is such that the Government will have to remove promptly all of their branch roads of secondary importance which can be made available. Steps are now being taken in the case of two of them.

Such being the case, it is again urgently represented to your Excellency that the necessity of assisting the W. & M. R. R. with iron without delay is imperative. The Road must stop, & that soon without such assistance. It is further & earnestly represented that after due enquiry the Government does /urgently/ need the iron called for & every pound besides it can obtain in South Carolina /& all the other States/ from secondary Roads to enable it to keep up the transportation on the main lines of rail road of the Confederacy; under these circumstances, it has been determined to ask your reconsideration of the views expressed in your letter, in the earnest hope that you will find reason to change them.

With sentiments of the highest respect I am Sir

> Your most obt. servt.
> J. F. Gilmer.
> Maj. Genl & Chf Bur

[1]In this volume.

Proclamation by ZBV   A&H:GLB

By the Governor of North Carolina
A Proclamation

Whereas, it is reported to me that many soldiers from the troops of this State have deserted their colors and comrades, and are now lurking in the woods and mountains, some of them subsisting by forcing their friends to violate the laws by aiding them and others by violent depredations upon peaceable citizens, entailing shame and obloquy upon themselves and their posterity, outraging the laws and the peace of society, and damaging the cause of their hard pressed country.

And whereas, Genl. Robt. E. Lee, in General Orders No. 54, Augt. 10th. 1864, has promised to deal leniently with all who promptly return to duty, though they may have incurred the penalties of desertion by prolonged absence without authority. No[w], therefore, I, Zebulon B. Vance, Governor of the State of North Carolina, do issue this my proclamation, urging most earnestly upon all such misguided men to wipe out from their once respected names the foul stain of desertion by promptly returning to the post of duty in accordance with said General order No. 54, promising to all such who voluntarily return or surrender themselves to the proper authorities a full and free pardon, or the infliction of only the mildest penalties of the military law, except those who have been guilty of capital felonies against the lives and property of the citizens, and this promise shall hold good for thirty days from the date hereof. And I hereby warn all such who refuse to comply with these terms that the utmost power of this State will be exerted to capture them or drive them from the borders of a country whose high honor and spotless renown they disgrace by refusing to defend, and that the extremest penalties of the law will be inforced without exception when caught, as well as against their aiders and abetters in the civil courts. Simultaneously with this proclamation orders will issue to the entire Militia of the State to turn out for their arrest, and I hope <that> by timely submission they will spare me the pain of hunting down like guilty felons many brave and misguided men who have served their country well and could do so again. Deserters from other States who hide in our woods and assist in giving our State a bad name, I can do nothing for, but to the erring soldiers of North Carolina I confidently appeal. I earnestly call on all good citizens to assist me in making this appeal effectual, both by their exertions as militia soldiers and their influence as men, to take pains to seek out all deserters of their acquaintance, put this proclamation in their hands, or in the hands of their relatives and friends and urge upon them to return to the path of duty, which is also the path of safety and of honor. If every good and loyal citizen would set about to reclaim or capture one deserter by every means in his power, he would succeed and he will have rendered a most valuable and patriotic service to his state and country. Civil magistrates are also exhorted to be diligent in proceeding against all such as violate the statute against harboring, aiding or abetting deserters and warning is hereby given that in all cases where either civil magistrates or militia or home guard officers refuse or neglect to faithfully perform their duty in this respect, upon proper evidence submitted to me, the Executive protection extended to them under Acts of Congress shall be withdrawn, as I cannot certify that officers civil or military, who refuse to perform their duties are "necessary to the due administration of the laws," which they will not execute.

Given under my hand and the Great Seal of the State, at Raleigh, this 24th. day of August 1864.

Z. B. Vance

ZBV *to William Smith* A&H:GLB

State of North Carolina
Executive Department
Raleigh Augt. 25th. 1864

His Excellency
Gov. Wm. Smith
Richmond

Dr. Sir

I must apologize for the long delay in answering your letter[1] and complying with your request. Maj. Dowd[2] my Qr. Master has orders to send you the cloth desired, which I would prefer you should consider a *loan*, should it be convenient to repay it in the course of twelve months. I hardly think I would be justified in selling it, as I cannot tell to what straits I may come in regard to clothing. Accept my thanks for your kind congratulations in regard to my re election. It is really [a] matter of congratulation to the whole country, as evincing the thorough loyalty of our tried and suffering people.

Very Respectfully
Yr. obt. Svt.
Z. B. Vance

[1]Not extant.
[2]Henry A. Dowd. Maj. Dowd formerly had been a colonel in the Fifteenth Regiment North Carolina Troops. Manarin et al., *North Carolina Troops*, 5:502.

ZBV *to John White*   A&H:GLB

State of North Carolina
Executive Department
Raleigh Augt. 25th. 1864

John White Esqr.
Commissioner &c
London

Sir

The holders of our "Rosin Bonds" have sent an Agent, Mr. Joseph V. Snedley to this country to investigate and report on the state of their interest here. Mr. Snedley was not authorized to conclude any definite arrangement and in conversation with him I was careful not to make any *proposition* or commit myself in any way. You will bear this in mind in any interview you may have with these bond holders as the Agent in his report may give them the impression whether designedly or not that an offer was made by me, none such was made nor any thing approaching it. Four queries were discussed between us. 1st. At what price can the bonds be bought for cash. 2d. How many brls. of Rosin delivered in Bermuda, Nassau or Halifax will be received in extinguishment of the claim for 228,000 brls. to be delivered under the terms of the bonds. 3d. At what price per pound will they rate Cotton delivered in Nassau, Bermuda or Halifax. 4th. At what price will they rate Cotton delivered in Wilmington, say on sixty days notice. The first, second, & third propositions you will at once perceive come to about the same thing as when Cotton or Rosin is once safely on the other side it has a fixed and well known value and may be regarded as cash. When the second question was propounded Mr. Snedley mentioned 50,000 brls. as an amount that might meet the views of the bond holders. These figures were his own and were not assented to by me. You are aware that under the existing regulations it is impossible to export Rosin during the war. And if the consent of the Department in Richmond could be obtained it would then be too slow a business for me to undertake it. Even 20,000 brls. could not be put in the Islands short of thirty trips of a vessel drawing the same water as the "Advance." For these reasons I do not desire to entertain any proposition based on a delivery in the Islands. Since I saw you investigation has convinced me that at an expense of not more than £75,000, I can deliver the 228,000 Rosin but it cannot be done until the close of the War. When the risk of holding and the other expenses consequent on delivery and safe keeping are taken into account I am confirmed in my limit given verbally to you of 100 per ct. advance on the bonds if they can be bought for that figure or anything in its neighborhood. I wish you to use your utmost efforts to purchase both these and the Cotton bonds for cash as it would gratify me much to be able to feel that the whole affair on the other side would be closed within a reasonable period. Should the holders of the bonds incline to take Cotton in Wilmington I should not be willing to put the Cotton at a lower rate than 5 pence. I would impress on you the necessity of advising me of your action in the matter of these Rosin bonds as speedily as possible. Should I buy the Rosin or any part of it, or should you make an arrangement by which the bond holders will receive Cotton, I should have to draw on you for the funds and I should like information as to the time at which you would prefer these drafts drawn. In the absence of advice I shall draw at 60 days sight. I shall await with anxiety advices from you as to the progress of negotiations with Messrs. Collie or others relating to the purchase of a steamer. I am much hampered by the existing regulations and shall be very glad to be relieved as soon as it can be done on favorable terms

> Very Respectfully
> Z. B. Vance

ZBV to Patrick H. Winston   A&H:GLB

> State of North Carolina
> Executive Department
> Raleigh Augt. 26th. 1864

P. H. Winston Esq.[1]
Richmond Va.

Dr. Sir

I send to you by Express to care of Lancaster & Co one hundred & Eighty thousand dollars old issue, equal to one hundred & twenty thousand dollars. It is due to Stuart Buchanan & Co for Salt and will be called for by Mr. Geo. B. Parker their Agent and partner. Please deliver & take his receipt as enclosed and notify me by telegraph if its all right.

> Yrs. Respectfully
> Z. B. Vance.

[1]Patrick Henry Winston, financial agent for North Carolina. *Dictionary of North Carolina Biography*, s. v. "Winston, Patrick Henry."

ZBV to Jeptha M. Israel   A&H:GLB

State of North Carolina
Executive Department
Raleigh Augt. 26th. 1864

J. M. Israel[1] Esq.
Saltville Va.

Dr. Sir

I have paid to Geo. B. Parker on the contract with Stuart Buchanan & Co one hundred and twenty thousand dollars. Receive all you can get and ship as fast as possible. Drop some at Max Medows depot for the border counties and notify me. If you can hire engines & trains, I will see that they are not impressed. The funds you receive for the sale of this Salt must not go into your general Salt Works funds but must be kept separate and returned to the Treasury. The Salt Works must stand on their own bottom apart from this contract.

Very Respectfully Yrs
Z. B. Vance

[1]Jeptha M. Israel, assistant agent and secretary and treasurer of North Carolina salt works, Saltville, Va. See Johnston and Mobley, *Papers of Vance*, 1:8n, and Jeptha M. Israel to ZBV, August 22, 1864, A&H:GP.

ZBV to Robert E. Lee   A&H:GLB

State of North Carolina
Executive Department
Raleigh Augt. 27th. 1864

Gen R. E. Lee

Dr. Sir

Your letter[1] in regard to desertion from the Army enclosing one from Brig Genl Scales has been duly recd. Previous to its reception I had adopted the best means within my power, as I conceived, to clear the State of deserters. I issued my proclamation promising all a pardon or mild punishment (except those guilty of capital felonies) who would return within thirty days and at the same time ordered the entire Militia force of the State into the field for sixty days to search for them. I should not have done so had I known that you disapproved of further clemency and yet I believe it will be attended with the best results and it is almost impossible to catch them otherwise in our vast forests swamps & mountains. Genl Martin[2] too commending near one half the State had published a similar order and I thought it might as well be general. I enclose a copy of my proclamation[3] for your information. The information of our great victory at Reams Station has caused general rejoicing. It is peculiarly gratifying to our State pride, as it seems to have been achieved in great part by North Carolina troops. I am General

> Most respectfully & truly
> Z. B. Vance

[1]Not extant.

[2]James G. Martin, who had transferred to Virginia in May to reinforce the defenses at Richmond. See William H. C. Whiting to ZBV, April 22, 1864, in this volume.

[3]See proclamation of August 24, 1864, in this volume.

Robert E. Lee to ZBV   A&H:GP

> Hd. Qrs. Army of Northern Va
> 29 August 1864

His Excy. Z. B. Vance
Governor of No. Ca.
Raleigh

Governor

The recent success of the enemy at Mobile[1] may induce him to attack Wilmington, and the importance of that port is such that every effort should be made to defend it. As you are aware, the strength of the enemy's armies in Virginia and Georgia will prevent the detachment of any part of our forces opposed to them, and our chief reliance for the protection of Wilmington must be placed upon the reserves and local troops of the State.

I think if an attack should be made, the enemy will be obliged to employ raw troops to a great extent, and I believe the local and reserve forces with the present garrison sufficient to hold the place, if they will come forward freely.

I respectfully ask the cooperation of your Excellency to induce them to do so, and the aid of your influence and authority to provide means for the most obstinate defence.

I have frequently been called upon to mention the services of North Carolina soldiers in this Army, but their gallantry and conduct were never more deserving of admiration than in the engagement at Ream's Station on the 25th. inst.

The brigades of Generals Cook, McRae and Lane, the last under the temporary command of Genl. Connor,[2] advanced through a thick abattis of felled trees under a heavy fire of musketry and artillery and carried the enemy's works with a steady courage that elicited the warm commendation of their Corps and Division Commanders and the admiration of the Army.

On the same occasion, the brigade of Genl. Barringer[3] bore a conspicuous part in the operations of the cavalry which were not less distinguished for boldness and efficiency than those of the Infantry.

If the men who remain in North Carolina share the spirit of those she has sent to the field, as I doubt not they do, her defence may be securely entrusted to their hands.

> I am with great respect,
> Your obt. servant
> R E Lee
> Genl

[Endorsed] Copy

ZBV

[1]On August 5, 1864, a U.S. fleet commanded by Rear Admiral David G. Farragut had captured control of Mobile Bay at the port city of Mobile, Alabama. Faust et al., Encyclopedia of Civil War, 503-504.

[2]John Rogers Cooke, William MacRae, James H. Lane, and James Connor. Faust et al., Encyclopedia of Civil War, 159-160, 163-164, 424, 466.

[3]Rufus Barringer. Current et al., Encyclopedia of the Confederacy, 1:133-134.

William N. H. Smith to ZBV   A&H:GP

Murfreesboro Aug 29 1864

Gov Z. B. Vance

Dear Sir

I deem it of the very highest importance to the future defence and quiet of this part of the State that there should be additional Iron Clads constructed like the Albemarle. I wrote accordingly to the Navy Department to urge upon the Secretary the policy of, at once, proceeding with the building of two others. I assured him of my belief that iron for their armor could be procured from some of our rail road track, if the boats were constructed. I transmit his letter[1] for your perusal assured that we shall find a readiness on your part to cooperate heartily in the enterprise. It occurs to me that portions of the iron below Kinston could be taken without detriment to any public interest, and this could be made available. Mr. [*Gilbert*] Elliot[t], I am informed, has some partial if not full understanding with the proprietors or officers of the road to this effect. It is apparent no place presents equal safety and such facilities for the prosecution of the work as the banks of the Roanoke. And it must not be forgotten that an effective fleet of iron-armed boats will not confine their operations to the Albemarle Sound and its tributaries, but may reasonably be expected to expel the enemy from all our sea coast and liberate our entire inland waters—a result worthy of any expenditure and sacrifice. Be kind enough to return Mr. Mallory's letter.

> Very respectfully &c
> Your obt. Servt
> W. N. H. Smith

[1]Not extant.

William Smith to ZBV   A&H:GP

State of Virginia
Executive Department
Richmond
Sept 1 1864

Gov. Vance

Dr. Sir:
I desire to say in answer to your favor of the 25th. ultimo:[1] that I shall want cloth for about seventy five (75) men, and would much prefer to get it as a purchase than as a loan. I imagine that so small a quantity will hardly be missed in your large stocks or affect your ability to clothe the soldiers of N.C. As, however I am expecting a <supply> small supply from Europe, I shall return what I get from you upon being informed that your necessities required it. I am, Governor,

Very Resply
Yr. obdt. Servt.
Wm Smith

[*Endorsed*] File & copy

Z B V

[1]In this volume

ZBV to George Davis   A&H:GLB

Ex. Dept. of N.C
Raleigh Sep 1, 1864

Hon. Geo Davis
Atto. Genl. C S.

Dr Sir
Permit me to ask your attention to a matter that has bred some confusion and is likely to breed more.

Until recently the Governor of North Carolina commissioned all officers of the line in the Regiments from this State originally inlisted for the War, and known as "State troops" in contradistinction to the "Volunteers" or twelve months men.[1] This was by virtue of an ordinance of the Convention, which gave the Governor also authority to Commission all officers in both classes of troops. The authority of the President to Commission any of the N.C. troops was derived I take it from the first Conscription act which was held to operate only upon the twelve months men. Accordingly the Governors claim to commission them was surrendered, and he Continued to Commission only the Regiments Originally "for three years or the War," with the consent & approbation of the Confederate Govt. Latterly Adjutant General Cooper has notified me that he will recognize no commission issued by this State whatsoever. Now where does the President get the right to commission the troops from N.C. not affected by either the first or the last acts of Conscription? Many of our regiments were originally enlisted for the period of the war, and could not possibly be so affected, and it seems to me the right remains with the Governor to Commission them. Practically it is better they were all equally subjected to our laws, and I make no objection on that score. But I dont feel at liberty to surrender both a right & a duty committed to me by the State unless Satisfied that the law has done it for me. Please let me hear from you.

Very Resptly Yours
Z. B. Vance.

[1]Before North Carolina entered the Civil War, an extant state law allowed twelve-month volunteers to enlist into state military service. But an act of the secession convention of May 20, 1861, enrolled volunteers as state troops for three years or the duration of the war. Barrett, *Civil War in North Carolina*, 20.

ZBV to Pierre G. T. Beauregard   A&H:GLB

Raleigh Sept 5th. 1864

Gen. Beauregard
Petersburg Va,

Most of the Home Guard for whom I had any arms are now in the field hunting deserters and can be easily concentrated at any desired point. Please see my letter to Gen Lee of this date.[1] Can any more arms be sent here

Z B. Vance

[1]In this volume.

ZBV *to Robert E. Lee*   A&H:GLB

State of North Carolina
Executive Department
Raleigh Sep. 5th. 1864.

Gen. R. E. Lee
Army of N. Va.

Genl.

Your letter[1] in relation to the defence of Wilmington has been recd. Every aid that I can render with the militia shall be given, though I will have arms for only a portion of them. A large part of those sent me from Richmond were unservisable but I am having them repaired as rapidly as possible.

Allow me to make a few suggestions touching the Defence of that important Seaport. Their are two regiments there the 36th. & 40th. N.C.T. and Youngs battalion[2] numbering about 2600 effective men. They are well drilled & disciplined but have never been under fire, and recent events in Mobile & elsewhere demonstrate their inefficiency to hold their own under the fierce cannonade of the enemys fleet. I would respectfully suggest the policy of sending them to the field & supplying their places with veteran troops. A less number of tried men I feel assured would be far more efficient, though I do not wish the garrison lessened of course. In case a real attack should be made upon Wilmington I earnestly urge that Genl. Beauregard should be sent there, and this not only because of the great Confidence felt in him, but also because of the very little repose in Gen Whiting. Since the affair at Petersburg the good opinion formed of that officer here, by the apparent skill evident in the construction of the works around Wilmington has been dissipated to a painful extent. Genl. Beauregard was intrusted with the defence of Charleston with the happiest results and it cannot be denied that Wilmington is now of far more importance to the Confederacy.

A great portion of my Home Guard is now in the field and will be easily transferred to any point where desired. I am happy to say that several hundred Deserters have already been apprehended or surrendered, and I trust to be able to get most of them in without again asking for regular soldiers.

I am, General, Very truly &
Respectfully
Yr. Obt. Servt.
Z. B. Vance

[1] August 29, 1864, in this volume.
[2] Tenth Battalion North Carolina Heavy Artillery, commanded by Maj. Wilton L. Young. Manarin et al., *North Carolina Troops*, 1:512.

ZBV to William H. Harrison   A&H:GLB

State of North Carolina
Executive Department
Raleigh Sept 6th. 1864

Col. W. H. Harrison
Mayor of Raleigh

Dr Sir

Dr Hawkins[1] President of the R. & G. Rail road informs me that during the suspension of through freight and travel on his road he could bring any quantity of wood for the use of the City this winter if it were only cut and placed by the road side. In view of the prospective scarcity and the suffering of the poor for fuel, I respectfully recommend that the City Commissioners take immediate steps for cutting a supply, and I will guarantee its prompt transportation.

Very respectfully yours
Z. B. Vance

[1] William Joseph Hawkins, a physician and president of the Raleigh and Gaston Railroad. *Dictionary of North Carolina Biography*, s. v. "Hawkins, William Joseph."

James A. Seddon to ZBV   A&H:VanPC

Confederate States of America,
War Department,
Richmond, Va. Sept. 7th. 1864

His Excy
Z B Vance
Raleigh N. C

Dear Sir

I am truly grateful for the confidence manifested by your communication of the 1st. Inst[1] and am gratified to be confirmed in my undoubting convictions, that whatever discontent you may, as I must think without adequate cause, unhappily have with the Confederate administration, you will never falter in firm adherance to our great cause, nor be wanting in contributing whenever occasion allows to the defeat of all machinations against the union and faithful Cooperation of all the states in attaining Independence and peace.

Some suspicions, founded on vague indications & intimations had been felt by me that designs of the kind you reveal were entertained by the Governor and some other leading men in Georgia but I had supposed they were only contemplated as a vessel in future contingencies and had not imagined initiatory measures towards their execution had been adopted. I still hope the steps taken were designed as merely a game of discreditable and dishonest Diplomacy under a delusive idea of affecting northern Sentiment and action towards peace, or at the least as [*illegible*] tentative in view of future possibilities <*illegible*>. Even in this most favourable view they indicate a spirit and a selfish unscrupulousness that must awaken the indignation of every true patriot and <must> should arouse the solicitude and vigilance of the Government. I wish much it were consistent with your sense of Honor and duty (of which however I recognize your capacity to best Judge) to reveal <both> the name of your informant and even more—that of the Deluded emissary or agents of the Govr. of Georgia. It is almost impossible without such information to follow out the mazes of this Intrigue or plot and counteract its baneful developments. The <*illegible*> recent reverses in Georgia[2] may stimulate and aid such schemes into most mischievous effects and it is therefore most important the Government should at once possess the fullest information attainable and stand prepared to expose and baffle this scheme and schemers. Warned by your timely information, limited as it is, some means will be taken to probe the matter and to guard against the apprehended mischief, but you will readily appreciate what facilities would be afforded and what additional service you would render by fuller communication, if allowable.

> With assurances of high esteem
> Truly yrs
> James A Seddon
> Secy of War

[1]Not extant. But apparently ZBV had written about rumors of a plot in Georgia to negotiate a separate peace with the Federal government.

[2]The Union army under the Command of Gen. William T. Sherman had recently captured Atlanta.

Ralph P. Buxton to ZBV   A&H:GP

Albemarle, N.C.
8 Sept 1864

Hon. Z. B. Vance
Governor of North Carolina

Dear Sir:

Six months ago a free negro boy, named *Wesley McDaniel* was tried and convicted at Montgomery Court upon a charge of Burglary, with intent to commit a Rape. I prosecuted the case with great reluctance, as I was by no means satisfied that the facts alleged by the prosecutrix made out the crime charged. Under this impression, I had sent a Bill to the Grand Jury charging a simple Assault & Battery, but afterwards was induced by the importunity of the girl's friends to send the Bill, upon which he was convicted. Immediately after the trial, I volunteered to sign a petition to your Excellency in the prisoner's behalf—before making application for Executive clemency, his counsel thought it their duty to have the Judgment of the court below revised by the Supreme Court, which was done at the June Term last, when the Supreme Court affirmed the Judgment of his Honor Judge French,[1] who tried the cause.

Last week, at Montgomery Court, it became the duty of Judge Gilliam,[2] who is riding this Circuit, to sentence the prisoner, which he did, appointing the 21st of October as the day of his execution. A petition for the pardon of the boy has been gotten up, numerously and respectably signed—I have endorsed the application, as I had offered to do, and it will no doubt soon be placed in your Excellency's hands.

Being more fully persuaded in my own mind, by subsequent reflection, that McDaniel's case is one calling for the interposition of the pardoning Power, not only on account of the youth of the prisoner (he was barely 16.) but also for the reason that he desisted voluntarily from the consummation of offense, and on account of the singular and unsatisfactory statement of his conduct on the occasion, as made by the witness and as correctly set forth in the Petition, I have thought it right not to content myself with barely indorsing the application for Executive Pardon, but to make to your Excellency a representation of the circumstances of the case, and in a distinct communication, *earnestly* to *ask* and to *urge* your Excellency to pardon this boy.[3]

Very Respectfully
Your Obdt Servt.
Ralph P Buxton
Sol. 5th Circuit

[1]Robert S. French, superior court judge. Cheney, *North Carolina Government*, 362, 371n.

[2]Robert B. Gilliam, superior court judge and former speaker of House of Commons. Williams, Hamilton, and Peacock, *Papers of Graham*, 5:117n.

[3]ZBV pardoned Wesley McDaniel on September 8, 1864, with the stipulation that the defendant receive "thirty-nine lashes on two several occasions with one weeks intermission between them." See pardon by ZBV, September 8, 1864, A&H:GLB.

ZBV to Joseph E. Brown A&H:GLB

Raleigh Sep 8th.

Gov. Brown
Milledgeville Ga.

Is there any possible chance to move two thousand bales of Cotton belonging to this State on your South Western [*Rail*] Road towards Augusta? I shall be greatly obliged to have it done.

Z. B. Vance

Robert E. Lee to ZBV A&H:GP

[*Telegram*]

Dunns Hill 9 Sept 1864

To His Ex Z B Vance

What amount of arms do you require

R. E. Lee

[*Endorsed*] ansd. 3,000

Z B V

Joseph E. Brown to ZBV A&H:GP

[*Telegram*]

Macon 9 Sept 1864

To Gov Z B Vance

The Rail Road Stock which escaped the Raid of the Enemy is Greatly needed in transporting of military supplies I have every disposition to aid you and hope I can in two (2) or three 3 weeks—if you will send agents to look to shipments the South Western Road is not threatened immedy I think I can get it out for you in time to save it.

Joseph E. Brown

ZBV to Jeremy F. Gilmer A&H:GLB

[*With enclosure*]

State of North Carolina
Executive Department
Raleigh September 10th. 1864

Maj Genl J F. Gilmer
Chief of Engr Bureau

Genl
Your letter of the 23d. ultimo[1] in regard to the removal of a portion of the rail from the Wilmington Charlotte & Rutherford R R. has been duly received and its contents considered. In reply I must say that desirous as I am and ever have been to aid the Confederate States Government in every way that I can, consistently with my duty as Chief Magistrate of North Carolina, I can see no good reason why I should grant that consent to the removal of said rails, which I withheld in my note to you of the 18th. of August last.[2] You seem Genl to entertain the opinion that this Road is one of merely "local interest." But in this you are surely /very/ much mistaken as you will no doubt readily concede when you have all the facts before you. It is upon supplies of provisions carried down by this road that the people of Wilmington, in a large degree depend for subsistence, and without which they would probably starve, and the place be lost to the State and the Confederate States, for all

the purposes of business. This Road moreover carried down more than one half of the supplies needed for the Army at that point, at a time when there were many more troops at Wilmington than at present. It seems to me in the highest degree impolitic, Just now, when an attack on Wilmington at an early day is deemed probable, to cripple this road which furnishes the only certain means of retreat to both citizens & soldiers in case of disaster. And I am informed that it is now doing a large amount of Government work which the Chief Engineer of the Department[3] declares to be indispensable to the defence of the place. Nor is this all, the State has at great expense erected Salt Works below Wilmington upon which its citizens largely depend for this indispensable article, which cannot be procured in sufficient quantities to answer the necessary demands of the community from any other place. These works are dependent upon this very road for all their supplies and if it is mutilated or destroyed, they will be destroyed with it, and the citizens of the whole State suffer also. This I submit is something more than a merely "local interest," indeed one of sufficient magnitude to render it expedient to undergo the comparatively trifling inconvenience of transporting rails a little greater distance from some of the branch roads further South, rather than sacrifice it. These branch roads in South Carolina we were told, several months ago, as now were upon the point of being torn up to repair the main trunk, but they still remain intact. But even if it were impracticable to bring iron from other Roads, I would remind you that the Genl. Superintendent of the Wilmington & Manchester R. R. in his report of the condition of his road in October last, said that, "in this particular (meaning the condition of the railing) we are probably in no more critical situation than most roads on the main line of business" So it would seem that the road cannot become unserviceable before the Company can, enriched as they have been by its large earnings, and owning a large interest in a Steam ship for running the blockade, import the iron necessary to repair the Road and leave uninjured the large interests involved in the continued operations of the Wilmington /Charlotte/ & Rutherford Road. You lay some stress in your letter upon the fact that "it is not proposed to remove all the Eastern Division of the Road." You cannot be aware of the fact that the Company is operating under a charter granted by the Genl Assembly of the State which requires that the road shall be finished by sections at stated times, and upon a failure to comply the charter is forfeited, so that the removing of the portion of the road proposed would be equivalent to the removal of the whole, as it would render the forfeiture of the charter inevitable. The State moreover is by the terms of the Charter, largely interested in said Road, and would by its destruction, lose millions of money. Again Colonel Garnett,[4] several months ago took some steps toward the removal of the rail from the same portion of this road, when his proceedings were stopped by an injunction from Judge [*William H.*] Battle, one of the Justices of our Supreme Court, and this injunction is still in force and cannot now be ignored by me, even if there were not other sufficient reasons for me to withhold my consent to the removal of the rails.

I herewith enclose a letter to you from Robt. H. Cowan, President of the road, to which I would invite your careful attention.

> I am very Respectfully
> Your obt servant
> Z B. Vance

P.S. I propose to submit the whole matter to the Legislature which will assemble in about six weeks I do not believe I have the power to surrender this iron without the consent of that body as whole is mortgaged to the State.

> Z. B. V.

¹In this volume.
²In this volume.
³Brig. Gen. William Henry Chase Whiting.
⁴Charles F. M. Garnett, chairman of the Confederate Iron Commission, created to "examine and advise on what Railroads in the Confederate States the iron on their track can best be dispensed with." Robert C. Black, *The Railroads of the Confederacy* (Chapel Hill: University of North Carolina Press, 1952), 275. See also Robert H. Cowan to ZBV, February 13, 1864, A&H:GLB.

[*Enclosure*]

Robert H. Cowan to Jeremy F. Gilmer   A&H:GLB

> Office Wilmington Charlotte &
> Rutherford
> R.R. Co. Laurenburgh N. C. Sept 5th.
> 1864

Maj. Genl. J. F. Gilmer
Chief Engineer Bureau
Richmond Va.

General

I have been furnished, by His Excellency Gov Vance, with a copy of your correspondence with him upon the subject of the removal of the iron from a portion of the track of my road.

The "Wilmington & Manchester R R. Co." have had ample means and every opportunity to furnish their road, and to keep it furnished. Other Roads have done so, but they have preferred to rely upon their position in the main line of communication to force the Government to use its power to impress from their neighbors.

The time has passed when this Company might have purchased the material necessary to keep their track in the best condition. But even now, by the exercise of energy and liberality, and by refusing to transport for those who are speculating upon the necessities of the country, they can perform all the transportation which the Government may require of them and put their track in comparatively good order. The only assistance necessary from the Government will be permission to import iron in their blockade running Steamers, such small quantities in such steamers as will not interfere with their regular freight. As it is pronounced a military necessity the Government cannot refuse this. If the Company owns, as I understand they do, a large Interest in a Steam Ship Company it will not be required.

I propose therefore, if the managers of that road cannot do the work of the Government that you pass it over to me and my directors with proper authority in the premises and we will guarantee it shall be done.

If you have authority to take ten miles of my road, you have authority to take it all. If you have authority to take my road and give it to them you have authority to take their road and give it to me. If they cannot do your work, I can. My proposition, therefore, is reasonable, and, altho' submitted in self defense, is submitted in good faith.

I refer you to the Hon. Geo Davis, Attorney General, and Major Robert Strange of Genl. Bragg's Staff, for anything you may wish to know about me.

> I am very Respectfully,
> Your most obdt
> Robt. H. Cowan
> President

Robert E. Lee to ZBV   A&H:VanPC

Hd. qrs. Petersburg
10 Sept '64

His Excy. Z B Vance
Govr. Of State of N. Carolina
Raleigh

Govr.

Your letter of the 5th. Inst:[1] has been recd. I am much gratified at your readiness & ability to render all the aid in your power in the defence of Wilmington. Of the former I never doubted, & I think by Combining all the means of the Confederate & State Governments the security of the city may be ensured. Your suggestions touching its defence have in a measure been anticipated. Genl. Beauregard is now there with a view of examining into its defences, armament, & garrison. One of the objects of his visit is to see whether a portion of the latter at least cannot be replaced by troops of experience. It is uncertain yet whether the enemy will attack Charleston or Wilmington, but it is my desire to give to Genl. Beauregard the defence of whichever place may be attacked. I hope nothing may prevent his services being thus applied. As soon as I receive an answer to my dispatch as to the number of arms you require[2] for your State force, I will endeavor to furnish them. Please state to what point they must be sent. The prospect of peace & independence depends very much upon the success of this Campaign I need not therefore inform your Excy. of the importance of bringing & maintaining in the field all our available force. The life & safety of the people demand<s> it.

I am with great respect
Your Excy's obet Servt
R E Lee
Genl

[1]In this volume.

[2]See the telegram Robert E. Lee to ZBV, September 9, 1864, including ZBV's endorsement, in this volume.

ZBV to Sion H. Rogers   A&H:GLB

State of North Carolina
Executive Department
Raleigh Sep 12, 1864

Hon S H. Rogers,
Atto. Genl N C.

Dr. Sir

I enclose you the proceedings of Capt. J. H. Sands[1] C. S. Comr. in the case of certain prisoners captured at Plymouth accused of treason & treasonable transactions with the enemy, forwarded forwarded [sic] me by the Asst. Secty. of War with the request that I shall have them indicted for treason in the Courts of this State. Their names are J. R. Thompson, S. Cobb, F. Haywood, J W. Oliver, J. Patrick, H Basnight and S. Barker. Please give me your counsel and advice thereon.

Resply yours
Z. B. Vance

[1]The proceedings are not extant, but apparently Sands was a Confederate commissioner for the War Department who was investigating eastern North Carolinians ("Buffaloes") who had joined the Union regiments formed in North Carolina and then had been captured by Confederates at the Battle of Plymouth in April 1864. See Weymouth T. Jordan Jr. and Gerald W. Thomas, "Massacre at Plymouth: April 20, 1864," *North Carolina Historical Review* 72 (April 1995): 125-193, and Judkin J. Browning, " 'Little Souled Mercenaries'? The Buffaloes of Eastern North Carolina during the Civil War," *North Carolina Historical Review* 77 (July 2000): 337-363.

ZBV to Theophilus H. Holmes   Duke:Holm

State of North Carolina,
Executive Department,
Raleigh Sep 12 1864.

Lt. Gen T H Holmes[1]
Richmond

Gen'l

Please if you concur with me in its importance, urge upon the President the exchanging of the troops in Garrison at Wilmington for fire-tried veterans from the field—about which we had a talk before you left.[2] Also, that in case of attack Gen Beauregard should come to Wilmington and take command.

Very resptly. &c
Z. B. Vance

[1]Lt. Gen. Theophilus Hunter Holmes, a North Carolinian and former commander of the Trans-Mississippi Department and subsequently the District of Arkansas. In February, he had resigned the latter post in the West and returned to North Carolina, where he commanded the state's reserve troops until the end of the war. *Dictionary of North Carolina Biography*, s. v. "Holmes, Theophilus Hunter."

[2]To confer with the War Department in Richmond.

ZBV to James A. Seddon   A&H:GLB

Raleigh Sept. 13th.

Hon. J. A. Seddon
Secty of War,
Richmond,

Can I get transportation, two cars per week, for vegetables for soldiers from Danville to Petersburg? Please answer at once.

Z. B. Vance

Sewall L. Fremont to ZBV   A&H:GP

[*Telegram*]

Wilmington Sept 14

To Gov Vance
Raleigh

Genl Beauregard wants to see You on business on friday morning early will <for> arrive by <fr> early train from Goldsboro this is entirely confidential will you be at home

S L Fremont[1]

[1]Col. Sewall Lawrence Fremont, Confederate engineering officer and superintendent of the Wilmington and Weldon Railroad, who was in charge of the construction of coastal defenses around Wilmington. *Dictionary of North Carolina Biography*, s.v. "Fremont, Sewall Lawrence."

George Davis to ZBV   A&H:GP

Confederate States of America
Department of Justice,
Richmond, Va. 16, Sept 1864

Governor Z. B. Vance
Raleigh N C

Dear Sir

Your letter of 1st. inst[1] reached here during my absence on a brief visit to No Carolina, whence I returned only yesterday. I avail myself of the earliest opportunity to reply.

I do not understand your letter as asking of me an official opinion as to the legality of the position assumed by the War Department, asserting the right of the President, and denying that of the Governor, to appoint the officers of the regiments known as the "State Troops" of No. Carolina. Indeed under the law, and the uniform practice of this Department, I am forbidden to give such an opinion except upon the requirement of the President or the Secretary of War. I must therefore content myself with explaining to you that view of the law which has governed the War Department in its late action.

You are mistaken in supposing that the right of the President to appoint the officers of these troops is claimed under the Conscription acts, or either of them. It is derived from a higher source, and is considered, not as a right simply, but as an imperative duty.

I have not examined particularly into the history of these regiments, but am informed at the Adjt General's office that they were received into the service of the Confederate States under the general authority of the act "To make further provision for the public defence," approved 11th. May 1861. The constitution recognizes but two classes of troops in the service of the Confederate States to wit, the Army of the Confederate States, and the Militia. The appointment of the officers of the latter is reserved to the States; but the officers of "the army," like all other officers of the Confederate Government, are required to be appointed by the President, with the advice and consent of the Senate. This difference in the mode of appointing officers gave rise early in the war to a very important question—that is, <under> in which of these two classes are Volunteers, and troops furnished by the different States to be <classed> embraced?

In August 1861 Mr Benjamin,[2] then Attorney General, gave an official opinion that troops furnished by the States upon a requisition of the Confederate Government were Militia and their officers were to be appointed under the State laws. Under the authority of this opinion, and the belief that it covered the case of the No. Ca. State Troops, the appointment of the officers of those troops was yielded to the Governor.

In August 1862 the case of troops raised and organized under the State laws, and received into the service of the Confederate States under the said Act of 11 May 1861 was presented to Mr Attorney General Watts[3] for his opinion and he declared officially that such troops are a part of "the army of the Confederate States," and all vacancies among their officers are to be filled by appointment of the President, with the consent of the Senate. I send you a copy of so much of the opinion as relates to this point.

The view of the law declared in this opinion has been adopted by the Secretary of War upon the case of vacancies in the No. Ca. State Troops being directly presented to him. He feels that he is imperatively bound by the constitution that the appointments should be made by the President, and that he has no discretion any longer to acquiesce in an arrangement made by his predecessor under what he believes, and what has since been declared to be, an erroneous construction of the law.

This brief synopsis, with the copy of Mr. Watts's opinion, will advise you of the reasons by which the War Department has been governed, and enable you to judge of their validity. I express no opinion myself, being as I have said, precluded from so doing by the rules of my office.

>Very Respectfully
>Yours &c
>Geo. Davis

[1]In this volume.
[2]Judah Philip Benjamin, appointed attorney general of the Confederacy in February 1861 and served in that post until September 17, 1861, when he was named secretary of war. He remained in that position until March 1862 when be became secretary of state. Faust et al., *Encyclopedia of Civil War*, 54.
[3]Thomas Hill Watts, appointed attorney general in March 1862 and served in that office until he resigned in September 1863 to become governor of Alabama. Faust et al., *Encyclopedia of Civil War*, 808.

Extract.

Assuming that these regiments and Legion were received into the Confederate Service, under the Act of the 11th of May, 1861, *as organized bodies*, the question is still how are vacancies in the offices to be filled? This Act expressly declares, that volunteer forces accepted under it shall be organized in accordance with and *subject to all the provisions of the Act entitled* "An Act to provide for the public defence." The fifth section of the latter act declares, that the officers of companies, squadrons, battalions, and regiments *"shall be appointed in the manner prescribed by law in the several States to which they shall severally belong,* but when inspected, mustered and received into the service of the Confederate States, said troops shall be regarded, in all respects, as a part of the Army of the Confederate States, according to the terms of their respective enlistments."

It is distinctly declared that the *appointment* of the officers of companies, squadrons, battalions and regiments shall be according to the law of the States from which they come. This may well be done, if, *in raising armies,*" Congress can Constitutionally authorize the reception of organized companies, battalions and regiments as well as the enlistment of single individuals. As Congress is unrestricted in this respect, in the *mode* of raising armies, I have no doubt that this can be done.

But when such troops are received into the service of the Confederate States, and are then to be regarded in all respects as a part of the Army of the Confederate States, the mode for the appointment of officers declared in the Constitution must prevail. The officers afterwards appointed for the companies, battalions and regiments are officers of the Confederate States. The Constitution, in the 2d clause, of 2d Section, 2d Article declares, that the President "shall nominate, and by and with the advice and consent of the Senate, shall appoint Ambassadors, other public ministers and consuls, Judges, of the Supreme Court, and all other officers of the Confederate States, whose appointments are not otherwise provided for, and which shall be established by law. But Congress may, by law, rest the appointment of such inferior officers as they may think proper, in the President alone, in the Courts of law, or in the Heads of the Departments."

When these troops became a part of the Army of the Confederate States, Congress not having vested the appointment of the officers in the President alone, or otherwise provided for such appointment, the vacancies can only be filled by the President's nomination and appointment, by and with the advice and consent of the Senate, as provided in the 9th section of the Act "For the establishment and organization of the Army of the Confederate States."

James A. Seddon to ZBV   A&H:GP

[*Telegram*]

Richmond 17 Sept. 1864

To His Excelly Vance
Raleigh

Col [*Frederick W.*] Sims informs me he has replied to your telegram[1] that after necessary army supplies are transported every facility will be offered for the transportation of vegetables for soldiers from Danville to Petersburg

J. A. Seddon

[1]ZBV to James A. Seddon, September 13, 1864, in this volume.

Jeremy F. Gilmer to ZBV   A&H:GP

Confederate States of America,
War Department,
Engineer Bureau,
Richmond, Va.
17 Sept. 1864.

To his Excellency—
Z. B. Vance
Governor of N. Ca.
Executive Office
Raleigh N.C.

Sir:

I have the honour to acknowledge your letter of the 10th. Inst.[1] in regard to the removal of the iron from a portion of the track <of the track> of the Wilmington, Charlotte & Rutherford R. Rd.

I beg leave again to remind your Excellency that it was never contemplated to dismantle that portion of the road in question which is used in the transportation of supplies to Wilmington and in the distribution of Salt from the State works near that city. Only ten miles of iron were proposed to be taken; and it was designed, by taking that amount altogether from beyond the Company work-shops at Laurinburgh, to meet the pressing wants of the Government without breaking up the road or even seriously impairing its general usefulness.

I would add that the iron from the branch roads in South Carolina that may be despoiled will be required in a short time for the repair of the Charlotte & South Carolina R. Rd. and of other main connexions in that state. Some small part may be given to the Wilmington & Manchester R. Rd., but not enough to supply its absolute wants.

The letter of Robt. H. Cowan Esqr. President of the Wilmington, Charlotte & Rutherford R. R. Co. enclosed in your own, has been carefully considered. The difficulty of importing R. R. Iron, either on account of Government or of private corporations, is at present so great, that his suggestions must, under existing circumstances, be regarded as impracticable. The repair of the Wilmington & Manchester R. Rd. is not designed as a favour to the Company, but is to be considered as an imperious military necessity. The administration & policy of the Company may, as is asserted, have been faulty: but it is to be borne in mind that, in consequence of the heavier transportation required, the main trunk-lines must, from natural causes and without fault on the part of any concerned, have become more rapidly & more seriously impaired than other less important roads.

In view of the extreme importance, in a military & national point of view, of a prompt and thorough repair of the Wilmington & Manchester R. Rd. and of the danger likely to result even from a temporary or partial interruption of transportation upon that line, I deeply regret that your Excellency has arrived at a decision which exposes us, as a people, to serious consequences. I remain very resp'y

> Your Obdt. Servant
> J. F. Gilmer
> Maj. Genl. & Chf. Eng'r. Bur.

[1] In this volume.

ZBV *to Pierre G. T. Beauregard*   A&H:GLB

> State of North Carolina
> Executive Department
> Raleigh Sept 17th. 1864

Genl Beauregard
Petersburg

Genl.

I regret that I forgot to mention during your short stop here[1] the condition of the State Salt Works at Wilmington. Gen Whiting has seized the boats by which they were supplied with wood and otherwise so embarrassed them as to virtually compel them to stop. He says they must be removed from Masonboro Sound, that the operators are disloyal communicate with the enemy &c. The removal my superintendent informs me would occupy thirty days time, cost $75000 and decrease the quantity & increase the cost of the salt 100 per cent.

I offered to discharge the disloyal men if pointed out, not acceded to; to send a company of State Troops to guard them but two companies are required which I have not to spare, what can be done? The State has already lost by the delay some $50.000 in money to say nothing of Salt. As you know salt is /absolutely/ indispensable—the people and the army will both suffer if these works are not resumed. Why cant one Company guard the works? How can the works there or anywhere else endanger the town? Why is it that

Gen Whiting is permitted to seize the property of the State treat her authority with such disrespect and damage her natural interests so vitally? If you can provide any possible relief I shall be greatly obliged

> Very Respectfully yours
> Z B Vance

[1]See Sewall L. Fremont to ZBV, September 14, 1864, in this volume.

Jefferson Davis to ZBV   A&H:GP

Circular Letter

> Executive Office,
> Richmond, 19th. Sept. 1864.

His Excellency Z. B. Vance,
Governor of the State of North Carolina,
Raleigh.

Sir:

I have the honor to call your attention to a matter of public interest in which harmony of action between the State and Confederate authorities is essential to the public welfare.

In some of the States executive proclamations have been issued requiring all aliens within their limits to render military service or to depart from the State within a specified period. The language of these proclamations has been so general as to seem to admit of no exceptions and their effect has been in some instances to alarm alien mechanics and laborers employed in the Confederate workshops and factories, to induce them to abandon their employment and to demand passports in order to return to their country.

Skilled workmen, experts in various mechanical pursuits indispensable in the foundries, laboratories, arsenals, machine shops and factories, have been engaged in Europe under contracts which guarantee to them immunity from the obligation of bearing arms, and many immigrants are now on their way to the Confederacy, on the faith of these contracts.

It is not doubted that the Governors of the several States who have issued such proclamations entertained no intention of interfering with mechanics and workmen in the Confederate military service. Men who are employed in manufacturing and preparing munitions of war and military supplies are as effectively engaged in the defence of the Country and should be as free from interference by the State authorities, as the soldiers in the field. But the failure to indicate in the proclamations already issued that such men as are thus employed in the Confederate service are not intended to be embraced within the terms of the proclamations, has already given rise to the abandonment of work indispensable to the army. I have therefore respectfully to request that in all cases where such proclamations have been or may hereafter be issued, the necessary notice be given that they do not apply to this class of aliens.

In addressing to you this communication it is my purpose carefully to avoid raising any question that could produce conflict between the general and State governments, and I therefore refrain from the expression of an opinion on the constitutionality of such exercise of power as is involved in these proclamations. It may not however be improper to invoke your consideration of the policy of banishing from our country at a time when the services of every man are particularly valuable, such aliens as have not acquired the residence which would subject them to military service, but who are willing to serve our country as artisans during the war. It is plain that the labor of all such as are usefully employed in the Confederate work-shops, factories, and laboratories must be performed by some one, and if these undomiciled foreigners are driven away, their places must be supplied, (if indeed they could be supplied at all) by men detailed from the army; and the action of the State authorities would thus result in an effect precisely the reverse of that intended by them; it would diminish instead of increasing the strength of the armies. Those aliens even who are laboring elsewhere than in the service of the government are efficiently aiding our cause by services of great value in furnishing to our people many necessary articles, such as shoes, clothing, machinery, agricultural implements and the like, which it is now so difficult to obtain from abroad. It is submitted that sound policy would require us to encourage during the war rather than prohibit the residence of such persons among us, even though they be not available for service in the field.

> I am, Sir, very respectfully,
> Your obedient servant,
> Jefferson Davis

ZBV *to James A. Seddon*   A&H:GLB

State of North Carolina
Executive Department
Raleigh Sep 19, 1864

Hon J. A. Seddon
Secy. of War

Sir

The State of North Carolina has contracted with nearly all the Cotton and woolen mills within her borders for a certain per cent of their productions. I have imported material & machinery for them and so far have supplied our troops with their fabrics at half the price paid by Confederate Agents. Gen Lawton has however conceived the idea that the whole business of this State supplying her own troops must be broken up no doubt for the reason that it is done better & cheaper than it could be done by him, accordingly details for hands in the factories have been refused and they are being sent to camp unless they will break their contracts with the State and enter into others with Gen Lawton. I am in receipt of a letter announcing the suspension of an extensive factory, this morning for that cause. I presume from the way in which I was treated about running the blockade and the many impediments thrown in the way of the State Q Masters Dept generally, that Gen Lawton['s] attempts to seize the whole business receives the countenance of the Confederate Administration. If so I would be glad to have it honestly avowed. If the Confederate and State Governments are reduced to the disreputable position of scheming against each other and of oppressing whenever one may happen to have the power over the other, I want to understand it when my time comes. North Carolina long ago made a contract with the C.S. to furnish her own troops in the field, and to enable her to do this it was agreed that her own resources should be surrendered to her own agents. Notwithstanding this was immediately disregarded, and we have to contend with Confederate agents in every market for every article. Yet it is our boast and pride that we have nobly fulfilled the contract. It does not suit our convenience in notions of duty toward our soldiers to surrender everything now to Mr Lawton and allow him to seize our mills by force after all that we have done to keep them up. Nor have we ever refused to loan the surplus to the C.S. after supplying our own troops.

I will not undertake to show the impolicy of such a course the millions saved the Confederacy by the enterprise of this State the comfort added to the hard lot of our soldiers nor any considerations of that character. But I beg you to pause before permitting Gen Lawton to oust N.C. of her resources to cloth her troops in this manner. It will not be submitted to by

> Very resply yr obt svt
> Z. B. Vance

ZBV to John White   A&H:GP

> State of North Carolina,
> Executive Department,
> Raleigh, Sep 21 1864.

Mr. John White,

Dr. Sir,

   The AdVances invoices signed by Power Lowe & Co. show that the six bales of cotton, accounted for by Mr. Flanners letter 18th. July '64[1] belonged to Dr. E. Warren & weighed 3348 lbs. and the five bales in the same letter belonged to me & weighed 2657 lbs.—Please have the funds separated. I enclose you copy of P. Leons recpt for Two bales per "Annie" weight 4861 lbs. Please get copy of receipts from Mr. E [*Warren*] at Wilmington for thirteen bales more per Collie's Steamers. Dispose of all & any more I may ship to best advantage & deposit to my order—

> Yrs
> Z. B. Vance

P.S. Two more bales sent by AdVance where Primrose went, weight upwards of 1000 lbs, will get it exactly from manifest—making in all Thirty bales—for my ac't

> Z B V

[1]Not extant.

Sion H. Rogers to ZBV   A&H:GP

Raleigh Sept 22nd 1864

To His Excellency
Gov Vance:

Sir:

The papers in the case of Joshua A Hill[1] and Seth W Laughlin[2] in the letter of Capt Sloan[3] have been received. The laws of Congress in relation to exemptions are clear as far as the cases here are concerned.

The act approved Oct 1st. 1864[3] exempts a great many persons & classes and then proceeds as follows—"and all persons who have been and now are members of the Society of Friends" &c *"Provided* Members of the society of friends &c shall furnish substitutes or pay a tax of five hundred dollars each into the public Treasury." This act was repealed by the last exemption act[4] <except> with some exceptional cases therein stated and among them I find in sec 4 of said last act the following proviso. "Provided, that no person, heretofore exempted on account of religious opinions and who has paid the tax levied to relieve him from Service, shall be required to render /military/ service under this act."

These last two questions are presented in these cases. Are they members of the Society of Friends, Nazarenes, Mennonists [*Mennonites*] or Dunkards, and have they paid the tax or furnished substitutes. If so they should at once be discharged. If not you have no right to demand their discharge—

I am with great respect

Sion H. Rogers
Att Genl

[1]Quaker conscript in the Twenty-seventh Regiment North Carolina Troops who deserted to the enemy on or about September 29, 1864, and was imprisoned in Washington, D.C. He was released on October 1, 1864, after taking the oath of allegiance. Manarin et al., *North Carolina Troops*, 8:98.

[2]Quaker conscript in the Twenty-seventh Regiment North Carolina Troops who died on December 8, 1864, in a Richmond hospital. Manarin et al., *North Carolina Troops*, 8:57.

[3]Capt. John A. Sloan, Company B, Twenty-seventh Regiment North Carolina Troops. Manarin et al., *North Carolina Troops*, 8:20; John A. Sloan to ZBV, September 6, 1864, A&H:GP.

[4]June 4, 1864. See Moore, *Conscription and Conflict in the Confederacy*, 89.

ZBV to James A. Seddon A&H:GLB

State of North Carolina
Executive Department
Raleigh Sept 22d. 1864

Hon J A. Seddon
Secy. of War

Sir

I learn that Lt. Col. W H H Cowles[1] 1st. N.C. Cavalry has been recommended for Brigadier of Chambliss'[2] Brigade by his superiors. I beg leave most cordially and earnestly to second the recommendation of this gallant and most accomplished young officer

In addition to rewarding merit & promoting the good of the service, the promotion of Lt. Col. Cowles would furnish grateful evidence to our people of the intention of the War Department to promote North Carolinians when deserving, to the command of troops from other States to which we have submitted reversed so long

Very Resply
Z. B. Vance

[1]William H. H. Cowles did not receive promotion to brigadier general and command of his brigade. He continued as a lieutenant colonel in the Ninth Regiment North Carolina State Troops (First Regiment North Carolina Cavalry) and was wounded, captured, and finally paroled in April 1865. After the war, he practiced law, became an influential power in the Democratic Party, and served in Congress. Manarin et al., *North Carolina Troops*, 2:7; *Dictionary of North Carolina Biography*, s.v. "Cowles, William Henry Harrison."

[2]Brig. Gen. John Randolph Chambliss Jr., who was wounded near Richmond and died on August 16, 1864. Faust et al., *Encyclopedia of Civil War*, 126.

Pierre G. T. Beauregard to ZBV   A&H:GLB

[*With enclosure*]

Hd. Qrs. Dept. N.C. & So. Va.
Sept. 22nd. 1864.

To his Excellency
Govr. Z. B. Vance,

Sir:

I have the honor respectfully to acknowledge the receipt of your communication of the 17th. inst.[1] relative to the seizure of the boats belonging to the State Salt Works, and removal of persons connected therewith on alleged disloyalty by Genl Whiting.

I have no information from General Whiting of his action on this subject, but will immediately call upon him for a report of the grounds on which his action is based. The seizure of the boats may have been induced by some controlling military necessity of which I have no knowledge and therefore, at present cannot judge of the propriety of the act. If not dictated by some such controlling cause, the boats will be restored. With regard to the removal of disloyal men, I enclose you a copy of a letter from the War Office to General Whiting on this subject. The instructions therein embodied must govern and control his action.

Until further informed by the report of General Whiting, I cannot give instructions, more than to restore the boats, if not absolutely inconsistent with the public interests, and to be governed in the other matter by the letter from the war office.

As far as my power extends, it will afford me much pleasure, to give you any aid to protect the rights and interests of your noble State.

I am Governor
With sentiments of great respect
Your Obt. Servt.
G. T. Beauregard
General

[1]In this volume.

[*Enclosure*]

H. L. Clay to William H. C. Whiting   A&H:GLB

> Confederate States of America
> War Department
> Adjt. & Inspr. Genls. Office
> Richmond June 18th. 1864.

Maj Genl. W H C. Whiting
Thro' Genl. Beauregard

General:

In reference to your communication of the 2nd. inst relative to disloyal persons residing on the Sound, and requesting instructions, I am directed by the Secretary of War to inform you, that the power of the Military Commander applies to remove those persons from their homes to a place in which they will not do mischief, if there were actual operations going on in that portion of the Department and it was necessary. But in the absence of such operations, the better mode of proceeding would be to call in the Civil Authorities, by making a specific charge against them, that they were holding intercourse with the enemy, or rendering to them aid and comfort, and obtaining their judgement on the matters charged. Any intercourse with persons of the description mentioned in the communication, involves a responsibility upon the part of the officer doing it, and any action must rest, not upon suspicion or surmise, but well authenticated facts to be supported. If there be such facts, the General would be justified in imposing such restraints as would prevent mischief. This, however, does not extend to sending them from the country.

> Very Respectfully Genl.
> Your Obt. Servt.
> H. L. Clay
> A. A. General

ZBV to David L. Swain   A&H:VanPC

Raleigh, Sept 22d. 64

Gov. Swain.

My dear Sir,

Your information concerning the condition of the forts on the Cape Fear has caused me to initiate enquiries which may do some good. I am however, inclined to doubt its accuracy. Such glaring deficiencies no General could be pardoned for suffering to exist a moment, and could hardly escape the eye of Gen Beauregard who assured me recently that the defences of Wilmington principally needed *men*.

I would be glad if I could have a long talk with you. I never before have been so gloomy about the condition of affairs. Early's defeat in the Valley I regard as the turning point of this campaign & confidentially, I fear seals the fate of Richmond though not immediately. It will require our utmost exertions to retain our footing in Va. until 1865 comes in. McLellands defeat[1] is placed among the facts & abolitionism is rampant for four years more. The Army in Georgia is utterly demoralized; and by the time the President, who has gone there, displays again his obstinacy in defying public sentiment and his ignorance of men in the change to a still worse commander, its ruin will be complete. They are now deserting by hundreds per diem. Gov Brown is a *humbug* & can do nothing but get in the way. He shant if the enemy pushes his luck till the close of the year we shall not be offered any terms at all.

The signs which discourage me more than all else, is the utter demoralization of the people. With a base line of communication 500 miles in Shermans rear, through our own country, not a bridge has been burnt, a car thrown from its track nor a man shot by the people whose country he has desolated! They seem every where to submit when our armies are drawn off. What does this show Governor? It shows what I have always believed that the great *popular heart* is not now & never has been in this war! It was a revolution of the *politicians* not the *people*; was fought at first by the natural enthusiasm of our young men, and has been kept agoing by state & sectional pride assisted by that bitterness of feeling produced by the cruelties & brutalities of the enemy.

I am not out of heart. As you know, I am of a hopeful & bouyant temperament—Things may come around yet. Gen. Lee is a *great man*, and has the remnant of the best army on earth, bleeding, torn & overpowered though it be. Saturday night may yet come to all of our troubles and be followed by the blessed hours of rest. God grant it. "Lord I believe, help

Thou mine unbelief"—in final success & independence. I fain would be doing. How can I help to win the victory? What can I do to secure a retreat? How shall I guide this suffering & much oppressed Israel that looks to me through the tangled & bloody pathway of the wilderness wherein our lives have fallen?

Duty called me to resist to the uttermost the dissolution of the Union; duty calls me to stand by the new union "to the last gasp with truth & loyalty." This is my consolation. The beginning was bad. I had no hand in it; should the end be bad I shall with Gods help be equally blameless. They never shall shake their gory locks at me & say that I did it!

I hope when you come down—you will give yourself time to be with me a great deal.

Mrs. Vance is almost restored & joins me in regards to your family. Please consider the greater part of my letter as Confidential

I am dear sir

Very truly yours
Z. B. Vance

[1]Former U.S. major general George B. McClellan, the Democratic Party's candidate for U.S. president in 1864. McClellan ran on a peace platform, but apparently ZBV considered his defeat by incumbent Abraham Lincoln in the November elections a foregone conclusion. See Phillip Shaw Paludan, *The Presidency of Abraham Lincoln* (Lawrence: University of Kansas Press, 1994), 283-291.

Joseph E. Brown to ZBV   A&H:GP

[*Telegram*]

Milledgeville
Sept 23 1864

Gov Z B Vance
Raleigh

If you will send out an agent to Look to it I think I can furnish you a train in a few days to carry your state cotton to Augusta

Jos E Brown

[*Endorsed*] Do not move the cotton unless it can be brought to Charlotte

---

ZBV to Milledge L. Bonham A&H:GLB

State of North Carolina
Executive Department
Raleigh Sept. 23d. 1864.

His Excellency
Gov. M. L. Bonham
Columbia S. C.

Dear Sir

The Legislatures of the various States will soon be in Session. It will become them to take such steps in aid of the common cause as the perillous and straightened condition of the country demands. The great evil of desertion must be broken up, if possible, provisions must be made to feed the poor, and the feeble and desponding must be encouraged and inspired with hope; and beyond all else, *men must be sent to the armies of Gens.* [Robert E.] *Lee and Hood.*[1] To find where and how to get these men is the great object of inquiry. Large numbers, no doubt, are in the various departments of the Confederate Government, who could be sent to the field, and their places filled by non-combatants. It will be for the Confederate Government to look after these. There are also numbers engaged in the various State Departments /who/ might be spared. And there is yet a large class of State officers in all the States withheld from service, not only on account of the necessity for them in administering the governments but also because the principle of state sovereignty rendered it improper to allow the Confederate Government to conscript them. This latter class I suppose to be quite numerous in all the States; and could there be a way prescribed to put, at least, a portion of them into service without injuring the efficiency of the State Governments, and without infringing upon the rights of the States and their dignity /as sovereigns,/ they would constitute quite a material reinforcement to our hard pressed armies. It seems indeed desirable.

Beyond doubt however, it is especially desirable, that action on this and all kindred matters should be uniform, or as nearly so as possible. It would avoid much discontent, for every man to know that he was required to do only that, which every one else has to do, and that, the burdens of the war are fairly distributed.

In order to obtain this uniformity, as well as to consult on any other matter of public concern which might present itself, I beg leave respectfully to suggest a meeting of all the Southern Executives on this side of the Mississippi at some such point as Augusta Ga. during the coming month of

October when and where some general plan of action might be agreed upon for the relief of the Country, and recommended to our several Legislatures.

Should such a suggestion meet with favor at your hands, I would be greatly pleased to hear from you in regard to the time and place of meeting. Any time so far as I can now see will suit me, and any place within three days travel by rail.

> I am Gov.
> Very respectfully
> Your obt. Serv't.
> Z. B. Vance

Letters of the same tenor with the preceeding one were today sent to the governors of Georgia, Alabama, Florida, Mississippi, Tennessee, and Virginia.

[1]John Bell Hood, commanding the Confederate Army of Tennessee against the campaign of Gen. William T. Sherman, who had recently captured Atlanta and subsequently began his march to the sea and eventually into the Carolinas. Current et al., *Encyclopedia of the Confederacy*, 2:789-791.

William H. C. Whiting to ZBV   A&H:GP

> Hd qrs. Wilmington
> Sept. 24, 1864.

To his Excellency Gov. Vance,
Raleigh,

Sir,

Can you do anything for Wilmington in the way of labor? I have most important work to do on Bald Head & at Caswell—work that is essential to the safety of the place. In the Spring all negroes, the whole of the very small force sent here were taken away & 4 months of precious time were lost. Of the free negroes ordered to be enrolled, I have been able to get but 800, & many of these have deserted & many are down in sickness.

If you can do anything to aid in this matter, I beg you will do it quickly.

There is another sort of help wanted. We must have troops here. All the labor & all the fortifications & all the Engineering skill in the country will not be able to save this place without an adequate force. At no time since the war began, has the force to defend Wilmington been so small as it is now.

At no time has it been in greater danger. You know the position of our two great armies—and what our chance is of receiving aid by detaching troops from them. Even if we could expect that, it might and probably would come too late—or at any rate *after* the enemy might have secured his foothold, perhaps even cut off the forts from the town. It is perfectly possible to do this. It can only be prevented by the presence of troops in force.

If the enemy should be enabled to cut off the forts, no amount of gallantry or endurance on the part of the garrisons could save them, for they would eventually starve. It is no more practicable to protect a position like this by its garrison alone from a combined land & naval attack, than to protect Richmond or Petersburg by their fortifications without the presence of Genl. Lee's army.

I am informed on good authority, that there are 10,000 men in N.C. between the military ages, not in service. Will not many of them come forward at this time to aid in the defence of their own homes? While it is the duty of the Confederate Government to provide for the safety of all vital points, no one can help seeing that as events have gone lately, all its force will have to be concentrated in the two great armies. We must do our best here to help ourselves.

If North Carolina can provide any aid, I beg that it may be done at once. It is time for all troops that are to be here to be gathering. One half the number before the event will do what double may not be able to affect after the enemy makes his appearance. Let these 10,000 men come out for 3 months until the winter may release some of the veterans. Their very presence may avert attack.

I have been laboring now for nearly two years to procure guns & put up forts. Neither guns nor forts will avail, nor Engineering without men.

> Very respectfully
> W. H. C. Whiting
> Maj. General—

P.S. Since writing the above, I have received a letter from Gen'l Lee, handed me by Gen'l Beauregard who has just passed through south in which he says the force of negroes *must* be increased. He says further that I "must rely for reinforcements from the Reserve forces of the State & the increase to your rank & file from the conscripts."

The case is before you now for such aid as you render.

ZBV to Nicholas W. Woodfin   A&H:GLB

State of North Carolina
Executive Department
Raleigh Sept 26th. 1864.

N. W. Woodfin Esqr.

Dr. Sir,
    I have been anxiously expecting you to go to Saltville for some months. Every thing is going badly there, judging from the tenor of my information. We cannot get a bushel shipped from the works, though private parties continue to ship a great deal. The suspension of our works at Wilmington renders it doubly important, that those at Saltville should be pushed with all possible vigor. If it should be out of your power to return there at once, please let me know it.

Very respectfully yours
Z. B. Vance

David L. Swain to ZBV   A&H:VanPC

Chapel Hill, 26 Sep. 1864.

His Ex. Gov. Vance.

My dear Sir,
    Your esteemed favour of the 22d.[1] was delivered to me by Col. Whitaker on Saturday.
    A successful defence of Atlanta, which I cannot but suppose would have been made if Johnston had remained at the head of the army,[2] and a decisive victory over Grants armies in Virginia would probably have given such an impetus to the Peace party at the North, as would have resulted in an early armistice and subsequent peace. But the evacuation of Atlanta inclines the seat in the other direction, and we are now in a situation that admits of no alternative, but to "watch and wait" I have always entertained the opinion that the most disloyal portion of the Confederacy was Northern Georgia, the northeastern angle of S. C. the South western of N. C. the Southeastern of Ala. and East Tennessee. The population of these several sections, making in the aggregate, an area of fertile soil, sufficiently extensive to form a respectable

state, is homogeneous and substantially non slaveholding, originally opposed to secession and at present favoring reconstruction. A continued succession of victories would have made them, our friends, all present indications point to neutrality if not hostility. The country from Nashville to Chatanooga is covered and from Chatanooga to Atlanta virtually subjugated. The population on the entire line from Nashville to Atlanta is sturdy hardy and heroic, and if it had the heart to rise as one man, might not merely cut off the supplies, demolish the defences, but wipe out Shermans army in twenty days. Nothing but the will is wanting, but I fear that upon the part of the majority this is entirely wanting. If this apprehension is well founded, and the events of the next three weeks will settle the question, Sherman will not merely hold Atlanta, but secure the command of the Macon road, and cut off all communication with the gulf states. This will leave us with a pay roll of half a million, dependent on the tithes and taxes, of ¾ of Georgia, 5/6 of S. C. ¾ of Virginia and 7/8 of N. C. With you I have unlimited confidence in Genl. Lee. He will do all that man can do, but he must almost work miracles to retrieve our failing fortunes, and yet I cannot but hope that God will enable him to do it. I regret that truth and conscience compel me to present so sombre a picture. I hope to be with you in about a week, and perhaps events may transpire within that brief period, to change the present gloomy aspect of affairs and inspire hope and confidence. In the mean time, as already stated I can perceive nothing to be done that you are not doing but "to watch and wait" Your proclamation inviting the return of deserters was timely and has proven efficient. The Confederate authorities, may call a small army of officials, in many instances nuisances, when they [*illegible*], to the rescue and it may be well, to sound the alarm in the ears of Mr. Seddon, "Awake, arise or be forever fallen" The newspapers in some instances, are urging most importunately, an immediate call of the General Assembly, the repeal of exemptions, to military officers, Justices of the Peace &c &c. If this were done, it would not I suspect, add as materially to the strength of the army, as the immediate march of supernumerary officials to the front, and the campaign will probably close, before the Genl. Assembly, could meet and organize new levies. Reserving further remarks upon public topics, until we meet, permit me to call your immediate attention, and request similar aid to that so promptly and effectually rendered in securing supplies for the Faculty of the University a year ago.

I see from a notice in the newspaper that Maj. S. M. Finger[3] whose Head Quarters are at Charlotte is Controlling Quarter Master for N. C. You probably know him personally, and can bring personal and official influence to bear upon him, which neither I nor any one else can. I either know or have heard or read of some one of /members of most of/ the leading families in N. C. but that Majors names is entirely new to me.

Will you do me the favour as President of the Board of Trustees to enable the President of the Faculty to provide substance for himself and assist some of his brethren to submit and recommend to the favourable consideration of the Major the following proposition, viz that on the delivery to the Quarter Master of Pitt or Edgecombe whichever may be most convenient 300 barrels of corn, more or less, and the fodder stripped from it, I may be permitted to receive an order on the Quarter Master of Orange, to allow the delivery of a like quantity of corn and fodder by the tithe payers in the immediate neighborhood of Chapel Hill, and also on the delivery of 50 barrels of corn & 50 bushels of wheat at Asheville, the same quantity here. Such an arrangement I suppose will be decidedly to the advantage of the government as well of as the University and myself. Corn grows on good land in Pitt and in Buncombe is superior in quality to the small ears and nubbin collected for us last year, from the hilly land around here. My place in Pitt is within 12 miles of Tarboro, which connects with the Wilmington and Weldon Rail Road at Rocky Mount, and can be transported to any point when it will be needed with more care and at less expense than from this place. If I receive a favorable answer I will go down to Raleigh about a week hence. I have appointed to meet a friend at Tarboro on the 7th. Oct. You will perceive therefore the necessity of an immediate application to Maj. Finger.

Your old Friend
D. L. Swain

[1] In this volume.

[2] In July Gen. John B. Hood had replaced Gen. Joseph E. Johnston in command of the Army of Tennessee opposing the advance of Gen. William T. Sherman. Faust et al., *Encyclopedia of Civil War*, 400.

[3] Sidney Michael Finger. As Confederate quartermaster for the eighth congressional district, he was responsible for tax in kind in North Carolina. After the war he served in the state legislature and as superintendent of public instruction. Paul D. Escott, "Poverty and Governmental Aid for the Poor in Confederate North Carolina," *North Carolina Historical Review* 61 (October 1984): 476n.

William Smith to ZBV   A&H:GP

State of Virginia,
Executive Department,
Richmond,
Sept 27, 1864

To His Excellency
Z B Vance,
Raleigh N. C.

Sir:

I received on yesterday yours of the 23rd. Inst.,[1] suggesting the propriety of the Governors of the [*illegible*] Mississippi States meeting at some convenient point at an early date, in order that we may unite in such general recommendations as we may agree to be proper to the Legislatures of our several states, shortly to be assembled.

In the general objects of your letter I cordially concur. While it may be, that a meeting such as you propose may give rise to much misrepresentation, I can see no solid objection to it, but can well see that great good may result from it.

I would respectfully suggest that Columbia be selected as the place at which we shall assemble, and that an Early day be fixed therefor. I propose to convene the Legislature of Virginia upon the first Monday in November, if not earlier.

I am

Very Respectfully
Yr. obdt. Servt.
Wm Smith

[1]See ZBV to Milledge L. Bonham, September 23, 1864, in this volume.

Milledge L. Bonham to ZBV   A&H:GP

State of South Carolina,
Executive Department,
Columbia September 28th. 1864

His Excellency Z. B. Vance
Governor of North Carolina

Dear Sir:

I have received your letter[1] proposing a meeting at Augusta, Georgia, of the Governors of the Southern States, during the coming month of October, with a view of securing some uniformity of action for filling the ranks of our Army, and your proposition meets my entire approval. Augusta is a very suitable place and possibly the most central for us all. The day should be as early as practicable, but the danger in making it so is, that we will not have present the Governors West of the Mississippi. This, I fear, will not be practicable under two months, which would be too late for the approaching sessions of our Legislatures—that of this State meeting on the fourth Monday in November next. In assenting to your proposition, it is proper that I should state, that in South Carolina no persons are reserved to the State but all have gone into Confederate Service from the classes of Militia officers, Magistrates, Deputy Clerks and Deputy Sheriffs, (except in one or two cases where the Confederate Government has detailed or Exempted them) and several other classes, all of which classes, I have understood in several of the States, have been reserved by the States or by the Executives thereof. Whilst I think each State should have a permanent force of its own, as matters now stand, it is better that every one who can be spared should go into Confederate service—but the most important thing now to be done, in my judgment, to fill our ranks and secure the greatest harmony and satisfaction among our people, is the placing in service the Army of Efficient officials and detailed men scattered through the Confederacy, whose duties can as well, or better, be performed by infirm men, disabled officers and soldiers, citizens exempted by Confederate law from service in the field and persons over fifty years of age.

Very Respectfully and truly yours
M. L. Bonham

[*Endorsed*] Copy & file

Z B V

[1]September 23, 1864, in this volume.

ZBV *to James G. Martin*   A&H:GLB

State of North Carolina
Executive Department
Raleigh Sept. 28th. 1864.

Gen. J. G. Martin
Morganton, N.C.

The troops at Asheville having gone to Tennessee, the citizens are very uneasy at their exposed situation. If you think it necessary you may send over a portion of Hinton's[1] Regiment temporarily to their assistance.

Very respectfully yours
Z. B. Vance

[1]James W. Hinton, Sixty-eighth Regiment North Carolina Troops. Clark, *Histories of Regiments from North Carolina*, 3:713-728.

ZBV *to William H. C. Whiting*   A&H:GLB

State of North Carolina
Executive Department
Raleigh Sept 28th. 1864

Genl. Whiting
Wilmington

Genl.

Your letters of the 24th. inst.[1] in relation to the defence of Wilmington have been received, and have my earnest consideration. I regret to learn that the defence of Wilmington depends alone upon the Militia forces of the State. If this be so, the place might as well be surrendered on the first summons of the enemy. The entire force I could send you for three months would not exceed five thousand men, raw and untrained. It was my intention to send every one promptly when the crisis comes, and the reason why I cannot send them and have not sent them heretofore in order that you might drill and to some extent discipline them is twofold. First, nearly all of the militia subject to my control are farmers. They are now saving forage, making molasses, and sowing wheat. I have had them out for thirty days, drilling, organizing, and arresting deserters, about 1000 of whom have been returned to duty. Were these men kept out all the time, and not permitted to sow wheat, the loss to both people and Army would be incalculable This is part of the programme military commanders are apt to forget. Now, if I were to send you the negroes and the Home Guard, having already the Junior & Senior Reserves, what labor would be left to do any thing at all?

I admit that almost any thing is preferable to the capture of Wilmington, but destitute as the country is of labor, I had earnestly hoped that the militia would be spared till the last moment. Secondly, I respectfully submit that I am entitled to judge of the necessity which calls these men to the field. It has been the habit of Confederate Commanders in N.C. to conduct all matters connected with our defence without reference to me whatever, with the exception of Gen. G. W. Smith,[2] and calls are constantly made upon me for the militia without putting me in possession of any facts other than the opinion of the officers upon what the necessity of the call is predicated. In the Spring Gen. [*Matt W.*] Ransom telegraphed me from Weldon to call out the Militia, and to my inquiry what for, he made no reply. Gen [*Laurence S.*] Baker wrote me from Goldsboro to the same effect, some weeks ago. And even now I have not been informed of one single circumstance showing why Wilmington is about to be attacked. Your opinion is, of course, to be respected; but I should be much better satisfied to make these people lose their crops, if my own judgement had an oportunity of concurring with yours as to its immediate necessity. I now say to you, General, that if convinced of its being absolutely necessary to the safety of Wilmington, I will make any sacrifice that may be required, even to the risk of starvation. I will send you every man I can control in the State, except from a few counties on the Western border, will appeal to every other ablebodied man to go, and will go myself.

You have already the power under Act of Congress to impress slave labor, and for various reasons I prefer you should do it unless I had the power of returning them when I thought proper.

> I am Genl.
> Very Respectly. yours
> Z. B. Vance

[1]In this volume.

[2]Gustavus Woodson Smith, who earlier in the war had commanded for a short time the Department of North Carolina and Southern Virginia. Boatner, *Civil War Dictionary*, 771-772. See also ZBV to Jefferson Davis, February 2, 1863, in Johnston and Mobley, *Papers of Vance*, 2:39-40.

Joseph E. Brown to ZBV   Har:Brown

Executive Department
Milledgeville Oct 1st. 1864

His Excellency Z B Vance

Dear Sir

Your communication of 23d. Sept.[1] came to this office by last mail.

While your remarks in reference to State officers are not applicable to this State, where every officer civil and military who can possibly be spared and keep the State Govmnt in existence, is, and for months past has been in military service as part of the militia of the State, they may be and probably are applicable to other States.

The questions you present for consideration are grave ones, and are well worthy of a consultation on the part of the governors of the respective States.

It will therefore afford me great pleasure to meet you and the other Governors at such time and place as may be agreed upon.

As the Legislature of this State meets the first Thursday in November and as it is important that I be at home for a few days prior to the meeting to prepare for the session, I respectfully suggest that the meeting be held in Augusta on the 17th. of this month. As your letter will probably be received by each before this reaches you, it may be easy to learn by Telegraph whether this time will be agreeable. If not, I will if in my power conform to the wish and convenience of others.

I do not know where to send the letter you enclosed for Gov. Caruthers[2] of Tennessee, I have sent it to Brig. Genl M. J. Wright of Tennessee who commands the post at Macon in this State with request that he forward

It is probably not known to you that Gov Caruthers has never been inaugurated and that Gov Isham G Harris is still the governor of Tennessee. His address is Macon care of Genl Wright who I believe is his brother in law.

I am Very truly [&c.]
Joseph E. Brown

[1] Not extant to Brown, but see ZBV to Milledge L. Bonham, September 23, 1864, in this volume.

[2] Robert L. Caruthers, who was elected—with a small vote—Confederate governor of Tennessee in 1863, when Isham G. Harris did not stand for election because state law prohibited him from succeeding himself. Caruthers was never inaugurated because the Federal military government led by Gov. Andrew Johnson controlled the government in Tennessee. Harris remained the nominal Confederate governor until April 1865, when Unionist William G. Brownlow was elected

governor. W. Buck Yearns, ed., *The Confederate Governors* (Athens: University of Georgia Press, 1985), 193-194, 271n; Faust et al., *Encyclopedia of Civil War*, 118, 344.

ZBV to James A. Seddon   A&H:GLB

State of North Carolina
Executive Department
Raleigh October 3d. 1864

Hon James A. Seddon
Secretary of War

Dear Sir

I have received a recent letter from Major Genl W H C Whiting, suggesting that the sending to sea of the Confederate Steamers Tallahassee and Chickamauga now fitting out at Wilmington would only excite the enemy to increase the number of the blockading squadron to such an extent as to render it almost impossible for vessels running the blockade to escape them, and that the public interest would be the better served by retaining them for the defence of the place.

These suggestions have in my opinion much weight and meet my decided approval. Should they meet the approval of your judgement, I earnestly request that you will use your influence to have them carried into effect.

With sentiments of much respect

Your obedient servant
Z. B. Vance

William H. C. Whiting to ZBV   A&H:VanPC

Hd. Qrs. Wilmington
Oct. 4, 1864.

Private.

To His Excellency Gov. Vance
Raleigh

Sir,

There are several matters to which you allude in your letter of the 28th.[1] entirely independent of those personal to myself which satisfy me that you have been seriously imposed upon by information received as to my administration here. For the first time I am informed that "citizens have been shot down wantonly in the streets by my patrols"—There has been no such case.

As to the trains which you complain of as being frequently seized—You should not attribute this to me—I never interfere with the R R. except upon the direct & special order of the War Dept, & in each and every case where any R R transportation has been taken in this command, it has been done on orders from Richmond—

With regard to the Salt Works we are at issue; but only as to the mode & place of supply—Both my correspondence & action were endorsed by my comdg. Generals & still your Salt works are permitted to go on though I as well satisfied of their prejudicial effect now as ever, of the disloyalty of the operatives, of their constant communication with the enemy, who land nightly & prowl even to the vicinity of the city—Put yourself in my situation, held responsible not only by your own people but the whole country & satisfied that near your capitol there was a dangerous & disloyal organization carried on by men who ought to be in the ranks, especially when the old & young are called out, I really don't think you would hesitate long in your line of action—

Your boats have been prohibited in these sound because all boats are dangerous there—I would not trouble the Salt works if I had any troops at all & I never did while the War Dep't. kept a proper force here—Since Martins' & Clingman's brigades have been taken away, the enemy are constantly coming in & constantly securing information—The newspapers which reach them they get every other day & only one day old—

With regard to the pilot of the A. D. Vance it was /at/ the instance of your own people & agents that he was taken off—It was evident to all on the A. D. Vance that the man Morse was determined not to take the ship out; he came back from the bar time after time, till all her passengers left her— He was frequently the subject of complaint from your agent for outrageous & unpatriotic extortion—Finally he was a detailed man in the service of the gov't, detailed by myself & sent to you, as the best pilot we had—Such he continued until he became too rich & too greedy—He was taken from the A. D. Vance, at the instance of the State Agents & because I thought & think still that he deserves severe punishment—The ship was in no way compromised by any action of mine—Her loss was due to the substitution of N. C coal for your English coal in four of those Naval expeditions against which I so earnestly & vainly protested & which will yet work far greater havoc to the State of N. C than the loss of the A. D. Vance. If her loss was not due to this it was to treachery in her English crew who were reported as greatly dissatisfied at the removal of their cotton from her—

I shall be much obliged if any one will inform me of any single usurpation of civil authority here on my part—The civil authority here at best is weak—I have many times been called on to aid in restraining the crowds of drunken foreign sailors that infest the streets & the negros who are a disgrace to the civil authority; but usurpation no—

I do not say anything more of the last subject of difficulty mentioned, than that I do not know to what your informants allude unless to some strong expressions of dissent in matters entirely political & which no doubt an informer would distort into personality—

I have only written this letter to put myself right in matters as to which I have been misrepresented & abused—None of the people in the district which I command have suffered by the war the hundredth part of what a very large portion of the community has had to endure & they have no right to complain—I have been compelled to adopt many measures which are harsh & hard—but it has been by law & called for by the unavoidable necessities of the war—It has been done without favor & with the constant endeavor to press as little as possible upon the people—Those who are unwilling to make any sacrifice & who expect to [live] just as in peace time, & who in this city are devoted to extortion & speculation, are the only persons who could have so unjustly & so shamefully attempted to abuse your Excellency's mind in regard to my course here—It is natural & nothing else is expected of such.

I am satisfied as to Your Excellency's good feeling & only desire here to remove impressions which may very naturally have grown up & can readily be accounted for, & I remain

> With great respect
> Yr. obt. Sevt.
> W. H C Whiting

[1]Not extant. Apparently Whiting is referring to a letter other than the one of September 28 that appears in this volume.

ZBV to Fenner B. Satterthwaite   A&H:GP

State of North Carolina,
Executive Department,
Raleigh, Oct 5th. 1864.

Hon F. B. Satterthwaite
Prest Council of State

Sir

Your communication informing me of the assembling of a quorum of your body and your readiness to proceed to the consideration of any business which I may submit has been received. Accept my thanks for your prompt attendance.

The first matter which I shall bring to your consideration is the filling of the vacancies in the Board of Internal Improvement caused by the resignations of Joseph H Flanner Esqr now absent in Europe, and Montford McGeehee Esqr a member elect from the County of Caswell to the next General Assembly. I respectfully recommend for the filling those positions Capt John D Hyman of Henderson County and Henry Nutt Eqr of New Hanover County.

There are two vacancies in your own body, caused by the resignations of R. P. Dick Esqr. and Jesse R. Stubbs Esqr., both members elect to the Legislature. I respectfully recommend <for these positions> Alfred G. Foster Esq of the County of Randolph <and> for the position made vacant by the resignation of R. P. Dick Esqr and for the other vacancy I respectfully present the names of P H Winston Jr Esqr and Major H. A Gilliam, either of whom would be entirely acceptable to me. I will take occasion during your session to address you a communication upon the subject of the condition of the country.

very respectfully
Your obedient servant
Z. B. Vance

David G. Worth to ZBV   A&H:GLB

Wilmington N C.
Oct 5th. 1864.

To His Excellency
Gov Z. B. Vance
Raleigh N.C.

Dr. Sir

During the month of September the State Salt Works at this place produced about 2600 bushs Salt. This is at least 3000 bushs—short of what might have been made had the whole of the works been running. This Salt has been sold at $14 per bush, which is less than it actually cost. The works are still laboring under the same disadvantage & drawbacks that they have since June last. I am compelled to haul all the wood I consume at least four miles & the force of teams at my command is inadequate to supply one half the works with wood. As stated in former reports by the use of flats to transport wood I was enabled to discharge about one hundred head of mules in the Spring. (After the seizure of the flats by Genl Whiting I had to fall back on the old mode of hauling wood. I then could not replace the teams I had discharged & if I could have done so, could not have fed the mules owing to scarcity of grain &c.) The loss in production of salt has been not less /than/ 10000 bush, which could have been sold at not over $12 per bushel, then has there been a loss to the people of the State, of not only the Salt, but there would have been a saving to them if they could have got it, as compared with the market price at this place of about $180,000. There has besides, in my endeavor to keep the price down & in the cost of building these flats, been an actual loss in cash of full $40,000.

If the works are not likely to be reestablished soon, I /would/ advise that a portion of the hands be discharged as there are more of them on the rolls than are actually needed for carrying on the works on their present footing. At present nearly all of them are sick with chills & fever. So that I am almost stopped on that account

I have abundant supplies of provisions on hand for two months to come. So that I have abandoned all apprehensions of starvation. The calls for Salt are increasing daily. I am not able to supply one fourth of the demands on me.

Very resply,
Your obt se'vt.
D G. Worth. S.S. Comr

Fenner B. Satterthwaite to ZBV   A&H:GP

Council Chamber
6 Oct 1864

His Excellency
Gov Vance

The Council of State have received and maturely considered your communication of yesterday in which you ask our advice as to anticipating the regular assembling of the General Assembly

The Council are agreed with one dissenting opinion that the absolute necessity required by law does not at the present time sufficiently appear to warrant an extra call of the General Assembly.

They unanimously concur with your Excellency as to the proposed conference at Augusta and assure your Excellency that they will be happy to assemble again at the earliest possible moment should events occur which in your Excellency's opinion require it.

The Council beg to tender their sympathy to your Excellency in the present heavy labors and responsibilities of your situation and to state that in their opinion every possible object of public benefit or advantage is being accomplished under your Administration of the State Government.

Respectfully
F B. Satterthwaite
Prest. Council

Robert E. Lee to ZBV   A&H:VanPC

Hd. Qrs. Chaffins
8 Oct '64

Confidential

His Exel. Z. Vance
Govr. of N.C. Raleigh

Govr.

It is necessary that this Army should be increased. The enemys greatly superior numbers enable him to extend his flanks in both directions, until at last if not prevented, he will envelop us. He is also daily recg. reinforcements, & I wish to draw to me every man I Can. I have written to Genl Holmes to endeavour to replace the 50th N.C. at Plymouth & Washn. by reserves, & the 67th N.C. at Kinston also. The 68th N.C at Morganto<w>n as far as I know is not now required there. The two last named regts. are in the State Service, but the former I believe is in the Confederate. If there is an objection to turning over the 67th & 68th regts. to the Confate. Govt. will Circumstances permit your assigning them to duty under me till the active Campaign Ceases? Have you not some battns. of State Cavry. that could relieve the 65th N.C. (Cavry.) at Kinston? These four regts would be of the greatest benefit to me. I requested Genl. Beauregard on his late visits to Wilmington & Charleston, to exchange portions of the garrisons at each, so that we could have a part of the garrison at least at Wilmington that had served under fire. The breaking out of the yellow fever at Charleston, & the assignment of Genl Beauregard to duty in the S.W. will prevent this arrangement. I know now no way of accomplishing this desirable object but to send some of the regts. of this Army to Wilmington & draw from there some with which it is garrisoned. Do you think the regts. from this army, which are much depleted Could be filled up at Wilmington & that in the meantime the deficit in numbers be supplied by reserves. Another difficulty arises in the character of troops. The troops at Wilmington are mostly Arty. while those I have are Infy. If Youngs & Moores battns. with any unassigned Comps. were organized into a regt. under some good officer, say Major Riley, this regt. with the 36th & 40th (Heavy Arty.) might be replaced as I have suggested, provided instruction could be obtained for /the regts. replacing/ them, & their ranks [recruited]. I believe Wilmington would be better defended by the arrangement. I fear however there will be great difficulty in making it. I will write to Genl Whiting on the subject & see what are the objections. I have not forgotten your anxiety on the subject of the Commdg. officer at Wilmington. I share it in an equal degree, but I can find no one whom I deem better. He is a man of unquestionable ability, versed in the particular knowledge suited to his position, but whether he would be able at the required time to apply those qualifications, & to maintain the Confidence of his Command, is with me questionable. I derived much Comfort from the report of the Condition of things by Genl Beauregard. He found everything in good order, much work had been done & saw no evidence of the Cause that excites my anxiety. At that time as I informed your Excy., it was my intention to place Genl Beauregard in Command of the Port in the event of an attack. His having been placed on duty in Georgia will now prevent, & I have no one to send in his place

>I am with great respect
>Your Obt Servt
>R E Lee
>Genl.

John Milton to ZBV   A&H:GLB

>Executive Department
>Tallahassee
>October 11th. 1864

His Excellency Z. B. Vance
Governor of North Carolina

Dear Sir

Yrs. 28th. ulto.[1] is before me. It arrived during my absence from here. The object you propose to accomplish by a Convention of Governors, are vastly important and are cordially approved by me. I will at any time appointed, meet you in Convention at Augusta Ga. or at any point more convenient and agreeable to others, when notified, if in my power to do so; but we are so constantly threatened with raids in different parts of the State, that my presence here seems to be almost indispensable.

>I have the honor to be
>Respectfully
>John Milton[2]

[1]Not extant, but see ZBV to Milledge L. Bonham, September 23, 1864, in this volume.

[2]Governor of Florida. Faust et al., *Encyclopedia of Civil War*, 496.

William H. C. Whiting to ZBV A&H:GLB

Hd. Qrs. Wilmington
Octo. 11th. 1864.

Confidential

His Excellency
Gov Vance
Raleigh

Sir

The Secretary of War informs me that in Richmond the Governor & the War Department concurring *all men capable of bearing arms are organized for the defence of the City* & asks me if I cannot obtain your consent to make the same arrangement here—If possible I beg that you will agree to this. Let them have their own officers their own hours & the understanding that they will be required only when all business is suspended. What I want is to know upon what I can rely & that these parties of whom there will be a thousand at least, may know that they are expected and if necessary will be obliged to do something for their homes. Can you give me a favorable answer? I have information direct from New York that Farragut[1] is now busy preparing his expedition. I think you had better commence at least to send forward reinforcements. Two thousand men would be a God Send to me now, though I shall want more. I have not enough just to keep the negroe laborers from running away. I give you the information which is direct from New York. I hope you will repeat to the President himself a remonstrance against that ill omened expedition leaving this port.[2] Fortunately they have not been able to get out this moon, but they are still impressing Coal & thereby endangering all the Ships in port precisely as they caused the loss of your noble ship.[3] Including her we have paid for the cruise of the Tallahassee by 10 vessels already. The sentiment of the Community and the Army & Navy is bitterly opposed to it and unanimously, including even those engaged in the expedition. There will be time for you to use your influence, if you agree with me and I am assured you do, before the expedition can go. I am thus urgent because we need and N.C. needs these men and guns here at our own doors, especially on the eve of Farraguts approach.

Very Respectfuly,
W. H. C. Whiting
Maj. Gen.

[1]Vice Admiral David Glasgow Farragut of battles of New Orleans and Mobile Bay fame. Ill health prevented him from participating in an attack on Fort Fisher and the port of Wilmington. Faust et al., *Encyclopedia of Civil War*, 254.

[2]A raid on Federal ships by Confederate gunboats *Chickamauga* and *Tallahassee*. Lindley S. Butler, *Pirates, Privateers, and Rebel Raiders of the Carolina Coast* (Chapel Hill: University of North Carolina Press, 2000), 194, 199-200.

[3]*Advance*, which was captured on September 10, 1864. Wise, *Lifeline of the Confederacy*, 286.

ZBV *to Edward J. Hale*   A&H:Hale

Private

Raleigh, Oct 11th. [1864]

E J Hale Esq
Fayetteville
N C

My dear Sir,
    You will have noticed that my Council refused to recommend convening the Legislature. It is represented to me that Gen Lee's army is in most desperate straits and must abandon Petersburg if not reinforced. Most urgent appeals for men have been made to me. I convened my Council & proposed to call the Legislature & submit to it the propriety of sparing some of our state officers or empowering me to send the H Guards beyond the State in case of emergency. After some little chaffing they refused out & out. I think I shall have to cut loose from some of the old fogies & rely for counsil & advice from men nearer my own age & notions of things—but I regret the necessities of my situation. I do not know that the state will surrender any of its officers, but I want the Legislature to take the responsibility of refusing. What do you think of it?
    Some two weeks ago, I invited all the Southern Governors east of the Miss River, to meet me at Augusta, Ga. on the 17th. inst. to consult on this and other questions connected with the reinforcing of our armies. Smith, Bonham, Brown & Clark[1] have responded favorably & there is no doubt but that Harris Watts & Milton[2] will also. I leave here for the place of meeting on Friday. Cant you write before I leave or to Augusta? giving me your views of what I should say & propose to this conference? My intention is to compare notes, see how many men each State has retained in its service, how many it can spare & agree upon some common plan to be submitted

to our several Legislatures. Will I damage myself by taking this course, and, what is more important, can I benefit the country? Ought the States to be further [*burned*] I confess I have my misgivings since the recent orders from Richmond stripping off details, farmers &c. I think however I might pledge N Carolina to submit to whatever others will submit to. Gov Graham thinks I might go thus far safely.

Should I call my<self> Council again on my return it will be with the view of submitting to it our proposed action at Augusta, and I would be glad if you could favor it in yr columns.

I am in good health and my spirits are improving.

Accept assurances of my high esteem.

Very sincerely yours
Z. B. Vance

[1]William Smith, Milledge Luke Bonham, Joseph Emerson Brown, and Edward Clark, Confederate governors of Virginia, South Carolina, Georgia, and Mississippi, respectively. Faust et al., *Encyclopedia of Civil War*, 70, 83-84, 142-143, 698.

[2]Isham Green Harris, Thomas Hill Watts, and John Milton, Confederate governors of Tennessee, Alabama, and Florida, respectively. Faust et al., *Encyclopedia of Civil War*, 344, 496, 808.

ZBV to Jefferson Davis   A&H:GLB

State of North Carolina
Executive Department
Raleigh Octo. 12th. 1864.

His Excellency
Jefferson Davis

Sir

In answer to your circular letter of a recent date respecting the foreigners in our midst I have to say that I concur in the suggestion advanced by you. No laws have been passed in this State oppressive of this class of persons and no edicts of expulsion have been or will be adopted.

I am Sir

Very respectfully
Yr. obt. Servt.
Z. B. Vance.

ZBV to James A. Seddon   A&H:GLB

Raleigh Oct. 13

Hon. J. A. Seddon
Secty. of War
Richmond

Jasper W. Davis, Clerk & Master of the Court of Equity for Stokes Co. No. Ca. while on a visit to Richmond recently was seized and put in the trenches. Please order his immediate release. He is needed as a necessary State officer.

Z. B. Vance.

Daniel H. Hill to ZBV   A&H:VanPC

Davidson College N C
Oct 13th. 1864

His Excellency Z. B. Vance
Governor of N C

There seems to be a common impression that Wilmington is to be attacked and probably the State invaded. I think that I could be useful in such a juncture and would once more renew my tender of service to you. I wrote to you some eight months ago that Mr. Davis would give me no further employment as I had offended him in a private interview. He promised the N C Delegation to give me a command as soon as I reported for duty. This was a most disingenuous quibble as no law or regulation requires a relieved officer to report at all. However, I complied with his condition & reported. Three days after my Report was recd & filed, Genl Early telegraphed to Richmond that he wished me to command Breckinridge's Division in the fight at Lynchburg (Genl. B being sick). The reply came, "Genl Elesy[1] will be sent to you tomorrow, B, Bragg Genl"

Davis has officially & privately said again & again that he has no fault to find with me & no military delinquency to attribute to me & yet he has done all that he could do to degrade me.

If I had the strength to carry a musket, I would have gone into the ranks long ago. I have no pride about position. Tis with me simply a question of physical ability

If you would really like to have my services in any capacity however humble, I would propose that you write to Davis & ask him to tell you frankly whether he intended to give me a command again; that you needed me & that need must plead the excuse for asking the question

He could scarcely disregard the letter of the Gov of a State, which was furnishing half the troops guarding his sacred person & capital

I regret the necessity for troubling but I dont want to be idle when others are employed, but especially when my own State is threatened

Yours truly
D H Hill

[*Endorsed*] Say that I have written the Prest. & will write again when his reply is recd. File private

Z B V

[1]Arnold Elzey, commanding local defense troops in Virginia. Faust et al., *Encyclopedia of Civil War*, 242.

Edward J. Hale to ZBV   A&H:VanPC

Fayetteville, Oct. 13, 1864

My Dear Sir:

I regret that your letter of the 11th.[1] was delayed, only reaching me to-day, of course too late for an answer to reach you before you start for Augusta, even if I had had time to write to-day, as I had not.

You do not state by *whom* it is represented to you that Lee's army is in desperate straits & must abandon Petersburg if not reinforced. I suppose, however that it is officially represented by the proper authority. If so, & if you have any <*illegible*> forces that you can send them to reinforce him, it seems to me that it will be wise policy not only for the Confederacy but for the State, to send them forthwith. The defence of North Carolina is now being made at Petersburg & Richmond. Reinforcements might, & no doubt could, make that defence effective; and save No. Ca. from the incalculable loss & evil of being made the battle ground, & being desolated as Virginia has been. I really have not the data upon which to found a reliable opinion upon the point of what further reinforcements the State can spare. It does seem to me, however, that there are a great many men still in this State; some of whom might well be spared, including many of the Justices & Militia officers. It seems to be admitted that there is great dissatisfaction in the army at the withholding of these men from the field.

I suppose, but the opinion may be founded only upon popular clamor, that No. Ca. has been more effectually conscribed than any other State. This, if so, is discreditable to the other States, or to those who administer the law in them, or to both; but it by no means exonerates us from the *full* performance of our duty. I have never allowed myself to be influenced by a consideration of what others do, nor should a State. <But> We are too much & deeply interested in this matter of the defence of Va. to stand upon what others have done or failed to do.

Entertaining these views, I think, if I were in your place, I would go further than Gov. Graham advises: What I *could* do I would *propose* to do, & endeavor to induce the other Governors to do also—not by way of *submitting* to what they would submit to, but as a free offering to the country in its necessities.

As to your Council, it seems to me not a little strange that the very men you have just appointed should vote against your proposition to call the Legislature. (I take it for granted that they were nominated by you to the Council to fill the vacancies.)

Another reason why we have not spoken in the Observer in regard to the call of the Legislature is that we have no means of knowing what would be the feeling of that body. If it should refuse to do anything, the effect would be very bad—better that it should not meet at all. And is there not reason to fear that they will lack the nerve to conscribe any class, especially such influential classes as the Justices & Militia officers? If the Legislature will refuse, better that they should not meet. But could you not expect to influence them by your own strong convictions of the necessity, as stated to you?

But again: We did not know that you desired the Legislature to meet. The Conservative had taken ground against it.

I think most favorably of your meeting of Governors, & hope great good from it. Should it result in an agreement to pursue a concerted line of policy, advise me. The Observer will second any movement calculated to promote the success of the great cause.

> In haste, but always,
> Yours truly
> E. J. Hale

[1] In this volume.

ZBV to James A. Seddon   A&H:GLB

[*Telegram*]

Raleigh Octo. 14th. 1864

Hon J. A. Seddon
Secty of War
Richmond Va.

I am informed that my hands at the State Salt Works, Saltville Va. are conscribed. Can you not forbid it? You have stopped my works at Wilmington, for Gods sake dont deprive this whole community of the means of living for the sake of 40 men.

Z. B. Vance

ZBV to Anna Pritchard   SHC:Van

Raleigh—Oct 14th 64

Mrs. Pritchard,

Your very sensible and well timed letter concerning your little son was duly received. I thought so highly of it that I took the liberty of having it published, suppressing names &c. for which I trust you will pardon me. I hope it may do good—It has already been highly spoken of. Your son can not be conscribed until he is 17 years old, and the object of enrolling him I suppose originated in a fancy of Gen. Holmes to ascertain how many recruits he could have one year hence—He had no kind of authority to do so by law—

I am Madam
Very resply. yr. obt. Svt.
Z. B. Vance

ZBV to Jefferson Davis Har:Van

Ex. Dept. of N C
Raleigh Oct 14, 1864

His Excellency
Jefferson Davis
Prest. &c. &c.

Sir,

I beg leave to enter my most respectful and earnest remonstrance against the sailing of the two privateers from the port of Wilmington.[1] Ten or twelve valuable Steamers have already been lost in consequence of the cruise of the Tallahassee & among /them/ the noble Steamer Ad-Vance, which alone, I respectfully submit has been of far more value to the Confederacy than all of our privateers combined. For these and other obvious reasons, I hope these two vessels may remain in the Cape Fear to assist in its defence.

Respectfully
Yr. obt. svt.
Z. B. Vance—

[1]See William H. C. Whiting to ZBV, October 11, 1864, in this volume.

James A. Seddon to ZBV A&H:GP

[*Telegram*]

Richmond Oct 15 1864

Raleigh Oct 15
Gov Z B. Vance

In present exigency I cannot relax call on any liable by Law to Military service in field I do not believe however your Salt making will be stopped.

J. A. Seddon
Secty War

Robert E. Lee to ZBV A&H:GP

[*Telegram*]

Hd Qrs Gen Lee
[Oct] 17 1864

Gov Z B Vance

I have teleghed to Richmond for the arms you ask if they can be spared they will be sent

R E Lee

Van Thomas to ZBV A&H:VanPC

Richmond Va.
Oct. 18th. 1864

Hon Z. B. Vance

Dear Sir—

I left Fort Delaware ten days ago. I was a room mate of your brother Gen R. B. Vance. He requested me to write to you & state the following facts. The General has been suffering from a continued consterpation for several months, resulting from the sameness of diet & long & close confinement. He is of the opinion that if he is not soon Exchanged his health will be very materially impaired. He wishes you to make every effort to have him specially exchanged for some Federal General whom we hold, or if an exchange can not be effected he thinks you can make an arrangement by which some Yankee General can be paroled & sent North, in consideration of *him* being paroled & sent South. The General does not wish you to make application directly to the Government your self, but to Gen Beauregard or Hood, through Gen Bate,[1] who is Gen Vance's intimate & personal friend & will doubtless take great pleasure in rendering him any service in his power.

I herewith send you a communication[2] signed by Lieuts. Smith and Bristol, with a watch chain made by these young gentlemen, & sent as a present to yourself.

The General would have written himself but I was taken away very unexpectedly & he had no time to write. I leave here in the morning for

Mobile where I expect to remain for several days. I would be happy to hear if you receive this.

> Respectfully
> Your obt Servt.
> Van Thomas
> Adjt.

[1]William Brimage Bate, Army of Tennessee. Faust et al., *Encyclopedia of Civil War*, 44.

[2]Not extant.

ZBV to John White   A&H:GP

> Ex. Dept. of N.C.
> Raleigh Oct 22d. 1864

It is hereby agreed between Govr. Z B Vance and John White of Warrenton, heretofore appointed Special Agent and Commissioner of the State to Europe, for purposes indicated in his instructions, that the latter is to receive three hundred & fifty dollars in specie or its equivalent per month, for his services and his necessary expenses incurred in such business.

> Z. B. Vance
> Gov. of N.C.

[*Endorsed*] The above contract was made the 10 or 12th. July, & I considered myself in the service of the state from that term. I left Warrenton to embark for England on the 2nd. of August, remained at Wilmington from the 5th. of August till after the middle of Septr. trying to get out on the S.S. Advance, not succeeding returnd. to Raleigh, & left again in Octr. at which time this contract was reduced to writting—I claim pay from the 15th. July 1864 to the 1st. October 1865, making 14 ½ months @ $350. is $5075.00

> J. White

Robert Ould to ZBV   A&H:VanPC

Confederate States of America,
War Department,
Richmond, Va. Oct 24th. 1864

His Excellency Z. B. Vance
Governor No. Ca

Sir,

Your letter of the 21st. Inst[1] has just been received.

Within the past few days I have entered into an agreement with the Federal authorities, which allows either Government to send clothing, blankets, bread, meat, sugar, coffee, pickles, vinegar, &c to the prisoners held by the adverse party. I take it for granted this arrangement will include the several States. We are allowed to make our purchases either in Europe or the Northern cities. I see no difficulty in your uniting with the Confederate Government in making purchases at the North or sharing in any other plan which it may take for the relief of our prisoners.

Please let me know in detail what you consider the best means to adopt for the relief of North Carolina soldiers under this agreement. It will give me pleasure to further and aid your views. Individuals can also send any contributions (not contraband) through flag of truce boats, to their friends or relatives. I receive many such from day to day.

Respectfully
Yr obt. Svt.
Ro. Ould
Agent of Exchange

[1]Not extant.

Braxton Bragg to ZBV   A&H:GP

[*Telegram*]

Wilmington
Oct 25 1864

Gov Z. B. Vance

Information just recd Justifies the belief that a traitorous communication is kept up with the enemy Some parties at the State Salt works I deem it of the utmost importance to the safety of this position & the state that this be immediately arrested and it can only be done by removing the operations it is impossible with our force to prevent the evil by Guarding the Coast I earnestly hope you will promptly <accquiesce> /acquiesce/ in this suggestion

Braxton Bragg[1]

[1]Commanding the Cape Fear District and the defense of Wilmington. Soon made commander of the newly formed Department of North Carolina, which included the Wilmington defense. Chris E. Fonvielle Jr., *The Wilmington Campaign: Last Rays of Departing Hope* (Campbell, Calif.: Savas Publishing Co., 1997), 88-89.

Jefferson Davis to ZBV   A&H:GP

Richmond, Va.
Oct. 25th. 1864

Gov. Z. B. Vance
Raleigh, N.C.

Sir,

Your letter of 14th. Inst.[1] entering your "Most respectful and earnest remonstrance against the sailing of the two privateers from the port of Wilmington," has been received. The two vessels referred to are the Steam Sloops "Tallahassee" and "Chickamauga," regularly commissioned and officered vessels of the Prov. Navy of the C. States and not "privateers.["]

From an official list before me I find but four instead of "ten or twelve" disasters off the port of Wilmington from the sailing of the "Tallahassee" to the date of your letter, and the cause of the loss of some of them is known to be independent of the cruise of this Ship.

Our cruisers though few in number, have almost swept the enemy's foreign commerce from the Seas.

Though the "Tallahassee" captured thirty one vessels, her Service is not measured by, nor limited to, the value of these Ships and cargoes, and the number of her prisoners; but it must be estimated in connection with other results: the consequent insecurity of the U.S. coastwise commerce, the detention and delay of vessels in port, and the augmentation of the rates of Marine insurance, by which millions were added to the expenses of commerce and navigation, and the compulsory withdrawal of a portion of the blockading force from Wilmington, in pursuit of her.

A cruise by the "Chickamauga" and "Tallahassee" against Northern coasts and commerce would at once withdraw a fleet of fast Steamers from the blockading force off Wilmington in pursuit of them, and this result alone would render such a cruise expedient.

It is the presence of these vessels in port which increases the rigor of the blockade. In case of an attack upon Wilmington they could avail nothing against the land attack and very little against an attack by vessels of War. Before sailing however Genl. Bragg has been directed to confer fully with the Naval Commander upon this subject and they no doubt will use their discretion as may best subserve the public interest.

> I am Sir,
> Very Respectfully,
> Your Obt. Servant,
> Jefferson Davis

[1]In this volume.

ZBV to Jefferson Davis   A&H:GLB

> State of North Carolina
> Executive Department
> Raleigh Octo. 25th. 1864

To His Excellency
Jefferson Davis

Gen. D. H. Hill an officer whose abilities in the field are highly esteemed in North Carolina is now at home without employment. I would be greatly pleased if he could be put in command of the Eastern portion of the Department of N. Ca. where there are a few regular troops and many Militia now assembling. Should it not be your pleasure to give him this or some other command, I propose giving him such employment myself as I can find for him to do. Like a good and gallant soldier, he expresses to me his great desire to serve anywhere or how his country

> Very Respectfully
> Z. B. Vance

ZBV to George A. Trenholm   A&H:GLB

State of North-Carolina
Executive Department
Raleigh Oct. 25th. 1864

Hon G. A Trenholm
Secty. of the Treasury
Richmond Va.

Dear Sir

I am forced to call your attention to a matter which is causing the greatest inconvenience to the Treasury of this State, and to beg that you will issue such orders as will correct the evil. Under the contract which this State has entered into with the C.S. to furnish with clothing her own troops, large sums are constantly due to our Treasury. Owing, as I must believe to an intention on the part of Genl. Lawton to force an abandonment of the arrangement, he has continued to interpose every possible obstacle to the settlement of this claims, which have heretofore generally been audited and settled without hesitation. Recently an account has been allowed to reach the sum of $2,400,000 to the 1st. Sept./64 before a settlement could be obtained; and that after months of unremitting importunity by our Agent Mr. Winston. Adjustment was however at length made and four checks of half a million each were prepared & sent to Maj Pearce Q.M. at this place for our benefit. Maj. Pearce pays one to my Q.M. appropriates one to his own purposes and retains the other two alleging that he will pay them when the money comes to hand: This is the way we are paid. The inconvenience is very great. The money we receive for clothing & supplies is immediately invested in the purchase of more, the State acting in fact as the Agent of the Q.M. Genl. for our own troops. When payment is refused or delayed, the Treasury of the State has to issue its own notes or borrow to keep the contract working, the loss by depreciation or otherwise falling of course upon us. Now Sir, in order to render justice and greatly facilitate me in clothing one half of the troops who defend Richmond, let me ask you to amend this evil, and cause prompt settlements to be made of my accounts from month to month. And also to give such orders as will prevent Maj. Pearce from applying to other purposes, funds specifically appropriated to the payment of North Carolina. When the other three drafts will be received it is impossible to tell. We are almost at a dead lock now for want of the money.

Very Respectfully
Yr. obt. svt.
Z. B. Vance

ZBV to Theophilus H. Holmes   A&H:GLB

State of North Carolina
Executive Department
Raleigh Oct. 25th. 1864

Gen. Holmes

Dear Sir

Maj. [*Henry A.*] Dowd informs me that you have instructed him that all applications for the detail of hands in factories working for the State must be submitted to Maj Chisman. A portion of these applications have already recd. the approval of the regular conscript authorities including yourself. The others I now enclose for your approbation also, and desire to accompany them with an explanation.

Though I have heretofore submitted to apply for details for the State as other parties, I deny the right of the Government to seize any person working for and in the employ of North Carolina in any department provided for by Law. The Q.M. Genl. Lawton has for a long time been endeavoring to force me to abandon the States contract for furnishing its own troops, and every possible effort for this purpose has been resorted to. The last device was the attempt to conscribe the hands in all the factories which had contracts with the State and would not abandon them for Confederate Contracts. More than one instance of an open and avowed attempt of the kind can be cited long before the recent order revoking details. The order from Richmond directing these applications to be submitted to Maj Chisman is, I have no doubt, a continuation of the same plan. I shall not submit to it. Whilst I am willing that *every* man shall go and *every thing* stop at the decisive hour, I am not willing that Gen Lawton should break down the State of North Carolina in this way and deprive her of the power to clothe her armies in the field. Should these details therefore be unreasonably refused, I shall have to try tilts with the Confederate Govt.

Very Respectfully Yours
Z. B. Vance

ZBV to Theophilus H. Holmes   A&H:GLB

State of North Carolina
Executive Department
Raleigh Oct 26th. 1864.

Gen T. H. Holmes

Present

Gen'l

I respectfully but earnestly invoke your attention and that of the whole Dept. to the absolute necessity of retaining at least a limited number of the Mechanics, Millers, Tanners, &c who are going off under recent orders. Anxious as I am to reenforce the Army, I am fully convinced that the Govt. is going too far in stripping the country of this class of persons, that it is weakening the government, producing real danger of starvation next year, and causing general alarm throughout the country. Taken in connection with the fact the Senior Reserves & Home Guards are also called out, I think real distress may be expected, & I hope you will urge the Dept. to forbear, at least to some extent. I shall be compelled to make large Details from the Home Guards, if the Government will do nothing. Heretofore I have exempted very few indeed.

Respectfully Yours
Z. B. Vance

ZBV to Braxton Bragg   A&H:GLB

[*Telegram*]

Raleigh Oct. 26th.

Gen. Bragg
Wilmington N.C.

Do what you think best with the Salt Makers until I go down which will be in a day or two.

Z. B. Vance

David G. Worth to ZBV   A&H:GP

Wilmington N.C.
Oct 27th 1864

To His Excellency
Govr. Z. B. Vance
Raleigh N.C.

Dr. Sir—

In making a selection of men whom you directed me to surrender, I have chosen principally those who are now absent on sick furloughs. There are a few of them, (perhaps 20), at the works. I write to know if I shall allow these to go home say on a ten (10) day furlough, with orders to report to the enrolling officers of their counties when the time expires. Most of these have more or less bedding, clothing & cooking utensils which they desire to take home to their families. I hope you will allow them to go—

I enclose the list, & have also advised the enrolling offices of each county of the names & whereabouts of each man—with directions to them to have them enrolled & forwarded to camp—

Very Res'fully
Your obt Servt
D. G. Worth S S comr

[*Endorsed*] He may discharge them & notify the enrolling officer—I can not grant furloughs after they are discharged—I want half a doz coopers, if he has them save them

ZBV

File

ZBV to James A. Seddon   A&H:GLB

[*With enclosure*]

State of North Carolina
Executive Department
Raleigh October 27th. 1864

Hon. Jas. A. Seddon
Secretary of War
Richmond Va.

Sir

I enclose you a copy of a letter, this day received from Messrs H. A. Gilliam[1] & Thos. Bragg[2] in relation to the imprisonment of Mr. William Adkinson in Richmond Va. for crimes alleged to have been committed in this State. I have therefore to demand of you that said Adkinson may be immediately returned to this State that his case may be investigated according to the due course of law.

Very Resply.
Yr. obt. Servt.
Z. B. Vance

[1]Henry A. Gilliam of Washington County, a former legislator and Whig colleague of ZBV. As a major in the Seventeenth Regiment North Carolina Troops, he had been captured at the fall of Hatteras in August 1861 and subsequently paroled. See Henry A. Gilliam to ZBV, September 24, 1862, in Johnston and Mobley, *Papers of Vance*, 1:223.

[2]Thomas Bragg was a lawyer, a state senator, governor, and Confederate attorney general. *Dictionary of North Carolina Biography*, s.v. "Bragg, Thomas."

[*Enclosure*]

Henry A. Gilliam and Thomas Bragg to ZBV   A&H:GP

Halifax N.C.
Octo. 25th. 1864

His Excellency
Hon. Z. B. Vance
Govr. of N. Carolina
Raleigh N.C.

Governor,

About the first of September past Mr. William Adkinson Jr. a citizen of Washington County, in this State was arrested in the /County of/ Bertee by order of Col Geo Wortham commanding at Plymouth N.C. and confined there, 'till about the 5th. of the present month when he was sent to Goldsboro, where he was confined until about the 10th. and then sent to Richmond and is now confined in Castle Thunder. We are informed and believe that he was arrested upon the charge of trading with the public enemy. We were employed by Adkinson as counsel, and supposing that his case would be investigated before Judge Biggs[1] at the Octo. Term of the District Confederate Court which was held at this place on the 11th. Inst, we caused witnesses to be summoned for his defence. As he was not brought to this place for trial, the residence of the party being within this district and supposing he was in Jail at Goldsboro, a writ of habeas corpus was issued by Judge Biggs to have this party brought before him, at the District Court at Goldsboro on the 4th. Nov. next. This time was agreed upon between ourselves and Geo. V. Strong Esq, the District Attorney. We desire for the accused an investigation of the facts. We ask that you will cause the party to be returned to this State, that that investigation may be had.

Very Respectfully
Your Obt. Servants
H. A. Gilliam
Ths. Bragg

[1]Asa Biggs, Confederate district judge and ardent secessionist. *Dictionary of North Carolina Biography*, s.v. "Biggs, Asa."

ZBV to William Smith   A&H:GLB

State of North Carolina
Executive Department
Raleigh Octo. 27th 1864

His Excellency
Wm. Smith
Richmond Va.

Govr.

You mentioned during our recent trip to Augusta that you thought you could sell me some Salt and deliver it by means of your State trains within my reach.

Please inform me if you can send me 30,000 bushels at what price & where delivered? If not delivered this side of Lynchburg it would do me no good.

I have not forgotten your cloth which will turn up in a few days.

Most truly Yours
Z. B. Vance

Robert B. Vance to ZBV   A&H:VanPC

Fort Delaware Del
Oct 27th 1864.

Hon Zeb B. Vance
Raleigh N.C.

My Dear Bro:

Lt Howard, long my mess mate, goes through on exchange and I send you a note. Yours of 11th.[1] reached me the day before yesterday. I was much pleased to learn of Sister Hattie's convalescence, as my wife wrote me of her illness. I approve of your determination to appeal to Caesar about the exchange. I am well satisfied now that I shall (even if there is a general exchange) be held here 'till the last. I am no favorite and yet I am sure I have tried to behave myself, but have spoken freely always for my country, and particularly against *oath takers* Lt Howard, if he has opportunity, can explain fully some things which have occurred here. You said nothing, whatever, of

Chambers? What became of him? Did you get the chain [Lush] and Bristol made?[2] I wish you to see Mr J. W. Crowder about organizing a subordinate Christn Association at Raleigh—I have written him. Please send Hattie's note[3] on to her, as I enclose it in your envelope. Write me as often as you can, as I feel the need of home letters & good words to cheer me. My anxiety for exchange grew out of the fact that I had been *unfortunate*. God bless you all

Bro Robert

[1]Not extant.
[2]See Van Thomas to ZBV, October 18, 1864, in this volume.
[3]Not extant.

ZBV to Robert Ould   A&H:GLB

State of North Carolina
Executive Department
Raleigh October 28th. 1864

Judge Ould
Comr. of Exchange

Dr. Sir
   Your letter[1] is received giving me the gratifying information that arrangements have been made for supplying our prisoners North with necessary comforts for the winter, and that we would be allowed to purchase supplies in the Northern Cities. I desire immediately to make arrangements for supplying the troops of this State, which I can do very readily having funds in Europe. If I can have an Agent North, I should greatly prefer having my brother Genl. Vance for this purpose, if the authorities will consent. He is now at Fort Delaware and his health is daily giving away from his confinement. As it seems /that/ he cannot be exchanged I would be much gratified if our Government would grant him this privilege and procure the consent of the enemy. No better man could be found to dispense the bounty of N. C. or the Confederate Government. Please let me know immediately.

Very Respectfully Yours
Z. B. Vance.

[1]October 24, 1864, in this volume.

Milledge L. Bonham to ZBV   A&H:GLB

[*Telegram*]

Columbia Octo. 28th. 1864

Gov. Z. B. Vance

Can you loan me until I can replace them or sell me at cost & charges about five thousand Blankets for South Carolina Troops. Answer.

M. L. Bonham

ZBV to Milledge L. Bonham   A&H:GLB

Raleigh
Octo. 29th. [1864]

Gov. Bonham
Columbia S.C.

In consequence of having to furnish the Home Guards and Reserves of this State now out for defence of Wilmington, I fear I shall not have the Blankets to spare you. Will know certainly in a few weeks when done issuing to the N.C. Troops for the Winter.

Z. B. Vance

Robert E. Lee to ZBV   A&H:GLB

Hd. Qrs. Army N. Va.
29th. Octo. 1864

His Excy. Z. B. Vance
Governor of N. Carolina
Raleigh

Governor

I have the honor to acknowledge the receipt of your letter of the 25th. inst.[1] and while I regret the facts you state I thank you for your efforts in our behalf.

I am gratified to hear what you say of the Home Guards and Reserves and trust that you will bring out as many as possible. With reference to the 67th. & 68th. regts. I understand that one is in Western N.C. I hope that the troops under Col. [John B.] Palmer are sufficient for the necessities of that region, especially as he is now cooperating with Genl. Breckenridge so as to prevent the advance of the enemy from E. Tenn. I would therefore advise that whichever one of the regts. above referred to is in West N.C. be sent to Wilmington to aid in the defence of that place.

> Very Respectfully
> Your obt. Servt.
> R. E Lee
> Genl

[1]Not extant.

ZBV *to John C. Breckinridge*   A&H:GLB

> State of North Carolina
> Executive Department
> Raleigh Oct. 29th. 1864

Genl. J. C. Breckinridge—
Comdg. Dpt. S. W. V.

Genl.

I beg leave to call your attention to the very distressing state of affairs in the Mountains of Western North Carolina and to ask your assistance in the effort to remedy it. I learn that in certain localities, particularly in Cherokee County & the region bordering, the warfare between scattering bodies of irregular troops is conducted on both sides without any regard whatever to the rules of civilized war or the dictates of humanity. The murder of prisoners and non combattants in cold blood, has I learn become quite common and in fact almost every other hour incident to brutal and unrestrained soldiery. I desire by all means to put an end to these things. The troops on our side are all commissioned and regularly authorized Home Guards or Militia are under my control and can be made to conform to the usages of war, provided a similar control can be exercised over our enemies. They are mostly tory renegades from both No. Carolina & Tennessee and pretend to be acting under regular Federal authority. If so can we not by regular systematized retalliation force them into terms? If not under Federal control, can they not be induced for the sake of humanity to assume such control of these bands of lawless men? I suggest the propriety of your communicating with the Federal General Comdg. East Tennessee to ascertain if some check cannot be given to the passions of men whose thirst for murder & robbery disgraces the name of Soldiers, and if no relief can be afforded innocent non combattants from these inhuman outrages.

I will not stop to show that any acts of violence on our part are more than provoked & justified by the atrocities of the enemy, as I am not seeking to exculpate my own people, or to inculpate those of the Federals. I desire only if possible to check the evil. Maj. M. L. Brittan of the Cherokee Home Guards & some of his Battalion were recently captured and were carried off as I learn with the avowed intention of murdering them. I shall of course retaliate & at the rate of two for one, if this is done & so there is no end of it. Please make an effort to save this officer & his men if you can hear of them. Should you be able to effect any thing in this regard, I beg you will communicate with Col. J. B. Palmer, Comdg. at Asheville N.C. and give him such instructions as you may think best for bringing about the desired end. I shall be pleased to hear from you at your earliest convenience

> I am General
> Very respectfully & truly
> Yr. obt. svt.
> Z. B. Vance

Robert Ould to ZBV   A&H:GP

> Richmond
> Oct 31st '64

Gov. Z. B. Vance
Raleigh N.C.

My dear Sir,

I have not yet had an opportunity of perfecting the details of the agreement.[1] I expect to do so in a few days. There will be no difficulty in obtaining the consent of the Federals that Gen. Vance should superintend and certify the distribution of supplies &c at the camp or depot where he may be. Whether they will go to the extent you desire, I cannot now say. I will make all endeavours to consummate your wishes—

> Yours truly
> Ro. Ould
> Agent of Exchange

ZBV to Alexander Collie   A&H:GLB

State of North Carolina
Executive Department
Raleigh Nov. 2d. 1864

Alexr. Collie Esqr.
17 Leadenhall Street
London

I forward to you this morning duplicate copies of a letter addressed you in August last[1] which I fear was lost on the Advance. I had acquired so great confidence in that Steamer that I neglected to forward copies [by] other Steamers. Mr White who is again made the Agent of North Carolina, has at length got out and I trust will reach you safely.

To him I refer you not only for general news, but for all information connected with our business and my wishes in regard thereto. Things continue so uncertain with regard to blockade running that I am at a loss what to do since the loss of the Advance.

In general terms I may say that I dont desire to run the Vessels in which we are joint owners under the present "Regulations" and shall trust to you and Mr White to make such arrangements with the Steamers as may be deemed best. Another earnest effort will be made this winter to repeal these "Regulations" and upon the result will greatly depend my future action.

A private letter[2] written you some time since expressing my thanks for many acts of personal kindness on your part, having also miscarried, I fear, I beg you to accept a renewal of them now and to say that Mr White is requested to offer them in person also.

Very Respectfully
Yr. obt. svt.
Z. B. Vance

[1]Not extant.
[2]Not extant.

ZBV to Theophilus H. Holmes   A&H:GLB

State of North Carolina
Executive Department
Raleigh Novr. 2d. 1864

<To> Genl. T. H. Holmes

Genl.

In conformity with your request[1] I enclose you a list[2] of the classes of persons whom I have claimed as necessary State officers and agents to be exempt from conscription together with a copy of a joint resolution of the Legislature as to authority for my claim. To these I only desire to add that I claim any and all persons in the actual employment of the State in every department where the law enjoins duties to be done which requires the employment of such persons. Without such power to employ any needful agents, no department of this government could be carried on for a moment and the State would be shorn of its sovereignty and crippled in all its operations. Since our conference on the subject you will have learned of the decision of our Supreme Court in Johnson vs Mallett in which it is laid down as law that my certificate in behalf of an officer is not material, that all officers and Agents provided by the Constitution or the laws made in pursuance thereof are, without regard to any action of the Congress, exempt from conscription.

I regard this as settling the whole question and shall be governed by it accordingly. Feeling as deeply interested in the filling up of our armies as any one can be, I have only to say in conclusion that it shall be my purpose to aid you by filling as far as possible all the departments under my control with non conscripts and turning over all able bodied men who can be spared.

Very Respty Yours
Z. B. Vance

[1]Not extant.
[2]Not extant.

ZBV to Robert E. Lee   A&H:GLB

State of North Carolina
Executive Department
Raleigh Nov 2d. 1864

Genl. Robt. E. Lee
Commanding Army No. Va.

General

I have the honor to acknowledge the receipt of your letter of the 30th. Ultimo.[1] The 68th. regiment North Carolina Troops is at Salisbury guarding prisoners of War. I have twice ordered it to Wilmington since the 20th. ultimo, but in each instance the order has been suspended by the officer in command and authority asked to detain the Regiment until a proper guard can be collected and organized to relieve it. Brig. Genl. [James G.] Martin promises that this shall be done in a few days. I regret that I have no cavalry to spare for the purpose mentioned in your letter. There are but two small Companies in the State service, Wynn's Battalion east of the Mountains. They are north of the Roanoke River acting under the orders of the Commanding Officer at Weldon, where their services are said to be very necessary. Every effort will be made to strengthen General Bragg should it become necessary. At present he does not seem to apprehend an attack.

With great respect
Your obt. servt.
Z. B. Vance

[1]Actually October 29, 1864, in this volume.

James A. Seddon to ZBV   A&H:VanPC

War Department
Richmond Va
Novr. 2nd 1864

His Excellency, Z. B. Vance
Governor of North Carolina

Sir

Your letter of the 27th. Ult.[1] enclosing a copy of a letter from H. A. Gilliam & Thomas Bragg relative to the imprisonment of Wm Adkinson &

in which you *"demand"* "that said Adkinson may be immediately returned to North Carolina, that the case may be investigated according to the due course of law," has been recd. Wm. Adkinson is a citizen of Maryland living in Queen Anne Co., /where his family now are./ He had a store in Plymouth and was doing business there when the same was in the possession of the U.S. forces.

At the fall of Plymouth last spring, he escaped and went to Beaufort, N.C. then in possession of the U.S. troops. From thence, he sent a message to one Halley to exchange goods for cotton & tobacco & loaded a vessel for that purpose & proceeded to Edenton N.C with her; & from that place went to Halleys house where he was arrested. There are several charges against Adkinson, of having given aid & comfort to the Enemy & having taken mules from a citizen but the fact being apparent that he is an *alien enemy* & being captured by the military authorities of the Confederacy, he is held as such. The facts I have detailed appear in a report submitted by the officer in whose custody he is & which recommended this disposition of him, & was approved the 14th Ult. It is quite apparent that Your Excellency has no ground for any intervention in this matter

> Very Respectfully
> Your obt svt
> James A Seddon
> Secy of War

[1]In this volume.

George A. Trenholm to ZBV   A&H:GP

> Treasury Department, C.S.A.,
> Richmond Nov 5 1864

To His Excellency
Govr. Z. B. Vance
Raleigh N.C.

Sir,

I have the honor to acknowledge your letter of 25th. ulto,[1] which has been attentively perused. The threatening attitude assumed by the enemy early last month, rendered it necessary for the great body of Clerks in the several Departments to be sent to the trenches, and the recent order revoking all details has prevented the return of most of them. These circumstances combined with others to produce the delay in making the payments to North Carolina of which you complain. It was proper to submit your letter to the Quarter Master General, and /is/ just to that Officer to state, that he disclaims all conduct calculated or intended to delay a settlement; that on the contrary he had tendered the payment of what was due up to 1st April (about $900,000) but being in old issue, it was refused by the State authorities.

I find the facts of the case at present to be that three of the requisitions referred to have been satisfied viz

Sep 10	Warrant	No.	6234	500,000
" 20	Warrant	No.	6325	500,000
Nov 1	Warrant	No.	6693	500,000

I hope the money for these will have been received before this letter reaches your hands; and the remaining requisition I will satisfy next week.

I remain Sir

YrmoobtServt
G A Trenholm
Secy of Treasy

[Endorsed] Copy & file

ZBV

¹In this volume.

ZBV to John R. Winston   A&H:GLB

State of North Carolina
Executive Department
Raleigh Nov. 5th. 1864

Col. Jno. R. Winston
Commanding 45th. Regt. N.C.T.

Colonel

I have received the "battle flag" of the gallant Regiment which you command, which has been borne with such conspicuous gallantry upon so many bloody fields. It will afford me much pride and pleasure to place it among the sacred relics of the State as an evidence of the valor and heroism of our troops

> With sentiments of great respect
> Your obedient Servt.
> Z. B. Vance

William Smith to ZBV   A&H:GP

> State of Virginia,
> Executive Department,
> Richmond,
> Novr. 12th. 1864

Gov Vance

Dear Sir

The cloth you kindly sent me[1] has been received, for which you will please accept my thanks.

I have now to ask that you will permit me to pay for it. By sending me the bill, I will promptly remit you the amount.

> In haste
> Very truly yrs
> Wm Smith

[1]See ZBV to William Smith, October 27, 1864, in this volume.

B. F. Alttend to ZBV   A&H:GP

[*With Enclosure*]

> State of South Carolina,
> Executive Department,
> Columbia Novr. 12, 1864

His Excellency
Z. B. Vance
Governor of North Carolina

Sir:

I am directed by his Excellency the Governor to send you the enclosed copy of a correspondence between himself and Mr. Trenholm.

He desires to express the hope that he has properly understood and represented the views entertained by the Governors recently assembled at Augusta.

He would write himself, but is quite unwell.

> I have the honor to be
> Very Respectfully
> Your Obt. Servt.
> B. F. Alttend
> Private Secretary

[*Enclosure*]

Milledge L. Bonham to George A. Trenholm   A&H:GP

> State of South Carolina,
> Executive Department,
> Columbia Novr. 12th 1864

Hon. G. A. Trenholm
Secretary of the Treasury

Sir:

Your letter of the 28th. of October was received several days since but owing to the pressure of other matters and to sickness, I have been unable to answer it sooner.

So far from its being their wish to embarrass the Government in its commercial operations for procuring shoes, clothing and other army supplies, it is believed by the Governors who assembled at Augusta, that the States would facilitate the Government in procuring those articles, by running, without restriction, chartered vessels as well as those owned exclusively by themselves. The troops of those States which have run vessels on their own account, unmolested, have been far better clad, than those from States which have not enjoyed the same advantages. Moreover, the first named States have been enabled to supply their people with the needful agricultural implements for raising supplies for themselves and for the Army. The States would necessarily, in all their importations, prove auxiliaries to the Government. I do not see "that the common object will be impeded instead of promoted" by the States chartering vessels unless (which I cannot think probable) the States should charter vessels with the view of excluding the Government. I confess I think every State should run the blockade with one or more vessels upon her own account—I suppose no State would run more than two—and if she charters them, I see no good reason why they should not be allowed to run them without restriction.

I cheerfully send a copy of your communication to each of the other Governors with whom I was associated, with a copy of this reply.

>Very Respectfully
>Your obedient servant
>M. L. Bonham

David G. Worth to ZBV   A&H:GLB

[*With enclosure*]

>Wilmington N.C.
>Nov. 15th. 1864

To His Excellency
Gov. Z. B. Vance
Raleigh N.C

Dear Sir

I am just in receipt of the enclosed order from Genl Whiting. This conflicts with the written & verbal orders I recd. from you on the 10th. inst.[1] I have been exerting my utmost efforts to execute your commands of that date and should have completed the work on tomorrow or at furthest on Thursday. Genl Whiting's order not only requires the removal of the teams & property by *sundown* today—which is a physical impossibility, but also directs that the employees, on arrival, be sent to the Enrolling Officer. I leave him to execute the order. I do not, in the face of the orders & instructions I have from you feel called on to obey his commands.

If he takes *all* the men I shall be left helpless with a large am't of property & effects uncared for and unprotected. You informed me on the 10th. inst that the men now unemployed at the works should not be interfered with till action should be taken in the premises by the Legislature. I stated this fact to the Genl. and also showed him your written orders to me & informed him that I had not yet completed the work. He replied that in any event his orders would be executed. I know of no special reason for this order outside of the one which has been influencing the Genl in all his orders in connection with these works for the past six months. Your telegram[2] directing me to go the coast of South Carolina, if I could leave, and look out a location for the works, has just been recd. I will go immediately after the present troubles are settled.

> Very Respectfully
> Yr. obt. Servt.
> D. G. Worth S. S. Comr.

[1]Not extant.
[2]Not extant.

[*Enclosure*]

William H. C. Whiting to David G. Worth   A&H:GLB

Copy

Hd. Qrs. Wilmington
Nov. 15th. 1864

Mr. Worth
Supt. State Salt Works
Present.

Sir

I am directed to inform you that it has become necessary to cause the removal of all Salt Works upon the Sound. Please to have your teams and movable property and all men belonging to State Salt Works moved at once—*today*. Notification has already been sent by telegraph to Cols. Tansill & Jackson to see to the execution of this order. After sun down today none but troops will be allowed outside the city lines. Send the employees on arrival to the Enrolling Officer. If it will be of any aid or advantage to the State the Qr. Mr. Dept. will forage your teams for their temporary use for such time as you may suggest. It is of importance that no time be lost.

> Very Respecfully
> W.H.C. Whiting.
> Maj. Gen.

ZBV to Jefferson Davis A&H:GLB

State of North Carolina
Executive Department
Raleigh Nov. 15th. 1864

To His Excellency
Jefferson Davis

Sir

I deem it my duty to address you in regard to the situation of Wilmington. I have just returned from a visit to the works below that City and find them all in excellent condition so far as I am able to judge, there seems to be nothing wanting but *troops*. If attacked in strong force I humbly conceive that its capture is inevitable unless strengthened by at least two brigades of veteran troops. The militia assembled & to assemble there, I fancy will be totally inadequate to resist a land attack in the rear of Fort Fisher which seems to be the point of real danger. In view of all the facts in the case, of which I presume the Commanding General keeps you sufficiently informed, I respectfully submit that Genl Lee should spare a few veterans as a nuclus for the raw troops defending Wilmington notwithstanding the great pressure upon his lines. Except for the moral effect involved in losing our Capital I cannot see that Richmond itself is of any greater importance to us now than Wilmington. To leave it entirely in the hands of Militia except the garrison I deem extremely injudicious.

Very Respectfully
Yr. obt. Servt.
Z. B. Vance.

David G. Worth to ZBV A&H:GP

[*Telegram*]

Wilmington Nov 16th 1864

To Gov Z B. Vance

The order for conscription of my men comes from War Dept The men are all here Genl Bragg will allow only the teamsters to return to Sound to move property. The balance will be in the way here what shall I do with them and the state & private teams

D G Worth
S S Comr

ZBV *to David G. Worth*   A&H:GLB

[*Telegram*]

Raleigh Nov. 16th. 64

D. G. Worth
Wilmington N.C.

The men shall not be conscribed without my consent. Inform Genl. Bragg that you have my orders to retain the men and to send as many as may be necessary to remove the property. If he prevents you by force let me know immediately

Z. B. Vance

ZBV *to Braxton Bragg*   A&H:GLB

[*Telegram*]

Raleigh Novr. 16th. 64

Genl Bragg
Wilmington

I learn with surprise that you have seized my salt hands and refuse to permit [*them*] to return to [*the*] sound to remove [*property*] This is altogether different treatment from what I expected and I inform you candidly I shall resist by every means in my power. These hands are not subject to conscription by the laws of our State

Z. B. Vance

Braxton Bragg to ZBV   A&H:GP

[*Telegram*]

Wilmington Nov 17th. 1864

To Gov Z B Vance

You are misinformed My only action was that reported to you <to N> in my letter of the fifteenth inst[1] Yesterday upon the report of your agent[2] that he was prevented by a Junior officer[3] from saving all the state property I gave the necessary orders to effect this object suspend any action until you hear from me in writing and I am sure you will have no cause to complain

Braxton Bragg

[1]Not extant.
[2]David G. Worth.
[3]William H. C. Whiting.

Braxton Bragg to ZBV   A&H:GLB

[*With enclosures*]

Hd. Qrs. Dept of N.C.
Wilmington 17th. November 1864.

His Excellency Z. B. Vance
Governor of N.C.

Sir.

Your dispatch of yesterday is just received and I have replied by telegram to correct the report which seems to have reached you

I enclose herewith a copy of my first instructions to Maj Genl. Whiting dated the 15th. At the time of giving those instructions I notified you by mail.

After doing so, I was gratified to learn you had previously given similar orders and that the removal was already in progress.

Yesterday evening your Agent called and informed me he had not secured all the State property when he was required to remove his hands. I gave him a written permission to send a guard back immediately, and at the same time directed that he be allowed to continue the operation of removal until all property was saved.

Upon the receipt of your dispatch of the morning which you will see has been based on erroneous information I caused the enclosed note, No 2, to be addressed to General Whiting.

I trust, Governor, you will find in my action, the best assurance that I can give, of a desire to avoid all cause of complaint, and to secure your cordial support instead of resistance.

> I am Sir:
> Very respectfully
> Your obt Servt.
> Braxton Bragg
> Genl. Comdg.

[Enclosure 1]

Francis S. Parker to William H. C. Whiting   A&H:GLB

> Hd. Qrs. 3d. Mil. Dist.
> Dept. of N.C. & So. Va.
> Wilmington N.C.
> Nov. 15th. 1864.

Major Gen. W. H. C. Whiting
Commanding &c. &c.
Wilmington.

General:

General Bragg directs that the State Salt Works on Masonboro Sound be suspended from operation and the personnel and material there of be removed for the present to a position of safety near this city.

> I am, General,
> Very Respectfully
> Your obt. Svt.
> Frank S. Parker
> Major & A.A.A.G.

[*Enclosure 2*]

Francis S. Parker to William H. C. Whiting   A&H:GLB

Hd. Qrs. 3d. Mil. Dist.
Dept. of N.C. & So Va.
Wilmington N.C
17th. Nov. 1864.

Major Genl. W. H. C. Whiting
Commanding &c. &c.
Wilmington

General:

I am directed to enclose you a copy of a dispatch[1] just received from his Excellency Governor Vance.

General Bragg desires that you will confine your official action in this matter to the removal of the men and material as required. in my communication of the 15th. inst. and he hopes you will extend every facility for the safe removal of all property. I am further instructed to say that the question of the conscription of these men is one beyond the jurisdiction of the military commander and must rest where the law and regulations place it, with the enrolling officer.

Very respectfully, General
Your obt. Svt.
Francis S. Parker
Major & A.A.A.G.

[1]ZBV to Braxton Bragg, November 16, 1864, in this volume.

David G. Worth to ZBV   A&H:GP

Wilmington N C
Novr. 18th. 1864.

To His Excellency
Govr. Z B Vance
Raleigh N C

Dr Sir—

The hands were allowed to return to the Sound yesterday to finish removing the property.

I now have nothing for the men to do except hauling wood. What shall I do with the surplus hands. It is expensive to feed them here unless they could be profitably employed. Would it not be well to allow them to go home for a few days?

I should like to have time to finish hauling the wood to the River. It is very much needed here. The town is bare of wood & no means of getting much brought here—

Very Res'fully
D. G. Worth S S comr

[*Endorsed*] Ansd. by telegraph

Z B V

Mary F. Lutterloh to ZBV   A&H:GP

Fayetteville Nov 19th 1864

To His Excellency Gov Vance

My dear Sir,

I have thought it not improper for me as President of the Cumberland Hospital Association to appeal to you in behalf of our poor working women, who have looked to the Association for employment, which they have received by means of a Contract entered into with the State to furnish Soldiers Shirts to the Department at Raleigh.

The exorbitant prices of provisions induced us to apply for a corresponding advance in the price of labor to save our Poor from suffering.

Hitherto our Cutter has been allowed 3 *cts* each for a shirt, and our seamstresses 75 cts each for making—The expense of baling and hauling has been defrayed by the Association—We think it but fair and just that the State should pay all the expenses connected with the Contract.

In reply to our appeal for an advance in the price of labor Mr. Dowd[1] writes that he will allow 5 cts a shirt for cutting and baling and $1. for making.

My dear Sir the Association has been paying 7 cts to our Cutter for cutting and baling—3 cts of which were paid by the state and 4 cts were added by the Association to save her from suffering, and we now ask for an advance, and also that the state shall pay all the expense.

I beg to assure you Sir that I have made the foregoing statement with no view of reflecting upon the a q m[2] who I doubt not is actuated by a sense of duty, but with an earnest desire that our noble old state should be more noble and more liberal to the dependants of our gallant soldiers now in the field.

I trust I need not assure you Sir, I have no personal interest to subserve in this matter, but have written in behalf of our seamstresses, who are seriously affected by the low price of labor.

I beg in the name of the County of Cumberland that a more remunerative price be allowed them.

Your kind attention to this Communication will much oblige

Yours very Respectfully
Mary F. Lutterloh, Pres't
Cumbd. Hosp. Association

[*Endorsed*] Maj Dowd—

Z B V

[F ansd. &c.]

[1]Maj. Henry A. Dowd, state quartermaster.
[2]Dowd.

Jefferson Davis to ZBV   A&H:VanPC

Richmond Va. Nov: 21, 1864

His Excellency
Z. B. Vance

Governor:
I have the honor to acknowledge the receipt of your letter of the 15th Inst:,[1] relative to the defences of Wilmington, and to inform you that proper attention shall be giveing to your suggestions, which the Secretary of War has been directed to communicate to Genl. R. E. Lee.

very respectfully & truly
Jeffn Davis

[1]In this volume.

ZBV to Joseph E. Brown   A&H:GLB

[*Telegram*]

Raleigh Nov. 22d.

Gov. Brown
Milledgeville Ga.

Can you sell or charter me an Engine and ten cars five feet guage? Please reply immediately and state the price.

Z. B. Vance

ZBV to Laurence S. Baker   A&H:GLB

State of North Carolina
Executive Department
Raleigh Nov. 22d. 1864

Brig. Genl. L. S. Baker

Dear Sir
I am informed that you have issued an order directing the owners of slaves, impressed to work on fortifications, that have run away to return said slaves or others in their place; and that upon a failure to do so, a guard will be sent to arrest said slaves. I have received information from the most reliable sources, that the effect of attempting to execute the order, will be to run the slaves from their owners and in many instances to the enemy. I deem it my duty to call your attention to the matter and to urge upon you the importance of so modifying the order as to prevent the happening of the result to which I have alluded.

Yours Very Respectfully
Z. B. Vance.

ZBV to Theophilus H. Holmes   A&H:GLB

State of North Carolina
Executive Department
Raleigh Nov. 23d. 1864

Genl. T. H. Holmes

Dr. Sir

Large numbers of exchanged N.C. prisoners of war are arriving here every day destitute of clothing and every other comfort. Maj. Pierce[1] refuses to issue to them any clothing although he has an abundance derived from the State for the supply of our own troops. As I cannot see these men suffer I have been giving them all supplies, though we may not receive any pay for them. Is there any reason why Maj. Pierce cannot supply them himself? It is worse than cruel to turn them off.

Very respectfully
Yr. obt. Servt.
Z. B. Vance

[1]Maj. W. W. Peirce, Confederate quartermaster stationed in Raleigh to issue clothing to returning Confederate prisoners of war. Tucker, *Zeb Vance*, 425.

William A. Graham to ZBV   A&H:VanPC

Richmond
Nov 29th 1864

His Excelly Z. B. Vance

Dear Sir

I have read your message[1] in some haste, but in general, think your recommendations wise and appropriate. I think it of great importance, that in any regulations on the subject of troops furnished to the Confed. Govt. there shall be a respectable body guard reserved of the sovreignty of the state. I write mainly to say, that I have heard of the introduction into our Legislature, of Resolutions[2] proposing negotiations for peace, through the agency of comrs. appointed by the States. I regret this movement, especially at a time when the enemy seems to have gained an advantage in Ga., and are overrunning a portion of that state. It will be seized upon by the enemy as a declaration favorable to them and will dispirit our own people, as a confession of despondency. I hope there is no danger of the resolution receiving the approbation of the Legislature. Such a proceeding /must/ lead to embarrassment here, and very seriously embroil the state with the Confed. Govt. It will also awaken jealousies in the other states, which will operate to the injury of the common cause.

It is difficult to divine the future, but I am not without hope, that after the termination of this campaign, say between New Year and March, the enemy will very seriously consider whether it is expedient to prepare for expeditions next year upon the grand scale necessary to success—and that after the opening of Congress at Wash'g'ton, /we/ may see overtures of peace. I regret, that our Govt. seems so little inclined to make offers to take the initiative, which I think it might do with propriety, but if the enemy move, I trust it may lead to good results.

Mr. Henry[3] of Ten. made a speech today on his resolutions, defining position, and the subject was referred to the Committee on Foreign relations.

The state of affairs in Ga. occasions some gloom here, and it is somewhat added to by a most inopportune and illconsidered application for a general suspension of Hab. Corp., which I fear is to be granted.

I write in haste & remain

very truly Yours
W. A. Graham

[1]Not extant.

[2]Resolutions introduced in the state Senate by John Pool and in the House by Daniel Fowle "to initiate negotiations for an honorable peace." The resolutions were not passed. See *Journal of the Senate of North Carolina, 1864-65*, 26-27, 38, and *Journal of the House of Representatives of North Carolina, 1864-65*, 55. See also William A. Graham to ZBV, November 29, 1864, in Hamilton, Williams, and Peacock, *Papers of Graham*, 6:195-197.

[3]Gustavus Adolphus Henry, Confederate senator from Tennessee, a strong supporter of Jefferson Davis and a Confederate "ultra nationalist." Current et al., *Encyclopedia of the Confederacy*, 2:763-764.

William Smith to ZBV   A&H:GP

[*With enclosure*]

State of Virginia,
Executive Department,
Richmond,
Nov. 30, 1864

Gov. Z. B. Vance

Dear Sir:

I regret that we cannot supply you with the salt you want.[1] The enclosed letter from the Salt Agent of the State will furnish the explanation.

I am very anxious to get your bill for the cloth you kindly furnished my State. Oblige me by forwarding it without delay.

Very truly Yours
Wm Smith

[1]See ZBV to William Smith, October 27, 1864, in this volume.

[*Enclosure*]

John N. Clarkson to William Smith   A&H:GP

Saltville 25th. Nov. 1864

Hon Wm. Smith
Gov of Va.

Dear Sir

I have delayed answering your letter and telegram because I had hopes of being able to furnish some Salt for the Governor of North Carolina.

You are aware of my difficulties during this year. My litigation with Chs. Scott & Co, the burning of New River Bridge and the Other Bridges and the total suspension of transportation on the Road, prevented me from making salt. I am much behind with my contracts with the State and the Confederate Government, so that I cannot spare any salt from my own Works.

Stuart Buchanan & Co owe me on the contract with the Joint Committee of the General Assembly of Va. about 5000 bushels of Salt, which I was in hopes, I could turn over to you. I have been negotiating with them for the delivery of it, but find that I cannot get it.

I am therefore reluctantly compelled to say that it is out of my power now to deliver any Salt to the Governor of North Carolina.

> Yours truly
> Jno N Clarkson
> Supt Salt Works.

James A. Seddon to ZBV   SHC:Car

[*Telegram*]

Richmond
Nov 30 1864

To His Ex Z B Vance

There is urgent need for more forces to meet the advance of Genl Shermans army & to prevent its junction with Forces being landed & threatening movement near Pocotaligo latest accounts make it still doubtful whether Sherman is not marching on Augusta Genl Wheeler has just telegraphed that the infantry of the enemy have <burned> hurried to A road leading to that city Genl Bragg has suggested that as the movements near Pocotaligo frees Wilmington from the danger of attack the reserves from North Carolina should be sent to him & the matter is now under Genl Lees consideration it would be as well as patriotic on the part of North Ca. To give all assistance possible to defie or frustrate the design of Sherman while remote from her borders Genl Beauregard Telegraphs his opinion that Shermans ultimate design [is] to reinforce Genl Grant

> Jas A Seddon
> Secty War

ZBV to P. B. Hawkins   A&H:GLB

[*Telegram*]

Raleigh Dec. 1st.

P. B. Hawkins[1]
Saltville Va.

Dont have a bushel for any body but N. Ca. Wait for orders

Z. B. Vance

[1]North Carolina's representative for the delivery of salt. It is uncertain why Vance referred to him as "general." See ZBV to J. G. Dent, Dec. 2, 1864, in this volume.

ZBV to William Smith   A&H:GLB

[*Telegram*]

Raleigh Dec. 1st.

Gov. Smith
Richmond Va.

Being unable to get any salt hauled from Saltville, I have at length hired foreign trains and sent there. Your Board of Public Works have ordered them to haul one fourth for Confederate Govt. or lay off on side track. I respectfully ask to be relieved from this. You have two trains running in the State. Answer immediately.

Z. B. Vance

ZBV to William Smith   A&H:GLB

[*With enclosure*]

State of North Carolina
Executive Department
Raleigh Dec. 2d. 1864

His Excellency
Gov. William Smith
Richmond Va.

Gov.

Our State Salt Works at Wilmington are broken up by the Confederate
Authorities and we have been unable to get any Salt transported over the
Roads in your State till I hired trains and forwarded, hoping by this means
to procure this indispensible article. But it seems from Telegrams, Copies
of which I enclose to you herein, that even this last resort is not to avail
us. Is the action indicated in these Telegrams by virtue of the authorities
of Virginia? If so, I deem it exceedingly unneighborly and unkind. I hope
however that it is not so, and that the Authorities of your State will, instead
of interfering to obstruct, see to it, that we shall be permitted to bring away
our Salt, upon such terms as it becomes good neighbors to grant and receive

Very Respectfully
Yr. obt. Servt.
Z. B. Vance

[*Enclosure*]

P. B. Hawkins to ZBV   A&H:GLB

[*Telegram*]

Saltville
Dec 2d. 1864

Gov. Vance

Besides hauling a fourth (¼) Salt am notified that our train must haul
wood to the Virginia works to make Salt for the C. S. Government. In
consequence of their interference our trains have left us.

P. B. Hawkins

ZBV to J. G. Dent A&H:GLB

Null[1]

State of North Carolina
Executive Department
Raleigh Dec. 2d. 1864

J. G. Dent Esqr.

Sir

You are hereby authorized to act as Agent for the transportation of Salt for the State of North Carolina from Saltville to Danville. The terms on which you will render this service are as follows: You will take at Saltville one half of the load of each train to be delivered at Danville and the State of North Carolina will pay one half of the expenses of the trip. This arrangement to continue so long as the parties to it have any Salt at Saltville. The above arrangement to be subject to the approval of Genl. P. B. Hawkins and to be inoperative until approved by him.

Respectfully
Z. B. Vance

[1]The word "Null" was written across the letter-book document.

ZBV to P. B. Hawkins A&H:GLB

Null[1]

State of North Carolina
Executive Department
Raleigh December 2d. 1864

Genl. P. B. Hawkins

My Dr. Sir

Mr. J. G. Dent has applied to me with some propositions for the transportation of Salt, and I have given him an appointment in accordance with them which appointment I have made subject to your approval. I am unable at this distance to take any control of the Details of this business and can only say to you that your approval or disapproval of Mr. Dents Agency must be based on knowledge in your possession as to the facts of the case.

If you can by any means in your power secure a train to transport all of our Salt in good time you will do so at once. You will also see that the expense (½ the trip) are no greater than the State would otherwise have to pay. With these remarks I leave the matter to your judgement

Respectfully
Z. B. Vance

[1]The word "Null" was written across the letter-book document.

ZBV to James A. Seddon   A&H:GLB

[*Telegram*]

Raleigh Decr. 5th. 1864

Hon. J. A. Seddon
Richmond Va.

Having broken up my Salt Works at Wilmington, you have now conscribed my hands at Saltville,[1] and stopped those there. Please inform me where N.C. is to get Salt or how people can live without it?

Z. B. Vance

[1]For more details, see Jeptha M. Israel to ZBV, December 4, 1864, A&H:GP.

ZBV to Robert Ould   A&H:GLB

State of North Carolina
Executive Department
Raleigh Decr. 5th. 1864

Judge Ould
Agt. Of Exchange
Richmond Va.

Dr. Sir
There is a proposition before our Legislature to appropriate £5,000 Stirling, for the relief of N.C. prisoners of war. It is supposed the arrangement

made by the C. States will be sufficient. Please inform me if you think it will? Or if not sufficient to make all of our prisoners comfortable can this State get the privilege of shipping one hundred bales to N. York for this purpose and save our exchange? An early answer will oblige.

Very resply Yrs
Z. B. Vance

William Smith to ZBV   A&H:GP

State of Virginia,
Executive Department,
Richmond,
Dec. 6, 1864

To His Excellency
Gov. Vance

Sir:

I have yours of the 2nd Inst:,[1] in reference to the embarrassments in obtaining salt for your State. I regret the existence of these difficulties, and will endeavor to have them removed.

I have the honor to be
Most resply. Yours
Wm Smith

[*Endorsed*] File & copy

Z B V

[1]In this volume.

John C. Vaughn to ZBV   A&H:GLB

Hd. Qrs. Cavy. Forces E. Tenn
Greenville Tenn Dec. 6th. 1864

To His Excellency Gov. Vance
Raleigh N.C.

Dear Sir

Information has just reached me that two young men by name, Nathaniel Miller and George Collins while on their way to this command some three weeks since were cut off from a detachment under the command of Capt. Atkinson—by bushwackers, and while passing through Ashe County were arrested by the Civil Authorities (I presume) and lodged in Jefferson Jail accused of taking some horses in an illegal way. Shortly after their confinement they were taken out of jail by three men—two of whose names are Norris /citizens/ of Watauga County, and the other Petty said to be a deserter from some Georgia Regt. and were murdered in a most brutal and inhuman way.

Young Miller was a member of the first Tenn Cavy, joined it when he was fifteen years of age and has been a noble and gallant soldier ever since. He was beloved and respected by every member of his Regt. Young Collins had just made his way out through the Federal lines to join the army and was only Sixteen years old. So far as his friends and acquaintances in this army (and there are many who have known him from infancy) know naught could be said against his character and reputation in any way. These young men situated as they were, cut off and chased in a strange country by bushwackers may have taken the horses as they were accused and it may be that it was necessary for their personal safety, but be that as it may their execution was most heinous and brutal, and the vile perpetrators of this deed deserve to be executed by fire. I know you have no sympathy with such offenders, and the recital of this deed is no doubt as horrifying to your feelings as it was to mine. But I hope through you that your civil officers will have these offenders arrested and speedily brought to the justice they so much deserve. Believing therefore that you will take such steps as will insure the arrest and close confinement of these men and all those who have been accessory in any way to the murder of these innocent boys and hoping soon to hear of the arrest and punishment of the vile perpetrators of this crime, I have the honor to be—

Very Respectfully,
Yr. obt. svt.
John C. Vaugn,[1]
Brig Genl. C.S.A.

[1]John Crawford Vaughn, commanding Confederate forces in East Tennessee. Ezra J. Warner, *Generals in Gray: Lives of the Confederate Commanders* (Baton Rouge: Louisiana State University Press, 1959), 316-317.

ZBV *to James A. Seddon*   A&H:GLB

State of North Carolina
Executive Department
Raleigh Decr. 8th. 1864

Hon. James A. Seddon
Secty. at War
Richmond Va.

I have to call your attention again to a violation of the rights of citizens of this State in their arbitrary arrest by the military and transportation beyond the State for impressment. Henry P. Retter late a Surgeon in the 8th. N. C. T. and a citizen of Camden Co. N.C. was arrested a few days since by Col. Gillead Comdg. at Weldon on suspicion of disloyalty and sent to Richmond for incarceration without entering at all into the question of his guilt or innocence. I think I am clear in saying that such removal beyond the limits of this State is an infraction of his legal rights, and an infringment of the jurisdiction of North Carolina. In a letter addressed by yourself to me in January 1863 responding to the demand of the Legislature of North Carolina for the return of one J. R. Graves[1] then held in Richmond on a charge of disloyalty, you admitted fully the impropriety and illegality of arresting a citizen of this State and transporting him to Virginia. In speaking of the reasons in possession of the Department for supposing the said Graves a spy you say, "As such (that is a citizen of No. Ca.) while amenable to arrest as a spy on sufficient grounds, or even as a traitor, he could with no propriety or legality be removed from the State, but should be handed over to the appropriate authorities civil or military in that State to be dealt with according to law" and again "that there can be neither prudence nor justification for not promptly admitting the error committed by his removal and rectifying it by his immediate return and delivery under your Excellency's demand." Extremely gratified as I was at this prompt and full concession of the rights of North Carolina's citizens, I have been constantly pained and irritated by an almost weekly repetition of the offence until it has become no longer tolerable. I have therefore respectfully to demand that the said Henry P. Retter be returned to the jurisdiction of North Carolina to be dealt with by due course of law, and to request that you will cause such orders to be issued to military commanders in N.C. as will in future prevent such arbitrary and illegal proceedings so well calculated to disturb that harmony which should exist between the two Governments. I am Sir

> Very Resply
> Yr. obt. Servt.
> Z. B. Vance.

[1]Not extant, but see ZBV to George V. Strong, January 1, 1863, in Johnston and Mobley, *Papers of Vance*, 2:1-3.

ZBV to Washington C. Kerr   A&H:GLB

> State of North Carolina
> Executive Department
> Raleigh Decr. 10th. 1864

Prof W. C. Kerr[1]
State Geologist
Davidson College N.C.

In confering upon you the appointment of State Geologist vice Prof Emmons decd.[2] it was not my intention to have you continue the survey on the Scale designed & pursued by your predecessor, the situation of the country rendering that in my opinion undesirable at present.[3] You are desired to confine yourself principally to such operations as will conduce to the selection of proper locations for the establishment of manufactories of steel, iron, blue stone, copperas, mineral medecines and the various articles of indispensible domestic necessity. Of course it is not intended that any such factories shall be established at the expense of the State, as all such should be self sustaining. You will therefore expend as little of the appropriation as possible. I am Sir,

Very resptly yours
Z. B. Vance.

[1]Washington Caruthers Kerr, professor of chemistry, mineralogy, and geology at Davidson College, 1857-1862. ZBV appointed him state geologist in 1864, but hardships prevented him from granting Kerr a regular salary or work. Gov. Jonathan Worth reappointed him in 1866. *Dictionary of North Carolina Biography*, s.v. "Kerr, Washington Caruthers."

[2]Ebenezer Emmons, geologist, educator, and physician from Massachusetts, who was Kerr's predecessor as head of the North Carolina Geological Survey. He served in that office from 1852 to his death in 1863. *Dictionary of North Carolina Biography*, s.v. "Emmons, Ebenezer."

[3]See Washington C. Kerr to ZBV, December 1, 1864, A&H:GP.

Robert Ould to ZBV   A&H:GP

Richmond
Dec 13th 1864

Hon. Z. B. Vance

Dear Sir

Your letter of the 5th inst.[1] has just been received. I hope and believe the efforts of the Confederate Government will be Sufficient to Supply the wants of all our Soldiers in captivity. At the Same time I See no objection to your good old State contributing what quota of means She chooses to aid the Confederate fund. I do not think the U. S. authorities will allow *you* to ship the cotton. The Confederate authorities will however make a shipment on a U. S. vessel from Some port hereafter to be designated. You can Send on the Same vessel what cotton you may name. You however will experience great difficulty in distributing the proceeds of the Sale amongst North Carolina Soldiers. They are Scattered amongst all the Federal prisons, Some twenty in number. It will give me pleasure to aid you in any endeavours you may make for the relief of your people.

Respectfully
yr. obt. svt.
Ro. Ould
Agent of Exchange

¹In this volume.

ZBV *to James A. Seddon*   A&H:GLB

State of North Carolina
Executive Department
Raleigh Decr. 13th. 1864

Hon James A. Seddon
Secty. At War

Dr. Sir

I earnestly desire to secure your action in behalf of the mountain country of Western N. Carolina now under the command of Col J.[*John*] D. [*B.*] Palmer. There are troops enough there to afford ample protection both against the enemy and the tories and deserters, who throng the mountains murdering and robbing the citizens, if under proper control and management. Col [*William Holland*] Thomas is worse than useless, he is a positive injury to that country. His command is a favorite resort for deserters, numbers of them I learn are on his rolls, who do no service, he is disobedient of orders and invariably avoids the enemy when he advances. Col. Palmer is a good bureau officer but I think unfitted for field service, especially of the peculiar character required in that country.

I respectfully and earnestly recommend that you ask the President to appoint Collett Leaventhrope [*Leventhorpe*] late Colonel of the 11th. N.C.T. a Brigadier and place him in command of that District. This gallant officer is now a Brigadier of Home Guards in the service of this State and has the universal confidence of our people civil and military. I am earnest in the opinion that he more than any other man could restore quiet and order in that country, I am Sir,

Very Respectfully
Yr. obt. svt.
Z. B. Vance

James A. Seddon to ZBV   A&H:GP

War Dept. Decr. 15th. 64

His Excy Z. B. Vance
Govr. of N.C

Sir

I have instructed Major J. Blair Hoge of the Adj Genl's department, whom I would commend to your special consideration, to visit Raleigh and confer with you with the view of obtaining from you for the immediate supply of the Forces in Virginia and North Carolina any commissary stores you may have at command. From various causes, which Major Hoge will more fully explain, there is at present lamentable Deficiency of provisions, especially of meat for the supply of those forces and there is imminent danger, that unless unusual sources of supply can at once be commanded, the armies, on which the defence and safety of both states depend, cannot be maintained in service. This is naturally the season of severest trial on the Commissariat, and several untoward circumstances, concurring with the depreciation of our currency, have materially enhanced the difficulties of that <Commissariat> / Branch of Service/. Understanding that you had accumulated, both at Home and in the Islands, considerable stores of provisions, I do not hesitate, relying on your sagacity and patriotism to perceive and appreciate the emergency and its necessities, to appeal to you to sell or lend to the Department all such stores as you can command. Major Hoge is fully authorized to arrange with you the terms of transfer either as an accommodation or a sale, and I would earnestly request that you will view his proposition with favor and enter into some satisfactory arrangement with all practicable dispatch.

Very Truly Yrs
James A Seddon
Secy of War.

[*Endorsed*] Write informing the Sec'y that we have given him half what we had here & transferred all our bacon at the islands &c Copy & file

ZBV

Regret that we had not more

James A. Seddon to ZBV   A&H:GP

Richmond Va.
War Department
15th Decr. 1864

His Excellency Z B Vance
Govr. of North Carolina

Sir.

The Hon Mr. [*William N. H.*] Smith of N.C. called the attention of the department to the case of Mr. Ritter[1] on the 10th Inst & requested that an investigation might take place, which was ordered. The result of the investigation was an order for his discharge

Very Respectfully
Your obt svt
James A. Seddon
Secy of War.

[1]See ZBV to James A. Seddon, December 8, 1864, in this volume.

ZBV to Jefferson Davis   A&H:GLB

State of North Carolina
Executive Department
Raleigh Dec 16th. 1864

His Excellency
Jefferson Davis
President C.S.A.

Dear Sir

I inclose you a copy of a communication[1] informing me that the House of Commons of the General Assembly of this State has passed a resolution requesting me to correspond with your protesting against the cruel and inhuman manner in which slaves conscribed from our citizens, are now treated, and request that the evil be immediately remedied.

Rumors and statements are constantly arriving here, that the slaves conscribed and assigned to labor on the works at and near Wilmington are treated with great cruelty and inhumanity, by being overworked, almost starved, not half clad and lodged without shelter, by reason of which they are suffering great mortality. Not only the interest of their Masters and the Country, but also humanity forbids the continuance of such a state of things. And I cannot doubt that as soon as your attention is called to it, you will take the necessary steps to remedy the evil complained of.

> Very Respectfully
> Your obt. servt.
> Z. B. Vance

[1]See Richard S. Donnell to ZBV, December 16, 1864, A&H:GP.

ZBV to James A. Seddon   A&H:GLB

Raleigh Dec 17th. 1864

Hon J. A. Seddon
Richmond Va.

What arrangement can be made with C.S. for paying and clothing the Troops of this State not turned over? They serve all the time under Confederate authority and the Legislature desire to avoid the expense. Please reply today.

> Z. B. Vance

ZBV to John C. Vaughn   A&H:GLB

Ex. Dept. of N. Ca.
Raleigh Decr. 17th./64

Brig Gen J. C. Vaugn
Abingdon Va.

Dear Sir

I have the honor to receive your letter of the 6th inst.[1] and take the earliest moment to reply. I regret exceedingly the circumstances you mention of the murder (for such in legal contemplation it is) of Miller and Collins of your command of which I had heard something before. Upon making such enquiry as was possible since the reception of your letter, I learn that the young men stole two horses from a Mrs. Norris the mother of the young men who followed and arrested them. They were placed in Jail in Jefferson and there taken out soon after by one Capt. Long a a [sic] Militia officer in company with the two young Norris' under pretence of carrying them to the Jail of Wataga [Watauga] County for safe keeping and were killed on the way. My informants an entirely reliable & loyal gentleman, says that the young Norris' were instigated entirely by Long who is regarded as being to blame for the whole matter. Long was subsequently arrested by an officer (name unknown to me) and fifteen men from your command and taken off no one knowing his fate. I beg to remind you that should he be executed by your men, as was threatened, it would be also murder. If returned to me I will have him & the Norris' dealt with by the Civil law. Otherwise I shall not feel called upon to move in the matter. And now General I am glad of an opportunity to say a word to you on this matter of horse stealing & general plundering of the citizens by the Cavalry. No one can more sincerely deplore this *quasi* warfare between the troops and the citizens than myself. But Sir, the conduct of many of your men & those of the late Genl. Morgan[2] in parts of our mountain country has been sufficient to drive our people to desperation. The stories of robbery & outrage by them would fill a volume, and would fully justify the immediate & indiscriminate slaughter of all men caught with the proofs of their villainy. From looking upon them as their gallant protectors, thousands in their bitterness of heart have come to regard them as their deadliest enemies & to wonder no longer at the recital of Yankees atrocities. How much of all this is due to the lawless soldiery, or how much to the permission & connivance of their officers I cannot say. I have been a Soldier myself & knowing the difficulties even of restraining infantry, I do not wish to be uncharitable to any gentleman holding a Confederate Commission. But when men are required to mount themselves and having no horses today parade on good ones tomorrow, it is difficult to believe that their officers do not know how their men get horses. Hence a general stealing of horses & an occasional slaughter of the thief. I am frank to say that I approve of it & regret that it occurs so seldom. With ample powers to impress & the enemy's country so often in the reach of our Cavalry, it seems to me General that that [sic] the system is utterly indefensible on any grounds whatever. Discipline might avoid it, but death to the offender certainly will. I have the honor to be, Genl,

Very Respectfully
Yr. obt. svt.
Z. B. Vance.

¹In this volume.

²John Hunt Morgan, Kentuckian, brigadier general, and guerrilla, whose cavalry raided into Tennessee. He was killed in that state in September 1864. Current et al., *Encyclopedia of the Confederacy*, 3:1086-1087.

William H. C. Whiting to ZBV   A&H:GP

[*Telegram*]

Wilmington 18 Dec 1864

To Gov Z. B Vance
Raleigh

A very large fleet very formidable under Porter¹ with very large land forces twenty thousand 20,000 under Butler² left Fortress Monroe on Friday to attack Wilmington the advance squadron is already at Beaufort.

W. H. C. Whiting
Maj Genl

¹Rear Adm. David Dixon Porter commanding a Federal naval expedition that launched an unsuccessful attack on Fort Fisher near Wilmington on December 23-24, 1864. Current et al., *Encyclopedia of the Confederacy*, 2:611-612; Faust et al., *Encyclopedia of Civil War*, 594.

²Maj. Gen. Benjamin Franklin Butler commanding the land forces in the unsuccessful attack on Fort Fisher on December 23-24, 1864. Current et al., *Encyclopedia of the Confederacy*, 2:611-612; Faust et al., *Encyclopedia of Civil War*, 98-99.

James A. Seddon to ZBV   A&H:GP

[*Telegram*]

Richmond Dec 18 1864

To Gov Z B Vance

I regret to have no authority to pay or clothe the State troops to which you refer¹ a special act of Congress will be necessary

J A Seddon
Secy of War

[*Endorsed*] Copy & file

ZBV

[1]See ZBV to James A. Seddon, December 17, 1864, in this volume.

Braxton Bragg to ZBV   A&H:GP

[*Telegram*]

Wilmington 20 Dec 1864

His Excellency Gov Vance

a heavy fleet off armed steamers & transports now assembling off New Inlet[1] all the assistance you can give us is now needed

Braxton Bragg

[1]Located north of Smith's Island, New Inlet was the most important of two navigable passages to the Cape Fear River and the port of Wilmington. Fort Fisher protected the inlet. Barrett, *Civil War in North Carolina*, 245-246.

ZBV to Alexander R. Lawton   A&H:GLB

State of North Carolina
Executive Department
Raleigh Dec 20th. 1864

Genl. A. R. Lawton Q. M. G.
Richmond

General

I have the honor to inform you that I have purchased in the Eastern part of the State twenty thousand (20,000) bushels of Corn. This Corn I desire to have transported to this place. As the question of transportation is one of some importance in the present state of our rail roads may I ask that you order Capt. S. W. Venable A. Q. M. at Weldon to receive this corn at that place and also that you order Capt. W. E. Price, A. Q. M. Raleigh to turn

over to my Quarter Master at Raleigh the quantity of corn receipted for by
Capt Venable from the tithe corn which will be delivered to Capt. Pierce.

Very Respectfully
Z. B. Vance
Govr. &c

Proclamation by ZBV   A&H:GLB

By the Governor of North Carolina
A Proclamation

Whereas the long expected attack upon our only remaining seaport is
now about to be made, and our State is also likely to be invaded at other
points by an enemy to whom mercy & civilization are alike unknown and
unregarded; and whereas all the organized forces of the State already ordered
to the front may still be insufficient to roll back the tide which threatens
us with worse than death, and to drive from our doors a fate horrible to
contemplate:

Now, therefore I, Zebulon B. Vance, Governor of the State of North
Carolina, relying upon the loyalty and devotion of her Citizens, do issue this
my proclamation, commanding and abjuring all good people, whether by law
subject to military duty or not, who may be able to stand behind breastworks
and fire a musket of all ages and conditions, to rally at once to the defence
of their country and hurry to Wilmington. And I do appeal to every man
who has the spirit of a freeman in his bosom who has a spark of the fire or a
drop of the blood of the heroes of the great army of the great captain in his
veins to come and come at once. The man who hangs back now because the
law does not compel him go and consoles himself with the much abused and
mean spirited plea that he can "be more useful at home" will find it hard to
make us believe that he is not pleading the cause of cowardice or disloyalty.
The country needs their help *now*, and that help must be given in this hour
of distress, or they must own that their souls are only fitted to enjoy the
freedom purchased with other men's blood. For a few days all men physically
able are needed at the front and especially do we need the example of all
those who aforetime panted for the fray, while it was yet at a distance, and
snuffed the battle while it was yet afar off. Let every man physically able
then hurry with his blanket to Wilmington, where arms and rations will
be furnished, and let those left behind mount themselves and patrol their

counties, looking after the women and children and preserving order. Your Governor will meet you at the front and will share with you the worse.

Given under my hand and the Great Seal of the State. Done at our City of Raleigh, on the 20th. day of December 1864

Zebulon B. Vance

ZBV to James A. Seddon   A&H:GLB

State of North Carolina
Executive Department
Raleigh Dec 21st. 1864

Hon James A Seddon
Secty of War

Sir

I enclose to you a copy of a joint resolution[1] passed by the General Assembly of this State, requesting me to "bring to the attention of the proper Confederate authorities" the fact that "many citizens of this State, pronounced by the proper Medical Examining Boards unfit for field service, have nevertheless been required to perform such service in the Battalion commanded by Maj. H /(Hahr) F. J./[2] have contrary to law and without necessity." In obedience to the dictates of law and the principles of humanity involved, no less than the Resolution referred to, I have to express the hope that you will see that those men, thus placed in their present position contrary to law and where their well ascertained unfortunate physical condition renders it impossible for them to be of service to their country be forthwith released.

Very Respectfully
Your obt. Servt.
Z. B. Vance

[1]Not extant.

[2]F. J. Hahr, commander of the Nineteenth "light duty" Battalion, served at Wilmington from October 1864 until January 1865. Clark, *Histories of Regiments from North Carolina*, 4:383.

ZBV *to James A. Seddon*   A&H:GLB

State of North Carolina
Executive Department
Raleigh Dec. 21st. 1864

Hon James A Seddon
Secretary of War
Richmond Va.

Sir

I have the honor of inclosing to you a copy of a Resolution of the House of Commons of the General Assembly of this State[1] requesting me to communicate with the Authorities at Richmond, with a view to relieving our unfortunate maimed and disabled veterans from the cruelties consequent upon rigid enforcement of an order recently issued by the Adjutant and Inspector General by which all wounded and sick soldiers, who can without /serious/ detriment to their health, are required to report to their respective commands. In doing so you will permit me to express the confident belief that there can be no hesitation in relieving these noble veterans who bear in their persons the permanent marks of their devotion to their country from those hardships and indignities which are too great to permit me to believe they could have been intended by said order, but which must necessarily follow the rigid inforcement of all its provisions.

Very Respectfully
Your obt. Servt.
Z. B. Vance.

[1]See Richard S. Donnell to ZBV, December 19, 1864, A&H:GP.

Inaugural Address by ZBV   A&H:VanPC

Fellow Citizens
<Gentlemen,>

Two years ago I was inaugurated Chief Magistrate of our honoured State in the midst of war and /all/ its <confusing consequences> /attending confusion./ I was called from the army, untried, and untrammelled by pledges or promises, to this responsible and embarrassing position. The generous confidence of my countrymen took for granted my abilities and my patriotism. For my elected term I have gone in and out before them, in the zealous & faithful performance of my imposed duties during such a time, and under such circumstances of trial, as none of my predecessors have been called on to endure. The most unanimous verdict ever rendered in favour of a public servant by the people of N. Carolina, has testified /alike to/ their approbation and their forbearance, and placed me here to renew my stewardship. Surely I have been fortunate and my countrymen have been generous.

Again I make no new promises, lay down no new principles. The thing that has been is the thing that shall be, God helping me. As I have laboured so will I labour, for the renown and substantial good, of the people who have trusted me. The principles evolved by my public acts in the past, shall continue to guide me in the future. Elected without regard to party, I shall endeavor to know no man after the manner of a partizan, except in so far as it may become necessary to distinguish between those who would forward & those who would thwart my principles & aims. My friends shall be the friends of my country; my foes shall be my countrys enemies. But as the difficulties of my position are still greater than when I first assumed its duties, as the darkness which obscures the statesman path is even blacker than before, I can but sincerely hope that your charity may increase accordingly. No living man could hope to avoid censure in times like these, with issues of life and death resting upon his hands from which he may not, dare not shrink. I trust however in the reflecting generosity of those who placed me under these heavy burdens. So long as they will beleive that I am patriotic, that I am sincerely and with singleness of heart devoted to the land of my birth and of my unchangable love, so long shall my path be smoothed and my labours lightened by that spirit which hopeth all things, and with all things.

Should I live to meet, at the close of this tempestuous and troubled period of office upon which I am now entering, the same mead of approbation as that with which the passing one has been honored, then indeed <should> / shall/ I be satisfied that God has /been with me &/ aided me to be useful to my country in the darkest hour of her history. Events are with Him; let us, let all men, exert our utmost strength for the honour & independence of our country.

There is one great danger against which I earnestly pray our people to /be/ warned. Disunion, distraction, division; of sentiment & aim; leading to civil [feuds], domestic violence and political death. If crushed by overwhelming numbers on the field of battle we are guiltless of the unavoidable result. But we can surely avoid, if we will, internal violence & self destruction. There is no greater enemy of his country & of his race than him who would foment <the> /our/ passions to this end. Let all of our movements whether of peace

or war, be in solid column; our people at home as our brothers at the front /
standing/ *in line of battle, facing one way & together*! Then victory is not
only doubly assured but thrice glorious, and defeat will be robbed of half its
calamities.

[*Endorsed*] *Private* Gov. Vance's Inaugural Address delivered on Thursday
the 22d. Dec. 1864

Robert E Lee to ZBV   A&H:GP

[*Telegram*]

Hd. Qrs A. N. V. via Petersburg
Dec 23 1864

Gov Z B. Vance
Raleigh

Can you aid Genl Bragg to subsist troops sent to Wilmington

R. E. Lee

William A. Graham to ZBV   A&H:VanPC

Private—

Richmond
Decr. 23rd 1864.

His Excely. Z. B. Vance

Dear Sir

I had intended to defer a reply to your letter of the 16th. inst.,[1] untill I
should reach home, (as I supposed tomorrow), but being detained here, a day
by accident I avail myself of the leisure to write you.

I deeply deplore the dissensions among friends which your letter reveals,
and which is easily to be inferred from the reports of proceedings of the
General Assembly. In the varying aspects of our affairs, there is much room
for difference of opinion, & much occasion for charity & toleration. I
regard the salvation of this country, if saved it can be, as in the hands of the
conservative men, who opposed the revolution, while there was a chance
to avert it, but when it became inevitable, have nobly done their duty in

endeavoring to give it success. I regret any division among them, because of their power to do good, and the sincerity of their patriotism in endeavouring to take care of the country—and this the more, because their opponents have been from the beginning and are now united as a party with their old animosities, political and almost personal, unabated, and their spirit of proscription whenever there [is] a crumb of patronage <unabated> as intense as ever. The advent of the conservatives to power in North Carolina, was the spontaneous effusion of the popular will, designed to rebuke faction and proscription, <will> /while/ determined to stand by the country in the dreadful struggle through which it was destined to pass. I would exhort those therefore /who/ have been as brethren heretofore to bear and forebear much, before coming to a final estrangement.

The country is now in an agony of trial. That it becomes us, not to quail, but to act manly parts, is the dictate not only of patriotism, but of interest to render to the common cause, our due need of service, but not in so doing, to surrender the sovereignty or safety of the state. Self defence is the first law of nature, and our first best country ever is at home." It is wise therefore to retain that force, which is exempted from conscription by law, for the purposes of the state itself—and still wiser to abstain from intestine divisions which may lead to the shedding of fraternal blood. At the same time, the common cause must be supported, disorder must be suppressed and society made safe. While these general principles, should in my opinion, guide our action, you in your public position which you hold by almost the unanimous voice of the people, can afford to be tolerant, without any danger /of the imputation/ of yielding from unworthy motives, and in fact not yielding at all any vital principle. Criticism from friends as well as adversaries is to be expected in public life. When it exceeds just bounds & becomes personal, every one is the best judge in his own case, of the notice to be taken of it. So far as may depend on my counsels, you may be assured, in case of difference of the remonstrances of friendship, rather than the cavilling of enmity. I shall spend a week at home, and may possibly visit Raleigh for a day, and see you.

The military situation is threatening. No official accounts as yet from Hood.[2] If the reality be as bad as the report in the northern papers, the expedition is a disastrous failure, and the hope of recovering Tennessee is lost. Lee's army here is sufficient for defence. Nothing for three or four days, from Savannah & Sherman. Raids reported north of this on the central R. Road, and a formidable expedition beyond Lynchburg towards the salt works. Hab. Cor. [habeas corpus] will be shorn of much of its former hideousness, but is still unnecessary & offensive. The amelioration has been gained by the discussion of the subject since last winter. The enemy seems bent on active operations during the winter. I had hoped there would be such a cessation, as would allow some effort at negotiation. Both Govts. seem to me sadly deficient in tact on this head.

> I remain very faithfully yours
> W. A. Graham

[1]Not extant.
[2]Commanding the Confederate Army of Tennessee, Gen. John Bell Hood defended against the expedition of Gen. William T. Sherman in Georgia. Rather than oppose Sherman's march to the sea, Hood attacked northward into Tennessee to strike's Sherman's army in the rear and cut its supply line. The maneuver failed, however, and Hood lost a large portion of his army. Current et al., *Encyclopedia of the Confederacy*, 2:789-790.

Braxton Bragg to ZBV   A&H:GP

[Telegram]

Sugar Loaf [Dec.] 26 [1864] 8PM
Gov Vance
Thank you for the offer of ammunition will call for it when needed. We have reopened communication with [Fort] fisher and the condition is decidedly better. The enemy is lying close entrenching under cover of his gunboats. We lost one hundred and fifty reserves last night surrendered outside of Fisher from incapacity of commanders

> Braxton Bragg
> Genl

ZBV to Harriett Espy Vance   A&H:GP

[Telegram]

Wilmington 27 Dec 1864
Mrs Vance[1]
The Enemy reembarked today—No Yankees on shore near Wilmington will probably land at some other point.

> Z B Vance

[1]ZBV's wife, Harriett Espy Vance.

ZBV *to Mrs. James Spence*   A&H:GLB

Hd. Qrs Forces. Of N.C.
Wilmington Dec 27th. 1864

To Mrs. James Spence
Liverpool, England

Honored Madam.

I have received only recently a copy of the "Albion" newspaper containing an authentic account of the great Southern Bazar held in your City in the month of October for the benefit of Confederate Soldiers in Federal prisons. From this source I learn that you Madam did my State the honor to preside over the Stall dedicated to it, in company with Mrs. F. Worthington and assisted by Miss. Spence, Miss. E. Spence, Miss Hope, Miss. Norton, Miss Balman, and the Misses Worthington. Cares of engrossing character have prevented me from sooner making my grateful acknowledgements for this goodness. Now that this city is attacked and that there is a possibility at least of our only available seaport being closed, I can no longer delay the pleasurable task even though the roar of artillery shakes the city as I write, of the generous sympathy which conceived this humane undertaking, or of its magnificent results I will not particularly speak. Womanly kindness and womanly sympathy for the suffering is the same in both hemispheres. You and your colleagues in this noble work are but the Sisters of those here who are this day dressing the wounds and wiping away the death-damp from the brows of perishing southern soldiers. I cannot adequately praise and bless this gentle sister-hood of charity and mercy which lends a brightness and <a> glory to civilization or give you an idea of that it has done for our bleeding and devoted soldiery. From my own dear Countrywomen it was of course expected, but when such manifestations come to us from beyond the seas, from strangers, breaking through the forms of diplomacy, it makes ones heart to burn with pride and gratitude in an unwonted measure. I may never be able to see much less to repay you my dear Madam and those who acted with you, for this kindly interest in our suffering soldiers, But I beg to assure you all that though rendered poor by the calamities of war, The people of North Carolina are yet rich in gratitude and "thanks to the exchequer of the poor," are hereby through me their chief magistrate rendered with all the abundance of overflowing hearts. May God forever bless you, my dear Madam and all your colleagues in mercy and goodness, for your efforts in behalf of a suffering people, struggling as they are to assume their rightful position among the nations.

With assurances of the highest consideration and esteem which I beg you will accept for yourself and convey to all others concerned,

I have the honor to be

Very Sincerely Yours
Zebulon B. Vance
Govr. of N.C.

Stephen R. Mallory to ZBV					A&H:GP

Confederate States of America.
Navy Department,
Richmond, December 28 1864

His Excellency
Z. B. Vance
Governor of North Carolina
Raleigh N C

Sir,

Confident that you will be pleased to correct any error of statement into which you have been inadvertently led, I beg leave to invite your attention to the following extracts from your recent message,[1] and to the subjoined copies of official papers upon the subjects to which these extracts refer.

"After losses by detentions, the surrender of cargo space &c of not less than two hundred thousand dollars in gold, I regret to have to announce the loss of the Steamer Advance during the month of September. This noble vessel the pride of the State, and benefactor of our soldiers and people was captured by the enemy after she had successfully made her way through the blockade squadron, in consequence of the seizure of her coal for the use of the cruiser Tallahassee, compelling her to put to sea with North Carolina coal. This being unsuited to her furnaces and machinery rendered her incapable of making more than half her usual speed, and left behind her a dense volume of black smoke, by which she was followed and captured. So obviously is her loss attributable to unwarranted seizure of her coal that I trust you will memoralize for compensation. The unwise policy of making our only remaining seaport a resort for our cruizers cannot be too strongly condemned. It has doubled the stringency of the blockade, has already caused the loss of many valuable steamers, and will ultimately provoke the utmost efforts of the enemy to capture Wilmington. It is no exaggeration to say that the Advance alone in solid benefits has been worth more than all the cruizers we have ever had afloat. Why it should be the policy of our Government to compel the state to quit the importation of supplies for the common benefit, and then pursue a course with our armed vessels so well calculated to crush all importations whatever is to me inexplicably strange."

Captain [*Robert F.*] Pinkney, CS Navy, in command of the naval forces at Wilmington, and under whose direction coals were obtained for the Tallahassee and Chickamauga, forwards the following report on the subject:

"Flag Officer R. F. Pinkney
Comdg &c &c

Sir

In reply to your verbal enquiry in reference to the impressment of coal in this station for the use of the C S Steamers that have recently sailed from this port, I have the honor to state, that not one particle of coal was taken from the Steamer Advance, nor one pound impressed to which the State, or any of the joint owners of that steamer had the slightest claim. When the steamers Let her B, and Florie were being fitted out a portion of the coal necessary for the supply of those steamers was taken from the wharf of Mess Power Low & Co, the agents and part owners of the Advance; but I was distinctly informed by a member of that firm, that this coal belonged to three different steamers not then in port. To one of these steamers I had lent about twenty tons of N C Coal to be returned in English coal, and the quantity taken from her just satisfied my claim. The other two steamers as I have said were not then in port and the coal that belonged to them was lying there waiting their return. It is now alledged by the Agents of the Advance that as they had control of this coal, it might have been available for the Advance, if the Government had not impressed it. This, however, is a mere probability as other steamers belonging to this firm might in the mean time have come in short of fuel, to which this coal would undoubtedly have been given. At any rate it did not belong to the Advance, nor was it retained for her exclusive use, and its being appropriated to her use depended upon a mere contingency—namely, her not being preceded into port by other vessels with an insufficiency of coal for their outward voyage. It will then be seen that the extraordinary statement ventured upon by Gov Vance in his late annual message, that the loss of the Advance is attributable solely to the impressment of coal by the C.S. Government has very little foundation in fact.

> Very respectfully
> Your obt servt
> J A Willard.
> Naval Coal agent

Forwarded by
R. F. Pinkney
Capt. &c.

You will perceive from this report that your statement as to coals taken from or belonging to the Advance was an error.

I deem it proper to advert particularly to the following paragraphs of your message. "These cruizers sally forth with coal seized from steamers engaged in bringing in supplies of vital importance, thus ensuring their capture, destroy a few insignificant smacks which only serve to irritate the enemy, and then steam back to Wilmington to seize more coal, bringing down upon the inlets a new swarm of the enemy's gunboats."

It is not my purpose to discuss questions of policy, but simply to correct errors of fact, and I deem it unnecessary here to express an opinion upon the views which your message presents relative to the use made of the port of Wilmington by confederate cruisers. Nor, in reference to your remark as to the "course of the Government with our armed vessels so well calculated to crush all importations whatsoever," is it necessary to say more than that the number of vessels engaged in the blockade trade of Wilmington was never greater than at this time.

It is proper to apprise you that no information of the loss of any steamer resulting from the impressment of her coals, other than that presented in your message, has ever reached this Department; nor have I reason to believe that any vessel was ever lost from the cause stated in the foregoing extract. Under the orders of this Department but one day's fuel could be taken from any steamer and the North Carolina coals substituted for the quantity thus taken could be burned at night without disadvantage or danger from its smoke.

To enable you to correct so much of your statement as limits the captures by the cruizers to "a few insignificant smacks," I enclose a list[3] of the captures made by the Tallahassee and Chickamauga, from which you will perceive that their captures were not only more important than is consistant with your statement, but that nineteen of the forty six were square rigged vessels.

> I have the honor to be
> very respectfully
> your obt serv.
> S R Mallory
> Secretary of the Navy

[1]Not extant, but abstracted in this correspondence.
[2]"List of vessels captured by the C. S. Steamer Tallahassee, Comdg J Taylor Wood," enclosed in this correspondence, A&H:GP.

Robert E. Lee to ZBV   A&H:GLB

> Hd. Qrs. Army N. Va.
> 28th. Dec. 1864

His Excy. Z. B. Vance
Governor of N. Carolina
Raleigh

Governor

I beg leave to call the attention of your Excellency to the great danger we incur from the condition and management of our railroads, with the hope that you may be able to remove some of the difficulties under which we labor. Genl. Hoke's division was ordered to Wilmington as soon as it was known that the enemy was threatening that place. The first brigade left Richmond by the Danville road on Tuesday morning 19th. inst. The other brigades followed as soon as they could be marched from below Richmond and placed on the trains. The first brigade did not reach Wilmington until the 25th. & by the afternoon of the 26th. only four hundred men of the second brigade of two thousand had arrived. At that time Gen Bragg telegraphed that the remainder of the division had passed the Piedmont road, where most of the delay occurred and would arrive rapidly. Yet he reported yesterday evening that up to that time only the first two brigades were with him below Wilmington and that the rest had probably reached the city. Your Excellency will readily perceive the danger we were exposed to. Fortunately the delay was not fatal as it might well have been. I have requested an investigation of this matter with a view to ascertain whether the unprecedented delay was occasioned by any circumstance within the control of the military authorities, but I have thought that the State authorities can do something to aid us. I am informed that freight & passengers are shifted at Greensboro from the trains of the Piedmont road to those of the Greensboro road & vice versa, occasioning much inconvenience and unnecessary delay, as the two roads have the same gauge. I trust that your Excellency will endeavor to ascertain what can be done to facilitate transportation by rail, and give all the assistance in your power. The delay is not only dangerous and injurious, but has given rise to painful suspicions which in justice to those connected with the management of the roads, should be removed.

> With great respect
> Your obt. servt.
> R. E. Lee
> Genl.

James A. Seddon to ZBV A&H:GP

Confederate States of America,
War Department,
Richmond, Va. Dec. 31 1864

His Excellency Z. B. Vance,
Governor of North Carolina,
Raleigh, N.C.

Sir,

I have just received your letter of the 20th. inst.1 stating that, in response to my request through Major Hoge, you have ordered all the bacon you have at the Islands, and one-half of the quantity on hand in North Carolina, to be transferred to this Department.

This liberality on your part is highly appreciated and gratefully acknowledged by me. Your generous response to my appeal proves I did not err in the belief, that you would cheerfully lend from the stores accumulated by you, supplies greatly needed for the support of the army. It is hoped the interruption of railroad transportation will be temporary, and that the

Commissariat will soon be in a condition to replace what has been so promptly and cheerfully tendered as a loan.

> Very Respectfully
> Your obdt. servt.
> James A. Seddon
> Secretary of War

[*Endorsed*] File—& copy

Z B V

[1]Not extant, but see ZBV's endorsement in James A. Seddon to ZBV, December 15, 1864, in this volume.

ZBV to Stephen R. Mallory   A&H:GLB

> State of North Carolina
> Executive Department.
> Raleigh Jany. 3d. 1865.

Hon S R. Mallory.
Secy of the Navy.
Richmond Va.

Sir,

Your letter of the 28th. ult.[1] with enclosures relative to the loss of the Steamer Advance has been recd. You do me no more than justice in expressing your confidence in my willingness to "correct any errors of statement into which you (I) may have been inadvertantly led." It would afford me great pleasure to correct the supposed erroneous statement contained in my recent message attributing the loss of Steamer Advance to the appropriation of her coal for the steamers of the Government were I conscious of any error. Even from the proof submitted by Capt. Pinkney's letter an extract from which you enclose, were I to retract my statement, I fancy I should be deliberately committing a greater error than the one which you are kind enough to attribute to inadvertency. I made the statement of which you complain deliberately and upon authority which I regard as reliable, and think I have been sustained by the facts. Power Low & Co were the part owners and Agents of the Vessels; it was their duty to accumulate coal for the use of our Vessels by taking small quantities from each one which had a surplus for supplying those which were short. To this common heap the Advance contributed as others and when she came to sail this heap destined as well for her and the others of the line had been taken by the Navy Dept. & she had to go with N.C. Coal. The enclosed certificate[2] of OReilly[3] and Harriss[4] will show how much was taken, wherefrom and that it was actually applied to the use of the Tallahassee as I charged. The argument of Capt Pinkney to show that the Advance *might not* have got the coals and therefore could have no interest in a thing she might fail to get is a subterfuge more becoming a lawyer than a gallant high minded sailor, as is his reputation. The coals were reserved for her or any other vessel of the firm that might come in short of enough to return with. They *were* taken by the Navy Dept, the Advance failed to get therefore what she was entitled to by the action of the Confederate authorities and hence her capture. I am willing that the public should judge of the error from these statements.

I beg leave further to call your attention to the certificate of Mr. Savage, Collector at Wilmington showing that there was no gold on the Advance when she was captured, I do this because of the appearance of an article in the Richmond Sentinel said to have been written under the auspices of the Navy Dept. in which it was alleged that there was a large amount of Gold on this Vessel the non appearance of which was supposed to account in part for her capture. From this it will be seen that in order to convict me of "venturing upon an extraordinary statement" some parties connected with the Navy Dept., have ventured upon a rather ordinary one.

Like you Sir, I do not desire to discuss the policy of the Govt in regard to our armed cruisers & blockade running generally. If I did I might /well/ cite the recent formidable attack upon Wilmington from which alone we were delivered by the Providence of God, as a full confirmation of my opinions. And I might well ask if one of the three vessels which lately entered that port laden with bacon was not of greater benefit to the Confederacy even though it was the enterprise of "gamblers" than the destruction of all the enemys vessels at sea mentioned in the list you enclose. My opposition to the policy of the Govt. is not based upon anything factious or any regard for the interest of men who have been making fortunes by running the blockade whether native or foreign. I never made objection to their being placed under such restrictions as the Govt. thought proper; but why a State struggling for the common good to clothe and provide for its troops in the public service should meet with no more favor than a blockade gambler passes my comprehension.

> Very Respectfully,
> Yr. Obt. Servt.
> Z. B. Vance—

[1]December 28, 1864, in this volume.

[2]Not extant, but see Stephen R. Mallory to ZBV, January 28, 1865, in this volume.

[3]J. T. O'Reilly, in charge of the wharves and warehouses of Power, Low and Co., Wilmington.

[4]George Harris, wharf and warehouseman.

William H. C. Whiting to ZBV   A&H:GP

Hd. Qrs. Wilmington
January 4th., 1865

His Excellency Gov. Vance
Raleigh

Sir,

While our recollection of Christmas day & Ft Fisher is fresh, let me beg your aid & cooperation in getting immediately as large a force of free negros as possible. I need labor always now especially. We must not let our last place go for want of work still less because we have foiled the enemy's first effort must we fold our arms & say enough has been done. In every department I need a free laboring force. I am earnestly desirous of releasing all slaves, especially in view of the complaints I learn relative to clothing them. That is not my fault: I have done all in my power to provide clothing for negros even to overstepping the limits of my authority. It has been literally due to want of money & material. Still the reports are greatly exaggerated for many negros have been sent here totally unprovided in the first instance by their masters. But at all times I am unwilling to impress. The act provides for the conscription of free negros before impressing the slaves & I hope with your aid & that of your militia organization to obtain a sufficient number of free negros & to get back those that have deserted. An enrolled corps of 1200 to 1500 free negros properly organized into companies according to regulation entitled to furlough at proper times, fed clad & paid & retained in service would relieve the people of the state of all use of their slaves for the defence here. With my works so well advanced I can preserve their condition & provide all I want of new construction with such a force.

If we can get it in the State, I will guarantee the exemption of the Slave labor as far as we are concerned here. Please to let me hear from you.

I have written to Col Mallett.

Very Respy.
W. H. C. Whiting
Maj. Genl.

Jefferson Davis to ZBV   A&H:GP

Richmond, Va. Jany. 6, 1865

His Excellency
Z. B. Vance
Governor of North Carolina

Dear Sir,

Your letter[1] asking that Genl. D. H. Hill be assigned to duty in North Carolina "or should it not be the purpose of the Department to assign him, that you propose giving him some employment," was received some time since. Various causes have prevented an earlier reply.

In the meantime Genl. Hill has been ordered to report to Genl. Beauregard for duty at or near Charleston So. Ca.

I am very respectfully
Your Obdt. Svt.
Jeffn. Davis

[1]ZBV to Davis, October 25, 1864, in this volume. See also ZBV's endorsement (the only surviving portion) of Daniel H. Hill to ZBV, December 24, 1864, A&H:VanPC. ZBV states: "Say that I did not know until after my return from Wilmington That the Prest. took no notice of my letter asking him to be assigned to command in NC."

ZBV to Robert E. Lee   A&H:GLB

State of North Carolina.
Executive Department.
Raleigh January 6th. 1865.

General Robert E. Lee
Commanding Army of Northern Virginia

General.

I have received your letter[1] calling my attention to the dangers to the public service arising "from the condition and management of our railroads" and asking my assistance in endeavoring to facilitate transportation and to prevent dangerous and injurious delays. I was made painfully aware of the delays of which you so justly complain during the recent attack upon

Wilmington and I assure you that you shall have my hearty cooperation in producing such reforms as can be effected on North Carolina roads. I have no control whatever over the Piedmont road.

> With sentiments of great respect.
> Your obedient servant.
> Z. B. Vance

[1]December 28, 1864, in this volume.

Robert E. Lee to ZBV   A&H:GP

[*Telegram*]

> Head Quarters [*January*] 7, 1865
> Via Petersburg

To His Ex Z. B. Vance
Your telegram of 6th[1] recd to what Commands do the men whos execution you wish delayed belong

> R. E. Lee

[1]Not extant.

ZBV to Jefferson Davis   A&H:GLB

> State of North Carolina.
> Executive Department.
> Raleigh Janry 7th. 1865.

His Excellency
President Davis.

Sir,
I beg leave most cordially to join in the recommendation which I take for granted has been made by his superiors, of Col. Lamb Comdg. Fort Fisher for promotion. I was near by during the recent attack upon the defences of Wilmington and people and soldiers alike were enthusiastic in praise of his skill and gallantry. Presuming that the official reports have done justice to

his soldiery qualities, I mainly desire to assure you that our people would gladly see him made a Brigadier from North Carolina though not a citizen thereof.

> I have the honor to be Sir
> Very Respectfully.
> Yr. Obt. Servt.
> Z. B. Vance

Robert E. Lee to ZBV   A&H:GP

[*Telegram*]

Head Qrs Jany 9th. 1865

To His Ex Z. B. Vance

Execution has been suspended by order of War Dept

R. E. Lee

ZBV to James A. Seddon   A&H:GLB

[*With enclosure*]

> State of North Carolina.
> Executive Department.
> Raleigh Janry. 9th. 1865.

Hon. J. A. Seddon
Secty. Of War.

Dr. Sir,
  I respectfully ask your attention to the enclosed copy of a letter from Mr. Andrew Barnard a citizen of Clay Co. N.C. for whose loyalty and respectability I readily vouch. It details a transaction not at all rare or uncommon, and I should not deem it worth while to trouble you with it except that it identifies the thief and traces him to the promise and leaves him under the protection of his Commanding General. There is therefore presented a fair opportunity for punishment of the offender, and for making an example not only of him but of officer or officers who connive at and permit these outrages. Should such an opportunity be permitted to pass unimproved the conclusion will be forced upon our people that their

Government officially countenance rapine and robbery, or else is too weak to inflict punishment for these crimes, a suspicion which has already done more to demoralize our people and weaken our cause than all other causes together. I venture to hope that prompt punishment will be inflicted and that the Quarter Master at Athens, Ga. may be ordered to pay Mr. Bernard and the other sufferers full value for their property.

Very Respectfully,
Z. B. Vance—

[*Enclosure*]

Andrew Barnard to ZBV   A&H:GLB

At home Clay County N.C.
Dec 30th. 1864.

Gov. Vance

D. Sir

The small acquaintance and your plain friendly manner encourages me to write you a few lines hoping that you will hear and consider my complaint and assist me in obtaining justice from the public authorities. My case is this Sir, on the night of the 8th. inst. a band of Confederate Soldiers (9 in number) rode up to my premises into my horse lot and commenced trying to bridle some young horses that had never been used they was wild and stout /and/ hard to manage, but they finally succeeded in getting two. They then took two of my using horses, four in all, and left. (me remonstrating all the time) but they heeded not, said their officers had sent them to get horses and they was agoing to have them wherever they could find them, I then asked the officer of the squad his name and some showing that I could get pay for my stock, he refused to give it more than that they belonged to Maj. Grahams Battalion then camped near Athens Ga. that the property was for the use of the Government and there would be a man along next day who would settle with and give me a certificate that man has not yet appeared. I have since learned there was one hundred and fifty scattered over the country engaged in the same business, they gathered through the night between 30 & 40 head in this & adjoining county in Geo. Some was rescued, but they made their escape with 25 or 30 head mine of the number, they was accosted next day /by/ a man in towns cty and asked for his authority, he presented an order signed by Gen Reynolds[1] for Capt Thompson to proceed to North East Geo. and western N.C. and take horses from disloyal men. Now Sir my self and sons have never been accused of being disloyal that I know of and as an evidence I had four sons went into the Confederate Service early in the War. One died at Richmond in 62 the other three is still in /the/ service, one in the 2d. N.C. Cavalry now lying at Petersburg, the other two at Kinston N.C. Col Folks Reg.[2] Now Sir, three of the horses forced from me belonged to two of those sons left under my care and protection, one a favorite animal left for the use of his wife who is staying with me. I was so much hurt at the loss of the property, that myself and some others of my neighbors followed them to Atkins, thinking that Gen Reynolds would perhaps restore our stock, we went before him with a good recommendation as loyal citizens, he received us kindly, we stated our business, he exclaimed loudly against the conduct of his men and wished we had killed half of them and assured us we should have our stock back, if we could find it, gave us an order to Maj Grahams camp to get our stock if it was there, we went and searched the camp, but could not find a horse we knew. We could get no satisfaction out of Graham, or his men, so we returned to the Gen quarters, he then said he could do nothing more for us in the mean time we met Capt Thompson the officer of the thieves who took our stock. We told the Gen so and urged him to make him bring up the stock he brought from our County, for we believed the stock was run off or hid out of our reach. The Gen refused, said they was a wild reckless set that he could not control. So ended our mission. Now Gov. I wish to know if there is any way to obtain legal redress and if you will assist us, for if we cant regain our stock, we want pay for it and we think it will have to be through you if we ever get anything, if not we would like to know if our sons and neighbors is to be kep at a distance to keep back the common enemy, while thieving scoundrels is sent out by government officers to rob them of their property left at home, if so we are a gone people, for there will soon be nothing left to fight for, the old men and boys left at home is not able to contend by force against those marauding parties for we have neither arms or ammunition and as for the home guard we can never get them on the track until it is cold. Our fighting material is away, so we have to suffer. Now Sir, if you think us old men and helpless women and children worthy of any part of your attention and care you will please assist in getting pay for the property already lost and send us at least a few men that will shoot highway robbers when they come amongst us and ever oblige.

Yours Truly & c.
Andrew Barnard

[1]Alexander Welch Reynolds. Faust et al., *Encyclopedia of Civil War*, 625.
[2]Sixty-fifth Regiment (Sixth Cavalry) North Carolina Troops, commanded by Col. George Nathaniel Folk. Manarin et al., *North Carolina Troops*, 2:457.

Robert E. Lee to ZBV   A&H:VanPC

Hd. Qrs. A N Va
9th. Jany 1865

His Excy. Z B Vance
Governor of N Carolina
Raleigh,

Governor,
I beg leave to ask your assistance to prevent any allusion by the papers of Raleigh, or any others in your State to certain commercial transactions which will probably occur on the rivers of eastern N Carolina, particularly the Chowan. These transactions are of great importance to the Army & may be of such magnitude as to attract attention. Any reference to them reaching the enemy may & probably will put and end to them at once, to our great injury.
You will know best how to accomplish this object so as not to make the matter public, and I respectfully request your aid.

With great respect
Your obt. servt.
R E Lee
Genl

Braxton Bragg to ZBV   A&H:GP

[*Telegram*]

Sugar Loaf via Wimington
[*January*] 14, 1865

To His Excellency Gov Vance
The Enemy has landed a heavy force and evidently intends making a strong effort. We need all your assistance and as soon as you can send it.
Bombardment of fort fisher yesterday was heavy but damage and loss slight

Braxton Bragg
Genl

ZBV to William A. Graham   A&H:GLB

State of North Carolina.
Executive Department.
Raleigh January 14th. 1865.

Hon. Wm. A. Graham
Richmond Va.

Dear Sir.

I have the honor to transmit to you copies of Resolutions passed by the General Assembly of this State, one entitled a "Resolution in relation to the expenses incurred in the execution of the Conscription Laws," and the other entitled "Resolutions relating to Brigading certain North Carolina Regiments."

I fully concur in the propriety and justness of these demands and most respectfully request that you will urge their adoption. The report of the Adjutant General Shows that the State on the 2d. day of December 1864 had expended the sum of Two hundred and forty one thousand, nine hundred & forty 85/100 Dollars ($241,940 85/100) in executing the Conscription laws and in arresting deserters from the Army.

Yrs. Very Respectully.
Z. B. Vance

P.S. Also a resolution of instruction to our Senators and Representatives in Congress in regard to disabled soldiers.

Copy of above letter has today also been sent to,[1]

W. N. H. Smith	W. T. Dortch
Robt R. Bridgers	Josiah Turner Jr.
T. C. Fuller	John A. Gilmer
J. T. Leach	J. M. Leach
J. G. Ramsay	G. W. Logan
B. S. Gaither	

[1]Members of the Confederate Congress from North Carolina.

Braxton Bragg to ZBV   A&H:GP

[*Telegram*]

Sugar Loaf 1 K A.M. /Jan/ 16, 1865

To Gov Vance

I am mortified at having to report the unexpected capture of Fort Fisher with most of its Garrison about 10 oclock tonight particulars not yet known

Braxton Bragg
Genl

ZBV to Sion H. Rogers   A&H:GLB

State of North Carolina.
Executive Department.
Raleigh Jany. 16th. 1865.

Hon S. H. Rogers
Atto Genl of N.C.

Dr. Sir,

The General Assembly has passed a resolution requesting me to take such steps as I "may deem proper" for the suppression of distillation in the State by the Confederate Govt.

Will you please to inform me, if in your opinion the parties engaged therein are amenable to the law of this State against distillation?

Very Respectfully,
Yr. obt. svt.
Z. B. Vance

ZBV to William Smith   A&H:GLB

State of North Carolina.
Executive Department.
Raleigh January 17th. 1865.

His Excellency William Smith
Governor of Virginia.

Dear Sir;

The General Assembly of this State at its recent session passed the following resolution and directed me to notify you of its adoption. "Resolved that his Excellency the Governor be directed to notify the Governor of Virginia *forthwith* that the conduct of the Authorities of Virginia in diverting to the use of the latter, one engine and two trains of cars, hired to this State for the transportation of salt from Saltville to Danville, is regarded by the General Assembly now in Session as a serious departure from the courtesy of States and as an act of mischief and injury to the people of North Carolina."

In communicating the foregoing resolutions of the General Assembly I deem it my duty as the Executive of the State, to say that I deeply regret the action of the Board of Public Works of your State, which in my opinion rendered the passage of said resolution eminently right and proper, and at the same time to express the hope and belief that the wrong will be repaired, and that courtesy which has hitherto charactarized the entire course between the two states, whose interests are so ultimately blended will be immediately restored.

Upon learning the proceedings of your Board of Public Works I deemed it my duty to forbid the exportation of articles of Virginia upon the rail roads of the State, not by way of retaliation, but as a precautionary measure rendered necessary by the deficiency in the supply of Salt which would be thus produced. That restriction shall be most cheerfully withdrawn whenever your authorities shall revoke the unprecedented order in regard to our trains. I was much pleased to see that in your message you referred to this action of the Board of Public Works with disapprobation. Hoping and believing that your Board of Public Works will, upon having this matter called to their attention see the injustice and wrong which is likely to follow from it, and that the two States may in the future, as in the past, move on harmoniously.

I am Governor with much respect,
Your Obedient Servant
Z. B. Vance

ZBV to James A. Seddon A&H:GLB

State of North Carolina.
Executive Department.
Raleigh January 17th. 1865.

Hon. James a. Seddon,
Secretary of War.

Dear Sir;

The General Assembly of this State has authorized me to purchase two hundred thousand dollars worth of Cotton or Tobacco and to make all possible efforts to ship the same in connection with the shipments of the Confederate Government for the relief of prisoners of War. This fund is intended to be additional to that which has been provided by the Confederate Government. In view of the great suffering and wants of our brave and noble soldiers now confined in Northern prisons, I am exceedingly anxious to effect the wishes of the General Assembly and most respectfully request your cooperation.

With much respect,
Your obedient Servant,
Z. B. Vance—

Sion H. Rogers to ZBV A&H:GP

Raleigh Jan 18th. 1865

His Excellency,
Gov. Vance:

Dear Sir:

Your letter of the 16th. Inst[1] informing me of the action of the General Assembly in reference to the "distillation of spiritous liquors in this state by the Confederate Government and whether the parties engaged therein are amenable to the laws of this state against distillation" has been received.

I am of opinion that they are not. The Constitution of the Confederate states empowers the Congress thereof "to raise and support armies." There is no limitation upon this power except <as> so far as is necessary to protect the existence of the state and what is contained in the constitution.

To show how full this power is I refer you to the Amendments of the United States Constitution, Article 5: the last paragraph, in reference to private property.

> I am with great respect
> Your obt servant
> Sion H. Rogers
> Att Genl

[1]In this volume.

ZBV *to James A. Seddon*   A&H:GLB

> State of North Carolina.
> Executive Department.
> Raleigh January 18th. 1865.

Hon. James A. Seddon.
Secretary of War.

Dear Sir.

One of my Agents at Saltville in Virginia informs me that since the movement of the enemy upon that place, about eight hundred bushels of Corn, belonging to this State, have been consumed by the commands of Generals [George Blake] Cosby and [Basil Wilson] Duke and Col. Gittner.[1]

This Corn was absolutely necessary to enable us to carry on the business of making salt and I hope that you will cause a like quantity to be returned immediately.

> With sentiments of great respect
> Your obedient servant,
> Z. B. Vance—

[1]Confederate commanders in southwest Virginia and east Tennessee. Faust et al., *Encyclopedia of Civil War*, 186, 229.

ZBV *to Andrew G. Magrath*　　　　　　A&H:GLB

State of North Carolina.
Executive Department.
Raleigh January 18th. 1865.

Gov. A. G. Magrath[1]
Columbia, So. Ca.

Governor,

Your communication[2] by the hands of Col. Mullins Aid de Camp, has been recd. and carefully considered. I regret that the press of weighty and harassing matters at this moment upon me will prevent my replying so fully as I desire. I have however conversed fully and freely with Col. Mullins and being /able/ only to reply in outline he will be able to fill up and explain minutely.

I think the crisis demands particularly the skill of the politician, perhaps more than that of the great General. In other words judging from my own people I regard our danger now as arising more from our moral than our physical weakness. The spirit of our people must be revived, their patriotism aroused anew and a determination to suffer be enfused if we are to hope for ultimate redemption. How is this to be done? The success of our arms would certainly beget hope and confidence, but the former can hardly be expected without the latter going before. I can hardly give you an adequate conception of the general despondency and gloom which prevails among us, or of the importance of preventing its extension to the Army.

In regard to your first proposition concerning the Militia, I most fully concur in the wisdom of your suggestions. The same were brought forward by me in the meeting of Governors at Augusta and were urged upon the Legislature of this State in my last message to that body. I failed however in convincing them of the propriety of removing the restrictions alluded to and in the present unhappy situation of Wilmington it will hardly be possible to get them to reverse their judgment. Rest assured however, that I will not cease to struggle for that amicable and harmonious state of things as regards the mutual help to be afforded each State by the other, which you desire.

I concur most heartily also in your suggestion concerning the restoration to command of Genl. J. E. Johns[t]on, I go further and will unite with you and others in asking that Genl. Lee /shall/ be invested with full and absolute command of the military forces of the Confederacy, which I take it for granted would result in the restoration of Generals Johns[t]ons, G. W. Smith[3] and other distinguished officers now in retirement. I propose in these matters to unite with you and sign a communication to President Davis which you shall prepare setting forth our opinions and wishes.

In regard to the calling of State Conventions I have been long committed against them as involving revolution within revolution as your express it and as incurring also the danger of domestic violence and civil feuds. I do not think such a measure can be carried in North Carolina, though it will be attempted unless the great State of Georgia should set the example, I shall write my views /and/ opinions fully to Gov Brown on this subject and hope that that State whose example did so much to persuade this State into the revolution will not be the first to forsake her. The letter[4] to Gov Brown I send by Col. Mullins unsealed that you may peruse it and will be glad if it meets your approbation.

The great evil of desertion is one that has engaged my attention for the past two years. There are enough soldiers absent from their commands without leave to render the armies of the Confederacy irristable and triumphant if they were all returned. How can this be done? I invite your earnest attention to the subject and would gladly hear any further suggestions you may have to offer thereon. It is certainly worthy of the highest efforts of Statesmanship.

Referring you again for particulars to Col. Mullins /and/ assuring you of my hearty concurrence and earnest cooperation in your efforts for the common good.

I am Governor
Very Respectfully Yours
Z. B. Vance

[1]Andrew Gordon Magrath, who on December 14, 1864, had succeeded Milledge L. Bonham as governor of South Carolina. Faust et al., *Encyclopedia of Civil War*, 468.

[2]Not extant.

[3]Gustavus Woodson Smith, who had been a favorite of ZBV, had resigned his commission and command of the Department of North Carolina and Southern Virginia in February 1863. See ZBV to Jefferson Davis, February 2, 1863, in Johnston and Mobley, *Papers of Vance*, 2:39-40.

[4]See ZBV to Joseph E. Brown, January 18, 1865, in this volume, immediately following this correspondence.

ZBV to Joseph E. Brown   A&H:GLB

State of North Carolina.
Executive Department.
Raleigh January 18th. 1865.

Gov. J. E. Brown—

Governor,

The present condition of affairs makes it proper that I should again seek communication with my brother Governors for the purpose of mutual consel and assistance.

The march of Sherman through Georgia his threatened advance through So. Carolina and the recent disasters involved in the defeat of Genl Hood and the fall of the principal defensive work of Wilmington, have necessitated the desire of a State Convention for vague and indefinable purposes. I do not think however that a Convention can be called in North Carolina unless your State should lead in the movement, and I see many indications of such an intention among your people, I suppose you are aware of my opinion in regard to the danger of such a movement. I expressed them to you by letter last spring and had the happiness to receive your concurrance in my conclusions then, I regard it as simply another revolution and by which we would incur not only the danger attendant upon a disunited Confederation, but also of domestic strife and bloodshed. For I have no idea that a severance of our existing relations could possibly be so unanimously effected as to prevent a considerable minority backed by the Army from inaugurating a State of anarchy more horrible than anything we have yet endured or may expect to endure. Judging by my own people, I regard such a deplorable result as morally certain. It seems to me that the State Governments through their Executives and Legislatures will have all the necessary moral weight and can accomplish every desired object short of revolution, and that by calling a convention we can have no other object in view except revolution. I frankly confess to you that I regard it our chief aim at this time to hold the demoralized and trembling fragments of society and law together and prevent them from dropping to pieces until the rapidly hastening end of our struggle shall be developed. To do this is not only humane and in every respect our duty but also puts off the evil day and keeps us in position to take advantage of any fortunate circumstance tending to redeem our losses, to inspire our people with hope or even to secure better terms in case all should be lost.

Besides the tenor of my advices from Richmond of late is to the effect that President Davis is inclined to make earnest efforts for peace on a basis as modest as I suppose you or I could willingly agree to. I am anxious therefore to see this the legitimate and proper channels fairly tried and thoroughly exhausted before we take matters in our own hands and inaugurate revolutionary measures. I earnestly hope therefore that Georgia will not set an example which I fear would be fatal to North Carolina. The latter was greatly influenced by the former in the beginning of this revolution and the Secession of the Empire State of Georgia after mature deliberation had more influence in determining the fate of North Carolina than any other State in the Confederation except perhaps our great Northern neighbor Virginia. Both these latter were exceedingly loath to quit the old Union and embark their sober & cautious people upon the bloody waves of war in the face of such tremendous odds. They hesitated no longer when our Southern Sisters plunged in and cried for help. How they have helped—how they have bled and suffered none will more cheerfully acknowledge than the people of Georgia by the side of whose gallant sons their blood has been spilled and their sufferings endured. I appeal to you then Governor in all candor and honour to ask if Georgia should not in this great matter show due deference to the opinions and wishes of her Northern Sisters, who moved mainly out of sympathy for those who got first into trouble? I believe she will /hope s[h]e will/ not only for the sake of the cause, but for the sake of humanity, and that our action to the last may be harmonious, cordial, sympathetic. Please let me hear your opinions as soon as your convenience may serve and believe me to be,

> Very Respectfully and
> Sincerely Yours,
> Z. B. Vance

James A. Seddon to ZBV   A&H:VanPC

> Confederate States of America,
> War Department,
> Richmond, Va. Jan 18 1865

His Excellency Z. B. Vance,
Governor of N.C.
Raleigh, N.C.

Sir,

I have received the application of Joseph J. Neave, a Quaker from England, for permission to come within the Confederate lines, referred by your Excellency.

A similar application, addressed directly to the Confederate authorities, was, after advisement, declined. It was deemed inexpedient to grant such permission, because the Quakers were, from their profession, known to be inimical to our slave institutions, and to advocate nonresistance. Besides, the parties came immediately from the country of the enemy after association with them, and by their sanction. It was not considered advisable to admit these missionaries to free intercourse with our people, and circumstances would seem more strongly now than then to forbid it.

> Very Respectfully
> Your obt. servt.
> James A. Seddon
> Secretary of War

ZBV to Robert Ould   A&H:VanPC

Private

> State of North Carolina,
> Executive Department.
> Raleigh, Jany 21 1865.

Judge Ould,
Comr. of Exchange,

Dr. Sir,
    A recent letter from my brother Gen Vance informs me that if our Govt. will parole his equivalent to go North he can be exchanged or paroled to come South.
    Can this be done?

> Respectfully yours
> Z. B. Vance

[*Endorsed*]   Jan 26th. '65

Respectfully returned to His Excellency Gov. Vance. If the Federal authorities will send Gen. Vance by flag of truce, I will simultaneously deliver to them his equivalent. It is contrary to our practice and against good policy to send an officer on special parole to secure the release of any one. We ought not to do anything which would put any officer in a better position than that occupied by others. The Yankees ought not to ask of us any thing more than a readiness to deliver the equivalent when we receive the prisoner. This we offer to do in any and every case. As the enemy have twice as many officers as we have, if all that we have were sent North on parole to secure the exchange of particularly named parties, when we got through, more than two thousand of our officers would be in their hands. What would they and their friends say, after their companions had been selected for exchange and they left behind? I am happy to inform you that Gen. Vance has been selected to assist Gen Beall[1] in N. York city in the matter of purchasing and distributing supplies. He is on parole.

Ro. Ould
Agent of Exchange

[*Endorsed*] File-private

ZBV

[1]Confederate general William N. R. Beall, who had been captured at Port Hudson in 1863. Imprisoned at Johnson Island, he was paroled at New York City in 1864 to sell cotton and purchase supplies for Confederate prisoners of war. Current et al., *Encyclopedia of the Confederacy*, 1:145-146.

David L. Swain to ZBV   A&H:VanPC

Raleigh [*sic*] 21 Jan 1865

His Excellency,
Gov Vance

My dear Sir,

I write to you this morning to thank you for the eminent service rendered in sending me the medicine which Mr. McCauls brought up night before last. It came to my hands at 12 yesterday—A delay of six hours might have produced most distressing results. Anna[1] will never cease to thank you for kindness exhibited, at such a crisis. I believe I may add with much confidence that her most earnest prayers will be constantly offered for blessings upon you and those near and dear to you.

The weather is most inclement, or I might attempt to go over to Raleigh this evening. I would be glad now to have the "long talk" [invited] in your letter of the 22d. Sep.[2] Your remark "the great popular heart is not now and never has been in this war"—"that it is revolution of the politicians and not of the people," has been [mournfully] and fully verified by Sherman's triumphant march, his almost *royal progress*, from Atlanta to Savannah. We can all understand what submission and extermination mean, but the intermediate term, subjugation, is of more difficult definition. Is Maryland subdued? is Missouri? is Kentucky? No one of the three is likely to offer resistance to the Federal Government, unless what is not likely to occur, the presence of the great invading army shall summon to the rescue. Their's are cases of submission or subjugation and neither has any more inclination to undergo the martyrdom of extermination than N.C. Of the condition of Texas, Arkansas, Florida, Alabama, Mississippi and Louisiana, I know almost nothing. They must I suppose stand or fall of themselves. Now that Hood has fallen eminently in his attempt to redeem Georgia and Tennessee, these two states may be considered virtually in the same category with Maryland, Missouri and Kentucky—or rather as in the [transition] state between the decidedly loyal states, as N.C. and the disloyal Maryland. Congress has resolved with entire unanimity I believe that Virginia shall never be [disarmed] and that we will accept no terms short of independence. The public idea is a counterfeit one.

> "Still forever better—
> Though each man's life blood were a river
> Better be, where the unconquered Spartans still are free
> In their proud charnel at Thermopylae"[3]

Notwithstanding all this, I suppose that even South Carolina, will stop short of extermination in efforts to free Maryland and New Virginia against their will. The war is to be maintained henceforth mainly by S.C., N.C. and /Old/ Virginia. Georgia and Tennessee will do nothing of themselves. We have no General like Lee, no veteran army like his to march to their relief.

Now that our only port of entry is sealed up all foreign supplies of arms, ammunition and subsistance cut off, all domestic supplies for Lee dependent for transmission upon the Piedmont road, the naked question seems to present itself, are we prepared to submit to martyrdom? The world has exhibited in past ages, but one Thermopylae, will N.C., S.C., or old Va. present another? Is Independence now within our reach? In September I echoed your ejaculation most heartily. "Lord I believe, help thou mine unbelief." I suspect that neither of us can make the asseveration at present. I have made no reference to foreign intervention because /I can perceive/ no grounds on which we can hope for acceptable succor from England or France. The idea of enrolling and arming slaves, and concilliating the world by abolition of slavery, meets with little favor in this quarter.

What then can be done? If Clay, Calhoun & Webster could be summoned from the grave, it might task their /combined/ statesmanship to the uttermost to devise a remedy. How is it "among the ranks of living man." Gov. Graham, Col. [James L.] Orr and Mr. [William C.] Rives by united counsels might [possibly] given the proper [article] on public opinion, but I fear that combination on their part is not probable at a sufficiently early day. In N.C. much, very much, perhaps everything depends upon the course which you shall persue. Call your friends around /you/, consult them freely, keep your own counsels, and at the proper moment, strike where duty calls, and unity of sentiment and consert of action may render the blow effectual.

As this hastily written note, is virtually a reply to your confidential letter of the 22 September, you will of course consider it as confidential.

> I am with much true respect
> Affectionately Yours
> D. L. Swain

[1]Swain's daughter and oldest child, who died in 1867.
[2]In this volume.
[3]Swain is quoting from Lord Byron's "Ode on Venice" (1819); however, Byron's phrase was "extinguished Spartans."

N.C. Soldiers of Lee's Army to ZBV   A&H:GP

> Richmond Virginia
> January 24th 1865

To His Excellency,
Z. B. Vance
Governor of N.C.

Sir

It is with much reluctance that we address a letter of this tone to you, knowing as we do, that your mind is already heavily taxed with many grave and important matters which this war gives rise to. We know that Your Excellency would carry out Good Old North State gallantly, and with undimmed honor through this struggle for liberty; and we believe that no one is more able to do so than yourself.

We have been to the front endeavoring to keep the Enemy back for the past three or four years, (against great odds too) and would still fight them to the last, hoping to conquer in time, but those at home must look to the wants, and ameliorate the suffering of our wives and little ones there.

Very many of our wives were dependent on our labor for support before the war, and when articles of food and clothing could be obtained easier than now. At this time they are alone, without a protector, and cannot by hard and honest labor, obtain enough money to purchase the necessaries of life. We had hoped that something would be done to render the currency better, but it seems to get worse. Many of us have left our wives and children at home in the country upon little tracts of land, and who are now suffering for want of help to raise bread and meat.

It is not in the power of Yankee armies to cause us to wish ourselves at home, we can face them, and can bear their shot and shell without being moved; but, Sir, we cannot hear the cries of our little ones and stand. We must say something, /must/ *make an effort to relieve them*, and would do it through you, believing it to be the best way. We suffer much ourselves for food & clothing. Our rations are *too small*, and appear to be decreasing. Our clothing is not sufficient to shield us from inclement weather, but in health we would not complain of this, but when we are sick and compelled to go into hospitals, we do not receive food which is proper for us to eat. It is as course as that issued to us in the field, and worse prepared.

Something should be done to remedy these evils. But it is not of *ourselves* that we would complain, it is of our *wives and little ones* at home, who are necessituous.

Do something for them and there will be less desertion, and men will go into battle with heartier good will. *But it is impossible for us to bear up under our many troubles*, the greatest of which is, the suffering of our wives and little ones at home.

We beg your pardon for bothering you with this, but *something must be done, speedily.*

We remain with much respect
And Obedience
N.C. Soldiers of Lee's Army

To
The Governor of Our State

David L. Swain to ZBV   A&H:VanPC

Chapel Hill, 25 Jan 1865.

My dear Sir,

I wrote you a hasty letter[1] last week in which I had occasion to speak of the present perilous condition of our public affairs. At the time I did so I had no knowledge that propositions for the call of a convention were before the General Assembly, or any expectation that such measures would be proposed. I had not then seen the remarks of Mr. Orr[2] of Miss. on the article and editorial comment in the Richmond Sentinel headed Treason!—These proceedings in the Gen. Assembly and in Congress, indicate that there is in both bodies a large minority anxious for peace on the best terms that can be had, and of this minority no inconsiderable proportion would probably prefer reconstruction to an alliance (coupled with the abolition of slavery) with England and France.—My reference to Gov. Graham, Col. Orr of S.C., and Mr. Rives of Va. looked to the combined action of the most conspicuous statesmen in the three states, on which the prosecution of the war mainly depend.

I enclose you a magazine article,[3] the whole of which busy as you may be, you may think worthy perusal. I call your attention more particular however, to the few first pages as showing that the present are not the *only dark days* known to our history. The remarkable similarity in our condition in 1780 to the /present/ state of our affairs must strike you most forc[e]ably. It may serve to marshall you in the way that you are going. Mr. Neathry the State Printer was the publisher of the magazine and extracts from this article under the head of *History Repeating Itself, or North Carolina in 1780 and 1865*, might be reproduced with advantage in the Conservative.

My opinion is that the Gen. Assembly will not pass the convention bill. If it should do so, however, the people will vote it, in my opinion, by a decided majority.

I repeat the estimate heretofore given that your situation is one of great delicacy and difficulty, and calls for careful consultation with those on whose friendship and patriotism you can rely.

Yours affectionately,
D. L. Swain

Mr. Hill's[4] Christian name should be spelled Whitmel not Whitmill as printed.

[1]January 21, 1865, in this volume.
[2]Jehu A. Orr, a former secessionist Democrat, a jurist, a former U.S. Congressman, and a member of the Confederate Congress. William C. Harris, *The Day of the Carpetbagger: Republican Reconstruction in Mississippi* (Baton Rouge: Louisiana State University Press, 1979), 155-156.
[3]Possibly Swain's "Life and Letters of Whitmill Hill," *University of North Carolina Magazine* 10 (March 1861).
[4]Whitmel Hill, Revolutionary War officer, government official, and delegate to the Continental Congress. *Dictionary of North Carolina Biography*, s.v. "Hill, Whitmel."

James A. Seddon to ZBV   A&H:GP

CSA, War Dept.
Richmond, Va, Jany 26th. 65

His Excellency Z B Vance
Gov of North Carolina
Raleigh, N.C.

Sir:

In reply to your letter of the 21st. Dec. last[1] transmitting copy of the Resolutions of the Legislature of North Carolina relative to an order of the Adj & Insp Genl, requiring sick and mutilated soldiers to report to their commands, I have the honor to say that modification will be made in the order to relieve as far as practicable the evils complained of.

Very Respectfully
James A. Seddon
Secy. of War

[1]In this volume.

Andrew G. Magrath to ZBV   A&H:GP

State of South Carolina,
Executive Department.
26 January 1865.

Governor:

At my return from Charleston, Col. Mullins gave me your letter.[1] I am at once gratified and honored with your concurrence in the suggestions I ventured to make to you. Confirmed in my purpose by your approval, I am preparing and will dispatch without delay to the Governors of Alabama, Mississippi and Florida similar suggestions to those which were addressed to you. And supported as they will be by your endorsement I have no doubt of speedily securing that united and concerted action which I hope and believe will accomplish all that we desire. At the earliest moment and in anticipation of the response from the Governors of the States I have named, I will prepare and submit to you the draft of such a paper as I think calculated fitly to express the opinions we have formed.

I have written to Governor Brown in acknowledgment of his reply to me and also to the Hon. A. H. Stephens; to the latter addressing myself particularly to the consideration of the great danger of calling the people of Georgia into a Convention: assuring him of my hope and belief that without incurring the great dangers involved in the call for a Convention, all that we desire to secure can be accomplished without it; and most strongly urging him to use the authority of his name and the influence of his position against that proposition.

It is to me a proposition of incontestable correctness that the great source of the evils under which we labor is to be traced to the dependent position which the State Governments have been content to assume, in the progress of a war which in its large proportions has called forth the exercise of those powers, which were reserved to the States; but which Congress has attempted to use; and in that attempt the State Governments from patriotic, but as events have shown, not wise motives have acquiesced.

Starting from principles directly antagonistic, the Government of the United States and the Government of the Confederate States, have practically arrived in matters of administration at the same result. In both the suggestions of convenience, have been regarded as the sanction sufficient for any conduct they might adopt. And the most ill-omened cry throughout the Confederation is the one so frequently heard, that the force of law is suspended; and the pressure of the War has borne down the authority of the Constitution.

In the United States such a principle harmonized with the political dogmas there professed. In the Confederate States it was in violent opposition to the tenets for the vindication of which these States seceded. The arbitrary course of the former Government was therefore the natural consequence of its doctrines: while such a course in our Government was utterly inconsistent with its purposes or its powers. We have therefore presented in the whole progress of the war, the startling contradiction of States united in a league, for the support of their separate independence; called on to ignore if not abjure that independence. A compact of carefully guarded powers, expanding into a Government without limitation or responsibility. Guarantees for the liberty of person and protection of property, not only not respected; but so recklessly invaded, that the retention of such prerogatives now seem rather a mockery than a guaranty.

Whenever there has been an invasion of those guarantees of personal liberty and property, the citizen was paralyzed by the acquiescence of his State in the assumption by the common Government of its prerogative: and if the State did manifest a purpose to assert its dignity and its rights; the cry that the arm of the Common Government would be thereby paralyzed forced it to abandon its purpose and trust to the hope that a speedy termination of the war would terminate the forced and unnatural, I will not say, undignified condition, in which it had been placed.

As might have been expected, the exercise of powers which were never intended to be conferred upon the Common Government, has necessarily called forth, an equally unauthorized administration of them. Impressment, for the sake of illustration, has supplied the place of the contract. The order of a Bureau, accomplishes what Congress itself would not venture to do. The functions of a Judge are transferred to some military officer. And the court of Justice is closed by the denial to a magistrate of the power to enquire into the cause of a commitment. Arrests are made by order: detention is secured by command: and a power more gigantic than any crowned head in Europe would exercise, is presented to us as the means by which we are to insure success in a struggle to establish a Free Government.

It is thus that we have dried up the openings from which new courage and fresh impulse could have been given to our people in this protracted contest in which they have been engaged. We taught them to know their States as their country; and in the defence of that country we have blotted out and hidden from their view those states which are that country.

Unhappily for us the lapse of time which has but served to multiply the cases in which the State Governments have acquiesced in this wide departure from the standards of right and justice; have also so much increased the dangers of defeat and so much intensified the desire for repose, that it will require something of firmness to sustain the State Government in its proper position. But if there is difficulty and however great may be that difficulty it is to be more than counter-balanced by the plain truth, that it is only by restoring the State Governments to their proper condition, that our success in this war can be secured.

Unless military successes shall give to it new life, the credit of the Confederate Government is gone: with the loss of its credit its resources of course are also gone. Fortunately the credit of the States is unimpaired. The question therefore is looming up directly before us: shall the Confederate Government administer our credit, as it has our supplies and warlike appliances which we have given to it? I may well suppose that to this proposition there will be but one answer. If so, it will furnish the occasion, and that according to all probability not far distant, when we must understand better than we have done, the relations of the States to the Common Government at Richmond.

If I look forward to this or any other circumstance which is likely to bring us back to our true position, it is because in that position alone, can I find assurance of our certain success. We still have men enough to make an army able to win our deliverance: We still have resources sufficient to carry us safely through all our difficulties. But we have no more men to lose: We have now no resources to waste. The States, as States seceded: the States as States are to fight out this bloody war. They are the realities of this grand drama: all else is but the appendage. It is the political condition of each State which is to be lost or won. It is the life, liberty and property of the citizens of each of those States, which are staked upon the issue of the contest. If we save these, we save the Common Government these states have framed. And those States are held together not because they have so written and signed; but because they recognize in all of their relations, the evidence of a common destiny. Let us not forget in dealing with this great war, that we find our strength in the comprehension of the great principles of human conduct and action.

I have been led away by the consideration which press upon me farther I fear than your patience will allow: and will only delay you until I assure you of the respects of

> Your obedient servant
> A. G. Magrath

[1]January 18, 1865, in this volume.

Stephen R. Mallory to ZBV   A&H:GP

> Confederate States of America.
> Navy Department,
> Richmond, January 28th. 1865

His Excellency
Z. B. Vance
Governor of North Carolina
Raleigh N.C.

Sir,

I regret that the pressure of public business and my serious indisposition have delayed a response to your letter of the 3rd. instant.[1]

The distinct question at issue between us was raised by the statement of your message in reference to the Advance, that "the seizure of her foreign coals for the 'Tallahassee,' compelling her to put to sea with North Carolina Coals," was the cause of her loss. This question I distinctly met in my previous communication, and I desire to adhere to it. You will pardon me therefore for declining discussion upon other points which you raise as to whether the "Advance" had gold on freight &c, and which are unnecessary to the determination of this single question of fact.

In reference to your allusions to an anonymous article published in the "Sentinel," said to have been written under the auspices of the Navy Department; and to your statement that "From this it will seem that in order to convict me (You) of venturing upon an extraordinary statement, some parties connected with the Navy Department have ventured upon a rather ordinary one," it is only necessary to say that they are not only irrelevant but erroneous; and that the article in question was neither /written/ under the auspices, nor with the knowledge of this Department.

The policy of the Government with regard to its cruizers and the commerce of Wilmington, the influence of this policy upon the enemy to attack Fort Fisher, and the comparative value of a single cargo of bacon and a certain number of the enemy's ships destroyed at sea, all touched upon in your letter, invite discussion, but as their investigation would throw no light whatever upon the question of fact at issue, I refrain from further reference to them.

Your statement was, "This noble vessel, the pride of the State and benefactor of our soldiers and people, was captured by the enemy after she had successfully made her way through the blockading squadron in consequence of the seizure of her foreign Coals for the use of the cruizer 'Tallahassee,' compelling her to put to sea with North Carolina coal."

The obvious inference from this language is, that not only were coals taken from the "Advance" for the "Tallahassee," but that they were so taken when the "Advance" was about to "put to sea," compelling her to proceed with North Carolina coal and it was to correct a statement which I supposed had been entered upon unadvisedly that I furnished you with the formal report of the Coal Agent of this Department at Wilmington, made to Capt. Pinkney, the Chief Naval Officer in command there, that not only had no coal been taken from the "Advance," for the "Tallahassee," but that when coals were taken for the "Florie" and "Let her B," a portion of which, as alleged by Mr. Harris, was subsequently transferred to the "Tallahassee," and to which coals your statement refers, the "Advance" was not in the port of Wilmington. The coal agent says "that not one particle of coal was taken from the steamer "Advance," nor one pound impressed to which the State, or any of the joint owners of that steamer had the slightest claim."

Subsequent to the date of my former communication the following dispatch was received from Capt. Pinkney.

"Wilmington Decr. 29th. 1864

Hon. S. R. Mallory,

No coal was taken from the Advance, nor any belonging to her for the Tallahassee or any other vessel. I sent a report to this effect from the Coal Agent here some time ago.

(Signed) R. F. Pinkney
Comdg &c &c."

I regarded this report as conclusive and doubted not that you would so regard it, for I could not suppose that these agents could have seized the coals of the "Advance" and compelled her to "put to sea with North Carolina coal" without being aware of the fact. Your letter of the 3rd. however, not only reiterates the statement of the message, but it presents the following certificate in support of it.

"Wilmington N.C. Dec. 6. 1864.
I J. T. O'Reilly having charge of Messrs. Power Lowe & Co's wharf and Warehouse, do certify that on the 9th. July last, the Navy Department took from said Wharf 1170 barrows of Welsh coal being by weight 179 60/2000 Tons, which were placed on board St. Ship 'Let her B,' said ship having hauled to the wharf for that purpose.

I further certify that no coals have ever been returned in place of those taken as above described by said or any other Department of the Confederate States.
(Signed) J. T. O'Reilly."

This certificate that in July last coals were taken by the Navy Department from the wharf of Power Low & Co for the steamer "Let her B" is produced in proof of the statement that the loss of the "Advance" in the following September was "in consequence of the seizure of foreign coal for the cruizer 'Tallahassee' compelling her to put to sea" &c.

The following is the second certificate:

"Wilmington N.C. Decr. 6th. 1864.
I certify that on the afternoon of the 28th. or 29th. ult. I was present at a conversation between Mr. J. A. Willard Navy Agent and Eli Murrary Esqr. Agt. of State of No. Ca. at this place. I asked Mr. Willard the question what became of the coal taken from Messrs. Power Low & Co and others which he alledged had been placed on board the Stmr. 'Florie' and 'Let her B' after the expedition upon which these vessels were destined had been abandoned he replied 'what had not been consumed in going up and down the river had been transferred to the Stmr. Tallahassee.'

(Signed) Geo. Harris"

This certificate shows that Mr. Willard the Naval Coal Agent stated that the coal taken in July last from Power Low & Co, and referred to by Mr. O'Reilly, was used for the Steamers "Florie" and "Let her B," and that after the abandonment of the expedition for which they were designed, what had not been consumed in going up and down the river had been transferred to the "Tallahassee."

In addition to the evidence of these certificates in support of the statement made, you inform me that "Power Low & Co were part owners and agents of the vessel; it was their duty to accumulate coal for the use of our vessels by taking small quantities from each one which had a surplus for supplying those which were short. To this common heap the 'Advance' contributed as others and when she came to sail this heap destined as well for her and the others of the line had been taken by the Navy Department" &c.

Thus it appears that the Navy Department neither took coal from the "Advance" nor any coal belonging to her or designed for her exclusive use, but that the coal which it took from Power Low & Co for the "Let her B" in July last, might /possibly/ have been used for the "Advance" in the following September, if other vessels, equally entitled to it, had not in the meantime consumed it.

With all respect for your own convictions upon the subject I am unable to perceive that the charge advanced in your message is sustained by the certificates or by the foregoing explanation now presented.

In my previous communication I adverted to that statement in your message in which the captures /made by/ our cruizers out of Wilmington were characterized as "a few insignificant smacks," and, presuming that so strange an error of fact, and one so unjust to the officers and men of these cruizers, could only have found a place in your message from want of information upon the subject, and that its correction would promptly follow a presentation of the facts, I invited your attention to it, and submitted a schedule of the captures in question, numbering forty six, (46) & embracing nineteen (19) square rigged vessels. I regret that while your derisive reference to a "few insignificant smacks" is being circulated throughout the country, its correction, with the facts before you, has escaped your attention.

I have the honor to be with great respect

> Your Obt. Servt.
> S. R. Mallory
> Secretary of the Navy

[*Endorsed*] Copy & File

ZBV

[1]In this volume.

William A. Graham to ZBV   A&H:VanPC

Richmond
Jany. 28th 1865.

His Excely. Z B. Vance

My Dear Sir

I hasten to advise you that an informal commission consisting of,

A. H. Stephens
R. M. T. Hunter
J. A. Campbell,[1]

has been appointed by the President to proceed to Washington, and confer on the differences between the Northern and Southern States. This is so important a movement, and as it has obtained publicity here, I have felt at liberty to communicate it to you. It has no doubt been occasioned by the visits of Blair[2] who is again here, said to have been detained by the ice in the river today.

What will be result no one can foresee, but to all it is a fountain of good hopes.

I remain
very truly yours
W. A. Graham

[1]Alexander Hamilton Stephens, Confederate vice-president; Robert Mercer Taliaferro Hunter, Confederate senator and former secretary of state; and John Archibald Campbell, Confederate assistant secretary of war and former U.S. associate supreme court justice. On February 3, 1865, the three commissioners attended the so-called Hampton Roads Conference, held with Federal delegates in the hopes of negotiating a peaceful conclusion to the war. The conference failed primarily because the Federal government refused to recognize Confederate independence. Faust et al., *Encyclopedia of Civil War*, 108, 335-336, 376.

[2]Francis Preston Blair Sr., influential political advisor to President Abraham Lincoln. He proposed the negotiations that led to the Hampton Roads Conference, hoping that the Federal and Confederate governments would declare a truce and then combine in military operations to drive the French from Mexico. Faust et al., *Encyclopedia of Civil War*, 65.

William Smith to ZBV   A&H:VanPC

Private

State of Virginia.
Executive Department.
Richmond.
Jan'y 28. 1865

Gov. Vance
Raleigh

Dear Governor:

We are full of peace rumors here. The sketch of Blair's declarations in the *Enquirer*, is without foundation. The only result of his last interview with the President was the assurance, that Lincoln would receive commissioners to treat of peace. They have been appointed informally, and left this morning. Some quite interesting incidents occurred in connection with their appointment. It is understood that the President and Stephens have not been on good terms for some eighteen months or two years. On this occasion however, the former sent for Stephens, and they had a long, and as I understand frank and satisfactory, interview. The President having determined to send three commissioners, called upon Mr. Stephens to select the first one. He named Judge Campbell. The President then selected R. M. T. Hunter, and added "allow me to hope, Mr. Stephens, that you will accept the position of the third," which he did and as I have said, they are off this morning. This was handsome, and has given, I think, a good deal of satisfaction here.

I have no idea however, that anything will come of the movement, Except a clear demonstration that we can get no terms from Lincoln which we can accept with honor or safety. And so far it will do us good. God knows, I am anxious for peace, but more so for independence, and willingly as I would live to see the End of this bloody struggle, and to unite in putting up our fences, after it shall be over, I am not willing to survive the liberty and independence of my country

Very truly yours
Wm Smith

ZBV to Braxton Bragg   A&H:GLB

Raleigh Jan 3[0, *1865*]

Genl Bragg.
Wilmington.

Can I with safety disband the Home Guard for a few weeks? They have to be reorganized under the new law and I think this as good time as any.

Z. B. Vance—

ZBV to Anonymous   A&H:VanPC

Raleigh, Jany 31 [*1865*]

Dear Sir,

Your letters have been and read. I wish I had time to answer them as their importance deserves. I can not however, having only a moment in my office. Events as you will see are hurrying rapidly to a crisis. Our Commissioners to Washington[1] have gone on and the whole Country is in a ferment. Rumour after rumour reaches us from Richmond, gold is going down down, North & South, and the impression here seems to have taken hold of every body that the fighting is over, and the Legislature seems disposed to omit every preparation for the public defense. Never was there a greater error. It is most unwise to suspend our preparations in the hour of negotiations. We should really double our dilligence, & present to our enemies the energetic determination of a great people, driven to the wall in the last stages of desperation and ready to dare every thing! But alas! Alas! We hail the first step of our enemies toward negotiation, on any terms, as an act of gracious condescension and tacitly accept our degradation beforehand! I wish I could give you my opinions in full of this peace movement. It is a great swindle, and we are so anxious to be duped that we can never plead *rape*. I believe however it will result in peace but such a peace as I for one will blush to accept. Well, well! Come down & see me.

Most sincerely yours
Z B Vance

[1]Commissioners to Hampton Roads Conference: Stephens, Hunter, and Campbell.

ZBV to Bradley T. Johnson   A&H:GLB

State of North Carolina
Executive Department
Raleigh Feb 1st. 1865

Genl Bradley T. Johnson[1]
Salisbury N.C.

Most distressing accounts reach me of the suffering and destitution of the Yankee prisoners under your charge. If the half be true it is disgraceful to our humanity and will provoke severe retaliation. I hope however it is not so bad as represented, but lest it be so, I hereby tender you any aid in my power to afford to make their condition more tolerable. I know the great scarcity of food which prevails, but shelter and warmth can certainly be provided and I can spare you some clothing if the Yankees will deliver as much to N.C. Troops in Northern prisons.
Please let me hear from you.

Respfly Yrs
Z. B. Vance

[1]Bradley Tyler Johnson, commandant of the Confederate prison at Salisbury, North Carolina. Faust et al., *Encyclopedia of Civil War*, 396-397.

ZBV to James A. Seddon   A&H:GLB

State of North Carolina,
Executive Department
Raleigh Feby. 1st. 1865

Hon J A. Seddon
Secy of War

Dr. Sir,
I beg leave to call your attention to the condition of the Federal prisoners of war at Salisbury N.C. Accounts reach me of the most distressing character

in regard to their suffering and destitution. I earnestly request you to have the matter enquired into and if in our power to relieve them that it be done. If they are wilfully left to suffer when we can avoid it, it would be not only a blot upon our humanity, but would lay us open to a severe retaliation. I know how straightened our means are however, and will cast no blame upon any one without further information.

> Very respectfully,
> Yr. obt. Servt.
> Z. B. Vance

Frederick W. Seward to ZBV   A&H:GP (Holden)

[*With enclosure*]

(*Duplicate*)

Department of State
Washington, February 2, 1865

To his Excellency
The Governor of the State of North Carolina.
Raleigh, N.C.

Sir:

I transmit an attested Copy of a Joint Resolution of Congress, approved on the 1st. instant, proposing to the Legislatures of the several States a Thirteenth Article to the Constitution of the United States. Your Excellency is requested to cause the decision of the Legislature of North Carolina to be taken upon the subject. An acknowledgment of the receipt of this communication is requested by

> Your Excellency's
> Most obedient Servant,
> F. W. Seward
> Acting Secretary.

[Enclosure]

Resolution by William H. Seward

(Duplicate)

United States of America.
Department of State,
To all to whom these presents shall come, Greeting:

I certify, That annexed is a true copy of a Joint Resolution of Congress, entitled "A Resolution submitting to the Legislatures of the several States a Proposition to amend the Constitution of the United States," approved February 1, 1865; the original of which is on file in this Department.

In testimony whereof, I, William H. Seward, Secretary of State of the United States, have hereunto subscribed my name and caused the seal of the Department of State to be affixed.

Done at the City of Washington, this second day of February, A. D. 1865, and of the Independence of the United States of America the eighty-ninth.

William H. Seward

A Resolution submitting to the Legislatures of the several
States a Proposition to amend the Constitution of the United States.

Resolved by the Senate and House of Representatives of the United States of America in Congress assembled, (two thirds of both Houses concurring,) That the following article be proposed to the legislatures of the several States as an amendment to the constitution of the United States, which, when ratified by three fourths of said legislatures, shall be valid, to all intents and purposes, as a part of the said Constitution, namely:

Article XIII.

Section 1. Neither slavery nor involuntary servitude, except as a punishment for crime whereof the party shall have been duly convicted, shall exist within the United States, or any place subject to their jurisdiction.

Section 2. Congress shall have power to enforce this article by appropriate legislation.

Approved, February 1, 1865.

G. W. *Booth to* ZBV   A&H:GP

Hd. Qrs. Post Salisbury
3d. February 1865.

To His Excellency
Governor Z. B. Vance

Sir,

Your communication of 1st. inst.[1] in reference to the condition of the Federal prisoners at this Post has been received. General Johnson has been absent for the week or so past, detained in Virginia by the illness of his wife and I will endeavor to furnish your Excellency a short statement. General Johnson will on his return, which is expected tomorrow or at most the first of next week, answer at more length.

The C.S. Prison when established at this place was contemplated for Confederate prisoners only. Buildings and sufficient ground being purchased for that purpose. About the fifth of November 1864, a large number prisoners of war—some 8,000 were suddenly sent here, the Govt. having no other place to send them. The grounds were enlarged and such preparations as could be made were arranged for their reception. A short time after their arrival tents were issued and now they are all under shelter of some sort. The number of prisoners confined here has reached as high a figure as 10000. When sent here they were in extremely bad condition.

Wood in sufficient quantity is issued them. Only two days have they been without and then unavoidable circumstances prevented its issue. The issue of wood is regulated in a measure by the weather. In extreme days they receive more than when the weather is mild. As evidence that they have plenty—they offer to sell and do sell to the sutler wood for his store in exchange for Tobacco. He informs me that more is offered him than he buys or has use for.

The matter of food receives the earnest attention of the Commanding Officers. They regularly receive One lb. good bread, One pint soup, besides small issues of Meat or Sorghum—sometimes small quantities of both. Enclosed please find a mem a/c[2] showing the number of prisoners and the articles given them, for the past fifteen days. As to clothing their condition is truly deplorable—most of them having been prisoners some 6 or 9 mos. The Confederate Govt. cannot issue clothing to them, and none has been received at this Post from the North. Gen. Johnson, in a communication to Comr. Ould, in early part of January, called attention to their condition in this respect, which he set forth in the fullest terms, and requested his paper be forwarded to the Federal Authorities. Your generous proposition will no doubt be readily agreed to by the Fed. Govt. As soon as the Genl. returns I will lay your communication before him and he will do all he can to effect its consum/m/ation.

Ten wells are in the Prison, which afford them water, in addition they are permitted every day to bring water in barrels from a neighboring creek. No stream of water runs thro' the Prison—this is unfortunate, but a removal of prisoners to Columbia is contemplated and all improvements—building &c has been prohibited by Genl. Winder.[3] Genl. York[4] who has visited most of the Prisons south recruiting, assures me of the superiority of this. In consequence of the lack of transportation and the damages to the R. Roads of late, the energy of the Officers of the Com & Q.M. depmts. has been subjected to no mean test, but the prisoners have not suffered for wood or rations. An Inspector from your Excellency will receive every facility to visit the Prison.

In regard to a former communication[5] from your Excellency in reference to the Senior Reserves, a reply to which has been delayed by the Generals absence, I most respectfully state—Every indulgence consistent with the service has been afforded them. Furloughs for seven days with the addition of the time required to reach their homes, are granted at the rate of six to the One hundred arms bearing men present for duty. The duty is onerous on them, but is caused by the frequent and numerous desertions.

> I have the honor to be
> Very Respectfully
> Your Excellency's
> Obdt. svt.
> G.W. Booth
> Capt. & a.a.g.

P.S. Since writing the above a telegram has been recd. stating that shoes, blankets, &c have been shipped from Richmond and Federal officers are now here to superintend their distribution

> G W Booth
> A A G

[1]ZBV to Bradley T. Johnson, in this volume.
[2]Not extant.
[3]In February 1864, John H. Winder had become commissary general for all Confederate prisons east of the Mississippi. Faust et al., *Encyclopedia of Civil War*, 836.

[4]Zebulon York, a Louisiana brigadier recruiting foreign-born Federal prisoners of war to fight for the Confederacy. Current et al., *Encyclopedia of the Confederacy*, 4:1751-1752.

[5]Not extant.

ZBV to Calvin H. Wiley   A&H:Wiley

State of North Carolina,
Executive Department,
Raleigh Feb 3 1865.

Rev C H Wiley[1]

My dear Sir,

Your very interesting letter[2] has been recd. and read carefully by myself & Mrs. Vance. I have not time to answer it as its importance deserves and reckon you hardly expected me to do so now.

I am free to confess that I have long entertained views somewhat similar to yours with regard to the amelioration of our system of slavery. Years ago, when the furor in behalf of slavery was so strong in consequence of Northern aggression, that the boldest among us did not dare to say a word against any part of the system, I have been deeply impressed with the opinion that it was our duty to reform & correct it, for the very cause's sake.

Nothing would afford me greater pleasure than to begin now, if there was any opening. I fear indeed that the fatal blow is about to be stricken which shall abolish it at once, to the great injury of both races. No time, I feel sure, will be allowed for doctoring or reforming, for whether we reconstruct the Union or establish our independence with foreign aid I am quite certain that the price we pay will be *abolition*. But should I be disappointed, should God permit me to see my country established in peace again with slavery preserved, I shall deem it a duty I owe to Him to assist my countrymen in effecting these great reforms demanded alike by policy, humanity, and religion.

I can not write more now. We are almost in a state of chaos here, many seem to regard peace as already come & are disposed to abandon every preparation for defence.

With many thanks for your undeniable manifestations of regard

I am very truly yours
Z B Vance

[1]Calvin Henderson Wiley, state superintendent of common schools. *Dictionary of North Carolina Biography*, s.v. "Wiley, Calvin Henderson."

[2]January 25, 1865, A&H:VanPC. In his letter, Wiley maintained that the sin of mistreating slaves—separating families, refusing to teach them to read and write, etc.—had resulted in God's retribution and the impending collapse of the Confederacy. A deeply religious man, Wiley advocated schooling for slaves.

ZBV *to James A. Seddon*   A&H:GLB

State of North Carolina
Executive Department
Raleigh Feb. 6th. 1865

Hon. James A. Seddon
Secy. of War

Dear Sir.

I have received information from numerous citizens of Burke County that certain persons profess to have authority from the Confederate Government to distil grain into Whiskey in that county, and that they have and now are buying up grain at high prices for that purpose. The citizens from whom I receive this information represent that grain is very scarce in that section of the State and that the families of Soldiers and the poor and needy will require all the surplus which can be spared from the Army. It is also stated that the whiskey when so distilled is to be converted into vinegar and is not to be used for hospital purposes. I am informed that it has been urged upon the Confederate Authorities as a reason for granting such privileges that large quantities of pork can be received from the swill of these distilleries, but surely such a reason could not influence their action. If the object is to raise pork, it can be much better effected by feeding the grain directly to the swine. Knowing as I do the wants of the community whose interest is thus to be effected, I most earnestly insist that if such permission has been granted it be immediately revoked. With sentiments of much respect,

Your obedient Servant,
Z. B. Vance-

John C. Breckinridge to ZBV   A&H:GP

Confederate States of America
War Department
Richmond February 8, 1865

His Excellency Z. B. Vance
Governor of N. Carolina
Raleigh N.C.

Sir

Your letter of the 1st inst[1] calling attention to the suffering condition of
the Federal prisoners at Salisbury, has been received.

I have the honor to inform you that I have directed the Adjt General
to cause an inspection to be made of the prison at Salisbury and have such
instructions given to the Inspecting Officer as will enable him to correct the
evils complained of.

Very Respectfully
John C Breckinridge[2]
Secretary of War

[1]ZBV to James A. Seddon February 1, 1865, in this volume.

[2]John Cabell Breckinridge, whom President Davis had recently appointed
secretary of war following James A. Seddon's resignation. Current et al., *Encyclopedia
of the Confederacy,* 1:213-215.

ZBV to Stephen R. Mallory   A&H:GLB

State of North Carolina,
Executive Department,
Raleigh, Feby 9th. 1865

Hon S. R. Mallory,
Secty. of the Navy

Sir;

Your communication of the 28th. ult.[1] has been received, in regard
to what you are pleased to term "a question of fact" between yourself
and me. I have not the slightest objection to your proposed adherence

to the statements made in your former communication. I only desire to be admitted a similar privilege, of adhering to my own allegations in regard to the loss of the Advance. Nor do I care to argue the "question of fact" so gravely made upon me involving only a quibble as to whether coal in the possession of my Agent was in my possession. The distinction between that kind of possession which is required to support an indictment for larceny and that required to sustain an act of trespass *vi et armis*[2] might be learnedly discanted upon here, but as you very properly observe in reference to my allusion to the supposed gold on board the Advance it would be "unnecessary to the determination of the single question of fact."

But though such is my susceptibility to reason I may be induced to forego an argument on the question of the possession of my agent being my possession, I confess I am not quite ready to admit that the possession of A.B. abstractly considered is not the possession of A.B. or that other remarkable proposition that the legal and undisputed possession of an article affords not "the slightest claim" of property. And yet such doctrine I understand you to advance when acknowledging that Power Lowe & Co were part owners of the Steamer Advance, that your Agents took one hundred & sixty nine tons of coal from them, you yet assert that not one particle of coal was taken from the Steamer Advance, nor one pound impressed to which the State or any of the joint owners of that Steamer had the slightest claim!!

Now in the name of Blackstone, Coke and all the lawyers at once from Moses to Capt. Pinkney, who *did* have any claim to that coal? who *was* its owner?

But really my /dear/ Sir, I think this correspondence had better close and leave the public and the proper committee in Congress to determine the question between us. If the taking from my Agent of coals collected by him for the use of my vessel & his did not justify me in my statements to the Legislature, then I am content they should say so. I desire of course no difficulty with the Navy Dept or any other branch of the government struggling & straining as they are in the public defense. I was induced more particularly to make this public complaint because it was not the first time that the coals for my Steamer had been seized by the Confederate authorities in Wilmington, and for the further reason that from the first I met with nothing but opposition from all sides in my efforts to clothe the troops of North Carolina. I mentioned those other matters to which you allude as irrelevant to the present question, simply because I considered the general policy of my message on this head as assailed by you, and as I have assailed the policy of the Govmt. Now that the fall of the defences of the Cape Fear and the closure of our last port[3] have given a melancholy confirmation to my strictures, I have no more to say.

Very respectfully,
Your obt. servt.
Z. B. Vance-

[1]In this volume.

[2]With force and arms.

[3]A joint Federal army and navy operation had captured Fort Fisher near Wilmington on January 15. That capture ended blockade-running out of the Cape Fear port. U.S. troops occupied the town of Wilmington on February 22. Faust et al., *Encyclopedia of Civil War*, 273, 831.

ZBV to Stephen R. Mallory   A&H:GLB

State of North Carolina.
Executive Department,
Raleigh Feb 11th. 1865.

Hon S. R. Mallory,
Secretary of the Navy.

Sir:

On examining a printed copy of your letter to me of the 28th. Dec. ult,[1] sent me by a member of Congress, I find that I had committed the mistake of attributing to Capt. Pinkney, certain offensive expressions which were only used by one J. A. Willard, Naval Coal Agent. I was led into this by the following language in your letter, "Capt Pinkney C.S. Navy &c. forwards the following report," and by not noticing the signature closely at the end of the quotation. I have the honor therefore to beg that you will consider the correspondence, on my part, amended by striking out the words "Capt Pinkney" wherever they occur and the insertion of "Willard," and also by striking out any words of respect or praise in my first letter, qualifying the words "Capt Pinkney," as not applicable to the word "Willard," for I should as greatly regret the waste of civility on the latter, as I do the unintentional or mistaken application of any censure to the former.

I am Sir,
Very Respectfully
Your obt. Servt.
Z. B. Vance

[1]In this volume.

Bradley T. Johnson to ZBV   A&H:GP

Hd Qrs. Post. Salisbury NoCa
Feby 12 1865

His Excellency Z. B. Vance
Governor of NoCa

Governor

On arriving yesterday I found yrs of 16th. ulto[1] & 1st. inst[2] which have heretofore been replied to by Capt Booth AAG.

I avail myself of my first time to acknowledge personally your liberal offer. Col. Hoke[3] informs me that the condition of the Reserves is greatly ameliorated but they still want clothes.

I think (350) three hundred & fifty out fits will do. Jackets, pants, shirts, drawers, shoes, stockings & caps.

Please to order them sent to Capt Goodman Post Quarter Master & have an invoice sent me also, so that I can see they are properly applied to your Reserves exclusively.

No one can feel more acutely than I do the condition of the prisoners of war here. It is disgraceful to our country. Capt Booth's letter showed you that as to food & fuel they were well supplied but they suffer for clothes & shelter. Genl Winder proposed removing them before Xmas. & therefore forbade any buildings to be erected here. A large percent have therefore lived *in holes in the ground.* Were I to attempt to erect Barracks here Spring wd. come on before they cd. be finished. I must therefore try to get Tents. Can you lend me or procure for me in Raleigh 150 or 200 Wall tents. If so pray send them on at once. I recently visited Richmond for the main purpose of pressing on our authorities our duties to ourselves & these people, laying before them the terrible suffering & mortality among them. I have procured from the Federal officer for distributing goods in Richmond 3500 Blankets which will be here tomorrow. With the tents their condition will be tolerable, but nothing will alleviate it but speedy exchange.

In Richmond & since from Vice Prest. Stephens I learned that Genl Grant is willing to receive from us 3000 per week. I have telegraphed Genl Gardner[4] at Richmond urging him to press the immediate delivery of all the prisoners in North & South Carolina at Wilmington. This could be done from Florence & Columbia South Carolina by the Manchester Road & from here by way of Raleigh without encumbering our transportation. If this is not done speedily, the prisoners from Columbia will have to be moved up here or to Greensboro & those from <Columbia>/Florence/

towards Raleigh, & thus NoCa will have to subsist 20,000 more men, eating up supplies which should go to Richmond. In case of the evacuation of Wilmington no distant contingency, & the possession of Columbia by the enemy, equally possible the Prisoners at Florence are cut off, & can only be extricated by a march thro central NoCa on Raleigh which will expose yr people to more depredations than from the march of a hostile column. These considerations will, I doubt not induce your Excellency to join with me in urging the Confederate authorities to consent to an immediate delivery of these prisoners at the most convenient point.

Grant proposes to take his men & deliver ours—both parties to be on *parole*. I think he never intended to exchange them so as to allow our men to go back to our Army. On this our authorities may stick—but we ought to agree to it at once. The prisoners here eat our rations & keep men out of the field to guard them. They are a terrible burthen—it wd. be better to send them home at once on parole. But the men we get back, will go home, reinvigorate the population for the War, work, help to raise provisions, & in case of emergency, *defend themselves*, by guerrilla war, of which right no parole can deprive them.

It wd. be better to have them in our Army, but failing that, let us have them at the plough with the rifle in the fence corner.

I press this upon you, for if these people are not turned over to their own authorities, they will be pressed back into No Ca who will have to subsist three Armies—the Confederate, the Federal & the *Neutral*, more terrible than either.

> Yr obt svt
> Bradley T. Johnson
> Brig. Genl

[*Endorsed*] File & Copy

ZBV

[1]Not extant.

[2]In this volume.

[3]John Franklin Hoke, commander of Fourth Regiment of North Carolina Reserves assigned to guard prisoners of war. *Dictionary of North Carolina Biography,* s.v. "Hoke, John Franklin."

[4]William Montgomery Gardner, Confederate commandant of military prisons east of the Mississippi River. Faust et al., *Encyclopedia of Civil War.*

William A. Graham to ZBV   A&H:VanPC

Confidential

Richmond
Feb. 12th 1865

His Excell Z. B. Vance-

My dear sir

Your telegram[1] was received today, in which you request that I shall solicit Mr. Stephens[2] to take Raleigh in his way home, and make a public address there on the state of the country.

In reply I have to state, that Mr S. left this city last Wednesday evening for Ga. that he declined to make any speech here after his return from the interview with Lincoln & Seward,[3] and I have reason to believe, that he does not design to address the people of his own state, as the papers of this city have announced, but without authority. He had had no intercourse with the President during this session of Congress untill within a few days before the appointment of the commission to confer with the U.S. Govt. They were brought together by the interposition of friends, and held two long consultations: at the end of which he was appointed on the commission. After his return from Hampton roads they met again: but having an opinion, that the President is not conducting our affairs wisely, he refused to take part in any public demonstration, as to the course to be pursued in the future, and is said to have left here in much despondency as to future prospects. A deep anxiety pervades the minds of others, not so much on account of the termination of the negotiations, as of the military situation. Grant is understood to have been heavily reinforced, so as to confine to this section all of Lee's army: and Sherman threatens to overrun S.C. and perhaps our own state at no distant day. The speeches at public meetings here and the inflammatory leaders in the newspapers brought out no volunteers, but degenerated into an advocacy of the fatal policy of appealing to our slaves for assistance against the enemy. Subsistence for Lee's army is also jeoparded by the occupation of the S.C. Railroad by Sherman, and every advance he makes in this direction. The forces we have, in that quarter do not seem to be concentrated, but are divided out between Charleston, Augusta, Columbia and I know not what other localities, with jarring counsels among our Generals.

No one advises the acceptance of the terms offered by Lincoln, but the question is being considered, what is to be done to resist his armies, and whether reunion, by which ten states may defeat the proposed amendment to the Constitution & retain slavery be not preferable to the triumph of his arms, and the subjection of every thing to his power. Whether a solution can be given to these problems by the agency of this Govt. or the interposition of the states, is also matter of consideration. The President is not in favor with Congress, and is believed not to possess the wisdom required for the emergency. His administration could be easily made powerless, but that would be to weaken the cause of the country. The Sect. State[4] is very unpopular and was struck at by the Va. delegation in their request for a general change of Cabinet, by which Sedden was induced to resign. This delegation in a body was the only one consulted, before the introduction of the suspension of Hab. Corpus: and you will see from the Presidents reply to Sedden that a pretty quarrel now exists between them.

The Commissioners represent Lincoln & Seward as apparently courteous, kind, and anxious for peace, but earnest /in/ stating their terms, and seemingly confident in their power to enforce them.

No one can foresee what turn events may take. Congress will be in session for two or three weeks yet, and I will endeavor to keep you advised of their progress. There is said to be deep depression in the army or portions of it. In the late battle near Pet.bg certain troops (Va. I believe) refused to charge untill Genl. Lee rode forward to lead them in person, and in doing so had a button shot from his coat.

The employment of slaves as soldiers has again been brought before the senate & referred to committee. I look upon it as a fatal measure if adopted, and Mr Hunter believes, the agitation of this subject in the Prests message was the cause of the proposed amendment to the Constitution U.S. to abolish slavery.

I have thus given you something of the undercurrents of events, and conversations here, pertaining to /the/ serious crisis which is now upon us, and have to beg, that you will observe proper discretion among those to whom you may think proper to confide them.

Very truly yours
W. A. Graham

[1]Not extant.

[2]Alexander H. Stephens, Confederate vice-president.

[3]On February 3, at Hampton Roads, Virginia, Lincoln and his secretary of state, William Henry Seward, met to discuss peace terms with Confederate commissioners Alexander H. Stephens, John A. Campbell, and Robert M. T. Hunter, all critics of Jefferson Davis. The conference failed quickly when the Confederate commissioners learned that Lincoln would not compromise on his stipulations that the Confederate states lay down their arms, renounce their independence, and accept the emancipation of their slaves. Current et al., *Encyclopedia of the Confederacy*, 2:732-733.

[4]Judah P. Benjamin.

ZBV *to Tod R. Caldwell*　　　　　　　A&H:GLB

State of North Carolina,
Executive Department,
Raleigh Feb. 13th. 1865

Todd R. Caldwell Esq.[1]
Morganton N.C.

Dear Sir;

The board of which you were chairman, to investigate the condition of the rail-roads in N.C. having never made any report of their proceedings, and a similar committee having been appointed by the last session of the Legislature, said Board is dissolved, and your commission, with those of your associates is hereby revoked.

Very respectfully,
Your obt. servt.
Z. B. Vance-

[1]Tod Robinson Caldwell, lawyer, state legislator, postwar governor, and one of the founders of the Republican Party in North Carolina. *Dictionary of North Carolina Biography*, s.v. "Caldwell, Tod Robinson."

ZBV *to William Smith*　　　　　　　A&H:GLB

State of North Carolina,
Executive Department,
Raleigh Feb. [*ca. 14*] 1865.

His Excellency Gov. Smith.

Dear Sir,

Your letter[1] in answer to mine[2] enclosing a resolution of the Genl. Assembly of this State, in relation to the subject of the transportation of salt, has been received, covering statement of Mr. J. N. Clarkson Supt. &c.

The General Assembly was on the point of adjourning when it was read, and therefore could take no action in regard thereto. The special committee on salt, however, to whom I submitted your communication, desired me to express for them their satisfaction as to its explanations and to say that they considered their previous action as hasty. I desire, Governor, to add expressions of my own regret, for any hasty condemnation of the action of the constituted authorities of your State, calculated to impair those friendly and intimate relations which have and should exist between N.C. & Virginia. Whilst I cannot say that the requirement levied upon foreign trains by your Board of Public Works to transport salt for the Confederate States is unreasonable, it is yet open to the objection that, as we understand it Virginia is furnishing the Confederacy salt by *contract*, and that we should not be required to assist in filling Virginia's contracts, and further, that the trains we sent there to haul for N.C. were hired at a cost of $200 per day, and we were compelled to pay full freight on every bushel of salt beside. This you will acknowledge would render it peculiarly hard on us unless the State of Virginia or the Confederate Government would pay all expenses of the fourth load of what we could not complain. Again, one of one of [sic] the trains hired by this State, was required to haul wood for the furnaces of the Virginia works, and in case of refusal, was forbidden to run at all: so my agent informs me, of this no explanation was offered, and I must suppose escaped your attention altogether. It seems to me that this requisition was entirely unreasonable, and not to be allowed. I agree with you in the opinion that there may be private axes to grind in this matter of transportation of salt, but have not been able to ascertain precisely where the fault lies. It is due to you to be informed however, that considerable quantities of salt have been sold in various towns in this State by a Mr. Gilchrist said to be a partner or agent of Col. Clarkson, whether it be the salt of that gentleman or of the State of Virginia, I submit that its transportation here shows a capacity of the Virginia Roads to transport more salt from Saltville than is required either by her citizens or the Confederate Govt. and to the extent that this salt prevents North Carolina salt from coming forward we have the right to complain. In regard to the order which I gave that no supplies should go from this State to Virginia, I regret that you regard it so harsh and unneighborly. I did nothing more than verbally request our rail-roads not to transport provisions from this State to yours, which I thought warranted by the orders of your Board of Public Works, prohibiting our salt from coming over your roads even on our own trains except upon such conditions as we deemed unjust. Had I applied it only to supplies belonging to the State and going in your State trains, the order would have been precisely similar and I must be pardoned for adding, just. I shall however take great pleasure in revoking it, and shall hereafter require trains from your State to do only the amount of transportation here as is imposed upon ones in Va. I make no allusion to the constitutional question raised in your letter, as a *tu quoque*[3] is a poor argument, and I earnestly desire that our relations should have a deeper & more friendly foundation than the requirements of the constitution, sacred as they should be. To make some definite arrangement of this matter, I have authorized Mr. Woodfin our Supt. to call and see you, and to make any accommodation which may be just and right. He is fully posted as to my /own/ views and thoroughly conversant with the matters, in hand, and I hope he may be able to suggest such terms as will be acceptable to you, and profitable to both parties.

> I am, Governor,
> Very respectfully yours,
> Z. B. Vance

[1]February 13, 1865, A&H:GP
[2]January 17, 1865, in this volume.
[3] "You also"—one doing what one criticizes in others.

Proclamation by ZBV   A&H:GLB

By the Governor
A Proclamation to the People of North Carolina

Whereas It is incumbent on me by virtue of the high trust your partiality has conferred upon me to watch with vigilence over your welfare, guard with fidelity your interests; and warn you of every approaching danger, Now therefore I Zebulon B. Vance, Governor of the said State, actuated by a sacred sense of duty and love of country, do deem it necessary to address you in this manner in regard to the dangers and duties of the present time, earnestly praying that it may be conducive to harmony and good will, wherein only is to be found a safe and honorable deliverance from all our troubles. It is known to you all, that in the beginning of these troubles North Carolina was so decidedly opposed to initiating the secession of her Southern sisters that any attempt to force her to do so by even a majority of her people prior to the Proclamation of Lincoln in 1861, would most likely have resulted in civil war, among our own citizens. It pleased God, however, to prevent this calamity and to calm all the fierce passions of party bitterness, and to cause the most perfect unanimity by means of that Proclamation which placed before us the dire necessity of either assisting or slaughtering our own brothers and friends. Interest, honor, and sympathy combined to decide us upon resistance to what all united in condemning as a cruel and wicked war upon the homes and liberties of the South. With unexampled zeal we entered into the war, rushed forward our bravest sons, and poured out our richest treasures. With immense sacrifices, and varying fortunes we continued the struggle, still with great unanimity for years. About the end of the third year, however, a portion of our people in common with many others throughout the South, seeing how our best citizens were falling, and how our fairest lands were desolated, began to urge that peace should be sought for by negotiations as well as by the sword. They argued that our Confederate authorities, moved by pride of opinion and embittered by the length and fierceness of the conflict, had not made a sufficient trial of statesmanship as a means of stopping the war, that no doubt if properly approached either by commissioners, appointed by our common government, or by the states separately, supposing diplomatic reasons would prevent the enemy, from treating with the former, that our enemy would grant us better terms than we had supposed, and promising that if a fair and honest effort at negotiations should be spurned by the enemy or rejected then all classes and conditions of men in the South would, unite in an earnest prosecution of the War. This was the first serious approach to a division among our people. Sympathizing with the reasonableness of this demand, though not with all the reasons given for believing in its efficiency, and being as sincerely desirous as it was possible for man to be, to stop the war on honorable terms, I as your Governor addressed President Davis in December 1863, and urged this course upon him. In answer thereto, he assured me that three separate and distinct efforts had been made to treat with the enemy, without obtaining even a hearing and that he did not see how a fourth one could be initiated without humiliation to ourselves and injury to our cause. Trusting that Providence would yet open the way the matter rested here for another year. Many, however of our people who advocated peace upon such vague and ill-defined terms as to cause doubt of their good faith and loyalty, continued sedulously to disseminate the oppinion that our own government alone was to blame for the continuance of the war, going so far in some instances as to threaten revolutionary measures for wresting the treaty-making power from its hands, and negotiating with the enemy ourselves, alleging that we could certainly get such terms if the States would act in their sovereign capacity, as would secure our property and slaves, by reconstruction. Since the beginning of the present year however two individuals from the North having visited Richmond on a peace mission, by the authority of President Lincoln, and having as our President supposed opened the way for another effort at negotiations, it was promptly made. He immediately sent a delegation through, the lines for that purpose, consisting of Vice President Stephens, Judge Campbell late of the Supreme Court of the United States, and the Hon. R. M. T. Hunter Confederate States Senator from the State of Virginia, men all eminent for their abilities, public services, and the long continued confidence and respect of their countrymen. The first two are well known to have opposed the beginning of this war, and to sympathize with the general desire for negotiations. They were met at Fortress Monroe by President Lincoln, and Mr Seward, his Secretary of State, who without allowing them to leave the boat on which they arrived, told them what appears in the following official report

Richmond Feb. 5, 1865.

To the President of the Confederate States:

Sir,

Under your letter of appointment of commissioners of the 28th. <we> we proceeded to seek an informal conference with Abraham Lincoln President of the United States upon the subject mentioned in your letter. The Conference was granted, and took place on the 3d. inst, on board a steamer anchored in Hampton Roads where we met President Lincoln and Hon. Mr. Seward Secretary of State for the United States. It continued for several hours, and was both full and explicit. We learned from them that the message of President Lincoln to the Congress of the United States in December last explains clearly and distinctly his sentiments as to the terms, conditions and mode of proceeding by which peace could be secured to the people, and we were not informed that they would be modified or altered to obtain that end. We understood from him that no terms or proposals of any treaty or agreement looking to an ultimate settlement would be entertained or made by him with the authorities of the Confederate States because that would be a recognition of their existence as a separate power which under no circumstances would be done, and for like reasons that no such terms would be entertained by him from States separately, that no extended truce or armistice as at present advised would be granted or allowed without a satisfactory assurance in advance of the complete restoration of the authority of the Constitution and Laws of the United States over all places within the States of the Confederacy; that whatever circumstances may follow from the re-establishment of that authority must be accepted out and out. Individuals subject to pains and penalties, under the laws of the United States, might rely upon a very liberal use of power confided to him, to remit these pains and penalties, if peace be restored during such conference. The proposed amendments to the constitution adopted by Congress on the 31st. ult were brought to our notice. These amendments provide that neither slavery nor involuntary servitude except for crime should exist within the United States, or in any place within its jurisdiction, and Congress should have power to enforce the amendments by appropriate legislation, of all the correspondence that prece/e/ded the conference herein mentioned and leading to the same, you have heretofore been informed.

Very Respectfully Your obt Servt.
A. H. Stephens
R. M. T. Hunter
J. A. Campbell

Thus you see that neither terms nor conditions were spoken of in the interview but only subjugation offered us, the mere details of which they proposed to settle at one blow. All our hopes in the humanity and moderation of our enemies were dashed to the ground. No terms or proposals of a treaty coming either from the Confederate States, or any one of the States would be entertained, but a complete, absolute and unconditional submission to the Constitution and laws of the United States is required as a preliminary step to any, even the slightest cessation of hostilities. Seeing then that we can treat with the enemy, neither by the authorities of the Confederate States, nor by separate State action, what will be result if we submit, as we are required to do? This we can partly judge by examining that constitution and those laws, to which we are required to yield obedience. That constitution is not the one we left. In addition to the changes it has undergone by corrupt and violent interpretation by Black Republican judges its wording has been changed as to decree immediately and forever the abolition of slavery. The "laws" to whose tender mercies we are referred provide most minutely and particularly for the punishment of death by the halter, of every man, soldier, sailor or marine, civilians and others, who have been engaged in what they term rebellion. Not ceasing to punish with the death of the offender, the "laws" of the United States also provide that all his property, real and personal, shall be confiscated. The only mitigation of the vigor threatened by these laws is contained in Mr. Lincoln's proclamation accompanying his annual message in December 1863, in which he proposes to hang only those above the rank of Colonel in the Army and Lieutenant in the Navy, and all civil and diplomatic officers or agents of the Confederate Government, and various other classes therein specified, coupled with a vague intimation to our commissioners in their recent interview, that whilst we must prepare to accept all the pains and penalties of the laws, we might rely on a liberal use of the pardoning power, vested in him. He also informs us that the terms set forth in his recent message of December last, wherein he re-endorses the above mentioned proclamation will be rightly adhered to. Now then, we can sum up, in some sort, the consequences of our submission. Four million slaves, two hundred thousand of whom have been in arms against us, turned loose at once in our midst, our lands confiscated, and sold out to pay the cost our subjugation or parcelled among negro soldiers as the reward of the slaughter of their masters; our women, children and old men reduced to beggary, and driven from their once happy homes, our mutilated and diseased soldiers, starving in rags from door to door, spurned by even pensioned negro soldiers, whilst the gallows grows weary under the burden of wisest statesmen and bravest defenders, to say nothing of universal financial ruin and the intolerable oppression of a rapacious and vindictive foe in the hour of conquest! Great God! is there a man in all this honorable, high spirited and noble commonwealth, so steeped in every conceivable meanness, so blackened with all the guilt of treason, or so damned with all the leprosy of cowardice, as to say yes, we will submit to all this! and whilst there yet remains a half million men amongst us able to resist! And who says the enemy will give us anything better? Not Mr. Lincoln; and do the weak and the vacillating among us, know better than he does, what he will do for us? Having made therefore a fair and honest effort to obtain peace by negotiation, and knowing now precisely, from the lips of the President of the United States, what we are to expect, what are we to do next? There is only one thing left for us to do. We must fight my countrymen to the last extremity, or submit voluntarily to our own degradation. Let no man mistake the issue now. The lines of distinction will be drawn plainly between those who are for their country, and those who are against their country. There is no half-way home upon the road. The purifying fire is even now burning throughout the land, and its consuming flames must separate the dross from the true metal. Degradation, ruin and dishonor on the one hand, liberty, independence and honor, if our souls be strong, on the other. Is it not worth another honest and manly /effort/? Aye, another, and another, and another, and a thousand efforts of our whole people. As North Carolinians, decendants of revolutionary heroes, and fathers and brothers of the noblest dead and living soldiers, that ever drew a blade for human freedom, we cannot tolerate the thought of such bare and infamous submission. Should we willfully throw down an organized Government, disband our still powerful armies, and invite all these fearful consequences upon our country, we would live to have our children curse our gray hairs for fastening our dishonor upon them. I trust and believe that there will be little difference of opinion in North Carolina as to the propriety of continued resistance. The great argument which will be brought forward to shake your honor and intended to incite you to despair will be that successful resistance is no longer possible. Some will tell you that we are already subdued: that the enemy outnumbers us, that our fighting men are all slain, our resources all exhausted and we might as well submit now. This, my countrymen, is false, and as frequently proceeds from a craven or a traitorous, as from an honest but mistaken spirit. Great as our calamities have been, straitened as we are for all supplies both of men and materials, I tell you in all candor, that when I survey our condition by the light of human history, I see no danger which threatens to be fatal to our cause, except this depression of spirit among the people and the still more fearful risk of internal dissension. So long as we remain one and determined, it is not in the power of our enemies to subdue us "But except these abide in the ship ye cannot be saved." All things may be supplied if we were but possessed of that bold and manly spirit of resistance to tyranny, of which liberty and independence are born. That alone can fill the widow's barrel and still the orphans cry, can cast cannon and build ships of war: can raise up armed men from the dust of the dragons teeth, can wrest tangible realities from the very jaws of impossibility. Without it, numbers but add to the ignominy, of certain defeat, even as the Persian millions were whipped and ashamed by the three hundred in the mountain pass. Are our men all slain? Over four hundred thousand names yet stand upon the muster rolls of the Confederacy, to say nothing of the many thousands who shirk. Where are they? Thousands upon thousands absent without leave, are lurking in the woods, and swamps of the South. Are our provisions all gone? Hundreds of thousands of bushels of grain now rot at the various depots of the South for want of transportation, and this transportation cannot be protected because these absent soldiers are not at the post of duty. Oh! my countrymen! If you would but rise to entreat, to shame, to drive them back to their country's standard. Has our territory been overrun? It has, but how much of it has been held? The enemy marched triumphantly through the heart of our sister Georgia, and is she conquered? Except for the garrison at Savannah and the ashes of desolation on their track through the interior, Georgia has neither enemy nor the sign of enemy on her soil. So of most portions of the South which space does not permit me to enumerate. For four years, their countless legions have gnawed at the vitals of Virginia, yet today they claim not even all of her territory which is swept by their cannon. The cities they garrison, the land their armies actually stand upon, and the waters ridden <upon> by their fleets, are all that they really hold, or ever can hold except by our ignoble consent. Let the balance of our cities go, Mobile, Charleston, Wilmington, Richmond, all, and if we are determined to be free our subjugation is quite as distant as ever. For thank God, the Confederacy does not consist in brick and mortar, or particular spots of ground however valuable they may be in a military point of view. Our nationality consists in our people. Liberty dwells in the heart of her votaries, and the ragged, barefooted soldiers standing in the depths of the forest, or in the shadow of the mountain, can offer her sacrifices, which will be as sweet and as acceptable as those proffered in gorgeous temples in the midst of magnificent cities. So if our country and its cause, like to the Kingdom of God, be enthroned in our hearts, then indeed am I persuaded, that neither principalities nor powers, nor things present nor things to come, nor height nor depth nor life nor death, nor any other creature shall be able to separate us from that independence and honor for which our people have suffered and our sons have died. Therefore, my countrymen, having warned you of this danger which is upon us, I now appeal to you by everything held sacred among men, to bear yourselves as becomes your high lineage and future hopes: I implore you to lay down all party bitterness, and to be reconciled to your neighbor for the sake of your country, to use every possible exertion to restore absentees to the Army: to divide of your abundance freely with the poor and the suffering; to strengthen the arms of your rulers and to sustain your soldiers and their Generals; and to give cheerfully your aid physical, mental, and moral, in whatever sphere you may be, to prevent the degradation of your country, and the ruin of its people. For the purpose of determining the best means of accomplishing this as well as for giving expression to your opinions, I earnestly recommend that you assemble in primary meetings in every county in the State, and let the whole world and especially our enemies see how a free people can meet a proposition for their absolute submission to the will of their conquerors.

Given under my hand and the great seal of the State in our city of Raleigh, on the 14th. day of February A.D. 1865.

Z. B. Vance

John A. Gilmer to ZBV   A&H:VanPC

Confidential

House of Reps.
February 14th. 1865

Govr. Vance-

Dear Sir,

Yours of the 8th.[1] was handed to me by Mr. [*Nicholas W.*] Woodfin last evening.

I answered promptly your telegram in relation to Mr. [*Alexander H.*] Stephens, that he had left here for home before it arrived.

Upon the failure of our Commissioners[2] there burst forth from Congress, and the Soldiers and citizens in this section a demonstration of vigor, spirit and determination. How far this patriotic spirit may extend I cannot say.

A time of great trial is upon us. I have every confidence that, if our people can be cheered up and fully aroused, we can yet under the blessing of Providence secure our Independence, and save the Country from utter ruin, disgrace and degradation. But I assure you that I am beginning to doubt whether we have inherited the undaunted courage of our Revolutionary sires. The discouraging spirit of despondency, is to be dreaded more than the power of the Enemy.

As matters now stand, how any fair minded, rational man, can for a moment with composure, think of the consequences and results of Submission, is to me most surprising.

I had an interview with Mr. Stephens after he returned. He was very reticent. He was urged by his friends to speak here before he left. From this he excused himself. He intimated no disposition to speak, & did not promise to speak when he got home. I am informed that on his way to Danville, at Scottsville (27 miles from Danville) a crowd called on him for a speech, but he did not show himself.

I do not feel cheered at many letters which I receive from N.C.

I am in no way encouraged at the reluctance of Congress, shown in voting for a good & efficient tax bill. Without the passage of such a bill, I anticipate increased troubles in our finances.

If things progress as they now do, I fear that our assembly in May will call a convention, & that this body will repeal the Ordinance of Secession, make arrangements to go back into the Union, with the hope of driving the other Southern States into the same action, and in time to vote against the abolition Amendment, proposed to the Constitution of the U.S.

Between us in the fullest confidence I say I think I can already /see this/ breaking out. I fear the effort will be made, and will result in a great failure, and engulf the Southern States, and Especially good old N.C into a state of ruin horror, and misery, that cannot be described. Too grievous to be borne.

God only knows our fate. By submission there is no hope. By a manful united, spirited and determined defence there certainly is some hope.

You will see a brief of my speech on the 9th. here, in the Richmond Dispatch of the 10th.

Congress will adjourn in about two weeks. When I get home I wish you would bring up to my House Mrs. V. and the children, & stay with me a week or two, so that we might talk over matters.

Please accept assurances of my high esteem, & tender my regards to Mrs. V. of yours.

Truly
John A Gilmer

[1]Not extant.
[2]At the Hampton Roads conference.

P. H. *Langdon to* ZBV   A&H:VanPC

Confederate States of America,
Quarter Master's Office,
<Richmond, Va.>/Weldon, N.C./
February 15th. 1865

His Excellency,
Z. B. Vance, Governor.

Gov,

I desire to call your attention to the condition of free negroes, enrolled and put in the service, "under the Act of Congress."[1] These negroes receive only Eleven Dollars per month, and clothing and one ration, each. Many of them have very small farms with large families dependent entirely upon them for support. It is almost impossible, under the circumstances, to prevent them from deserting from any work on which they are employed. Cannot something be done to encourange them to remain and serve the Country faithfully, by making some provision for their families? The Counties make certain provision for Soldiers families, but these poor creatures have nothing, in the abscence of the patriotic stimulus of the white man, to encourage them to be steady & faithful: thus, otherwise a useful class of labor, is rendered invalid. I submit with great deference the matter for your consideration.

I am, Governor,
Very Respectfully,
Yr. Obt. Servt.
P. H. Langdon
Capt. A.Q.M.

[*Endorsed*] I am not authorized by law to give them any thing. I know of no way except to appeal to the Counties—It certainly ought to be done

Z B V

[1]Passed in February 1865, the act ordered free black men between the ages of eighteen and fifty to be impressed as laborers. They received the same pay and rations as white soldiers. Current et al., *Encyclopedia of the Confederacy*, 2:642-644.

Robert E. Lee to ZBV   A&H:GP

[*Telegram*]

Richmond 16 Feby 1865

To His Ex Gov Vance

Genl Hoke[1] reports arrival of one division of Schofields[2] Corps at fort fisher More are believed to have reached Morehead City Genl Bragg[3] leaves for Raleigh tomorrow to see you I can send no more forces from this army please bring every man from the State

R E Lee

[1]Robert F. Hoke, commanding troops in defense of Wilmington.
[2]Union general John McAllister Schofield, recently given command of the U.S. Department of North Carolina. Faust et al., *Encyclopedia of Civil War*, 661.
[3]Braxton Bragg, in overall command of the defenses at Wilmington.

Robert E. Lee to ZBV   A&H:GP

[*Telegram*]

Richmond Feby 19 1865

To Gov Vance

What assistance can you give Genl Bragg Supplies of all kinds should be at once moved from route of Enemy thoroughly and Completely Horses mules stock <of> of all kinds should be driven off Genl Beauregard[1] thinks Sherman is moving on Charlotte to make junction with Schofield at Raleigh or Weldon This cannot be done if all supplies are removed or destroyed.

R E Lee

[1]Now commanding troops in South Carolina and Georgia against Gen. William T. Sherman's northward advance.

ZBV to Robert E. Lee   A&H:GLB

[*Telegram*]

Raleigh, Feb. 20th.

Genl. R. E. Lee
Richmond Va.

Your dispatches[1] recd. I will give Gen Bragg all the assistance in my power. Have called out every man liable to duty in the State. I cant destroy provisions without a force of Cavalry.

Z. B. Vance

[1]February 16, 19, 1865, in this volume.

Jefferson Davis to ZBV   A&H:GP

[*Telegram*]

Richmond 21 Feby 1865

To Gov Z B Vance

I thank you for your patriotic proclamation[1] and trust you may promptly bring large auxiliary force in to the field time is all importance to a success— Which will revive confidence

Jeff Davis

[1]February 14, 1865, in this volume.

ZBV to Pierre G. T. Beauregard   A&H:VanPC

Feb 23rd. 65

Gen Beauregard

Genl,

If not inconsistent with the good of the service, I have the honour to ask that Capt Jno A. Lindsay 45th. NC Regt. (Retired list) now on provost duty be ordered to report to me for sixty days. I desire his aid in [*illegible*] militia & state forces.

> Very resply.
> Yr obt svt
> Z. B. Vance

Robert E. Lee to ZBV   A&H:GP

> Hd. Qrs. C.S. Armies
> 24th. Febry 1865

His Excy. Z B Vance
Governor of N. Carolina
Raleigh.

Governor,

The state of despondency that now prevails among our people is producing a bad effect upon the troops. Desertions are becoming very frequent, and there is good reason to believe that they are occasioned to a considerable extent by letters written to the soldiers by their friends at home. In the last two weeks several hundreds have deserted from Hill's Corps, and as the divisions from which the greatest number of desertions have taken place, <contain> are composed chiefly of troops from N Carolina, they furnish a corresponding proportion of deserters. I think some good can be accomplished by the efforts of influential citizens to change public sentiment, and cheer the spirits of the people. It has been discovered that despondent persons represent to their friends in the army that our cause is hopeless, and that they had better provide for themselves. They state that the number of deserters is so large in the several counties that there is no danger to be apprehended from the home guards. The deserters generally take their arms with them. The greater number are from regiments from the western part of the State.

So far as the despondency of the people occasions this sad condition of affairs, I know of no other means of removing it than by the counsel and exhortation of prominent citizens.

If they would explain to the people that the cause is not hopeless, that the situation of affairs though critical, is critical to the enemy as well as ourselves, that he has drawn his troops from every other quarter to accomplish his designs against Richmond, and that his defeat now would result in leaving nearly our whole territory open to us, that this great result can be accomplished if all will work diligently and zealously, and that his successes are far less valuable in fact than in appearance. I think our sorely tried people would be induced to make one more effort, to bear their sufferings a little longer, and regain some of the spirit that marked the first two years of the war. If they will, I feel confident that with the blessing of God, what seems to be our greatest danger, will prove the means of deliverance and safety.

Trusting that you will do all in your power to help us in this great emergency,

I am very respectfully

> Your obt. servt.
> R E Lee
> Genl

John C. Breckinridge to ZBV   A&H:GP

> Confederate States of America
> War Department
> Richmond February 24 1865

His Excellency
Z B Vance
Governor of North Carolina
Raleigh N.C.

Sir

This will be handed to you by Major Hoge of the Adjt Genl's Depmt who also bears a letter[1] from Brig Genl St John[2] the Commissary General. To the latter I beg leave to ask your particular attention and to invoke in aid of his plans your cordial and effective cooperation, from which he and I, anticipate such good results as your energy and zeal are calculated to produce

> Very Respectfully Yr Obt Svt
> John C. Breckinridge
> Secretary of War

[1]February 24, 1865, A&H:GP, requesting that ZBV appeal to North Carolinians to sell or "loan . . . their reserve supplies" to the Confederate government for the war effort.

[2]Isaac Munroe St. John, who had replaced Lucius B. Northrop as commissary general on February 16, 1865. Current et al., *Encyclopedia of the Confederacy*, 3:1361.

ZBV to Pierre G. T. Beauregard   A&H:GLB

[Telegram]

Raleigh Feb. 25th.

Gen Beauregard,
Charlotte.

Please advise me of Shermans movements. If he comes by Charlotte I wish to move a large lot of Q. Masters Stores.

Z. B. Vance

ZBV to Braxton Bragg   A&H:GLB

[Telegram]

Raleigh Feb. 25 [1865]

Genl Bragg[1]
Magnolia.

Please inform me of progress of enemy. I desire to move stores and am waiting for information.

Z. B. Vance

[1]Moving his troops westward toward Goldsboro, following the fall of Wilmington on February 21. Barrett, *The Civil War in North Carolina*, 283-284, 290.

Joseph E. Johnston to ZBV   A&H:GP

[Telegram]

Charlotte 28 Feby 1865

To His Excelly Gov Z B Vance

Should Sherman Come this way I reccommend the neighborhood of Danville Should he turn towards Fayetteville Salisbury would be safe.

J. E. Johnston[1]

[1]Now in command of Confederate force opposing Sherman's advance into North Carolina, having replaced Beauregard, who, along with Bragg, was then subordinate to Johnston. Barrett, *The Civil War in North Carolina*, 290, 296. Apparently Johnston was recommending to ZBV sites to which the governor could evacuate quartermaster stores. See ZBV to P. G. T. Beauregard, February 25, 1865, in this volume.

ZBV to John White   A&H:GLB

State of North Carolina
Executive Department
Raleigh Feb. 28th. 1865

Mr. John White
Comr of N. Ca. Care of A. Collie & Co.
17 Leadenhall St. London

Dr. Sir;

You will before this reaches you, have learned of the capture of Wilmington and the consequent stoppage of our blockade running business. The course proper for you to pursue under the changed aspect of affairs has I presume suggested itself to you. Nothing remains but to *close up* our affairs as completely as possible and wait for a change. Our accounts in England I suppose can easily be reduced to shape and what funds we have should be placed in safety to aid in the final adjustment of our indebtedness. Our goods on hand, whether in Europe or the Islands, I leave you to dispose of in any way deemed best, consulting Mr. [*Joseph H.*] Flanner and Mr. [*Alexander*] Collie. You may also relieve Mr. Flanner of his agency from this date, and will please reduce your own expenditures on State account as far as practicable. Not being able to export any more cotton, of course it becomes us to exercise the most rigid economy. There is upwards of a thousand pounds sterling due us from the Confederate Govt. for freight brought in on the Advance by Mr. Flanner which I presume he forgot to collect whilst in this country. Please see him & try to get it. Majr. Walker the Confederate agent at Bermuda gave receipts for it. Mr. Wm. Collie who kindly bears this will give you the military news. It is bad enough, God knows. Your family are well. I have recd. nothing from you since Halifax.

Truly Yours,
Z. B. Vance

Address by ZBV   A&H:GLB

To the People of North Carolina.

Fellow citizens;

The necessities of our country as represented by our Confederate authorities, impel me again, to appeal to your generosity. You are aware that in consequence of interruption to our railroad communications by recent movements of the enemy, the subsistence of Genl. Lee's army has become greatly jeopardized. For at least a few months that Army will have to rely for subsistence upon North Carolina and Virginia alone. I am informed by the Commissary Department that the usual methods of collecting supplies will be insufficient for the purpose. In reference to this point I need only cite the authority of Genl. Lee himself who writes as follows in regard to a similar appeal to the people of Virginia, "I cannot permit myself to doubt that the people will respond to it, when they reflect upon the alternative presented to them. They have simply to choose whether they will contribute such Commissary and Quartermaster stores as they can possibly spare to support an army which has already borne and done so much in their behalf, or retaining their stores, maintain the army of the enemy engaged in their subjugation. I am aware that a general obligation of this nature rests lightly on most men—each being disposed to leave his discharge to his neighbor— but I am confident that our citizens will appreciate their responsibility in this case, and will not permit an army, which by God's blessing and their patriotic support has hitherto resisted the efforts of the enemy, to suffer now, through their neglect." It seems, therefore, that our all depends upon the voluntary action of the people of North Carolina and Virginia, and trusting that whatever you have to spare, will be promptly and patriotically brought forward for the use of your country in its hour of trial: the following plan is submitted, which is being acted upon in the State of Virginia with the best results. It is understood also, that provisions will be received either as sales, loans or donations. 1st. Let every citizen who can, pledge himself to furnish the rations of one soldier for six months, without designating any particular soldier as recipient of the contribution. 2d. Let those thus pledging themselves furnish, say 80 pounds of bacon and 180 pounds of flour, or their equivelent in beef or meal, to be delivered to the nearest commissary agent.

3d. Let the donor bind himself to deliver one half of the amount above stated, viz. 40 pounds of bacon and 90 pounds of flour (or its equivelent) immediately, and the remainder at the end of three months, unless he prefer to adopt the better plan of advancing the whole amount pledged, at once.

4th Let the pledge of each individual, subscribing and furnishing the rations of one Soldier for six months, be made the basis of larger subscription. Those whose generosity, and whose means will enable them to do so, may obligate themselves to provide the rations of 5, 10, 20 or any number of soldiers for six months, while even the poor, who could not afford to supply the rations of one man, may combining authorize one of their number to make the designated subscription of at least one ration for one man for six months. To effect this, I earnestly recommend that county and neighborhood meetings, be immediately held in every portion of the State, at which subscriptions may be taken up, and that a committee of responsible and reliable gentlemen be appointed by such meetings, to wait on those who do not attend, and ascertain what can be raised at the earliest possible moment. And rest assured, that no patriot can better serve his country, than in so doing. By this means every possible ounce of provisions which can be spared for the support of our Army, may be made available. Should you not, Fellow Citizens, respond to this call, you may calculate, not only upon seeing your own sons in the Army suffer and be defeated in the field, for want of those supplies, but you will have the mortification to behold them seized and appropriated to the support of the enemy who comes to destroy us. Advancing as he does, through the interior of the land, without either water or rail-road communications in his rear, he is now subsisting by the plunder and the and the [sic] ruin of the people of South Carolina, and must necessarily do so, when he enters our State. Be assured, therefore, that every pound of bacon and beef, and every bushel of meal which you withhold from your own Army, is a certain contribution to the maintainance of that of the enemy. You have, therefore, to choose whether you will feed your sons, who are bleeding in our defence, or our ruthless enemy who arms our slaves and lays waste our country. To show you, fellow citizens, the earnest impression I have of the necessity of this action, and that I will call upon you to make no sacrifice which I shall not share with you, I have tendered to the Commissary Department one half of my entire years' supply, and expect to put my own family upon the limited rations allowed to our soldiers, regretting that I have so little to offer. That which is left me to subsist upon will be doubly sweet because it will be the bread of honor and independence. Confidently relying upon the generosity and patriotism of a people to whom I have often appealed and never appealed in vain, I am fellow citizens,

> Your obedient Servant,
> Z. B. Vance
> [n.m.n.d.]

ZBV to Joseph E. Johnston   A&H:GLB

[*Telegram*]

Raleigh, March 1st. 1865.

Genl. Johnson
Charlotte

How far do you wish to bring the wide guage? I do not want it further east than Salisbury unless great necessity requires it.

Z. B. Vance

ZBV to Jeremy F. Gilmer   A&H:GLB

Raleigh March 1st. 1865.

Maj. Genl. Gilmer
Charlotte N.C.

How far do you wish to alter the guage of N.C. Roads. I object to its being done east of Salisbury. I don't wish the connection broken with the West.

Z. B. Vance

ZBV to Henry A. Gilliam   A&H:VanPC

State of North Carolina,
Executive Department.
Raleigh, March 1 1865.

Maj H A. Gilliam

Dr. Sir,

You are hereby authorized to make an investigation into the matter of the alleged illegal arrest of H. P. Ritter by the authority of Confederate officers, in accordance with a resolution of the General Assembly ratified the 6th day of Feb 1865, and report the result of your investigations to me as soon as practicable.

Very Resptly
Yr obt svt
Z. B. Vance

Joseph E. Johnston to ZBV   A&H:GP

[*Telegram*]

Charlotte 2d. Mch 1865

To His Ex Z B Vance

I find that not the War Dept but Genl Beauregard ordered the widening of the Rail Road I consider the extension of the work to Danville a military necessity

J. E. Johnston

[*Endorsed*] Copy & file

Z B V

Robert E. Lee to ZBV   A&H:GP

[*Telegram*]

Hd Qrs. ANVa Mar 2d. 1865

To His Ex Z B Vance

The Q M Genl & I agree with Genl Johnston in thinking it all important that the widening of the <the guage> guage should continue to Danville if possible

R E Lee

[*Endorsed*] Copy & file

Z B V

ZBV to Robert E. Lee   A&H:GLB

State of North Carolina,
Executive Department.
Raleigh March 2d. 1865.

Genl. R. E. Lee.

Dr. Sir:

Yours[1] has been received giving me the distressing intelligence of the increase of desertion from our armies. I had had [sic] heard from other sources of this defection of our troops, and was already too well aware that the cause of it was to be found in the general public despondency. I inaugurated a series of public meetings in this State by my recent proclamation,[2] for the purpose of reviving public sentiment, and though many have been held and many more will be held, yet the near and triumphant approach of the enemy has so alarmed the timid and so engrossed the loyal in preparation for his coming that I fear they will hardly have their proper effect. I have myself been so busy in trying to organize my Militia and secure my vast public stores that [I] have only been able to address the people at two or three points. Rest assured however General that I am fully alive to the importance of the crisis and whatever man can do in my situation shall be done. I shall now order out in every County that class of the Home Guard not subject to duty in the field and put them to work arresting deserters. In many Counties however they are necessarily inefficient from the great number of the deserters and the natural fear of the destruction of their property &c. If you could send me as many as two regiments of Cavalry, by quartering them in the midst of these disaffected districts and foraging upon the friends of the deserters, they could not only arrest many but could recruit themselves and horses, restore confidence and inspire with courage the local forces. I earnestly recommend this action, General, and think in the long run it would not weaken your Army. I think our people will respond liberally to the appeal for supplies[3] which I have just published this morning at the instance of the Secretary of War. The first answer made to it two hours after its appearance in the morning papers, was from a poor widow of this city, who hard pressed to live in these distressing times, as I know she is, came yet to offer me two pieces of bacon and a barrel of meal. Such offerings on the sacred alter of country, hallow our cause, and I hope will secure God's blessing upon it.

Very truly yours
Z. B. Vance

P.S. I send you a copy of my appeal to the people of my State.

Z.B.V.

[1]February 24, 1865, in this volume.
[2]February 14, 1865, in this volume.
[3]February 28 or March 1, 1865, in this volume.

Pardon by ZBV   A&H:GLB

The State of North Carolina.
Zebulon B. Vance,
Governor, Captain General and
Commander-in-chief of the State of
North Carolina.

To all who shall see these Presents, Greeting.

Whereas, Slave Aleck, property of Benjamin Thorp at the Fall Term, One thousand eight hundred and sixty four of the Superior Court of Law of Granville County, was convicted of the murder of Slave Cornelius property of Peterson Thorp of said County and by the judgement of the said Court was sentenced to be hung & whereas on appeal to the Supreme Court said judgment was affirmed, And whereas it has been made to appear to me that the case is one fit for the exercise of Executive clemency. Now Therefore, in consideration of the premises, and by virtue of the power and authority in me vested by the Constitution of the State; I do by these presents, pardon the said Alick, of said judgement and offence upon the condition that the owner of said Alick pay all cost in his case incurred, And upon the further condition, That this pardon shall not extend to any other offence whereof the said Alick may have been guilty.

Given under my hand, and attested by the Great Seal of the State. Done at the City of Raleigh, this the 2d. day of March, One thousand eight hundred and Sixty five, and in the Eighty ninth year of our Independence.

Z. B. Vance

ZBV *to Calvin H. Wiley*   A&H:Wiley

State of North Carolina,
Executive Department.
Raleigh March 2 1865

Rev C. H. Wiley

Dr Sir,

In ansr. to yours of the 28th. ult,[1] I advise you to pack up your records &
move them to north west by wagon in case it should become necessary. I do
not think however they would harm you or your records, but it may be best
to get them out of the way. I do not know yet when Sherman will strike,
though upon it depends the salvation of my own vast stores.

I agree with you in the importance of not adding to the general panic
& will not let my own family remove west on that account, though what
little we have will be ready to remove in case of necessity. That much is but
ordinary prudence.

Very truly yours,

Z. B. Vance

[1]Not extant.

Joseph E. Johnston to ZBV   A&H:GP

[*Telegram*]

Charlotte 3d Mch 1865

To His Excelly Z B Vance

to make a prompt movement to meet the Enemy threatening your
Capital I need fifty additional good wagons & teams to transport supplies
to meet the emergency Can you assist me by having them collected in the
vicinity of Raleigh & Smithfield at that earliest possible moment.

J. E. Johnston

John C. Breckinridge to ZBV   A&H:GP

War Dept March 3d. 1865

Gov Z B Vance
Raleigh N C

It is of great importance to have the guage widened through to Danville,
and I respectfully urge you to consent that it may be widened from Salisbury
to Greensboro.

John C Breckinridge
Sec of War

[*Endorsed*] Copy & file

Z B V

ZBV to Jeremy F. Gilmer   A&H:GLB

[*Telegram*]

Raleigh March 3d. 1865.

Gen. Gilmer.
Charlotte N.C.

I positively object to wide guage coming East of Salisbury, unless I am
permitted the same control over the forage trains which the law gives me
over the N.C. Roads. I write by mail.

Z. B. Vance

ZBV to Jeremy F. Gilmer   A&H:GLB

State of North Carolina.
Executive Department.
Raleigh March 3d. 1865.

Genl. Gilmer,
Charlotte N.C.

Sir

My reason for objecting to the widening of the guage of the N.C. Road East of Salisbury is two fold.

1st. It breaks my connection with the West where I must remove my stores and public records in case Raleigh is threatened, compelling me to break bulk twice and leaving me no power of controlling transportation in the hands of the new Company who will occupy the Road.

2d. Should Sherman, as is most likely, unite with Schofield and advance upon Greensboro from this direction, all of the rolling stock in N.C. crowded upon Greensboro for safety would be destroyed, whilst the S.C. stock would be safe, having the road open behind it. I do not understand that it is the interest of N.C. to make the sacrifice of her own property to save that of S. Carolina.

I cannot see how the extending of the wide guage to Greensboro is a "military necessity." The rolling stock of this State it seems to me is amply sufficient to transport everything desired between Salisbury and Greensboro, and by widening the guage so far you will render idle as much stock as you would gain, and endanger much more, until further reasons are assigned therefor I must adhere to my objection.

Very Respectfully,
Yr. obt. Servt.
Z. B. Vance

ZBV to Braxton Bragg A&H:GLB

State of North Carolina.
Executive Department.
Raleigh March 3d. 1865.

Genl. B. Bragg
Goldsboro, N.C.

Genl,

I hope you will induce all slave owners in Duplin New Hanover and Onslow to remove immediately all able-bodied slaves in this direction, and will afford them all necessary aid in so doing. If necessary, I will sustain you <in> removing by force all such slaves as will likely afford recruits to the enemy. If the owners cannot support them the Govt can usefully employ them.

Very Resply
Your obt. Servt
Z. B. Vance

ZBV to Joseph E. Johnston A&H:GLB

[*Telegram*]

Raleigh March 4th. 1865.
Genl. J. E. Johnston.
Charlotte N.C.

I can have fifty waggons (mostly two horse) by this day week, if you will give authority to impress a few country waggons for post duty. State has no authority to impress.

Z. B. Vance

Braxton Bragg to ZBV   A&H:GP

[*Telegram*]

Goldsboro 6 Mch 1865

To His Ex Z B Vance

I thank you for your kind offer to feed the passing Troops & have instructed operator as suggested

Braxton Bragg

ZBV to Braxton Bragg   A&H:GLB

[*Telegram*]

Raleigh March 7th. 1865.
Genl. Bragg.
Goldsboro.

If the Govt. will furnish 22 miles of iron, and a few hundred hands, the R.R. to deep river can be finished in 15 days. I advise the iron be taken below Magnolia and that the effort be made.

Z. B. Vance

ZBV to Commandant   A&H:GLB

[*Telegram*]

Raleigh March 8th.
Commandant
Fayetteville.

You have taken the liberty of impressing my wagons without my permission. I send them back for State <State> goods and notify you to keep your hands off them.

Z. B. Vance

Joseph E. Johnston to ZBV   A&H:GP

[*Telegram*]

Fayetteville Mch 9 1865

To His Ex Z. B. Vance

Genl Bragg reports that he attacked enemy yesterday four (4) miles beyond Kinston & drove him back three miles taking Several hundred prisoners and killing & wounding a large number our loss comparatively small. Col Sale at Goldsboro reports this morning <ten> one thousand (1,000) prisoners arrived and five hundred (500) coming Maj Gen Cox[1] who was at Wilmington commander federal troops Genl Bragg extols Maj Gen Hill and Hoke and their troops

J. E. Johnston

[1]Jacob Dolson Cox. Faust et al., *Encyclopedia of Civil War*, 188.

Robert E. Lee to ZBV   A&H:GP

Hd. Qrs. C S Armies
9th. March 1865

His Excy. Z B Vance
Governor of N. Carolina
Raleigh.

Governor,

I received your letter of the 2nd. inst.[1] and return you my sincere thanks for your zealous efforts in behalf of the army and the cause. I have read with pleasure and attention your proclamation and appeal to the people, as also extracts from your addresses. I trust you will infuse into your fellow citizens the spirit of resolution and patriotism which inspires your own action. I have now no cavalry to spare for the purpose you mention, and regret that I did not receive the suggestion at an earlier period. I think it a very good one, and would have been glad to adopt it. I have sent a force of infantry under Brig Gen Johns[t]on (R D)[2] to guard the line of the Roanoke [*River*], and operate as far as practicable in the adjacent counties to arrest deserters.

Another detachment of five hundred men under Col McAllister[3] has been sent to Chatham & Moore counties, in which the bands of deserters were represented to be very numerous. They will however operate in other quarters as occasion may require. They are instructed to take no prisoners among those /deserters/ who resist with arms the civil or military authorities. I hope you will raise as large a force of local troops to cooperate with them as you can, and think that the sternest course is the best with the class I have referred to. The immunity which these lawless organizations afford is a great cause of desertion, and they cannot be too sternly dealt with.

I hope you will be able to aid Gen [Joseph E.] Johnston who needs all the reinforcements you can give him. If he can check the progress of Gen Sherman the effect would be of the greatest value. I hope the late success of Gen Bragg near Kinston will revive the spirits of the people, and render your labors less arduous.

The conduct of the widow lady whom you mention deserves the highest commendation. If all our people possess her spirit, our success I should feel to be assured.

> Very respectfully
> Your obt. servt.
> R E Lee
> Genl

[1] In this volume.
[2] Robert Daniel Johnston.
[3] Lt. Col. Alexander C. McAllister, originally of the Forty-sixth Regiment North Carolina Troops, in command of the special force since February 27, 1865. Manarin et al., *North Carolina Troops*, 11:134.

Patrick H. Winston Jr. to ZBV   A&H:GP

> Council Chamber
> March 13 1865.

His Excellency Z B Vance
Governor of North Carolina

In accordance with your summons the Council of State have met and organized by the appointment of P H Winston Jr their President and A M McPheeters their Secretary

They are now in session and prepared to receive and act upon any communication or matter which you may submit to their consideration

> Very Respectfully
> P H Winston Jr
> Prest. of the Council.

Patrick H. Winston Jr. to ZBV   A&H:GP

> Council Chamber
> 14 March 1865.

His Excellency Z B Vance
Governor of North Carolina

Your communication of yesterday[1] has been received.

The Council of State unanimously confirm and ratify the appointments therein made by you to wit

Henry A Nutt & John D Hyman for the Board of Internal Improvements and Prof. Richard Stirling L. C. Edwards & W J Yates for the Literary Board

The Council have maturely considered the communication of your Excellency in regard to the approach of the enemy to our Capital.

The Act of the Legislature locating the Seat of Government at Raleigh permantly and unalterably is the paramount law until changed by the power which made it.

The Council think that the resolution of the Legislature directing the removal of the valuable effects of the State in the discretion of the Governor furnished some guidance at least at the present juncture

After much consultation we are of opinion and so advise

1 That the Governor shall at the proper time proceed to remove from each and every department of the Government all the certainly valuable and important papers and effects of the State consulting in each case the head of the department in question.

2 That the Governor and Treasurer accompany said effects. As to the other officers it is not so important but should the Governor in his discretion think their removal necessary it is probably their duty to go according to the aforesaid resolution of the Legislature

3 That those officers who do not leave shall remain in their rooms in the building as they usually do in their daily business.

4 That the Governor with such officer or officers as attend him shall with said valuable effects retire to some point west of Raleigh their location to be selected by the Governor and changed by him when necessary

The Council after conferring with Mr. [*Jonathan*] Worth the Treasurer advise that he burn all the State Treasury notes fundable immediately, all of less denomination than one dollar except one thousand dollars & all notes fundable 1 Jany 1866 and to be fundable 1 Jany 1876 except <three> /Five/ hundred thousand dollars which he can burn hereafter if necessary

The Council regret that in the nature of the case they cannot be more specific than in some cases they have been. They are satisfied that the opinions of your Excellency aided by the other Executive officers will be more likely to be prudent and correct as events happen than any advice in advance by the Council.

We beg to tender to your Excellency our sincere sympathies in the heavy labors and responsibilities of your present position.

> Respectfully
> Yr obt Servant
> P H Winston Jr.
> Prest. of the Council

[1] Not extant.

ZBV *to Joseph E. Johnston*   A&H:GLB

> State of North Carolina.
> Executive Department
> Raleigh March 14, 1865.

Gen J. E. Johnston
Present.
Genl;

Great disorders are already coming from the selling of spirits to the soldiers in the City and the evil may be expected to increase as the number of soldiers increases. It is somewhat embarrassing for Civil officers to assume authority to remove or destroy private property, & I therefore have to request you in the name of the loyal and orderly citizens of this city to issue orders for the immediate removal or destruction of all liquor in this place, except such small quantities as may be necessary for family & medical purposes.

> Very Respy.
> Yr. obt. Servt.
> Z. B. Vance

ZBV to John C. Breckinridge   A&H:GLB

[*Telegram*]

Raleigh March 18 1865.

Gen. Breckinridge,
Secty. of War.
Richmond.

I cannot possibly consent to the widening of the guage of N.C. Road East of Salisbury. It will be ruinous to the State & I can see no real necessity for it. Please stop it until the matter can be consulted upon.

Z. B. Vance

John C. Breckinridge to ZBV   A&H:VanPC

[*With enclosure*]

War Dept March 21 1865

Hon Z Vance
Gov of N C
Raleigh

Dear Sir

I return your letter that you may see the endorsements upon it. I may mention that my communication to the President covering a correspondence between Gen Lee and myself, and other papers, related wholly to the military situation, and the wants of this Dept in the matters of money, subsistence &c. &c. It was intended to advise the legislative Dept of the Govt fully as to the condition of affairs, but had no reference to any thing beyond the proper business of my Dept—nor did the President in communicating the papers to Congress do more than call special attention to them. His published message embraces all that has occurred touching the question of peace.

I shall be happy to hear from you at any time and will be pleased to confer fully. I am obliged this morning to write in great haste, but Major Foote will be able to supply any omissions in this note.

Very truly yours
John C. Breckinridge
Sec of War

[*Enclosure*]

ZBV to John C. Breckinridge

State of North Carolina,
Executive Department.
Raleigh, March 17 1865.

Hon. Jno. C. Breckinridge
Sec'y at War
Richmond Va.

Dr. Sir,

I have been informed that certain communications, of the utmost importance to the Cause of the Confederacy, have been submitted to Congress in secret session by the President and the several heads of Depts. I have also been informed that their nature was such as to render it entirely proper & indeed rightful, that I as Governor of North Carolina should be informed of their contents. I have therefore the honour to most respectfully request a copy of said papers if not deemed inconsistent with the public good, and have sent the bearer Major James H. Foote, A.A.G.N.C. a discreet and loyal gentleman to receive them should you deem it advisable to comply with my request.

I am Sir,
Very resptly. & truly
Yr obt svt.
Zebulon B. Vance

[*Endorsed*] War Dept March 20 1865. Respectfully submitted to the President, for his decision. It is supposed that the Communications referred to by Gov Vance are those accompanying my letter to you of the 13d. inst.

John C. Breckinridge
Sec of War

[*Endorsed*] Secty of War. A secret message to either house of Congress cannot be communicated to others until the injunction of secresy is removed. But we can and should give the Govr. any information which may be useful and serve in our cooperation for the public defence. 20 March 65.

Jeffn Davis

John C. Breckinridge to ZBV   A&H:GP

[*Telegram*]

Richmond 24 Mch 1865

To Gov Z. B. Vance

I requested Maj Foote to confer with you fully about change of guage East of Salisbury under the late law. I may be compelled to take possession of some of the roads and increase the rolling stock to secure supplies. I will agree to restore old guage as soon as the emergency is past. Please answer as the matter is urgent.

John C. Breckinridge
Secy War

[*Endorsed*] Copy of Answer Raleigh March 25 Genl J. C. Breckinridge Secretary of War. Richmond I do not wish to make unreasonable opposition to change of guage east of Salisbury, but have asked various officers for reasons for so doing & received none. It will greatly damage the State & before consenting should like to be shown that its indispensible to Confederacy

Z. B. Vance

ZBV to Joseph E. Johnston   A&H:VanPC

(*Copy*)

Raleigh March 25th.
Gen J. E. Johnston
Smithfield N.C

If this city is uncovered I should be glad to have some of the reserve Artillery ordered here to assist in defending the place against raids. Hundreds of stragglers are round about here who ought to be brought in

Z. B. Vance

Patrick H. Winston Jr. to ZBV A&H:GP

State of North Carolina
Council Chamber
28 March 1865

His Excellency Z B Vance
Governor of North Carolina

Sir

The Council have received and maturely considered your communication of to day[1] in reference to convening the General Assembly before the day to which that body had adjourned.

There are but four members of the Council present two of whom are opposed to any call of the Legislature at the present time. The other two favor the call at such conveniently early day as your Excellency may select.

The Council regret that they are not more unanimous.

Very respectfully
Yr obt Servant
P H Winston Jr
Prest. of the Council

[1]Not extant.

Joseph E. Johnston to ZBV A&H:GP

[*Telegram*]

Smithfield Mch 28 1865

To His Excellency Z. B. Vance.

If the perpetrators of illegal impressments are pointed out they shall be punished. If the property so impressed is identified it shall be restored. The aid of the people of the country is necessary & I ask yours. I am anxious to protect citizens against Robbery.

J E Johnston

[*Endorsed*] Copy & file

Z B V

ZBV to Joseph E. Johnston   A&H:VanPC

Raleigh, Mch 28th. 1865

Genl. Johnston
Smithfield

Much distress is caused by illegal impressments in this neighborhood. Officers often taking every horse a farmer has. The act of Congress should be strictly adhered to except in immediate front of the Enemy. Please order all horses so taken to be restored.

Z. B. Vance

ZBV to Joseph E. Johnston   A&H:VanPC

Raleigh. Mch. 28, 1865

Genl. J. E. Johnston
Smithfield

The outrages of the straggling are becoming intolerable in this & adjoining Counties. Can you not make an example of some of them?

Z. B. Vance

ZBV to Joseph E. Johnston   A&H:VanPC

Raleigh March 30 [1865]

Genl. Johnston
Smithfield

It is represented to me that Col. Kempers[1] artillery are doing much wanton damage near Hillsboro, burning fences around wheat fields &c. Please take measures to stop it.

Z. B. Vance

[1] Identity unknown.

ZBV to General A&H:VanPC

[Raleigh N.C.]
[31st. March 1865]

Genl,

Since my last note Gen Bragg has recd. later information from Gen Bradly Johnson at Salisbury, confirming first accounts & locating Stoneman[1] with his whole force in valley of the Yadkin near Wilksboro. Send to him for a copy; I have none.

Resply
Z B Vance

[*Endorsed*] File

[1]Federal cavalry general George H. Stoneman raiding North Carolina from the west. Barrett, *The Civil War in North Carolina*, 350-366.

John C. Breckinridge to ZBV A&H:GP

[*Telegram*]

Richmond 1st. Apl 1865

To Gov Z. B. Vance

The object in continuing change of guage to Danville is to receive the assistance [of] the wide guage rolling stock now south of Salisbury for the Danville South side & Virginia and Tennessee R roads on which Genl Lees army is so dependent & secure the use of the trains of the latter road in case of disaster for the roads further south which are all of the same guage with them The losses of wide guage stock have been so serious in the last few months that all now remaining should be capable of transfer promptly to whatever section of the country the movements of our Army may require. I consider this matter of very great importance & hope to hear from you with regard to it.

John C. Breckinridge
Secy War

ZBV to William T. Sherman   SHC:Spen

State of North Carolina,
Executive Department,
Raleigh, April 11th, 1865.

Genl. Wm. T. Sherman
Commding U.S. Force

General

His Honor Mayor Wm. H Harrison is authorized to surrender to you the City of Raleigh. I have the honor to request the extension of your favor to its defenseless inhabitants generally and especially to ask your protection for the charitable Institutions of the State located here filled as they are with unfortunate inmates, most of whose natural protectors would be unable to take care of them in the event of their destruction.

The Capitol of the State with its Libraries, Museum and most of the public records is also left in your power. I can but entertain the hope that they may escape mutilation or destruction in as much as such evidence of learning and taste could advantage neither party in the protection of the war whether destroyed or preserved.

I am General
Very Respectfully
Z. B. Vance

Jefferson Davis to ZBV   A&H:GP

[Telegram]

Greensboro 11th. April 1865

To Gov Z B Vance

I have no official report but scouts said to be reliable and whose statements were circumstantial and corroborative report the disaster as extreme. I have not heard from Genl Lee since sixth inst and have little or no hope from his army as an organized body. I expected to visit you at Raleigh but am accidentally prevented from executing that design and would be very glad to see you here if you can come at once [or] to meet you elsewhere In North Carolina at a future time. We must redouble our efforts to meet present disaster. An army holding its position with determination to fight on and manifest ability to maintain the struggle will attract all the scattered soldiers and daily and rapidly gather strength. Moral influence is wanting and I am sure you can do much now to revive spirit and hope of the people.

Jeffn Davis

William T. Sherman to ZBV   A&H:VanPC

Head-Quarters Military Division
of the Mississippi, in the Field,
Gulleys Station NC
April 12, 1865.

To his Excellency,
Z. B. Vance, Governor of North Carolina

Sir,

I have the honor to acknowledge receipt of your communication of this date,[1] and enclose you a safeguard for yourself and any members of the State Government that choose to remain in Raleigh. I would gladly have enabled you to meet me here, but some interruption occurred to the Train by the orders of General Johnston after it had passed within the Lines of my Cavalry advance, but as it came out of Raleigh in good faith it shall return in good faith, and will in no measure be claimed by us.

I doubt if hostilities can be suspended as between the Army of the Confederate Govt. and the one I command but I will aid you all in my power to contribute to the end you aim to reach, the termination of the existing war.

I am truly your obt Servant,
W. T. Sherman
Maj Genl.

[1]Not extant.

William T. Sherman to ZBV   A&H:VanPC

Head-Quarters Military Division
of the Mississippi, in the Field,
Gullys Station
Apr 12, 1865.

Governor Vance,

If you conclude to remain in Raleigh you had better send some one out by the train to me as quick as possible, that I may make orders that will prevent any unnecessary confusion resulting from several head of Column, with necessary skirmishers coming in & through the City at the same time. As the Confederate Army is our only Enemy, I must take all possible precautions as you are aware that they do not recognize you as an agent to commit them.

Yrs truly
W. T. Sherman
Maj Genl.

ZBV to William J. Hardee   SHC:BattFM

State of North Carolina,
Executive Department,
Raleigh, April 12, 1865.

Gen Hardee[1]
Comdg &c

Genl,

Mr. Battle the bearer is Prest. of the Chatham R. Rd. Company and has only two horses which are absolutely necessary to his business. An officer of Wheeler's[2] is trying to seize one of them. Our citizens have suffered enough in this way & I beg you to order that it shall not be carried further.

Resptly.
Z. B. Vance

[1]William Joseph Hardee, under Joseph E. Johnston's command. Faust et al., *Encyclopedia of Civil War*, 338.

[2]Maj. Gen. Joseph Wheeler, commanding Confederate cavalry. Current et al., *Encyclopedia of the Confederacy*, 4:1707.

Pierre G. T. Beauregard to ZBV   A&H:GP

Greensboro April 15 [*1865*]
Shops.[1]

Gov Z. B. Vance

President Davis left this afternoon on horseback for Salisbury. He regretted not having seen you.

G. T. Beauregard

[1]Company Shops, an Alamance County railroad terminal and repair facility, present-day town of Burlington.

James Sloan to ZBV   A&H:GP

Greensboro April 15/65
Shops

Gov Vance

I am nearly ruined [by] a raid on my state stores this day from passing troops. The guard killed one man and several wounded, all are again quiet. Lost by pilfering very many good[s]. What shall I do. I am issueing to N.C. Troops. Do I beg you come to my assistance. Answer.

Jas Sloan
Maj & C S

ZBV to Joseph E. Johnston   A&H:VanPC

Greensboro 16th. Apl [*1865*]

Gen. J. E. Johnston

Genl,

I have a quantity of Quarter Masters stores here under the control of Majr. Sloan, and I learn that Col McMicken has assumed control of them

& is dealing out to suit himself. I respectfully request that you forbid this and place a guard around them to prevent pillage. My stores in Raleigh to the amount of nearly 10,000 suits were freely given this army, my stores of leather blankets &c at Graham were pillaged and I confess I am getting tired of it. Having shown every disposition to be liberal & patriotic in dividing my means, I should be much pleased to be permitted to dispose of the remainder as I see proper.

> Very resptly.
> Yr obt svt.
> Z B Vance

[*Endorsed*]

> Hd. Qrs &c &c
> Greensboro N.C. Apl 16/65

Respectfully referred to Col McMicken for explanation. The issue of the Qr Mr's stores referred to by Gov Vance must be stopped at once until the matter is investigated.

> G. T. Beauregard
> Gen. 2nd. Comd.

[*Endorsed*]   April 16th. 1865

Respectfully returned. The stores referred to by Gov. Vance as being taken from Grahams station are now on the cars or in wagons they were removed from Grahams station by Order of Gen'l Johnston to prevent their /being/ pillaged by soldiers or falling into the hands of the enemy.

The stores at this place were placed at my disposal by Maj Sloan for issue to this Army, giving preference to the extent of their wants to the North Carolina troops, stating to my assistant Maj Vardell that he was unable to issue it, or protect it. There has been but a small quantity issued. As I had ordered the distribution to be made to the Corps. In obedience to the Orders of Gen'l Beauregard I have stopped the further issue, and placed all the stores in charge of Maj Sloan, but request that Govr. Vance will transfer the cloth and clothing to the Army

> M. B. McMicken

[*Endorsed*]   Hd. Qrtrs. &c &c &c

Greensboro N.C. April 16, 1865
Resply. forwarded to Gov. Vance for his information

G. T. Beauregard
Genl

ZBV to James Sloan   A&H:VanPC

Greensboro
April 16 1865

Majr Sloan,
    Will issue clothing for the N C Troops in Gen Hardee's Corps upon the requisitions of the proper officers. Also to any other N C Troops under similar regulations. I will turn over the remainder to Col McMicken for the army generally

Z B Vance

John C. Breckinridge to ZBV   A&H:VanPC

Private

April 17th. 51/2 P M [*1865*]

Gov Z B Vance

Dear Sir
    At request of Gen Johnston just recd I start as soon as a locomotive can be fired up to meet him near Hillsboro. Will it be agreeable to you to go along?

Yours Truly
John C Breckinridge

Thomas Webb to ZBV   A&H:VanPC

Company Shops
Apl 18th. 65

Gov Vance

I had no one to send after you. I had the whistle sounded again and again and waited more than three quarters of an hour and you would not come. You ought to have stayed when you were at the Depot. An Engine will start for you at twelve 12 oclock. Go to Depot & be ready to come back immedy

Thos Webb[1]
Prest

[1]Thomas Webb, Hillsborough lawyer and president of the North Carolina Railroad. Allen W. Trelease, "The Passive Voice: The State and North Carolina Railroad, 1849-1871," *North Carolina Historical Review* 61 (April 1984): 186n.

Jonathan Worth to ZBV   A&H:VanPC

Shops, Apl. 19/65

Govr. Vance

I have reason to believe that I have lost every horse and mule. The necessity of getting home to procure others and plant corn without delay has impressed on me the great importance to the general welfare that a pacification be made in season to plant corn, now rapidly passing away. Can you not disband the State troops?

The security of the valuables in my care imperatively requires that they be placed in the capital at the very earliest period possible. I need not state the reasons. In the midst of graver matters the importance of getting the State archives out of the way of marauders quickly may escape you & I therefore desire to impress on you the importance of procuring a permit to pass the lines as soon as possible.

I would not have you take time to reply, but only wish to make these suggestions knowing you will give them due consideration.

Yours very truly
Jonathan Worth

ZBV to Joseph E. Johnston   A&H:VanPC

Copy

State of North Carolina
Executive Office
Greensboro 19th. April 1865.

Gen Joseph E. Johnston
Commanding &c

General

The troops under your command having forcibly seized all of the property belonging to the State from Haw River Depot to this place are now threatening to sack the Cars now at the shops in which are placed the archives and funds of the State Treasury and State Banks. It seems impossible to control them. Inasmuch as Genl Sherman has offered a safe guard to all the Officers, and property of the Civil Departments of the State on their returning to Raleigh I have the honor to request permission for the Hon. Jonathan Worth Treasurer of North Carolina, and his assistants and others in charge of /the/ property above mentioned to return to Raleigh in the Cars now occupied by them, the names of the persons will be given if required.

Very Respectfully
Yr Obt Servt
Z.B.V.

Joseph E. Johnston to ZBV   A&H:VanPC

Greensboro' April 19th. 1865.

His Excy. Z B Vance
Governor of North Carolina.

Sir,

I have just received the letter of this date in which you state that the troops under my command having "forcibly seized all of the property belonging to the State, from Haw River depot to this place, are now threatening to sack the cars at the Shops in which are placed the Archives & funds of the State Treasury & State Banks," & requesting permission to send the Treasurer & his assistants with the property abovementioned, to Raleigh, General

Sherman having offered safe gaurd in such cases.

If application had been made, a special gaurd for the State property referred to, would have been furnished. I order it now by Telegraph. If I find reason to think the Confederate authority insufficient, I shall be unable to oppose your proposition.

You will oblige me greatly by enumerating the State property seized by Confederate troops, & also by giving any information of circumstances that you may have.

> Most respectfully
> Your Obt. Srvt.
> J. E. Johnston
> General.

ZBV to Joseph E. Johnston   A&H:VanPC

Copy

> State of North Carolina
> Executive Department
> \<Raleigh> /Greensboro/
> 19th. April 1865

Genl. Joseph E. Johnson
Commanding &c

General

Being totally uninformed of the condition of affairs in this State and being unable to obtain from any one a statement of what is going on or what the Government of the Confederate States intends to do, I respectfully request permission to send by flag of truce a letter to Genl Sherman commanding forces of United States in North Carolina, which shall be submitted to your perusal.

I am induced to take this course for the reason that the people of my State are now suffering all the horrors of rapine and anarchy and I feel it my duty, in the absence \<of the proper authorities> of other authority on whom it might more properly devolve to use my best exertions to protect them.

> Very Respectfully
> Yr. obt. Servt.
> Z. B. Vance

Joseph E. Johnston to ZBV   A&H:VanPC

Greensboro' April 19th. 1865.

His Excy. Z B Vance
Governor of North Carolina

Sir,

I have just received the letter in which you say that "being totally uninformed of the condition of affairs in this State, & being unable to obtain from any one a statement of what is going on, or what the government of the Confederate States intends to do" you request permission to send a letter to General Sherman by Flag of truce.

It was expected by the Secretary of War & myself that you would <come> join us at Hillsboro' last night. when we intended to show you the agreement entered into with General Sherman. Your letter informs me of your arrival in Greensboro, the bearer says, three hours ago. You can not, therefore, I think, regard me as negligent in not having communicated with you on the subject. I need not remind you that I was not one of those to whom you applied for /the/ information you desire. Had you done so, be assured that every thing concerning North Carolina that I know would have been communicated to you.

A basis of negotiations was agreed upon yesterday, as well as a suspension of hostilities to give time for their conclusion. I have not a copy of the paper with me, but will be glad to show it to you & hear your opinion when it is returned to me.

Most respectfully
Your obt. Servt.
J. E. Johnston
General.

ZBV to Joseph E. Johnston   A&H:VanPC

Copy

State of North Carolina
Executive Department
Greensboro 19th. April 1865.

Genl Joseph E. Johnston
Commanding &c

General

Your letter of this date is just received. The reason why I did not join you last night at Hillsboro was that the President of the Rail Rd. & Genl Breckinridge both agreed to send for me when the train arrived there, it being uncertain at what time it would leave Genl Hampton's Hd. Qrs.[1] As it was I waited at the Depot from 4 o'clock to the time designated by you until Eight P.M. In this however I make no complaint of you. <Night>

Night before last I was invited by Genl Breckinridge to go down to where you were to participate in the consultation there to take place and as I supposed & deserved to accompany the flag of truce to a conference with Genl Sherman, thinking very naturally that I was entitled to know something of and participate in proceedings which arise <vitally> more immediately to affect my people than those of any other State in the Confederacy.

You cannot be ignorant of the part which I was invited to take at Genl Hampton's Hd. Qrs. Feeling therefore that I was to be excluded from a voice in the decision of the fate of my own people, I thought I could reasonably expect to be informed of the conclusion arrived at by others and make such provision as remained in my power for the welfare of the State. Such was the object of my note of this morning.

From reading your reply I am at a loss to determine whether you refuse permission for me to communicate with the enemy or wish me to infer that you desire I should suspend my request until a copy of the paper containing the result of yesterdays proceedings between you & Genl. Sherman shall have been submitted to me. I shall be glad to be informed on this point.

Very Respectfully
Yr. obt. Servt.
Z B Vance

---

[1]The headquarters of Confederate cavalry general Wade Hampton, near Hillsborough. Barrett, *The Civil War in North Carolina*, 383.

Joseph E. Johnston to ZBV   A&H:VanPC

Greensboro
April 19th. 1865

His Excy. Z. B. Vance
Governor of North Carolina

Sir:

Your letter in reply to mine of to-day, is just received.

I do not think that the omissions of Genl. Breckinridge /& Mr Webb/ ought to be laid at my door. As a mere military officer arranging an armistice, I do not think that it would have <proper> been proper on my part, to invite any civilian to join in the conference. Had I been determining the terms on which negotiations were to be based, there is no gentleman whose aid I would have sought sooner than yours. But I had nothing to do but to learn the views of the president, & they were not fully communicated until after my meeting with Genl. Sherman.

I supposed that after reading the accompanying paper, which contains all the information to be had on the subject, you would not desire to correspond with Genl. Sherman, & therefore made no reference to that matter. Should you at any time desire to hold such correspondence, I will refer the subject by telegraph to the Secretary of War.

Most respectfully
Your obt. Sevt.
J. E. Johnston

ZBV to William A. Graham   A&H:GraPC

Greensboro
Apl 19 1865

Gov Graham

Bring in your carriage for the president.

Z. B. Vance

W. G. Vardell to M. B. McMicken   A&H:VanPC

Head Quarters Johnstons Army
Greensboro N.C. April 20th. 1865

Maj M B McMicken
Chief Qr Mr

Maj

In obedience to your directions of this date, I have the honor to report amount of, and circumstances under which property of the state of N.C. was removed by me from Graham &c, and also transferred to me at this point by Maj Sloan.

I arrived at Graham on Thursday afternoon April 13th, found everything in great confusion ascertained that Mr Oliver, Agent of the State of No Ca had a lot of stores he was desirous to be rid of. I called upon him and he proposed that I should take possession of the stores upon my own responsibility. I refused. He then requested me to receive them from him on the ground that he was unable to move them and feared that the stragglers from Lee's Army would break into his storeroom and rob him. He reported some 20 bales of blankets 10,000 lbs leather & 7,000 pairs pants. I told him I would only receive the pants as I could not carry anything more. To this he consented. I instructed Maj Roy Qr Mr to receive the pants, which he did & gave Mr Oliver a regular receipt for the same. On Friday night I reported to Genl Johnston, informed him of what I had done & also that the blankets & leather remained in store under charge of Mr Oliver. He directed me to put the same in R Road depot under charge of an officer for shipment by R Road to Greensboro N.C. Capt A Stephens AQM Stewarts[1] Corps was instructed accordingly. I arrived within 2 1/2 miles of Greensboro on Saturday April 15th at about 1 P.M and rode into Greensboro about 4 P M a mob of citizens and soldiers crowded the streets laden with shoes cloth & clothing. I went to Maj Sloans office & found the cloth &c being given out to all applicants. I applied to him to know if I could obtain some clothing for Johnstons Army. He replied that the cloth &c was the property of the state of No Ca and was to be given to her troops. I remarked that I was satisfied a larger portion of the clothing was passing into unworthy & unentitled hands. I requested him to communicate with Gov Vance on the subject. he informed me that Gov Vance was in the town. On inquiry I found that this was a mistake. I returned to Maj Sloan and requested him to telegraph Gov Vance upon this subject. he said he would do so, but had telegraphed the Gov already in reference to these stores and had received no reply. On Sunday morning April 16th about 9 A M I called upon Maj Sloan and asked him if he had received a reply to the telegram he answered he had not but that the Military had taken the matter out of his hands, that Maj Holmes Commandant of the post, would give me all the information. I then called upon Maj Holmes, he stated that he wished three or four Qr Masters to take charge of issue the stores properly and requested me to furnish them. I replied that I could do so but would like to see Maj Sloan with him, as I could not consent to take charge of, and issue the property of the State of No Ca unless some person representing the state consented thereto or requested it. We called upon Maj Sloan together who remarked that as long as the stores were there it offered an inducement for the mob to pillage and commit acts of violence and he would like the stores distributed as rapidly as possible, he had received no orders from Gov Vance as to the disposition of the stores and would like me to take charge of & issue the same. I replied, "I take this matter in charge at your request & will follow your directions." It was agreed the troops from No Ca should be served first & the remainder be divided in the Army. I then asked for a report of the stores on hand. I was told that the goods had been sent there without invoices & he supposed there was about 7000 blankets 1700 prs pants 900 Jackets and 6900 Yards Grey cloth. I proceeded to distribute these stores "pro rata" to the Army with instructions to the Corps Qr Masters to fully equip the N.C. troops in their commands and then divide the remainder amongst the other troops. I had issued about 1200 Yds to Lee's[2] Corps when a communication was received by you from Genl Beauregard in reference to a letter received from Gov Vance respecting the issue of these stores. I immediately ceased issuing I then received an order from you to cease issuing any property of the state of No Ca & to place all stores &c belonging to the state of No. Ca in the hands of Maj Sloan. I thereupon issued an order to Maj Roy Qr Mr to turn into Maj Sloan all the pants he had brought from Graham by wagons, also one to Capt Stephens AQM Stewarts Corps to turn in all he had brought by Rail from Graham. Also instructed Maj George Qr Mr Lee's Corps to return the 1200 Yds Grey Cloth he had received, when he informed me it had already been issued. On Thursday 18th. April Col Cole informed me that Gov Vance had directed him to turn over to the Army of Tenn a certain portion of cloth & clothing which I received and divided as per list enclosed each Qr Master receipting for his portion. These vouchers & one from a N.Ca Regt are I am informed the only vouchers that have been given the state of No Ca for all the property she has issued excepting some sales to officers.

> I have the honor to be
> Very Respectfully Your Obt Servt
> (Signed) W G Vardell

Maj & Qr Mr

[1] Lt. Gen. Alexander Peter Stewart. Current et al., *Encyclopedia of the Confederacy*, 4:1545.

[2] Lt. Gen. Stephen Dill Lee. Faust et al., *Encyclopedia of Civil War*, 431.

ZBV *to Joseph E. Johnston*   A&H:VanPC

State of North Carolina
Executive Department
Greensboro 20th. Apl. 1865.

Genl Joseph E. Johnston
Commanding &c

General

In your first note of yesterday in reply to mine alleging that certain property of the State had been seized by Confederate troops &c, you say, "You will oblige me greatly by enumerating the State property seized by Confederate troops and also by giving any information of circumstances that you may have."

It is impossible particularly to comply with your request. Maj James Sloan Chief State Qr. Master of this Post reports that he had on hand on the arrival of the troops at this place, two hundred & forty three (243) Bales of Blankets, cloth and ready made clothing, averaging respectively, <one hundred> (100) Blankets and <five hundred yards> /500 yds/ of cloth to the bale and also <four thousand> /(4000)/ pairs of pants, <six hundred> (600) jackets and a small quantity of leather. Of this amount there was issued to the troops <Thirteen> 16,028 yds. cloth, 4458 pairs pants, 2000 pairs socks, 1143 Jackets. /Nearly/ All the remainder, certainly much over half of the whole was violently seized or issued miscellaneously under the threats of the mob to avoid seizure. At the same time the books, papers and private property of the Qr. Master were stolen & destroyed. A small quantity of blankets and home made cloth yet remains on hand.

Capt. Oliver, Qr. Master at Graham N.C. reports that he delivered under pressure of the mob of soldiers 6300 pairs of pants 7000 lbs. leather, 21 bales Blankets (100 to the bale) ten coils Rope & 2000 yds. of Jeans Cloth. There was actually taken by the mob 5000 lbs. leather, & <three> 3000 yd. cloth, in which the citizens participated. In addition to these statements of my Qr. Masters, I myself saw the conclusion of th[e] sacking of a train at McLeans station yesterday morning by Soldiers laden with blankets & leather, the cars had just been emptied as I got there and the <rode> /road/ side &

the woods were crowded with soldiers staggering under heavy loads of the plunder. It seemed to be an understood & permitted matter as officers of nearly all grades were standing quietly around.

The hardship complained of in all this General, is, that there remains no one to make reparation to the State. Whilst the arrears of pay due the soldiers from the Confederacy, would justify the delivery to them of any stores <to them> belonging to the Confederate States, it is peculiarly hard on North Carolina alone to be thus compelled to pay off the soldiers of all the other States. The debt contracted in Europe by the purchase of these supplies will of course be shared by none of the other States, and in this respect the voluntary issues amount in reality to a mere gift. North Carolina having done five times over more than any other State for the clothing of the Confederate army, I think I can appeal the more strongly to you to protect her against plunder & pillage.

In all this I have made no reference to a system of the most complete and outrageous robbery of private citizens now going on to a most distressing extent, and which I do not know that it is in your power to prevent.

When all this is considered I am sure that you will pardon me for urging upon you, the /adoption of/ most stringent measures in your power for the protection of my State and people against the lawless <violence> /license/ of an army about to be disbanded.

> Very Respectfully
> Yr obt Servt
> Z. B. Vance

ZBV to Joseph E. Johnston   A&H:VanPC

Copy

> State of North Carolina
> Executive Department
> Greensboro 20th. Apl. 1865.

Genl Joseph E. Johnston
Commanding &c

General

Your second note of yesterday in reply to mine of the same date in reference to a <permit for the treasurer of North Carolina to return to Raleigh was recd. yesterday evening.> /permit to send a letter by flag of truce to Genl Sherman was recd. yesterday afternoon./

I regret General, that the correspondence should have assumed the phase of a mere personal complaint on my part, though I felt so a<c>utely what I thought to be exceedingly uncourteous treatment on the part of some one, toward myself, that I perhaps improperly referred to it in a letter the intention of which was simply to procure a <passport for Mr. Worth> permit to send a letter to Raleigh. And though I do not lay the omissions of Genl Breckinridge and Mr. Webb at your door, as you will see disclaimed in my second note of yesterday, yet I think <you> upon reflection you cannot fail to agree with me, that after having received an invitation to attend a conference with yourself & others at Genl Hampton's Hd. Qrs., whither I should not have thought of intruding myself unasked, to be <left> excluded entirely from said conference, rendered my position exceedingly embarrassing, which was in no wise relieved by being left on the return to this place.

You are correct in supposing that after reading the paper[1] which you enclosed me yesterday containing a memorandum of the basis of agreement written by yourself & Genl Sherman, for the termination of the war, I would not desire to communicate with the latter. I am content of course to await the issue of these negotiations.

Very Respectfully
Yr. obt. Servt
Z. B. Vance

[1]Not extant.

ZBV to Joseph E. Johnston   A&H:VanPC

State of North Carolina
Executive Department
Greensboro 21st. April 1865

Genl Joseph E. Johnston
Commanding &c

General,
   On the 16th. Inst. a Maj. Y. S. Patton, representing himself as Chief Quarter Master of Genl. Hardie's Corps, called upon me with a requisition for

six thousand suits of clothes for Genl. Hoke's Division. I gave him an order to Maj. Sloan to supply that Division, a copy of which is enclosed, upon which he obtained the stores mentioned in the within copy of requisitions,[1] which I beg to call to your attention with Maj Sloan's endorsement thereon. I learn from Genl. Hoke that only a very small portion of said Stores were delivered to his Division, the greater part having been issued to the remainder of Hardee's Corps. I respectfully request that justice be done in the premises. The obtaining of these stores by Maj. Patton under false pretences I regard as much less respectable than the seizure of them by a mob would have /been/.

> Very Respectfully
> Yr. obt. Servt.
> Z. B. Vance.

[1]Not extant.

ZBV *to Joseph E. Johnston*   A&H:VanPC

Copy

> State of North Carolina
> Ex. Dept.
> Greensboro 21st. April 1861 [*1865*]

Genl Joseph E Johnston
Commanding &c

General

The following dispatch has just been recd. from Capt. White A.Q.M. at Salisbury, to wit, "Salisbury April 20th. Gov. Vance xxxx. The Confederate Authorities here are taking off some of the State Bacon this A.M. Brig Genl Johnston says it is done by order of Genl J. E. Johnston; to be returned. I cannot prevent it. Let me hear from you. Signed T. White A.Q.M."

Please let me know if you have issued any such order.

> Very Respectfully
> Yr obt Servt
> Z. B. Vance

E. J. Harris to ZBV   A&H:VanPC

Hd. Qrs. Army of Tenn.
Near Greensboro, No. Ca.
April 21st. 1865.

His Excellency
Z. B. Vance
Govr. of North Carolina

Governor:

Genl. Johnston desires me to inform you that the Inspector of Field Transportation reports in his possession about two hundred (200) unservicable animals, and also a number of unservicable waggons, harness &c—all of which, upon your promise to have them distributed to worthy citizens of the State of North Carolina, will be turned over to such parties, and at such times, as you may designate.

Be good enough to communicate with me on the subject.

Very Respectfully
Yr. Obdt. Servt.
E. J. Harris
Col. & Inspect. Genl. A. T.

ZBV to E. J. Harris   A&H:VanPC

Copy

State of No. Ca.
Executive Dept.
Greensboro 21st. Apl. 1865.

Col. E. J. Harris
Inspect. Genl. Army Tenn.

Colonel

Your note of this date /<is to hand>/ informing me that "the Inspector of Field Transportation reports <two> in his possession about two hundred (200) unservicable animals & also a number of unservicable wagons, harness &c" all of which Genl Johnston proposes to be turned over to me to be distributed to worthy citizens of this State, is to hand. I will very gladly accept them and will appoint an Agent to receive them at such time and place as may be convenient to you.

> Very Respectfully
> Yr. obt. Servt
> Z. B. Vance

ZBV to Thomas White   A&H:VanPC

Copy

Greensboro April 21st. [*1865*]

Capt. Thos. White
Salisbury

Do not give up your Stores to any one. Tell Genl. Johnston that I forbid his touching my property without my consent.

> Z. B. Vance

Joseph E. Johnston to ZBV   A&H:VanPC

Greensboro' April 21st 1865

His Excy. Z. B. Vance
Governor of North Carolina

Sir,

I had the honour to receive your note[1] reporting that bacon belonging to the State had been seized by the commanding officer at Salisbury, who professed to act under my authority. I gave no such order, & as soon as your note was received directed Brigr. Genl. Johnston by telegraph to return the bacon.

> Most respectfully
> Your obt. sert.
> J. E. Johnston
> General

[1]April 21, 1865, in this volume.

James Sloan to ZBV   A&H:VanPC

Greensboro N.C.
Apl 21st 1865

To his Excellency
Gov Z. B Vance,

Greensboro NC

In obedience to your enquiry of this date as to the quantity of Quarter Master's Stores stolen & issued at this place during the past six days, I have the honour to report that I recd. from Col [*Henry A.*] Dowd q.m. on Storage, and had on hand at the time, Two hundred & forty three (243) Bales, Blankets, Cloth, Flannel & Clothing, no invoice accompanying, the several shipments, I was necessarily ignorant of the contents.

From Graham, I recd by Genl Johnstons Waggon train some four thousand (4000) pair Pants & some Six hundred (600) Jackets together with a small quantity of upper & sole Leather

To the army of Tennessee, I issued Thirteen thousand yds Flannel (13000) Three thousand & twenty Eight yds. Cloth (3028) Four thousand four hundred & fifty Eight Pr Pants (4458) Two thousand pair Wool Socks (2000) Eleven hundred & forty three Jackets (1143). The remainder of the Cloth, Flannel, Jackets, Pants &c was stolen & issued to N.C. soldiers, the Home Guard & parolled prisones returning from Genl Lee's army.

The raid on my office & ware houses on Saturday last, resulted in the destruction of my personal effects, Books, papers, some 1200 to 1500 lbs English & Domestic upper & sole Leather, & some three hundred Pair Shoes (300) &c. & a quantity of Cloth Clothing & Blankets.

The destruction of my books vouchers &c is irrepairable. At the time it occurred, a heavy rain was falling, streets very muddy, Papers, books, &c trodden under foot of man & beast, and the raid was not quelled intill a squad of a few men from the 7th N.C. Regt fired on the mob, killing one, & mortally wounding some three others.

Should I be so fortunate as to recover my books & papers, carried away, I may at a future day, be able to submit a more satisfactory return.

I have remaining in the fire proof ware house of the State, Ninty (90) Bales Blankets, of one hundred each (100), some (25) Twenty five Pieces Tates Jeans averageing some (25) Twenty five yd. each, some Four hundred lbs upper & Sole Leather (400) In the shed, near my office, there is stored Thirty (30) Bales, Cotton, liable to be destroyed /or stolen/ at any moment, unless an <in>efficient Guard is kept over the same.

Permit me in conclusion, to say that we are indebted to the efficient command of Gen'l Brantly,[1] for the protection and safe keeping of the State Goods after the memorable Saturday of last week.

I know nothing of the quantity or Value of the Goods destroyed at Company Shops or Graham, or on the Rail Road. To Col Cole and his untiring assistants we are indebted for the distributing and issueing, under circumstances of the most embarrassing and unpleasant character.

Your order is respectfully solicited as to the disposition to be made of the stores remaining on hand.

> Very Respectfully
> Your Obdt Servt
> James Sloan
> Majr & Q.M.

[1]Brig. Gen. William Felix Brantley. Faust et al., *Encyclopedia of Civil War*, 77.

ZBV to William A. Graham   A&H:GraPC

Greensboro,
April 21. [*1865*]

Dear Governor,

The terms agreed upon by Johnston & Sherman, embrace substantially,

1. Truce, suspension of hostilities east of the Miss. Indefinitely, not to be broken except upon 48 hours notice.

2d. The disbanding of all C.S. Armies, their arms to be turned over & deposited in Capitols of each State &c.

3d. Recognition of State Govts intact upon Governors taking oath of allegiance, & disputed State Govts to be decided by Supreme Court of U.S.

4. General amnesty—no man to be disturbed in *person* or property for crime of rebellion &c.

5. Restoration of Courts & authority to U.S. in full over the Country.

I believe these are the principal points. The paper is signed by both Generals, who add, "that not having complete authority they agree to procure the ratification of their principals as soon as possible."

I fear that there may be a delay which will cause our own troops to do us more damage than the enemy could. The greatest state of anarchy & confusion prevails here.

The terms are better than I expected & I hope may be made final.

I would write more but write with great trouble & haste and don't know that I can get this to you.

Truly yours,
Z. B. Vance

ZBV *to John C. Breckinridge*   A&H:VanPC

Copy

State of No. Ca.
Executive Office
Greensboro, Apl 22d. 1865.

Hon Jno. C. Breckinridge
Secty. of War

Dear Sir

As you are perhaps aware, the State of No. Ca. has made large issues of both Quarter Master's & Commissary Stores to the Confederate State's Armies, other than her own troops. Several millions of dollars are now due and have been due for twelve months past. Recently the entire Army of Tennessee has not only been supplied with clothing, by issues, but large amounts have also been taken violently. As there remains no one to whom we can look for payment in the future, and as it bears peculiarly hard upon North Carolina, to be compelled alone to pay the debts in Europe contracted for the purchase of the most of these articles which have inured to the common benefit of all the States, I am exceedingly anxious to know if some arrangement cannot be made by which in part the state may be indemnified.

I would respectfully suggest that there is a considerable amount of public property of various kinds, and especially of Cotton which might be delivered to me for this purpose in case of the restoration of peace. I think Sir, you will agree with me in saying, that justice and equity demand something of this kind. North Carolina came forward with her own credit and not only furnished her own troops but with a lavish hand furnished large supplies to the Army at large, and she should not be left to suffer, when there /are/ any means in the power of the Government to indemnify her. Over seven hundred thousand dollars ($700,000) are borrowed in Europe on Cotton and Rosin Warrants, which were expended in Army supplies. Much of the Cotton bought to redeem them has been destroyed by the enemy or to prevent its falling into their hands, and I hope and believe it to be just, that you will order delivered to me Cotton in this or any other State sufficient to <assist> /enable/ me in redeeming these warrants. Please let me hear from you on this subject at an early day.

> Very Respectfully
> Yr. obt. Servt.
> Z. B. Vance

ZBV to Joseph E. Johnston   A&H:VanPC

Copy

> State of North Carolina
> Executive Department
> Greensboro April 22nd 1865.

Gen Joseph E. Johnston
Comdng &c

Genl,

In view of the large amount of stores recently turned over by the State of North Carolina to the Confederate army for which there remains but little possibility of payment, I respectfully suggest that in case of the successful termination of pending negotiations the public property in possession of the Confederate States be delivered to me in partial extinguishment of said claim provided the said public property is not disposed of otherwise by any treaty to be concluded.

The heavy debt, incurred by North Carolina in the purchase and accumulation of these stores, <which is> payable in gold, <and> which have been distributed for the common benefit renders it peculiarly hard upon this state; and no other way of securing even partial payment suggests itself to me.

Perhaps this should have been more properly addressed to the Secretary of War and if so not knowing his whereabouts and having no means of communicating with him I shall feel obliged to you to give it the proper reference.

> Very Respectfully
> Your obedt Servt
> Z. B. Vance

E. J. Harris to ZBV   A&H:VanPC

Hd. Qurs. Army of Tenn.
Greensboro, N.C. Apl 22nd. 1865.

His Excellency
Z. B. Vance,
Governor of North Carolina.
Greensboro, N.C.

Governor:

In reply to your communication,[1] just now received, Genl. Johnston directs me to <say> request the name of your agent, and where he can be found. It would be more convenient to have him here, in Greensboro, that the matter might be at once disposed of. The Genl. would be pleased to have some authorized agent appointed, that receipts might be taken for the property turned over to him.

Can you conveniently reply to me this evening?

Very Respectfully,
Your obdt. Servt.
E. J. Harris
Col. & Inspr. Genl. A. T.

[1]April 21, 1865, in this volume.

Jefferson Davis to ZBV   A&H:GP

[*Telegram*]

Charlotte Apr 23 1865

To Gov Z B Vance

I had hoped to have seen you before this date. Is it convenient for you to come here at this time. I desire to confer with you as heretofore Expressed.

Jeffn Davis

Joseph E. Johnston to ZBV A&H:VanPC

Camp near Greensboro'
April 24th 1865

His Excy. Z. B. Vance
Governor of N. Carolina

Sir,

I had the honour to receive your two letters of the 20th[1] on that day.

My object in asking you for minute information of the robberies of which you complain was, to get the means of restoring the State property & punishing the robbers. I have postponed replying until now in order, before doing so, to obtain more minute accounts of the matter in question than you had given. In that connection, I enclose the statements of Major McMicken, Chief Qr Master, Major Jas Sloan Qr Mr. N.C.A. & Major Vardell.[2] They justify me, I think, in asking you to acquit "the troops under my command" of the charge of having "forcibly seized all the property of the State from Haw River depot to this place."

The only robberies mentioned in these papers, were committed by a mob in Greensboro', on the 15th. The only troops that I know of then in the town, were N. Carolina reserves, placed there by Lieut. Genl. Holmes. Those under my command <encamped> marched that day but 10 or 12 miles from Haw River bridge. You may remember that we passed there on the 16th. & left then encamping a mile & a half from the town. It is, therefore, not unreasonable to say that any Confederate soldiers concerned in seizing public property in Greensboro' on the 15th, must have belonged to the Army of Virginia, not that of Tennessee.

Major McMicken explains the occurrence you witnessed on the 19th at McLeans Station thus: Major Melton, Qr Mr of Genl Hampton's corps, was that morning receiving stores <stores> for the cavalry, including blankets, at that place. He had no vehicles, & the different articles were taken from the cars by the men of the party he had brought for the purpose.

Great outrages are committed on your people by Confederate soldiers, I know. But they are the disbanded men of the Army of Northn. Va. I regret this as much as you do, but can not, with my little force, prevent it. Indeed this army has probably suffered as much, proportionally, as the people of the State. For crowds of these disbanded soldiers seize our subsistence stores wherever they find them.

Most respectfully
Your obt. sert.
J. E. Johnston
General

[1]In this volume.
[2]See W. G. Vardell to M. B. McMicken, April 20, 1865, and James Sloan to ZBV, April 21, 1865, in this volume; and James Sloan to M. B. McMicken, April 21, 1865, and M. B. McMicken to Joseph E. Johnston, April 23, 1865, A&H:VanPC.

Joseph E. Johnston to ZBV   A&H:VanPC

Camp near Greensboro'
April 24th 1865

His Excy. Z. B. Vance

Governor,
I have had the honour to receive the letter of the 22d instant,[1] in which you propose to me, in the event of "a successful termination of pending negotiations," to deliver to you the Confederate property in North Carolina, on account of the debt of the Confederacy to your State.

I will readily do all I properly can to secure to North Carolina the sum due her from the Confederate government. But the course you propose seems to me impracticable. I believe that every other State of the Confederacy has a claim similar to that which you state, & think, therefore, that it would be just to divide any means available for the payment of those debts, proportionally.

Most of the public property in the possession of the army was impressed. Frequently with the condition that it should be returned. I intend, as far as practicable, to return it to its proper owners. A very large portion of it was obtained in this State, & I shall confidently ask your excellency's assistance in its restoration.

Most respectfully
Your obt. Sert.
J. E. Johnston

[1]In this volume.

Joseph E. Johnston to ZBV   A&H:VanPC

Camp near Greensboro
April 24th 1865

His Excy.
Z. B. Vance

Governor,
I have, this evening, been informed by Major General Sherman that our agreement of the 18th instant is not approved by the U.S. government. He has, consequently, given me notice of the termination of the armistice to-morrow.

Most respectfully
Your obt. servt.
J. E. Johnston
General

Jonathan Worth to ZBV   A&H:VanPC

Shops 25 Apl [1865]

Gov Vance
It is believed here that hostilities are to be commenced in this event what can I do with the State archives must I move west or remain where I am

J Worth

ZBV to William T. Sherman				A&H:VanPC

State of North Carolina,
Executive Department,
\<Raleigh\>
Greensboro' April 27th., 1865.

Major Genl. W. T. Sherman
Comdg. U.S. Forces in N.C.

General:

The Honorable Jonathan Worth who bears my letter of this date to you, desires to confer with you as Treasurer of this State, in regard to the removal of the effects under his charge & belonging to the several departments of the State government.

Under the circumstances attending the disbanding of an army it is considered highly important that these effects, most of which are records simply should be restored to their usual place of deposit in the Capitol at Raleigh, & your safe-guard Mr. Worth is authorized to solicit for this purpose.

I have the honor to be

Very respectfully yr. obt. Servant
(Signed) Z. B. Vance

ZBV to William T. Sherman				A&H:VanPC

State of North Carolina
Executive Office
Greensboro, April 27th. 1865

Major General W. T. Sherman
Comdg U.S. Forces in N.C.

General:

Having been \<unavoidably\> prevented from communicating with you /for reasons which I will explain should we meet/ at an earlier day I have now again the honor to request a personal interview with yourself. As I did not receive your communication of the 12th. inst[1] \<until\> enclosing a safe conduct until I had reached Hillsboro' & as it contemplated my remaining in Raleigh I am doubtful whether you would consider it as still holding good. I shall therefore be obliged to you if you will either renew the safe conduct or grant me an interview under a Flag of Truce, at an early a day as practicable. The objects to be obtained can be more fully set forth when we meet; but I will <merely> intimate that they refer more particularly to the immediate convening of the Legislature of the State & the adoption of prompt measures to save the people from a condition of anarchy which now threatens them.

> I am General, very respectfully
> Your Obedient Servant
> (Signed) Z. B. Vance

[1]In this volume.

Jonathan Worth to ZBV   A&H:GP

[*Telegram*]

Raleigh 28 Apl 1865

To Gov Vance

Genl Sherman has left Genl Schofield declines the interview you solicit here but says you can see him in a few days in Greensboro. He directs me to bring here the state records.

I send a telegram to Maj Harvey to go after them. I will go up by next train.

J. Worth

Proclamation by ZBV   A&H:VanPC

State of North Carolina.
Executive Department,
Greensborough, April 28th, 1865.

By the Governor of North Carolina
A Proclamation.

Whereas, by the recent surrender of the principal armies of the Confederate States, further resistance to the forces of the United States has become vain, and would result in a useless waste of blood; and whereas, all the natural disorders, attendant upon the disbanding of large armies arc upon us, and the country is filled with numerous bands of citizens and soldiers disposed to do violence to persons and property:

Now, therefore, I, Zebulon B. Vance, Governor of the State of North Carolina, in the sincere hope of averting some of the many evils which threaten us, do issue this my Proclamation, commanding all such persons to abstain from any and all acts of lawlessness, to avoid assembling together in crowds in all towns and cities, or doing anything whatsoever calculated to cause excitement; and earnestly appealing to all good citizens, who are now at home, to remain there, and to all soldiers of this State to retire quietly to their homes, and exert themselves in preserving order. Should it become necessary for the protection of citizens, I also appeal to the good and true soldiers of North Carolina, whether they have been surrendered and paroled or otherwise, to unite themselves together in sufficient numbers in the various counties of the State, under the superintendence of the civil magistrates thereof, to arrest or slay any bodies of lawless and unauthorized men who may be committing depredations upon the persons or property of peaceable citizens, assuring them that it will be no violation of their parole to do so. And I would assure my fellow citizens generally, that, under God, I will do all that may be in my power to settle the government of the State, to restore the civil authority in her borders, and to further the great ends of peace, domestic tranquility and the general welfare of the people. Without their aid I am powerless to do anything.

Z. B. Vance.

By the Governor:
A. M. McPheeters, Private Secretary,

ZBV to John M. Schofield   A&H:Whit

Greensboro' April 30th 1865

Major Gen Schofield
Raleigh N.C.

A large number of trains belonging to the Atlantic and N.C. Rail Road and other Roads in the eastern part of the State, have been accumulated near this place. Can they be permitted to return and resume operations, under their present organization and if not what disposition do you propose to make of them.

Z. B. Vance

Rufus S. Tucker to ZBV   A&H:VanPC

Raleigh NC
May 1, 1865.

Gov Z. B. Vance

My Dear Friend

Your very kind letter[1] has been received by Capt Guthrie, and I was most happy to receive it and will treasure it as one of the most important private papers of the day.

I have read it to most of our friends, and we all approve the sentiments therein expressed, and the course you pursued on leaving here. Your true friends are still true: the Union of the States is now what you & I and good Citizens will work for, without vituperation & abuse: and we all regret the course the papers of Raleigh are pursuing in singling out & abusing certain men: & we still further regret the *Ultra* position they take in all matters.

B. F. Moore,[2] Dick Donnald[3] and others do not join in the above, but are representing the true Conservative feeling of the Country.

My mother, Brother William, Wife & all join me in much love to yourself & family.

We are all quiet, but doing nothing to make a living.

Your friend truly

R. S. Tucker[4]
Would write more but am hurried.

[1]Not extant.

[2]Bartholomew Figures Moore, lawyer, former legislator and state attorney general. He had opposed secession, and after the war he participated in the state Constitutional Convention of 1865 and practiced law in the Federal courts. *Dictionary of North Carolina Biography*, s.v. "Moore, Bartholomew Figures."

[3]Richard Spaight Donnell, lawyer, banker, legislator, and state Speaker of the House, 1863-1865. After the war, he attended the Constitutional Convention of 1865. *Dictionary of North Carolina Biography*, s.v. "Donnell, Richard Spaight."

[4]Rufus Sylvester Tucker, Confederate officer in 1862, assistant adjutant general in 1863, and principal clerk in state House of Commons in 1864-1865. After the war, he became a wealthy businessman, railroad magnate, and director of the Institute of Deaf, Dumb, and Blind in Raleigh. *Dictionary of North Carolina Biography*, s.v. "Tucker, Rufus Sylvester."

Thomas White to ZBV   A&H:GP

[*Telegram*]

Salisbury, May 2d. 1865

To Gov. Z. B. Vance

Records are stored in Clerk & Masters office Will be hard to get private storage Will that place do?

Thos. White

Bedford Brown to ZBV   A&H:VanPC

Caswell Cy, N.Ca.
<April> May 2d. [18]65

His Excellency Gov Vance

Dear Sir

I have just received the letters[1] of Gov Graham & yourself, proposing, that I should form one of the Commission, composed of Gov Graham and Mr [*John A.*] Gilmer, to proceed to Washington and confer with the authorities of /the/ United States, in reference to the policy to be pursued, in regard to N. Carolina. I regret, that I am compelled by the state of my health to decline this flattering request, which otherwise I should most cheerfully comply with. Appreciating this manifestation of respect most highly, I most [surely] hope those distinguished gentlemen will proceed on their mission in a matter of such vast importance to the State of N. Carolina and remain

Very truly,
Yours
Bedford Brown

[1]Not extant.

Harriett Espy Vance to ZBV   A&H:VanPC

Statesville May 19th. 1865

My dear Husband:

I /have/ received both of your letters[1] written from Raleigh, the latest one relieved my anxiety very greatly. It is truly encouraging to know you are accompanied by such men as Gov Swain & the others mentioned in your letter. I shall feel more at ease about you on account of your having acquaintances, tho' I know the same Almighty Friend is just as able & willing to sustain you when left alone under trials, as when surrounded with friends; still human friendship & sympathy is not to be despised, but to be cherished. You know My dear, that my trust is in the Lord, for "in the Lord Jehovah is everlasting strength." put your trust in Him. You remember one of old said, "I was brought low & the Lord helped me." His sustaining grace has supported me under this heavy affliction, I can truly say.

We all continue quite well & meet kindness from every source. I feel very grateful to the Federal Officers who had charge of you, for their kindness & politeness. they will never have cause to regret it, I am sure, the people of North Carolina will ever remember them & appreciate them on account of it. I am continuly receiving assurance of the deep sympathy of the good people of our noble old state. May the Good Lord reward them for their devotion to you.

Our dear boys send much love to Papa. the servants too desire to be remembered—are very kind to us indeed. Mr Bradley & Zebbie send regards. I will send this letter to Raleigh to Maj Wilson who goes down in the morning & will get him to mail it to you from there. I know you will continue to write every opportunity. I have been greatly favored in hearing from you, for which I feel very thankful. You have doubtless reached Washington City before this & have learned too for what you were arrested. Of course I am anxious to know, in the mean time I will endeavor to hope for the best. "The Lord God omnipotent reigneth & will do right." into His hands I commit you My dear one. May His everlasting armes be around you. Dont suffer yourself to be uneasy about us. We are getting along very well & are hoping to have you return to us before long. All your friends here desire kindest remembrances. I wrote Brother Robert last evening, have heard nothing from him as yet. Again God bless you My dear good Husband. Believe me most truly.

Your affectionate wife

Hattie Vance

P.S. Maj Wilson did not leave on Saturday as expected, so I just add a line or two this morning to assure you of our continued welldoing. Cousin Sophionia Pearson & Ann Lizzie came down on Friday to see me. Cousin S. goes back this morning. Ann Lizzie will remain with me. they both desire much love to you. I havent time to write more this morning as the Maj has sent for the letter. The boys all send love & believe me dearest

Your devoted wife
Hattie

[1]Not extant.

Edward Warren to ZBV   A&H:VanPC

Baltimore May 26th. 1865.

My Dear Sir:
    I write a line to assure you of my continued friendship, and of my deep interest in your welfare and that of your family.
    If I can serve you in any manner, consistent with my obligations to the Government, do not hesitate to call on me.
    I shall immediately communicate with your wife and children for the purpose of assuring them that they have in me a friend who is anxious to prove his gratitude and <friendship> affection.
    Your have been kind to me in better days, and I shall never forget it. I have taken the oath as a matter of duty; and I sincerely trust that it may enable me the better to conduce to your comfort and relief. As this letter is dictated by notions of personal friendship alone and by no political feelings, ties or objects, I sincerely hope it may reach its destination.

Yours very truly
Edward Warren

Harriett Espy Vance to ZBV   A&H:VanPC

Statesville June 5th. 1865

My dear Husband,
    I received your letter[1] of the 24th. of May this morning & one from Gov Swain of the 27th. yesterday, which relieved my anxiety in a great measure,

being the first reliable intelligence I have had from you since you left Raleigh. The state of suspense I have been in, has been very trying upon me, but the sustaining grace of God has been my source of comfort & consolation. May this precious grace be given you My dear one, to strengthen & sustain you under the trying circumstances with which you are surrounded. The mercy seat is the only place we can meet now. this is certainly a great privilege. May it be often resorted to, by us both. I am truly thankful to learn you <are> have all necessary comforts & are able to exercise on account of your health. Dont allow yourself uneasiness on account of "loved ones at home"—We are well cared for. Indeed the kindness I have received at the hands of the people of Statesville & surrounding country is unbounded. their concern for your welfare & that of your family will ever be appreciated by both of us. I will remain in their midst as I am very comfortably situated & can get news from you so much more readily than at Asheville. I act thus upon the advice of Maj Wilson & Mr. Simonton. The articles pertaining to the Executive Mansion have all been delivered upon demand of the military authorities & others placed in the house by the kind & good people of this community for our comfort. It is a great relief to me to have the responsibility of the Government House property off me as you know. Isaac & Julia have left, greatly to my satisfaction as they were trying me <greatly> not a little. Hannah is still with me & never did so well in her life, indeed I never kept house with less trouble. Ann Lizzie (*our true friend*) is with me /also/ & is a very great comfort—will remain with me during your absence. Sends much love & says tell you, every thing in her power shall be done for the comfort of your dear ones. Cousin Sophionia came down to see me as I wrote you & she, cousin Robert & all the family will do what they can; so you see we are surrounded with friends. I am continuly receiving assurance from the people generally, of their earnest desire to render us any & every assistance. I have heard nothing from Asheville since your arrest. am daily expecting brother Robert down, tho' he writes it is not altogather safe for persons to leave their homes, or at least he wrote this some three weeks since. I guess he can come now. Alfred Baird came & spent several days with us—heard of your arrest after leaving Asheville & just came on to see us at once, returned last week & said he would stay with brother Robs family when he got home, that he might come to us, so I think he will be here this evening & advise me what is best. In the mean time write me to this place, care of Maj Wilson who is very kind, as is every body. All <my> /our/ friends advise me to remain here & I know you would consider it best if you knew all the circumstances. Zebbie is still with me & Uncle Dolph is willing he should remain. he desires kindest remembrances. So do all your friends & they are legion. Our dear boys are all well & talk much about their dear Papa. Again let me assure you of our well doing in every respect. I will write as often as possible. Gov Swain's letter encouraged me to hope for your early release. he wrote from Washington City. I am in hopes he will write me immediately, upon his arrival at home. I am glad to hear you have Gov. Brown as a companion, I trust you will be a mutual benefit to one another in a spiritual as well as temporal point of view. your other companions are doubtless agreeable too. I wrote once before this & trust you have received the letter, as Genl Cooper was kind enough to send it on for me. I will write every opportunity. The children send much love, I hope to be able to write more particularly of Mother & our other friends at Asheville in my next. They were all well when brother Rob wrote on the 17th. of May. Into the hands of our most merciful & kind Father in heaven, would I commit you My dear one. He doeth all things right. Let us trust in Him doing our own duty & all will be well.

> *Ever Yours*
> Hattie Vance.

[1]Not extant.

Harriett Espy Vance to ZBV   A&H:VanPC

Statesville June 9th. 1865

My dear Husband;

I wrote you on Monday /the/ 4th. just after receiving yours of the 24th. of May, the only letter I have had from you since you left Raleigh. I hope you have been permitted to receive my letter by this time. Col Haynes came over last evening & told me Col Murry would leave Salisbury for Washington City tomorrow & would no doubt take a letter for me; so I avail myself of the opportunity of /informing you of/ our well doing. I am anxiously hoping to hear from you again *very soon*—you know my anxiety is great. but I strive to hope for the best.

Since writing the above I have learned through Mr John D. Brown, Judge Pearson & others that the papers state that you are paroled & allowed the privileges of the City. I trust it is so, tho' I dont permit it to influence me too much, fearing it may not be so. If it is, I will hope to see you before a great while. In the mean time, dont let yourself be unnecessarily uneasy about your "loved ones at home"—We are getting on quite as well as we could, with you away from us. Meet kindness from every source. Charley & David have gotten their Pony at last & are delighted of course. Charlie attends to it himself. I had a letter from Brother Robert a few days ago—neither sister

Harriett or himself were well—said he would go on to see you, if he had permission. Mother & the rest of our friends at Asheville were quite well. I let Zebbie Baird go home day before yesterday on a visit, he will return in a short time. I will remain here for the present as I wrote you on Monday, being able to hear from you so much more direct than at Asheville. I am anxiously hoping to hear from you through Gov. Swain. I know he will write me as soon as he returns home. he wrote me such a kind letter, with regard to you from Washington City. What a true friend he is & a noble one too. Ann Lizzie & the children send much love. Hannah is still with us. Julia & Isaac, I wrote you, had left. I know not what has become of them.

Marion wrote to Hannah he would come up for her to go to Raleigh, if she wished to go. she doesnt seem to want to leave me, but wants to be with her husband, which is very right. She wrote him to come up & they could then decide what was best. I will offer to hire him for what is considered proper until your return home. I get on very well indeed, never kept house with so little trouble. Am satisfied I have always had too many servants about me. Hannah does the work with Ann Lizzie & my help without any difficulty. If I could only have you at home My dear one, the darkies might all go. You know I have always contended we would be better off without them. the poor creatures are themselves much more to be pitied than we are tho' they may not agree with us. I do sincerely trust their condition may be much better than it is at present, for in some instances it is lamentable. I guess I had better stop writing or they may not allow my letter to reach you if you are still a prisoner & I fear you are. May the rich blessings of Our kind & Merciful Father in heaven rest upon you My dear husband is the sincere prayer of

Your devoted
Hattie

My dear Cousin,

I have begged cousin Hattie to allow me a small space, in her letter, only to say, that I am doing every thing in my power, to make your "dear ones" happy. I think very often of you, and hope soon to see the face, of my dear cousin Zeb.

Yours with affection,
Ann Lizzie Pearson

William H. H. Cowles to ZBV   A&H:VanPC

Raleigh June 26/65

Gov Vance

My Dear Sir

We hear it here that you decline taking the *Oath*, and thereby return to your State, if its the Oath we see in the papers, I think you should take it, provided you can return home, to stand out longer is *useless*, we are powerless, and we should make the best of our condition, submit and yield, obedience to the powers that be, for they are ordained of God. Though if we were to doubt any portion of the Bible, it seems a reasonable doubt might be raised as to the ordaining.

Gov Holden[1] is appointing Magistrates, and such Magistrates. Your former neighbour, Mark Williams, Jackson Moss, and Parker Overby, I understand have been appointed.

B. F. Moore has been nominated for Gov in Franklin County.

Mr. Merryman [*Merrimon*] of Asheville is here and says things are quiet in the West. Mr. M thinks you ought to take the Oath and come home to your family and friends, it would do us all good to know you were in the State, and we want you to come this way and make us a talk, on the times, our condition, prospects, rights and duties.

Every body has taken the Oath that could, and I understand [*Duncan K.*] McRae has applied for *pardon*.

Gov Holden has shut up the Banks, saying I understand, we have forfeited our Charters, and that we can do "no act of Banking" fortunately Gov H is not an Oracle in law if he was in politics.

Col. Little[2] and [*David A.*] Barnes I understand paid their respects to Gov H and family.

I have written hastily, excuse me for offering you advice.

Genl. Cox[3] who has taken Genl. Schofields place is boarding with me, I find him a reasonable, conservative christian gentleman, and would be glad for you to make his acquaintance, by stoping with us as you come home.

Mr. Worth will give you particulars as to matters and things generally.

I am Sir
Your friend
W H Cowles

[1]President Andrew Johnson had appointed William W. Holden as provisional governor of North Carolina.

[2]George Little, former aide to ZBV.

[3]Federal general Jacob Dolson Cox, who had come to North Carolina with the Twenty-third Corps near the end of the war. Faust et al., *Encyclopedia of Civil War*, 188.

ZBV to Harriett Espy Vance   A&H:VanPC

Old Capitol Prison
Washington June 30th. [*1865*]

My dear wife,

As Mr. [*Robert R.*] Bridgers has not left yet, I write again by him thinking you will be more likely to get it by him than by the mails which are yet quite uncertain. Yesterday I recd. yours of the 23d. inst[1] and was much pleased at its contents, glad to know that you were doing so well. You must make my special thanks to Hannah for her faithful conduct to you which shall not go unrewarded when I get home. I am still quite well, have put in my application for a pardon and am anxious to return to you as soon as possible. My kind love to Cousin Ann Lizzie, and my blessings to our dear children.

Again my dear wife, believe me as ever most affectionately

Your husband
Z.B.V.

[1]Not extant.

CALENDAR OF PAPERS NOT PRINTED IN THIS VOLUME

1864-1865

Correspondents	Date	Subject	Repository
Nicholas W. Woodfin to ZBV	Jan 1	salt	A&H:GP
Theodore Andreae to ZBV	Jan 1(1)	cotton	A&H:GP
Theodore Andreae to ZBV	Jan 1(2)	cotton	A&H:GP
Power, Low & Co. to ZBV	Jan 1	cotton	A&H:GP
Millege L. Bonham to ZBV	Jan 1	cotton	A&H:GP
Solomon A. Cohen to ZBV	Jan 1	service offer	A&H:GP
H. L. Brinkley et al. to ZBV	Jan 1	conscription	A&H:GP
Collett Leventhorpe to ZBV	Jan 1	fires	A&H:GP
An Old Friend to ZBV	Jan 1	peace	A&H:GP
E. D. Mathews to ZBV	Jan 1	hardship	A&H:GP
Henry E. Colton to ZBV	Jan 1	appointment	A&H:VanPC
Paul F. Faison to ZBV	Jan 2	atrocities	A&H:GP
Henry E. Colton to ZBV	Jan 2	resin & tin	A&H:GP
Cotton Blevins to ZBV	Jan 2	gift	A&H:GP
J. J. L. Harden to ZBV	Jan 2	conscription	A&H:GP
Gilliam Jones to ZBV	Jan 2	atrocities	A&H:GP
John A. Gilmer to ZBV	Jan 2	conscription	A&H:GP
Sion H. Rogers to ZBV	Jan 2	special court	A&H:GP
George Davis to ZBV	Jan 2	resignation	A&H:GLB
James A. Seddon to ZBV	Jan 2	passport	A&H:VanPC
ZBV to David L. Swain	Jan 2	peace	SHC:Swain
Thomas J. Sumner to ZBV	Jan 3	wood	A&H:GP
W. S. Fowler to ZBV	Jan 3	transfer	A&H:GP
Mrs. William A. Graham to ZBV	Jan 4	husband	A&H:GP
D. McD. Lindsey to ZBV	Jan 4	permit	A&H:GP
S. M. Ingram to ZBV	Jan 4	appointment	A&H:GP
M. S. Wiggins to ZBV	Jan 4	appointment	A&H:GP
Theodore Andreae to ZBV	Jan 4	Don	A&H:GP
Charles Manly to ZBV	Jan 4	UNC supplies	A&H:GP
S. H. Williams to ZBV	Jan 4	transfer	A&H:GP
R. C. Wormouth to ZBV	Jan 4	complaint	A&H:GP
Daniel M. McGugan to ZBV	Jan 4	conscription	A&H:GP
John Q. Winborne to ZBV	Jan 5	troop company	A&H:GP

Correspondents	Date	Subject	Repository
A. Rebel to ZBV	Jan 5	civil unrest	A&H:GP
W. P. Perry to ZBV	Jan 5	appointment	A&H:GP
George Donnell to ZBV	Jan 5	slave impressment	A&H:GP
John Winston to ZBV	Jan 5	slave impressment	A&H:GP
Jesse R. Stubbs to ZBV	Jan 5	new brigade	A&H:GP
William J. Clarke to ZBV	Jan 6	Federal threat	A&H:GP
S. H. Williams to ZBV	Jan 6	transfer	A&H:GP
Theodore Andreae to ZBV	Jan 6	*Don*	A&H:GP
W. H. Wheeler to ZBV	Jan 6	impressment	A&H:GP
William A. Graham to ZBV	Jan 6	Senate appointment	A&H:GP
S. W. Whitaker to ZBV	Jan 6	conscription	A&H:GP
N. Bowen to ZBV	Jan 6	clothing	A&H:GP
William F. Porter to ZBV	Jan 6	desertion	A&H:GP
Elisabeth Magness to ZBV	Jan 6	visit north	A&H:GP
J. H. Johnson to ZBV	Jan 6	cloth	A&H:GP
Thomas Coston to ZBV	Jan 6	cotton	A&H:GP
Theodore Andreae to ZBV	Jan 6	*Don*	A&H:GP
Sion H. Rogers to ZBV	Jan 6	Confed. tax	A&H:GP
S. J. Wiggins to ZBV	Jan 6	discharge	A&H:GP
Sarah A. Elliott to ZBV	Jan 6	cotton	A&H:GP
John W. Cameron to ZBV	Jan 6	Rich. Bradley	A&H:VanPC
Henry A. Dowd to ZBV	Jan 6	pork price	A&H:VanPC
Theodore Andreae to ZBV	Jan 7	steamers	A&H:GP
John D. Shaw to ZBV	Jan 7	conscription	A&H:GP
John Blevins et al. to ZBV	Jan 7	detail	A&H:GP
Clement Dowd to Ralph P. Buxton	Jan 7	distilling	A&H:GP
David G. Worth to ZBV	Jan 7	salt	A&H:GP
C. L. Banner to ZBV	Jan 7	W. W. Holden	A&H:GP
George Davis to D. Kahnweiler	Jan 7	letter	A&H:VanPC
John Shaw to ZBV	Jan 8	civil unrest	A&H:GP
Theodore Andreae to ZBV	Jan 8	*Don*	A&H:GP
Thomas J. Candler to ZBV	Jan 8	deserters	A&H:GP
William T. Muse to ZBV	Jan 8	*Don*	A&H:GP
Nancy Sparks to ZBV	Jan 8	discharge	A&H:GP
Jefferson Davis to ZBV	Jan 8	peace	A&H:VanPC
William T. Muse to ZBV	Jan 9	coal	A&H:GP
G. W. Bristol to ZBV	Jan 9	taxation	A&H:GP
G. H. White to ZBV	Jan 9	conscription	A&H:GP
Alexandria Wallis et al. to ZBV	Jan 9	conscription	A&H:GP
George Davis to D. Kahnweiler	Jan 9	letters	A&H:VanPC
Elinder Goodin to ZBV	Jan 10	destitution	A&H:GP
James Whitaker Jr. to ZBV	Jan 10	destitution	A&H:GP
Avabella Davis to ZBV	Jan 11	destitution	A&H:GP
John F. McKesson to ZBV	Jan 11	impressment	A&H:GP
A. M. Veazey to ZBV	Jan 11	cotton cards	A&H:GP
J. S. Lemmon to ZBV	Jan 11	cotton	A&H:GP

Correspondents	Date	Subject	Repository
M. S. McCurry to ZBV	Jan 11	conscription	A&H:GP
John B. Tapscott to ZBV	Jan 11	cloth	A&H:GP
D. H. Willard to ZBV	Jan 11	transfer	A&H:GP
Alexander R. Lawton to ZBV	Jan 11	harness	A&H:GP
James A. Seddon to ZBV	Jan 11	impressment	A&H:GP
James A. Seddon to ZBV	Jan 11	*Don*	A&H:GP
James T. Hendley to ZBV	Jan 11	desertion	A&H:GP
Henry E. Colton to ZBV	Jan 11	appointment	A&H:VanPC
William Gaither to ZBV	Jan 12	son	A&H:GP
H. H. Hinnant to ZBV	Jan 12	cotton cards	A&H:GP
Samuel B. French to ZBV	Jan 12	Jackson statue	A&H:GP
Seth M. Barton to ZBV	Jan 12	W. H. Marshall	A&H:GP
J. Jarratt to ZBV	Jan 12	W. A. Chatham	A&H:GP
John H. Shaw to ZBV	Jan 12	conscription	A&H:GP
Theodore Andreae to ZBV	Jan 12	money drafts	A&H:GP
Otis F. Manson to ZBV	Jan 12	meat	A&H:GP
W. Hooper to ZBV	Jan 12	conscription	A&H:GP
David L. Swain to ZBV	Jan 12	Senate appointment	A&H:GP
John D. Hyman to ZBV	Jan 12	newspaper	A&H:VanPC
H. Fitzhugh to ZBV	Jan 13	*Advance*	A&H:GP
James W. Cromartie to ZBV	Jan 13	desertion	A&H:GP
Theodore Andreae to ZBV	Jan 13	*Hansa*	A&H:GP
Power, Low & Co. to ZBV	Jan 13	*Advance*	A&H:GP
Paul F. Faison to ZBV	Jan 13	distilling	A&H:GP
J. E. Robertson to ZBV	Jan 13	furlough	A&H:GP
John D. Whitford to ZBV	Jan 13	pork	A&H:GP
S. A. P[er]kins to ZBV	Jan 13	special court	A&H:GP
Thomas W. Ritter to ZBV	Jan 13	John Maness	A&H:GP
John A. Bradshaw to ZBV	Jan 13	"negroes"	A&H:GP
J. C. Pegram to ZBV	Jan 13	meat	A&H:GP
Andrew C. Cowles to ZBV	Jan 13	peace movement	A&H:GP
Eliza Rothrock to ZBV	Jan 13	conscription	A&H:GP
Robert Ould to ZBV	Jan 14	prisoners	A&H:GP
William H. C. Whiting to ZBV	Jan 14	Salisbury	A&H:GP
Ralph P. Buxton to ZBV	Jan 14	Moore County	A&H:GP
William L. Lowrance to ZBV	Jan 14	soldier	A&H:GP
J. Cline to ZBV	Jan 14	House vacancy	A&H:GP
A. F. Williams to ZBV	Jan 14	conscription	A&H:GP
C. Anderson et al. to ZBV	Jan 14	discharge	A&H:GP
Charles R. Wilson to ZBV	Jan 14	cotton	A&H:GP
David L. Swain to ZBV	Jan 14	election	A&H:VanPC
Margaret Godwin to ZBV	Jan 14	deserters	A&H:GP
R. R. Heath to ZBV	Jan 15	special court	A&H:GP
Thomas B. Power to ZBV	Jan 15	*Advance*	A&H:GP
James W. Hinton to B. F. Butler	Jan 15	prisoners	A&H:GP
William H. McKee to ZBV	Jan 15	conscription	A&H:GP

Correspondents	Date	Subject	Repository
W. H. Holderness to ZBV	Jan 15	conscription	A&H:GP
John D. Whitford to ZBV	Jan 16	pork	A&H:GP
E. A. Temple to A. B. Romano	Jan 16	pass	A&H:GP
B. E. Blanton to ZBV	Jan 16	peace	A&H:GP
S. Galloway to ZBV	Jan 16	"negroes"	A&H:GP
Luke Blackmer to ZBV	Jan 16	disaffection	A&H:GP
W. P. Carson to ZBV	Jan 16	pass	A&H:GP
J. Leighton Wilson to A. Sinclair	Jan 16	appointment	A&H:GP
Thomas Crabtree to ZBV	Jan 16	transfer	A&H:GP
Alexander Collie to ZBV	Jan 16	trade	A&H:GP
Theodore Andreae to ZBV	Jan 16	finances	A&H:GP
Thomas Carter to ZBV	Jan 16	*Hansa*	A&H:GP
James Sloan to ZBV	Jan 16	conscription	A&H:GP
ZBV to Sheriffs	Jan 16	elections	A&H:GLB
Thomas Draper to ZBV	Jan 17	letter	A&H:GP
S. J. Westall to ZBV	Jan 17	destitution	A&H:GP
W. N. Bilbo to ZBV	Jan 17	attrocities	A&H:GP
Rowland Best to ZBV	Jan 18	conscription	A&H:GP
P. F. Lehman to ZBV	Jan 18	conscription	A&H:GP
Theodore Andreae to ZBV	Jan 18	*Hansa*	A&H:GP
William H. C. Whiting to ZBV	Jan 18(1)	*Advance*	A&H:GP
William H. C. Whiting to ZBV	Jan 18(2)	*Advance*	A&H:GP
Mary Newberry to ZBV	Jan 18	conscription	A&H:GP
Joseph D. Flanner to ZBV	Jan 18	*Advance*	A&H:GP
Power, Low & Co. to ZBV	Jan 18	*Advance*	A&H:GP
John H. Haughton to ZBV	Jan 18	habeas corpus	A&H:GP
R. G. Bangus to ZBV	Jan 18	deserters	A&H:GP
A. R. Smith to ZBV	Jan 18	cotton cards	A&H:GP
James A. [Mutt] to ZBV	Jan 18	distilling	A&H:GP
Robert A. Bost to ZBV	Jan 18	transfer	A&H:GP
M. [?]erle to ZBV	Jan 18	R. B. Vance	A&H:VanPC
E. L. Kinney[?] to ZBV	Jan 18	new reg'ts.	A&H:VanPC
D. Kahnweiler to ZBV	Jan 18	papers	A&H:VanPC
George Davis to D. Kahnweiler	Jan 18	papers	A&H:VanPC
Joshua Hill to ZBV	Jan 18	detail	A&H:VanPC
J. H. Crawford to ZBV	Jan 19	export	A&H:GP
Sion H. Rogers to ZBV	Jan 19	special court	A&H:GP
Ralph P. Buxton to ZBV	Jan 19	special court	A&H:GP
Henry A. London to ZBV	Jan 19	meeting	A&H:GP
Report of J. H. Carrington (1863)	Jan 19	Eli Swanner	A&H:GP
ZBV to Robert R. Heath	Jan 19	special court	A&H:GLB
Henry C. Colton to ZBV	Jan 19	peace convention	A&H:VanPC
R. R. Heath to ZBV	Jan 20	permit	A&H:GP
Thomas Carter to ZBV	Jan 20	*Advance*	A&H:GP
J. H. Everitt to ZBV	Jan 20	destitution	A&H:GP
J. N. Watkins to ZBV	Jan 20	destitution	A&H:GP

Correspondents	Date	Subject	Repository
George H. Faribault to ZBV	Jan 20	peace movement	A&H:GP
ZBV to Orange Co. Shff.	Jan 20	Senate election	A&H:GLB
ZBV to Horatio Seymour	Jan 20	prison clothing	A&H:GLB
Otis F. Manson to ZBV	Jan 20	meeting	A&H:VanPC
Edward Warren to ZBV	Jan 21	*Advance*	A&H:GP
S. L. Jones to ZBV	Jan 21	cotton	A&H:GP
Wilkes Co. to ZBV	Jan 21	invitation	A&H:VanPC
W. W. Peirce to ZBV	Jan 21	clothing	SHC:Clar
E. J. Thompson to ZBV	Jan 22	cotton cards	A&H:GP
James Longstreet to ZBV	Jan 22	R.B. Vance	A&H:GP
C. C. Henderson to ZBV	Jan 22	cotton cards	A&H:GP
Power, Low & Co. to ZBV	Jan 22	*Advance*	A&H:GP
David L. Swain to ZBV	Jan 22	conscription	A&H:GP
J. Edgar Newsom to ZBV	Jan 23	appointment	A&H:GP
George Little to ZBV	Jan 23	*Advance*	A&H:GP
Landon C. Haynes to ZBV	Jan 23	son	A&H:GP
James Sinclair to ZBV	Jan 23	letter	A&H:GP
Tolivar Davis to ZBV	Jan 23	disaffection	A&H:GP
B. W. Cooper to ZBV	Jan 23	cloth	A&H:GP
V. Ripley to ZBV	Jan 23	poor relief	A&H:GP
Thomas A. Nicholson to ZBV	Jan 23	conscription	A&H:GP
John A. Young to ZBV	Jan 23	Federal raid	A&H:GP
W. H. Hatch to ZBV	Jan 23	gold	A&H:VanPC
Power, Low & Co. to ZBV	Jan 24	Wylie & Co.	A&H:GP
William Lamb to ZBV	Jan 24	*Advance*	A&H:GP
Francis E. Shober to ZBV	Jan 24	disloyalty	A&H:GP
Daniel H. Hill to ZBV	Jan 24	appointment	A&H:GP
George Little to ZBV	Jan 24(1)	*Advance*	A&H:GP
George Little to ZBV	Jan 24(2)	*Advance*	A&H:GP
R. F. Hackett to ZBV	Jan 24	disloyalty	A&H:GP
W. H. [Humley] to ZBV	Jan 24	R. B. Vance	A&H:GP
Robert Ould to Ethan A. Hitchcock	Jan 24	prisoners	A&H:GP
Power, Low & Co. to ZBV	Jan 25	*Advance*	A&H:GP
James Cordill et al. to ZBV	Jan 25	atrocities	A&H:GP
R. H. Maury to ZBV	Jan 25	bonds	A&H:GP
W. H. Hatch to ZBV	Jan 25	prisoners	A&H:GP
Lizzie E. Cheek to ZBV	Jan 25	poor relief	A&H:GP
J. T. Moore to ZBV	Jan 25	cotton yarn	A&H:GP
Anonymous to ZBV	Jan 25	distilling	A&H:GP
An Old Friend to ZBV	Jan 25	states' rights	A&H:GP
Edwin M. Holt to ZBV	Jan 25	cloth	A&H:GP
Burgess S. Gaither et al. to ZBV	Jan 25	peace negotiations	A&H:GP
Thomas W. Ritter to ZBV	Jan 25	atrocities	A&H:GP
Benjamin F. Butler to James W. Hinton	Jan 26	atrocities	A&H:GP

Correspondents	Date	Subject	Repository
C. Walker to ZBV	Jan 26	steamers	A&H:GP
E. Kidder to ZBV	Jan 26	arrival	A&H:GP
David A. Barnes to Robert Ould	Jan 26	passport	A&H:GP
J. T. Murray to ZBV	Jan 26	conscription	A&H:GP
J. [T]. Hoke to ZBV	Jan 26	cotton cards	A&H:GP
Henry A. Dowd to ZBV	Jan 26	supplies	A&H:GP
Peter A. Ray to ZBV	Jan 26	cotton yarn	A&H:GP
Roland Best to ZBV	Jan 26	detail	A&H:GP
Marcus [?] to ZBV	Jan 26	peace convention	A&H:VanPC
Richard C. Gatlin to James W. Hinton	Jan 26	regt. officers	SHC:Yel
Kidder & Flanner to ZBV	Jan 27	arrival	A&H:GP
J. W. Winstead to ZBV	Jan 27	detail	A&H:GP
Many Citizens to ZBV	Jan 27	conscription	A&H:GP
Gilbert Elliott to ZBV	Jan 27	Albemarle	A&H:GP
J. W. Rabon to ZBV	Jan 27	detail	A&H:GP
J. T. Pretlow to ZBV	Jan 27	son	A&H:GP
Paul C. Cameron to ZBV	Jan 27	mowing blades	A&H:GP
A. J. Ervin to R. H. Chilton	Jan 27	transfer	A&H:GP
William Hale et al. to ZBV	Jan 27	appointment	A&H:GP
Thomas M. Jones to ZBV	Jan 27	desk	A&H:GP
James W. Cooke to ZBV	Jan 28	gunboats	A&H:GP
Robert M. Henry to ZBV	Jan 28	cloth	A&H:GP
Augustus S. Merrimon to ZBV	Jan 28	habeas corpus	A&H:GP
James Johnson to ZBV	Jan 28	distilling	A&H:GP
W. W. Peirce to ZBV	Jan 28	transcript	A&H:GP
Jesse Revis to ZBV	Jan 28	substitution	A&H:GP
Charles F. M. Garnett to ZBV	Jan 28	roads	A&H:GP
John M. Guyther to ZBV	Jan 28	new company	A&H:GP
Calvin H. Wiley to ZBV	Jan 29	common schools	A&H:GP
H. B. Reese to ZBV	Jan 29	cotton cards	A&H:GP
Mrs. A. E. Smith to ZBV	Jan 29	destitution	A&H:GP
Duncan McKay to ZBV	Jan 29	substitution	A&H:GP
Theodore J. Hughes to ZBV	Jan 29	*Advance*	A&H:GP
T. Edw. Hamilton Jr. to ZBV	Jan 29	*Don*	A&H:VanPC
J. L. Wilson to ZBV	Jan 30	permit	A&H:GP
Z. B. Moore, affidavit	Jan 30	distilling	A&H:GP
Warner Lewis to ZBV	Jan 30	substitution	A&H:GP
Julia Gilmer to ZBV	Jan 30	cards	A&H:GP
Thomas W. Ritter to ZBV	Jan 30	conscription	A&H:GP
Arthur C. Smith to ZBV	Jan 30	D. G. Worth	A&H:GP
— Weaver to ZBV	Jan 30	Buncombe court	A&H:VanPC
John D. Hyman to ZBV	Jan 30	peace petition	A&H:VanPC
Joseph G. Lockhart to ZBV	Jan 30	skirmish	SHC:Van
Gustavus W. Smith to ZBV	Jan 30	priv. freight	SHC:Van
John R. Williams to ZBV	Jan 31	transfer	A&H:GP
James Calloway to ZBV	Jan 31	Wilkes visit	A&H:VanPC

Correspondents	Date	Subject	Repository
J. T. Evans to ZBV	Jan 31	Federal advance	SHC:Van
M. Mosland et al. to ZBV	Jan n.d.	peace convention	SHC:Set
Thomas B. Power et al. to ZBV	Feb 1	*Advance*	A&H:GP
Humble citizen to ZBV	Feb 1	peace	A&H:GP
C. L. Harris to ZBV	Feb 1	desertion	A&H:GP
W. Murdock to ZBV	Feb 1	son	A&H:GP
John J. Guthrie to ZBV	Feb 1	*Advance*	A&H:GP
Temperance Tise to ZBV	Feb 1	son	A&H:GP
Z. Lamb to ZBV	Feb 1	appointment	A&H:GP
L. N. Caddell to ZBV	Feb 1	discharge	A&H:GP
Edward [?] Mallett to David L. Swain	Feb 1	transfer	A&H:VanPC
Robert E. Lee to ZBV	Feb 1	Jas. F. Taylor	A&H:VanPC
J. J. Erwin to ZBV	Feb 1	cotton cards	A&H:VanPC
James A. Seddon to ZBV	Feb 1	conscription	A&H:VanPC
L. N. Caddell to ZBV	Feb 2	discharge	A&H:GP
Power, Low & Co. to ZBV	Feb 2	J. J. Guthrie	A&H:GP
Thomas B. Power to ZBV	Feb 2	*Advance*	A&H:GP
Thomas Carter to Henry A. Dowd	Feb 2	cargo	A&H:GP
J. W. Swann to ZBV	Feb 2	*Advance*	A&H:GP
R. Strange to ZBV	Feb 2	Robert Cowan	A&H:GP
E. P. Jones to ZBV	Feb 2	New Bern	A&H:GP
H. E. Colton to ZBV	Feb 2	speech	A&H:GP
J. A. Hogue to ZBV	Feb 2	slaves	A&H:GP
[Woodbury] Wheeler to ZBV	Feb 2	colonial documents	A&H:GP
W. Howard to ZBV	Feb 2	flour	A&H:GP
Warren Lewis to ZBV	Feb 2	F. M. Vogel	A&H:GP
C. M. Andrews to ZBV	Feb 2	promotion	A&H:GP
Thomas J. Boykin to ZBV	Feb 3	cotton	A&H:GLB
J. E. Johnston to ZBV	Feb 3	capture	A&H:GP
J. B. Carpenter to ZBV	Feb 3	peace	A&H:GP
Edward Warren to ZBV	Feb 3	New Bern	A&H:GP
Thomas Carter to ZBV	Feb 3	cargo	A&H:GP
[?] to ZBV	Feb 3	messages	A&H:GP
John H. Haughton to ZBV	Feb 3	peace	A&H:VanPC
James W. Hinton to ZBV	Feb 4	gunboat iron	A&H:GP
Theodore Andreae to ZBV	Feb 4	cargo	A&H:GP
Thomas Carter to ZBV	Feb 4	cargo	A&H:GP
Frank J. Wilson to ZBV	Feb 4	*Advance*	A&H:GP
Edward Warren to ZBV	Feb 4	troops	A&H:GP
John D. Whitford to ZBV	Feb 4	Kinston	A&H:GP
Joel R. Griffin to ZBV	Feb 4	Unionism	A&H:GP
James W. Hinton to ZBV	Feb 4	Federal raid	A&H:GP
Power, Low & Co., list	Feb 5	cotton	A&H:GP
Joseph H. Flanner to ZBV	Feb 5	*Advance*	A&H:GP
Warren Lewis to Thomas Settle	Feb 5	passport	A&H:GP
Power, Low & Co. to ZBV	Feb 5	*Advance*	A&H:GP
John [Rutherford] to ZBV	Feb 5	mules	A&H:GP

Correspondents	Date	Subject	Repository
John J. Guthrie to ZBV	Feb 5	*Advance*	A&H:GP
John L. McDowell to ZBV	Feb 5	*Advance*	A&H:GP
Joseph H. Flanner to ZBV	Feb 5	*Advance*	A&H:GP
A. H. McAlister et al. to ZBV	Feb 5	promotion	A&H:GP
W. B. Griffin et al. to ZBV	Feb 5	hospitals	A&H:GP
Frank K. Alexander to ZBV	Feb 5	impressment	A&H:GP
Edwin G. Reade to ZBV	Feb 5	ships	A&H:VanPC
R. H. Abernathy to ZBV	Feb 5	cotton cards	A&H:VanPC
J. H. [Forest] to ZBV	Feb 6	Home Guard	A&H:GP
John Hielman to ZBV	Feb 6	peace	A&H:GP
Thomas Carter to ZBV	Feb 6	cargo	A&H:GP
Mrs. J. H. Hawley to ZBV	Feb 6	conscription	A&H:GP
Quincy F. Neal et al. to ZBV	Feb 6	speech	A&H:GP
John D. Whitford to ZBV	Feb 6	New Bern	A&H:VanPC
James A. Seddon to ZBV	Feb 6	conscription	A&H:VanPC
R. F. Hackett to ZBV	Feb 7	speech	A&H:GP
Theodore Andreae to ZBV	Feb 7	blockade	A&H:GP
Murdock to ZBV	Feb 7	disloyalty	A&H:VanPC
H. J. Horton to ZBV	Feb 8	transfer	A&H:GP
T. C. Cooper to ZBV	Feb 8	cotton cards	A&H:GP
B. B. Tomlinson to ZBV	Feb 8	transfer	A&H:GP
T. Warner to ZBV	Feb 8	conscription	A&H:GP
J. M. Parrott to ZBV	Feb 8	pork	A&H:GP
G. Marshall to ZBV	Feb 8	peace	A&H:GP
John A. McArthur to ZBV	Feb 8	conscription	A&H:GP
James W. Osborne to ZBV	Feb 8	special court	A&H:GP
James Sloan to ZBV	Feb 8	flour	A&H:GP
Thomas Carter to ZBV	Feb 8	*Don, Hansa*	A&H:GP
Matt W. Ransom to A. L. Rives	Feb 8	promotion	A&H:GP
A. U. Powell to ZBV	Feb 8	clothing	A&H:GP
ZBV to Theodore Andreae	Feb 8	*Don*	A&H:GLB
A. B. Romano to ZBV	Feb 9	pass	A&H:GP
Daniel G. Worth to Robert H. Cowan	Feb 9	r.r. iron	A&H:GP
Joshua Bonor to ZBV	Feb 9	Home Guard	A&H:GP
James C. Davis to ZBV	Feb 9	discharge	A&H:GP
A. J. H. [Letterhill] to ZBV	Feb 9	distilling	A&H:GP
C. S. McKinney to John W. Cameron	Feb 9	supplies	A&H:GP
John Hancock to ZBV	Feb 9	conscription	A&H:GP
J. M. Goff et al. to Bryan Grimes	Feb 9	execution	A&H:GP
G. W. Logan to ZBV	Feb 9	impressment	A&H:GP
Jesse J. Yeates to ZBV	Feb 9	allegiance	A&H:GP
[James A. Seddon] to ZBV	Feb 9	conscription	A&H:VanPC
John Dawson to R. H. Cowan	Feb 10	railroads	A&H:GP
J. A. E. Mebane to ZBV	Feb 10	cotton cards	A&H:GP
Power, Low & Co. to ZBV	Feb 10	*Don*	A&H:GP

Correspondents	Date	Subject	Repository
G. West to ZBV	Feb 10	conscription	A&H:GP
L. R. Gibson to ZBV	Feb 10	peace	A&H:GP
Tod R. Caldwell to ZBV	Feb 10	conscription	A&H:GP
T. McGee to Henry A. Dowd	Feb 11	*Don*	A&H:GP
Theodore Andreae to ZBV	Feb 11	*Don, Hansa*	A&H:GP
H. Cabiness to ZBV	Feb 11	conscription	A&H:GP
A. J. Cole to ZBV	Feb 11	transfer	A&H:GP
James W. Hinton to ZBV	Feb 11	atrocities	A&H:GP
R. A. Russell to ZBV	Feb 11	transfer	A&H:GP
Joseph H. Flanner	Feb 11	*Advance*	A&H:GP
John [Robinson] to ZBV	Feb 11	Nova Scotia	A&H:GP
J. M. Barton to ZBV	Feb 11	bacon	A&H:GP
ZBV, commission	Feb 11	special court	A&H:GP
C. W. Styron to John W. Cameron	Feb 11	supplies	A&H:GP
D. W. Lile to ZBV	Feb 11	conscription	A&H:GP
Commission to William M. Shiff	Feb 11	special court	A&H:GLB
ZBV to Theodore Andreae	Feb 11	imports	A&H:GLB
David L. Swain to ZBV	Feb 11	Edward Mallett	A&H:VanPC
C. B. Poindexter to ZBV	Feb 12	*Don*	A&H:GP
S. V. Perkins to ZBV	Feb 12	Federal raid	A&H:GP
F. W. J. Hurst to Power, Low & Co.	Feb 12	*Advance*	A&H:GP
[?]	Feb 12	*Advance*	A&H:GP
H. C. Jones to ZBV	Feb 12	speech	A&H:GP
R. S. Abrams to ZBV	Feb 12	court seal	A&H:GP
James A. Seddon to A. T. Davidson	Feb 12	conscription	A&H:GP
D. R. Ambrose to ZBV	Feb 12	captured slaves	A&H:GP
William Gray to ZBV	Feb 12	appointment	A&H:GP
Thompson Allan to David A. Barnes & Geo. Little	Feb 12	tax exemptions	A&H:GP
John D. Hyman to ZBV	Feb 13	W. W. Holden	A&H:GP
J. A. McDonald to ZBV	Feb 13	conscription	A&H:GP
N. L. Williams to ZBV	Feb 13	desertion	A&H:GP
Joseph H. Flanner to ZBV	Feb 13	*Advance*	A&H:GP
D. C. Clark to ZBV	Feb 13	appointment	A&H:GP
A. T. Davidson to J. L. Henry	Feb 13	command appeal	A&H:GP
John A. Burnett to ZBV	Feb 13	distilling	A&H:GP
William H. C. Whiting to ZBV	Feb 13	*Hansa, Don*	A&H:GP
James A. Seddon to ZBV	Feb 13	muskets	A&H:GP
Report and manifest	Feb 13	cargo	A&H:GP
Alexander Collie to ZBV	Feb 13	blockade	A&H:GP
Alexander Collie to ZBV	Feb 13	war support	A&H:GP
Robert H. Cowan to ZBV	Feb 13	WCRRR	A&H:GLB
[Jon] R. Grist to ZBV	Feb 13	lard & bacon	A&H:VanPC
John A. Gilmer to ZBV	Feb 14	conscription	A&H:GP
Henry E. Colton to ZBV	Feb 14	peace	A&H:VanPC
Calvin J. Cowles to ZBV	Feb 14	Wilkes visit	A&H:VanPC

Correspondents	Date	Subject	Repository
Joseph A. Brown to George [Hammis]	Feb 15	supplies	A&H:GP
T. F. Powell to Turner	Feb 15	money	A&H:GP
John W. Cameron to Robert H. Cowan	Feb 15	supplies	A&H:GP
John A. Bradshaw to ZBV	Feb 15	impressment	A&H:GP
George A. Duncy to ZBV	Feb 15	conscription	A&H:GP
C. D. Smith to ZBV	Feb 15	Home Guard	A&H:GP
William Johnston to ZBV	Feb 15	CSCRR	A&H:GP
Otis F. Manson to ZBV	Feb 15	departure	A&H:GP
J. A. Reagan to ZBV	Feb 15	peace / cards	A&H:GP
J. M. Wood to ZBV	Feb 15	brigade transfer	A&H:GP
R. F. Simonton to ZBV	Feb 15	speech	A&H:VanPC
W. C. Strong to ZBV	Feb 15	cotton	A&H:VanPC
W. A. Gillespie to ZBV	Feb 16	conscription	A&H:GP
A. [G.] Breni[z]er to ZBV	Feb 16	muskets	A&H:GP
Clement Dowd to ZBV	Feb 16	deserters	A&H:GP
Richard C. Gatlin, special order	Feb 16	court martial	SHC:Sha
Abner Saul to ZBV	Feb 17	sons / corn	A&H:GP
Robert H. Scales to ZBV	Feb 17	cotton cards	A&H:GP
William M. Shiff to ZBV	Feb 17	court business	A&H:GP
[J.] C. Armstrong to ZBV	Feb 17	poor relief	A&H:GP
R. H. Maury & Co. to ZBV	Feb 17	account	A&H:GP
M. J. McSween to ZBV	Feb 17	prisoners	A&H:GP
E. B. Drake to ZBV	Feb 17	speech	A&H:GP
Arabella Davis to ZBV	Feb 17	soldier relief	A&H:GP
John L. Stanfield to ZBV	Feb 17	appointment	A&H:GP
Willie Mitchell to ZBV	Feb 17	conscription	A&H:GP
John J. Guthrie to ZBV	Feb 17(1)	*Advance*	A&H:GP
John J. Guthrie to ZBV	Feb 17(2)	*Advance*	A&H:GLB
William H. C. Whiting to ZBV	Feb 17	*Advance*	A&H:VanPC
Edwin G. Reade to ZBV	Feb 17	conscription	A&H:VanPC
Alex Barrett to ZBV	Feb 18	pardon	A&H:GP
Power, Low & Co. to ZBV	Feb 18	*Advance*	A&H:GP
N. H. McGee to ZBV	Feb 18	transfer	A&H:GP
C. W. L. Neal to ZBV	Feb 18	conscription	A&H:GP
David G. Worth to ZBV	Feb 18	salt works	A&H:GP
ZBV to William A. Graham	Feb 18	election	A&H:GLB
ZBV to Edwin G. Reade	Feb 18	appointment	A&H:GLB
Thomas M. Crofoau to ZBV	Feb 18	visit	A&H:VanPC
Power, Low & Co. to ZBV	Feb 19	cargo	A&H:GP
W. H. Bailey to ZBV	Feb 19	county justice	A&H:GP
D. A. Montgomery to ZBV	Feb 19	conscription	A&H:GP
Noah Gibson to ZBV	Feb 19	conscription	A&H:GP
Leonidas F. Siler to ZBV	Feb 19	Federal raids	A&H:GP
Theodore Andreae to ZBV	Feb 19	*Advance*	A&H:GP

Correspondents	Date	Subject	Repository
Lizzie Pearson Bullock to ZBV	Feb 19	promotion	A&H:VanPC
R. V. Welch to ZBV	Feb 20	cotton cards	A&H:GP
Power, Low & Co. to ZBV	Feb 20	*Advance*	A&H:GP
L. F. Bates to ZBV	Feb 20	speech	A&H:GP
William N. Bolling to Robert H. Cowan	Feb 20	r.r. iron	A&H:GP
S. D. Wallace to David A. Barnes	Feb 20	*Advance*	A&H:GP
Thomas R. Miller to ZBV	Feb 20	legislature	A&H:GP
A. C. Williamson et al. to ZBV	Feb 20	visit	A&H:GP
G. B. Hamilton to ZBV	Feb 20	speech	A&H:GP
J. H. [Forest] to [K. C.] Chisman	Feb 21	desertion	A&H:GP
G. C. Powell to ZBV	Feb 21	transfer	A&H:GP
James G. Bailie to ZBV	Feb 22	cotton cards	A&H:GP
A. R. Bryan to ZBV	Feb 22	election/peace	A&H:GP
H. Harrill et al. to ZBV	Feb 22	visit	A&H:GP
John Berry to ZBV	Feb 22	election	A&H:GP
R. R. Bearden to ZBV	Feb 22	appointment	A&H:GP
J. B. Carpenter to ZBV	Feb 22	appointment	A&H:GP
James W. Terrell to ZBV	Feb 22	desertion	A&H:GP
E. W. Herndon to ZBV	Feb 22	R. B. Vance	A&H:GP
Peter Johnson to ZBV	Feb 22	distilling	A&H:GP
John Berry to ZBV	Feb 22	resignation	A&H:GLB
P. W. Hairston to ZBV	Feb 23	speech	A&H:GP
W. B. March et al. to ZBV	Feb 23	speech	A&H:GP
J. M. Israel to ZBV	Feb 23	tax	A&H:GP
Edward Kidder to ZBV	Feb 23	recommendation	A&H:GP
James G. Burr to ZBV	Feb 23	recommendation	A&H:GP
T. W. Swann to ZBV	Feb 23	apppointment	A&H:GP
Alexander Collie to ZBV	Feb 23	*Constance*	A&H:GP
Power, Low & Co. to ZBV	Feb 23	*Advance*	A&H:GP
A. J. Galloway to Henry A. Dowd	Feb 23	cargo	A&H:GP
[S. S. Henry] to ZBV	Feb 23	war progress	A&H:GP
D. H. Starbuck to David A. Barnes	Feb 23	conscription	A&H:GP
Alexander Collie to ZBV	Feb 23	cotton	A&H:VanPC
W. L. Quarles to ZBV	Feb 23	comm. officer	SHC:SWBatt
Charles F. M. Garnett to ZBV	Feb 24	railroads	A&H:GP
R. Bradbury to ZBV	Feb 24	conscription	A&H:GP
D. Snider & W. A. [Prescott] to ZBV	Feb 24	transfer	A&H:GP
Reuben Saunders to ZBV	Feb 24	conscription	A&H:GP
Samuel C. Bryson to ZBV	Feb 24	peace	A&H:GP
James K. Gibson to ZBV	Feb 24	cotton	A&H:VanPC
T. George Walton to ZBV	Feb 25	conscription	A&H:GP
Calvin H. Wiley to ZBV	Feb 25	conscription	A&H:GP
J. W. Strange to ZBV	Feb 25	appointment	A&H:GP
W. B. Lowe et al. to ZBV	Feb 25	A. E. Jackson	A&H:GP
Edwin G. Reade to ZBV	Feb 25	court	A&H:GP

Correspondents	Date	Subject	Repository
James A. Seddon to ZBV	Feb 25	conscription	A&H:VanPC
J. S. Lemmon to ZBV	Feb 26	steamers/cargo	A&H:GP
Elizabeth M. McGee to ZBV	Feb 26	destitution	A&H:GP
John A. Gilmer to ZBV	Feb 26	conscription	A&H:GP
[L. B.] Stone to ZBV	Feb 26	cotton cards	A&H:GP
Election Writ	Feb 26	state House	A&H:GP
Thomas Carter to ZBV	Feb 27	coal	A&H:GP
Power, Low & Co. to ZBV	Feb 27	*Advance*	A&H:GP
Luke Blackmer to ZBV	Feb 27	habeas corpus	A&H:GP
D. [S]oftin to ZBV	Feb 27	habeas corpus	A&H:GP
James W. Wilson to ZBV	Feb 27	departure	A&H:GP
Lauchlin McKinnon to ZBV	Feb 27	discharge	A&H:GP
Owen R. Kenan et al. to ZBV	Feb 27	speech	A&H:GP
M. M. Jones to ZBV	Feb 27	prisoners	A&H:GP
J. A. Lineback to ZBV	Feb 27	leave request	A&H:GP
Jonathan Worth to ZBV	Feb 27	finances	A&H:GP
Thomas J. F[orlan] to ZBV	Feb 27	conscription	A&H:GP
S. S. Wall to ZBV	Feb 27	conscription	A&H:GP
S[amuel] Wilkins to ZBV	Feb 27	speech	A&H:GP
L. L. Steward et al. to ZBV	Feb 27	peace	A&H:GP
ZBV to James A. Seddon	Feb 27	r.r. iron	A&H:GLB
L. J. Rains to ZBV	Feb 28	discharge	A&H:GP
Thomas Carter to ZBV	Feb 28	*Advance*	A&H:GP
Peter Mallett to ZBV	Feb 28	habeas corpus	A&H:GP
Francis E. Shober to ZBV	Feb 28	appointment	A&H:VanPC
S. V. Pickens to ZBV	Feb 29	battalion service	A&H:GP
Thomas B. Power to ZBV	Feb 29	*Advance*	A&H:GP
Jacob Briant to ZBV	Feb 29	desertion	A&H:GP
Power, Low & Co. to ZBV	Feb 29	*Advance*	A&H:GP
Thomas J. Boykin to ZBV	Feb 29	*Advance*	A&H:GP
Benjamin H. Boi[ssan] to ZBV	Feb 29	army company	A&H:GP
J. Russell to ZBV	Feb 29	flour	A&H:GP
B. [H.] Sorsley to ZBV	Feb 29	conscription	A&H:GP
G. C. Moses to ZBV	Feb 29	friendship	A&H:GP
James D. Long to ZBV	Feb 29	conscription	A&H:GP
James H. Greene to ZBV	Feb 29	conscription	A&H:GP
William Murdock to ZBV	Feb 29	Confed. raids	A&H:GP
John A. Taylor to ZBV	Feb 29	conscription	A&H:GP
W. G. Barbee to ZBV	Feb 29	speech	A&H:GP
John J. Guthrie to Capt. Wyle	Feb 29	*Advance*	A&H:GP
Robert H. Cowan to C. F. M. Garnett	Feb 29	WMRR iron	A&H:GP
Israel P. Sorrels to ZBV	Feb n.d.	peace	A&H:GP
Joshua Boner to ZBV	Feb n.d.	desertion	A&H:GP
J. M. [Haffolah] to ZBV	Feb n.d.	conscription	A&H:GP
Power, Low & Co. to ZBV	Mar 1	*Advance*	A&H:GP

Correspondents	Date	Subject	Repository
James Sinclair to ZBV	Mar 1	cotton	A&H:GP
W. P. Mast to ZBV	Mar 1	conscription	A&H:GP
Francis E. Shober to ZBV	Mar 1	conscription	A&H:GP
Thomas J. Boykin to ZBV	Mar 1	steamers	A&H:GP
R. K. Fields to ZBV	Mar 1	state troops	A&H:GP
James R. Grist to ZBV	Mar 1	conscription	A&H:GP
D. H. Starbuck to ZBV	Mar 1	conscription	A&H:GP
Will L. Scott to ZBV	Mar 1	conscription	A&H:VanPC
R. A. McLaughlin, certification	Mar 2	court case	A&H:GP
John C. Broadhurst to ZBV	Mar 2	discharge	A&H:GP
Joshua Boner to ZBV	Mar 2	discharge	A&H:GP
S. A. Sharpe to ZBV	Mar 2	visit	A&H:GP
L. M. Scott to ZBV	Mar 2	conscription	A&H:GP
Rufus Y. McAden to David A. Barnes	Mar 2	conscription	A&H:GP
Lucie A. Ellington to ZBV	Mar 2	cotton cards	A&H:GP
George V. Strong to ZBV	Mar 2	passage	A&H:GP
N. H. D. Wilson to ZBV	Mar 2	conscription	A&H:GP
Philip Leon to ZBV	Mar 2	*Annie*	A&H:GP
Rufus Barringer to ZBV	Mar 2	appointments	A&H:GP
James A. Seddon to ZBV	Mar 2	cotton / r.r.	A&H:GLB
Henry E. Colton to ZBV	Mar 2	speech	A&H:VanPC
Hall C. Lindsay to ZBV	Mar 3	conscription	A&H:GP
John H. Winder to ZBV	Mar 3	ZBV's note	A&H:GP
Joseph H. Flanner to ZBV	Mar 3	*Alpha*	A&H:GP
W. K. Webb to ZBV	Mar 3	transfer	A&H:GP
"The People" to ZBV	Mar 3	conscription	A&H:GP
W. P. Caldwell to ZBV	Mar 3	conscription	A&H:GP
Power, Low & Co. to ZBV	Mar 3	*Advance*	A&H:GP
Thomas Carter to ZBV	Mar 4	*Hansa*	A&H:GP
James Sheeter to ZBV	Mar 4	supplies	A&H:GP
James T. Rogers to ZBV	Mar 4	appointment	A&H:GP
G. C. Moses to ZBV	Mar 4	gub. election	A&H:GP
R. B. Ellis to ZBV	Mar 4	conscription	A&H:GP
[Sam.] S. Mc[T]ate to ZBV	Mar 4	W. W. Holden	A&H:GP
David M. Furches to ZBV	Mar 4	habeas corpus	A&H:GP
W. H. Neave to ZBV	Mar 4	commission	A&H:GP
James R. Love to ZBV	Mar 4	Thomas Legion	A&H:GP
William H. James to ZBV	Mar 4	r.r.	A&H:GP
Charles F. M. Garnett to ZBV	Mar 4	r.r.	A&H:GP
Mrs. W. Smith to ZBV	Mar 4	*Advance*	A&H:VanPC
George C. Stedman to ZBV	Mar 4	speech	A&H:VanPC
William H. C. Whiting to ZBV	Mar 5	black labor	A&H:GP
Thomas Carter to ZBV	Mar 5	*Don, Annie*	A&H:GP
John M. Davidson to ZBV	Mar 5	clothing	A&H:GP
John Berry to ZBV	Mar 5	resignation	A&H:GP

Correspondents	Date	Subject	Repository
W. P. Caldwell to ZBV	Mar 5	habeas corpus	A&H:GP
T. T. Slade to ZBV	Mar 5	support	A&H:GP
W. D. Lawson to ZBV	Mar 5	desertion	A&H:GP
W. G. Morisey to ZBV	Mar 5	conscription	A&H:GP
A. Mitchell to ZBV	Mar 5	habeas corpus	A&H:GP
Robert H. Cowan to ZBV	Mar 5	r.r.	A&H:GP
Henry Watson to ZBV	Mar 5	Home Guard	A&H:GP
ZBV to James A. Seddon	Mar 5	cotton	A&H:GLB
James A. Seddon to ZBV	Mar 5	conscription	A&H:GLB
John A. Gilmer to ZBV	Mar 5	conscription	A&H:VanPC
W. J. S. Miller to ZBV	Mar 5	disaffection	A&H:VanPC
William L. Dortch to ZBV	Mar 5	speech	A&H:VanPC
William A. Graham to ZBV	Mar 5	Raleigh visit	A&H:VanPC
James M. Leach to ZBV	Mar 5	substitution	A&H:VanPC
William B. Rodman to ZBV	Mar 5	speech	A&H:VanPC
J. A. Burke to ZBV	Mar 5	exports	A&H:VanPC
Robert Tansill to ZBV	Mar 5	speech	A&H:VanPC
D. M. Carter to ZBV	Mar 5	speech	A&H:VanPC
Thomas Webb to ZBV	Mar 5	departure	SHC:Van
Thomas L. Clingman to ZBV	Mar 6	Jefferson Davis	A&H:GP
Aaron Bass to ZBV	Mar 6	transfer	A&H:GP
Charles F. Mitchell to ZBV	Mar 6	free blacks	A&H:GP
Joseph J. Young to ZBV	Mar 6	speech	A&H:VanPC
Thomas L. Clingman to ZBV	Mar 6	Jefferson Davis	SHC:Van
William A. Carrington to ZBV	Mar 7	hospital	A&H:GP
William J. Headen to ZBV	Mar 7	conscription	A&H:GP
R. V. Blackstock to ZBV	Mar 7	conscription	A&H:GP
F. George, J. W. Ellis to ZBV	Mar 7	petition	A&H:GP
M. M. Fry to ZBV	Mar 7	conscription	A&H:GP
Clement Dowd to ZBV	Mar 7	W. W. Holden	A&H:GP
L. N. Durham to ZBV	Mar 7	cotton cards	A&H:GP
Jesse Hargrave to ZBV	Mar 7	conscription	A&H:GP
R. C. Puryear to ZBV	Mar 7	black labor	A&H:GP
M. London to ZBV	Mar 7	appointment	A&H:GP
C. A. Boon to ZBV	Mar 7	habeas corpus	A&H:GP
N. Hunt to ZBV	Mar 7	speech	A&H:GP
ZBV to James A. Seddon	Mar 7	conscription	A&H:GLB
R. G. H. Kean to ZBV	Mar 8	ZBV telegram	A&H:GP
William H. C. Whiting to ZBV	Mar 8	W. F. Lynch	A&H:GP
Nathaniel Boyden to ZBV	Mar 8	conscription	A&H:GP
William B. Flanner to Henry A. Dowd	Mar 8	*Hansa*	A&H:GP
J. H. Judkins to ZBV	Mar 8	conscription	A&H:GP
John H. Webster et al. to ZBV	Mar 8	free Negro	A&H:GP
William A. Lo[ve] to ZBV	Mar 8	conscription	A&H:GP

Correspondents	Date	Subject	Repository
Lakey Justice to ZBV	Mar 8	conscription	A&H:GP
Thomas Rollins to ZBV	Mar 8	conscription	A&H:GP
W. H. Bailey to ZBV	Mar 8	conscription	A&H:GP
John M. Worth to ZBV	Mar 8	deserters	A&H:GP
J. C. Blackburn to ZBV	Mar 8	conscription	A&H:GP
Christopher G. Memminger to ZBV	Mar 8	citizen attacks	A&H:GP
H. E. Benton to ZBV	Mar 8	blockade	A&H:GP
Christopher G. Memminger to ZBV	Mar 8	citizen attacks	A&H:GLB
James A. Seddon to ZBV	Mar 8	citizen attacks	A&H:GLB
Jason C. Harris to ZBV	Mar 8	speech	A&H:VanPC
Henry J. Ryals to ZBV	Mar 8	speech	A&H:VanPC
James M. Leach to ZBV	Mar 8	peace	A&H:VanPC
William S. Harris to ZBV	Mar 8	speech	A&H:VanPC
Virginian to ZBV	Mar 8	speech	A&H:VanPC
James W. Hinton to ZBV	Mar 9	peace	A&H:GP
W. H. Wheeler to ZBV	Mar 9	commissions	A&H:GP
W. A. Lillay to ZBV	Mar 9	deserters	A&H:GP
L. C. Edwards to ZBV	Mar 9	Mr. Hester	A&H:GP
Theodore Andreae to ZBV	Mar 9	steamers	A&H:GP
Theodore Andreae to ZBV	Mar 9	cotton	A&H:GP
M. Fetter to ZBV	Mar 9	transfer	A&H:GP
"Many Citizens" to ZBV	Mar 9	conscription	A&H:GP
Thomas M. Garrett to ZBV	Mar 9	supplies	A&H:GP
Joseph E. Rives to ZBV	Mar 9	conscription	A&H:GP
Judah P. Benjamin to ZBV	Mar 9	court decision	A&H:VanPC
Theodore Andreae to ZBV	Mar 10	steamers	A&H:GP
B. F. Arthur to ZBV	Mar 10	ZBV telegram	A&H:GP
A. J. Sikes to ZBV	Mar 10	furlough	A&H:GP
M. W. Simmons to ZBV	Mar 10	conscription	A&H:GP
James Johnson et al. to ZBV	Mar 10	transfer	A&H:GP
W. W. Patterson et al. to ZBV	Mar 10	furlough	A&H:GP
D. B. McSween to ZBV	Mar 10	M. J. McSween	A&H:GP
W. F. Beasley to Mr. Winston	Mar 10	state troops	A&H:GP
J. S. Call to ZBV	Mar 10	poor relief	A&H:GP
P. K. Dickinson to ZBV	Mar 10	r.r.	A&H:GP
John F. Miller to ZBV	Mar 10	speech	A&H:VanPC
Virginian to ZBV	Mar 10	speech	A&H:VanPC
[ZBV] to Theodore Andreae	Mar 10	payment	SHC:Van
D. H. Starbuck to ZBV	Mar 11	conscription	A&H:GP
H. W. Fries to ZBV	Mar 11	A. C. Vogler	A&H:GP
J. R. Hargrove to ZBV	Mar 11	Salisbury	A&H:GP
Ezekiel Joines to ZBV	Mar 11	conscription	A&H:GP
L. D. Childs to ZBV	Mar 11	W. W. Holden	A&H:GP
L. C. Edwards to ZBV	Mar 11	H. Hester	A&H:GP
Joanne Wylie to Power, Low & Co.	Mar 11	*Advance*	A&H:GP

Correspondents	*Date*	*Subject*	*Repository*
R. S. Cooke to ZBV	Mar 11	conscription	A&H:GP
Theodore Andreae to ZBV	Mar 11	cargo space	A&H:GP
Kemp P. Battle to ZBV	Mar 11	cargo space	A&H:GP
ZBV to William H. C. Whiting	Mar 11	slave labor	A&H:GLB
D. N. Neill to ZBV	Mar 11	speech	A&H:VanPC
Isaac M. St. John to ZBV	Mar 11	nitre	A&H:VanPC
Alexander R. Lawton to ZBV	Mar 12	r.r. supplies	A&H:GP
S. T. Jones to ZBV	Mar 12	appointment	A&H:GP
George F. Pate to ZBV	Mar 12	conscription	A&H:GP
Lawrence A. Adams to ZBV	Mar 12	Junius Tate	A&H:GP
J. M. Young et al. to ZBV	Mar 12	troop speech	A&H:GP
J. C. Gaines to ZBV	Mar 12	troop speech	A&H:GP
David G. Worth to ZBV	Mar 12	salt	A&H:GP
David G. Worth to ZBV	Mar 12	salt	A&H:GLB
M. M. Gaines to ZBV	Mar 12	speech	A&H:VanPC
A. H. McCleod to ZBV	Mar 13	conscription	A&H:GP
Francis E. Shober to ZBV	Mar 13	conscription	A&H:VanPC
Alfred G. Foster to ZBV	Mar 13	speech	A&H:VanPC
John A. Gilmer to ZBV	Mar 13	conscription	A&H:VanPC
William T. Nicholson et al. to ZBV	Mar 14	troop speech	A&H:GP
A. Mitchell to ZBV	Mar 14	conscription	A&H:GP
Henry A. London to ZBV	Mar 14	visit	A&H:GP
C. McN. Blue to ZBV	Mar 14	M. J. McSween	A&H:GP
A. G. Foster to ZBV	Mar 14	conscription	A&H:GP
W. P. Pope to ZBV	Mar 14	gift	A&H:GP
J. T. W. Davis to ZBV	Mar 14	conscription	A&H:GP
R. H. Winborne to ZBV	Mar 14	Buffaloes	A&H:GP
William A. Allen to ZBV	Mar 14	speech	A&H:GP
Augustus S. Merrimon to ZBV	Mar 14	appointment	A&H:GP
James F. Summers to ZBV	Mar 14	discharge	A&H:GP
Alexander Collie & Co. to ZBV	Mar 14	steamers	A&H:GLB
P. Hough to ZBV	Mar 14	speech	A&H:VanPC
Power, Low & Co to ZBV	Mar 15	*Advance*	A&H:GP
W. H. Newberry to ZBV	Mar 15	conscription	A&H:GP
R. A. Jenkins to ZBV	Mar 15	peace	A&H:GP
E. F. B. Koonce to ZBV	Mar 15	transfer	A&H:GP
Cameron Smith to ZBV	Mar 15	desertion	A&H:GP
S. W. Reid to ZBV	Mar 15	conscription	A&H:GP
E. [R.] Liles et al. to ZBV	Mar 15	speech	A&H:GP
Sarah A. Barden to ZBV	Mar 15	husband	A&H:GP
Robert L. Abernathy to ZBV	Mar 15	election	A&H:GP
W. S. M. Davidson et al. to ZBV	Mar 15	distilling	A&H:GP
William Duffes to ZBV	Mar 16	conscription	A&H:GP
Daniel [S.] Hill to ZBV	Mar 16	speech	A&H:GP
C. L. Cook to ZBV	Mar 16	conscription	A&H:GP

Correspondents	Date	Subject	Repository
Alexander Collie to ZBV	Mar 16	cotton	A&H:GP
Seaton Gales to ZBV	Mar 16	troop speech	A&H:GP
James F. Summers to ZBV	Mar 16	conscription	A&H:GP
Samuel H. Walkup to ZBV	Mar 16	troop speech	A&H:GP
Cook's Brigade to ZBV	Mar 16	troop speech	A&H:GP
D. W. Bagley to ZBV	Mar 16	speech	A&H:VanPC
D. McNeil to ZBV	Mar 17	conscription	A&H:GP
A. R. McDonald to ZBV	Mar 17	habeas corpus	A&H:GP
Lineberger & Co. to ZBV	Mar 17	clothing	A&H:GP
G. M. Lea to ZBV	Mar 17	black labor	A&H:GP
John H. Weller to ZBV	Mar 17	conscription	A&H:GP
Joseph H. Flanner to ZBV	Mar 17	Liverpool	A&H:GP
Samuel B. French to ZBV	Mar 17	clothing	A&H:GP
George W. Munford to ZBV	Mar 17	Va. resolution	A&H:GP
R. L. Beale to ZBV	Mar 17	distilling	A&H:GP
Tod R. Caldwell to ZBV	Mar 18	poor relief	A&H:GP
W. C. Erwin to ZBV	Mar 18	impressment	A&H:GP
S. S. Thompson to ZBV	Mar 18	conscription	A&H:GP
A. S. McNeely to ZBV	Mar 18	visit	A&H:GP
Elititia Eatman to ZBV	Mar 18	destitution	A&H:GP
W. C. Tate to ZBV	Mar 18	poor relief	A&H:GP
Clark M. Avery to ZBV	Mar 18	visit	A&H:GP
George N. Folk to ZBV	Mar 18	New Bern	A&H:GP
D. A. G. Palmer to ZBV	Mar 18	speech	A&H:GP
David Coleman to ZBV	Mar 18	conscription	A&H:GP
H. J. Harris to ZBV	Mar 18	appointment	A&H:GP
Hannah Hardin to ZBV	Mar 18	conscription	A&H:GP
S. O. Dean to ZBV	Mar 19	disaffection	A&H:GP
Joseph H. Flanner to ZBV	Mar 19	Liverpool	A&H:GP
John D. Hyman to ZBV	Mar 19	speech	A&H:VanPC
James L. Henry to ZBV	Mar 20	Home Guard	A&H:GP
D. [P.] Shoaf to ZBV	Mar 20	conscription	A&H:GP
J. C. Duckworth to ZBV	Mar 20	speech	A&H:GP
Eward J. Warren to ZBV	Mar 20	Eli Swanner	A&H:GP
Robert S. Gilmer to ZBV	Mar 20	endorsement	A&H:GP
Francis E. Shober to ZBV	Mar 20	appointment	A&H:GP
Milledge L. Bonham to ZBV	Mar 20	cargo space	A&H:GLB
Marshall Hildreth to ZBV	Mar 21	conscription	A&H:GP
T. T. Slade to ZBV	Mar 21	slave	A&H:GP
Jesse G. Shepherd to ZBV	Mar 21	promotion	A&H:GP
William H. C. Whiting to ZBV	Mar 21	black labor	A&H:GP
L. Blackmer to ZBV	Mar 21	conscription	A&H:GP
Donald MacRae to ZBV	Mar 21	appointment	A&H:GP
George W. Jones to ZBV	Mar 21	appointment	A&H:GP
E. F. Ashe et al. to ZBV	Mar 21	W. W. Holden	A&H:GP

Correspondents	*Date*	*Subject*	*Repository*
Isaac Jarrett to ZBV	Mar 21	destitution	A&H:GP
P. Leon to ZBV	Mar 21	cargo space	A&H:GP
Osborne Stacy to ZBV	Mar 21	discharge	A&H:GP
Richard Harris to ZBV	Mar 21	speech	A&H:GP
David Stephenson to ZBV	Mar 21	detail	A&H:GP
ZBV to James A. Seddon	Mar 21	impressment	A&H:GP
William H. C. Whiting to ZBV	Mar 21	black labor	A&H:GLB
T. C. Westall to ZBV	Mar 21	speech	A&H:VanPC
Walter L. Steele to ZBV	Mar 21	speech	A&H:VanPC
J. A. Lineback to ZBV	Mar 22	cotton	A&H:GP
David Kahnweiler to ZBV	Mar 22	impressment	A&H:GP
May Wheat Shober to ZBV	Mar 22	brother	A&H:GP
Peter Mallett to ZBV	Mar 22	David Mahaley	A&H:GP
Peter Mallett to ZBV	Mar 22	David Mahaley	A&H:GLB
Thomas A. Noment to ZBV	Mar 23	speech	A&H:GP
William A. Smith to ZBV	Mar 23	conscription	A&H:GP
John Webb to ZBV	Mar 23	son	A&H:GP
A. M. McPheeters to ZBV	Mar 23	book publishing	A&H:VanPC
Richard H. Smith to ZBV	Mar 24	slave labor	A&H:GP
W. M. Hardy to ZBV	Mar 24	clothing	A&H:GP
Luke Blackmer to ZBV	Mar 24	disaffection	A&H:GP
A. J. Fordham to ZBV	Mar 24	tax in kind	A&H:GP
W. M. Hardy et al. to ZBV	Mar 24	reelection	A&H:GP
Love A. Hall to ZBV	Mar 24	join regt.	A&H:GP
A. C. Murdock to ZBV	Mar 25	prisoner	A&H:GP
L. H. Durham to ZBV	Mar 25	petition	A&H:GP
Samuel B. French to ZBV	Mar 26	cotton cards	A&H:GP
A. E. Jackson to ZBV	Mar 26	robbery	A&H:GP
John White to R. C. [Gatton]	Mar 26	supplies	A&H:GP
Ralph P. Buxton to ZBV	Mar 26	extradition	A&H:GP
W. F. Leak to ZBV	Mar 26	visit	A&H:GP
A. H. Joyce to ZBV	Mar 26	conscription	A&H:GP
Jefferson Davis to ZBV	Mar 26	cargo space	A&H:GLB
James A. Seddon to ZBV	Mar 26	impressment	A&H:GLB
Henry Heth to ZBV	Mar 27	troop visit	A&H:GP
Francis E. Shober to ZBV	Mar 27	habeas corpus	A&H:GP
Americus B. Burr to ZBV	Mar 27	application	A&H:GP
H. G. Spruill to R.H. Bank	Mar 27	disloyalty	A&H:GP
J. R. McDonald et al. to ZBV	Mar 27	speech	A&H:GP
Nancy Tooper to ZBV	Mar 27	desertion	A&H:GP
J. R. Murchison et al. to ZBV	Mar 28	troop speech	A&H:GP
D. M. Carter to ZBV	Mar 28	invitation	A&H:GP
J. A. Sanders to ZBV	Mar 28	cotton cards	A&H:GP
Andrew H. Hodges to ZBV	Mar 28	discharge	A&H:GP
J. C. McCrae to ZBV	Mar 28	appointment	A&H:GP
Milton Terry to ZBV	Mar 28	speculation	A&H:GP

Correspondents	Date	Subject	Repository
R. H. Finney to ZBV	Mar 28	visit	A&H:GP
Almand A. McKay et al. to ZBV	Mar 28	speech	A&H:GP
W. Musson to ZBV	Mar 28	gift	A&H:VanPC
J. L. Henry to ZBV	Mar 29	desertion	A&H:GP
Sydney Pristwood to ZBV	Mar 29	murder	A&H:GP
John Paris to ZBV	Mar 29	troop visit	A&H:GP
William W. Avery to ZBV	Mar 29	impressment	A&H:GP
W. F. Williams to ZBV	Mar 29	travel	A&H:GP
Stuart Buchanan, contract	Mar 29	salt & corn	A&H:GP
Wharton J. Green to ZBV	Mar 30	prisoners	A&H:GP
George W. Logan to ZBV	Mar 30	conscription	A&H:GP
William Murdock to ZBV	Mar 30	appointment	A&H:GP
S. M. Silver to ZBV	Mar 30	clemency	A&H:GP
Burgess S. Gaither to ZBV	Mar 30	conscription	A&H:VanPC
Wharton J. Green to ZBV	Mar 30	prisoners	SHC:Gree
Thomas L. Clingman to ZBV	Mar 31	troop speech	A&H:GP
H. G. Spruill et al. to ZBV	Mar 31	visit	A&H:GP
Nicholas W. Woodfin to ZBV	Mar 31	salt	A&H:GP
O. P. Taylor to ZBV	Mar 31	conscription	A&H:GP
John W. Cameron to ZBV	Mar 31	visit	A&H:GP
H. C. Horton to ZBV	Mar 31	conscription	A&H:GP
R. [C.] Pearson to ZBV	Mar 31	Scotland trip	A&H:GP
Ed Wooten to ZBV	Mar 31	appointment	A&H:GP
M. L. Davis to ZBV	Mar 31	taxes	A&H:GP
Whitman J. Hill to ZBV	Mar 31	conscription	A&H:GP
John H. Addington to ZBV	Mar 31	conscription	A&H:GP
S. D. Wallace et al. to ZBV	Mar 31	visit	A&H:GP
[P. Leon] to ZBV	Mar 31	Advance, Annie	A&H:GP
William L. Love to ZBV	Mar 31	Home Guard	A&H:VanPC
Thomas J. Boykin to ZBV	Mar n.d.	political support	A&H:VanPC
William C. Tate to ZBV	Apr 1	conscription	A&H:GP
E. W. Hunt to ZBV	Apr 1	volunteer	A&H:GP
A. J. Dargan to ZBV	Apr 1	appointment	A&H:GP
Power, Low & Co. to ZBV	Apr 1	Advance	A&H:GP
William H. C. Whiting to David A. Barnes	Apr 1	Advance	A&H:GP
Power, Low & Co. to George Little	Apr 2	Advance	A&H:GP
Nathaniel A. Boyden to ZBV	Apr 2	Home Guard	A&H:GP
J. [Bruton] to ZBV	Apr 2	conscription	A&H:GP
H. G. Spruell to R. H. Bank	Apr 2	ZBV	A&H:GP
J. N. Bryoon to ZBV	Apr 2	speech	A&H:GP
George Setzer to ZBV	Apr 2	speech	A&H:GP
John N. Whitford to ZBV	Apr 3	visit	A&H:GP
Susan C. W[eeler] to ZBV	Apr 3	poor relief	A&H:GP
James M. Patton to ZBV	Apr 3	detail	A&H:GP
A. H. Joyce to ZBV	Apr 3	conscription	A&H:GP

Correspondents	Date	Subject	Repository
Sallie Fitzgerald to ZBV	Apr 3	poor relief	A&H:GP
T. Davis to ZBV	Apr 4	speech	A&H:GP
Calvin J. Cowles to ZBV	Apr 4	impressment	A&H:GP
Thomas J. Sumner to ZBV	Apr 4	NCRR	A&H:GP
Thomas W. Groves, certification	Apr 4	Geo. W. Pinnix	A&H:GP
Walter W. Lenoir to ZBV	Apr 4	W. W. Holden	A&H:VanPC
J. B. Fitzgerald to ZBV	Apr 5	blacksmith	A&H:GP
Elizabeth G. Richmond to ZBV	Apr 5	office job	A&H:GP
George Coggin & John T. McKinnon to ZBV	Apr 5	speech	A&H:GP
Edward J. Warren to ZBV	Apr 5	visit	A&H:GP
Ralph P. Buxton to ZBV	Apr 5	extradition	A&H:GP
Archibald McLean to ZBV	Apr 5	visit	A&H:GP
James M. Leach, circular	Apr 5	ZBV support	A&H:VanPC
W. H. Wise to ZBV	Apr 6	poor relief	A&H:GP
Samuel McD. Tate to ZBV	Apr 6	visit	A&H:GP
Robert H. Cowan to ZBV	Apr 7	r.r. tools	A&H:GP
William H. C. Whiting to ZBV	Apr 7	*Advance*	A&H:GP
Thomas Bragg to Robert F. Hoke	Apr 7	J. A. Everitt	A&H:GP
Cyrus P. Mendenhall to ZBV	Apr 7	cards/clothing	A&H:GP
R. E. Wilson to John B. Griswold	Apr 7	J. A. Everitt	A&H:GP
W. B. Stipe to ZBV	Apr 7	conscription	A&H:GP
Nicholas W. Woodfin to ZBV	Apr 7	salt	A&H:GP
James C. Brown to ZBV	Apr 7	"noble woman"	A&H:GP
Nicholas W. Woodfin to ZBV	Apr 7	salt	A&H:GP
Frank G. Ruffin to ZBV	Apr 7	purchasing agents	A&H:GP
C. S. Holleman to ZBV	Apr 8	conscription	A&H:GP
R. W. Best to ZBV	Apr 8	Sallie Taylor	A&H:GP
John E. Brown et al. to ZBV	Apr 8	visit	A&H:GP
S. D. Pool to ZBV	Apr 8	J. A. Everitt	A&H:GP
William J. Long to ZBV	Apr 8	speech	A&H:GP
R. G. A. Love to ZBV	Apr 8	release	A&H:GP
John A. Richardson to ZBV	Apr 8	women	A&H:GP
Ann H. Hays to ZBV	Apr 9	desertion	A&H:GP
Sewall L. Fremont to ZBV	Apr 9	*Advance*	A&H:GP
E. B. Freeman to ZBV	Apr 9	passport	A&H:GP
A. W. Palmer et al. to ZBV	Apr 9	speech	A&H:GP
B. B. Bulla to ZBV	Apr 9	speech	A&H:GP
ZBV to Stuart Buchanan & Co.	Apr 9	N. Woodfin	A&H:GLB
William M. Shipp to ZBV	Apr 9	speeches	A&H:VanPC
William A. Graham to ZBV	Apr 9	support	A&H:GraPC
R. R. Bearden to ZBV	Apr 10	cotton	A&H:GP
K. H. Williams to ZBV	Apr 10	shoemaker	A&H:GP
John Grissom to ZBV	Apr 10	transfer	A&H:GP
Peter S. Moody to ZBV	Apr 10	conscription	A&H:GP
Mary Smith to ZBV	Apr 10	prisoner	A&H:GP

Correspondents	*Date*	*Subject*	*Repository*
Allen T. Davidson to ZBV	Apr 10	W. W. Holden	A&H:VanPC
Thomas King to George Little	Apr 11	poor relief	A&H:GP
Power, Low & Co. to ZBV	Apr 11	*Advance*	A&H:GP
Thomas Carter to ZBV	Apr 11	T. J. Boykin	A&H:GP
Joannes Wylie to ZBV	Apr 11	*Advance*	A&H:GP
Thomas J. Boykin to ZBV	Apr 11	*Advance*	A&H:GP
John R. Burney et al. to ZBV	Apr 11	poor relief	A&H:GP
G. W. Blacknall to ZBV	Apr 11	speech	A&H:GP
H. H. Blount to ZBV	Apr 11	speech	A&H:GP
Edward J. Hale to ZBV	Apr 11	visit	A&H:GP
James S. Evans et al. to ZBV	Apr 11	speech	A&H:GP
H. Fitzhugh to ZBV	Apr 11	*Advance*	A&H:GP
Nat to Operator	Apr 11	*Primrose*	A&H:GP
Philip Leon to ZBV	Apr 11	*Annie*	A&H:GP
J. W. Green to ZBV	Apr 11	conscription	A&H:GP
John K. Potts to ZBV	Apr 11	W. W. Holden	A&H:VanPC
H. Fitzhugh to ZBV	Apr 12	cotton	A&H:GP
Power, Low & Co. to ZBV	Apr 12	cotton	A&H:GP
J. W. Wilson to ZBV	Apr 12	cotton	A&H:GP
T. A. Griffin to ZBV	Apr 12	free black	A&H:GP
Calvin Pippen to ZBV	Apr 12	impressment	A&H:GP
David G. Worth to ZBV	Apr 12	conscription	A&H:GP
John A. Thompson to ZBV	Apr 12	detail	A&H:GP
J. M. Taylor to ZBV	Apr 12	salt	A&H:GP
J. L. Morehead et al. to ZBV	Apr 12	speech	A&H:GP
Philip Leon to ZBV	Apr 12	cargo	A&H:GP
Philip Leon to ZBV	Apr 12	*Annie*	A&H:GP
Thomas J. Boykin to ZBV	Apr 12	soldiers	A&H:VanPC
Philip Leon to ZBV	Apr 13	cargo	A&H:GP
G. W. Ellis et al. to ZBV	Apr 13	women	A&H:GP
J. W. Thomas to ZBV	Apr 13	conscription	A&H:GP
Joseph F. Houck to ZBV	Apr 13	detail	A&H:GP
George Little to ZBV	Apr 13	steamer	A&H:GP
Thomas Carter to ZBV	Apr 13	cotton	A&H:GP
Luke McLean to ZBV	Apr 13	commission	A&H:GP
A. M. Pepper to ZBV	Apr 13	conscription	A&H:GP
Christopher G. Memminger to ZBV	Apr 13	Confed. cargo	A&H:GP
William Smith to ZBV	Apr 13	cotton	A&H:GP
ZBV, pardon	Apr 13	women	A&H:GLB
George Little to ZBV	Apr 14	*Advance, Annie*	A&H:GP
Philip Leon to ZBV	Apr 14	meeting	A&H:GP
Tilman Vance to ZBV	Apr 14	tobacco	A&H:GP
William J. Colvert to ZBV	Apr 14	machinery	A&H:GP
J. M. Bullock to ZBV	Apr 14	slave labor	A&H:GP
L. J. Haughton to ZBV	Apr 14	speech	A&H:GP
James Calloway to ZBV	Apr 14	desertion	A&H:GP

Correspondents	*Date*	*Subject*	*Repository*
E. Cranor to ZBV	Apr 14	destitution	A&H:GP
Lirrie L. Leach to ZBV	Apr 14	peace	A&H:VanPC
H. Fitzhugh to ZBV	Apr 14	*Advance*	A&H:VanPC
Philip Leon to ZBV	Apr 15	*Edith*	A&H:GP
Joseph H. Flanner to ZBV	Apr 15	*Advance*	A&H:GP
Philip Leon to ZBV	Apr 15	departure	A&H:GP
Stephen R. Mallory to ZBV	Apr 15	*Advance*	A&H:GP
William H. C. Whiting to ZBV	Apr 15	gun	A&H:GP
Thomas Carter to ZBV	Apr 15	gun	A&H:GP
J. H. Forest to ZBV	Apr 15	visit	A&H:GP
David A. Barnes to Thomas Bragg	Apr 15	arrests	A&H:GP
Joseph H. Flanner to ZBV	Apr 15	London	A&H:VanPC
Richard C. Gatlin, special order	Apr 15	discharge	SHC:Sha
David A. Barnes to Peter Mallett	Apr 16	David Mahaley	A&H:GP
C. C. Whitehurst to ZBV	Apr 16	*Advance*	A&H:GP
Thomas Bragg to ZBV	Apr 16	arrests	A&H:GP
R. V. Blackstock to ZBV	Apr 16	W. B. Cheek	A&H:GP
M. S. Sherwood to ZBV	Apr 16	conscription	A&H:GP
Musentin Sparks to ZBV	Apr 16	conscription	A&H:GP
Thomas Bragg to ZBV	Apr 16	arrests	A&H:GLB
ZBV to James A. Seddon	Apr 16	conscription	A&H:GLB
Wittkowsky & Saltzberg to ZBV	Apr 16	gift	A&H:VanPC
Phillip Leon to ZBV	Apr 16	tea & coffee	A&H:VanPC
Edward J. Hale to ZBV	Apr 17	speech	A&H:VanPC
E. Childs to ZBV	Apr 18	tories	A&H:GP
J. C. Keener to ZBV	Apr 18	impressment	A&H:GP
Thomas Carter to ZBV	Apr 18	*Advance*	A&H:GP
J. J. Barrentine to ZBV	Apr 18	conscription	A&H:GP
W. R. Aiken to ZBV	Apr 18	conscription	A&H:GP
Fenner B. Satterthwaite to ZBV	Apr 18	disaffection	A&H:GP
George C. Alexander to ZBV	Apr 18	impressment	A&H:GP
M. W. Simmons to ZBV	Apr 18	distilling	A&H:GP
James O. Simmons to ZBV	Apr 18	distilling	A&H:GP
W. P. Caldwell to ZBV	Apr 18	conscription	A&H:GP
D. M. Carter to ZBV	Apr 18	recommendation	A&H:GP
Henry T. Clark to ZBV	Apr 18	visit	A&H:GP
Henry T. Clark et al., resolution	Apr 18	visit	A&H:GP
C. R. King to ZBV	Apr 18	distilling	A&H:GP
B. B. Horton to ZBV	Apr 18	impressment	A&H:GP
W. H. Mills, affidavit	Apr 18	impressment	A&H:GP
G. A. Dancy, certificate	Apr 18	appointment	A&H:GP
Robert V. Blackstock to ZBV	Apr 18	conscription	A&H:VanPC
Peter E. Hines to ZBV	Apr 19	patient	A&H:GP
Mrs. S. Eaves to ZBV	Apr 19	son	A&H:GP
E. K. Walsh to ZBV	Apr 19	transfer	A&H:GP
Peter Mallett to ZBV	Apr 19	James F. House	A&H:GP

Correspondents	Date	Subject	Repository
A. D. McLean et al. to ZBV	Apr 19	visit	A&H:GP
Isaac Scott to ZBV	Apr 19	bonds	A&H:GP
William H. C. Whiting to ZBV	Apr 19	slaves	A&H:GP
William H. C. Whiting to ZBV	Apr 19	shoes	A&H:GP
W. H. Neane to ZBV	Apr 19	gratitude	A&H:GP
B. H. Goode to ZBV	Apr 19	just. peace	A&H:GP
William H. C. Whiting to ZBV	Apr 19	Private Leary	A&H:GP
R. R. Bearden to ZBV	Apr 19	Isaac Scott	A&H:GP
Robert S. Gilmer to ZBV	Apr 19	cards & labor	A&H:GP
ZBV to James A. Seddon	Apr 19	David Mahaley	A&H:GLB
H. Watson to ZBV	Apr 20	commissioner	A&H:GP
Thomas W. Graves to ZBV	Apr 20	conscription	A&H:GP
Jackson Johnston to ZBV	Apr 20	Jacob Siler	A&H:GP
John Lingle to ZBV	Apr 20	conscription	A&H:GP
James [K.] Gibson to ZBV	Apr 20	clothing	A&H:GP
B. A. Casschart to ZBV	Apr 20	speech	A&H:GP
W. H. A. Speer to ZBV	Apr 20	visit	A&H:GP
David A. Barnes to S. A. Sharpe	Apr 20	conscription	SHC:Sha
H. K. Thomas et al. to ZBV	Apr 21	conscription	A&H:GP
H. [R.] Strong to ZBV	Apr 21	prisoners	A&H:GP
J. F. Wooten to ZBV	Apr 21	prisoners	A&H:GP
Joannes Wylie to ZBV	Apr 21	*Advance*	A&H:GP
George Setzer to ZBV	Apr 21	conscription	A&H:GP
A. B. Fry to ZBV	Apr 21	transfer	A&H:GP
J. H. Forest to ZBV	Apr 21	Peter Mallett	A&H:GP
Thomas B. Power to ZBV	Apr 21	*Advance*	A&H:GP
Samuel B. French to ZBV	Apr 21	Va. request	A&H:GP
J. F. Owens et al. to ZBV	Apr 21	reprieve	A&H:GP
Calvin J. Cowles to ZBV	Apr 21	Home Guard	A&H:VanPC
James M. Ray to ZBV	Apr 22	Burnsville	A&H:GP
R. E. A. Love to ZBV	Apr 22	conscription	A&H:GP
J. F. E. Hardy to ZBV	Apr 22	passport	A&H:GP
J. R. Tucker to ZBV	Apr 22	G. N. Saunders	A&H:GP
Christopher G. Memminger to ZBV	Apr 22	cotton	A&H:GP
John E. Deans to ZBV	Apr 22	black labor	A&H:GP
S. Lander to ZBV	Apr 22	gift	A&H:GP
James W. Johnston to ZBV	Apr 22	slave labor	A&H:GP
David G. Worth to ZBV	Apr 22	salt	A&H:GLB
James W. Ferrell, memorandum	Apr 22	iron & straw	A&H:VanPC
M. L. Bullain to ZBV	Apr 22	poor relief	A&H:VanPC
D. D[ovey] & E. 3. Morris to ZBV	Apr 23	distilling	A&H:OP
David G. Worth to ZBV	Apr 23	salt	A&H:GP
L. C. Wilson to ZBV	Apr 23	postmaster	A&H:GP
N. A. McLean to ZBV	Apr 23	visit	A&H:GP
William J. Clark to ZBV	Apr 23	Plymouth flag	A&H:GP
Lloyd T. Jones to ZBV	Apr 23	discharge	A&H:GP

Correspondents	*Date*	*Subject*	*Repository*
J. H. Johnston to ZBV	Apr 23	passport	A&H:GP
A. H. Joyce to ZBV	Apr 23	discharge	A&H:GP
M. T. Smith to ZBV	Apr 23	black labor	A&H:GP
John [H.] Haughton to ZBV	Apr 23	habeas corpus	A&H:GP
Bedford Brown to ZBV	Apr 23	slave labor	A&H:GP
James A. Seddon to ZBV	Apr 23	conscription	A&H:GLB
Virgil A. Wilson to Edward J. Hale & Sons	Apr 23	Yadkin County	A&H:VanPC
John M. Otey to David A. Barnes	Apr 24	ZBV's return	A&H:GP
John R. Williams to ZBV	Apr 24	petition	A&H:GP
H. B. Hardy to ZBV	Apr 24	passport	A&H:GP
S. W. Smith to ZBV	Apr 24	women	A&H:GP
Mary E. Shearing to ZBV	Apr 24	poor relief	A&H:GP
William R. Campbell to ZBV	Apr 24	desertion	A&H:GP
George Little to ZBV	Apr 25	slave labor	A&H:GP
Mrs. Charles W. Skinner to ZBV	Apr 25	visit	A&H:GP
Edward A. Pollard to ZBV	Apr 25	passport	A&H:GP
David G. Worth to ZBV	Apr 25	loyalty	A&H:GP
E. B. Drake & son to ZBV	Apr 25	pass	A&H:GP
J. L. Price to ZBV	Apr 25	desertion	A&H:GP
N. A. Ramsey to ZBV	Apr 25	Home Guard	A&H:GP
Samuel L. Sadler to ZBV	Apr 25	horse	A&H:GP
Joshua Tyson et al. to ZBV	Apr 25	clemency	A&H:GP
Mary V. Jacobs to ZBV	Apr 25	conscription	A&H:GP
David G. Worth to ZBV	Apr 25	conscription	A&H:GP
M. W. Johnston to ZBV	Apr 25	black labor	A&H:GP
W. A. Houck to ZBV	Apr 25	conscription	A&H:GP
J. M. Israel to ZBV	Apr 25	conscription	A&H:GP
George Hillyer to ZBV	Apr 26	ZBV letter	A&H:GP
J. M. Bullock to ZBV	Apr 26	shovels	A&H:GP
William Howard to ZBV	Apr 26	A. McCoy	A&H:GP
A. H. Van Bokkelen to ZBV	Apr 26	hospital	A&H:GP
E. P. Jones et al. to ZBV	Apr 26	speech	A&H:GP
William H. C. Whiting to George Little	Apr 26	black labor	A&H:GP
W. D. Floyd to ZBV	Apr 26	military company	A&H:GP
John A. Young to ZBV	Apr 26	conscription	A&H:GP
Eli P. Martin to ZBV	Apr 26	shirking	A&H:GP
John H. Haughton to ZBV	Apr 27	ZBV letter	A&H:GP
Thomas C. Fuller to Richard H. Battle	Apr 27	Cong. election	A&H:GP
Fenley Shain to Lyndon Swain	Apr 27	justice of the peace	A&H:GP
James M. Morris to ZBV	Apr 27	depredation	A&H:GP
Jordan Womble to David A. Barnes	Apr 27	N. Woodfin	A&H:GP
James M. Leach to ZBV	Apr 27	elections	A&H:VanPC

Correspondents	Date	Subject	Repository
B. F. Petty to ZBV	Apr 28	cotton tax	A&H:GP
Lineberger & Co. to ZBV	Apr 28	clothing	A&H:GP
Joseph G. Carraway to ZBV	Apr 28	discharge	A&H:GP
Soldier to ZBV	Apr 28	conscription	A&H:GP
John Yancey to ZBV	Apr 28	disaffection	A&H:GP
Richard B. Pascall et al. to ZBV	Apr 28	Cong. election	A&H:GP
[John] McCormick to ZBV	Apr 28	poor relief	A&H:VanPC
J. M. Sikes et al. to ZBV	Apr 29	hospital	A&H:GP
John M. Rose to ZBV	Apr 29	r.r. business	A&H:GP
W. B. Gulick to ZBV	Apr 29	state funds	A&H:GP
R. R. Bearden to ZBV	Apr 29	steamers	A&H:GP
Robert V. Blackstock to ZBV	Apr 29	Burnsville	A&H:GP
Priscilla Miller to ZBV	Apr 29	horse	A&H:GP
William H. C. Whiting to ZBV	Apr 29	salt works	A&H:GP
Ezekiel Wilson to ZBV	Apr 29	slave labor	A&H:GP
J. C. Mills to ZBV	Apr 29	destitution	A&H:GP
C. B. Curler et al. to ZBV	Apr 29	distilling	A&H:GP
S. C. Allison to ZBV	Apr 29	discharge	A&H:GP
James A. Seddon to ZBV	Apr 29	Thomas's Legion	A&H:VanPC
James T. Harris to ZBV	Apr 30	slave labor	A&H:GP
William Sparks to ZBV	Apr 30	conscription	A&H:GP
W. A. Caldwell to ZBV	Apr 30	appointment	A&H:GP
E. [Mauny] to ZBV	Apr 30	slave labor	A&H:GP
W. H. Croom to ZBV	Apr 30	discharge	A&H:GP
J. F. Pegram et al. to ZBV	Apr 30	visit	A&H:GP
A. A. Patille to ZBV	Apr 30	slave labor	A&H:GP
Bryan Tyson to ZBV	Apr 30	war progress	A&H:GP
J. H. Greene, certificate	Apr 30	tax	A&H:GP
James A. Seddon to ZBV	Apr 30	western N.C.	A&H:VanPC
Robert Primose to ZBV	Apr n.d.	Mr. Carter	A&H:GP
George V. Strong to David A. Barnes	Apr n.d.	letter	A&H:GP
W. A. Philpott to ZBV	Apr n.d.	constables	A&H:GP
S. H. Williams to ZBV	Apr n.d.	appointmnet	A&H:GP
D. Lewis et al. to ZBV	Apr n.d.	women	A&H:GP
Lenoir County, resolution	n.m.n.d.	support ZBV	A&H:GP
J. D. Ramseur to ZBV	May 1	troop morale	A&H:GP
John A. Nicholson to ZBV	May 1	conscription	A&H:GP
Jonathan Worth to ZBV	May 1	W. W. Holden	A&H:VanPC
ZBV to George Little	May 2	D. K. McCrae	A&H:GP
Martin Lipps to Calvin J. Cowles	May 2	disaffection	A&H:GP
Joseph H. Flanner to ZBV	May 2	cotton	A&H:GP
Joseph H. Flanner to Alexander Collie & Co.	May 2	shipments	A&H:GP
John Scott, certificate	May 2	election	A&H:GP
G. W. Nicholson to ZBV	May 2	salt works	A&H:GP

Correspondents	Date	Subject	Repository
Delia Upchurch to ZBV	May 2	destitution	A&H:GP
Woodbury Wheeler to ZBV	May 2	father	A&H:GP
Power, Low & Co. to ZBV	May 2	cotton	A&H:GP
Allen T. Davidson to ZBV	May 2	cavalry raids	A&H:GP
William L. Love to ZBV	May 2	press	A&H:VanPC
William L. Love to ZBV	May 2	support	A&H:VanPC
Sterling, Campbell, & Albright to ZBV	May 2	purchase	A&H:VanPC
J. S. Lemmon & Co. to ZBV	May 3	cargo	A&H:GP
John M. Tate to ZBV	May 3	gift	A&H:GP
John H. Hyman to ZBV	May 3	appointment	A&H:GP
Murdock J. McSween to ZBV	May 3	prison term	A&H:GP
James A. Seddon to ZBV	May 3	slave labor	A&H:GLB
C. Moore to ZBV	May 4	conscription	A&H:GP
Donald McRae to ZBV	May 4	appointment	A&H:GP
Francis E. Shober to ZBV	May 4	conscription	A&H:GP
Daniel T. Carr to ZBV	May 4	conscription	A&H:GP
Luke Blackmer to ZBV	May 4	visit	A&H:GP
Parmy Johnson et al. to ZBV	May 4	destitution	A&H:GP
Eugene Grissom to ZBV	May 4	transfer	A&H:GP
William C. De Journett to ZBV	May 4	cavalry abuse	A&H:GP
James P. Dillard to ZBV	May 4	slave labor	A&H.GP
Rufus Barringer to ZBV	May 4	brigadier general	A&H:VanPC
Calvin J. Cowles to ZBV	May 5	cavalry abuse	A&H:GP
Lyra York to ZBV	May 5	cavalry abuse	A&H:GP
Frances S. Pittman to ZBV	May 5	taxes	A&H:GP
Lydia C. Hines to ZBV	May 5	destitution	A&H:GP
Collett Leventhorpe to ZBV	May 5	resignation	A&H:GP
P. G. T. Beauregard to ZBV	May 5	N.C. reg't.	A&H:GP
Joseph E. Brown to ZBV	May 5	letter	A&H:GP
Luke Blackmer to ZBV	May 5	speech	A&H:VanPC
Power, Low & Co. to ZBV	May 6	cotton	A&H:GP
W. H. Hampton to ZBV	May 6	W. W. Holden	A&H:GP
Jesse J. Yeates to ZBV	May 6	visit	A&H:GP
Stephen Johnson to ZBV	May 6	conscription	A&H:GP
J. Irvin to ZBV	May 6	slave	A&H:GP
David G. Worth to ZBV	May 6	salt	A&H:GLB
William L. Love to ZBV	May 6	newspaper	A&H:VanPC
W. W. Gaither to ZBV	May 7	Wilderness	A&H:GP
B. A. Kitrell et al. to ZBV	May 7	visit	A&H:GP
W. L. Glass to ZBV	May 7	visit	A&H:GP
J. C. Barnhardt to ZBV	May 7	slave labor	A&H:GP
James C. Pinnix to ZBV	May 7	slave labor	A&H:GP
John [H.] [Pi]nder to ZBV	May 7	prisoner	A&H:GP
L. P. Warren to ZBV	May 7	Col. Jones	A&H:GP
William P. Bynum to ZBV	May 7	election	A&H:VanPC

Correspondents	Date	Subject	Repository
W. H. Webster to ZBV	May 8	membership	A&H:GP
Leon F. Sensbaugh toZBV	May 8	reputation	A&H:GP
W. H. Wheeler to ZBV	May 9	conscription	A&H:GP
Samuel P. Horton to ZBV	May 9	speech	A&H:GP
A. W. Cummings to ZBV	May 9	W. W. Holden	A&H:GP
W. F. Sutch to ZBV	May 9	sterling	A&H:GP
John W. Harper to ZBV	May 9	transfer	A&H:GP
George H. Round to ZBV	May 9	passport	A&H:GP
Margaret E. Love to ZBV	May 10	destitution	A&H:GP
Mary Corah to ZBV	May 10	husband	A&H:GP
J.[C.] Harper to ZBV	May 10	conscription	A&H:GP
James Walker to ZBV	May 10	slave	A&H:GP
A. W. Ingold & Co. to Dr. Warren	May 10	ZBV speech	A&H:GP
Power, Low & Co. to ZBV	May 10	*Advance*	A&H:GP
R. F. Williams to ZBV	May 10	slave labor	A&H:GP
D. McNeill to ZBV	May 10	Home Guard	A&H:GP
Lieutenant to ZBV	May 10	militia officers	A&H:GP
Thomas J. Boykin to Power, Low & Co.	May 11	John J. Guthrie	A&H:GP
Duncan K. McRae to ZBV	May 11	rosin bonds	A&H:GP
R. R. Grayn to ZBV	May 11	Capt. Kilpatrick	A&H:GP
John D. Hyman to ZBV	May 11	printer	A&H:GP
Yancy Turrentine et al. to ZBV	May 11	speech	A&H:GP
Gilbert Elliott to ZBV	May 11	r.r. iron	A&H:GP
Power, Low & Co. to John J. Guthrie	May 11	note	A&H:GP
Nicholas W. Woodfin to ZBV	May 11	salt works	A&H:GP
F. J. Person et al. to ZBV	May 11	Josiah Powell	A&H:GP
A. J. Roberts to ZBV	May 12	arrest	A&H:GP
A. W. Ezzell to ZBV	May 12	troops speech	A&H:GP
John Wimbish & E. H. Hicks to ZBV	May 12	speech	A&H:GP
Frances Gales to ZBV	May 12	discharge	A&H:GP
M. W. Moore to George Little	May 12	correspondence	A&H:GP
John H. Haughton to ZBV	May 13	election	A&H:GP
W. H. Thomas to ZBV	May 13	destitution	A&H:GP
Alexander Collie & Co. to Duncan K. McRae	May 13	steamers	A&H:GP
Joseph H. Flanner to ZBV	May 13	steamers	A&H:GP
T. Ruffin to ZBV	May 14	death claims	A&H;GP
Elisha Banner et al. to ZBV	May 14	speech	A&H:GP
Amos N. Hall to ZBV	May 15	appointment	A&H:GP
S. V. Pickens, report	May 15	inspection	A&H:GP
James M. Pipkin to ZBV	May 15	prisoner	A&H:GP
William L. Love to ZBV	May 15	newspaper	A&H:VanPC
Kinc[hin] K[erry] to ZBV	May 16	slave	A&H:GP
S. R. Chisman to ZBV	May 16	Danville	A&H:GP
Thomas G. Ferrell to ZBV	May 16	commission	A&H:GP

Correspondents	*Date*	*Subject*	*Repository*
J. E. Reaves to ZBV	May 16	conscription	A&H:GP
William L. Henry to ZBV	May 16	poor relief	A&H:GP
Simon Hall to ZBV	May 16	desertion	A&H:GP
Charles C. Clark to ZBV	May 16	female prisoner	A&H:GP
J. C. Norman to ZBV	May 16	speech	A&H:GP
Thomas Carter to ZBV	May 17	cargo	A&H:GP
S. R. Chisman to ZBV	May 17	*Advance*	A&H:GP
Geroge Tunstall to ZBV	May 17	pass	A&H:GP
J. E. Reeves to ZBV	May 17	appointment	A&H:GP
R. C. Puryear & N. L. Williams to ZBV	May 17	impressment	A&H:GP
Cyrus P. Mendenhall to ZBV	May 17	passport	A&H:GP
John J. Guthrie to ZBV	May 17	salary	A&H:GP
James W. Hinton to ZBV	May 17	conscription	A&H:GP
Romulus M. Saunders, commission	May 17	court	A&H:GLB
James W. Hinton to ZBV	May 17	bacon	A&H:VanPC
J. W. Cooke to ZBV	May 18	r.r. iron	A&H:GP
W. O. Harrison to ZBV	May 18	election	A&H:GP
J. R. Cole to ZBV	May 18	Danville	A&H:GP
Joseph E. Brown, proclamation	May 18	conscription	A&H:GP
Willie J. Palmer to ZBV	May 18	fund increase	A&H:GP
N. A. Stoman & Thomas McDaniel to ZBV	May 18	distilling	A&H:GP
George Little to Richard S. Donnell	May 18	conscription	A&H:GP
G. B. Harris to ZBV	May 18	Union cavalry	A&H:GP
Luke Blackmer to ZBV	May 18	David Mahaley	A&H:GP
R. A. Jenkins to ZBV	May 18	tobacco & slave	A&H:GP
Richard S. Donnell to ZBV	May 18	peace proposals	A&H:GP
James W. Hinton to ZBV	May 18	conscription	A&H:VanPC
Giles Mebane to House speaker	May 19	justices of the peace	A&H:GP
Henry R. Strong to ZBV	May 19	citizen prisoners	A&H:GP
G. C. Moses to ZBV	May 19	W. W. Holden	A&H:GP
M. D. Holmes to ZBV	May 19	speech	A&H:GP
Calvin H. Wiley to ZBV	May 19	cotton cards	A&H:GP
Joseph A. Worth to ZBV	May 19	distilling	A&H:GP
ZBV to James A. Seddon	May 19	D. L. Russell	A&H:GLB
Calvin C. Jones to ZBV	May 19	W. W. Holden	A&H:VanPC
George M. B[uis] to ZBV	May 20	transfer	A&H:GP
Thaddeus S. White to ZBV	May 20	conscription	A&H:GP
George N. Folk to ZBV	May 20	sheriff's complaint	A&H:GP
George N. Folk to ZBV	May 20	citizen prisoners	A&H:GP
John D. Williams et al. to ZBV	May 20	distilling	A&H:GP
Otis F. Manson to ZBV	May 20	W. H. Haywood	A&H:GP
W. J. Long to ZBV	May 20	speech	A&H:VanPC
Joseph E. Brown, proclamation	May 21	conscription	A&H:GP
W. A. Smith to ZBV	May 21	correspondence	A&H:GP
G. E. Pierce to ZBV	May 21	slave runaways	A&H:GP

Correspondents	Date	Subject	Repository
James A. Seddon to ZBV	May 21	impressment	A&H:GP
[H. M.] Blount to ZBV	May 21	speech	A&H:GP
B. S. Young to ZBV	May 21	poor relief	A&H:GP
W. A. Smith to ZBV	May 22	old men release	A&H:GP
A. H. Joyce to ZBV	May 22	speech	A&H:GP
James Glove to ZBV	May 23	poor relief	A&H:GP
James Calloway to ZBV	May 23	attacks on citizens	A&H:GP
William L. Love to ZBV	May 23	Home Guard	A&H:GP
W. H. Hatch to George Little	May 23	sterling bills	A&H:GP
Richard S. Donnell to ZBV	May 23	war information	A&H:GP
Thomas J. Boykin to ZBV	May 23	imports	A&H:GP
James K. Gibson to ZBV	May 23	John C. Vaughn	A&H:VanPC
Walter L. Steele to ZBV	May 24	W. W. Holden	A&H:GP
John B. S. Dimitry to ZBV	May 24	conscription	A&H:GP
T. A. Bell to ZBV	May 24	distilling	A&H:GP
G. M. Roberts to ZBV	May 24	conscription	A&H:GP
Henry T. Clark to ZBV	May 24	conscription	A&H:GP
James H. Foote to Tyre Glen	May 24	unlawful arrest	A&H:GP
Andrew MacFarlan, account	May 24	freight charges	A&H:VanPC
J. A. Pemberton to ZBV	May 25	conscription	A&H:GP
M. J. McSween to ZBV	May 25	prisoners	A&H:GP
Julia Goulet to ZBV	May 25	visit	A&H:GP
Edward Warren to ZBV	May 25	skirmish	A&H:GP
B. F. Hooks to ZBV	May 26	reserves	A&H:GP
Tyre Glen to ZBV	May 26	unlawful arrest	A&H:GP
S. T. Speer to ZBV	May 26	Tyre Glen	A&H:GP
Webb Hill to ZBV	May 26	detail	A&H:GP
James A. Seddon to ZBV	May 26	battle flag	A&H:GLB
A. S. Kemp to ZBV	May 27	appointment	A&H:GP
Sion H. Rogers to ZBV	May 27	conscription	A&H:GP
William A. Caldwell to David A. Barnes	May 27	conscription	A&H:GP
Giles Mebane et al. to ZBV	May 27	blockade merchants	A&H:GP
Sion H. Rogers to ZBV	May 27	conscription	A&H:GLB
Richard S. Donnell & Giles Mebane, resolution	May 28	Mallett's battalion	A&H:GP
John Dawson, petition	May 28	merchants	A&H:GP
G. W. Alexander to David A. Barnes	May 28	Eli Swanner	A&H:GP
Sion H. Rogers to ZBV	May 28	slave felonies	A&H;GP
B. F. Little to ZBV	May 28	speech	A&H:GP
James W. Hinton to ZBV	May 28	W. W. Holden	A&H:VanPC
John H. Winder to ZBV	May 29	advice	A&H:GP
J. K. Curtis et al. to ZBV	May 29	transfer	A&H:GP
L. M. Allen to ZBV	May 29	conscription	A&H:GP
William McQueen to ZBV	May 29	speech circulars	A&H:GP
Thomas J. Boykin to ZBV	May 29	blockade merchants	A&H:GP
Stephen D. Pool to ZBV	May 29	Senior Reserves	A&H:VanPC

Correspondents	Date	Subject	Repository
G. C. Moses to ZBV	May 30	visit	A&H:GP
O. G. Parsley to ZBV	May 30	blockade merchants	A&H:GP
W. T. Howard to ZBV	May 30	assistance	A&H:GP
O. G. Parsley to ZBV	May 30	state agent	A&H:GP
William N. H. Smith to ZBV	May 30	Mallett's battalion	A&H:GP
A. L. Hendrix to ZBV	May 30	impressment	A&H:GP
L. C. Edwards to ZBV	May 30	conscription	A&H:GP
Goodman Durden to ZBV	May 30	justices of the peace	A&H:GP
Otis F. Manson to ZBV	May 30	hospital conditions	A&H:GP
O. P. Carson to ZBV	May 30	conscription	A&H:GP
ZBV to Samuel L. Fowle et al.	May 30	appointments	A&H:GLB
William Robinson to ZBV	May 30	political enemies	A&H:VanPC
A. G. Logan et al. to ZBV	May 31	conscription	A&H:GP
O. G. Parsley to George Little	May 31	state agent	A&H:GP
Joseph Walch to ZBV	May 31	conscription	A&H:GP
William N. H. Smith to ZBV	May 31	Mallett's battalion	A&H:GP
James A. Seddon to William N. H. Smith	May 31	Mallett's battalion	A&H:GP
A. J. Battle to ZBV	May 31	destitution	A&H:GP
W. D. Walters to ZBV	May 31	conscription	A&H:GP
Wilson Faircloth to ZBV	May 31	desertion	A&H:GP
R. F. Pinkney to ZBV	May 31	gunboat iron	A&H:GP
John K. Gilliat & Co., account	May 31	freight charges	A&H:VanPC
James A. Seddon to ZBV	May 31	detail	A&H:VanPC
John G. Ferrell to ZBV	Jun 1	assistance	A&H:GP
Jesse R. Stubbs to H. A. Gilliam	Jun 1	votes	A&H:GP
W. N. Tillinghast to ZBV	Jun 1	power of attorney	A&H:GP
W. J. L. Miller to ZBV	Jun 1	speech	A&H:GP
John D. Whitford to ZBV	Jun 1	r.r. iron	A&H:GP
C. C. Pitts to ZBV	Jun 1	harvest	A&H:GP
General Assembly Act	Jun 1	taxes	A&H:GP
George Davis to ZBV	Jun 1	resignation	Har:Dav
Catherine S. Johnson to ZBV	Jun 2	desertion	A&H:GP
W. P. Wilkins to ZBV	Jun 2	appointment	A&H:GP
Robert W. Best to ZBV	Jun 2	speech	A&H:GP
Richard Hanes to ZBV	Jun 2	speech	A&H:GP
Eugene Gressom to ZBV	Jun 3	habeas corpus	A&H:GP
Thomas A. Deniell to W. E. Deniell	Jun 3	poor relief	A&H:GP
John J. Hedrick to ZBV	Jun 3	appointment	A&H:GP
Peter Mallett to ZBV	Jun 3	salt workers	SHC:Mall
James Sinclair to ZBV	Jun 3	disaffection	A&H:GP
Joseph H. Hyman to ZBV	Jun 4	misconduct	A&H:GP
John Barden to ZBV	Jun 4	conscription	A&H:GP
H. J. Harris to ZBV	Jun 4	election	A&H:GP
ZBV to David A. Barnes (see ZBV's endorsement)	Jun 4	exemption	A&H:GP

Correspondents	Date	Subject	Repository
J. R. Stubbs to ZBV	Jun 4	loyalty oath	A&H:GP
Samuel Smith to ZBV	Jun 4	conscription	A&H:GP
H. A. Gilliam to David A. Barnes	Jun 4	loyalty oath	A&H:GP
Evey S. Jackson to ZBV	Jun 5	harvest	A&H:GP
James L. Henry to George Little	Jun 5	transfer	A&H:GP
J. T. Leach to ZBV	Jun 6	peace	A&H:GP
John Cox to ZBV	Jun 6	transfer	A&H:GP
William H. C. Whiting to supt. salt works	Jun 6	salt works	A&H:GP
William H. C. Whiting to Richard C. Gatlin	Jun 6	salt works	A&H:GP
William Pickett to ZBV	Jun 6	conscription	A&H:GP
Walter Preston to ZBV	Jun 6	arms contract	A&H:GP
R. A. Forbes to ZBV	Jun 6	speech	A&H:GP
David G. Worth to David A. Barnes	Jun 6	salt workers	A&H:GP
David Kahnweiler to ZBV	Jun 7	shoes	A&H:GP
A. G. Carter et al. to ZBV	Jun 7	speech	A&H:GP
A. M. Powell to ZBV	Jun 7	speech	A&H:GP
William H. C. Whiting to ZBV	Jun 7	salt works	A&H:GP
Tom Weaver to ZBV	Jun 7	election	A&H:GP
Richard S. Donnell to ZBV	Jun 7	commission	A&H:GP
W. F. Henderson to ZBV	Jun 7	conscription	A&H:GP
William H. C. Whiting to ZBV	Jun 7	salt works	A&H:GLB
Murdock J. McSween to ZBV	Jun 8	habeas corpus	A&H:GP
J. J. Buxton to ZBV	Jun 8	appointment	A&H:GP
A. A. Willard to ZBV	Jun 8	cloth	A&H:GP
N. A. Ramsey to ZBV	Jun 8	appointment	A&H:GP
J. N. Hunter, certification	Jun 8	justice of the peace	A&H:GP
Jesse G. Drew, certification	Jun 9	standard keeper	A&H:GP
Henry F. How to George Little	Jun 9	cotton	A&H:GP
John M. [Otey] to George Little	Jun 9	salt works	A&H:GP
W. Herring to ZBV	Jun 9	conscription	A&H:GP
Jesse E. Barden to ZBV	Jun 9	conscription	A&H:GP
C. P. Gibson to ZBV	Jun 9	poor relief	A&H:GP
William Church et al. to ZBV	Jun 9	Home Guard	A&H:GP
Henry F. How to George Little	Jun 9	cotton	A&H:GLB
Thomas Carter to George Little	Jun 10	cargo	A&H:GP
R. Y. McSel[ers] to George Little	Jun 10	conscription	A&H:GP
David G. Worth to George Little	Jun 10	salt works	A&H:GP
James H. Hill Special Order	Jun 10	suspension	A&H:GP
William E. Mann to ZBV	Jun 10	gift	A&H:GP
James W. Osborn to ZBV	Jun 10	disaffection	A&H:GP
Joseph H. Flanner to ZBV	Jun 11	*Advance*	A&H:GP
Amos M. Herring to ZBV	Jun 11	conscription	A&H:GP
Edward Warren to David A. Barnes	Jun 11	money	A&H:GP

Correspondents	Date	Subject	Repository
Otis F. Manson to ZBV	Jun 11	supplies	A&H:VanPC
Nancy Gordon to ZBV	Jun 12	harvest	A&H:GP
Cleveland Sawyer to ZBV	Jun 12	conscription	A&H:GP
J. Cline to ZBV	Jun 12	speech	A&H:GP
Joseph H. Flanner to ZBV	Jun 13	steamers	A&H:GP
Fred G. Roberts to ZBV	Jun 13	election	A&H:GP
David L. Swain to ZBV	Jun 13	election	A&H:GP
William Smith to ZBV	Jun 13	supplies	A&H:GP
Joseph H. Flanner	Jun 13	cotton	A&H:GLB
"An Act to Amend . . ."	Jun 14	tax laws	A&H:GP
J. F. Martin to ZBV	Jun 14	J. A. Boyden	A&H:GP
David G. Worth to David A. Barnes	Jun 15	conscription	A&H:GP
J. M. Galloway to ZBV	Jun 15	conscription	A&H:GP
Jonathan Charles to ZBV	Jun 15	harvest	A&H:GP
Leonard Godwin to ZBV	Jun 15	pardon	A&H:GP
Nathaniel Boyden to ZBV	Jun 15	J. A. Boyden	A&H:GP
J. W. Hall to ZBV	Jun 15	J. A. Boyden	A&H:GP
George Little to Peter Mallett	Jun 15	salt workers	A&H:GP
John H. Garrett to ZBV	Jun 15	Federal raid	A&H:GP
J. W. Hall to ZBV	Jun 15	J. A. Boyden	A&H:GP
George Little to Peter Mallett	Jun 15	salt workers	A&H:GP
John H. Garrett to ZBV	Jun 15	Federal raid	A&H:GP
C. C. Peacock to ZBV	Jun 16	distilling	A&H:GP
B. B. Bulla to ZBV	Jun 16	special court	A&H:GP
A. M. Nesbitt to ZBV	Jun 16	J. A. Boyden	A&H:GP
J. W. Jones to ZBV	Jun 16	J. A. Boyden	A&H:GP
S. R. Chiseman to ZBV	Jun 16	Home Guard	A&H:GP
William Johnston to ZBV	Jun 17	supplies	A&H:GP
Alexander Collie, account	Jun 17	cotton	A&H:VanPC
David G. Worth to ZBV	Jun 18	salt works	A&H:GP
Westly Yarber to ZBV	Jun 18	desertion	A&HGP
Andrew C. Cowles to ZBV	Jun 18	promotion	A&H:GP
W. C. Lee to ZBV	Jun 18	desertion	A&H:GP
David G. Worth to ZBV	Jun 18	salt works	A&H:GLB
William Horton et al. to ZBV	Jun 20	civil unrest	A&H:GP
G. Holmes to ZBV	Jun 20	secret party	A&H:GP
W. H. Furman, superior court document	Jun 20	slave trial	A&H:GP
E. D. [M.] to ZBV	Jun 20	election	A&H:GP
William H. Bagley to ZBV	Jun 20	Federal raids	A&H:GP
William Horton to ZBV	Jun 21	election	A&H:GP
William Horton to ZBV	Jun 21	conscription	A&H:GP
A. A. Willard to Calvin H. Wiley	Jun 21	cloth	A&H:GP
Samuel F. Phillips to ZBV	Jun 21	resignation	A&H:GP
Samuel F. Phillips to ZBV	Jun 21	resignation	A&H:GLB
Otis F. Manson, requisition	Jun 21	medicine	A&H:VanPC

Correspondents	Date	Subject	Repository
Otis F. Manson to ZBV	Jun 21	supplies	A&H:VanPC
[E.] F. Arendell to ZBV	Jun 22	Federal raid	A&H:GP
W. F. Henderson to ZBV	Jun 22	civil law	A&H:GP
"Regulations and Additional Instructions"	Jun 22	taxes	A&H:GP
J. L. Hines to ZBV	Jun 22	election	A&H:GP
J. M. Galloway to ZBV	Jun 22	conscription	A&H:GP
Josiah Jones to David A. Barnes	Jun 23	conscription	A&H:GP
A. McBride to ZBV	Jun 23	harvest	A&H:GP
Alfred G. Fos[ter] to ZBV	Jun 23	election	A&H:GP
M. S. Turner et al. to ZBV	Jun 23	impressment	A&H:GP
A. B. Grigg to ZBV	Jun 23	discharge	A&H:GP
William Eaton Jr. et al. to ZBV	Jun 23	slave trial	A&H:GP
Jere Pearsall to ZBV	Jun 23	conscription	A&H:GP
William J. Chapel to ZBV	Jun 24	discharge	A&H:GP
William H. Bagley to ZBV	Jun 24	election	A&H:GP
R. M. [L]apilan to ZBV	Jun 24	desertion	A&H:GP
Calvin H. Wiley to ZBV	Jun 24	cloth	A&H:GP
M. A. Chambers to ZBV	Jun 25	desertion	A&H:GP
William Hicks to ZBV	Jun 25	claim	A&H:GP
Thomas Carter to ZBV	Jun 25	cotton	A&H:GP
A. W. Davis to ZBV	Jun 25	furlough	A&H:GP
Calvin H. Wiley to ZBV	Jun 25	conscription	A&H:GP
William F. Jewell to ZBV	Jun 25	furlough	A&H:GP
Joseph F. Flanner to ZBV	Jun 25	affection	A&H:VanPC
John D. Whitford to ZBV	Jun 25	r.r. board	A&H:VanPC
James L. Henry to ZBV	Jun 25	arrest	A&H:VanPC
Robert R. Heath to ZBV	Jun 27	court case	A&H:GP
H. J. Harris to ZBV	Jun 27	election	A&H:GP
Dennis L. Singletary to ZBV	Jun 27	detail	A&H:GP
Thomas Carter to ZBV	Jun 27	cargo	A&H:GP
Sion H. Rogers to ZBV	Jun 27	r.r. directors	A&H:GP
William W. Mimson to ZBV	Jun 27	speech	A&H:GP
T. J. Hahn to ZBV	Jun 27	conscription	A&H:GP
William H. C. Whiting to ZBV	Jun 27	Plymouth	A&H:GP
Sion H. Rogers to ZBV	Jun 27	r.r. directors	A&H:GLB
Samuel W. Melton to ZBV	Jun 27	M. J. McSween	A&H:VanPC
L. E. Satterthwaite to ZBV	Jun 28	Federal raid	A&H:GP
John A. Gilmer to ZBV	Jun 28	Federal raid	A&H:GP
John A. Gilmer to ZBV	Jun 28	Federal raid	A&H:GP
Joseph W. Wilson to ZBV	Jun 28	Federal raid	A&H:GP
Ensly Council to ZBV	Jun 28	secret society	A&H:GP
Joseph H. Flanner to ZBV	Jun 29	*Advance*	A&H:GP
Peter Mallett to ZBV	Jun 29	conscription	A&H:GP
John A. Gilmer to ZBV	Jun 29	Federal raid	A&H:GP
Thomas Carter to ZBV	Jun 29	cargo	A&H:GP

Correspondents	Date	Subject	Repository
John D. Whitford to ZBV	Jun 30	r.r. iron	A&H:GP
M. Q. Waddith to ZBV	Jun 30	election	A&H:GP
John A. Gilmer to ZBV	Jun 30	Federal raid	A&H:GP
Alexander Collie, account	Jun 30	expenses	A&H:GP
Christopher G. Memminger to ZBV	Jun 30	western N.C.	A&H:VanPC
James W. Wilson to George Little	Jul 1	election	A&H:GP
Thomas Carter to ZBV	Jul 1	cargo	A&H:GP
Richard C. Gatlin, general order	Jul 1	Home Guard	A&H:VanPC
John M. Davidson to ZBV	Jul 1	appointment	A&H:VanPC
Sewall L. Fremont to ZBV	Jul 2	cotton	A&H:GP
C. Murray & Co. to ZBV	Jul 2	wharf	A&H:GP
R. F. Pinkney to Gilbert Elliott	Jul 2	r.r. iron	A&H:GP
James W. Wilson to ZBV	Jul 3	W. W. Avery	A&H:GP
William F. McKesson to ZBV	Jul 4	slave sale	A&H:VanPC
James C. McKesson to ZBV	Jul 5	transfer	A&H:GP
W. Collie to ZBV	Jul 6	*Annie*	A&H:GP
Joseph Brown to ZBV	Jul 6	certification	A&H:GP
Gilbert Elliot to David A. Barnes	Jul 7	r.r. iron	A&H:GP
John E. Goodwin to ZBV	Jul 7	conscription	A&H:GP
O. D. Cooke to ZBV	Jul 7	appointment	A&H:GP
Otis F. Manson to ZBV	Jul 7	supplies	A&H:VanPC
[R.] Gibbon to ZBV	Jul 8	cloth	A&H:VanPC
Alphonso C. Avery to ZBV	Jul 8	transfer	A&H:VanPC
Catherine Carson to ZBV	Jul 8	discharge	A&H:VanPC
[F.] George Walton to ZBV	Jul 9	conscription	A&H:GP
George W. Logan to ZBV	Jul 9	political support	A&H:VanPC
Robert S. [Gerber] to ZBV	Jul 11	ballots	A&H:GP
John [N.] Cunningham to ZBV	Jul 11	conscription	A&H:GP
James L. Henry to ZBV	Jul 11	arrest	A&H:VanPC
William R. McCaskill to ZBV	Jul 12	desertion	A&H:GP
Theophilus H. Holmes to ZBV	Jul 12	disaffection	A&H:GP
Jesse G. Shepherd to ZBV	Jul 12	appointment	A&H:GP
Matthew Shaw to ZBV	Jul 12	poor relief	A&H:GP
J. R. Fowle et al. to ZBV	Jul 14	destitution	A&H:GP
T. H. Satterthwaite to ZBV	Jul 14	election	A&H:VanPC
William A. Crocker to ZBV	Jul 15	election	A&H:GP
W. H. B. Taylor to ZBV	Jul 15	speech	A&H:GP
R. R. Heath, commission	Jul 15	special court	A&H:GLB
Alexander Collie, account	Jul 15	cotton	A&H:VanPC
E. J. Hardin to ZBV	Jul 15	Junior Reserves	A&H:VanPC
James A. Seddon to ZBV	Jul 16	conscription	A&H:GP
Moses L. Holmes to ZBV	Jul 16	speech	A&H:GP
[C. R. Keeling] to ZBV	Jul 16	transfer	A&H:GP
James A. Seddon to ZBV	Jul 16	conscription	A&H:GLB
L. J. Johnson to ZBV	Jul 17	election	A&H:VanPC
John J. Guthrie to ZBV	Jul 18	election	A&H:GP

Correspondents	Date	Subject	Repository
Robert E. Lee to ZBV	Jul 18	arms	A&H:GP
J. D. C. to ZBV	Jul 18	provisions	A&H:GP
William F. McKesson to ZBV	Jul 18	political support	A&H:VanPC
J. A. Fuqua to ZBV	Jul 19	train	A&H:GP
J. C. Court[eny] to ZBV	Jul 19	Federal raid	A&H:GP
Laurence S. Baker to ZBV	Jul 19	troops	A&H:GP
Laurence S. Baker to ZBV	Jul 19	train	A&H:GP
Laurence S. Baker to ZBV	Jul 19	ammunition	A&H:GP
Stephen D. Poole to ZBV	Jul 19	arms	A&H:GP
J. K. Wilson to ZBV	Jul 19	elections	A&H:GP
John R. Williams Jr. to ZBV	Jul 19	messages	A&H:GP
W. W. Harrison to ZBV	Jul 19	wheat	A&H:GP
Edward J. Hale to ZBV	Jul 19	transfer	A&H:VanPC
J. R. Stubbs to ZBV	Jul 20	cotton	A&H:GP
John A. Hawks to ZBV	Jul 20	desertion	A&H:GP
Richard H. Battle Jr. to ZBV	Jul 20	appointment	A&H:GLB
P. H. Langdon to ZBV	Jul 20	flag	A&H:GLB
John S. Daney to ZBV	Jul 20	flag	A&H:GLB
Guilford Coleman to ZBV	Jul 21	desertion	A&H:GP
James A. Seddon to ZBV	Jul 21	salt works	A&H:GP
John Devereux to John White	Jul 21	shoes	A&H:GP
Theodore Andreae to ZBV	Jul 21	contract	A&H:VanPC
C. L. Harris to ZBV	Jul 22	distilling	A&H:GLB
ZBV, proclamation	Jul 22	reward	A&H:GLB
George Little to James A. Seddon	Jul 25	passport	A&H:GLB
Charles F. M. Garrett to ZBV	Jul 26	r.r. iron	A&H:GP
R. F. Walker to ZBV	Jul 26	election	A&H:GP
Thomas M. Crossan to David A. Barnes	Jul 26	Capt. Hughes	A&H:GP
Hugh S. Cole to ZBV	Jul 26	election	A&H:VanPC
Phil L. Carson to ZBV	Jul 26	election	A&H:VanPC
David A. Barnes to C. L. Harris	Jul 27	distilling	A&H:GLB
T. J. Boykin to David A. Barnes	Jul 28	election	A&H:GP
Otis F. Manson to George Little	Jul 28	election	A&H:GP
Alfred M. Scales to ZBV	Jul 28	election	A&H:GP
J. B. [Lenor] to ZBV	Jul 28	election	A&H:GP
F. N. Freeman to ZBV	Jul 28	election	A&H:GP
William H. Richardson to ZBV	Jul 28	clothes	A&H:GP
John W. Reynolds to ZBV	Jul 28	election	A&H:VanPC
Robert D. Johnston to ZBV	Jul 28	election	A&H:VanPC
ZBV to John White	Jul 29	appointment	A&H:GP
D. M. Carter to ZBV	Jul 29	election	A&H:VanPC
W. H. Speer to ZBV	Jul 29	election	A&H:VanPC
Jesse R. Stubbs to ZBV	Jul 30	resignation	A&H:GLB
George W. Pinnix to ZBV	Aug 1	constable	A&H:GP
Henry Heth to ZBV	Aug 1	election	A&H:GP

Correspondents	Date	Subject	Repository
Robert P. Dick to ZBV	Aug 1	resignation	A&H:GP
David L. Swain to ZBV	Aug 1	appointment	A&H:GP
Josiah Turner to ZBV	Aug 1	legislator	A&H:VanPC
W. G. B. Garrett et al. to ZBV	Aug 2	reprieve	A&H:GP
Sophia C. Turner to ZBV	Aug 2	soldier's mother	A&H:GP
J. W. Blacknall to ZBV	Aug 2	appointment	A&H:GP
James L. Henry to ZBV	Aug 2	election	A&H:VanPC
H. H. Dawson to ZBV	Aug 3	soldiers' clothing	A&H:GP
J. A. Paschall to ZBV	Aug 3	appointment	A&H:GP
W. G. M. Davis & F. C. Fitzhugh to [John White]	Aug 4	*Advance*	A&H:GP
J. P. Hunt to ZBV	Aug 4	desertion	A&H:GP
W. S. Sharp to ZBV	Aug 4	election	A&H:GP
E. Marsh to ZBV	Aug 4	UNC library	SHC:Car
Jeremy F. Gilmer to ZBV	Aug 5	r.r. iron	A&H:GP
Sam C. Bryson & Samuel L. Love to ZBV	Aug 5	election	A&H:GP
Milledge L. Bonham to ZBV	Aug 5	slave murder	A&H:GP
R. V. B. to ZBV	Aug 5	election	A&H:VanPC
Richard C. Puryear to ZBV	Aug 5	election	A&H:VanPC
R. H. Northrop to ZBV	Aug 6	passport	A&H:GP
R. D. Hart to Kemp P. Battle	Aug 6	appointment	A&H:GP
P. K. O. G. to ZBV	Aug 6	peace	A&H:GP
Sidney B. Erwin to ZBV	Aug 6	election	A&H:VanPC
Thomas Carter to ZBV	Aug 6	*Advance*	A&H:VanPC
C. L. Cook to ZBV	Aug 6	election	A&H:VanPC
W. E. DeMill to ZBV	Aug 7	aid for father	A&H:GP
W. D. [Buell] to ZBV	Aug 7	abuse of citizens	A&H:GP
E. R. Liles to ZBV	Aug 7	Home Guard	A&H:VanPC
Andrew C. Cowles to ZBV	Aug 7	election	A&H:VanPC
David A. Barnes to J. P. Hunt	Aug 8	desertion	A&H:GP
Mrs. R. H. Duke to ZBV	Aug 8	poor relief	A&H:GP
John White & Thomas Boykin to ZBV	Aug 8	*Advance*	A&H:GP
Calvin W. Wooley to ZBV	Aug 8	Heroes of America	A&H:GP
Peter Adams to ZBV	Aug 8	W. W. Holden	A&H:GP
James H. Everett to ZBV	Aug 8	conscription	A&H:GP
Sewall L. Fremont to ZBV	Aug 8	conscription	A&H:GP
Philip Leon to ZBV	Aug 8	*Advance*	A&H:VanPC
Augustus S. Merrimon to ZBV	Aug 8	election	A&H:VanPC
John [White] to ZBV	Aug 9	*Advance*	A&H:GP
P. H. Langdon to Theophilus H. Holmes	Aug 9	appointment	A&H:GP
A. G. Brooks to ZBV	Aug 9	deserter clemency	A&H:GP
Jonathan Robbins to ZBV	Aug 9	conscription	A&H:GP
M. S. Sherwood to ZBV	Aug 9	conscription	A&H:GP

Correspondents	Date	Subject	Repository
John A. Gilmer to ZBV	Aug 9	conscription	A&H:GP
G. [M.] Worth to ZBV	Aug 9	deserters	A&H:GP
Daniel L. Russell to ZBV	Aug 9	impressment	A&H:GP
John H. Haughton to ZBV	Aug 9	deserters	A&H:VanPC
James W. Osborne to ZBV	Aug 9	election	A&H:VanPC
W. F. Leak to ZBV	Aug 10	deserters	A&H:GP
Power, Low & Co. to ZBV	Aug 10	*Advance*	A&H:GP
Nicholas W. Woodfin to ZBV	Aug 10	salt	A&H:GP
G. W. Blacknall to ZBV	Aug 10	hospital conditions	A&H:GP
W. W. Hampton to ZBV	Aug 10	deserters	A&H:GP
John A. Gilmer to David A. Barnes	Aug 10	conscription	A&H:GP
Robert H. Cowan to ZBV	Aug 10	r.r. supplies	A&H:GP
James A. Hague to ZBV	Aug 10	election	A&H:VanPC
R. P. Buxton to ZBV	Aug 11	conscription	A&H:GP
E. Murray to ZBV	Aug 11	blockade	A&H:GP
Thomas Jasper to ZBV	Aug 11	appointment	A&H:GP
William Thomas to ZBV	Aug 11	deserters	A&H:GP
Power, Low & Co. to George Little	Aug 11	ZBV's return	A&H:GP
Power, Low & Co. to John White	Aug 11	*Advance*	A&H:GP
Thomas Carter to ZBV	Aug 11	*Advance*	A&H:GP
William Smith to ZBV	Aug 11	cloth	A&H:GP
Thomas J. Boykin to ZBV	Aug 11	steamer	A&H:VanPC
P. J. Sinclair to ZBV	Aug 12	conscription	A&H:GP
John K. Boyden to ZBV	Aug 12	conscription	A&H:GP
D. P. Foust to ZBV	Aug 12	conscription	A&H:GP
James L. Henry to ZBV	Aug 12	cavalry attacks	A&H:GP
Milledge L. Bonham to ZBV	Aug 12	extradition	A&H:GP
Otis F. Manson to ZBV	Aug 12	hospital supplies	A&H:GP
W. W. McRackan to ZBV	Aug 12	conscription	A&H:GP
Noah Auman to ZBV	Aug 12	Heroes of America	A&H:GP
Jesse G. Shepherd to ZBV	Aug 12	John K. Riley	A&H:GP
John J. Garrett et al. to ZBV	Aug 12	conscription	A&H:GP
Milledge L. Bonham to ZBV	Aug 13	extradition	A&H:GP
Morning Post clipping	Aug 13	Federal deportation	A&H:GP
Joshua Miller to ZBV	Aug 13	conscription	A&H:GP
Fred Philips to ZBV	Aug 13	quartermaster	A&H:GP
Thomas M. Holt to ZBV	Aug 13	gift of flour	A&H:VanPC
Otis F. Manson to ZBV	Aug 13	R. B. Vance	A&H:VanPC
William H. Cowan to ZBV	Aug 15	speech	A&H:GP
M. L. McCorkle to ZBV	Aug 15	transfer	A&H:GP
S. F. Dougherty to ZBV	Aug 15	deserters & tories	A&H:GP
R. Taylor Bennett to ZBV	Aug 15	recommendation	A&H:GP
Mrs. Mc D. Lindsey to ZBV	Aug 15	votes list	A&H:GP
R. E. Cooper to ZBV	Aug 15	transfer	A&H:GP
James G. Cook to ZBV	Aug 15	appointment	A&H:GP
W. H. Clifton et al. to ZBV	Aug 15	pardon	A&H:GP

Correspondents	Date	Subject	Repository
Fannie Swann to ZBV	Aug 15	appointment	A&H:GP
H. Watson to ZBV	Aug 15	election	A&H:VanPC
Fred L. Roberts to ZBV	Aug 15	election	A&H:VanPC
Thomas Carter to ZBV	Aug 16	engineer	A&H:GP
David M. Sykes to ZBV	Aug 16	conscription	A&H:GP
Alex Richard to ZBV	Aug 16	conscription	A&H:GP
M. McKesson to ZBV	Aug 17	passport	A&H:GP
J. R. Williams to ZBV	Aug 17	deserter	A&H:GP
P. J. Sinclair to ZBV	Aug 17	conscription	A&H:GP
Soldier's widow to ZBV	Aug 17	poor relief	A&H:GP
Catherine T. Douglas to ZBV	Aug 17	wounded husband	A&H:GP
Robert F. Brach to ZBV	Aug 17	deserters	A&H:GP
D. Fraser to [?]	Aug 17	Liverpool passage	A&H:GP
R. N. Price to ZBV	Aug 17	paper request	A&H:GP
Jonathan Worth to ZBV	Aug 17	state finances	A&H:GP
George H. Taylor to ZBV	Aug 17	appointment	A&H:GP
Jonathan Worth to ZBV	Aug 18	card machinery	A&H:GP
Lewis George to ZBV	Aug 18	soldier's pass	A&H:GP
William McGee, affidavits	Aug 18	conscientious objector	A&H:GP
Power, Low & Co. to ZBV	Aug 18	*Advance*	A&H:GP
M. S. Robins to ZBV	Aug 18	secretary position	A&H:GP
James K. Gibson to ZBV	Aug 18	payment	A&H:VanPC
E. Garner to ZBV	Aug 19	election	A&H:GP
William L. Rogers to ZBV	Aug 19	discharge	A&H:GP
Mrs. McAulay to ZBV	Aug 19	appointment	A&H:GP
Blanton Duncan to ZBV	Aug 19	English support	A&H:GP
John A. Gilmer et al. to ZBV	Aug 19	conscription	A&H:GP
Louis Hebert to ZBV	Aug 19	*Advance*	A&H:GP
William W. Roberson to ZBV	Aug 19	election	A&H:VanPC
Julia A. Hott to ZBV	Aug 20	conscription	A&H:GP
James A. Seddon to ZBV	Aug 20	passport	A&H:VanPC
Richard C. Gatlin, order 78	Aug 20	Home Guard	SHC:Sha
William H. C. Whiting to ZBV	Aug 21	recommendation	A&H:GP
K. K. Barnhill to ZBV	Aug 22	transfer	A&H:GP
William H. C. Whiting to ZBV	Aug 22	Georgia troops	A&H:GP
John Robbins, affidavit	Aug 22	conscientious objector	A&H:GP
William T. Shipp to ZBV	Aug 22	election	A&H:GP
Braxton Craven to ZBV	Aug 22	import request	A&H:GP
C. J. Cochran to ZBV	Aug 22	Heroes of America	A&H:GP
Otis F. Manson to ZBV	Aug 22	hospital	A&H:GP
Thomas Miller to ZBV	Aug 22	deserters	A&H:GP
Jeptha M. Israel to ZBV	Aug 22	salt contract	A&H:GP
G. D. Hines to ZBV	Aug 22	r.r. fares	A&H:GP
K. J. [U.] Crow to ZBV	Aug 23	justice of the peace	A&H:GP

Correspondents	Date	Subject	Repository
R. F. Simonton to ZBV	Aug 23	r.r. vacancy	A&H:GP
Thomas B. Long to ZBV	Aug 23	Red Strings	A&H:GP
R. Williams to ZBV	Aug 23	transfer	A&H:GP
E. H. Britton to ZBV	Aug 23	conscription	A&H:GP
Philip Leon to ZBV	Aug 23	*Annie*	A&H:GP
Power, Low & Co. to ZBV	Aug 23	*Advance*	A&H;GP
Mary Ann Buie to ZBV	Aug 23	praise	A&H:GP
[J.] L. Brown to ZBV	Aug 23	introduction	A&H:GP
N. M. Hardy to ZBV	Aug 23	election	A&H:GP
William B. Gulick, certificate	Aug 23	state currency	A&H:GP
Stuart Buchanan & Co. to Nicholas W. Woodfin	Aug 23	salt contract	A&H:GLB
T. C. Allison to ZBV	Aug 23	satchel of Mrs. ZBV	A&H:VanPC
L. E. Satterthwaite to ZBV	Aug 23	conscription	A&H:VanPC
Henry A. Dowd to ZBV	Aug 23	gift	A&H:VanPC
William H. C. Whiting to ZBV	Aug 24	Federal ships	A&H:GP
Peter Mallett to ZBV	Aug 24	conscription	A&H:GP
J. L. Neagle to ZBV	Aug 24	Thomas Long	A&H:GP
Alfred W. Jackson to ZBV	Aug 24	deserter pardon	A&H:GP
A. M. McPheeters, statement	Aug 24	ZBV proclamation	A&H:GP
D. W. Neill et al. to ZBV	Aug 24	deserters & murder	A&H:GP
David L. Swain to ZBV	Aug 24	election	A&H:VanPC
James G. Burr to ZBV	Aug 24	appointment	A&H:VanPC
ZBV, proclamation (printed)	Aug 24	desertion	A&H:VanPC
Martha E. Drury to ZBV	Aug 25	husband's arrest	A&H:GP
C. B. Mallen to ZBV	Aug 25	Home Guard	A&H:GP
L. J. Williams to ZBV	Aug 25	transfer	A&H:GP
Elizabeth Thale to ZBV	Aug 25	prison pass	A&H:GP
John W. Hinsdale to ZBV	Aug 25	Home Guard	A&H:GP
Nancy King to ZBV	Aug 25	poor relief	A&H:GP
G. L. Carson to ZBV	Aug 25	poor relief	A&H:GP
Philip Leon to ZBV	Aug 25	*Advance*	A&H:GP
C. H. Wiley to ZBV	Aug 25	card factory	A&H:GP
R. L. Simonton to ZBV	Aug 25	r.r. vacancy	A&H:GP
Laurence S. Baker to ZBV	Aug 25	Wilmington defense	A&H:GP
R. W. Lassiter to ZBV	Aug 25	clemency	A&H:GP
W. Murdock to ZBV	Aug 26	invention	A&H:GP
W. C. Means to ZBV	Aug 26	discharge	A&H:GP
Edward J. Hale to ZBV	Aug 26	Home Guard	A&H:GP
James W. Pegram to Richard S. Ewell	Aug 26	soldiers hospital	A&H:GP
William Allen et al. to ZBV	Aug 27	conscription	A&H:GP
Power, Low & Co. to ZBV	Aug 27	*Advance*	A&H:GP
L. N. B. Battle to ZBV	Aug 27	Senior Reserves	A&H:GP
Jesse G. Shepherd to ZBV	Aug 27	Home Guard	A&H:GP
William Johnston to ZBV	Aug 27	conscription	A&H:GP

Correspondents	Date	Subject	Repository
John H. Haughton to ZBV	Aug 27	conscription	A&H:GP
Thomas McNeely, certification	Aug 27	conscription	A&H:GP
Z. McCowry to ZBV	Aug 27	conscription	A&H:GP
A. M. Powell to ZBV	Aug 27	cloth	A&H:GP
John Withers to ZBV	Aug 27	interstate commerce	A&H:VanPC
Emily A. Crump to ZBV	Aug 27	brother-in-law	A&H:VanPC
Alfred G. Foster to ZBV	Aug 27	conscription	A&H:VanPC
W. P. Moor to ZBV	Aug 28	discharge	A&H:GP
John W. McElroy to ZBV	Aug 28	appointments	A&H:GP
William T. Shipp to ZBV	Aug 28	W. W. Holden	A&H:GP
W. P. Caison to ZBV	Aug 28	medical treatment	A&H:GP
L. F. Bates et al. to ZBV	Aug 28	Home Guard	A&H:GP
J. W. Alspaugh to ZBV	Aug 28	disloyalty	A&H:GP
G. M. Hazell to ZBV	Aug 29	conscription	A&H:GP
Robert De Scheveinitz to ZBV	Aug 29	brother	A&H:GP
John M. Wright to ZBV	Aug 29	conscription	A&H:GP
John J. Whitehead to ZBV	Aug 29	conscription	A&H:GP
Thomas M. Holt to ZBV	Aug 29	conscription	A&H:GP
W. H. Drake to ZBV	Aug 29	conscription	A&H:GP
Patrick H. Winston to ZBV	Aug 29	money receipt	A&H:GP
C. R. King to ZBV	Aug 29	conscription	A&H:GP
Otis F. Manson to ZBV	Aug 29	soldiers hospital	A&H:GP
W. W. Williams to ZBV	Aug 29	arrest	A&H:GP
G. C. Moses to ZBV	Aug 29	desertion	A&H:GP
W. G. Brawly to ZBV	Aug 29	deserter clemency	A&H:GP
J. L. Bailey to ZBV	Aug 29	desertion	A&H:GP
Robert E. Lee to ZBV	Aug 29	Wilmington defense	A&H:GLB
J. H. Sands to Allen Jordan	Aug 30	desertion & murder	A&H:GP
F. M. Parker to ZBV	Aug 30	conscription	A&H:GP
Edward Warren, statement	Aug 30	surgeon general	A&H:GP
R. L. Periman to ZBV	Aug 30	departure	A&H:GP
Samuel [F.] Phillips to ZBV	Aug 30	Senior Reserves	A&H:GP
Edward Warren, statement	Aug 30	state money	A&H:GLB
Richard C. Gatlin, order 84	Aug 30	conscription	SHC:Shar
Terrence Freeman to ZBV	Aug 31	intruders	A&H:GP
Hosea Bradford to ZBV	Aug 31	discharge	A&H:GP
J. Jacob Shipton to ZBV	Aug 31	deserter	A&H:GP
James H. Foote to ZBV	Aug 31	clerk request	A&H:GP
Frank J. Drake to ZBV	Aug 31	appointment	A&H:GP
A. T. Semmay to ZBV	Aug 31	household items	A&H:GP
Francis H. Smith to ZBV	Aug 31	VMI	A&H:GLB
John A. Gilmer to ZBV	Aug 31	senate election	A&H:VanPC
J. E. Murphy et al. to ZBV	Aug n.d.	whiskey	A&H:GP
William S. Pitts to ZBV	Aug n.d.	Wilmington visit	A&H:GP
John White to A. M. McPheeters	Sep 1	*Advance*	A&H:GP
John White to ZBV	Sep 1	*Advance*	A&H:GP

Correspondents	Date	Subject	Repository
Francis E. Shober to ZBV	Sep 1	conscription	A&H:GP
James T. Roper to ZBV	Sep 1	desertion	A&H:GP
Wennie Reece to ZBV	Sep 1	passport	A&H:GP
John R. Roach to ZBV	Sep 1	desertion	A&H:GP
T. W. Sparrow to ZBV	Sep 1	conscription	A&H:GP
Bryan Tyson to ZBV	Sep 1	invitation	A&H:GP
G. A. Upchurch to ZBV	Sep 1	desertion	A&H:GP
Lucy T. James to ZBV	Sep 1	poor relief	A&H:GP
William Lee Davidson to ZBV	Sep 1	appointment	A&H:GP
James B. Ballard et al. to ZBV	Sep 1	free black clemency	A&H:GP
A. Kelsey to ZBV	Sep 1	election	A&H:VanPC
S. P. Smith to ZBV	Sep 2	Home Guard	A&H:GP
W. J. Palmer to ZBV	Sep 2	supplies	A&H:GP
John B. Ashcroft to ZBV	Sep 2	Home Guard	A&H:GP
James Marion Higgins to ZBV	Sep 2	venereal disease	A&H:GP
Tyre York to ZBV	Sep 2	deserter	A&H:GP
S. A. Walkup to ZBV	Sep 2	Home Guard	A&H:GP
G. Westman to ZBV	Sep 2	passport	A&H:GP
S. A. Sharpe to Richard C. Gatlin	Sep 2	Home Guard	A&H:GP
Joseph H. Flanner to ZBV	Sep 2	*Advance*	A&H:VanPC
J. C. Gay to ZBV	Sep 3	Home Guard	A&H:GP
John B. Lyon to ZBV	Sep 3	passport	A&H:GP
Morgreth Wesbrooks to ZBV	Sep 3	deserter pardon	A&H:GP
Charles C. Hackett to ZBV	Sep 3	desertion	A&H:GP
John R. Winston to ZBV	Sep 3	deserters	A&H:GP
Jesse J. Yeates to ZBV	Sep 3	"Buffaloes"	A&H:GP
S. E. Davis et al. to ZBV	Sep 3	conscription	A&H:GP
Thomas S. Hansley to ZBV	Sep 3	deserter pardon	A&H:GP
William H. Richardson to ZBV	Sep 3	VMI supplies	A&H:GP
Elizabeth Ryals to ZBV	Sep 3	poor relief	A&H:GP
Philip Leon, receipt	Sep 3	cotton	A&H:VanPC
Power, Low & Co. to ZBV	Sep 5	*Advance*	A&H:GP
S. A. Sharpe to ZBV	Sep 5	deserters	A&H:GP
James L. Henry to ZBV	Sep 5	promotions	A&H:GP
Jack F. Hill to ZBV	Sep 5	conscription	A&H:GP
William Howard to ZBV	Sep 5	furlough	A&H:GP
Otis F. Manson to ZBV	Sep 5	hospital	A&H:GP
J. R. Hargrave to ZBV	Sep 5	recommendation	A&H:GP
George A. Mott to ZBV	Sep 5	militia officer	A&H:GP
John S. E. Summy to ZBV	Sep 5	soldiers home	A&H:GP
Stephen Johnson to ZBV	Sep 5	discharge	A&H:GP
Robert H. Cowan to ZBV	Sep 5	r.r. iron	A&H:GP
David G. Worth to ZBV	Sep 5	salt works	A&H:GLB
M. Taylor Brown to ZBV	Sep 5	family news	A&H:VanPC
E. Murray & Co. to ZBV	Sep 5	*Advance*	A&H:VanPC
Edward J. Hale to ZBV	Sep 5	appointment	A&H:VanPC

Correspondents	Date	Subject	Repository
Alexander C. Cowles to ZBV	Sep 5	appointment	A&H:VanPC
J. S. Burr to ZBV	Sep 5	arrest	A&H:VanPC
John A. Sloan to ZBV	Sep 6	Quaker conscripts	A&H:GP
Stephen Lee et al. to ZBV	Sep 6	conscription	A&H:GP
Allen Jordan to ZBV	Sep 6	murder case	A&H:GP
John Spence to Dr. York	Sep 6	deserter	A&H:GP
James H. Everitt to ZBV	Sep 6	political support	A&H:GP
Giles Britt to ZBV	Sep 6	desertion	A&H:GP
David G. Worth to ZBV	Sep 6	salt works	A&H:GP
J. J. Young to ZBV	Sep 6	soldiers home	A&H:VanPC
A. Bodeker to ZBV	Sep 7	money	A&H:GP
John R. Respass to ZBV	Sep 7	loyalty	A&H:GP
Robert H. Cowan to ZBV	Sep 7	r.r. iron	A&H:GP
William D. Etheridge to ZBV	Sep 7	disloyalty	A&H:GP
Joseph M. Tate to ZBV	Sep 7	prisoner request	A&H:GP
James Calloway to ZBV	Sep 7	raid defense	A&H:GP
Joseph Cline to ZBV	Sep 8	conscription	A&H:GP
John Wilson et al. to ZBV	Sep 8	Senior Reserves	A&H:GP
William J. White to ZBV	Sep 8	conscription	A&H:GP
Luke Blackmer to ZBV	Sep 8	furloughs	A&H:GP
S. R. Hawly to ZBV	Sep 8	destitution	A&H:GP
S. F. Patterson to ZBV	Sep 8	conscription	A&H:GP
E. Murray & Co. to ZBV	Sep 8	transfer	A&H:GP
J. M. McCorkle to ZBV	Sep 8	Wesley McDaniel	A&H:GP
ZBV, pardon	Sep 8	Wesley McDaniel	A&H:GLB
Lewis E. Satterthwaite to ZBV	Sep 8	steamer	A&H:VanPC
W. H. Hatch to ZBV	Sep 8	prisoner exchange	A&H:VanPC
Robert B. Vance to ZBV	Sep 8	W. K. Handy	Mich:Han
Samuel P. Arrington to ZBV	Sep 9	conscription	A&H:GP
E. A. Alexander to ZBV	Sep 9	conscription	A&H:GP
Robert B. Gilliam to ZBV	Sep 9	Wesley McDaniel	A&H:GP
Robert B. Gilliam to ZBV	Sep 9	desertion	A&H:GP
Power, Low & Co. to ZBV	Sep 10	*Advance*	A&H:GP
W. S. Davidson to ZBV	Sep 10	clothing	A&H:GP
Francis E. Shober to ZBV	Sep 10	recommendation	A&H:GP
James A. Puttick to ZBV	Sep 10	transfer	A&H:GP
W. F. Holden to ZBV	Sep 10	detail	A&H:GP
William Hobson to ZBV	Sep 10	desertion	A&H:GP
Abner S. Williams to ZBV	Sep 10	conscription	A&H:GP
A. Hamilton Tolor to ZBV	Sep 10	deserters	A&H:GP
Jesse Wallin to ZBV	Sep 10	appointment	A&H:VanPC
D. D. Ferebee to ZBV	Sep 10	recommendation	A&H:VanPC
S. A. Sharpe to ZBV	Sep 11	Home Guard	A&H:GP
James Calloway to ZBV	Sep 11	Federal raid	A&H:GP
Clement Dowd to ZBV	Sep 11	deserters	A&H:GP

Correspondents	Date	Subject	Repository
E. Murry to ZBV	Sep 12	Mr. London	A&H:GP
Sophia C. Turner to ZBV	Sep 12	appointment	A&H:GP
James P. Cook to ZBV	Sep 12	deserter	A&H:GP
E. M. Welborn to ZBV	Sep 12	Home Guard	A&H:GP
Emma Keerans to ZBV	Sep 12	transfer	A&H:GP
James Hall to ZBV	Sep 12	deserters	A&H:GP
Lewis E. Harris to ZBV	Sep 12	r.r. stock	A&H:GLB
E. Murray & Co. to Philip Leon	Sep 12	cotton	A&H:VanPC
John A. D. Hampton to ZBV	Sep 12	Home Guard	A&H:VanPC
Thomas J. Boykin to ZBV	Sep 12	*Advance*	A&H:VanPC
Charles E. Shober to ZBV	Sep 13	passport	A&H:GP
Archibald McLean to ZBV	Sep 13	desertion	A&H:GP
M. L. Waddell to ZBV	Sep 13	magistrate	A&H:GP
David Weldon to ZBV	Sep 13	appointment	A&H:GP
T. M. Starr to ZBV	Sep 13	discharge	A&H:GP
A. S. Horney to ZBV	Sep 13	conscription	A&H:GP
Sewall L. Fremont to David A. Barnes	Sep 14	meeting	A&H:GP
John W. Dunham to ZBV	Sep 14	deserter	A&H:GP
Joshua Barnes to ZBV	Sep 14	deserter	A&H:GP
M. F. Freeland to ZBV	Sep 14	James S. Rickett	A&H:GP
George H. Haigh to [ZBV]	Sep 14	deserter	A&H:GP
W. J. Kelly et al. to ZBV	Sep 14	Home Guard	A&H:GP
C. A. Nichols to ZBV	Sep 14	illegible	A&H:GP
Jeremy F. Gilmer to ZBV	Sep 14	r.r. iron	A&H:GP
Bedford Brown to ZBV	Sep 14	appointment	A&H:VanPC
William W. Morrison to ZBV	Sep 15	Goldsboro	A&H:GP
Maury & Co. to ZBV	Sep 15	passport	A&H:GP
Phebe Crook to ZBV	Sep 15	militia & magistrates	A&H:GP
N. A. Powell to ZBV	Sep 15	conscription	A&H:GP
D. Whisnant et al. to ZBV	Sep 15	conscription	A&H:GP
Soldiers to ZBV	Sep 15	hospital	A&H:GP
Giles Mebane to ZBV	Sep 15	conscription	A&H:GP
John Sims to ZBV	Sep 15	detail	A&H:GP
M. London to ZBV	Sep 15	tobacco agent	A&H:VanPC
A. Mitchell to ZBV	Sep 16	Home Guard	A&H:GP
M. S. Robins to M. L. Waddell	Sep 16	appointment	A&H:GP
Samuel F. Phillips to ZBV	Sep 16	court martial	A&H:GP
Power, Low & Co. to ZBV	Sep 16	*Advance*	A&H:GP
Andrew C. Cowles to ZBV	Sep 16	favors	A&H:GP
Hosea Bradford to ZBV	Sep 17	conscription	A&H:GP
F. S. Parker to H. D. Craton	Sep 17	discharge	A&H:GP
C. L. Hunter to ZBV	Sep 17	passport	A&H:GP
D. W. Honeycutt to ZBV	Sep 17	detail	A&H:GP
H. G. Spruill to ZBV	Sep 17	medicine	A&H:GP
William Freeman et al. to ZBV	Sep 18	deserter	A&H:GP
Andrew C. Cowles to ZBV	Sep 18	deserters	A&H:GP

Correspondents	Date	Subject	Repository
J. M. Leach to ZBV	Sep 18	arrest	A&H:VanPC
David L. Swain to ZBV	Sep 18	Wilmington	A&H:VanPC
George W. Logan to ZBV	Sep 18	son's removal	A&H:VanPC
Thomas L. Clingman to ZBV	Sep 18	cloth	Har:Clin
W. W. Haddock to ZBV	Sep 19	enemy trade	A&H:GP
William M. Norman to ZBV	Sep 19	prisoners	A&H:GP
Sophia L. Turner to ZBV	Sep 19	transfer	A&H:GP
J. M. Shearer to ZBV	Sep 19	prisoner	A&H:GP
J. W. A. Young to ZBV	Sep 19	destitution	A&H:VanPC
Henry E. Colton to ZBV	Sep 19	House clerk	A&H:VanPC
E. Murray & Co. to ZBV	Sep 19	cotton	A&H:VanPC
Richard Anderson to ZBV	Sep 19	Home Guard	A&H:VanPC
James A. Seddon to ZBV	Sep 20	gov't vessels	A&H:GP
John D. Shaw, certification	Sep 20	deserter	A&H:GP
L. C. Latham to ZBV	Sep 20	conscription	A&H:GP
M. S. Robins to Archibald McLean	Sep 20	commands	A&H:GP
K. J. McCrow to ZBV	Sep 20	deserters	A&H:GP
A. E. Johns to ZBV	Sep 20	poor relief	A&H:GP
M. D. Craton to ZBV	Sep 20	discharge	A&H:GP
J. E. Reynolds to ZBV	Sep 20	Home Guard	A&H:GP
J. W. Townsend et al. to ZBV	Sep 20	Trinity College	A&H:VanPC
John A. Gilmer to ZBV	Sep 20	newspaper article	A&H:VanPC
James A. Seddon to ZBV	Sep 20	steamer passage	A&H:VanPC
J. [Keener], receipt	Sep 20	county seal	A&H:VanPC
Thomas Settle to ZBV	Sep 21	torture	A&H:GP
W. R. Bass to ZBV	Sep 21	conscription	A&H:GP
E. Murray & Co. to Philip Leon	Sep 21	cotton	A&HVanPC
James L. Henry to ZBV	Sep 21	John B. Palmer	A&H:VanPC
Archibald McLean to ZBV	Sep 22	murder case	A&H:GP
Caleb E. Barringer et al. to ZBV	Sep 22	prisoners	A&H:GP
W. B. P. Bigham to ZBV	Sep 22	soldier's pay	A&H:GP
J. W. McCurry to ZBV	Sep 22	detail	A&H:GP
Daniel W. Anderson to ZBV	Sep 22	transfer	A&H:GP
G. D. Good to ZBV	Sep 22	furlough	A&H:GP
James M. Leach to ZBV	Sep 22	disagreement	A&H:VanPC
S. T. Speer to ZBV	Sep 22	senator's death	A&H:VanPC
Power, Low & Co. to ZBV	Sep 23	meeting	A&H:GP
M. S. Robins to officer, 51st Reg't.	Sep 23	murder case	A&H:GP
Fenner B. Satterthwaite to ZBV	Sep 23	discharge	A&H:GP
Mont. Patton to ZBV	Sep 23	troops	A&H:GP
C. S. Brown to ZBV	Sep 23	passport	A&H:GP
E. S. Parker to ZBV	Sep 23	discharge	A&H:GP
John J. Owens to ZBV	Sep 23	furlough	A&H:GP
Edward J. Warren to ZBV	Sep 23	appointments	A&H:GP
James W. Burrows to ZBV	Sep 23	gift	A&H:VanPC
R. W. Lassiter to ZBV	Sep 23	appointment	A&H:VanPC

Correspondents	Date	Subject	Repository
T. McKesson to ZBV	Sep 24	appointment	A&H:VanPC
James A. Seddon to ZBV	Sep 24	detail denial	A&H:VanPC
Sophia Ivy to ZBV	Sep 25	husband	A&H:GP
D. Beck et al. to ZBV	Sep 25	transfer	A&H:GP
Thomas J. Boykin to ZBV	Sep 25	transfer	A&H:VanPC
Ladies of Nash to ZBV	Sep 26	militia	A&H:GP
Eli Pasour to ZBV	Sep 26	conscription	A&H:GP
William P. Leary to ZBV	Sep 26	appointment	A&H;GP
K. M. C. Williamson to ZBV	Sep 26	Home Guard	A&H:GP
William H. C. Whiting to ZBV	Sep 26	steamers	A&H:GP
David W. [Kinyoun] to ZBV	Sep 26	Gordon & Pruett	A&H:GP
T. P. Atkinson to ZBV	Sep 26	r.r. provisions	A&H:GP
N. S. Perkins to ZBV	Sep 26	discharge	A&H:GP
John A. Gilmer to ZBV	Sep 26	recommendation	A&H:VanPC
William A. Askew to ZBV	Sep 27	transfer	A&H:GP
Ed. C. Fisher to ZBV	Sep 27	asylum	A&H:GP
E. R. Norton to ZBV	Sep 27	distilling	A&H:GP
James M. Carter et al. to ZBV	Sep 27	pardon	A&H:GP
E. J. Aston to ZBV	Sep 27	Home Guard	A&H:VanPC
Lewis E. Harris to ZBV	Sep 28	r.r. transport	A&H:GP
Martha Hough to ZBV	Sep 28	Home Guard	A&H:GP
A. H. Polk to ZBV	Sep 28	cloth	A&H:GP
John Shiff et al. to ZBV	Sep 28	transfer	A&H:GP
M. Taylor Brown to ZBV	Sep 28	*Advance*	A&H:VanPC
David L. Swain to ZBV	Sep 28	habeas corpus	A&H:VanPC
James A. Hague to ZBV	Sep 28	W. W. Holden	A&H:VanPC
Tyrrell Brewer to ZBV	Sep 29	deserter	A&H:GP
William L. Morris to ZBV	Sep 29	prisoner	A&H:GP
James Calloway to ZBV	Sep 29	meeting	A&H:GP
Betsy Conner to ZBV	Sep 29	conscription	A&H:GP
Mary E. Anderson to ZBV	Sep 29	prisoner son	A&H:GP
George L. Hancock to ZBV	Sep 29	furlough	A&H:GP
H. M. Kithan to M. S. Robins	Sep 29	Alex Phares	A&H:GP
Joseph H. Hyman to ZBV	Sep 29	band instruments	A&H:GP
Milledge L. Bonham to ZBV	Sep 29	meeting	A&H:GP
J. R. Bulla et al. to ZBV	Sep 29	pardon	A&H:GP
Mont. Patton to ZBV	Sep 29	J. L. Henry case	A&H:VanPC
Andrew C. Cowles to ZBV	Sep 29	Home Guard	A&H:VanPC
Richard Sterling to ZBV	Sep 30	son	A&H:GP
G. W. Blacknall to ZBV	Sep 30	poor relief	A&H:GP
J. L. Henry to ZBV	Sep 30	deserters	A&H:GP
John L. Outlaw to ZBV	Sep 30	furlough	A&H:GP
Jesse G. Shepherd to ZBV	Sep 30	conscription	A&H:GP
Lewis S. Williams to ZBV	Sep 30	poor relief	A&H:VanPC
E. G. Greenlee et al. to ZBV	Sep 30	invitation	A&H:VanPC
Joseph H. Flanner to ZBV	Sep 30	*Advance*	A&H:VanPC

Correspondents	*Date*	*Subject*	*Repository*
Alfred Foster et al. to ZBV	Sep 30	deserters	SHC:Sha
Robert Murdock to ZBV	Sep n.d.	England letter	A&H:GP
Mary A. Hardy et al. to ZBV	Sep n.d.	discharges	A&H:GP
A. A. McBryde to ZBV	Sep n.d.	deserter	A&H:GP
"One Present" to ZBV	Sep n.d.	desertion	A&H:GP
William A. Coble to ZBV	Sep n.d.	gift	A&H:VanPC
Theodore J. Andreae, statement	Oct 1	cotton	A&H:GP
James B. Slaughter to ZBV	Oct 1	transfer	A&H:GP
Collett Leventhorpe to ZBV	Oct 1	Plymouth	A&H:GP
E. Murray to ZBV	Oct 1	J. R. Grist	A&H:GP
B. F. [Surm] to ZBV	Oct 1	conscription	A&H:GP
Calvin H. Wiley to ZBV	Oct 1	card machines	A&H:GP
David G. Worth to ZBV	Oct 1	J. R. Grist	A&H:GP
George Y. Freeman to ZBV	Oct 1	transfer	A&H:GP
Francis E. Shober to ZBV	Oct 1	WNCRR	A&H:GP
R. P. Buxton to ZBV	Oct 1	plunder raids	A&H:GP
Joseph E. Brown to ZBV	Oct 1	govs. meeting	A&H:GLB
Sion H. Rogers to ZBV	Oct 1	opinions	A&H:VanPC
E. Murray & Co. to ZBV	Oct 1	flour	A&H:VanPC
G. W. Logan to ZBV	Oct 1	son's removal	A&H:VanPC
J. R. Chambry to ZBV	Oct 1	Robert Vance	A&H:VanPC
David G. Worth to ZBV	Oct 1	salt	A&H:VanPC
F. L. Warren, estimate	Oct 2	tax in kind	A&H:GP
J. M. Taylor to ZBV	Oct 2	Silas Moore	A&H:GP
Isabella McDonald to ZBV	Oct 2	discharge	A&H:GP
Robert H. Cowan to ZBV	Oct 2	r.r. iron	A&H:GP
Henry H. Siler to ZBV	Oct 3	transfer	A&H:GP
V. Ripley et al. to ZBV	Oct 3	Home Guard	A&H:GP
Francis E. Shober to ZBV	Oct 3	endorsement	A&H:GP
W. A. Philpott to ZBV	Oct 3	jail break	A&H:GP
Calvin H. Wiley to ZBV	Oct 3	Literary Board	A&H:GP
Luke Blackmer to ZBV	Oct 3	P. A. Brown	A&H:GP
P. F. Mozingo to ZBV	Oct 3	desertion	A&H:GP
Robert H. Cowan to ZBV	Oct 3	r.r. iron	A&H:GLB
[?] S. Patterson to ZBV	Oct 3	Mountain Home	A&H:VanPC
David A. Barnes to Calvin H. Wiley	Oct 3	conscription	A&H:Wiley
W. A. Mitchell to ZBV	Oct 4	conscription	A&H:GP
William H. Harrison to ZBV	Oct 4	conscription	A&H:GP
Sion H. Rogers to ZBV	Oct 4	clemency	A&H:GP
Daniel F. Summey to ZBV	Oct 4	C. Leventhorpe	A&H:GP
Rufus K. S[haw] to ZBV	Oct 4	T. A. Garrett	A&H:GP
Stephen Johnson to ZBV	Oct 4	transfer	A&H:GP
Samuel R. Chisman to J. M. Wilson	Oct 4	r.r. freight	A&H:GP
John Robertson to ZBV	Oct 4	transfer	A&H:GP
J. J. Young to ZBV	Oct 4	resignation	A&H:GP
Thomas C. Fuller to ZBV	Oct 5	conscription	A&H:GP

Correspondents	Date	Subject	Repository
Clara B. Hoyt to ZBV	Oct 5	transfer	A&H:GP
W. P. Moore to ZBV	[Oct 5]	deserters	A&H:GP
June Mal[ern] to ZBV	Oct 5	conscription	A&H:GP
Thomas J. Sumner to ZBV	Oct 5	r.r. freight	A&H:GP
James W. Wilson to Samuel R. Chisman	Oct 5	r.r. freight	A&H:GP
John R. Winston to ZBV	Oct 5	flag	A&H:GLB
George Howard, commission	Oct 5	special court	A&H:GLB
Samuel McD. Tate to ZBV	Oct 5	state funds	A&H:VanPC
Jesse Hargrave to ZBV	Oct 5	deserters	A&H:VanPC
David M. Carter to ZBV	Oct 5	counties	SHC:Car
Stuart L. Johnston to ZBV	Oct 6	resignation	A&H:GP
John McRae to ZBV	Oct 6	appointment	A&H:GP
Sewall L. Fremont to ZBV	Oct 6	appointment	A&H:GP
Edward Kidder to ZBV	Oct 6	appointment	A&H:GP
E. Murray to ZBV	Oct 6	appointment	A&H:GP
W. H. McRary to ZBV	Oct 6	appointment	A&H:GP
David G. Worth to ZBV	Oct 6	appointment	A&H:GP
John Roberts to ZBV	Oct 6	justice of the peace	A&H:GP
Jesse G. Shepherd to ZBV	Oct 6	conscription	A&H:GP
Joseph G. Simmons to ZBV	Oct 6	conscription	A&H:GP
A. G. Foster to ZBV	Oct 6	arrival	A&H:GP
D. W. Hamlin to ZBV	Oct 6	militia	A&H:GP
George Davis to Gen. Kemper	Oct 6	discharge	A&H:GP
J. C. Fowler to ZBV	Oct 6	desertion	A&H:GP
Edward J. Warren to ZBV	Oct 6	conscription	A&H:GP
J. R. Waddy to ZBV	Oct 6	gifts	A&H:GP
ZBV, pardon	Oct 6	John Harwood	A&H:GLB
E. M. Bruce to ZBV	Oct 6	Gen. Martin	A&H:VanPC
William N. H. Smith to ZBV	Oct 6	Plymouth	LC:CSA
John M. Harris to ZBV	Oct 7	supplies	A&H:GP
Otis F. Manson to ZBV	Oct 7	dispatch	A&H:GP
J. W. & E. G. Thompson to ZBV	Oct 7	transfer	A&H:GP
Jesse J. Yeates to ZBV	Oct 7	Home Guard	A&H:GP
James W. Wilson to Samuel R. Chisman	Oct 7	r.r. freight	A&H:GP
Lucius H. Smith & R. H. Bristol to ZBV	Oct 7	praise	A&H:VanPC
R. Bradley to ZBV	Oct 7	McClellan	A&H:VanPC
Daniel L. Russell to ZBV	Oct 8	appointment	A&H:GP
Francis E. Shober to ZBV	Oct 8	conscription	A&H:GP
John H. Cook et al. to ZBV	Oct 8	conscription	A&H:GP
Hannah Parker et al. to ZBV	Oct 8	destitution	A&H:GP
W. H. Croom to ZBV	Oct 9	relief	A&H:GP
Philip Leon to ZBV	Oct 9	*Annie*	A&H:GP
Charles Clark to ZBV	Oct 9	meeting	A&H:GP

Correspondents	Date	Subject	Repository
George Howard to ZBV	Oct 9	appointment	A&H:GP
L. C. Benbury to ZBV	Oct 9	fishing	A&H:GP
Richard C. Gatlin, special order	Oct 9	H. H. Harris	SCH:Sha
M. S. Robins to Peter Mallett	Oct 10	conscription	A&H:GP
Robert R. Heath to Henry Berrier	Oct 10	court writ	A&H:GP
William Robinson to ZBV	Oct 10	conscription	A&H:GP
Joseph B. Coffield &			
William F. Doles to ZBV	Oct 10	clothing	A&H:GP
L. D. Chiles to ZBV	Oct 10	invitation	A&H:GP
Milledge L. Bonham to ZBV	Oct 10	meeting	A&H:GP
Charles Clark to ZBV	Oct 10	meeting	A&H:GP
William Smith to ZBV	Oct 10	dispatch	A&H:GP
J. W. Lash to ZBV	Oct 10	conscription	A&H:GP
J. W. Winstead to ZBV	Oct 10	slaves	A&H:GP
William H. C. Whiting to ZBV	Oct 10	troops	A&H:GP
M. A. Buie to ZBV	Oct 11	war conditions	A&H:GP
Mary P. Moore to ZBV	Oct 11	prisoner exchange	A&H:GP
Mary A. Manson to ZBV	Oct 11	conscription	A&H:GP
John Wilson to ZBV	Oct 11	meeting	A&H:GP
Sarah L. Johnston to ZBV	Oct 11	destitution	A&H:GP
Stephen D. Pool to ZBV	Oct 11	visit	A&H:GP
John Milton to ZBV	Oct 11	meeting	A&H:GLB
M Officer to [?]	Oct 12	ZBV answer	A&H:GP
Braxton Bragg to ZBV	Oct 12	information	A&H:GP
Milledge L. Bonham to ZBV	Oct 12	meeting	A&H:GP
William Smith to ZBV	Oct 12	meeting	A&H:GP
Joseph E. Brown to ZBV	Oct 12	meeting	A&H:GP
Duncan McIntyne to ZBV	Oct 12	transfer	A&H:GP
Ruth A. Allen to ZBV	Oct 12	appointment	A&H:GP
Samuel W. English to ZBV	Oct 12	prisoner exchange	A&H:GP
James A. McHerring to ZBV	Oct 12	transfer	A&H:GP
Isaac Jarrett to ZBV	Oct 12	distilling	A&H:GP
J. J. Young to ZBV	Oct 12	resignation	A&H:VanPC
J. H. Gibson to ZBV	Oct 12	cotton cards	A&H:VanPC
Thomas Carter to ZBV	Oct 13	John White	A&H:GP
B. J. Swe[r]t to ZBV	Oct 13	prisoners	A&H:GP
Thomas H. Watts to ZBV	Oct 13	meeting	A&H:GP
John N. Whitford to ZBV	Oct 13	letter	A&H:GP
Milledge L. Bonham to ZBV	Oct 13	fugitives	A&H:GP
J. [C]. D. Hackney to ZBV	Oct 13	impressment	A&H:GP
John H. Haughton to ZBV	Oct 13	conscription	A&H:GP
T. M. Angel to ZBV	Oct 13	civil unrest	A&H:GP
Richard H. Smith to David A. Barnes	Oct 13	impress slaves	A&H:GP
ZBV to James A. Seddon	Oct 13	conscription	A&H:GLB
Calvin H. Wiley to ZBV	Oct 13	card factory	A&H:VanPC
J. B. Balesley, certificate	Oct 14	WNCRR	A&H:GP

Correspondents	Date	Subject	Repository
W. F. Coldwell to ZBV	Oct 14	conscription	A&H:GP
W. C. Rencher, certificate	Oct 14	conscription	A&H:GP
John Withers to ZBV	Oct 14	conscription	A&H:GP
J. M. Fleming to ZBV	Oct 14	tobacco	A&H:GP
John D. Hyman to ZBV	Oct 14	conscription	A&H:GP
Samuel Musgrave to ZBV	Oct 14	tobacco	A&H:GP
John Milton to ZBV	Oct 14	meeting	A&H:GP
Thomas J. Boykin to ZBV	Oct 14	blockade	A&H:VanPC
Samuel B. Waters to ZBV	Oct 14	pass	A&H:VanPC
Lieut. Wiatt to ZBV	Oct 15	desertion	A&H:GP
John Dawson et al. to ZBV	Oct 15	poor relief	A&H:GP
David A. Barnes to James A. Seddon	Oct 15	conscription	A&H:GP
James A. Seddon to ZBV	Oct 15	conscription	A&H:GP
C. H. Dixon to ZBV	Oct 15	conscription	A&H:GP
Samuel R. Chisman to ZBV	Oct 15	WNCRR	A&H:GP
John A. Gilmer to ZBV	Oct 15	WNCRR	A&H:GP
Parrott Hardee to ZBV	Oct 15	conscription	A&H:GP
Joseph D. Summers to ZBV	Oct 16	conscription	A&H:GP
A. W. Swink to ZBV	Oct 16	conscription	A&H:GP
Luiser Powers to ZBV	Oct 17	conscription	A&H:GP
W. A. E. Roberts to ZBV	Oct 17	shoes	A&H:GP
G. W. Howell to ZBV	Oct 17	appointment	A&H:GP
A. M. Alexander to ZBV	Oct 17	arrest	A&H:GP
S. P. Dula to ZBV	Oct 17	petition	A&H:GP
Calvin H. Wiley to David A. Barnes	Oct 17	conscription	A&H:GP
Law F. Battle to ZBV	Oct 17	conscription	A&H:GP
J. L. Pool to ZBV	Oct 17	transfer	A&H:GP
Thomas H. Watts, petition	Oct 17	extradition	A&H:GP
H. T. Peake to "Conductor of Safe Train"	Oct 17	ZBV pass	A&H:GP
G. B. Harris to ZBV	Oct 18	desertion	A&H:GP
E. J. Blount to ZBV	Oct 18	slaves	A&H:GP
Eliza T. Evans to ZBV	Oct 18	destitution	A&H:GP
B. B. Bingham to ZBV	Oct 18	departure	A&H:GP
Phil B. Hawkins to George Little	Oct 18	conscription	A&H:GP
Henry C. Coe to ZBV	Oct 18	conscription	A&H:GP
A. E. Baird to ZBV	Oct 18	conscription	A&H:VanPC
Alfred M. Scales to ZBV	Oct 18	clothing	ECU:Scal
M. H. Cofer, r.r. ticket	Oct 19	ZBV	A&H:GP
M. H. Cofer, r.r. ticket	Oct 19	J. E. Brown	A&H:GP
George H. Blalock & David Allen to ZBV	Oct 19	transfer	A&H:GP
Richard C. Gatlin, special order	Oct 19	79th Reg't.	SHC:Sha
Philip Leon to ZBV	Oct 20	cargo share	A&H:GP
Thomas J. Boykin to ZBV	Oct 20	passports	A&H:GP
William F. Shinn to ZBV	Oct 20	suit	A&H:GP

Correspondents	*Date*	*Subject*	*Repository*
Herbert Gregory to ZBV	Oct 20	transfer	A&H:GP
Nancy Thomas et al. to ZBV	Oct 21	conscription	A&H:GP
A. Faw et al. to ZBV	Oct 21	Home Guard	A&H:GP
James H. Everett to ZBV	Oct 21	conscription	A&H:GP
Samuel F. Phillips to Henry A. Dowd	Oct 21	blockade account	A&H:GP
A. H. Roulston to ZBV	Oct 21	Baum case	A&H:GP
James W. Wilson to ZBV	Oct 21	WNCC	A&H:GP
O. L. Erwin to ZBV	Oct 21	Home Guard	A&H:GP
R. V. Blackstock to ZBV	Oct 21	impressment	A&H:GP
Jesse G. Shepherd to ZBV	Oct 21	conscription	A&H:GP
Augustus S. Merrimon to ZBV	Oct 22	Col. Henry	A&H:GP
ZBV, agreement	Oct 22	John White	A&H:GP
A. H. Roulston to ZBV	Oct 22	Baum case	A&H:GP
William J. Hardee to ZBV	Oct 22	truce boat	A&H:GP
J. D. Hutchison to ZBV	Oct 22	cards	A&H:GP
W. S. Harris et al. to ZBV	Oct 22	slaves	A&H:GP
E. S. Parker to ZBV	Oct 22	discharge	A&H:GP
Ransom Price et al. to ZBV	Oct 22	conscription	A&H:GP
[?] to Robert E. Lee	Oct 22	desertion	A&H:GP
William A. Bernard et al. to ZBV	Oct 22	transfer	A&H:GP
E. W. Herndon to ZBV	Oct 22	conscription	A&H:VanPC
Augustus S. Merrimon to ZBV	Oct 22	Henry case	Duke:Van
James M. White to ZBV	Oct 23	salt	A&H:GP
A. D. Hooper to ZBV	Oct 23	prison	A&H:GP
Anna C. Pearce to ZBV	Oct 24	troop support	A&H:GP
Martha A. E. Shelton et al. to ZBV	Oct 24	conscription	A&H:GP
Francis E. Shober to ZBV	Oct 24(1)	conscription	A&H:GP
Francis E. Shober to ZBV	Oct 24(2)	conscription	A&H:GP
Thomas H. Watts to ZBV	Oct 24	wine	A&H:GP
Stuart Buchanan to ZBV	Oct 24	certificates	A&H:GP
James T. Green to ZBV	Oct 24	conscription	A&H:GP
John A. Young to ZBV	Oct 24	appointment	A&H:GP
W. Murdock to ZBV	Oct 24	Home Guard	A&H:GP
E. J. Aston et al. to ZBV	Oct 24	conscription	A&H:GP
Thomas J. Boykin to ZBV	Oct 24	clothing	A&H:GP
ZBV, pardon	Oct 24	Moore & Phares	A&H:GLB
Robert B. Gilliam to ZBV	Oct 24	conscription	A&H:VanPC
J. F. Jones to ZBV	Oct 24	conscription	Duke:Van
Daniel L. Russell Jr. to ZBV	Oct 25	conscription	A&H:GP
W. P. Pope to ZBV	Oct 25	certificate	A&H:GP
T. W. Evans, receipt	Oct 25	John White	A&H:GP
John Dawson to ZBV	Oct 25	letter	A&H:GP
T. H. Warren to ZBV	Oct 25	Herbert Warren	A&H:GP
T. C. Davis to ZBV	Oct 25	Private Craig	A&H:GP
Eliza A. Thomas to ZBV	Oct 25	conscription	A&H:GP
A. A. McSwain to ZBV	Oct 25	conscription	A&H:GP

Correspondents	Date	Subject	Repository
Mary P. Moore to ZBV	Oct 25	W. E. Moore	A&H:GP
Fenner B. Satterthwaite to ZBV	Oct 25	conscription	A&H:GP
Henry A. Gilliam &Thomas Bragg to ZBV	Oct 25	habeas corpus	A&H:GLB
Braxton Bragg to ZBV	Oct 25	traitors	A&H:GLB
Neil McKay to ZBV	Oct 26	"articles"	A&H:GP
John A. Gilmer to ZBV	Oct 26	conscription	A&H:GP
M. C. Brown to ZBV	Oct 26	desertion	A&H:GP
W. P. Pope to ZBV	Oct 26	fish roe	A&H:VanPC
Thomas Rees to ZBV	Oct 27	conscription	A&H:GP
J. N. Perryman, certificate	Oct 27	A. F. Dodson	A&H:GP
Frost Snow, affidavit	Oct 27	conscription	A&H:GP
John White to ZBV	Oct 27	blockade	A&H:GP
George Harris to ZBV	Oct 27	conscription	A&H:GP
A. T. Summey to ZBV	Oct 27	disloyalty	A&H:GP
George A. Trenholm to Milledge L. Bonham	Oct 28	regulations	A&H:GP
George V. Strong to ZBV	Oct 28	conscription	A&H:GP
James P. Levy to ZBV	Oct 28	thefts	A&H:GP
R. C. Pearson to ZBV	Oct 28	artillery	A&H:GP
Joseph E. Brown to ZBV	Oct 28	George Harris	A&H:GP
Robert H. Cowan to ZBV	Oct 29	r.r. iron	A&H:GP
Thomas J. Sumner to ZBV	Oct 29	train	A&H:GP
M. M. Withers to ZBV	Oct 29	conscription	A&H:GP
W. W. Thornton to ZBV	Oct 29	wheat crop	A&H:GP
R. H. Graves to ZBV	Oct 29	conscription	A&H:GP
E. Murray and Co. to ZBV	Oct 29	John White	A&H:GP
W. R. Smith to ZBV	Oct 29	conscription	A&H:GP
Tod R. Caldwell to ZBV	Oct 29	conscription	A&H:GP
Thomas M. Holt & George W. Swepson to ZBV	Oct 29	conscription	A&H:GP
Robert H. Cowan to ZBV	Oct 29	r.r. iron	A&H:GLB
Alexander Collie to ZBV	Oct 29	cotton account	A&H:VanPC
C. L. Randolph to ZBV	Oct 30	cloth	A&H:GP
Nathaniel Boyden to ZBV	Oct 30	conscription	A&H:GP
David G. Worth to ZBV	Oct 30	conscription	A&H:GP
William Smith to ZBV	Oct 30	cloth	A&H:GP
Daniel Forest to ZBV	Oct 31	assignment	A&H:GP
Ebenezer Emmons Jr. to ZBV	Oct 31	grapes	A&H:GP
Jacob Siler to ZBV	Oct 31	Cherokee bonds	A&H:GP
[?] to ZBV	Oct 31	conscription	A&H:GP
Washington Baird to ZBV	Oct 31	Confed. Manual	A&H:GP
Jacob Siler to ZBV	Oct 31	Cherokee bonds	A&H:GLB
Ebenezer Emmons Jr. to ZBV	Oct 31	grapes	A&H:GLB
Robert Ould to ZBV	Oct 31	prison supplies	A&H:GLB
Alfred M. Scales to ZBV	Oct 31	exemptions	A&H:VanPC

Correspondents	Date	Subject	Repository
Mrs. L. O'B. Branch to ZBV	Oct 31	recommendation	A&H:VanPC
R. B. Wood to ZBV	Nov 1	Home Guard	A&H:GP
William H. C. Whiting to ZBV	Nov 1	Tallahassee, Chickamauga	A&H:GP
Nancy P. Richardson to ZBV	Nov 1	poor relief	A&H:GP
Braxton Bragg to Richard C. Gatlin	Nov 1	state troops	A&H:GP
Wiley T. Walker et al. to ZBV	Nov 1	conscription	A&H:GP
A. H. Baird to ZBV	Nov 1	deserters	A&H:GP
J. Ramsey Dills to ZBV	Nov 2	prisoners	A&H:GP
James W. Clark to ZBV	Nov 2	poor relief	A&H:GP
David G. Worth to ZBV	Nov 3	recommendation	A&H:GP
J. R. Neill to ZBV	Nov 3	Senior Reserves	A&H:GP
A. G. Foster to ZBV	Nov 3	conscription	A&H:GP
W. O. Harrelson to ZBV	Nov 3	conscription	A&H:GP
M. D. Craton to ZBV	Nov 3	conscription	A&H:GP
P. Leon to ZBV	Nov 4	impressment	A&H:GP
G. H. White to ZBV	Nov 4	poor relief	A&H:GP
William J. Green to ZBV	Nov 4	appointment	A&H:GP
Benjamin A. Moody to ZBV	Nov 4	prisoners	A&H:GP
Ralph P. Buxton to ZBV	Nov 4	impressment	A&H:GP
Calvin H. Wiley to ZBV	Nov 4	education	A&H:GP
Robert H. Chapman to ZBV	Nov 4	commission	A&H:GP
J. W. Cook to ZBV	Nov 5	certificate	A&H:GP
T. C. Westall to ZBV	Nov 5	detail	A&H:GP
W. H. Hold[eness] to ZBV	Nov 5	sorghum	A&H:GP
Sarah E. Jackson to ZBV	Nov 5	discharge	A&H:GP
J. D. Patterson to ZBV	Nov 5	horse thieves	A&H:GP
J. C. Whitson to ZBV	Nov 5	gift	A&H:GP
C. W. Trice to ZBV	Nov 5	appointment	A&H:GP
James W. Cooke to ZBV	Nov 5	liquor	A&H:GP
George A. Trenholm to ZBV	Nov. 5	cotton warrants	A&H:VanPC
James Sloan to ZBV	Nov 5	cloth	A&H:VanPC
T. H. Harrington to ZBV	Nov 6	impressment	A&H:GP
Q. A. Hartsfield to ZBV	Nov 6	conscription	A&H:GP
E. R. Liles to ZBV	Nov 6	Home Guard	A&H:GP
Louisa Gray to ZBV	Nov 7	conscription	A&H:GP
Eli W. Hall to ZBV	Nov 7	senate resignation	A&H:GP
Thomas Williams, certification	Nov 7	poor warden	A&H:GP
R. C. Holmes to ZBV	Nov 7	conscription	A&H:GP
James R. Powers to ZBV	Nov 7	prisoners	A&H:GP
Francis E. Shober to ZBV	Nov 7	Home Guard	A&H:GP
A. M. Powell to ZBV	Nov 7	gift	A&H:VanPC
C. Wooten to ZBV	Nov 7	gift	A&H:VanPC
Andrew S. Kemp to Jesse G. Shepherd	Nov 8	Home Guard	A&H:GP
Dagald Blue, certification	Nov 8	county solicitor	A&H:GP
Smith H. Powell to ZBV	Nov 8	soldiers' pay	A&H:GP

Correspondents	Date	Subject	Repository
R. F. Simonton to ZBV	Nov 8	Senior Reserves	A&H:GP
George A. Dancy, certification	Nov 8	card agent	A&H:GP
Allen T. Davidson to ZBV	Nov 8	cotton cargo	A&H:VanPC
Nancy Bird to ZBV	Nov 9	conscription	A&H:GP
George A. Dancy, certification	Nov 9	card agent	A&H:GP
D. T. Ashburn to ZBV	Nov 9	desertion	A&H:GP
James M. Spainhour to ZBV	Nov 9	Home Guard	A&H:GP
H. Cabiness to ZBV	Nov 9	appointment	A&H:GP
P. H. Winston to ZBV	Nov 9	Lincoln election	A&H:GP
H. D. Lee to ZBV	Nov 10	conscription	A&H:GP
William H. Maynard to ZBV	Nov 10	prisoners	A&H:GP
Eliza Evans to ZBV	Nov 11	hardship	A&H:GP
P. H. Winston to ZBV	Nov 11	appointment	A&H:GP
Thomas J. Wilson to ZBV	Nov 11	Home Guard	A&H:GP
J. K. Blankenship to ZBV	Nov 11	details	A&H:GP
Joshua Boner to ZBV	Nov 11	conscription	A&H:GP
J. H. Colfer to ZBV	Nov 11	conscription	A&H:GP
William Coker to ZBV	Nov 11	conscription	A&H:GP
John White to ZBV	Nov 12	blockade	A&H:GP
Nancy J. King et al. to ZBV	Nov 12	Home Guard	A&H:GP
S. P. Demlass to ZBV	Nov 12	Cliosophic Society	A&H:GP
Catherine Watson to ZBV	Nov 12	detail	A&H:GP
W. A. Coe to ZBV	Nov 12	application	A&H:GP
T. J. McMillen to ZBV	Nov 12	Salisbury	A&H:GP
William Smith to ZBV	Nov 12	cloth	A&H:GLB
Thomas J. Boykin to ZBV	Nov 12	steamer cargo	A&H:VanPC
W. J. Brown to ZBV	Nov 12	legal case payment	A&H:VanPC
A. A. Mitchell to ZBV	Nov 13	Senior Reserves	A&H:GP
E. Cranor to ZBV	Nov 13	robbery	A&H:GP
R. Bradley to ZBV	Nov 13	Wil. & Man. R.R.	A&H:GP
E. P. Moore to Uncle Robert	Nov 14	appointment	A&H:GP
B. T. Pearson to ZBV	Nov 14	appointment	A&H:GP
Francis E. Shober to Richard C. Gatlin	Nov 14	Home Guard	A&H:GP
Elijah Standly & P. R. Temple to ZBV	Nov 14	conscription	A&H:GP
Writ of election	Nov 14	senate vacancy	A&H:GLB
William H. Oliver to ZBV	Nov 14	gift	A&H:VanPC
Calvin H. Wiley to ZBV	Nov 15	education meeting	A&H:GP
Robert J. Townes, resolutions	Nov 15	Texas & peace	A&H:GP
Maria L. Samkin to ZBV	Nov 15	discharge	A&H:GP
Stuart Buchanan & Co. to ZBV	Nov 15	meeting	A&H:GP
J. D. Shaw to ZBV	Nov 15	conscription	A&H:GP
William Smith to ZBV	Nov 15	salt	A&H:GP
David G. Worth to ZBV	Nov 15	salt workers	A&H:GP
Braxton Bragg to ZBV	Nov 15	salt works	A&H:GLB
Milledge L. Bonham to ZBV	Nov 16	S.C. landholders	A&H:GP
Martha Lee to ZBV	Nov 16	tax	A&H:GP

Correspondents	Date	Subject	Repository
William M. Stevenson to ZBV	Nov 16	desertion pardon	A&H:GP
M. Fetter to ZBV	Nov 16	promotion	A&H:GP
Sarah F. Goodridge to ZBV	Nov 16	transportation	A&H:GP
Francis E. Shober to ZBV	Nov 16	freight restricted	A&H:VanPC
E. O. Wright to ZBV	Nov 17	devalued currency	A&H:GP
R. H. Small to Joseph Etheridge	Nov 17	cotton	A&H:GP
Richard Sterling to ZBV	Nov 17	poor relief agent	A&H:GP
Thomas M. Holt to ZBV	Nov 17	gift	A&H:VanPC
Sewall L. Fremont to ZBV	Nov 18	internal improvements	A&H:GP
James K. McDonald to ZBV	Nov 18	desertion pardon	A&H:GP
W. A. Houck to ZBV	Nov 18	conscription	A&H:GP
W. L. Archibald to ZBV	Nov 18	slave laborers	A&H:GP
Eli W. Hall to ZBV	Nov 18	senate resignation	A&H:GP
Bryan Smith to ZBV	Nov 18	desertion pardon	A&H:GP
Sam M. Hughes to ZBV	Nov 18	disaffection	A&H:GP
Robert Ould to ZBV	Nov 18	prisoners	A&H:VanPC
Lee Spach to ZBV	Nov 19	uniform cloth	A&H:GP
W. H. McNeil to ZBV	Nov 19	civil unrest	A&H:GP
J. G. Ferrell et al. to ZBV	Nov 19	prisoners	A&H:GP
Mrs. T. L. Skinner to ZBV	Nov 19	slaves	A&H:GP
Thomas J. Sumner to ZBV	Nov 19	r.r. rates	A&H:GP
B. R. Johnson to ZBV	Nov 19	cloth	A&H:VanPC
C. D. Smith to ZBV	Nov 20	Thomas's Legion	A&H:GP
Henry A. Gilliam to ZBV	Nov 20	appointment	A&H:GP
J. H. Brien to ZBV	Nov 20	Morganton	A&H:GP
N. F. Johnston to ZBV	Nov 20	prisoner exchange	A&H:GP
Francis Parker, extract	Nov 20	W. M. Stevenson	A&H:GP
Eady Herrick to ZBV	Nov 20	discharge	A&H:GP
Theophilus H. Holmes to ZBV	Nov 20	conscription	A&H:GP
Winston Fulton to Edward J. Hale	Nov 20	desertion	A&H:VanPC
Nathaniel A. Boyden to ZBV	Nov 20	salt	A&H:VanPC
James H. Everitt to ZBV	Nov 21	new reg't.	A&H:GP
A. D. Waddell to ZBV	Nov 21	slaves	A&H:GP
ZBV et al., endorsements	Nov 21	soldier's return	A&H:GP
J. Ramsay Dills to ZBV	Nov 21	prisoners	A&H:GP
T. V. Jordan to ZBV	Nov 21	appointment	A&H:GP
M. J. McSween to ZBV	Nov 21	apology	A&H:VanPC
William R. Utley to ZBV	Nov 22	conscription	A&H:GP
Jeremy F. Gilmer to ZBV	Nov 22	appointments	A&H:GP
John T. Beaman to provost marshal	Nov 22	disloyalty	A&H:GP
E. Murray & Co. to ZBV	Nov 22	steamers	A&H:GP
Theodore J. Hughes to John Devereaux	Nov 22	rosin & workers	A&H:GP
George H. Taylor to ZBV	Nov 22	clothing	A&H:GP
William Howard to ZBV	Nov 22	cotton & wool	A&H:GP

Correspondents	Date	Subject	Repository
W. W. Peirce to ZBV	Nov 22	impressment	A&H:GP
John D. Hyman to ZBV	Nov 22	meeting invitation	A&H:VanPC
George H. Faribault to ZBV	Nov 22	resignation	A&H:VanPC
Joseph Wileford to ZBV	Nov 23	impressment	A&H:GP
John A. Gilmer to ZBV	Nov 23	senate election	A&H:VanPC
William H. C. Whiting to ZBV	Nov 24	Wilmington	A&H:GP
Daniel [S.] Hill to ZBV	Nov 24	prisoners	A&H:GP
Fannie E. Mitchum to ZBV	Nov 24	impressment	A&H:GP
G. C. Moses to ZBV	Nov 24	Home Guard	A&H:VanPC
Drury Lacey to ZBV	Nov 24	recommendation	A&H:VanPC
Mrs. B. A. Capeheart to ZBV	Nov 24	gift	A&H:VanPC
J. G. Blackstock to ZBV	Nov 25	transfer	A&H:GP
J. H. Lee to ZBV	Nov 25	Salisbury	A&H:GP
W. A. Parham to ZBV	Nov 25	unlawful trade	A&H:GP
Stephen D. Wallace to ZBV	Nov 25	trade permission	A&H:GP
E. A. Vogler to ZBV	Nov 25	detail	A&H:GP
David G. Worth to ZBV	Nov 25	salt works	A&H:GP
J. F. Alderman to ZBV	Nov 25	flour	A&H:VanPC
Richard C. Gatlin, Special Order	Nov 25	Home Guard	SHC:Sha
Julian C. Hines to ZBV	Nov 26	appointment	A&H:GP
Samuel F. Phillips to ZBV	Nov 26	House clerk	A&H:GP
Watson P. Abram to ZBV	Nov 26	furlough	A&H:GP
Z. C. Hardin to ZBV	Nov 26	wounded soldiers	A&H:GP
W. A. Parham to ZBV	Nov 26	unlawful trade	A&H:GP
W. A. Gordon to ZBV	Nov 26	cadets	A&H:GP
Mrs. L. O'B. Branch to ZBV	Nov 26	son's appointment	A&H:GP
R. C. Pearson to ZBV	Nov 27	appointment	A&H:GP
William H. C. Whiting to ZBV	Nov 27	D. L. Russell	A&H:GP
Augustus S. Merrimon	Nov 28	J. L. Henry	A&H:GP
J. J. Whichard et al. to ZBV	Nov 28	prisoners	A&H:GP
Jeremy F. Gilmer to ZBV	Nov 28	N.C. reg't.	A&H:GP
Evengelical Tract Society, publication	Nov 28	donations	A&H:GP
W. C. Kerr to John C. Brown	Nov 28	salt works	A&H:GP
A. M. Powell to ZBV	Nov 28	foodstuffs	A&H:VanPC
Sallie E. Caudell to ZBV	Nov 28	Masons' charity	A&H:VanPC
W. P. Pope to ZBV	Nov 29	slaves & deserters	A&H:GP
Edward J. Hale to ZBV	Nov 29	senate election	A&H:VanPC
E. Murray & Co. to ZBV	Nov 29	*Advance*	A&H:VanPC
P. B. Hawkins to ZBV	Nov 30	salt transport	A&H:GP
E. C. Shaffner et al. to ZBV	Nov 30	band concerts	A&H:GP
Laurence S. Baker to ZBV	Nov 31[0]	recommendation	A&H:GP
T. Allen to ZBV	Nov 30	tax laws	A&H:GLB
John C. McMillan to ZBV	Nov n.d.	desertion pardon	A&H:GP
Washington C. Kerr to ZBV	Dec 1	state geologist	A&H:GP
John H. Haughton to ZBV	Dec 1	river meeting	A&H:GP
James G. Gibbs to ZBV	Dec 1	cloth & wire	A&H:GP

Correspondents	Date	Subject	Repository
Regimental lists	Dec 1	5th & 6th N.C. Reg'ts.	A&H:GP
Thomas C. Fuller to ZBV	Dec 2	information	A&H:GP
P. B. Hawkins to ZBV	Dec 2	salt	A&H:GP
P. B. Hawkins to ZBV	Dec 3	salt	A&H:GP
George W. Palmer to ZBV	Dec 3	gift	A&H:VanPC
Jeptha M. Israel to ZBV	Dec 4	conscription	A&H:GP
T. N. Ramsay to ZBV	Dec 4	transfer	A&H:GP
Mrs. James Southgate to ZBV	Dec 4	husband	A&H:GP
Jeptha M. Israel to ZBV	Dec 4	conscription	A&H:GP
A. Fulkerson to ZBV	Dec 4	prisoner	A&H:VanPC
Julius A. Lineback to ZBV	Dec 5	furlough	A&H:GP
Mary E. Mabry et al. to ZBV	Dec 5	furlough	A&H:GP
John Kimberly to ZBV	Dec 5	commission	A&H:GP
L. D. Childs to ZBV	Dec 5	conscription	A&H:GP
Henderson Jones to ZBV	Dec 5	pardon	A&H:GP
John W. Johnston, statement	Dec 5	conscription	A&H:GP
John M. Tate to ZBV	Dec 5	saddle	A&H:GP
S. P. Brittan to ZBV	Dec 5	distilling	A&H:GP
Ellen Poole to ZBV	Dec 5	husband	A&H:GP
Jeptha M. Israel to ZBV	Dec 6	conscription	A&H:GP
George Harris, certificate	Dec 6	coal	A&H:GP
L. P. Olds to ZBV	Dec 6	son	A&H:GP
J. T. O'Reilly, certification	Dec 6	coal	A&H:GP
Mrs. A. S. [Lirely] to ZBV	Dec 6	relief society	A&H:GP
Henry Savage to E. Murray	Dec 6	specie	A&H:GP
John A. Gilmer to ZBV	Dec 6	senate election	A&H:VanPC
Alex Keith, receipt	Dec 7	Robert B. Vance	A&H:GP
L. R. Cosby to ZBV	Dec 7	dispatch	A&H:GP
J. Rolen to ZBV	Dec 7	appointment	A&H:GP
P. B. Hawkins to ZBV	Dec 8	salt workers	A&H:GP
J. P. McPherson to ZBV	Dec 8	conscription	A&H:VanPC
W. Murdock to ZBV	Dec 9	western counties	A&H:GP
A. M. Powell to ZBV	Dec 9	mfg. industry	A&H:GP
P. B. Hawkins to ZBV	Dec 9	salt	A&H:GP
P. B. Hawkins to ZBV	Dec 9	governors & salt	A&H:GP
E. C. Brown to ZBV	Dec 9	detail	A&H:GP
James W. Wilson to ZBV	Dec 9	salt	A&H:GP
Samuel Jamison to ZBV	Dec 9	pardon	A&H:GP
James P. Leak et al. to ZBV	Dec 9	special court	A&H:GP
Augustus S. Merrimon to ZBV	Dec 9	special court	A&H:GP
Stuart Buchanan & Co. to ZBV	Dec 10	wood train	A&H:GP
J.W. Cole to ZBV	Dec 10	transfer	A&H:GP
Collett Leventhorpe to ZBV	Dec 10	Home Guard	A&H:GP
Collett Leventhorpe to ZBV	Dec 10	battle plans	A&H:GP
James B. Campbell to ZBV	Dec 10	clemency	A&H:GP

Correspondents	Date	Subject	Repository
Collett Leventhorpe to Richard C. Gatlin	Dec 10	reinforcements	A&H:GP
Collett Leventhorpe to ZBV	Dec 10	Federal retreat	A&H:GP
Collett Leventhorpe to ZBV	Dec 10	r.r. bridge	A&H:GP
C. R. Thomas, certification	Dec 10	salt	A&H:GP
Mary A. Mosby to ZBV	Dec 10	women & slaves	A&H:GP
J. W. Slocumb, certification	Dec 10	C. A. Guffy	A&H:GP
E. Murray & Co. to ZBV	Dec 10	cask	A&H:VanPC
J. Henderson Jones to ZBV	Dec 11	pardon	A&H:GP
James P. Leak to ZBV	Dec 11	court commission	A&H:GP
William H. C. Whiting to ZBV	Dec 11	reinforcements	A&H:GP
E. Murray to ZBV	Dec 12	coal	A&H:GP
H. H. Staples to ZBV	Dec 12	W. A. Grabowsky	A&H:GP
H. Hutt to ZBV	Dec 12	slave revolt	A&H:GP
William M. Shipp, commission	Dec 12	special court	A&H:GLB
John C. Mason to ZBV	Dec 13	James Cagle	A&H:GP
Robert DeSchweinitz to ZBV	Dec 13	Salem Academy	A&H:GP
John A. McArthur to ZBV	Dec 13	disloyalty	A&H:GP
J. B. [Tilghman] to ZBV	Dec 13	Roanoke Lit. Society	A&H:GP
Anonymous to ZBV	Dec 13	slave revolt	A&H:GP
E. Burke Haywood to ZBV	Dec 13	medical report	A&H:GP
H. Y. Gash to ZBV	Dec 13	prisoners	A&H:GP
Charles Manly to ZBV	Dec 13	recommendation	A&H:VanPC
L. E. Penland to ZBV	Dec 14	transfer	A&H:GP
Peter Mallett to ZBV	Dec 14	conscription	A&H:GP
Ralph P. Buxton to ZBV	Dec 14	special court	A&H:GP
Samuel F. Phillips to ZBV	Dec 14	impressment	A&H:GP
John A. Boyden to ZBV	Dec 14	gift	A&H:VanPC
S. E. Grandy to ZBV	Dec 15	clothing	A&H:GP
T. M. Jones to ZBV	Dec 15	provisions	A&H:GP
Robert S. French, commission	Dec 15	special court	A&H:GLB
W. D. Smith to ZBV	Dec 16	John White	A&H:GP
Robert R. Bridgers to ZBV	Dec 16	debt & bonds	A&H:GP
John Roberts to ZBV	Dec 16	cavalry raids	A&H:GP
Richard S. Donnell to ZBV	Dec 16	slave treatment	A&H:GP
James McCoy to ZBV	Dec 17	Union troops	A&H:GP
Julia E. Armstrong to ZBV	Dec 17	discharge	A&H:GP
R. S. McDonald to ZBV	Dec 17	slave revolt	A&H:GP
Robert E. Lee to ZBV	Dec 18	Wilmington	A&H:GP
James R. Love to ZBV	Dec 18	Federal raids	A&H:GP
William E. Earle to ZBV	Dec 18	deserters	A&H:GP
James A. Seddon to ZBV	Dec 18	clothing	A&H:GLB
Henry J. B. Clark et al. to ZBV	Dec 19	pardon	A&H:GP
George W. Munford to ZBV	Dec 19	salt regulations	A&H:GP
W. B. Wellons to ZBV	Dec 19	evangelical tract	A&H:GP
John R. Clements to ZBV	Dec 19	wives' visit	A&H:GP

Correspondents	Date	Subject	Repository
Robert H. Cowan to ZBV	Dec 19	r.r. resolutions	A&H:GP
Richard S. Donnell to ZBV	Dec 19	disabled veterans	A&H:GP
Richard S. Donnell to ZBV	Dec 19	naval stores	A&H:GP
William H. C. Whiting to ZBV	Dec 19	Wilmington	A&H:VanPC
Martin Leach to ZBV	Dec 20	furlough	A&H:GP
A. B. [Glenn] to J. H. Brown	Dec 20	resignation	A&H:GP
J. H. Abell to ZBV	Dec 20	surplus corn	A&H:GP
ZBV to Charles Phillips	Dec 20	export permission	A&H:GP
Robert E. Lee to ZBV	Dec 21	Wilmington troops	A&H:GP
B. B. Walker to ZBV	Dec 21	slave's defiance	A&H:GP
H. J. Dennis to ZBV	Dec 21	conscription	A&H:GP
L. P. Olds to ZBV	Dec 21	cotton stores	A&H:GP
William Murdock to ZBV	Dec 21	slaves in army	A&H:GP
J. Henry Smith to ZBV	Dec 21	pardon	A&H:GP
Henry B. Clark et al. to ZBV	Dec 21	pardon	A&H:GP
W. B. Gulick, memorandum	Dec 21	payment	A&H:GP
R. L. Coltrain et al. to ZBV	Dec 21	pardon	A&H:GP
Charles H. Newbold to ZBV	Dec 22	passport	A&H:GP
Collett Leventhorpe to ZBV	Dec 22	enemy landing	A&H:GP
Richard S. Donnell, resolution	Dec 22	salt transport	A&H:GP
G. C. Casy to ZBV	Dec 22	deserters	A&H:GP
Fred L. Roberts to ZBV	Dec 22	cotton transport	A&H:GP
Collett Leventhorpe to ZBV	Dec 23	gunboats	A&H:GP
Will L. [Scott] to ZBV	Dec 23	pardon	A&H:GP
Richard S. Donnell, resolution	Dec 23	prisoners	A&H:GP
W. L. Long to ZBV	Dec 24	pardon	A&H:GP
J. D. Patterson to ZBV	Dec 24	disloyalty	A&H:GP
Richard C. Gatlin to ZBV	Dec 24	transfers	A&H:GP
O. P. Meares to ZBV	Dec 24	troops trains	A&H:GP
Braxton Bragg to ZBV	Dec 24	Fort Fisher	A&H:GP
H. Walser to ZBV	Dec 24	furlough	A&H:GP
Stephen Frontis to ZBV	Dec 24	discharge	A&H:GP
A Southern Woman to ZBV	Dec 24	Home Guard	A&H:GP
Daniel H. Hill to ZBV	Dec 24	N.C. command	A&H:VanPC
W. W. Bramble to ZBV	Dec 25	transfer	A&H:GP
Thomas D. Hoge to ZBV	Dec 25	cotton, bacon	A&H:GP
[?] to ZBV	Dec 25	travel request	A&H:GP
Thomas J. Sumner to ZBV	Dec 25	troop trains	A&H:GP
S. R. Chisman to ZBV	Dec 25	supplies	A&H:GP
H. Hunt to ZBV	Dec 25	raids & slave revolts	A&H:GP
Archer Anderson to ZBV	Dec 26	Fort Fisher	A&H:GP
Braxton Bragg to Laurence S. Baker	Dec 26	C. Leventhorpe	A&H:GP
Richard C. Gatlin to ZBV	Dec 26	Kinston & Wilmington	A&H:GP
Richard C. Gatlin to ZBV	Dec 26	Goldsboro	A&H:GP
James L. Henry to ZBV	Dec 26	meeting	A&H:GP

Correspondents	*Date*	*Subject*	*Repository*
Stephen D. Pool to ZBV	Dec 26	troops	A&H:GP
T. D. Hogge to ZBV	Dec 26	bacon, ammunition	A&H:GP
T. D. Hogge to ZBV	Dec 26	ZBV message	A&H:GP
Patrick H. Winston to ZBV	Dec 26	ammunition	A&H:GP
Robert B. Gilliam to ZBV	Dec 26	conscription	A&H:GP
Augustus S. Merrimon to ZBV	Dec 26	reserve notes	A&H:GP
Will L. Scott to ZBV	Dec 26	pardon	A&H:GP
L. Hiatt to ZBV	Dec 26	J. H. Jones case	A&H:GP
George W. Swepson to ZBV	Dec 26	passport	A&H:GP
William W. Davis to ZBV	Dec 26	discharge	A&H:GP
James Calloway to ZBV	Dec 27	conscription	A&H:GP
Collett Leventhorpe to ZBV	Dec 27	Wilmington	A&H:GP
J. M. Atkinson et al. to ZBV	Dec 27	ambulance committee	A&H:GP
Richard C. Gatlin to ZBV	Dec 27	Goldsboro	A&H:GP
Collett Leventhorpe to ZBV	Dec 27	Goldsboro	A&H:GP
R. [Y.] McAdam to ZBV	Dec 27	pardon	A&H:GP
Jeptha M. Israel to ZBV	Dec 27	Saltville	A&H:GP
Mrs. Richard F. Drake to ZBV	Dec 27	conscription	A&H:GP
J. E. Cain to ZBV	Dec 27	appointment	A&H:VanPC
George Little to ZBV	Dec 28	J. H. Jones case	A&H:GP
William A. Graham to ZBV	Dec 28	Raleigh arrival	A&H:GP
J. G. Burr to ZBV	Dec 28	Masonboro Sound	A&H:GP
James M. Scruggs to ZBV	Dec 28	farming detail	A&H:GP
Giles Leitch to ZBV	Dec 28	special court	A&H:GP
Stephen Frontis to ZBV	Dec 28	discharge	A&H:GP
Mrs. Julius A. Robbins to ZBV	Dec 29	wool	A&H:GP
R. Street to ZBV	Dec 29	conscription	A&H:GP
A. Landis to ZBV	Dec 29	cotton & wool cards	A&H:GP
James H. Mayfield to ZBV	Dec 29	discharge	A&H:GP
Thomas J. Judkins to ZBV	Dec 29	furlough	A&H:GP
John M. Morehead to ZBV	Dec 29	doctor	A&H:GP
Harriet S. Briles to ZBV	Dec 30	conscription	A&H:GP
M. M. Jones to ZBV	Dec 30	loyalty	A&H:GP
Nina to ZBV	Dec 30	conscription	A&H:GP
Andrew Barnard to ZBV	Dec 30	horse theft	A&H:GP
J. McCormick to ZBV	Dec 30	appointment	A&H:GP
R. Bradbury to ZBV	Dec 30	transfer	A&H:VanPC
A. H. Merritt to ZBV	Dec 31	leave of absence	A&H:GP
R. Brantley to ZBV	Dec 31	appointment	A&H:GP
J. H. Brown to ZBV	Dec 31	S. B. Glenns	A&H:GP
Ralph Gonell to ZBV	Dec 31	discharge	A&H:GP
J. W. [Alspaugh] to ZBV	Dec 31	furlough	A&H:GP
J. H. Horner to ZBV	Dec 31	furlough	A&H:GP
William M. Tanner to ZBV	Dec 31	furlough	A&H:GP
Benjamin Larrier to ZBV	Dec 31	furlough	A&H:GP

Correspondents	Date	Subject	Repository
W. W. Bramble to ZBV	Dec 31	transfer	A&H:GP
Samuel McD. Tate to ZBV	Dec 31	poor relief	A&H:GP
Patrick H. Winston to ZBV	Dec n.d.	Petersburg trip	A&H:GP
Thomas J. Sumner to ZBV	Dec n.d.	Robert F. Hoke	A&H:GP
William H. C. Whiting to ZBV	n.m. 2	*Advance*	A&H:GP
Thomas Carter to David A. Barnes	n.m. 2	cotton cards	A&H:GP
Theodore Andreae to ZBV	n.m. 4	*Hansa*	A&H:GP
Power, Low & Co. to ZBV	n.m. 4	*Advance*	A&H:GP
Theodore Andreae to ZBV	n.m. 5	*Annie*	A&H:GP
Power, Low & Co. to ZBV	n.m. 8	*Advance*	A&H:GP
Theodore Andreae to ZBV	n.m. 8	*Don; Hansa*	A&H:GP
Robert H. Cowan to ZBV	n.m. 8	meeting	A&H:GP
Thomas Carter to ZBV	n.m. 9	*Advance*	A&H:GP
A. J. Harris to ZBV	n.m. 12	resignation	A&H:GP
W. L. Young to ZBV	n.m. 13	artillery	A&H:GP
Milledge L. Bonham to ZBV	n.m. 13	[boats]	A&H:GP
H. Fitzhugh to T. B. Power	n.m. 14	meeting	A&H:GP
W. L. Young to ZBV	n.m. 14	artillery	A&H:GP
Phillip Leon to ZBV	n.m. 14	*Hansa*	A&H:GP
H. J. Harris to ZBV	n.m. 15	telegram	A&H:GP
Power, Low & Co. to ZBV	n.m. 15	*Advance*	A&H:GP
Wilmington to Raleigh	n.m. 16	Capt. Farris	A&H:GP
John R. Lane to ZBV	n.m. 16	furloughs	A&H:GP
William H. C. Whiting to ZBV	n.m. 17	*Advance*	A&H:GP
Robert F. Hoke to ZBV	n.m. 17	H. Marshall; D. Bell	A&H:GP
R. H. Maury & Co. to ZBV	n.m. 17	Phillip Leon	A&H:GP
Phillip Leon to ZBV	n.m. 17	departure	A&H:GP
Power, Low & Co. to ZBV	n.m. 17	*Advance*	A&H:GP
Thomas Settle, statement	n.m. 17	slave murder	A&H:GP
T. G. Walton to ZBV	n.m. 18	Home Guard	A&H:GP
W. W. Poisson to ZBV	n.m. 18	speech	A&H:GP
Thomas H. Boykin to ZBV	n.m. 18	departure	A&H:GP
Henry A. Dowd to ZBV	n.m. 19	steamer cargo	A&H:GP
David A. Barnes to ZBV	n.m. 19	manifest	A&H:GP
Laurence S. Baker to ZBV	n.m. 19	troops	A&H:GP
James Longstreet to ZBV	n.m. 19	troop clothing	A&H:GP
Sewall L. Fremont to ZBV	n.m. 20	*Advance*	A&H:GP
Power, Low & Co. to ZBV	n.m. 20	Thomas Boykin	A&H:GP
Joseph D. Flanner to ZBV	n.m. 21	steamer cargo	A&H:GP
George Little to ZBV	n.m. 21	*Advance*	A&H:GP
David A. Barnes to ZBV	n.m. 21	Thomas Boykin	A&H:GP
Allen T. Davidson to ZBV	n.m. 21	Robert B. Vance	A&H:GP
Edward Warren to ZBV	n.m. 22	*Advance*	A&H:GP
Thomas M. Crossan to ZBV	n.m. 22	*Cape Fear*	A&H:GP
D. Kahnweiler to ZBV	n.m. 25	John H. Winder	A&H:GP
Joseph H. Flanner to ZBV	n.m. 26	cargo	A&H:GP

Correspondents	Date	Subject	Repository
G. C. Moses to ZBV	n.m. 28	conscription	A&H:GP
Sewall L. Fremont to ZBV	n.m. 28	*Advance*	A&H:GP
Theodore Andreae to ZBV	n.m. 29	*Advance*	A&H:GP
John J. Guthrie to ZBV	n.m. 29	*Advance*	A&H:GP
John H. Winder to David A. Barnes	n.m. 31	passports	A&H:GP
John White to ZBV	n.m. n.d.	Europe sales	A&H:GP
Poem	n.m. n.d.	Unionist sentiment	A&H:GP
J. M. Leach to ZBV	n.m. n.d.	election certificate	A&H:VanPC
J. M. Leach to ZBV	n.m. n.d.	gub. election	A&H:VanPC
Thomas L. Cotton to E. J. Hale & Sons	n.m. n.d.	conscription	A&H:VanPC
O. McMath to ZBV	n.m. n.d.	gub. election	A&H:VanPC
H. C. Jones to ZBV	n.m. n.d.	gub. election	A&H:VanPC
M. L. Wiggins to ZBV	Jan 1	discharge	A&H:GP
Amos Hildebrand et al. to ZBV	Jan 1	detail	A&H:GP
William B. Smith & Co. to ZBV	Jan 1	literary weekly	A&H:VanPC
ZBV to Robert S. French	Jan 2	special court	A&H:GLB
Bedford Brown to ZBV	Jan 3	Home Guard	A&H:GP
H. E. Colton to ZBV	Jan 3	appointment	A&H:GP
Alexander R. Lawton to ZBV	Jan 3	freight engines	A&H:GP
James B. Jordan to ZBV	Jan 3	prisoners	A&H:GP
W. Parham to ZBV	Jan 3	conscription	A&H:GP
Joshua Boner to ZBV	Jan 4	conscription	A&H:GP
A. H. Baird to ZBV	Jan 4	pants & boots	A&H:GP
Richard H. Scales to ZBV	Jan 5	Home Guard	A&H:GP
Sue O. Comly to ZBV	Jan 5	destitution	A&H:GP
J. Wilkes et al. to ZBV	Jan 5	conscription	A&H:GP
A. M. Alexander to ZBV	Jan 5	rent	A&H:VanPC
H. A. Davis to ZBV	Jan 6	detail	A&H:GP
George A. Trenholm to ZBV	Jan 6	Confed. debt	A&H:GP
J. T. Warden, certification	Jan 6	special court	A&H:GP
J. P. Mabry to ZBV	Jan 6	rifles	A&H:GP
Sophie L. Colton to ZBV	Jan 6	appointment	A&H:VanPC
R. [Bradbury] to ZBV	Jan 6	business applicant	A&H:VanPC
North Carolina soldier to ZBV	Jan 7	disaffection	A&H:GP
D. W. McGalliard to ZBV	Jan 7	transfer	A&H:GP
William Lamb to ZBV	Jan 7	battle flag capture	A&H:GP
E. [J.] Hine to ZBV	Jan 7	conscription	A&H:GP
Joseph Jones to ZBV	Jan 7	cavalry company	A&H:GP
Patrick H. Winston to ZBV	Jan 7	payment	A&H:GP
Julia A. Albright to ZBV	Jan 8	impressed slave	A&H:GP
Braxton Bragg to ZBV	Jan 9	Collett Leventhorpe	A&H:GP
Laban L. Harris to ZBV	Jan 9	coat & whiskey	A&H:GP
J. M. Davidson to ZBV	Jan 9	resignation	A&H:GP
J. E. Rheim to ZBV	Jan 9	conscription	A&H:GP
Joshua Boner to ZBV	Jan 9	conscription	A&H:GP
Augustus S. Merrimon to ZBV	Jan 9	special court	A&H:GP

Correspondents	Date	Subject	Repository
Obadiah Woodson to M. S. Robins	Jan 9	commission	A&H:VanPC
A. McDowell to ZBV	Jan 10	scripture & law	A&H:GP
Robert E. Lee to ZBV	Jan 10	Wilmington	A&H:GP
John White to Joseph H. Flanner	Jan 10	payment to Collie	A&H:GP
A. McDaniel to ZBV, resolutions	Jan 10	black marriage	A&H:GP
Mary C. Newton to ZBV	Jan 11	appointment	A&H:GP
J. C. Hill to ZBV	Jan 11	destitution	A&H:GP
William E. Earle to George Little	Jan 11	civil unrest & deserters	A&H:GP
William Lamb to ZBV	Jan 11	slave labor	A&H:GP
Andrew G. Magrath to ZBV	Jan 11	state militias	A&H:GP
R. L. Patterson to ZBV	Jan 11	disaffection	A&H:VanPC
Robert E. Lee to ZBV	Jan 11	supply transport	A&H:VanPC
H. R. Thomas to ZBV	Jan 12	conscription	A&H:GP
William R. Bass to ZBV	Jan 12	visit	A&H:VanPC
Edward Lawrence to ZBV	Jan 13	cotton & loan	A&H:GP
H. S. Parsons to ZBV	Jan 13	Fort Fisher	A&H:GP
Robert E. Lee to ZBV	Jan 13	Federal fleet	A&H:GP
John Dawson to ZBV	Jan 13	conscription	A&H:GP
J. G. Burr to ZBV	Jan 13	Wilmington	A&H:GP
Laurence S. Baker to ZBV	Jan 13	reinforcements	A&H:GP
Braxton Bragg to ZBV	Jan 13	Wilmington	A&H:GP
W. L. Smith to ZBV	Jan 13	Wilmington	A&H:GP
James Sloan to ZBV	Jan 13	Home Guard	A&H:GP
Richard Anderson to ZBV	Jan 13	deserter & thief	A&H:GP
W. W. Hampton to ZBV	Jan 13	recommendation	A&H:GP
David L. Swain to ZBV	Jan 13	morphine	A&H:VanPC
James L. Henry to ZBV	Jan 13	cavalry company	A&H:VanPC
J. G. Burr to ZBV	Jan 14	brigadier	A&H:GP
John A. Bradshaw	Jan 14	9th N.C. Reg't.	A&H:GP
Joshua Boner to ZBV	Jan 14	conscription	A&H:GP
Lee M. McAfee to ZBV	Jan 14	appointment	A&H:GP
Charles H. Winston to ZBV	Jan 14	geological report	A&H:GP
Ralph P. Buxton to ZBV	Jan 14	special court	A&H:GP
William H. Hamilton to ZBV	Jan 15	State Capitol	A&H:GP
Augustus S. Merrimon to ZBV	Jan 15	A. H. Jones	A&H:GP
J. G. Burr to ZBV	Jan 15	Wilmington	A&H:GP
S. A. Powell to ZBV	Jan 16	distilling	A&H:GP
J. J. Hines to ZBV	Jan 16	chaplain	A&H:GP
Mrs. James W. Hinton to ZBV	Jan 16	husband as prisoner	A&H:GP
Robert E. Lee to ZBV	Jan 16	eastern commerce	A&H:VanPC
James Sloan to ZBV	Jan 17	distilling	A&H:GP
Bayles M. Edney to ZBV	Jan 17	prisoner release	A&H:GP
Alfred Haney to ZBV	Jan 17	military service	A&H:GP
Robert S. French, commission	Jan 17	special court	A&H:GLB
David G. Worth to ZBV	Jan 18	J. R. Grist	A&H:GP

Correspondents	Date	Subject	Repository
J. G. Burr to ZBV	Jan 18	shovels	A&H:GP
William H. James to ZBV	Jan 18	shovels	A&H:GP
J. G. Burr to ZBV	Jan 18	Wilmington	A&H:GP
William M. Shipp, commission	Jan 18	special court	A&H:GLB
A. M. Alexander to ZBV	Jan 18	ZBV's property	A&H:VanPC
G. H. White to ZBV	Jan 19	poor relief	A&H:GP
M. S. Sherwood to ZBV	Jan 19	conscription	A&H:GP
A. E. Baird to ZBV	Jan 19	gratitude	A&H:VanPC
C. D. Smith to ZBV	Jan 20	peace	A&H:VanPC
Robert E. Lee to ZBV	Jan 20	mutiny	A&H:VanPC
Augustus S. Merrimon to ZBV	Jan 21	special court	A&H:GP
John D. Shephard to ZBV	Jan 21	gift	A&H:VanPC
H. F. Peedin to ZBV	Jan 22	deserter	A&H:GP
D. W. McGalliard to ZBV	Jan 23	organized company	A&H:GP
John A. Moore to ZBV	Jan 23	discharge	A&H:GP
B. Coffin et al. to ZBV	Jan 23	free black	A&H:GP
Phebe Norminger to ZBV	Jan 23	son's detail	A&H:GP
John N. Clarkson to William Smith	Jan 23	salt transport	A&H:GP
J. M. McGowan to ZBV	Jan 23	gift	A&H:VanPC
Richard H. Battle, endorsement	Jan 23	newspaper ad	A&H:VanPC
W. F. Ayres to ZBV	Jan 24	troop clothing	A&H:GP
Braxton Bragg to ZBV	Jan 24	captured troops	A&H:GP
Braxton Bragg to ZBV	Jan 24	morale	A&H:GP
Joshua Boner to ZBV	Jan 24	conscription	A&H:GP
Robert Strange to ZBV	Jan 24	desertion	A&H:GP
Calvin H. Wiley to ZBV	Jan 24	slavery	A&H:VanPC
Ed. W. Jones to ZBV	Jan 24	Confederacy	A&H:VanPC
Richard Chapman to ZBV	Jan 25	deserter	A&H:GP
Braxton Bragg to ZBV	Jan 25	Federal movement	A&H:GP
W. A. Parham to ZBV	Jan 26	Federal movement	A&H:GP
John D. Whitford to David A. Barnes	Jan 26	peas	A&H:VanPC
Otis F. Manson to ZBV	Jan 26	tobacco	A&H:VanPC
Otis F. Manson to ZBV	Jan 26	receipt	A&H:VanPC
R. C. Kerr to A. M. McPheeters	Jan 26	corrected bill	A&H:VanPC
A. C. Avery to ZBV	Jan 26	military organization	A&H:VanPC
C. A. Boon to ZBV	Jan 27	son's clothing	A&H:GP
W. A. Parham to ZBV	Jan 27	Federal troops	A&H:GP
Nathan Milaur to George Little	Jan 27	conscription	A&H:GP
Thomas J. Sumner to ZBV	Jan 28	wood transport	A&H:GP
Braxton Bragg to ZBV	Jan 28	Federal troops	A&H:GP
Power, Low & Co. to ZBV	Jan 28	cotton	A&H:GP
William Smith to ZBV	Jan 28	salt works	A&H:GP
Malcom B. McRae to ZBV	Jan 29	deserter	A&H:GP
Wittkowsky & Saltzberg to ZBV	Jan 29	gift	A&H:GP
J. D. [H.] Flanner to ZBV	Jan 30	recommendation	A&H:GP
Thomas A. Allison to ZBV	Jan 30	Home Guard	A&H:GP

Correspondents	Date	Subject	Repository
A. M. Johnson to ZBV	Jan 30	transfer	A&H:VanPC
Mrs. V. Atkinson to ZBV	Jan 31	buffaloes; slaves	A&H:GP
D. C. Richardson to ZBV	Jan 31	mechanic arrest	A&H:GP
James A. Seddon to ZBV	Jan 31	r.r. gauge	A&H:GP
James A. Seddon to ZBV	Jan 31	J. A. Teague	A&H:GP
James A. Seddon to ZBV	Jan 31	r.r. gauge	A&H:GP
B. C. Washburn to ZBV	Jan 31	salt	A&H:GP
J. J. Bruner to A. M. McPheeters	Jan 31	payment	A&H:VanPC
John Johnson to ZBV	Jan n.d.	arrest W. B. Fry	A&H:GP
J. J. Bruner to A. M. McPheeters	Jan n.d.	payment	A&H:VanPC
Henry Gregory, J. D. Skinner to ZBV	Feb 1	transfer	A&H:GP
J. E. Foster et al. to James A. Seddon	Feb 1	transfer	A&H:GP
John A. Stanly to ZBV	Feb 1	resignation	A&H:GP
Miss Perkins to ZBV	Feb 1	orphans; taxes	A&H:GP
John A. Gilmer to ZBV	Feb 1	peace resolutions	A&H:VanPC
James L. Henry to ZBV	Feb 1	army disaffection	A&H:VanPC
Wilkes Morris to E. Murray & Co.	Feb 1	cargo	A&H:VanPC
Richard S. Donnell, Giles Mebane, resolution	Feb 1	express thanks	A&H:VanPC
Mary A. Windsor to ZBV	Feb 1	transfer	A&H:VanPC
Will. S. Mullins to ZBV	Feb 1	manufacturing	A&H:VanPC
William A. Blount et al., invitation	Feb 2	tournament	A&H:GP
ZBV to William M. Shipp	Feb 2	special court	A&H:GLB
Amos W. Jackson to ZBV	Feb 2	deserter	A&H:VanPC
Samuel F. Phillips to ZBV	Feb 2	Home Guard	A&H:VanPC
J. L. Patton to ZBV	Feb 3	transfer	A&H:VanPC
Will. L. Scott to ZBV	Feb 3	conscription	A&H:VanPC
W. A. Parham to ZBV	Feb 4	cotton transport	A&H:GP
H. Cansler et al. to ZBV	Feb 4	special court	A&H:GP
Tod R. Caldwell to ZBV	Feb 4	distilling	A&H:GP
James W. Osborne, commission	Feb 4	special court	A&H:GLB
Sophia Johnson to ZBV	Feb 4	discharge	A&H:VanPC
Richard S. Donnell to ZBV	Feb 4	peace report	A&H:VanPC
ZBV, commission	Feb 4	special court	A&H:VanPC
Samuel Radford to ZBV	Feb 5	discharge	A&H:VanPC
E. C. Bartlett to ZBV	Feb 6	transfer	A&H:GP
William Kirkland to ZBV	Feb 6	Joseph Brown	A&H:GP
John D. Hyman to ZBV	Feb 6	appointment	A&H:VanPC
Braxton Bragg to ZBV	Feb 7	Federal troops	A&H:GP
J. McCormick to A. M. McPheeters	Feb 7	magistrates	A&H:VanPC
R. Bradley to ZBV	Feb 7	appointment	A&H:VanPC
Andrew G. Magrath to ZBV	Feb 8	code message	A&H:GP
Rufus Y. McAden to ZBV	Feb 8	appointment	A&H:VanPC
Thomas F. McKesson to ZBV	Feb 8	distilling	A&H:VanPC
J. G. Burr to ZBV	Feb 8	assistance	A&H:VanPC
David L. Swain to ZBV	Feb 8	assistance	A&H:VanPC

Correspondents	Date	Subject	Repository
Rations list	Feb 9	Salisbury Prison	A&H:GP
Samuel Cooper to ZBV	Feb 9	Hahn's Battalion	A&H:GP
Robert R. Heath, commission	Feb 9	special court	A&H:GLB
Robert S. French, commission	Feb 9	special court	A&H:GLB
Betty Whittington to ZBV	Feb 9	wool	A&H:VanPC
J. B. Kincaid, commission	Feb 9	justice of the peace	A&H:VanPC
W. Hardy to ZBV	Feb 10	shoes, clothing	A&H:GP
Robert F. Hoke to ZBV	Feb 10	Grant's movement	A&H:VanPC
R. C. Puryear to ZBV	Feb 10	slave	A&H:VanPC
W. W. Long to R. C. Puryear	Feb 10	slave	A&H:VanPC
J. Felton to ZBV	Feb 10	conscription	A&H:VanPC
John A. Gilmer to ZBV	Feb 11	Alexander Stephens	A&H:GP
J. W. Morris to ZBV	Feb 11	Federal forces	A&H:VanPC
Manliff Overman to ZBV	Feb 11	constable	A&H:VanPC
Ralph Gorrell to ZBV	Feb 11	Senior Reserves	A&H:VanPC
John A. Gilmer to ZBV	Feb 12	salt trains	A&H:GP
Nicholas W. Woodfin to ZBV	Feb 12	Stephens & Graham	A&H:VanPC
J. W. Morris to ZBV	Feb 12	Federal forces	A&H:VanPC
Robert S. Herring to ZBV	Feb 13	cloth	A&H:GP
George Tait to ZBV	Feb 13	mutiny	A&H:GP
Edward J. Hale to ZBV	Feb 13	meeting	A&H:GP
Robert F. Hoke to ZBV	Feb 13	meeting	A&H:GP
William Smith to ZBV	Feb 13	salt transport	A&H:GP
Henry E. Colton to ZBV	Feb 13	printing paper	A&H:VanPC
Mary Holder to ZBV	Feb 13	husband's murder	A&H:VanPC
Edward Warren to ZBV	Feb 13	Federal attacks	A&H:VanPC
G. C. Masey to ZBV	Feb 13	discharge	A&H:VanPC
Mont. Patton to ZBV	Feb 13	troop riot	A&H:VanPC
William Shipp to ZBV	Feb 13	special court	A&H:VanPC
John A. Boyden to ZBV	Feb 13	molasses	A&H:VanPC
John A. Boyden to ZBV	Feb 13	molasses	A&H:VanPC
David L. Swain to ZBV	Feb 14	Richmond meetings	A&H:VanPC
A. M. Powell to ZBV	Feb 14	r.r. iron	A&H:VanPC
K. Murchison et al. to ZBV	Feb 15	slave murderer	A&H:GP
Washington C. Kerr to ZBV	Feb 15	geological collection	A&H:GP
John C. Breckinridge to ZBV	Feb 15	passport	A&H:GP
T. B. Miller to ZBV	Feb 15	shoes, clothing	A&H:VanPC
A. G. Vance to ZBV	Feb 16	coffee & tea	A&H:GP
R. Radford to ZBV	Feb 16	speech	A&H:GP
M. A. Osborne to ZBV	Feb 16	commission	A&H:VanPC
B. A. Ernul to ZBV	Feb 16	farm equipment	A&H:VanPC
W. F. Parker to ZBV	Feb 16	cavalry	A&H:VanPC
William J. Hoke to ZBV	Feb 17	Federal forces	A&H:GP
Hattie Vance to ZBV	Feb 17	Hoke telegram	A&H:GP
H. Joyner to ZBV	Feb 17	Halifax arrival	A&H:GP
Bradley T. Johnson to ZBV	Feb 17	prisoners	A&H:GP

Correspondents	*Date*	*Subject*	*Repository*
J. H. Her[nnesa] to ZBV	Feb 17	distilling	A&H:VanPC
Joshua Roberts to ZBV	Feb 17	conscription	A&H:VanPC
George G. Wells to ZBV	Feb 18	departure	A&H:GP
W. J. Epps to ZBV	Feb 18	meeting invitation	A&H:GP
J. C. Benbow to ZBV	Feb 18	Quakers	A&H:VanPC
A. C. Murdock to ZBV	Feb 18	deserters	A&H:VanPC
P. G. T. Beauregard to ZBV	Feb 19	W. T. Sherman	A&H:GP
Laurence S. Baker to ZBV	Feb 19	Federal forces	A&H:GP
W. W. Rowland to ZBV	Feb 19	furlough	A&H:VanPC
Laurence S. Baker to ZBV	Feb 20	Federal forces	A&H:GP
Braxton Bragg to ZBV	Feb 20	assistance	A&H:GP
P. G. T. Beauregard to ZBV	Feb 20	coded telegram	A&H:GP
William J. Hoke to ZBV	Feb 20	arms, ammunition	A&H:GP
S. A. Harris to ZBV	Feb 20	Charlotte headquarters	A&H:GP
Thomas M. Crossan to ZBV	Feb 20	invitation	A&H:GP
P. G. T. Beauregard to ZBV	Feb 20	telegram	A&H:VanPC
Thomas M. Holt to ZBV	Feb 20	mill	A&H:VanPC
Gray Andrews to ZBV	Feb 20	furlough	A&H:VanPC
D. A. Davis to ZBV	Feb 20	recommendation	A&H:VanPC
Nelson P. Lindsay to ZBV	Feb 20	commission	A&H:VanPC
S. S. Ferguson to ZBV	Feb 20	furlough	A&H:VanPC
James L. Carson to ZBV	Feb 20	disaffection	A&H:VanPC
Robert E. Lee to ZBV	Feb 21	Sgt. Hart	A&H:GP
E. A. Drury et al. to ZBV	Feb 21	war support	A&H:GP
A. Carmichael to ZBV	Feb 21	assistant surgeon	A&H:VanPC
P. G. T. Beauregard to ZBV	Feb 22	W. T. Sherman	A&H:GP
A. McLean to ZBV	Feb 22	Home Guard	A&H:GP
Jo Williamson to ZBV	Feb 22	confiscation	A&H:VanPC
Lizzie Murdock to ZBV	Feb 22	father's death	A&H:VanPC
H. E. Colton to ZBV	Feb 23	transfer	A&H:GP
J. B. Jones et al. to ZBV	Feb 23	meeting invitation	A&H:GP
P. G. T. Beauregard, appeal	Feb 23	r.r. destruction	A&H:VanPC
W. B. Wright to ZBV	Feb 23	pardon	A&H:VanPC
H. E. Colton to ZBV	Feb 24	Fayetteville	A&H:GP
J. M. McCorkle to ZBV	Feb 24	Home Guard	A&H:VanPC
E. D. Hall to ZBV	Feb 25	assistance offer	A&H:GP
Braxton Bragg to ZBV	Feb 25	Federal advance	A&H:GP
F. G. De Fontaine to ZBV	Feb 25	printers	A&H:GP
A. C. Murdock to ZBV	Feb 25	speech	A&H:GP
Braxton Bragg to ZBV	Feb 25	Raleigh command	A&H:GP
P. G. T. Beauregard to ZBV	Feb 25	communication	A&H:GP
ZBV to John C. Breckinridge	Feb 25	Piedmont r.r.	A&H:GLB
L. C. Edwards to ZBV	Feb 25	Literary Board	A&H:VanPC
A. H. Baird to ZBV	Feb 25	resignation	A&H:VanPC
T. G. Croft to ZBV	Feb 25	deserters	A&H:VanPC

Correspondents	Date	Subject	Repository
John Beasley et al. to ZBV	Feb 26	impressment	A&H:VanPC
Irvin Thigpen, certification	Feb 26	John O. Oates	A&H:VanPC
J. G. Burr to ZBV	Feb 27	message	A&H:GP
Laurence S. Baker to ZBV	Feb 27	cavalry	A&H:GP
William Collie to ZBV	Feb 27	departure	A&H:GP
Collett Leaventhorpe to ZBV	Feb 27	Raleigh transport	A&H:GP
P. Murphy to ZBV	Feb 27	justice of the peace	A&H:VanPC
R. V. Blackstock to ZBV	Feb 27	desertion & r.r.	A&H:VanPC
Peter Adams to ZBV	Feb 27	NCRR	A&H:VanPC
Daniel S. Hill to ZBV	Feb 27	Home Guard	A&H:VanPC
David F. Caldwell to ZBV	Feb 27	r.r. gauge	A&H:VanPC
George Palmer to ZBV	Feb 27	wounded soldiers	A&H:VanPC
David A. Barnes to ZBV	Feb 28	Raleigh transport	A&H:GP
G. C. Moore to ZBV	Feb 28	destitution	A&H:VanPC
D. W. Lindsay to David A. Barnes	Feb 28	magistrate	A&H:VanPC
Thomas Webb to ZBV	Mar 1	trains	A&H:GP
Thomas J. Sumner to ZBV	Mar 1	r.r. gauge	A&H:GP
Joseph E. Johnston to ZBV	Mar 1	r.r. gauge	A&H:GP
Joseph E. Johnston to ZBV	Mar 1	r.r. gauge	A&H:GLB
Thomas C. Wallace to ZBV	Mar 1	orphan soldiers	A&H:VanPC
D. M. Lee to ZBV	Mar 1	ill son	A&H:VanPC
R. C. Cotton to ZBV	Mar 1	Home Guard	A&H:VanPC
S. J. Powell to ZBV	Mar 1	discharge	A&H:VanPC
Jeremy F. Gilmer to ZBV	Mar 2	r.r. gauge	A&H:GP
D. A. Lindsay to ZBV	Mar 2	transportation	A&H:GP
Laurence S. Baker to ZBV	Mar 2	cavalry orders	A&H:GP
J. W. Montgomery, contract	Mar 2	salt manufacturing	A&H:GP
Stuart Buchanan & Co., contract	Mar 2	salt manufacturing	A&H:GP
Joseph E. Johnston to ZBV	Mar 2	r.r. gauge	A&H:GLB
Jeremy F. Gilmer to ZBV	Mar 2	r.r. gauge	A&H:GLB
Robert E. Lee to ZBV	Mar 2	r.r. gauge	A&H:GLB
T. M. Walker to ZBV	Mar 2	distilling	A&H:VanPC
A. M. McPheeters to A. W. Ingold & Co.	Mar 2	newspaper bill	A&H:VanPC
A. M. McPheeters to A. W. Ingold & Co.	Mar 2	receipt	A&H:VanPC
John C. Breckinridge to ZBV	Mar 3	r.r. gauge	A&H:GP
Laurence S. Baker to ZBV	Mar 3	Maj. Shaw	A&H:GP
D. M. Lee to ZBV	Mar 3	transfer	A&H:GP
Robert D. Johnston to ZBV	Mar 3	military orders	A&H:GP
Nicholas W. Woodfin, contract	Mar 3	salt manufacturing	A&H:GP
Joseph E. Johnston to ZBV	Mar 3	supplies	A&H:GLB
James E. Allen et al. to ZBV	Mar 3	detail	A&H:VanPC
E. D. Hall to ZBV	Mar 3	military advice	A&H:VanPC
M. Q. Waddell to ZBV	Mar 3	robbery & violence	A&H:VanPC
Dennis D. Ferebee to George Little	Mar 3	resignation	A&H:VanPC

Correspondents	Date	Subject	Repository
A. P. Smith to ZBV	Mar 3	murder	A&H:VanPC
William Wellborn to ZBV	Mar 3	robbery & deserters	A&H:VanPC
Laura R. McDaniel to ZBV	Mar 4	Home Guard	A&H:VanPC
William F. Collins to ZBV	Mar 4	local defense	A&H:VanPC
Daniel S. Hill et al. to ZBV	Mar 4	speech	A&H:VanPC
George Tait to ZBV	Mar 4	furlough	A&H:VanPC
A. M. McPheeters to L. V. Blum	Mar 4	receipt	A&H:VanPC
James Sinclair to ZBV	Mar 4	cotton	A&H:VanPC
William Eaton to ZBV	Mar 5	council meeting	A&H:VanPC
James G. Cook to ZBV	Mar 5	Sinclair letter	A&H:VanPC
Robert H. Stinson to ZBV	Mar 5	robbery & deserters	A&H:VanPC
S. R. Chisman to ZBV	Mar 6	troop train	A&H:GP
H. G. Hugh to ZBV	Mar 6	D. M. Lee's son	A&H:VanPC
Calvin H. Wiley to ZBV	Mar 6	Home Guard exemption	A&H:VanPC
A. C. Murdock to ZBV	Mar 6	robbery & deserters	A&H:VanPC
Edward J. Hale to ZBV	Mar 6	Literary Fund	A&H:VanPC
J. B. Holman to ZBV	Mar 6	distilling	A&H:VanPC
John Thomson, contract	Mar 7	salt manufacturing	A&H:GP
H. E. Colton to ZBV	Mar 7	cotton	A&H:GP
John B. Sate to ZBV	Mar 7	Joseph E. Johnston	A&H:VanPC
Stuart Buchanan & Co., contract	Mar 8	salt manufacturing	A&H:GP
Joseph E. Johnston to ZBV	Mar 8	Kinston	A&H:GP
James Sinclair to whom it may concern	Mar 8	cotton	A&H:GP
John D. Whitford to ZBV	Mar 8	prisoners & artillery	A&H:GP
J. L. Ward to ZBV	Mar 8	salt	A&H:VanPC
L. V. Blum, receipt	Mar 8	ZBV proclamation	A&H:VanPC
John D. Whitford to ZBV	Mar 9	armies	A&H:GP
Joseph E. Johnston to ZBV	Mar 9	wagons	A&H:GP
B. H. Bryan to ZBV	Mar 9	Home Guard & food	A&H:GP
William Smith to ZBV	Mar 9	salt	A&H:GLB
J. A. Moore to ZBV	Mar 9	medicinal whiskey	A&H:VanPC
William Smith to ZBV	Mar 9	salt	A&H:VanPC
William F. Hilliard to ZBV	Mar 9	conscription exemptions	A&H:VanPC
Calvin H. Wiley to ZBV	Mar 9	robbery & deserters	A&H:VanPC
Thomas J. Sumner to ZBV	Mar 10	troop train	A&H:GP
Hughes to ZBV	Mar 10	transportation	A&H:GP
John D. Whitford to ZBV	Mar 10	transportation	A&H:GP
Braxton Bragg to ZBV	Mar 10	medical officers & supplies	A&H:GP
Thomas J. Sumner to ZBV	Mar 12	travel plans	A&H:GP
Robert F. Hoke to ZBV	Mar 13	C. Leventhorpe	A&H:GP
Thomas J. Sumner	Mar 13	return	A&H:GP
Bartholomew F. Moore to ZBV	Mar 13	Home Guard	A&H:VanPC

Correspondents	Date	Subject	Repository
Mrs. L. O'B. Branch to ZBV	Mar 13	flag	A&H:VanPC
Thomas H. Boyles to ZBV	Mar 13	appointment	A&H:VanPC
M. A. Caldwell to ZBV	Mar 13	poor relief	A&H:VanPC
T. B. Espy to ZBV	Mar 13	Espy family history	A&H:VanPC
J. [L.] Morehead to ZBV	Mar 14	gunpowder	A&H:GP
Thomas Webb to ZBV	Mar 14	troops	A&H:GP
C. R. Lewis to ZBV	Mar 14	invitation	A&H:VanPC
H. R. Hooper to ZBV	Mar 14	employee	A&H:VanPC
Jeptha M. Israel to Nicholas W. Woodfin	Mar 15	saltworks raid	A&H:GP
R. S. [Semontor] to ZBV	Mar 15	ZBV letter	A&H:GP
Operator to ZBV	Mar 15	departures	A&H:GP
Thomas J. Hughes to ZBV	Mar 15	gift	A&H:VanPC
J. M. Warren to ZBV	Mar 16	soldiers' families	A&H:GP
John T. Whaling, contract	Mar 16	salt	A&H:GP
Otis F. Manson to ZBV	Mar 17	soldiers' hospital	A&H:GP
A. J. Battle et al. to ZBV	Mar 18	impressment	A&H:GP
Thomas Webb to ZBV	Mar 18	board meeting	A&H:GP
William T. Dortch to ZBV	Mar 18	news	A&H:GP
W. J. Yates to A. M. McPheeters	Mar 18	departure	A&H:GP
A. M. McPheeters to W. J. Yates	Mar 19	travel instructions	A&H:VanPC
Laurence S. Baker to ZBV	Mar 20	Home Guard	A&H:GP
Thomas Webb to ZBV	Mar 20	departure	A&H:GP
Thomas Webb to ZBV	Mar 20	board meeting	A&H:GP
Nicholas W. Woodfin to ZBV	Mar 21	salt	A&H:GP
N. Kilny to ZBV	Mar 22	impressment	A&H:VanPC
John C. Breckinridge to ZBV	Mar 24	r.r. gauge & stock	A&H:GP
Joseph E. Johnston to ZBV	Mar 24	Robert E. Lee	A&H:GP
P. J. Coppidge to ZBV	Mar 27	appointments	A&H:GP
List	Mar 28	staff salaries	A&H:VanPC
List	Mar 28	warrants issued	A&H:VanPC
P. J. Coppidge to ZBV	Mar 30	appointments	A&H:GP
Arch. McLean to ZBV	Mar 30	provisions	A&H:VanPC
D. Coble to ZBV	Mar n.d.	robbery & violence	A&H:VanPC
William M. Shipp, commission	n.m. n.d.	special court	A&H:GLB
W. D. Reynolds to A. M. McPheeters	Apr 6	money	A&H:GP
Collett Leventhorpe to ZBV	Apr 7	bridges	A&H:GP
James Sloan to ZBV	Apr 11	state supplies	A&H:GP
John M. Otey to ZBV	Apr 12	Salisbury brigade	A&H:GP
William P. Johnston to ZBV	Apr 12	Gen. Hardee	A&H:GP
Thomas J. Sumner to ZBV	Apr 12	trains	A&H:GP
D. S. Ryan to ZBV	Apr 12	Robert E. Lee	A&H:GP
Archer Anderson to ZBV	Apr 12	Robert E. Lee	A&H:GP
David L. Swain to ZBV	Apr 12	Sherman letter	A&H:VanPC
William T. Sherman to officers	Apr 13	passage for ZBV	A&H:VanPC
Richard C. Gatlin to ZBV	Apr 14	arrival	A&H:VanPC

Correspondents	Date	Subject	Repository
Jonathan Worth to ZBV	Apr 14	travel route	A&H:VanPC
Collett Leventhorpe to ZBV	Apr 14	departure	A&H:VanPC
Thomas White to ZBV	Apr 17	supply raid	A&H:GP
Thomas White to James Sloan	Apr 17	state supplies	A&H:GP
Thomas White to ZBV	Apr 18	state supplies	A&H:GP
J. A. Boyden to ZBV	Apr 18	state mules	A&H:GP
Jefferson Davis to ZBV	Apr 18	continue war	A&H:GP
Richard C. Gatlin to ZBV	Apr 19	disband troops	A&H:VanPC
Thomas White to ZBV	Apr 20	troops	A&H:GP
George W. Thompson to ZBV	Apr 21	departure	A&H:GP
Bradley T. Johnson to ZBV	Apr 21	robbery	A&H:GP
Thomas White to ZBV	Apr 21	state supplies	A&H:GP
James Sloan to M. B. McMicken	Apr 21	state supplies	A&H:VanPC
J. W. Wilson to ZBV	Apr 22	family news	A&H:GP
Thomas J. Sumner to S. R. Chisman	Apr 23	train for ZBV	A&H:GP
Jefferson Davis to ZBV	Apr 23	arrival	A&H:GP
William L. Pitts to ZBV	Apr 23	rations	A&H:GP
M. B. McMicken to Joseph E. Johnston	Apr 23	state supplies	A&H:VanPC
Thomas J. Sumner to ZBV	Apr 24	train for ZBV	A&H:GP
J. [Hillshonner] to ZBV	Apr 24	property receipt	A&H:VanPC
R. G. Lindsay to ZBV	Apr 27	Sloan conference	A&H:GP
ZBV, proclamation	Apr 28	public cooperation	A&H:GP
Thomas Webb to ZBV	Apr 30	Graham departure	A&H:GP
Thomas White to ZBV	May 1	state records	A&H:GP
Frederick F. Low, proclamation	May 8	Abraham Lincoln	A&H:GP
J. S. McCubbins to ZBV	May 9	supply theft	A&H:VanPC
Henry G. Blasdel, proclamation	May 16	Abraham Lincoln	A&H:GP
J. N. Smith to E. Harlam	May 17	magistrates	A&H:GP
[G. M. Brooks] to Col. Johnson	May 24	magistrates	A&H:GP
U.S. authorities to ZBV	May 25	governor's furniture	A&H:GP
O. P. Stearns to Samuel A. Duncan	May 26	magistrates	A&H:GP
Thomas Cox, list	May 26	magistrates	A&H:GP
O. P. Stearns to Adj. General	May 26	magistrates	A&H:GP
[Frank P. Maniss] to ZBV	May 29	assistance offer	A&H:VanPC
Bryan Tyson to ZBV	May 29	assistance offer	A&H:VanPC
Gilbert J. [Drawn] to ZBV	Jun 3	kinship	A&H:VanPC
William H. Cowles to ZBV	Jun 8	Holden & Worth	A&H:VanPC
B. Morrison Harris to ZBV	Jun 10	assistance offer	A&H:VanPC
Robert B. Vance to ZBV	Jun 10	family & Asheville	A&H:VanPC
ZBV, account	Jun 15	Collie & Flanner	A&H:VanPC
R. J. Powell to ZBV	Jun 22	news article	A&H:VanPC
C. H. Hall to Maj. Turner	Jun 24	letters to ZBV	A&H:VanPC
Clara M. Knapp to Mr. Hall	Jun 24	letters to ZBV	A&H:VanPC
Clara B. [illegible] to ZBV	Jun 24	family & support	A&H:VanPC

Correspondents	Date	Subject	Repository
R. J. Powell to ZBV	Jun 26	pardons & property	A&H:VanPC
[G. Baldwin] to ZBV	Jun 27	assistance offer	A&H:VanPC
R. Tannahill to ZBV	n.m. 1	travel permission	A&H:GP
Braxton Bragg to ZBV	n.m. 7	slaves	A&H:GP
John M. Robinson to ZBV	n.m. 11	train	A&H:GP
Robert B. Vance to ZBV	n.m. 17	arrival	A&H:GP
C. P. Thompson to ZBV	n.m. 20	r.r. track	A&H:GP
William Johnston to ZBV	n.m. 28	pony & teams	A&H:GP

INDEX

A

B

D